I Hear America Singing

An Introduction to Popular Music

David Kastin

Prentice
Hall

Upper Saddle River, NJ 07458

Library of Congress Cataloging-in-Publication Data

Kastin, David
    I hear America singing : an introduction to popular music / David Kastin.
        p. cm.
    Includes discography, bibliographical references, and index.
    ISBN 0-13-353376-X
      1. Popular music—United States—History and criticism. I. Title.
    ML3477.K37 2001
    781.64'0973—dc21

                                                                    2001021690

This is dedicated—to the ones I love

For Laura and Alena

Acquisitions editor: Christopher T. Johnson
Production editor: Laura A. Lawrie
Manufacturing and prepress buyer: Benjamin D. Smith
Copy editor: Laura A. Lawrie
Editorial assistant: Evette Dickerson
Cover design: Bruce Kenselaar

This book was set in 10/12.5 AGaramond by Compset, Inc.
and was printed and bound by Banta Company.
The cover was printed by Phoenix Color Corp.

Printed in the United States of America

10 9 8 7 6 5 4 3 2 1 02 01 00

ISBN 0-13-353376-X

PEARSON EDUCATION Ltd., London
PEARSON EDUCATION AUSTRALIA PTY, Limited, Sydney
PEARSON EDUCATION SINGAPORE, Pte. Ltd
PEARSON EDUCATION NORTH ASIA LTD, Hong Kong
PEARSON EDUCATION CANADA, LTD., Toronto
PEARSON EDUCACIÓN DE MEXICO, S.A. de C.V.
PEARSON EDUCATION--Japan, Tokyo
PEARSON EDUCATION MALAYSIA, Pte. Ltd
PEARSON EDUCATION, Upper Saddle River, New Jersey

Contents

VII   PREFACE

CHAPTER 1   1   THE FOLK BALLAD:
                  STORYTELLING IN SONG

1   FORM FOLLOWS FUNCTION: THE ANGLO-AMERICAN FOLK BALLAD

2   FOLK SONG COLLECTORS AND BALLAD SCHOLARS: OUTSIDERS
     LOOK IN

3   BALLAD STORIES AND THE ORAL TRADITION

7   THE BROADSIDE BALLAD: JOURNALISM IN SONG

7   NEW COUNTRY, NEW BALLADS (AND A LOT OF OLD ONES, TOO)

10   FOLK BALLADS AND POPULAR CULTURE

12   THE AFRICAN-AMERICAN NARRATIVE SONG TRADITION

17   CORRIDOS: SPANISH BALLADS IN THE NEW WORLD

22   WOODY GUTHRIE: FATHER OF THE MODERN FOLK BALLAD

27   PROTEST AND PROPAGANDA

28   HOOTENANNIES AND THE HIT PARADE

30   THE FOLK REVIVAL OF THE SIXTIES

39   ACTIVITIES AND PROJECTS

CHAPTER 2   41   IN THE BEGINNING . . .
                  THERE WAS THE BLUES

41   THE BIRTH OF THE BLUES

44   THE COUNTRY BLUES: A REGIONAL GUIDE

48   BLUES LYRICS AND THEMES

57   THE CLASSIC BLUES: WOMEN IN THE SPOTLIGHT

58   RACE RECORDS

61   ENTER BESSIE SMITH AND MA: BLUES ROYALTY ON RECORDS

61   FIELD RECORDING: COUNTRY BLUES ON LOCATION

65   BLUES IN THE 1930s: OUT WITH THE OLD, IN WITH THE NEW

69   MUDDY WATERS AND THE BIRTH OF THE BIG CITY BLUES

72   PIONEERS OF ELECTRICITY

77   THE BLUES HAD A BABY AND THEY NAMED IT ROCK 'N' ROLL

79   ACTIVITIES AND PROJECTS

CHAPTER 3   81   JAZZ: THE SOUND OF A NEW CENTURY

81   NEW ORLEANS: BIRTHPLACE OF JAZZ

86   BUDDY BOLDEN: FIRST MAN OF JAZZ

88   1917: JAZZ ON RECORD AND ON THE MOVE

90   THE JAZZ AGE: PUTTING THE SIN IN SYNCOPATION

107   THE SWING ERA: SETTING THE STAGE

108   BENNY GOODMAN: KING OF SWING

113   DUKE ELLINGTON: IT DON'T MEAN A THING IF IT AIN'T GOT THAT SWING

115   COUNT BASIE: LAST OF THE BLUE DEVILS

117   LADY DAY

126   THE BEBOP REVOLUTION

132   CHANGES ON THE STREET

141   JAZZ AT MID-CENTURY: DIVERSITY AND DIVISIVENESS

150   THE AVANT GARDE: OUT OF THE MAINSTREAM

155   FUSION: JAZZ PLUGS IN

160   BACK TO THE FUTURE: WHYNTON MARSALIS AND NEOMAINSTREAM JAZZ

162   ACTIVITIES AND PROJECTS

CHAPTER 4   165   **R & B, ROCKABILLY, ROCK 'N' ROLL AND ROCK**

165   HAIL, HAIL ROCK 'N' ROLL

176   ELVIS PRESLEY: ENTER THE KING

187   THE DEATH OF ROCK 'N' ROLL: MYTH AND REALITY

193   THE MOTOWN EMPIRE: HITSVILLE, U.S.A.

197   ATLANTIC RECORDS AND THE STORY OF SOUL

200   STAX RECORDS: SOULSVILLE, U.S.A.

203   ARETHA FRANKLIN: THE QUEEN OF SOUL

206   JAMES BROWN: GODFATHER OF SOUL

208   THE TAMI SHOW: CELLULOID TIME CAPSULE (IN BLACK AND WHITE)

210   THE BRITISH ARE COMING . . .

215   THE FOLK REVIVAL: MUSIC WITH A SOCIAL CONSCIENCE

221   FROM ROCK 'N' ROLL TO ROCK

227   HIGH ART/BIG BUSINESS

233   SUPERGROUPS AND GUITAR HEROES

240   WOODSTOCK NATION: THREE DAYS OF PEACE AND MUSIC

247   ACTIVITIES AND PROJECTS

CHAPTER 5   249   **ROCK: FROM THE ME DECADE TO THE MILLENNIUM**

249   THE SEVENTIES: THE RISE OF CORPORATE ROCK

252   HEAVY METAL: THE DEVIL AND THE POWER CHORD

255   THE SINGER-SONGWRITER: POET LAUREATE OF THE ME DECADE

259   ART ROCK: NO LONGER A CONTRADICTION IN TERMS

CONTENTS

266   **Black Music in the Seventies: Many Nations Under a Groove**

272   **Rock at Mid-Decade: From the Mainstream to the Margins**

277   **Disco Fever**

281   **The Eighties and the Triumph of Pop**

292   **Girls Just Want to Have Fun**

299   **Metal Health in the 1990s**

304   **Alternative to What?**

310   **Rockin' at the End of the Millennium**

314   **Activities and Projects**

Chapter 6   317   **Rap: Talking Drum of the Global Village**

318   **To the Hip-Hop**

324   **Everybody's Rapping: From Rhythm to Rhyme**

326   **Rap on Wax: The First Generation**

329   **Hip-Hop Nation: Into the Mainstream**

336   **Gangsta Rap: Street Journalism or Action-Film Fantasy?**

342   **Rap Goes Pop**

343   **Rap Goes Co-Ed**

345   **Rap at the Millennium: Funerals and Fragmentation**

349   **Activities and Projects**

351   **Sound Sources**

353   **Bibliography**

357   **Glossary**

361   **Index**

Preface

THE PAST IS PROLOGUE . . .

Nowhere is the truth of this time-honored adage more striking than in the world of American popular music at the dawn of the new millennium. For example, just a few months before the turn of the twenty-first century, Moby (a.k.a. Richard Hall), long one of the leading figures of America's cutting-edge "techno" underground, released his latest dance-oriented collage of sound effects, free-form lyrics, and instrumental riffs. Yet, woven into these aural assemblages—made possible by the state-of-the-art technology of digital sampling—were soundbites from an assortment of obscure field recordings that preserved the vibrant voices of America's folk cultures.

Reviews of Moby's CD (entitled *Play*) often singled out the song "Honey" for special praise. Set off by a propulsive piano vamp and exuberant slide-guitar figures, the heart of the track is a sample of an a cappella vocal by Bessie Jones, a resident of one of the isolated sea islands off the coast of Georgia born during the first decade of the twentieth century. In fact, the traditional play-party song Moby appropriated for his composition had originally had been recorded on location by the pioneering American folk music collector and archivist, Alan Lomax back in the 1950s. Nor was Moby's the only fusion of technology and tradition to establish itself on the recent pop music landscape.

Back in the 1970s, first-generation hip-hop DJs such as Afrika Bambaattaa and Grandmaster Flash had claimed the title "master of records" by cutting and scratching their own multicultural mixes from crate loads of LPs (prompting rap historian David Toop to liken them to "librarians of arcane and unpredictable sound"). A decade later, rap groups such as Public Enemy were drawing on a repository of twenty thousand albums to construct complex sonic collages from the sampled shards of America's recorded history.

By the late 1990s, the *Billboard* charts had become a virtual archive of late-twentieth-century pop music as everything from classic rock (Puff Daddy recycles Led Zeppelin's "Kashmir") to R & B ballads (the Fugees' reprise Roberta Flack's "Killing Me Softly") to Broadway show tunes (rapper Jay-Z appropriates the chorus of "Hard Knock Life" from *Annie*) was resurrected on the latest Top Ten. Meanwhile, on critically acclaimed albums such as *Odelay* and *Midnight Vultures*, Beck wedded his surrealistic lyrics to a genre-busting array of samples drawn from folk and bluegrass music, country blues, fifties lounge music, and fusion jazz. So it is that the historian's favorite cliché seems finally to have been turned on its head; for in the realm of contemporary popular music, those who *know* the past don't just repeat it but reshape it.

A number of other windows into American pop music history also opened up during this period. With the advent of the CD, for example, the complete recordings of significant performers of the past (from Robert Johnson to Patsy Cline) were reissued on the new high-tech, rainbow-streaked disks. Soon an avalanche of increasingly elaborate, comprehensive boxed set retrospectives clogged the aisles of local record stores. About the same time, major label marketing strategists (riding a wave of premillennial nostalgia) had begun formulating a spate of all-star tribute albums on which contemporary recording artists covered the classic songs of Woody Guthrie . . . or Curtis Mayfield . . . or Cole Porter . . . or Tammy Wynette. Finally, a flurry of Hollywood movies aimed at the profitable youth audience mined yesterday's hit parade to create today's hip retro soundtracks.

Yet to a large extent, all of these recent phenomena only serve to reinforce a more fundamental reality, one that provides the framework for this exploration of America's musical legacy. For while it has continually presented itself in new guises, in every age the popular music of the day has been rooted in days gone by, just as in every generation, pop stars have been inspired by the performers who preceded them.

WHAT'S IN A NAME?

This book is an outgrowth of a course in American popular music and culture that I have been teaching for the past ten years. One of the central goals of my curriculum has been to forge connections between the world of contemporary popular music (with which my students are so intensely involved) and the historical foundation of this music (about which so many are entirely unaware). Before going any further, however, it is important to clarify the definition of "popular music" that has provided the framework for that inquiry, whether in the classroom or in these pages.

If a word-association experiment had been conducted among the American populace midway through the twentieth century, the phrase—*popular music*—would no doubt have elicited an astonishing array of images (diverging dramatically along racial, regional, and generational lines), among them:

- Frank Sinatra draped over a microphone stand in front of the Tommy Dorsey Orchestra
- Mambo King Perez Prado's band, launching a thousand dancers with his latest hit, "Cherry Pink and Apple Blossom White"
- Eddy Arnold singing "Bouquet of Roses" from the stage of the Grand Ole Opry
- Ella Fitzgerald at the Savoy Ballroom
- The Platters' crooning their sophisticated harmonies
- Doris Day in Technicolor

Just as in earlier eras such a survey might have conjured up names like George M. Cohan, Bert Williams, Sophie Tucker, Jimmie Rodgers, Bessie Smith, Irving Berlin, the Andrews Sisters, or Fats Waller. But for my students—and I suspect for most people coming of age during the past half-century—the concept of popular music has little meaning outside the context of "rock 'n' roll."

While rock has to varying degrees always adopted aspects of traditional pop's musical aesthetic—and adapted its finely tuned commercial mechanisms—the Big Beat had from the very beginning also derived much of its vitality and authenticity from America's diverse folk traditions. So, whereas this book devotes considerable space to an exploration of rock's evolution, it also seeks to trace its primal sources in Anglo-American ballads, African-American blues and gospel, and in the Spanish tinges that Jelly Roll Morton cited as an essential element in his own musical synthesis back at the turn of the twentieth century. Of course, the music Morton claimed to have created—jazz—is now enshrined in the conventional wisdom as "American's greatest contribution to world culture." It is only fitting, therefore, that jazz get its own comprehensive chapter in any chronicle of our nation's musical history.

FORM AND FUNCTION

With the advent of the Internet, a vast reservoir of information on every imaginable subject has become available at the click of a computer key. Since no single volume could hope to match the sheer scope, detail, and currency of the accumulated data poised to stream through cyberspace in the blink of an eye, more than ever before the textbook must provide a conceptual framework that will allow students to create meaning from the chaos of that "content." Therefore, in an effort to help students make sense of America's musical heritage, I have structured each chapter in the text around a central narrative that tells the story of a genre of popular music in the context of our nation's dynamic social and cultural history.

In order to preserve the integrity of these accounts, a significant portion of the information in each chapter is contained in supplementary boxes consisting of charts, maps, musical definitions, biographies, literary excerpts, or song lyrics. For example, boxes on such essential song forms as the ballad and blues are each illustrated with traditional examples, as well as by representative works by Woody Guthrie and Bob Dylan. These stand-along entries also serve as vehicles for important subjects (such as the minstrel show, Tin Pan Alley, and the griot tradition) that fall outside the parameters of the narrative sections.

Each chapter ends with an extensive selection of suggested projects (options include research-oriented topics, creative assignments, and "think pieces"). In order to facilitate further inquiry, I have produced a comprehensive bibliography and suggested sound sources for each genre. Here, too, an active learning experience was the primary consideration.

WORDS AND PICTURES

While popular music has had an influence on virtually all aspects of our culture, it has exerted a particularly powerful impact on twentieth-century American literature. For this reason, I have secured permission to reprint works by the following writers, all of whom have used music as a subject in their poems, novels, and essays:

- Ralph Ellison (an excerpt from an essay about blues shouter Jimmy Rushing)
- Michael Herr (an excerpt from *Dispatches* describing soldiers listening to Jimi Hendrix during the Vietnam War)
- Sterling A. Brown ("Ma Rainey," a poem about the Mother of the Blues)
- David Wohjan ("Mystery Train: Janis Joplin Leaves Port Arthur, for Points West, 1964," a poem about the doomed pop star)
- Jack Kerouac ("Charlie Parker," a poem composed immediately after Bird's death)
- Jayne Cortez ("I See Chano Pozo," a dynamic poem that captures the spirit of the Cubop legend).

In order to mirror the vitality of the music documented in the text, I have also included an array of photographs, as well as other graphic material such as album covers, posters, sheet music illustrations, broadside ballads, advertisements, and movie stills. In all, the book assembles approximately 125 evocative images, representing each musical style and historical era explored in the text.

ACKNOWLEDGMENTS

My journey through the dense and tangled history of American popular music would have been considerably more precarious if not for the achievements of those pioneering scholars and critics who first broke the trail and charted the way. In particular, I have benefited from the research, scholarship, and insights of the following: Alan Lomax, Eileen Southern, Gilbert Chase, Charles Hamm, John Storm Roberts, Le Roi Jones (Amiri Baraka), Paul Oliver, H. Wiley Hitchcock, Robert Palmer, Peter Guralnick, Nick Tosches, Americo Paredes, Marshall Stearns, Bill Malone, John Lovell, Jr., Albert Murray, Robert Walser, Samuel Charters, Ralph Ellison, Anthony Heilbut, and David Toop. I also would like to thank the reviewers of this book: Dick Weissman (University of Colorado), Dr. D. Royce Boyer (University of Alabama), and Jeffrey Magee (Indiana University).

On a more personal note, I would also like to acknowledge Norwell J. Therien, Jr. and Christopher Johnson at Prentice Hall for their patience and support, Lee Tanner (of The Jazz Image) for his beautiful photographs, Robert Walser (at UCLA) for his unwavering encouragement, Chris Strachwitz for the generous use of his photo collection and all his beautiful recordings (available from Arhoolie Records). For their various contributions, my appreciation also goes out to: Michael Schulman and Larry Schwartz at Archive Photo, Bernadette Moore and Claudia Depkin at RCA's photo archive, Valentina Morales and Loanne Rios Kong at Sony Music, Michael Brooks at Atlantic Records, David Sajnek at BMI Archives, Jazell Andujar at the *Village Voice*, Mark Medley at the Country Music Foundation, Terri Hinte at Specialty Records, Stephanie Smith and Jeff Place at Smithsonian/Folkways, Thea Munoz at the Rock and Roll Hall of Fame and Museum, as well as to the staffs of the MoMA film stills collection and the Library for the Performing Arts at Lincoln Center. Special thanks to my editor, Laura Lawrie, for her thoughtful attention and impeccable taste—and to my students, from whom I have learned so much.

1
The Folk Ballad: Storytelling in Song

Whether it was the saga of a great hero, a myth that explained the nature of the universe, or simply an account of the day's hunt, storytelling has been among the most ancient and pervasive of human activities. Although much about the origin of these archetypal stories will never be known, we do know that some of the earliest of them were not merely told but chanted or sung. One of the most enduring examples of such narrative songs is the folk ballad. Brought to the New World by early European settlers, the ballad tradition has been a dynamic presence in American popular music ever since.

Many traditional ballads can be traced back over a thousand years, and closely related versions of the same ballad have been found across Europe from Scandanavia and Germany to England, France, and Spain. But while it has proven impossible to determine with certainty either the circumstances that produced the ballad or the date they were first created, their rhythmic structure has suggested to many scholars that they may have originally been connected to ritual dances. The word ballad is, after all, derived from the Latin "ballare" (to dance).

While storytelling has, for the most part, become the turf of television and the movies, we can still find echoes of ancient ballads on the latest pop charts. And although most new narrative songs continue to draw on Anglo-American traditions passed down through the folk culture to succeeding generations of modern balladeers from Woody Guthrie and Bob Dylan to Bruce Springsteen and Tracy Chapman, more recently, pop performers have adopted other genres to fulfill this storytelling function. There are even those who argue that the age-old legacy of storytelling in song has found a new home in the hardcore scenarios of gangsta rap.

THE EVOLUTION OF THE BALLAD: FORM FOLLOWS FUNCTION

The ballad has been likened to some great tree whose trunk is rooted in a dark and distant past, and whose branches have spread through space and time bearing songs that share a number of distinctive qualities. In his authoritative 1932 study, *The Ballad of Tradition,* Princeton professor Gordon Hall Gerould itemizes the unique features that can serve as the defining elements of the species: "A ballad is a folk song that tells a story with stress on the central situation, tells it by letting the action unfold itself in event and speech, and tells it objectively with little comment or intrusion of personal bias."

Let's take a little closer look at each of these three hallmarks of the archetypal European ballad that provides the foundation of our own narrative song tradition:

1. Although they occasionally contain many verses, ballads are relatively concise in that they almost always focus on one particular event or scene. All prior or subsequent actions are referred to briefly at best.
2. Ballads take a show-don't-tell approach. Situations are presented dramatically rather than descriptively and dialog is used extensively to enhance the immediacy of the story.

3.   Events in a traditional folk ballad are allowed to unfold matter-of-factly and there is little heavy-handed characterization, nor does the narrative impose any moral judgment on the action.

These elements of narrative style are most often viewed as a direct consequence of the ballad's poetic and musical structure. Because it is organized into self-contained stanzas—each set to the same simple melody—the ballad is an example of the *strophic* form. And since each verse is shaped to fit a single repeated tune, there is a natural tendency for stories to develop as a series of compressed, dramatic scenes. As Gerould explains, "To each repetition of the melody would fall some little scene, some bit of dialogue or perhaps some longer speech. . . . A story composed to fit a recurrent melody, or composed simultaneously with such a melody, could not fail to have a dramatic quality. It would be forced into such a form by the circumstances of its performance."

In the Anglo-American ballad tradition that will be our focus, there are two primary stanza formats. The first (generally considered to represent an earlier mode) is made up of two lines with four beats per line (Example 1). The other (more common) form is made up of four lines in which both the first and third lines contain four beats and the second and final line each contain three beats (Example 2). In both type of stanzas there is a consistent pattern of alternating unaccented and accented syllables.

Example 1.   The elphin knight sits on yon hill.
He blaws his horn both lowd and shril.
(from "The Elfin Knight"—Child No. 2)

Example 2.   There lived a wife at Usher's Well,
And a wealthy wife was she;
She had three stout and stalwart sons,
And sent them o'er the sea.
(from "The Wife of Usher's Well"—Child No. 79)

For centuries, ballads flourished in oral form as an integral part of the social fabric of what is generally referred to as the "folk culture." As products of a rural, illiterate peasantry, these songs were either ignored or disparaged by the educated classes. While today we might be critical of this élitist attitude, in fact, it was the ballad's long isolation from most self-consciously literary or artistic intrusions that actually allowed for its natural evolution through the oral tradition to continue.

FOLK SONG COLLECTORS AND BALLAD SCHOLARS: OUTSIDERS LOOK IN

The folk ballad did eventually come to the attention of collectors, poets, scholars, and other members of the British literary élite, who were attracted by what they saw as its quaint charms. For example, both Walter Scott and Robert Burns not only became avid collectors of the ballads of their native Scotland, but they both were influenced greatly in their own writing by these songs. The English Romantic poets—including Wordsworth, Coleridge, and Keats—also embraced the native folk ballad and used it as a model for their own work. Other collectors were fascinated by the ballad as an artifact. For example, the personal library of the seventeenth-century diarist, Samuel Pepys, contained well over 1,500 examples in manuscript and printed form. But it was an American scholar who would be the first to make the serious study of the English folk ballad his life's work.

A Harvard University professor of English, James Francis Child, is credited with producing the most comprehensive and scholarly study of the folk ballads of the British Isles. Beginning in 1855 and continuing until his death in 1896, Child collected and collated hundreds of ballads and their "variants" (as different versions of a song are known); eventually the results of his efforts were published in a definitive five-volume edition entitled *The English and Scottish Popular Ballads*. Through painstaking analysis, Child established that there were a total of 305 narratives that—along with their numerous variants—formed the fundamental core of the entire British ballad canon. Although Child ignored the issue of ballad tunes (he dealt only with lyrics), his pioneering study remains the cornerstone of the field. To this day, whenever an Anglo-Scottish ballad is cited, it is with the number that Child assigned it in his massive collection (i.e., "The House Carpenter" [Child No. 243] or "Barbara Allen" [Child No. 84]).

Ironically, when it came time to conduct a comprehensive study of the folk ballad tradition in America, it was an Englishman—Cecil James Sharp—who made the first major contribution in this effort. On the basis of his research and extensive travels through the eastern United States, Sharp published *English Folk Songs of the Southern Appalachians* (1917). In this and other works, Sharp documented the survival and dynamic existence in America of scores of ancient ballads that British, Scottish, and Irish immigrants had brought with them from their homelands.

BALLAD STORIES AND THE ORAL TRADITION

So what were the stories that the so-called folk handed down through the generations and took across the Atlantic ocean? While studies of Anglo-American ballads do contain examples of heroic epics, legendary adventures, and supernatural thrillers, most ballads are not the equivalent of the latest Hollywood summer blockbusters. Instead, the overwhelming majority of the traditional ballads (collected in both the British Isles and the United States) deal with domestic concerns. Intimate and familial relationships—the dramas of everyday life—predominate. And of these, love stories are by far the most common. The passions and conflicts generated by romantic love have always been the primary subject of the ballad.

After a ballad had been adopted into the folk community, it was then subjected to an ongoing process of re-creation through the oral tradition. These variations suggest that a system of selectivity has been the key to the ballad's preservation. Although the nature of ballad variants is discussed in some detail elsewhere in this chapter, it is important to note here that these changes cannot simply be explained as a slip of memory or simple chance as was originally believed; for as one tracks the evolution of a particular ballad, invariably it is the most effecting detail and the most expressive turn of phrase that is retained. For this reason, the ballad has sometimes been compared to a stone passed from hand to hand, its rough edges becoming softly rounded, its surface gradually polished to a rich patina.

Meanwhile, even during this century, the extraordinary feats of memory exhibited by some members of the traditional folk culture have astounded researchers. As late as the 1920s, scholars and collectors have written of encounters with individuals who could perform dozens of ballads by heart or sing for hour on hour without repeating a single verse. For example, Cecil Sharp reported that while gathering specimens for his monumental study of the English folk song in America, one Virginia woman was able to sing from memory a total of sixty-four full-length ballads.

Although scholars have consistently stressed the "folk" origin of the British ballad—as well as its continual evolution through the oral tradition—they also acknowledge that, from the very beginning, important contributions to the ballad's development were made by a class of "professionals" who were at least one step removed from the folk culture: minstrels.

THE MINSTREL BALLAD

One of the most familiar inhabitants of our somewhat hazy image of medieval Europe is the wandering minstrel. A staple of those Hollywood epics of knights in shining armor and adventures of Robin Hood, minstrels have come to seem like figures of legend themselves; but, in fact, they were a reality of daily life in the Middle Ages. The minstrel's lyric poems and tales of courtly love—drawn from the great literary Romances and set to the shimmering strings of his harp—provided entertainment for members of the court, the manor, and the clergy, as well as for the common folk.

At local fairs or on market day, minstrels would attempt to win over their audience by singing their own versions of popular stories using the traditional ballad form. Writing about the role of the minstrel in her book

"Barbara Allen" (Trad.)

(Child No. 84)

Like the other entries in Child's collection of traditional folk ballads, "Barbara Allen" had been passed down for generations through the oral tradition. The earliest written reference to the song—from a diary entry dated January 2, 1666—suggests that the song was already quite familiar; for, returning home from a party that night, the well-known London social figure Samuel Pepys wrote in his diary that it had been a "perfect pleasure" hearing the actress Mrs. Knipp "singing her little Scotch song of 'Barbary Allen.'" The first broadside (printed) version of the ballad appeared in the mid-1700s.

The Lyrics

While the earliest versions of "Barbara Allen" established both the basic plot of the ballad and the heartless nature of its title character, later variants reflect the transformations that occur as a folk song is altered and reshaped over an extended period of time. The most common variations in the numerous versions of "Barbara Allen" involve the time of year in which the story is set, the name of Barbara's mistreated lover, and the identity of the town in which the events occurred.

Like so many ballads from the British Isles, "Barbara Allen" made its way across the Atlantic and was said to have been a particular favorite of George Washington. The following version is just one of the approximately 250 that have been collected in America:

Twas in the merry month of May
When green buds all were swellin';
Sweet William on his deathbed lay
For love of Barb'ry Allen.

He sent his servant to the town
To the place where she was dwellin',
Saying, "You must come to my master dear
If your name be Barb'ry Allen."

So slowly, slowly she got up
And slowly she drew nigh him;
And the only words to him did say
"Young man, I think you're dyin'."

He turned his face unto the wall
And death was in him wellin';
"Good-bye, good-bye to my friends all
Be good to Barb'ry Allen."

When he was dead and laid in grave
She heard the death bells knellin';
And every stroke to her did say,
"Hard-hearted Barb'ry Allen."

"On mother, Oh mother, go dig my grave
Make it both long and narrow;
Sweet William died of love for me
And I will die of sorrow."

"And father, father, go dig my grave
Make it both long and narrow;
Sweet William died on yesterday,
And I will die tomorrow."

Barb'ry Allen was buried in the old church yard
Sweet William was buried beside her;
Out of Sweet William's heart there grew a rose,
Out of Barb'ry Allen's a briar.*

They grew and grew in the old church yard
Till they could grow no higher;
At the end they formed a true lover's knot
And the rose grew 'round the briar.

*A plant with sharp thorns.

(Trad.)   Since folk ballads are products of a long and anonymous creative process, rather than an author's name, titles are typically followed by the abbreviation "Trad." (for traditional).

(Child No. 84)   This designation refers to the ballad's place in the collection of 305 English and Scottish ballads assembled by the Harvard University scholar Francis James Child.

(town)   At this point, the name of a particular town often appears. This phenomenon, referred to as "localization," helps scholars trace the history of each ballad. Variants of "Barbara Allen" include references to "London town," "Oxford town," "Scarlet town," "Knoxville," "Waco," and many other locales on both sides of the Atlantic.

(3rd verse)   The Romances of the Middle Ages (which were the source of many folk ballads) followed the code of "courtly love," in which the woman was idealized and worshiped from afar; a man dying of unrequited love was a common theme.

(final verse)   Similar endings are found in numerous ballads. Any standard element (which either begins or ends a folk ballad) is referred to as a "formula." These provide a familiar framework for the listener.

Refrains

Although they were initially ignored by the scholars who collected them (and often are omitted from printed collections), most folk ballads in the oral tradition included refrains. Often they were simply a series of lilting nonsense syllables placed between individual lines or verses (such as "Hey derry, derry, down" or "Fa la diddle, diddle"). In other cases, refrains may have represented a magical folk incantation, as in the flower refrains of some love ballads. One of these—"Parsley, sage, rosemary, and thyme"—was revived by Simon and Garfunkel for the title song of a 1966 album. Whatever form they took, such refrains provided a good opportunity for a group to join in the singing of a ballad during a performance.

The Music

The word "ballad" has a root in common with the word "ballet," suggesting that these songs probably originated as an accompaniment for folk dances. Eventually the story itself became the focus of the songs, but the tunes to which they were sung do retain a strong rhythmic quality that betrays their original role.

Ballad melodies varied from singer to singer, and changed according to the time period and geographical area. There were dozens of standard tunes based on ancient *modes* (rather than modern major or minor scales). Most often these were simple *pentatonic* (five-note) arrangements. Since the same tune accompanied each verse of the song, ballads are described as a *strophic* form.

Traditionally, folk ballads were performed *a cappella* (without the use of any musical instruments), and with no need to fit their voice to the fixed pitch or harmonies of an instrument, ballads were sung in a highly personal and richly ornamented style.

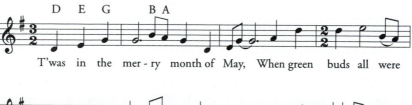

T'was in the mer-ry month of May, When green buds all were

Swell-in', Sweet William on his death-bed lay, For the love of Bar-bry Al-len.

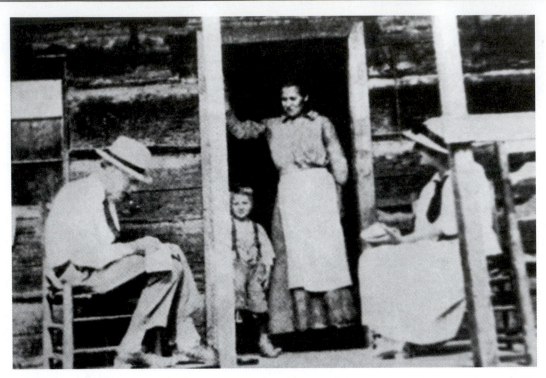

FIGURE 1-1.   Cecil Sharp and his long-time collaborator, Maude Karpeles, on one of their collecting trips to the Appalachian Mountains. Author's collection.

Cecil Sharp: British Ballads in America

On the basis of his visits to cabins like the one in Figure 1-1, Cecil Sharp discovered a treasure trove of traditional British ballads that had been kept alive for generations in the small and isolated communities of Kentucky and West Virginia. While many of the ballads he published in his book *English Folk Songs of the Southern Appalachians* (1917) retain the hallmarks of ancient European sources, others revealed the influence of their long evolution in America.

The Ballad Tree, the American scholar Evelyn K. Wells has explained that while minstrels "did not originate the ballad form, they undoubtedly adopted it for their tales of adventurous knights, ladies in distress, fabulous fairies, and monsters." In fact, most of the ballads that deal with such heroic subjects—including the approximately forty Robin Hood ballads that appear in Child's collection—do reveal the obvious hand of the minstrel.

Unlike the traditional folk ballads that were molded over generations through the oral tradition into models of simple, direct narrative (characterized by a cooly impersonal and fatalistic cast), the minstrel style is decidedly more self-conscious. Minstrel ballads are filled with poetic phrases drawn from the romances of courtly love; they directly solicit the listener's attention, repeatedly swear to their veracity, and often conclude with a neat moral judgment or sactimonious prayer.

Even though they often adapted local folk narratives for their own purposes, minstrels can be credited with helping to preserve many of the traditional ballads. Evelyn K. Wells expresses the attitude of most scholars, however, when she writes of the minstrel, "His constant reference to his noble and worthy audience, and to himself as a true teller of tales inspire neither our interest nor our confidence, and his stock epithets and turns of phrase, unlike those of the traditional ballad which keep their freshness, soon wear thin."

By the Elizabethan Age, minstrels were a dying breed. Times were changing and so was technology. During the sixteenth century, print had become the new medium of the ballad. This is not to say that the oral tradition was suddenly stilled. The folk continued to pass down the old songs, thereby maintaining the age-old evolutionary process. But with the rise of printing, the ballad form was adopted by the popular press as a vehicle for telling the true stories of the day. The age of the "broadside ballad" had arrived.

THE BROADSIDE BALLAD: JOURNALISM IN SONG

By the 1600s, the *broadside ballad* had become a familiar part of daily life in England. During the two centuries since Gutenberg's invention of the moveable-type printing press (in 1450), the uses for this powerful mass medium had expanded and filtered down from the nobility and clergy to much of the middle and lower classes. Literacy had become more common, and at a half-penny or a penny a copy, the broadside ballad was an affordable (and entertaining) way for virtually anyone to get the news of the day.

Printed on one side of a single sheet of paper—usually with a woodblock illustration at the top—the broadside ballad followed the basic form of the traditional folk ballads. Often there was even a note to the purchaser suggesting a well-known tune to which it could be sung. The favorite topics for the anonymous authors of these print ballads would not be unfamiliar to readers of today's tabloids: murders, fires, floods, executions, wars, assassinations, and all kinds of disasters both natural and manmade (although no one has yet uncovered a broadside telling the true "Ballad of My Alien Love Chyld").

Although their subjects were sometimes shocking and their style either sensational or sentimental, broadsides often do a good job of presenting the "five w's" of journalism. For example, a ballad written about the execution of a criminal would probably indicate when the evil-doer's hanging had occurred, where it took place, and what crimes had led him to his terrible fate; it might go on to describe the reaction of the crowd and possibly even quote his last words. In addition to the latest news stories, eventually most traditional ballads also found their way into print.

Some idea about the pervasiveness of broadsides can be gleaned from the lists of London's Company of Stationers (which was established in 1556 to license ballads for print). Although many printers undoubtedly bypassed the official bureaucracy, researchers have established that between 1557 and 1709, over three thousand broadside ballads were officially registered. On one particularly busy day (December 14, 1624), the Company of Stationers issued licenses for 128 ballads.

At this point, there begins a complex and fascinating dynamic within the folk tradition (one that persisted until well into the twentieth century), as ballads that had been handed down orally for centuries suddenly encountered printed versions of the same story. Often broadsides were simply absorbed into the folk stream where they too became subjected to the transformations of the oral process. Not only did this complex interaction take place after the introduction of print but, as we'll see, a similar interaction occurred again after the phonograph became the medium of choice for disseminating popular songs.

NEW COUNTRY, NEW BALLADS (AND A LOT OF OLD ONES, TOO)

By the time the first colonists set sail, the traditional British folk ballad had become as much a part of the heritage of England as the language itself. It didn't take long before the old songs took root in the new land and gradually they began to generate new, distinctively American branches. Having become a commonplace of daily life in the old country, the broadside ballad (and the habit of creating songs out of the events of the day) made its way across the Atlantic. Before long, Americans were creating their own songs out of the shared experience of people living together in a new environment: There were new ballads because there were new stories to be told.

Broadside Ballads: All the News That's Fit to Sing

This American broadside ballad about an incident during the Revolutionary War represents a unique form of popular journalism that had begun in England during the 1600s. As was the custom, this eighteenth-century example was printed on a single sheet of paper and was illustrated with a simple woodblock print.

Death of Major Andre.

COME all you brave Americans I pray you lend an ear,
I will sing you a short ditty your spirits for to cheer,
Concerning a young gentleman whose age was twenty-two,
He is fit for North America, with a heart that's just and true.

The British took him from his lodging and did him close confine
They in strong prison bound him & kept him there sometime,
But he being something valient resolv'd there not to stay,
He got himself at liberty and from them come away.

And when that he had returned home to his own country,
There was many a plan contriving to undo America;
Plotted by General Arnold, and his bold british crew,
They tho't to shed our innocent blood and America to undue.

It was of a scouting party that sail'd from Tarrytown,
They met a British officer of fame and high renown ;
And said to this young gentleman you are of the british core,
And I trust that you can tell me if the dangers are all o'er.

O then up steps John Spalding saying you must dismount,
And where you are agoing you must give a strict account ;
I am a British flag sir, I've a pass to go this way.
Upon an expedition in North America.

O then up steps John Spalding saying you must dismount,
And where you are agoing give me a more strict account ;
For I will have you searched before that you pass by—
On a strict examination he was found to be a British Spy !

" There take my gold and silver and all I have in store,
And when down to New. York I come will send you thousands
more !
I scorn your gold and silver, I've enough of it in store,
And when my money it is gone I will bodily fight for more.

O then he found that all his plans were like to be bro't to light,
He call'd for pen and paper and begged leave to write
A line to General Arnold to let him know his fate,
He begged of him assistance but alas, it was too late !

When Arnold he this letter read it made his heart relent,
He called for his barge, down to New York quickly went ;
There he is amongst the Britons a fighting for his king
He has left poor Major Andre on the gallows for to swing !

If you are a man from Britain with courage stout and bold,
I'le fear no man of valour tho' he be cloth'd in gold ;
This place it is improper our valour for to try,
And if we take the sword in hand one of the two must die !

When he was executed he being both meek and mild,
Around on the spectators most pleasantly did smile,
' fill'd each one with terror and caus'd their hearts to bleed,
They wished that Andre was set free and Arnold in his stead.

Success unto John Spalding, let his health be drank around,
Likewise to those brave heroes who fough: against the crown
Here is a health to every Soldier who fought for liberty,
And to the brave and gallant Washington of North America.

Printed and Sold at N0, 25, High Street, PROVIDENCE, where may be obtained 100 other kinds.

FIGURE 1-2. Courtesy of Brown University Library.

Early in the twentieth century, when the first serious ballad collectors began to gather narrative songs from the rapidly vanishing remnants of America's folk culture, they were amazed by how many ballads that appeared in the great Child canon had managed to survive in the Appalachian Mountains and the Maine woods. By most counts, approximately one-third of the 305 ballads that comprise the five volumes of *The English and Scottish Popular Ballads* had been successfully transplanted in the United States.

While many imported folk ballads did become a vital part of the evolving American culture, others seemed to quickly wither and die. In particular, those tales steeped in ancient superstitions or those filled with the archaic language and lore of courtly love had no place in the life of the new country, and they soon fell by the wayside. Of course, all the ballads that did take root in the American soil were subjected to a process of naturalization, as novel turns of phrase and local place names found their way into new variants of the old songs.

Certainly the most fertile traditional British ballad to make its way to these shores was "Barbara Allen." In the Archive of American Folk Song of the Library of Congress, which was established in the 1930s to serve as a storehouse and study center for our indigenous folk music, one can compare over 240 different versions of "Barbara Allen," collected from over half the states in the nation. Although American variants of the ballad typically retain the central focus on Barbara's characteristic cruelty, after the song crossed the Atlantic, the first thing singers did was to give the story an American setting.

Other imported folk ballads began to exhibit signs of America's democratizing influence. For example, the main character in the British ballad "Lord Randal" quickly lost his noble title, and, in one Virginia variant, he becomes known simply as "Johnny Randolph." In general, while Americans modernized, democratized, and localized the ballads of their ancestors, typically they continued singing them to the ancient modal melodies that would have been familiar to their great-great-great-grandparents.

WOMEN'S WORK

One of the more interesting theories about this process of retention and adaptation has been proposed by Alan Lomax (son of the pioneering American folk song collector, John Lomax, and a scholar of American musical history in his own right). According to Lomax, a surprising number of those ballads that were absorbed into the American folk tradition have a common theme. "For some considerable time, and especially in America," Lomax reminds us, "the ballads have been women's songs, attached to the household and the fireside." Understandably, he suggests, our American foremothers made "a selection from that lore of vehicles of fantasy, wishes, and norms of behaviour which corresponded . . . to the emotional needs of pioneer women in America."

So what were the themes of the ballads chosen by these women for whom, as Lomax describes it, "love and marriage meant grueling labour, endless childbearing and subservience?" Lomax believes that in their chosen ballads, "one can see the women turning to thoughts of revenge, to morbid death wishes, to guilt-ridden fantasies of escape." While they may have retained songs of fulfillment in which "the faithful and virtuous maiden gets her man," as Lomax points out, every story of "virtue rewarded has a darker twin." So it is that dozens of America's favorite ballads (like "The House Carpenter") centered not on the theme of romantic love but escape from romantic love (depicted in such songs as "a temptation that destroys women"). The American variant "Little Matty Groves" (Child No. 81), for example, is nothing less than a female revenge fantasy ending in spousal decapitation.

But the traumas borne by pioneer women living in a harsh and repressive environment did more than simply shape the American variants of old ballads. Lomax's own survey of our nation's ballads indicates that "the story of the pregnant girl murdered by her treacherous lover . . . has given rise to more than half of the ballads composed by white folk singers in America!" And, broadly speaking, the theme of sexual violence overwhelmingly dominates the new songs that began to emerge in the New World. One of the hundreds of such ballads is "Omie Wise," a ballad based on the murder of Naomi Wise by her lover Jonathan Lewis, which took place in Guilford County, North Carolina, in 1808. As the song describes, Lewis (who had taken up with another woman), makes his fiancée, Naomi, believe that he intends to elope with her, but instead he drowns her in a nearby spring. Although, as most versions of the ballad describe, Lewis was quickly arrested for the killing, he managed to break out of jail and head west. Years later he was apprehended and brought to trial, but was acquitted for lack of evidence.

An even more lurid example of this genre is the story of "Tom Dula." Supposedly written by Dula himself in the spring of 1868—shortly before he was hung for the murder of his former lover—this famous North Carolina ballad is a kind of musical confession ("I met her on the mountain,/I swore she'd be my wife,/I met her on the mountain,/And stabbed her with my knife"). While the ballad accurately details the specifics of the case including the name of his victim (Laura Foster) and the location of his execution (Statesville), Dula fails to mention either his accomplice or the motive for his murder. It seems that the killing was precipitated by the fact that Dula had passed on a venereal disease he had contracted from Foster to his new sweetheart, Ann Melton. According to the testimony of local residents, it was Melton who actually stabbed Foster and helped bury the body in a shallow grave.

Amazingly, in 1958 (almost a hundred years after the song was written), a clean-cut collegiate singing group who called themselves the Kingston Trio recorded a version of the old murder ballad titled "Tom Dooley." Within a few weeks of its release, it went to number one on the national pop chart, helping to usher in the folk revival of the 1960s. Over the next few years Joan Baez recorded dozens of Child ballads, and Bob Dylan (among other urban folkies) wrote his own broadside-style ballads about contemporary issues ranging from civil rights ("The Lonesome Death of Hattie Carroll") to the death of a boxer in the ring ("Who Killed Davey Moore?") to the story of a friend's conviction for vehicular homocide ("Percy's Song").

FOLK BALLADS AND POPULAR CULTURE

Without our own legacy of ancient legends, the dramas of daily life (both large and small) immediately became the basis of a flourishing broadside press. Beginning with ballads of Indian raids, snakebite victims, and witch trials, our collected narrative songs create a kind of ballad history of America. Among its pages are firsthand reports of the Revolutionary War, accounts of the notorious crimes of Wild West outlaws, reports of the sinking of the Titanic, and chilling depictions of the dust storms of the Great Depression. And from the very start, America's narrative songs were shaped by an ongoing dialog between the written and oral traditions—as well as through a complex interplay between the folk and popular cultures.

Although most of the ballads outlined above actually began their life as printed broadsides, those stories that struck a chord in the hearts of the people were often absorbed back into the existing oral tradition. Gradually some songs would take on a life of their own as they were handed down from generation to generation, moved from locale to locale, adapted to new environments, and adjusted to fit various moral values. Matters became even more complicated as ballads became the raw material for the colorful new world of American popular entertainment.

Take the song "Springfield Mountain" (generally recognized as America's oldest indigenous folk ballad), which tells the story of a young Massachusetts man named Timothy Myrick. According to one account written in the quaint spelling and syntax of the period, Myrick was "bit by a Ratel Snake on August the 7th 1761, and Dyed within about two or three ours, he being twenty two years." Soon after, there appeared a sentimental broadside ballad eulogizing the young man. Before long the song was absorbed into the oral tradition and disseminated throughout much of the country. At this point, things get even more interesting.

In about 1830, a professional performer (Lomax identifies him as George Spear) whose stock of American comic stereotypes included the New England "Yankee farmer," transformed the tragic ballad into a broad parody. Retitled "Love and Pizen," the ballad introduces a fictional fiancée into the true story. In her attempt to suck the venom from her lover's heel, she too falls victim to the poison ("But Molly had a rotten tooth,/Which the Pizen struck and killed 'em both"). Soon this parody came to supersede the original ballad, and over the next one hundred years, folk variants of "Love and Pizen" were collected from Vermont to Texas.

In the 1920s—during the early days of the "hillbilly" recording industry—many of the traditional Anglo-American ballads found their way onto 78 r.p.m. shellac discs. Among the rural Southern singers who introduced these old songs to the broader mainstream audience were Bradley Kincaid (whose version of "Barbara Allen" is particularly poignant), his fellow Kentuckian Buell Kazee (whose scholarly study of British ballad history added richness to his interpretations), and, of course, the Carter Family, whose distinctive versions of railroad disaster ballads, gospel hymns, and other traditional folk songs preserved a substantial portion of the American songbook (and earned them the designation of "The First Family of Country Music").

These pioneers of commercial country recording not only documented old ballads on a new medium, they served as a conduit for *professional* songwriters who were creating instant "folk songs" based on the news of the day. One writer who specialized in transposing the latest newspaper headlines (or radio broadcasts) into memorable verses was Carson Robinson, whose numerous ballads included a retelling of the Scopes "monkey trial."

FIGURE 1-3. The Carter Family: Alvin Pleasant ("A.P.") Carter; his wife, Sara (holding autoharp); and her sister, Maybelle (with guitar). Often referred to as "The First Family of Country Music," they helped preserve the past by transplanting ballads from the oral tradition to the mass media. Southern Folklife Collection. University of North Carolina at Chapel Hill.

The Carter Family: Old Songs, New Forms

Not content with performing their repertoire of traditional ballads and gospel songs at community picnics and dances, A. P. Carter dreamed of taking his family band into the brave new world of country music. So it was only natural that in 1927, the Carter Family would find its way to Bristol, Tennessee, where a Victor talent scout named Ralph Peer had set up a temporary recording studio.

Carter's years of song collecting had served him well. Starting with the six numbers that Peer cut on that August day in Bristol, the Carter Family launched a career that would span fifteen years and include over 250 recordings of traditional ballads, folk songs, and hymns.

With the assistance of Leslie Riddles—a black guitar player who served as a kind of human tape recorder—A. P. combined words and phrases from various songs and fused snatches of familiar melodies to create brand new variants. Although this could be seen as simply a continuation of a process that had been going on for centuries, this time the end result was preserved forever on a disk of black shellac.

Then there was Andrew Jenkins, who turned the story of a young man trapped in a Kentucky mine into a ballad entitled "The Death of Floyd Collins" that became a hit recording in 1925 for Vernon Dalhart, an early country music hitmaker. (For some reason, the Floyd Collins story has proven to be particularly adaptable; in addition to Robinson's ballad, the events also became the basis of a Hollywood film [*Ace in the Hole*, a.k.a. *The Big Carnival*, starring Kirk Douglas], a novel [*The Cave* by Robert Penn Warren], and, in the 1990s, an off-Broadway musical—*Floyd Collins*—by Adam Guettel.)

At first glance, these professionally composed "event songs"—whose subjects covered the usual array of tragic train wrecks, daring bank robberies, and assorted natural disasters—seemed no different from those ballads that had slowly evolved through the oral tradition. Unlike authentic "folk" songs, however, the commercial compositions of the hillbilly era were typically laced with self-conscious moralizing. For example, Carson Robinson's ballad about the Scopes trial ends by reminding the young teacher (convicted of espousing the heresy of evolution) that "the old religion's better after all," while Andrew Jenkins takes poor Floyd Collins to task for ignoring his father's advice. Ironically, as Bill Malone points out in his book *Country Music, U.S.A.*, "When later generations of folklorists moved into the byways and backwaters of the South . . . they collected such songs as 'The Death of Floyd Collins' as authentic specimens of the folk-produced songs of the region."

Ballads, however, have always done more than just tell a story; often they have taken a point of view, attempted to move us to terror or tears, or even called us to action. And when presented by a singer in a social setting, ballads can both entertain and enlighten. All these qualities account for the continued existence of the ballad tradition even after the rise of literacy and the development of newspapers, radio, and television. But the ballad legacy of the British Isles represents only one narrative style that took root in America. Other cultures also have made significant contributions to America's story in song.

THE AFRICAN-AMERICAN NARRATIVE SONG TRADITION

GRIOTS AND SONGSTERS

The storytelling traditions of Africa are as ancient and diverse as any on earth. In addition to a rich body of myths, many West African tribes had developed a unique form of oral narrative that was sung to the sound of gently plucked strings. Within these cultures, the combined role of storyteller and historian were embodied in the person of the *griot*.

It was the griot (also known as "jali" or "finah") who was responsible for both preserving the great events of the past and celebrating the accomplishments of the tribe and its heroes. Long narrative songs were memorized and passed down from one griot generation to the next. Accompanying themselves on instruments like the kora (a kind of multistringed harp made out of a large gourd), griots also turned current events into new songs and—for a suitable payment—either sang the praises of their patron or condemned his enemies.

While it is difficult to determine the exact extent to which elements of Africa's narrative songs found their way to America, over the generations African-Americans have imposed their own style of storytelling-in-song on the Anglo-American ballads created by their new countrymen. The result has been a body of songs so distinctive and appealing that as Gordon Hall Gerould (author of *The Ballad of Tradition*) wrote in 1932, "In many respects what the Negroes have done in adapting old songs to their uses and making new ones on the same general model is the most interesting thing in American balladry."

As with most other genres of African-American music, these narrative songs were stamped with the functional demands of the labors they had been created to accompany. In work songs, improvised phrases were set to the beat of a hammer or an ax, a washboard or a butter churn. Although the lyrics of work songs may have originated as random, unconnected statements shaped to the rhythm of a particular task, gradually the isolated phrases were linked into individual verses and then into stories. Over time, some of these stories were molded into the ballad form borrowed from descendants of the British, Irish, and Scottish immigrants who often shared with their black neighbors similar lives of economic deprivation (along with a heritage of oral literature and homemade music).

FIGURE 1-4.   Nyama Suso, a West African griot, accompanies his narrative songs on the kora. Photo by Samuel Charters.

The Griots: Bards of the Gambia (and Godfathers of Rap)

In every generation, it was the griot's task to memorialize the events of tribal history and to document the wars, disasters, and great deeds of village heroes. Thus, the griot's richly textured narratives can perhaps best be seen as a primary source for the African-American ballad whose accounts of legendary badmen (like Stagolee) and folk heroes (like John Henry) are also told in vivid verses to the accompaniment of plucked strings.

In fact, the hip-hop historian David Toop (among others) has also identified the griot as one of the godfathers of contemporary rap. In his pioneering study of the genre, *Rap Attack,* Toop suggests these figures provide an archetype for the inflated braggadocio and scathing "disses" of rap MCs: "Although they are popularly known as praise singers," Toop writes, "griots might combine appreciation of a rich employer with gossip and satire or turn their vocal expertise into an attack on the politically powerful or the financially stingy." In this way, he concludes, "hip-hop message and protest rappers had an ancestry in the savannah griots."

Although we can only speculate on the evolutionary process to which they were subjected, by the Reconstruction era the itinerant guitar-wielding "songsters" who provided the entertainment for rural black communities throughout the South had become a repository of narrative songs. Many of these employed the typical four-line ballad stanza, rhyme scheme, and strophic style (with its repeated melody) that are characteristic of the traditional ballads of the British Isles. Later some of the same stories also were recast in the form of oral poetry that came to be called the blues.

AFRICAN-AMERICAN BALLADS: FOLK HEROES AND BADMEN

While the ballads of the songster generally mirrored the classic Anglo-American style, they do show some qualities that distinguish them from the European models on which they were based. For example, African-American ballads place a much greater emphasis on character and dramatic imagery than on the narrative structure or chronology of the story they are telling. As might be expected, there is also an emphasis on the role of improvisation: Each singer is expected to add a personal dimension to the song. Finally, there is a less objective, journalistic style to most narrative songs in the African-American tradition; instead of focusing on specific details, the stress is placed on the emotional aspects of the story (thereby encouraging empathy and listener identification).

While the best estimates are that about one out of every ten American folk ballads is of African-American origin, by the time they were collected or documented on recordings during the 1920s these songs had already become part of an ongoing interracial dialog. As Harold Courlander explains in *Negro Folk Music, U.S.A.*: "Many ballads known to Negro singers are popular also among whites. Versions of 'John Hardy,' 'John Henry,' 'Casey Jones,' 'Railroad Bill,' 'Stagolee,' 'Frankie and Albert,' to name but a few, are sung by white mountaineer balladeers and played by mountain jug bands, and there obviously has been a good deal of interplay between white and Negro variants, both in style and content."

Just from the titles Courlander lists above, we can get some sense of the range of subjects that comprise the repertoire of singers within the black folk community. Not unlike their European counterparts, African-Americans celebrated the exploits of heroes (and anti-heroes) and recounted both crimes of passion and acts of courage. Like the ballads of the English settlers, they often turned reality into myth. This was certainly the case with the famous saga of "Casey Jones," a song that from its very creation stands as a classic example of the fundamentally heterogeneous racial ancestry of the American folk ballad.

Much of the drama of America's manifest destiny was played out on tracks of steel. Its leading men—and more than occasionally its tragic heroes—were the engineers at the throttle of the powerful locomotives that propelled settlers across the rapidly expanding nation. Among the countless songs that were composed about the great trains and their legendary engineers, perhaps the best known is the ballad of Casey Jones. Yes, there really was a "Casey" Jones, although that was a only a nickname John Luther Jones had picked up because his home town was "Caycee," Kentucky. On April 30, 1900—while trying to make up lost time on his run from Memphis to Canton, Mississippi—Casey was unable to stop when a freight train suddenly crossed his track. At the last moment, he ordered his fireman to jump, thereby saving his life. But Casey was killed in the horrific crash.

It was Wallace Saunders, a black worker in the Canton train yard, who is credited with creating the ballad honoring the martyred white engineer. While only fragments of the original song exist, Saunders seems to have attached the details of Casey's story to fragments of preexisting songs from both the black and white traditions. And as Courelander notes, while most later variants of the ballad "bear the brand of Negro songmakers," others reveal "a curious mixture of Negro idiom and imagery with non-Negro phrases." Over the course of many decades, the "The Ballad of Casey Jones" has been adapted by vaudeville songwriters, and recorded by both white country performers (like Fiddlin' John Carson) and black songsters (like Furry Lewis); it also provided the source of a sexually suggestive, double-entendre song ("J. C. Holmes Blues") by the greatest blueswoman of the 1920s, Bessie Smith.

While most African-American ballads have a similarly tangled history, not all of them are devoted to the theme of selfless heroism. In fact, if you're looking for the origins of rap music's violence-plagued narratives and larger-than-life anti-heroes, they had their start over one hundred years ago in so-called *badman ballads* such as

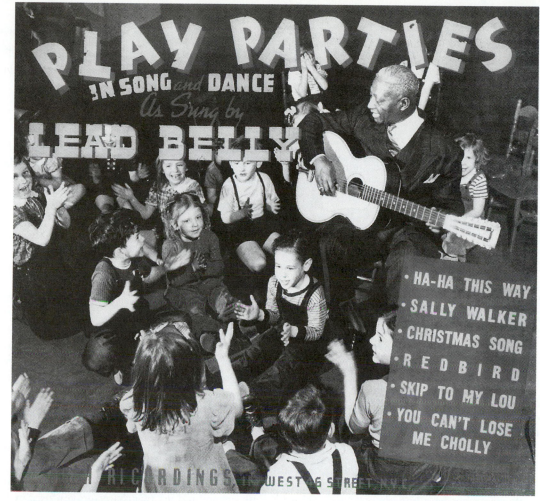

FIGURE 1-5. While he recorded definitive versions of blood-soaked badman ballads (like "John Hardy"), Huddie Ledbetter also delighted young audiences with the "play-party songs" he adapted from the African-American folk tradition. He has been a powerful influence on generations of performers from Woody Guthrie to Kurt Cobain. *Southern Folklife Collection. University of North Carolina at Chapel Hill.*

Leadbelly: Real Life Folk Hero

Billed as "The King of the Twelve-String Guitar"—the instrument he favored during his years of fame—Leadbelly not only wrote dozens of original blues and folk songs but can be credited with preserving and bringing to the attention of the public a vital part of our nation's culture that might otherwise have been lost forever. Among the best known of these songs are "Alberta," "Cotton Fields Back Home," "The Boll Weevil," "Pick a Bale of Cotton," "The Rock Island Line," and "Midnight Special." Along the way, he traveled the early folk-revival circuit with Woody Guthrie and became a folk hero on the scale of those about whom he sang.

A few years after his death (in 1949), the popular folk group the Weavers recorded a version of Leadbelly's signature song, "Goodnight Irene," that went to the top of the Hit Parade, and a quarter of a century later Led Zeppelin paid homage to Leadbelly by regularly performing his adaptation of an old British ballad, "The Gallows Pole," in their live shows. More recently, Nirvana frontman Kurt Cobain (who often declared Leadbelly his greatest influence) chose to end the band's *MTV Unplugged* appearance (aired shortly before Cobain's suicide) with a poignant cover of Leadbelly's "Where Did You Sleep Last Night?"

"Stagolee," "Frankie and Albert," and "John Hardy." But the truth is that the roots of gangsta rap go back a lot deeper than that. And while violence may be as American as cherry pie, its recipe didn't originate on this side of the Atlantic. For violence in all its guises has been a central theme of some of the earliest ballads in the European folk tradition.

Even a quick overview of the classic ballads from the British Isles would produce an anthology of horrors including murder, infanticide, rape, homicidal revenge, suicide, mutilation, poisonings, and patricide—and those are just the stories of domestic life. The ballads that document the battles, Scottish border raids, and other state-sanctioned combat offer an even bloodier panorama. Then there are the outlaw ballads, most prominently the dozens devoted to the not-so-sedate adventures of Robin Hood. Meanwhile, the vast collection of broadside ballads going back to the sixteenth century supply another treasure trove of tabloid brutality. Nor did things change much when the ballad began to tell the story of America.

Our narrative songs—those derived both from oral folk sources and from the broadside press—are a litany of sexual violation and general mayhem. While the Anglo-American tradition has produced more than its fair share of exciting "outlaw ballads" (stories of notorious criminals and cold-blooded killers), often these have retained the romantic rob-from-the-rich-give-to-the-poor aura that are so much a part of the Robin Hood legend. The anti-heroes of the African-American folk tradition, however, are often presented without this moralistic veneer. Typically, the protagonists of these badman ballads are not only unapologetic about their violent predilictions but actually revel in their brutal defiance.

So, when "that bad man Stagolee" catches Billy Lyons trying to steal his Stetson hat, Stagolee doesn't hesitate; instead, the song graphically recounts how Stagolee kills Billy despite his pleas for mercy on account of "my three little helpless babies/And one poor pitiful wife." Meanwhile, in the *badwoman* ballad "Frankie and Albert," Frankie (her real name was Frances) doesn't think twice about shooting the two-timing "Albert"; for as the song cooly declares, "He was her man, but he done her wrong." Although most variants portray "John Hardy" as a similarly heartless murderer (who takes the life of a fellow miner over a 25¢ bet), other versions of his ballad focus on Hardy's supposed gallow's conversion in which he renounces his evil ways.

Some scholars believe that this double-sided depiction of John Hardy's persona was the result of a tangled history that had inadvertantly linked this two-bit killer to the most celebrated hero in American balladry. As Alan Lomax explains, "Because he worked in the tunnels of the West Virginia mountains in the same epoch as John Henry, the two songs have sometimes been combined by folk singers, and the two characters confused by ballad collectors."

But while it may be an understable mix-up, it's also a particularly unfortunate one: For while John Hardy achieved his place in American folklore by pumping lead into a man in a barrelhouse crap game, John Henry earned his mythic martydom by driving steel "till he laid down his hammer and he died."

The "Ballad of John Henry" offers an excellent example not only of how a true event could be turned into a wonderful song but also how it could express the values and symbolic ideals of a culture. The actual story of the legendary hero who tested his own muscle against the power of the steam drill can be traced back to the construction of the Big Bend Tunnel on the Chesapeake and Ohio Railroad near Hinton, West Virginia, between the years 1870 and 1872 when new steel-driving machinery was being introduced.

Depictions of John Henry's epic struggle against the forces of modern technology clearly reflect such ideals as "courage in the face of enormous odds" and "the ability to endure in spirit even in the face of death"—which must have had special significance to the song's African-American creators. There are, however, a number of variants of the "Ballad of John Henry" that also use double entendres to create a sexual subtext. Certainly the bawdy humor conveyed by images of the steel-driving man's prowess with his enormous hammer was an important part of the song's appeal for its early audience. As Lomax explains, "The point of the jest, of course, was that John Henry died not from overwork at the tunnel, but from too much love-making."

As settlers moved west across the continent to Texas and California, they created new narrative songs that reflected their new environment (and celebrated a new American mythic hero—the cowboy). But along the way, they also encountered ballads from another cultural tradition that had taken a different route to the New World and that were sung in a different language.

CORRIDOS: SPANISH BALLADS IN THE NEW WORLD

Like the folk ballads of the British Isles, the traditional narrative songs of Spain also had their origins in the Romances of the Middle Ages. They were musical versions of those stories of brave knights and fair damsels that had fueled the fantasies of Don Quixote. And even before the earliest British colonists established their settlements in the New World, Spanish conquistadors and those who followed in their wake had transplanted these songs—along with the religion and language of their homeland—across a vast area they dubbed New Spain.

Like their English-speaking counterparts, Spanish settlers retained many of their cultural traditions while shaping them to a new environment and lifestyle. According to the folk song collector and author Americo Paredes, the heroes of the traditional *romances viejos* quickly faded, since "the new people who developed in what was to become Mexico were interested in their own historical events." So the narrative folk songs that would become a vital part of the evolving culture of Mexico took on new subjects and celebrated new heroes in a unique form of the ballad called the *corrido*.

The corrido shares many of the essential characteristics of the archetypal European folk ballad (and its British incarnation), including a strophic format, rhymed quatrains (called *coplas*), and a highly dramatic structure enhanced by the use of dialog. But it is the spare swiftness of the corrido narrative that actually gives the Mexican ballad its name. Rooted in the verb "correr"—to run or flow—the corrido is a model of unadorned action.

Among the other formal elements that have become associated with the corrido is a conventional introduction—known as *la llamada*—requesting the listener's attention (i.e., "Voy a cantar estos versos, pongan mucha atención todos"/"I am going to sing these stanzas, everyone pay much attention"), as well as a standard farewell referred to as *la despedida* (i.e., "Ya con esta me despido"/"Now with this I say farewell").

Typically the corrido is set to a correspondingly simple melody, most often with a strong triple-time rhythm such as $\frac{3}{4}$ or $\frac{9}{8}$. And while corridos (like other traditional ballads) were initially sung freely without the constraints of instrumental accompaniment, the use of the guitar—which has a long and intimate association with Spanish culture—was adopted relatively early in its evolution. At first, the instrument of choice for *corridistas* was the bajo sexto, a twelve-string bass guitar. Using a characteristic "corrido strum" (which accented the first beat of each three-beat phrase), the instrument provided a highly danceable rhythmic background for the simple, fast-paced narratives.

Like Anglo-American ballads, Mexican corridos were not only an important component of the oral folk song tradition but in their printed "broadside" versions also became a kind of people's newspaper. In fact, more than most other ballad styles, corridos have assumed a decidedly journalistic cast; both broadside corridos and those from the oral tradition typically focus on the specific dates, names, and other factual details of the events they recount. In most cases, however, the corrido's wealth of factual information actually serves as a foundation for a political message or statement of protest.

AMERICA'S BORDER BALLADS

During the early nineteenth century, Mexican settlers brought the corrido tradition into the oft-disputed territories of California, New Mexico, and the Rio Grande Valley, an area referred to by its inhabitants simply as "la Frontera"—the Border. In many ways, the corridos that were created here bear a striking similarity to the so-called border ballads that originated in the sixteenth century along the turbulent no-man's-land between England and Scotland—and for much the same reason.

As Americo Paredes explains in the introduction to his book about the songs of the Border culture, *A Texas Mexican Cancionero*, the "wild and unruly" region was more than simply fertile soil for outlaws and vagabonds. "To put it another way," Paredes writes, "it was a focus of intercultural conflict, based on the Borderer's resolve *de no ser dejado*, not to take it lying down." As he goes on to explain, this attitude continues to have resonance for Mexican-Americans and helps account for the vitality of the contemporary corrido: "For thousands of young Chicanos today, so intent on maintaining their cultural identity and demanding their rights, the Border corrido hero will strike a responsive chord when he risks life, liberty and material goods *defendiendo su derecho.*"

In fact, even in what is considered the earliest complete Mexican-American folk corrido, one can identify the smoldering resentment and fierce pride that would serve as a theme for so many that followed. Dating from about 1860, "El Corrido de Kiansis" ("The Ballad of Kansas")—also known as "El Corrido de los Quinientos Novillos" ("The Ballad of the Five Hundred Steers")—describes one of the first cattle drives on the Chisolm trail from Texas to the westernmost railhead in Kansas. This account of an episode that would be replayed in countless cowboy ballads and Hollywood films is told from the point of view of a *vaquero*—the Mexican cowboy—who rode alongside (and served as a model for) his American counterpart.

The corrido not only provides graphic descriptions of the dangers of the drive—the thundering hooves, spearlike horns, and swollen streams—but it also alludes to the subservient position of the vaquero (despite what the song suggests were his superior skills). The following is an excerpt from a variant of "Kiansis," which Americo Paredes collected in Texas more than three-quarters of a century after the events of the song (Paredes also supplied the prose translation):

Quinientos novillos eran, todos grandes y livianos, y entre treinta americanos no los podian emblar.	Llegan cinco mexicanos, todos bien enchivarrados, y en menos de un cuarto de hora los tenian encerrados.	Esos cinco mexicanos al momento los escharon, y los treinta americanos se quedaron azorados.
(Five hundred steers there were, all big and quick; thirty American cowboys could not keep them bunched together.)	(Then five Mexicans arrive, all of them wearing good chaps; and in less than a quarter-hour, they had the steers penned up.)	(Those five Mexicans penned up the steers in a moment, and the thirty Americans were left standing in amazement.)

There is a similar scene in what is unquestionably the most famous of all Border ballads, "El Corrido de Gregorio Cortez." Having eluded the forces of *los rinches* (a word derived from the local name for the Texas Rangers, but later generalized to refer to any authority figure viewed as hostile to Mexican-Americans), Cortez taunts the army of pursuers closing in on him with the lines that have become the most celebrated in the corrido canon:

Decía Gregorio Cortez con su pistola en la mano: –No corran, rinches cobardes, con un solo mexicano.–	(Then said Gregorio Cortez, with a pistol in his hand, "Don't run, you cowardly *rinches,* from a single Mexican.")

Based on actual events that took place in Karnes County, Texas, near the Mexican border at the beginning of the twentieth century, the ballad of Gregorio Cortez recounts the story of an innocent man who was falsely accused of being a horse thief and who, in an effort to escape, killed a sheriff. Pursued for ten days by hundreds of Texas lawmen and vigilantes, Cortez was finally captured on June 22, 1901. He was tried and convicted, and he spent eight years in prison before being pardoned. The story of Gregorio Cortez was extensively covered by newspapers on both sides of the border, but it also became the subject of numerous broadsides and folk corridos that combined elements of the classic badman ballad along with the sociopolitical consciousness that has come to characterize the Border corrido.

In his book-length study of the Cortez story and its corrido variants, *With His Pistol in His Hand,* Americo Paredes suggests that Cortez is the personification of the Border folk hero. Although there are examples of both macho badmen and Robin Hood figures in the corridos that originated in the American Southwest, Paredes explains that, like Cortez, the typical hero of the Border ballad is "not the highwayman or the smuggler, but the peaceful man who defends his right."

Naturally, the revolutionary ferment that convulsed Mexico during the second decade of the twentieth century (and whose powerful reverberations were felt across the border) inspired hundreds of corridos celebrating the exploits of such heroic figures as Pancho Villa and Emiliano Zapata. In fact, in his book *Tell Me a Story, Sing Me a Song: A Texas Chronicle*, William Owens even quotes a fragment of an old corrido in honor of Villa's horse, Adelita:

Caballo priento afamado	(The famed dark horse
que Pancho Villa montaba	which Pancho Villa rode
nomas vas un tren de carga	had only to see a freight train
se paraba y relinchaba.	he would rear and neigh.)

CONTEMPORARY CORRIDOS: INTO THE MAINSTREAM

During the 1920s and 1930s, corridos began chronicling the experiences of hardworking laborers coming north to work on farms and orchards in California and the Southwest. Others recounted the more colorful adventures of *tequileros* who smuggled alcohol across the border during Prohibition. It was also during this period that corridos once sung by ranch hands on horseback and by street corner *guitarreros* (or at family gatherings or in the local cantina) began to be commercially recorded. At the same time that so-called race labels such as Vocalion, Okeh, and Bluebird were setting up portable studios in storefronts and hotel rooms to record pioneering blues and hillbilly performers, field units made regular visits to San Antonio and El Paso to record corridos.

Like many early corrido recordings, the 1929 version of "Gregorio Cortez," by the *dueto* of Pedro Rocha and Lupe Martinez, filled both sides of a 78 r.p.m. disc. In this way, a complete, twenty-verse version of the song (the typical length of a corrido) could be recorded using all of the approximately six minutes total playing time available. During the 1940s, the vocal duo with its traditional two-part harmony and unadorned guitar accompaniment (which had been the most prevalent format during the first era of the recorded corrido) was replaced by the accordian-dominated *conjunto* or ensemble. Corridos celebrating the exploits of Mexican-American heroes of World War II—or of quick-witted smugglers—were infused with a contemporary rhythmic energy. Soon corridos would became a major part of the repertoire for the so-called Norteño groups that dominated Mexican-American popular music during the 1930s and 1940s.

After a period of decline, the Chicano Pride movement of the 1960s sparked a revival of interest in the corrido as a vehicle for social protest. Quickly recorded on 45 r.p.m. singles by small independent labels, the corrido became a kind of "electronic broadside." New corridos not only chronicled the struggles of Cesar Chavez and the migrant farm workers but also celebrated non-Hispanic heroes—like Martin Luther King and President John F. Kennedy—who were viewed as sympathetic to La Raza (The People). In fact, there have been at least two dozen different corridos devoted to Kennedy alone collected from this period.

Recently, the corrido has reentered the political arena. Prior to being appointed Secretary of Housing and Urban Development by President Clinton, Henry Cisneros was elected the first Mexican-American mayor of San Antonio, Texas. His campaign song was a corrido composed and performed by Santiago Jimenez, Jr., a Norteño accordianist and singer (whose father had been a pioneer of the style during the 1930s). By contrast, contemporary corridos also have resurrected folk heroes such as the *tequilero* (the Prohibition-era border smuggler)—whose contraband is now drugs rather than tequila. These (mostly) fictionalized, fast-paced epics are a fascinating blend of traditional corridos with imagery drawn from action movies.

Finally, just as elements from African-American badman ballads have morphed into the narratives of gangsta rap, the corrido's gun-wielding anti-heroes have been transposed into the hip-hop sagas of Latino rappers from East L.A. to East Harlem.

THE AMERICAN BALLAD'S SPANISH TINGE

While the corrido contributed its own separate linguistic and cultural chapter to America's story in song, some scholars also have explored the degree to which different ballad traditions may have merged as Anglo-American settlers made their way west.

Gregorio Cortéz, seated center, with his guard

FIGURE 1-6.   Gregorio Cortez (seated center) with members of the posse that had pursued him across southern Texas at the beginning of the twentieth century. Courtesy of Arhoolie Records.

Gregorio Cortez: Folk Hero of La Frontera

Corridos celebrating Gregorio Cortez as a peaceful man simply defending his rights first found their way into the oral tradition during the early 1900s, about the same time that the actual events of his story made their way into the nation's newspapers. The first recording of "El Corrido de Gregorio Cortez" (released by the blues and regional-music label Vocalion in 1929) took up both sides of a 78 r.p.m. disc.

Variants of the song have remained in the repertoire of Mexican-American performers throughout the decades; during the 1970s, Los Pinguinos del Norte (a popular Norteño band) recorded their version of the famous story, and a decade later a major Hollywood film, titled *The Ballad of Gregorio Cortez* (starring Edward James Olmos), made it to the big screen.

The distinguished corrido scholar Professor Americo Paredes has documented Cortez's story (and the corridos it inspired) in the book *With His Pistol in His Hand*. On the next page is an excerpt from one of the numerous variants Parades collected.

The Ballad of Gregorio Cortez

"Gregorio Cortez" is sung a bit more slowly than the average *corrido,* with the basses on the guitar strongly accented.

En el con - da - do de El Car-men mi - ren lo que ha su - ce - di - do,

mu - rió el Che - ri - fe Ma - yor, que - dan - do Ro - mán he - ri - do.

In the country of El Carmen, look what has happened;
the Major Sheriff is dead, leaving Román badly wounded.

En el condado de El Carmen
tal desgracia sucedió,
murió el Cherife Mayor,
no saben quién lo mató.

Se anduvieron informando
como media hora después,
supieron que el malhechor
era Gregorio Cortez.

Ya insortaron a Cortez
por toditito el estado,
que vivo o muerto se aprehenda
porque a varios ha matado.

Decía Gregorio Cortez
con su pistola en la mano:
—No siento haberlo matado,
lo que siento es a mi hermano.—

Decía Gregorio Cortez
con su alma muy encendida:
—No siento haberlo matado,
la defensa es permitida.—

Venían los americanos
más blancos que una amapola,
de miedo que le tenían
a Cortez con su pistola.

Decían los americanos,
decían con timidez:
—Vamos a seguir la huella
que el malhechor es Cortez.—

Soltaron los perros jaunes
pa' que siguieran la huella,
pero alcanzar a Cortez
era seguir a una estrella.

Tiró con rumbo a Gonzales
sin ninguna timidez:
—Síganme, rinches cobardes,
yo soy Gregorio Cortez.—

Se fue de Belmont al rancho,
lo alcanzaron a rodear,
poquitos más de trescientos,
y allí les brincó el corral.

Cuando les brincó el corral,
según lo que aquí se dice,
se agarraron a balazos
y les mató otro cherife.

Decía Gregorio Cortez
con su pistola en la mano:
—No corran, rinches cobardes,
con un solo mexicano.—

In the county of El Carmen
such a tragedy took place:
the Major Sheriff is dead;
no one knows who killed him.

They went around asking
  questions
about half an hour afterward;
they found out that the wrongdoer
had been Gregorio Cortez.

Now they have outlawed Cortez
throughout the whole of the
  state;
let him be taken, dead or alive,
for he has killed several men.

Then said Gregorio Cortez,
with his pistol in his hand,
"I don't regret having killed
  him;
what I regret is my brother's
  death."

Then said Gregorio Cortez,
with his soul aflame,
"I don't regret having killed
  him;
self-defense is permitted."

The Americans were coming;
they were whiter than a poppy
from the fear that they had
of Cortez and his pistol.

Then the Americans said,
and they said it fearfully,
"Come, let us follow the
  trail,
for the wrongdoer is Cortez."

They let loose the blood-
  hounds
so they could follow the trail,
but trying to overtake Cortez
was like following a star.

He struck out for Gonzales,
without showing any fear;
"Follow me, cowardly
  rinches;
I am Gregorio Cortez."

From Belmont he went to the
  ranch,
where they succeeded in
  surrounding him,
quite a few more than three
  hundred,
but he jumped out of the corral.

When he jumped out of their
  corral,
according to what is said here,
they got into a gunfight,
and he killed them another
  sheriff.

Then said Gregorio Cortez,
with his pistol in his hand,
"Don't run, you cowardly
  rinches,
from a single Mexican."

Music and Lyrics from *A Texas-Mexican Cancionero* by Americo Paredes. Courtesy of the University of Illinois Press.

Americo Paredes suggests that it was the dramatic events that took place in the 1830s—Indian raids, civil conflict, and guerrilla warfare against U.S. authority—that provided the inspiration for the earliest Border balladeers. In fact, Parades identifies this period as the beginning of a musical golden age that he has dubbed the "corrido century." Inevitably, as wagon trains filled with Anglo-American settlers moved across the continent, the songs of sodbusters and cowboys must have taken their place among those of the corridista and vaquero. Writing about this encounter in his book *The Latin Tinge* (which explores the impact of Hispanic music on American culture), John Storm Roberts offers the following hypothetical scenario:

> Mexican wagon trains traveling from Chihuahua or moving up the Santa Fe Trail to New Mexico commonly carried corrido singers known as *trovadores*. When two trains met and camped together, the trovadores from each would set up a song contest. Though Mexican and Anglo-American cowards were often at loggerheads, it seems improbable that there was no crossover during the entire period.

Roberts acknowledges that because of the common sources shared by the two ballad traditions (and the lack of sufficient documentary evidence) the exact degree to which the "songs of the Mexican-Americans of the Southwest influenced, or were influenced by, their American counterparts is not clear." It is just such cross-fertilizations, however, that have characterized American folk and popular music throughout our history. In fact, during the 1930s, a merging of the two styles could be heard clearly in the songs of a person who is considered America's greatest balladeer—and perhaps the most influential figure in the history of American folk music—Woody Guthrie.

WOODY GUTHRIE: FATHER OF THE MODERN FOLK BALLAD

In 1940, shortly after his arrival in New York City, Woody Guthrie was recruited to appear at a Depression-era benefit concert (organized by the "John Steinbeck Committee for Agricultural Workers"). Among those sitting in the audience was Alan Lomax. Having traveled the country from the time he was a teenager making field recordings of Mississippi blues singers, Appalachian balladeers, and Texas chain gangs, Lomax thought he had heard it all. But here's how Guthrie's biographer, Joe Klein, describes his reaction to Woody's New York debut:

> Off in the wings, Alan Lomax snapped to attention and felt a surge of adrenaline as he realized—quickly, viscerally, no question about it—that the little man onstage was someone he'd often thought about but feared he'd been born too late to meet: the great American frontier ballad writer.

Later, Lomax would declare Guthrie's performance the start of the "renaissance of American folk song," and he came to regard the scruffy little Oklahoman as "the best folk ballad composer whose identity has ever been known."

Woodrow Wilson Guthrie was born in the small ranching community of Okemah, Oklahoma, in 1912. His early life was shadowed by constant tragedy and, by the time he was sixteen, Guthrie had commenced the footloose rambling that would come to characterize his life. The first stop on this journey was the tiny town of Pampa, Texas. It was here that he learned how to play the guitar from his uncle, Jeff Guthrie, and soon Woody had become a member of Jeff's country and western string band (the Corncob Trio), playing the bar and roadhouse circuit of southern Texas.

It was during this period that Guthrie was probably first exposed to the Border corridos whose influence astute listeners such as John Storm Roberts have recognized in many of the hundreds of ballads Woody wrote and performed over the course of his career. These "Mexicanisms," as Roberts refers to them in *The Latin Tinge,* include the corrido-like guitar accompaniments he often employed, the detail-filled journalistic quality of his true-life ballads (with their highly charged political perspective), and the long swooping vocal ornamentations he often brought to the final phrases of his verses.

FIGURE 1-7. Woody Guthrie documented the life of America in over one thousand songs. While many of his songs expose injustice and dramatize the exploitation of the poor and powerless, he also is the author of "This Land Is Your Land," perhaps our nation's most stirring anthem of populist pride. *Courtesy of Smithsonian/Folkways.*

Woody Guthrie: Dust Bowl Balladeer

Woodrow Wilson Guthrie was born in 1912 in the small railroad junction town of Okemah, Oklahoma. At first the family's fortunes seemed full of promise, but suddenly a series of tragedies hit the Guthrie family. By the time he was sixteen, Woody was on his own. He painted signs and picked fruit and along the way he picked up a few chords on the guitar. It was the early 1930s and the nation was in the grip of the Great Depression. Millions of Americans were unemployed and throughout the Southwest dust storms and bank foreclosures forced thousands of small farmers off their land.

Guthrie joined the army of migrants heading west to what they believed would be a "Garden of Eden" in California. He also become a kind of Hillbilly Homer, recounting in his songs and ballads the epic odyssey of these "Dust Bowl refugees." Woody's genius was that he was able to create songs that not only made complex issues seem simple but also gave courage and hope to people whose lives seemed empty and prospects bleak. Yet, his own assessment of his role was that he was simply "the man that told you something that you already knew."

As for the melodies of his songs, those were also familiar. Describing his method for composing, Guthrie once said: "I mix up old tunes, I wheel and deal them and shuffle them out . . . use half of two tunes, one-third of three tunes and one-tenth of ten tunes." Throughout the 1940s, Woody recorded many of these songs for the Library of Congress Folk Song Archive, but it was during one of the sessions he did for Folkways Records during this period that Woody recorded his most famous song. For many, "This Land Is Your Land" remains our country's *unofficial* national anthem.

In the early 1950s, Woody began suffering the first symptoms of Huntington's disease (which had also prematurely taken his mother's life). He grew progressively weaker until he was virtually paralyzed. Guthrie remained a constant source of inspiration for new generations of singers and songwriters as much for what he stood for as for the songs he had written. Bob Dylan, who made a pilgrimage to visit him in the hospital in 1961, probably best described Woody's profound inspiration: "He was like a link in the chain for me. You could listen to his songs and learn how to live."

Woody died in 1967, but his songs have become indelibly woven into the fabric of America. In addition, his influence can be heard in dozens of contemporary performers. In 1989, when a Woody Guthrie (and Leadbelly) tribute album titled *A Vision Shared* was being assembled, singers and rock groups—including Dylan, Bruce Springsteen, John Mellancamp, U2, and Woody's son Arlo—eagerly lined up to contribute their own versions of his songs.

Many of the latest generation of folk-based performers (including Suzanne Vega, Tracy Chapman, Dan Bern, and Ani Di Franco, among others) also have acknowledged Guthrie's enormous impact and recorded his songs. In 1998, a collection of recently discovered Guthrie lyrics—set to music by new-wave British folkie Billy Bragg—was released on an album titled *Mermaid Avenue* (Woody's last home address before his final hospitalization).

Bound for Glory by Woody Guthrie

Woody Guthrie's voice seems to pour forth from the pages of his autobiography and the reader is immediately drawn into the story of his extraordinary life. In the following excerpt, Woody describes how he began his career as America's preeminent folk balladeer.

Things was starting to stack up in my head and I just felt like I was going out of my wits if I didn't find some way of saying what I was thinking. The world didn't mean any more than a smear to me if I couldn't find ways of putting it down on something. I painted cheap signs and pictures on store windows, warehouses, barns and hotels, hock shops, funeral parlors and blacksmith shops, and I spent the money I made for more tubes of oil colors. "I'll make 'em good an' tough," I said to myself, "so's they'll last a thousand years."

But canvas is too high priced, and so is paint and costly oils, and brushes that you've got to chase a camel or a seal or a Russian red sable forty miles to get.

An uncle of mine taught me to play the guitar and I got to going out a couple of nights a week to the cow ranches around to play for the square dances. I made up new words to old tunes and sung them everywhere I'd go. I had to give my pictures away to get anybody to hang them on their wall, but for singing a song, or a few songs at a country dance, they paid me as high as three dollars a night. A picture—you buy it once, and it bothers you for forty years; but with a song, you sing it out, and it soaks in people's ears and they all jump up and down and sing it with you, and then when you quit singing it, it's gone, and you get a job singing it again. On top of that, you can sing out what you think. You can tell tales of all kinds to put your idea across to the other fellow.

And there on the Texas plains right in the dead center of the dust bowl, with the oil boom over and the wheat blowed out and the hard-working people just stumbling about, bothered with mortgages, debts, bills, sickness, worries of every blowing kind, I seen there was plenty to make up songs about.

Some people liked me, hated me, walked with me, walked over me, jeered me, cheered me, rooted me and hooted me, and before long I was invited in and booted out of every public place of entertainment in that country. But I decided that songs was a music and a language of all tongues.

I never did make up many songs about the cow trails or the moon skipping through the sky, but at first it was funny songs of what all's wrong, and how it turned out good or bad. Then I got a little braver and made up songs telling what I thought was wrong and how to make it right, songs that said what everybody in that country was thinking.

And this has held me ever since.

FIGURE 1-8.   Self-portrait by Woody Guthrie.

A Woody Guthrie Sampler

"Dust Storm Disaster"

During the early 1930s, drought and erosion caused huge dust storms that covered over houses, buried cars, and darkened the sky across much of the Midwest. While photographers (like Arthur Rothstein) working for the Farm Security Administration were documenting these terrifying natural disasters in their black and white images, Woody Guthrie was composing a series of Dust Bowl ballads that recounted these same events with a combination of journalistic detail and poetic imagery.

On the fourteenth day of April
Of nineteen-thirty-five
There struck the worst of dust storms
That ever filled the sky.

You could see that dust storm coming
The cloud looked death-like black
And through our mighty nation
It left a dreadful track.

From Oklahoma City
To the Arizona line
Dakota and Nebraska
To the lazy Rio Grande.

It fell across our city
Like a curtain of black rolled down
We thought it was our judgment
We thought it was our doom.

The radio reported
We listened with alarm
The wild and windy actions
Of this great mysterious storm.

From Albuquerque and Clovis
And old New Mexico
They said it was the blackest
That ever they had saw.

In old Dodge City, Kansas,
The dust had rung their knell,
And a few more comrades sleeping
On top of old Boot Hill.

From Denver, Colorado,
They said it blew so strong,
They thought that they could hold out,
They did not know how long.

Our relatives were huddled
Into their oil-boom shacks,
And the children they were crying
As it whistled through the cracks.

And the family was crowded
Into their little room,
They thought the world had ended
And they thought it was their doom.

The storm took place at sundown.
It lasted through the night.
When we looked out next morning
We saw a terrible sight.

We saw outside our window
Where wheatfields they had grown,
Was now a rippling ocean
Of dust the wind had blown.

It covered up our fences,
It covered up our barns,
It covered up our tractors
In this wild and dusty storm.

We loaded our jalopies
And piled our families in,
We rattled down that highway
To never come back again.

FIGURE 1-9. "Dust Storm, Cimaron County, Oklahoma, 1936" by Arthur Rothstein. Courtesy of the Library of Congress.

"Pretty Boy Floyd"

In "Pretty Boy Floyd," Woody Guthrie takes the tradition of the "outlaw ballad" and makes it his own. The actual Depression-era bank robber was a notorious figure whose exploits were regularly reported in newspapers and on the radio. Guthrie's ballad turns Floyd into a latter-day Robin Hood, who literally steals from the rich and gives to the poor.

1 Come and gather 'round me, children,
A story I will tell
About Pretty Boy Floyd, the outlaw,
Oklahoma knew him well.

2 It was in the town of Shawnee
On a Saturday afternoon,
His wife beside him in the wagon,
As into town they rode.

3 There a deputy sheriff approached him
In a manner rather rude,
Using vulgar words of anger,
And his wife, she overheard.

4 Pretty Boy grabbed a log chain,
The deputy grabbed his gun,
And in the fight that followed
He laid that deputy down.

5 Then he took to the trees and timber
To live a life of shame,
Every crime in Oklahoma
Was added to his name.

6 Yes, he took to the river bottom
Along the river shore,
And Pretty Boy found a welcome
At every farmer's door.

7 The papers said that Pretty Boy
Had robbed a bank each day,
While he was setting in some farmhouse,
Three hundred miles away.

8 There's many a starving farmer
The same old story told,
How the outlaw paid their mortgage
And saved their little home.

9 Others tell you 'bout a stranger
That come to beg a meal,
And underneath his napkin
Left a thousand-dollar bill.

10 It was in Oklahoma City,
It was on a Christmas Day,
There came a whole carload of groceries
With a note to say:

11 "You say that I'm an outlaw,
You say that I'm a thief,
Here's a Christmas dinner
For the families on relief."

12 Yes, as through this world I've rambled
I've seen lots of funny men,
Some will rob you with a six gun,
And some with a fountain pen.

13 But as through your life you'll travel,
Wherever you may roam,
You won't never see no outlaw
Drive a family from their home.

"Plane Wreck at Los Gatos (a.k.a. "Deportees")

Although he is most closely associated with the era of the Great Depression, one of Woody Guthrie's best ballads was written in the late 1940s after he heard the news that a plane crash had taken the lives of a group of migrant workers being flown back to Mexico.

The crops are all in and the peaches are rotting.
The oranges are piled in their creosote dumps.
You're flying 'em back to the Mexican border,
To pay all their money to wade back again.

CHORUS:
Goodbye to my Juan, goodbye Rosalita,
Adios mis amigos, Jesus y María;
You won't have your names when you ride the big airplane,
All they will call you will be deportees.

My father's own father, he waded that river,
They took all the money he made in his life;
My brothers and sisters come working the fruit trees,
And they rode the truck till they took down and died.

Some of us are illegal, and some are not wanted,
Our work contract's out and we have to move on;
Six hundred miles to that Mexican border,
They chase us like outlaws, like rustlers, like thieves.

We died in your hills, we died in your deserts,
We died in your valleys and died on your plains,
We died 'neath your trees and we died in your bushes,
Both sides of the river, we died just the same.

The sky plane caught fire over Los Gatos canyon,
A fireball of lightning, and shook all our hills,
Who are all these friends, all scattered like dry leaves?
The radio says they are just deportees.

Is this the best way we can grow our big orchards?
Is this the best way we can grow our good fruit?
To fall like dry leaves to rot on my topsoil
And be called by no name except deportees?

The Latin tinges in Woody's music were just another layer in a personal style he assembled from all of America's diverse musical traditions. Growing up on the frontier in the early years of the twentieth century, the first songs Woody heard were the Anglo-American folk ballads that his mother sang around the house. In his 1943 autobiography, *Bound for Glory,* Guthrie recalled, "Mama taught us kids to sing the old songs and told us long stories about each ballad." He also picked up songs from Okemah's sizeable black population, most of whom had recently settled there after helping to complete a rail link to the town.

During the course of his long travels, Guthrie continued to absorb influences from blues, work songs, and "hillbilly" music; later he would learn still others directly from that great singing treasury of American folk music, Huddie Ledbetter (better known as Leadbelly), who he befriended in New York City. Woody Guthrie also created his songs according to an age-old folk process. Cutting across centuries and cultures, Guthrie often shaped his lyrics to old melodies, using his own unique turns of phrase and sharp-eyed observations to speak to a country he both celebrated and took to task.

So, while Woody could write "This Land Is Your Land," one of America's most stirring anthems of populist pride, he also created songs that depicted the struggles of Dust Bowl refugees and the hardships of Mexican migrants or that condemned the injustices suffered by the poor and powerless. In fact, there didn't seem to be any political or social issue that Guthrie's songs didn't dramatize, criticize, or poke fun at.

PROTEST AND PROPAGANDA

Throughout our nation's history, songs often have been used to arouse people's passions—whether to topple a tyrant or fight a war, or simply to elect a candidate. During the struggle for independence, colonial soldiers marched to the tune of "Yankee Doodle Dandy," whose verses mocked the British troops. And within days of the event, a song commemorating the Boston Tea Party ("Revolutionary Tea") was being sung up and down the Eastern coast. During the Civil War, former slaves marched into battle against the Confederacy singing freedom songs such as "No More Auction Block for Me," an anthem proclaiming their emancipation. Political campaign songs extolling one candidate (or denigrating his opponent) often were written to fit popular American folk tunes, and, with the approach of World War I, internationalists and isolationists alike often made their case in song.

In the early decades of the twentieth century, songs of protest and propaganda became a hallmark of the labor movement. The first group to use songs in its effort to create "One Big Union" was the Industrial Workers of the World (IWW). Shortly after the turn of the century, the IWW (or "Wobblies") began collecting their lyrics in a book titled *IWW Songs: To Fan the Flames of Discontent,* better known simply as the "Little Red Songbook." For the most part, however, Wobbly songwriters such as Joe Hill simply adapted popular hymns and the sentimental songs of the day to their own revolutionary purposes. It wasn't until the 1930s—when national unions began organizing the Southern textile workers and coal miners—that folk style ballads once again became a weapon for social change.

One of the first battles in the war to organize Southern workers occurred in 1929 at the Loray textile strike in Gastonia, North Carolina. Not only did the fiercely contested strike produce some of the earliest union ballads, but—when the most prolific composer of these songs, Ella May Wiggins, was shot down by vigilantes said to be on the company payroll—the modern protest movement also had its first martyr.

Ella May Wiggins had been singing traditional folk ballads from the time she was a little girl; during the strike, she turned her talent for storytelling in song to the struggle of the local workers. In one of her ballads, she had recounted the murder of a corrupt sheriff ("Chief Aderholt"); another described the sorrows of a working mother whose salary couldn't feed her hungry family ("The Mill Mother's Lament"). Eventually Wiggins's songs made their way into radical publications such as *New Masses,* where they would soon serve as a model for ensuing union campaigns in the coal mines of Kentucky.

It was the extreme violence that marked the strikes in Harlan County, Kentucky, during the early 1930s that earned the area its infamous nickname: Bloody Harlan. But the miners' futile efforts to unionize the mines also produced what is unquestionably the richest body of ballads of protest and propaganda to come out of the American union movement. Certainly the most powerful and enduring of these was created by Florence Reece, the wife of a union organizer. According to legend, it was after her family had been held at gunpoint by company thugs working with Sheriff J. H. Blair (who was looking for her husband) that Reece tore out a page from the calendar that hung on the cabin wall and wrote "Which Side Are You On?"

They say in Harlan County
There are no neutrals there;
You either are a company man
Or a thug for J. H. Blair.

Refrain: Which side are you on, boys?
Which side are you on?

Some of the best Harlan County ballads were produced by members of one extraordinary family. The half-sisters Sarah Ogan Gunning and Molly Jackson and their brother Jim Garland were members of the mining community and early and avid supporters of the union. One of their songs, "The Ballad of Harry Simms" (by Jim Garland), recounted the murder of a charasmatic teenage organizer, while the bitter and heartbreaking "Dreadful Memories" (by Sarah Gunning) described the psychological torment resulting from the deaths of so many of the impoverished miners' children ("Oh, how them little babies suffered!/I saw them starve to death and die").

"Aunt Molly" Jackson not only wrote songs (like "I Am a Union Woman") that were among the most potent anthems of the labor movement, she also documented specific events in the life of her community in hundreds of songs using the traditional ballad form ("Poor Miner's Farewell") or blues-based styles ("Hungry Ragged Blues"). During the 1930s, Aunt Molly went on a singing tour of thirty-eight states to raise money for union strike funds and, after relocating to New York, she became one of the primary inspirations for a new generation of urban "folk singers" being forged by Alan Lomax and Pete Seeger.

HOOTENANNIES AND THE HIT PARADE

Like Alan Lomax, Pete Seeger also was the son of one of the pillars of American folk song scholarship. Charles Seeger, a noted musicologist and professor, had not only published major studies of British ballads and Mexican-American corridos, he had collaborated with Alan and John Lomax on their popular collection, *Folk Song, U.S.A.* And by this time—like his friend Alan—Pete had also dropped out of Harvard; but rather than being content with just collecting songs, Pete took up the banjo in an effort to combine his love of traditional music with his driving need to be directly involved in the turbulent events of his time.

In fact, shortly after Woody Guthrie's debut at the agricultural workers' benefit concert, Pete and Woody left New York on a cross-country excursion during which they performed for unions and various progressive organizations. One of their stops was at a convention of local New Deal political clubs in Seattle, whose organizers had issued metal disks stamped "One Hoot" to serve in lieu of hard currency during the course of the event. So, when the visiting folk singers announced that they would be leading a communal songfest at the convention, someone got the idea to call it a "hootenanny."

When they returned home, the term was quickly adopted by New York City's rapidly expanding folk-music community. Soon Woody Guthrie, Pete Seeger, Leadbelly, Alan Lomax, and Aunt Molly Jackson were trading songs at hootenannies in union halls, auditoriums, and private homes all around town. It was also during this period that Seeger decided to form a folk music ensemble called the Almanac Singers, whose rotating membership included Woody, Leadbelly, Lee Hayes, Josh White, and the popular radio performer and actor Burl Ives. Although initially the Almanacs tended to appeal to a narrow base of union groups and Left-leaning organizations, during the early days of World War II, they achieved considerable mainstream popularity by singing their stirring anti-fascist ballads on major network radio shows.

The hootenanny itself became an established part of the folk scene for decades to come; in fact, during the folk revival in the 1960s, ABC television introduced a short-lived folk music program called "Hootenanny." The show's initial popularity quickly waned, however, when it was boycotted by most of the new generation of folkies including Bob Dylan, Joan Baez, and Peter, Paul, and Mary. The performers were protesting the fact that "Hootenanny" had refused to allow Pete Seeger to appear on the show. For, by the 1950s, Seeger—like many of the Depression-era folk singers who fused traditional ballads with "progressive" ideology—had become a victim of Cold

FIGURE 1-10. The Weavers (from left to right): Lee Hayes, Ronnie Gilbert, Pete Seeger, and Fred Hellerman. Courtesy of Vanguard Records.

The Weavers and the Folk Revival

During the early 1950s, when the Hit Parade was dominated by bland Tin Pan Alley pop songs, the Weavers defied the conventional wisdom by taking traditional folk songs they had first sung at Left-wing hootenannies to the top of the charts. Although they were arranged for maximum commercial appeal by their Decca producer, Gordon Jenkins, the songs themselves—including "Goodnight, Irene" (which they learned from Leadbelly) and Woody Guthrie's "So Long, It's Been Good to Know Ya"—helped inspire the folk revival of the 1960s.

Unfortunately, the political climate of the period (it also was the heyday of anti-Communist witch hunts) brought an abrupt end to the Weavers' career. After attracting the attention of some Congressional committees, the group abruptly lost its recording contract and the steady stream of invitations to appear on radio and television quickly dried up. Although loyal fans had continued to support them, the Weavers finally disbanded in 1963.

War politics. Ironically, Seeger's political demonization came at a time when he was just beginning to take folk music out of the arena of radical politics and onto the Hit Parade.

Following World War II, Pete Seeger formed a new folk quartet (along with Lee Hayes, Fred Hellerman, and Ronnie Gilbert) called the Weavers. After a spectacularly successful debut at New York's Village Vanguard, the Weavers were signed to Decca Records. During the early 1950s, they released a half-dozen top-ten hits, sold out concert halls across the country, and appeared on network radio shows, as well as on the new medium of television. Their repertoire mainly consisted of traditional folk songs from America ("On Top of Old Smokey") and from around the world ("Tzena, Tzena," "Wimoweh"). The Weavers were also the first to introduce a Leadbelly classic ("Good Night Irene") and one selection from Woody Guthrie's enormous folk song catalog ("So Long, It's Been Good to Know Ya") to a mass audience.

Although the group sold over four million records in 1952 alone, when their names began appearing on a number of McCarthy-era "blacklists" the Weavers lost their Decca contract; the invitations to appear on radio and TV dried up, and the group found itself traveling the country singing to a smaller (but even more devoted) audience of folk music fans until their eventual breakup in 1963.

Although they fell victim to the Cold War hysteria of the 1950s, the Weavers had actually jettisoned the overtly political messages that had been the raison d'être of the folk balladeers of the previous decades. In addition, their Decca recordings sacrificed musical "authenticity" (unadorned banjos and guitars) for producer Gordon Jenkins's slick string arrangements and choral background singers. Nevertheless, it was the Weavers who provided many members of the 1960s folk revival with their introduction to American traditional music. And, according to Serge Denisoff, author of *Great Day Coming,* it was the Weavers who "established the economic truth that folk music, after a proper orchestral polishing, was a saleable commodity."

THE FOLK REVIVAL OF THE SIXTIES

THE QUEST FOR AUTHENTICITY

If any one record can be said to have initiated the folk revival of the 1960s, it was surely the Kingston Trio's single "Tom Dooley." Within a few weeks of its 1958 release, the feel-good version of the true story of Tom Dula—who had been the protagonist in one of America's more sordid nineteenth-century murder ballads—was the number one pop hit in America, eventually selling over four million copies. Over the next four years, the Kingston Trio became the hottest pop act in the country and the group's record sales during the period—which totaled over $40 million—surpassed even those of their label's other biggest hitmaker, Frank Sinatra.

Not only did the group's enormous success generate a host of acoustic guitar and banjo-playing folk-trio clones (such as the Limeliters, the Chad Mitchell Trio, and Travelers 3), it did wonders for guitar sales across the country (which were reported to have more than doubled annually in the three-year period following the trio's debut). In the process, the Kingston Trio changed the face of popular music. As a 1961 *Look* magazine article reported, teenagers and college students were "[w]eary of the more and more juvenile level of pop music, frustrated by the dearth of good Broadway show tunes, and slightly befuddled by the growing complexity of jazz." So, propelled by the Kingston Trio, young America seemed—in the quaint words of the magazine—"ready to turn solidly folknik."

Among the millions who simply purchased a copy of "Tom Dooley," and the tens of thousands who went on to buy their own acoustic guitars, there were a few who found themselves powerfully and permanently affected not only by folk music itself but by its values. What folk music symbolized for a generation coming of age amid the Cold War tensions and consumerist fervor of the 1950s can be summed up in one word—authenticity. Inspired by the rousing harmonies of the Kingston Trio's ballads, hardcore "folkniks" began seeking out the more rough-hewn and obscure originals.

The principal touchstone for many of those who took up this quest for modern folk music's authentic sources was a six-record compendium of traditional blues, ballads, string band music, and folk-lyric songs that had been recorded back in the 1920s and 1930s. Issued in 1952 by the small independent Folkways Record company, *The Anthology of American Folk Music* had an incredible impact on the pioneers of the 1960s folk revival. As blues-and-jug-band revivalist, Dave Van Rock put it, "The *Anthology* was our bible. We knew every word of every song on it, including the ones we hated."

With the *Anthology* as a guide, serious young folkies left the commercial folk trios behind to seek out rare 78 r.p.m. recordings in junk shops and secondhand stores. They traveled to small local bluegrass festivals and gradually began to forge a community out of cheaply printed newsletters and folk song journals such as *Sing Out!* The more academically minded record collectors began writing articles about the music's pioneers; in the course of their research, however, they soon discovered that many of the performers who had seemed to them like figures from ancient myths were still alive. Among these living legends was the Tennessee mountain banjo player Clarence Ashley and

FIGURE 1-11. The *Anthology of American Folk Music,* a hugely influential set of recordings first released in 1952, was known as "the folkies' bible." Courtesy of Smithsonian/Folkways Records.

The Folkies' Bible

The *Anthology of American Folk Music* was a carefully assembled compendium of eighty-four blues, ballads, fiddle tunes, gospel songs, and other folk styles issued by Folkways Records. Unlike the commercial labels that had initially marketed these recordings, however, the *Anthology* dispensed with artificial, race-based musical classifications; instead, it was organized into three sets (of two LPs each)—"Ballads," "Social Music," and "Songs"—that highlighted the interweaving of black and white musical traditions.

A CD version of the *Anthology,* issued in 1998—almost a half-century after its original release—has made this rich heritage of American music available for future folk revivals.

the African-American songster Mississippi John Hurt, each of whose 1920s recordings had been collected on the *Anthology*.

While the footloose young folk scholars were out "rediscovering" the heroes of the past, a few of their more musically adept colleagues managed to hone their own guitar or banjo skills sufficiently to perform halting versions of what they had learned in concerts on college campuses and on a coffeehouse circuit that stretched from Berkeley to Boston to New York's Greenwich Village—the Folk Revival Capitol of America.

Under the mentorship of Pete Seeger and Alan Lomax, the new generation of folk revivalists and the newly rediscovered old timers began appearing together at an ever-expanding schedule of folk festivals across the country. Small independent labels such as Elektra and Vanguard joined Folkways in recording their music and—although the folk scene was still very much a homey little enclave existing on the fringes of the vast pop music landscape—it soon had its own version of the Big Time (the Newport Folk Festival), as well as its first stars (Joan Baez and Bob Dylan).

QUEEN OF THE FOLKIES . . . AND THE PRINCE OF PROTEST

In 1959, when Joan Baez appeared at the very first Newport Folk Festival, the eighteen-year-old singer was known only to a few fans who might have heard her perform in one of the clubs or coffeehouses in the Boston area where she was attending college. By the following year, she was one of the festival's headliners; but it wasn't until late 1960—after Baez recorded her self-titled debut album on Vanguard (filled with expressive versions of traditional American folk songs and Child ballads)—that she was heralded as the "Queen of the Folkies." In 1961, when her second LP (entitled, with appropriate austerity, *Joan Baez 2*) became the first album on an independent label to "go gold," the music industry suddenly sat up and took notice, and *Time* magazine put her on its cover.

Although the folk phenomenon had been attracting considerable (if rather bemused) media attention ever since "Tom Dooley," the genre's next dramatic breakthrough into the mainstream offered an even more direct challenge to the pop status quo. In 1962—four years after the Kingston Trio had taken a folk song to the top of the singles charts—another neatly pressed acoustic threesome pulled off the same trick; this time, however, it wasn't with a moldy old ballad, but with a contemporary song that combined folk music with a "message." Peter, Paul, and Mary's full-throated rendition of Pete Seeger's plea for racial equality and social justice—"If I Had a Hammer"—succeeded in forging a vital link between two generations of the folk revival and carried into the present the time-honored tradition of using folk music to address the important social and political issues of the day.

With the release of their follow-up single, "Blowin' in the Wind," Peter, Paul, and Mary not only scored another enormous hit, they provided the folk movement with its new anthem and introduced its new hero. More than anyone else, Bob Dylan became the personification of the Sixties folk revival, and 1963 was Dylan's year. As the song he had written was moving up the pop charts, Dylan was at Newport being hailed as the new "Prince of Protest." When festival headliners such as Joan Baez and Peter, Paul, and Mary performed his songs, they invariably preceded them with reverential introductions ("This song was written by the most important folk artist in America today," announced Peter Yarrow of Peter, Paul, and Mary) as they launched into "Blowin' in the Wind" to the delight of the almost fifty thousand young folkies.

Dylan also performed "Blowin' in the Wind" during his own Newport appearance, and on the evening of the festival's finale, Baez brought out the newly crowned folk prince (and her soon to be lover) for an encore that featured one of his latest and most scathing ballads, "With God on Our Side." The festival closed with Dylan literally and figuratively at center stage: his arms linked with Baez, Peter, Paul, and Mary, the Freedom Singers, and Pete Seeger, as they raised their voices in that secular spiritual of the civil rights movement, "We Shall Overcome." A few days later, Dylan would again sing and hear his songs sung at the historic March on Washington at which Martin Luther King, Jr., delivered his "I Have a Dream" speech.

Although meteoric in its speed and trajectory, the story of Dylan's journey to the Newport stage perfectly ecapsulates the experience shared by many members of the decade's folk revival. As a teenager of the mid-1950s growing up in the small town of Hibbing, Minnesota, Robert Zimmerman (the true identity of the future folk sensation) was caught up in the rock 'n' roll revolution that was sweeping America; he even joined a couple of high school rock bands (showing a special affinity for the music of Little Richard). But by the time he was ready to graduate, the Kingston Trio had kicked off the folk craze. So, within a few months of his arrival at the

FIGURE 1-12.   It was 1960, and nineteen-year-old Joan Baez had just released her first album of traditional American folk songs and Child ballads (including a haunting version of "Barbara Allen"). Soon Baez would appear on the cover of *Time* magazine as the "Queen of the Folkies." Courtesy of Vanguard Records.

Joan Baez: Queen of the Folkies

In addition to preserving the old tales of tender maids and milk-white steeds, Joan Baez also was instrumental in promoting the latest topical songs by a new generation of broadside balladeers. In fact, it was Baez who helped launch the career of the "Prince of the Protest Singers" when she invited Bob Dylan to join her onstage at the Newport Folk Festival. In 1969, Joan Baez infused the spirit of the folk revival into the counterculture by performing at Woodstock. She also has served as a model and inspiration for the next generations of female folk singers, from Janis Ian to Jewel.

University of Minnesota—now billing himself as "Bob Dylan"—he began performing a selection of Kingston Trio hits and old timey blues at local clubs and coffeehouses. Soon, however, he would add a whole new catalog of songs to his repertoire.

It was after a classmate gave him a copy of Woody Guthrie's autobiography, *Bound for Glory*, that Dylan's obsession with the great Dust Bowl balladeer first took hold. As another friend later told Dylan's biographer Anthony Scaduto, "He was just amazed by it. He fell in love with Woody Guthrie right away." He began carrying the book with him everywhere, reading passages to anybody who would listen and learning every Guthrie song he could. Finally, only a year after arriving in Minneapolis, Dylan was packing up and moving on. "Hold on to this stuff for me," he asked a friend. "I'm going to New York to see Woody."

Tragically, by the time Dylan arrived, Woody Guthrie had already been hospitalized for a number of years. He was suffering from the advanced stages of a paralyzing hereditary illness that had taken away his power to write and perform his songs and would, in 1967, finally take his life. But, true to his word, Dylan visited Guthrie and sang him some of his recent songs, including a heartfelt homage to his hero: "Song to Woody." Writing a postcard to his friends in Minnesota, Bob could bearly contain his exhilaration: "I know Woody. I know Woody. . . . I know him and I met him and saw him and sang to him. I know Woody—Goddamn." It was signed simply, "Dylan."

Two decades later, when he was interviewed (in conjunction with the release of the all-star Guthrie tribute album, *A Vision Shared*), Dylan was candid about the extent of Woody's early and enduring inspiration: "There was a time I did nothing but his songs," he admitted. "I mean he's written so many. I was like a Woody Guthrie jukebox. I was completely taken over by him; by his spirit or whatever." Dylan not only composed emotionally charged songs that addressed the dramatic events of his own time but, like Woody, also occasionally set his contemporary songs of social protest to traditional folk tunes or old time hymns. So, just as Woody coopted the Carter Family's version of the outlaw ballad "John Hardy" for his own Depression-era "Ballad of Tom Joad," Dylan adapted the melody of the African-American spiritual "No More Auction Block" for "Blowin' in the Wind."

Having been signed to a Columbia recording contract, Dylan's 1962 debut was made up of stripped-down weather-beaten versions of traditional American folk songs. But a year later when his follow-up album was released, it was comprised entirely of Dylan's original topical ballads. And, like Woody's, Dylan's songs addressed every conceivable topic—from the murder of a Southern civil rights activist ("The Ballad of Medgar Evers") to the tragedy of a boxer who died in the ring ("Who Killed Davey Moore?") to the paranoid hysteria of a Rightwing extremist group ("Talkin' John Birch Society Blues"). It was Dylan's insistence on singing this last song that got him bumped from appearing on what would have been his nationwide TV debut, Ed Sullivan's famous Sunday evening variety show.

One of the best of Dylan's ballads appeared on what would be his final album of predominantly topical material, *The Times They Are a' Changin'*, released in early 1964. A few months earlier, while in Washington to participate in Dr. King's massive civil rights rally, Dylan had read a small article about the trial in Baltimore of a wealthy young white man named William Zanzinger for the cold-blooded murder of Hattie Carroll, a fifty-one-year-old black barmaid. Taking the basic facts directly from the newspaper, Dylan wrote "The Lonesome Death of Hattie Carroll." Studded with poetic images and telling details, the song describes the events surrounding the murder, swiftly sketches the biographies of the two principal characters, and bitterly recounts the outcome: a six-month sentence.

While his songs of social consciousness endeared Dylan to Alan Lomax and Pete Seeger's generation of populist folkniks, and earned him a passionate following among the revivalists of the Sixties, Dylan was on the verge of initiating a stylistic transformation that would send shock waves through the folk community. Although he had returned to Newport in 1964 as the indisputed Prince of Protest, Dylan's concert was entirely made up of bitter and highly personal love songs from his latest (aptly titled) album, *Another Side of Bob Dylan*. As Dylan described his new direction to an interviewer, "There aren't any finger-pointing songs in here. Me, I don't want to write *for* people anymore. You know—be a spokesman. From now on I want to write from inside me."

Dylan's turn from protest to the personal was documented in a cinema verité film made on his final folk tour of England. Its title, *Don't Look Back,* neatly summed up what would remain Dylan's artistic credo for the rest of his career. True to his word, in 1965, he again stunned the Newport audience, this time by appearing with an electric guitar, a band, and a new repertoire of surrealistic rock tunes; according to some backstage observers, Pete Seeger had to be physically restrained from unplugging the electric cables that symbolized Dylan's rejection of folk music's cherished tradition of noncommercial purity.

Periodically, however, when provoked by some passion (or simply when he was inspired by what he saw as a good story), Dylan continued to write new ballads linked to the old tradition. In fact, one of the most potent topical songs of Bob Dylan's career, "Hurricane," a searing ballad about the false arrest and conviction of the middleweight boxer Rubin "Hurricane" Carter, appeared on his 1976 album, *Desire*. The same album also featured Dylan's latest addition to the outlaw ballad tradition: "Joey" was a ten-minute-plus narrative celebrating the life and career of a Brooklyn mobster named Joey Gallo.

WOODY'S CHILDREN . . . AND GRANDCHILDREN

During the early 1960s, when Bob Dylan was first making his way from the folk clubs and coffee house circuit of Greenwich Village into the pages of *Broadside* magazine and onto the stage of Newport, he was only one of a throng of young socially conscious folk singer/songwriters who Pete Seeger had dubbed "Woody's Children." While many of the civil rights and anti-war ballads that emerged from the period were politically naive and/or musically inept, a handful of the so-called protest singers managed to write songs that either transcended their narrow, propagandistic role or fulfilled it with some creative flair.

Among the best of the *Broadside* balladeers was Tom Paxton, who crafted both poignant, personal folk ballads ("Ramblin' Boy") and clever, topical songs ("What Did You Learn in School Today," "Lyndon Johnson Told the Nation"). By contrast, Phil Ochs, a former journalism major, was perhaps the most prolific and politically committed of the folk revival songwriters. A virtual singing newspaper, Ochs may not have been subtle, but he was an effective propagandist whose best songs were either stirring communal anthems ("I Ain't Marching Anymore," "There but for Fortune") or bitter diatribes ("Cops of the World").

Most of the women folk singers of the 1960s—including Joan Baez, Judy Collins, Mary Travers, and Odetta—tended either to perform the classics of the Anglo- (and African-) American folk repertoire or to cover songs by other contemporary folk revival writers. One exception was Buffy St. Marie, a Canadian-born performer of Cree Indian ancestry, who did compose a number of her own powerful songs that she sang in a throbbingly intense vocal style. Some of her compositions addressed issues related to her own culture ("Now That the Buffalo's Gone"), while others addressed the era's broader social themes, including war ("The Universal Soldier") and drugs "Cod'ine").

By the 1980s and 1990s, however, there would be a new generation of folk-based women performers whose original songs offered a unique (often feminist-oriented) perspective on a range of political and social issues. It was a diverse sisterhood that included both the traditionally minded (Tracy Chapman, Nanci Griffith, Lucinda Williams, and Michele Shocked) and the more adventurous (Jill Sobule, Suzanne Vega, and Ani Di Franco).

Meanwhile, Dylan's mid-1960s withdrawal from the ranks of the protest singers ("If you want to send a message, call Western Union," he once cracked) had drained much of the momentum from the movement. Although some political content was carried over into the songs of the so-called folk-rock era (which had been inspired by Dylan's own experiments with electricity), by the end of the decade, folk-oriented performers were embracing more personal themes. While they did accompany themselves on acoustic guitars (or were backed by low-voltage bands), the archetypal singer-songwriters of the 1970s (such as James Taylor, Harry Chapin, Leonard Cohen, and Joni Mitchell) almost completely rejected the political concerns of their folk-revival predecessors. It would take another ten years for the consciousness of the 1960s folk revival to re-emerge in the work of a new generation of performers who used their music to address the social issues of their time.

In 1980, after a media-hyped ascent to pop stardom (that began with his being labeled both the "New Dylan" and the "Future of Rock & Roll"), Bruce Springsteen turned away from the passionate, fuel-injected odes to hometown girls and the open road. As Ronald Reagan was completing a campaign for the presidency of the United States that sought to redefine American populism, Springsteen had just finished reading *Woody Guthrie: A Life*, Joe Klein's recently published biography of the Depression-era balladeer. Soon Springsteen had added Guthrie's "This Land Is Your Land" to his concerts, and he was writing his own socially conscious new songs

FIGURE 1-13.   Bob Dylan, circa 1961. Within a year of his arrival on the Greenwich Village folk scene, the nineteen-year-old Woody Guthrie protégé would be heralded as "The Prince of Protest." Author's collection.

Bob Dylan: Portrait of the Artist as a Young Folkie

As a high school kid in Hibbing, Minnesota, Robert Zimmerman had formed his own rock 'n' roll band, and his greatest musical hero was Little Richard. But, by 1959, when he entered the University of Minnesota, he was swept up in the post–Kingston Trio folk revival. Before long—billed as "Bob Dylan"—he was performing a rapidly expanding repertoire of traditional folk songs in local coffeehouses.

It also was during his brief college career that Bob Dylan discovered Woody Guthrie. According to Dylan, he was actually "taken over by Woody's spirit," but there's also no question that he consciously emulated the Depression-era balladeer's appearance, mannerisms, vocal style, and songwriting techniques. After arriving in New York City (on a quest to meet his hero), Bob began writing his own Guthrie-esque ballads about the social and political issues of the 1960s. Although Dylan would eventually turn on, plug in, and drop out of the folk revival, the mysterious echoes of American folk music have continued to inform Dylan's songs throughout his long and restless career.

Bob Dylan: Broadside Balladeer

On August 28, 1963, Bob Dylan joined a quarter of a million others who had come to the nation's capitol to attend the historic civil rights rally at which Martin Luther King, Jr., delivered his famous "I Have a Dream" speech. Along with Joan Baez (who led the crowd in "We Shall Overcome") and Peter, Paul, and Mary (who sang Dylan's "Blowin' in the Wind"), Bob Dylan performed one of his own recent indictments of Southern racism, "Only a Pawn in Their Game."

It also was during this weekend in Washington that Bob Dylan would come across a brief article in a local newspaper, the headline of which read: "Rich Brute Slays Negro Mother of 10." Drawing from the stark facts of the story, Dylan created one of his most powerful broadside ballads, "The Lonesome Death of Hattie Carroll."

The Lonesome Death of Hattie Carroll

WORDS AND MUSIC BY BOB DYLAN

William Zanzinger killed poor Hattie Carroll
With a cane that he twirled around his diamond ring finger
At a Baltimore hotel society gath'rin'.
And the cops were called in and his weapon took from him
As they rode him in custody down to the station
And booked William Zanzinger for first-degree murder.
But you who philosophize disgrace and criticize all fears,
Take the rag away from your face.
Now ain't the time for your tears.

William Zanzinger, who at twenty-four years
Owns a tobacco farm of six hundred acres
With rich wealthy parents who provide and protect him
And high office relations in the politics of Maryland,
Reacted to his deed with a shrug of his shoulders
And swear words and sneering, and his tongue it was snarling.
In a matter of minutes on bail was out walking.
But you who philosophize disgrace and criticize all fears,
Take the rag away from your face.
Now ain't the time for your tears.

Hattie Carroll was a maid of the kitchen.
She was fifty-one years old and gave birth to ten children
Who carried the dishes and took out the garbage
And never sat once at the head of the table
And didn't even talk to the people at the table
Who just cleaned up all the food from the table
And emptied the ashtrays on a whole other level.
Got killed by a blow, lay slain by a cane
That sailed through the air and came down through the room,
Doomed and determined to destroy all the gentle.
And she never done nothing to William Zanzinger.
But you who philosophize disgrace and criticize all fears,
Take the rag away from your face.
Now ain't the time for your tears.

In the courtroom of honor, the judge pounded his gavel
To show that all's equal and that the courts are on the level
And that the strings in the books ain't pulled and persuaded
And that even the nobles get properly handled
Once that the cops have chased after and caught 'em
And that the ladder of law has no top and no bottom.
Stared at the person who killed for no reason
Who just happened to be feelin' that way without warnin'.
And he spoke through his cloak, most deep and distinguished.
And handed out strongly, for penalty and repentance,
William Zanzinger with a six-month sentence.
Oh, but you who philosophize disgrace and criticize all fears,
Bury the rag deep in your face
For now's the time for your tears.

FIGURE 1-14.   Photo by Christine Alicino. Courtesy Elektra Entertainment.

Tracy Chapman: Talkin' 'bout a Folk-Revival Revival

Like earlier generations of folk-based performers, Tracy Chapman got her start singing on street corners and in coffeehouses. And, like her protest-song predecessors, she has often used her music to address contemporary social issues. Chapman's subjects have included poverty (her Top Ten breakthrough, "Fast Car"), radical politics ("Talkin' 'bout a Revolution"), and environmental genocide ("Rape of Our World"). And, maintaining another modern folk music tradition, she also has made regular appearances at benefit concerts for causes ranging from freedom of speech to the preservation of the rainforest.

documenting the lives of a new generation of the homeless and unemployed. He also began appearing at benefit concerts for political and social causes (including aid for farmers, against nuclear power, and in support of both Vietnam vets and Amnesty International). At his own concerts, he often rallied his fans to engage in social action, and he often donated part of the profit for performances to a local charity or union strike fund.

Although initially Springsteen grafted his Guthrie-esque vision to the exhilarating arena-rock style of which he was a master, in 1982 he gave his band a break and recorded a bleak, acoustic-based album titled *Nebraska*. In 1996, Springsteen delved even more deeply into the ballad tradition with "The Ghost of Tom Joad," which earned the hardcore rocker a Grammy for Best Contemporary Folk Album. The record's title song was a direct homage to Woody Guthrie who, half a century earlier, had written an extended ballad entitled "Tom Joad" based on the story of the main character of John Steinbeck's Depression-era novel, *The Grapes of Wrath*.

In the mid-1980s, Springsteen also joined a score of stars from the world of folk, country, and rock (including Dylan, Willie Nelson, Emmylou Harris, and Woody's son Arlo) on a Woody Guthrie (and Leadbelly) tribute album titled *A Vision Shared*. In an interview conducted at the time, Springsteen acknowledged the profound influence Guthrie had on his own personal and musical philosophy: "For me, Woody was that sense of idealism, along with a sense of realism that said, 'Maybe you can't save the world, but you can change the world.'"

Not only did the Irish band U2 participate in the Guthrie tribute album, but their own records made it clear that they shared his socially conscious vision. Although they had emerged from the nihilistic British punk movement, by 1982 U2 had begun to write songs with overtly political messages. Understandably, the first of these—"Sunday Bloody Sunday"—addressed the tragic conflict in their native country. They then turned their attention to the American civil rights movement by writing the stirring anthem "Pride (in the Name of Love)," dedicated to Martin Luther King, Jr. Over the years, they associated themselves with a variety of social causes and joined an ever-lengthening roster of rock performers at all-star benefits that recalled the idealism of the folk revivals of the 1930s and the 1960s.

While many contemporary pop performers publicly proclaimed their links to the folk tradition, paid homage to the pioneers of storytelling in song, and refocused the broadside ballad's politically charged perspective to address such contemporary issues as war, racism, and poverty, it took considerably more imagination to recognize the ballad's enduring influence when one was confronted with the tabloid-esque tales of gangsta rap. Yet, in these narratives of urban dysfunction with their cast of violent anti-heroes, knowledgeable listeners could hear echoes of the classic badman ballads of a hundred years ago. And as Public Enemy rapper Chuck D famously declared when he was chastised for the graphic imagery of his ghetto chronicles, rap was simply "the CNN of young black America."

Having transcended the constraints of tradition (and absorbed the contributions of America's diverse cultures), the long legacy of the folk ballad is alive and well. And—as we've seen—storytelling in song continues to fulfill a dynamic role even in our media-saturated era of C-SPAN and sound bites. With this in mind, it seems safe to predict that balladeers of the future will still be transposing the events and issues of their own age into musical narratives that entertain and enlighten, inform, and provoke.

Activities/Projects
Chapter 1: The Folk Ballad: Storytelling in Song

1. The phrase "the American Folk Ballad" can be decoded to reveal a great deal about the nature of our nation's tradition of storytelling in song. Create a project that explores both the "Americaness" of our ballads and the meaning of "folk" in the context of America's ballad history.

2. By referring to specific recorded examples, trace the evolution of the folk ballad's performance style over the course of its history in America. Identify the instruments that performers adopted, and describe how changing forms of accompaniment altered the ballad style.

3. Present an overview of the contributions of one of the following ballad scholar/collectors:
   a. Francis James Child
   b. Cecil Sharp and Maude Karpeles
   c. Charles Seeger
   d. John and/or Alan Lomax

4. Research the Anglo-American folk ballad's traditional modal structures and identify examples of these forms in the hillbilly/country recordings made during the 1920s.

5. Throughout the twentieth century, traditional folk tunes have been adapted to accompany new lyrics. Explore this process through specific songs by early country performers such as the Carter Family, as well as in the compositions of Woody Guthrie, Bob Dylan, and other folk/country performers.

6. a. Select a myth, folk tale, or romance and transpose it into a ballad that adheres to the traditional folk ballad structure and conventions.
    b. Select a recent news story and generate a broadside ballad based on the facts of the event. (Optional: Create a chorus expressing a personal opinion or point of view.)

7. Assemble an anthology of folk ballads in order to create a "ballad history of America." Compare the perspective offered in ballads with accounts of the same events provided in formal histories and textbooks.

8. Based on historical and modern accounts of the griot's role in the cultures of West Africa, explore the ways in which this figure can be seen as an influence on both traditional African-American ballads and contemporary rap.

9. Create a cross-cultural study examining black and white versions of the same ballads. Include in your discussion any significant changes in the lyrics (plot or characterization), music (melody, instrumental accompaniment), and performance style.

10. Present an overview of the border corrido that highlights the distinctive musical and lyric qualities of this tradition of storytelling in song.

11. Develop a comparative study of the "hero/anti-hero" in traditional Anglo-American ballads, African-American badman ballads, and Mexican-American border corridos.

12. Explore Alan Lomax's assertion that a significant percentage of traditional American folk ballads served as "vehicles of fantasy, wishes, and norms of behavior [reflecting] . . . the emotional needs of pioneer women in America."

13. Create an anthology of the ballads associated with the Dust Bowl era or the Southern labor movement of the 1930s and 1940s.

14. The turbulent social and political events of the 1960s provided the subjects for a new generation of "broadside balladeers." By citing specific songs by Bob Dylan, Tom Paxton, Buffy St. Marie, Phil Ochs, and others, describe how ballads depicted the important issues of the decade.

15. Survey the influence of the folk ballad on contemporary popular music (including folk-based styles, gangsta rap, and modern tejano performers).

2

In the Beginning . . . There Was the Blues

While we may never know the precise circumstances of its birth, the varied sources of the blues can be identified in such far-flung antecedents as the ancient chronicles of the West African griots, the rhythmic work songs of the chain gang, the tunes and texts of nineteenth-century spirituals, the haunting "hollers" of the cotton fields, and the slow-drag dance music of country string bands. And although this musical and cultural fusion had begun long before, it wasn't until the beginning of the twentieth century that encounters with what would be called "the blues" first begin to be documented.

By the 1920s, the blues had filtered out of the small-town street corners and backwoods juke joints where it began and made its way into the world of traveling tent shows and vaudeville theaters. After being formalized in the sheet music of African-American songwriters beginning with W. C. Handy ("The Father of the Blues"), it was recorded by Southern blues queens such as Ma Rainey ("The Mother of the Blues"). Over time, the blues not only became the foundation of American popular music but one of the pillars of American culture.

The blues served as the raw material for the improvisations of the first New Orleans jazzmen and when blended with other styles it became an essential ingredient of rock 'n' roll. The blues continues to supply the secret soul of country music and it even lurks in the rhymes and rhythms of rap. And having inspired a couple of generations of writers, artists, and composers, the blues remains an essential component of our national character. As one writer put it, "If you want to find out what America is and would like to be, the good and bad of it, listen to the music. Listen to the blues."

THE BIRTH OF THE BLUES

The traveling musicians who gradually molded the varied sources of the blues into its finished form were referred to as "songsters." Accompanying themselves on guitar, banjo, harmonica, or piano, songsters were the human jukebox for rural communities throughout the South from the end of slavery through the early years of the twentieth century. They would travel from town to town, playing their repertoire of ballads, breakdowns, and proto-blues on street corners, in rustic bars, at house parties, and in rural railway stations.

W. C. Handy, a trained musician and bandleader, got his first exposure to the folk sources of the music with which he would make his name (and his fortune) on a historic trip he made to the Mississippi Delta in 1903. As recounted in his autobiography, *The Father of the Blues,* it was while waiting for a train in the tiny town of Tutwiler in the heart of the Mississippi Delta that Handy recalls encountering what he described as the "weirdest music" he'd ever heard.

Handy reports that after awakening from a nap, he listened in amazement to the music of an itinerant musician clothed in rags, who slid a knife blade across the strings of a battered guitar, while singing the words of a song about "Goin' where the Southern cross the Yellow Dog." Using the colorful local slang that would become a part of the poetry of the blues, the singer was simply describing the intersection of the tracks of the "Southern" Railroad and the Yazoo Delta Railroad (known as the "Yellow Dog"), which was located at nearby Moorhead,

FIGURE 2-1.   The chain gang—an infamous symbol of the Southern penitentiary system—has kept alive the African-American work songs that died out elsewhere long ago. The call-and-response structure of these songs has been identified as one of the pillars of the blues. Collection of the Southern Folklife Center. University of North Carolina at Chapel Hill.

The Work Song: From Cotton Fields to the Chain Gang

In work songs, a leader establishes the specific rhythm suitable for a particular task with a forceful "call," while the group of workers "respond" with a short answer timed to coordinate their efforts. In Africa, however—where it flourished as nowhere else—the role of the work song went well beyond this basic organizational function. In the words of one Nigerian proverb, "If the trees are to be cut, you must sing. Without a song, the bush knife is dull."

Since enslaved Africans had been brought to America for only one reason—to work—it's no surprise that they would have maintained their ancient communal songs in their new land. Nor did the eventual elimination of slavery and the breakup of the plantation system bring an end to the work song tradition. During the 1930s, folk music collectors who visited Southern penitentiaries were startled to find dozens of antebellum work songs preserved within their stone walls.

More than a century ago, however, the work song's call-and-response emerged from the field. Now, with a guitar or banjo in hand (instead of a pick or hoe) singers established a rhythmic interplay between their voice and musical instrument that was private re-creation of the group work song structure. In this way, the work song became one of the essential ingredients of the blues.

Mississippi. It would take at least another decade, however, before this experience would reverberate in Handy's popular songwriting—and through him to the rest of America.

Ma Rainey claimed to have had a similar encounter with the blues at about the same time. She described hearing a young girl singing about being abandoned by her man back in 1902. The singer moaned the song with such mournful passion that Rainey found it unforgettable. Not only did she quickly adopt the style for her own performances on the Southern tent show circuit, but later Rainey would even take the credit for giving the music its name.

FIGURE 2-2.   Mississippi John Hurt was one of the last in a long line of performers known as "song-sters." During the second half of the nineteenth century, it was the songster who provided entertainment for rural black communities with a mixed bag of ballads, blues, and dance tunes. Center for Southern Folklife. University of North Carolina at Chapel Hill.

Mississippi John Hurt: Last of the Songsters

Although Hurt lived in the Delta, his gentle vocals and light, fluid guitar playing are a sharp contrast to the rough and intensely rhythmic style typical of the region. When the Race labels came to Mississippi in the late 1920s, Hurt got the opportunity to record his repertoire of traditional ballads such as "Frankie," "Stack O'Lee Blues," and "Spike Driver Blues" (a John Henry variant), as well as his popular double-entendre number, "Candy Man Blues." Thirty years after making these recordings—and fading into obscurity—Mississippi John Hurt was "re-discovered" and for a brief time he became one of the most beloved performers of the 1960s folk revival.

But it is only with the first published blues in 1912—and the earliest recordings of the music a few years later—that we can accurately document the development of this style. While there is evidence that by about 1910 songs had begun to exhibit some of the characteristic elements of the blues, it wasn't until 1912 that the first compositions officially bearing the word were actually issued. And in keeping with the initial looseness of the blues form, only one of the three self-proclaimed blues songs published that year—"Dallas Blues"—actually employed what would become the standard twelve-bar format. Because of its historical significance, the story behind the origin of this song bears retelling.

Hart Ward, who is credited as the composer of "Dallas Blues," was a white musician who had his own small dance orchestra in Oklahoma. It was while Hart was working on a new tune that a black porter who was sweeping nearby began whistling along to the appealing melody. When Ward finished playing, his homesick employee commented, "That gives me the blues to go back to Dallas." Later, when Hart was arranging for the song for publication, he adopted the porter's casual remark for his title, "Dallas Blues."

Ironically, although "Baby Seal's Blues" (by Arthur "Baby" Seals) and "Memphis Blues" (by W. C. Handy)—the other "blues" compositions published that same year—were the work of veteran *black* songwriters, these two songs simply merged blues elements into more conventional popular song forms. Soon however, Handy had not only adopted the traditional twelve-bar, A-A-B blues structure, but he became the key figure in setting off the blues craze that would forever change the course of American music. Yet, in a revealing passage of his autobiography, Handy takes a modest stance regarding his own contributions, while eloquently describing the vital role played by the traditional folk bluesmen who had originated the style:

> [The blues] was already used by Negro roustabouts, honky tonk piano players, wanderers, and others of their underprivileged but undaunted class from Missouri to the Gulf, and had become a common medium through which any such individual might express his personal feelings in a sort of musical soliloquy. My part in their history was to introduce this, the "blues" form, to the general public, as the medium for my own feelings and my own musical ideas.

THE COUNTRY BLUES: A REGIONAL GUIDE

The general name for the traditional blues to which Handy alludes above is the country blues (or folk blues). Although some of the pioneers of the genre were just local heroes, many of them were insatiable wanderers who rambled from town to town. Accompanying themselves on acoustic guitar, banjo, or harmonica, they played on street corners and in small backwoods bars called "jook (or juke) joints," and if they got the people dancing they might make enough in tips to buy themselves a bed and a meal.

For the most part, such men had turned their backs on the dead-end drudgery of sharecropping and on the respectable life of family, church, and community values. They were "bluesmen," with their own slang, style of dress, and nicknames (like Blind Lemon Jefferson, Mississippi John Hurt, Lightnin' Hopkins, Little Hat Jones, Funny Paper Smith, and Sleepy John Estes, to name just a few). While each singer put his own personal stamp on the blues, by the mid-1920s, when the country blues was first recorded, many distinctive regional styles—reflecting local musical traditions, economic and social conditions, and the physical environment itself—can be identified.

Many blues historians believe that it was on the huge cotton plantations that spread out along the rich flood plain of the Mississippi and Yazoo Rivers (an area that had the highest concentration of African-Americans in the South) that the blues originated. Known as the Mississippi Delta Blues, the style that emerged here—intensely percussive and with a narrow melodic range—retained more of an African musical aesthetic than any other blues region. No wonder W. C. Handy was so shocked when he heard it on his visit to the area back at the beginning of the century.

The distinctive, heavily textured vocals of the Delta bluesmen often break into high falsetto slurs that also can be directly traced to the melismatic highly individualized field hollers workers had originally developed during slavery as a form of personal communication. The guitar style of the Delta bluesmen is identifiable by the prevalent use of so-called bottleneck effects created by sliding a glass or metal object across the strings in an attempt to echo the varied timbres of their swooping vocals. The recordings of Charley Patton—who is often

Blues: Feeling and Form

The phrase "the blues" has been used since at least the sixteenth century to refer to a feeling of deep sadness or melancholy. But as a style of music, blues can only be traced back to about the turn of the twentieth century. And despite its linguistic roots, blues is not just a feeling, but a form.

Since the folk blues that emerged at the turn of the twentieth century evolved from various regional sources and combined both European and African traditions, musical analysis of specific tunes can be difficult. The following is simply a representation of the standard musical and lyric elements that make up the blues form.

Lyrics	"I got to keep movin'..."	"can't stay here no more" (A)	(instrumental accompaniment) ("break")	
Musical Structure	1 234	2 234	3 234	4 234
Harmony	I (tonic)	I	I	I (7)
	[—— "call" ——]		[— "response" —]	
	"I got to keep movin'..."	"can't stay here no more" (A)	(instrumental accompaniment ("break")	
	5 234	6 234	7 234	8 234
	IV (7) (subdominant)	IV (7)	I	I
	"Sunset'll find me..."	"Walkin' outa your door" (B)	(instrumental accompaniment)	
	9 234	10 234	11 234	12 234
	V (7) (dominant)	IV	I	I

FIGURE 2-3.

Lyrics

The typical blues stanza is made up of three lines. The first line (A) is repeated, and the third line (B) often provides a response or comment whose final rhyming word completes the verse.

I got to keep movin', can't stay here no more (A)
I got to keep movin', can't stay here no more (A)
Sunset'll find me walkin' outa your door (B)

The Twelve-Bar Structure

A typical blues verse is accompanied by twelve bars of music. Although every line of lyrics is alloted four bars (with approximately four beats to the bar), in reality each fits roughly within the first two bars of music. The remaining two bars are set aside for a short instrumental solo ("break"). In this way the blues conforms to the "call-and-response" pattern that is such a fundamental aspect of all African-based music, including the work song and spiritual.

Harmony

The imposition of a European harmonic structure on what is essentially an African-based musical style makes the blues a cultural hybrid. The basic harmonic structure of the blues is comprised of three chords as outlined below:

A.   The first line (A) is accompanied by the tonic, or first degree of the scale, represented by the roman numeral I.

A.   The second line (A) is primarily accompanied by the subdominant, or fourth degree of the scale, represented by the roman numeral IV. (There is a characteristic transition back to the tonic by the end of the line.)

B.   The third line (B) is accompanied by the dominant, or fifth degree of the scale, represented by the roman numeral V. (Typically, there is also a final transition [resolution] back to the tonic (I) at the conclusion of the stanza.)

Blue Notes

In keeping with African-derived musical principles, bluesmen altered standard European scales by lowering the third, fifth, or seventh note of the major scale one half step. These so-called blue notes contribute to the poignant, slightly dissonant, and suggestive sound that we instantly recognize as the blues.

referred to as the "Founder of the Delta Blues"—were among the first to document the gritty beauty of this profoundly influential style.

A very different style of country blues, however, emerged on the hard-baked farms and small-town sidewalks of East Texas. Reflecting the influence of a wide array of local music (including cowboy ballads, chain gang songs, rural dance music, and guitar rags), the Texas blues is characterized by a rhythmically free strummed guitar style that supplies a subtle accompaniment to the singer's clear high-pitched vocals, while detailed and complex guitar lines are typically created to bridge each lyric section. The music of Blind Lemon Jefferson with its interplay of plaintive vocals and brilliant, tightly arranged guitar responses is the embodiment of the Texas blues. It was the series of enormously popular recordings Jefferson released during the second half of the 1920s that made the Dallas-based performer the first country blues star.

Other important blues artists emerged along the East coast, from the more economically stable tobacco country of the Carolinas (known as the Piedmont area) to the commercial entertainment and recording center of Atlanta, Georgia. In the work of the great Atlanta-based twelve-string guitar player and singer, Blind Willie McTell, for example, one hears a lighter and more supple, harmonically rich strain of the blues that reflects the influence of the ragtime and minstrel shows that were part of the city's cultural environment. McTell's intricate blues guitar and "crying" vocals have a delicate beauty that is a world apart from the both the Texas and Mississippi Delta Styles.

But gradually as they traveled throughout the South from one country dance or juke joint to another, the bluesmen enriched their music with new lyrics and guitar licks. And, by the late 1930s, when Robert Johnson finally got the chance to make his historic records, his music not only embodied the Delta style he had absorbed directly through the oral tradition, but it reflected the influence of the other regional variations he had encountered on hundreds of blues recordings that had been issued during the previous decade. In this way, the regional accents of the blues began to lose their sharp distinctions.

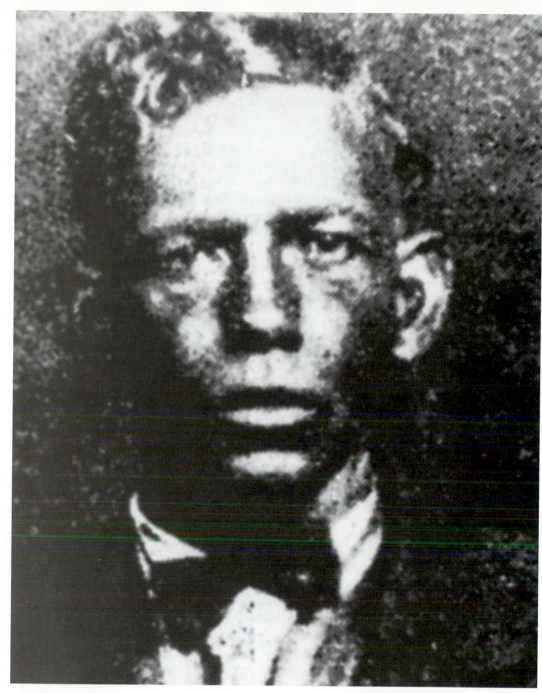

FIGURE 2-4.   This grainy portrait is the only known photograph of Charley Patton. Although he was one of a thriving community of folk musicians and songsters who forged the region's musical identity, Patton is often credited with being the "Founder of the Delta Blues." Center for Southern Folklife. University of North Carolina at Chapel Hill.

Charley Patton: Founder of the Delta Blues

Charley Patton's style is characterized by thickly textured vocals and propulsive, rhythmically flexible guitar accompaniments (often scarred with the abrasive sounds produced by a bottleneck or knife edge). Among Patton's most influential recordings are such erotically charged originals as "Pony Blues" and "A Spoonful of Blues," the poignant "Pea Vine Blues" (named for a local train), and his two-part masterpiece, "High Water Everywhere" (about a devastating Delta flood).

BLUES LYRICS AND THEMES

While the songs the bluesmen created may have reflected the environment and society in which they lived, the blues is primarily a medium of personal expression. And while the subjects of their songs often seemed to focus on hard drinking, hard loving, and hard traveling, country blues also explores a range of themes, including the mysteries of fate, the bitterness of racial prejudice, the world of magic and superstition, and the ever-changing aspects of nature. If ballads are a form of storytelling in song, then the blues is pure poetry, filled with haunting imagery that could be both beautiful and terrifying.

As a form of communication, the blues depends on the performer's ability to fuse a song's lyric content with an emotionally effective vocal delivery and an imaginative (and rhythmically potent) instrumental accompaniment into an artistically satisfying unity. It is only through the subtle interplay of each of these separate elements that the alchemy of the blues can be effected. On their own, however, the lyrics of blues songs often achieve the status of true folk poetry. Not only do they tell the story of black life in America in sharply etched vignettes, but the lyrics of the blues reveal in painful detail the most intimate of human relationships.

Although the blues often reflects an essentially tragic point of view, rarely does it become mired in pessimism or self-pity. In fact, it was the primary function of the blues performer to provide a kind of existential catharsis that transmutes pain into a life-affirming statement. In doing so, the blues can be seen not only as a vehicle for personal self-expression but as a medium for cultural survival.

The Western tradition of sung or chanted poetry can be traced back to ancient Greece, where concise expressions of personal experiences were set to the music of the lyre (a small stringed harp). On one level, therefore, blues can be viewed as a modern form of lyric poetry—even to the point of restoring the musical component that had been abandoned over time. And, as with most lyric poetry, a dominant theme of the blues is romantic love.

The social and economic pressures to which African-Americans were subjected took a devastating toll on personal relationships. For blues singers who were often alienated not only from the dominant society but (because of their peculiar lifestyle) from their own community as well, romantic ties were often tenuous at best. So even when blues songs do express genuine emotional commitment, love seems ultimately doomed (they don't call them "the blues" for nothing!).

In response to the physical constraints imposed on blacks during slavery, the freedom to travel freely—when it was finally realized—took on great symbolic significance. Countless blues songs celebrate the freedom of the road in all its forms; they pay homage to specific highways, train lines, and even the ubiquitous Greyhound buses that criss-crossed its dusty roads. And when the blues itself moved to the big cities of the North, lyrics clearly reflected the dramatic changes in the singer's environment and status.

Blues songs not only reflect the legacy of slavery (or depict responses to its demise); in some cases, they actually document intriguing retentions of African culture that had survived every attempt to eradicate them. Perhaps the most fascinating of these is the adaptation of West African spiritual beliefs and religious practice that became known as "hoodoo."

Blues lyrics are studded with allusions to hoodoo. Throughout the blues canon, specific references can be found to animal spirits, conjurers, gypsy women, or root doctors (who had the knowledge of such powerful charms as "High John the Conqueror root," "black cat's bones," "hot-foot powder," or "mojo hands"). There are even allusions to African deities such as Legba, a Yoruba god associated with the crossroad between the physical and spiritual planes of existence (a figure who gradually became intertwined with aspects of the devil that had been adopted from the Christian tradition).

It is in its treatment of sexual themes, however, that the blues has had the most profound influence on virtually every genre of popular song from Tin Pan Alley pop to rock and rap. Blues songs confronted every aspect of human sexuality with a frankness new to American music. Blues songs might approach the subject overtly or metaphorically; they are by turns raunchy or seductive, direct or insinuating, clever or titillating; but invariably—whether sung by men or women to audiences of blacks or whites—they were wildly popular.

FIGURE 2-5.   This advertisement for Blind Lemon Jefferson's "Matchbox Blues" was typical of those that "Race" labels placed in African-American newspapers during the 1920s. The song itself went to become the basis of a 1950s rockabilly hit for Carl Perkins ("Matchbox"), and was covered by the Beatles a decade later. Author's collection.

Blind Lemon Jefferson: First Star of the Country Blues

Blind Lemon Jefferson's rhythmically supple single-string arpeggios became the basis of a distinctive Texas guitar style that later would be taken up by other local bluesmen including Lightnin' Hopkins. Brought into the electric era by T-Bone Walker (who as a child had actually known Blind Lemon), the style would later be infused with a rock sensibility by Lone Star native Stevie Ray Vaughn.

Among Blind Lemon's eighty-odd recordings one can find both sly, double-entendre songs such as "Black Snake Moan" and "Oil Well Blues," as well as the deeply moving hymn, "See That My Grave Is Kept Clean" (which Bob Dylan recorded on his first album). In 1930, after one of his periodic Paramount recording sessions, Blind Lemon Jefferson walked out into a bitter Chicago snowstorm. The next day he was found frozen to death on a street corner, his guitar at his side.

The Geography of the Blues

At the beginning of the twentieth century, when it was still taking shape within the African-American folk culture, the blues embodied local musical traditions and reflected the social and economic conditions of its surroundings. During this formative period, bluesmen provided entertainment for isolated rural audiences and their music was marked by clearly defined regional styles.

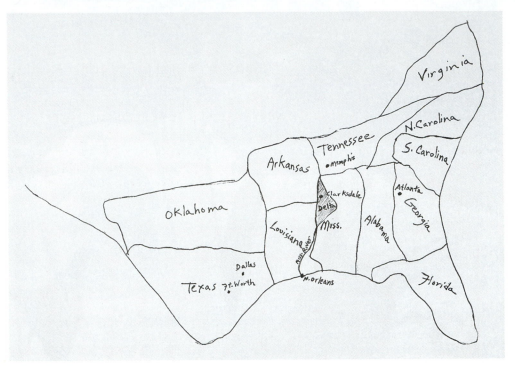

FIGURE 2-6.

I. Mississippi Delta Blues

Often cited as the birthplace of the blues, the "Delta" refers to the fertile flood plain created by the Mississippi and Yazoo Rivers, an area that stretches south from Memphis, Tennessee, to Vicksburg, Mississippi. This was a land of enormous cotton plantations and—at the turn of the twentieth century—an area with the highest concentration of African-Americans in the country. It was where W. C. Handy first encountered what he called the "weirdest music" he ever heard. The Delta was also home of both the notorious penitentiary known as "Parchman Farm" and the lonely crossroad where Robert Johnson is alleged to have made his deal with the devil.

CHARACTERISTICS

Rough, growling vocals are often set off by highly embellished falsetto slurs that had their origin in the melismatic hollers of the fieldworkers. Although the melodic range of the Delta blues is relatively narrow, a wide spectrum of vocal timbres adds to its emotional impact.

Guitar accompaniments are linked closely to the singer's vocals, creating a doubling effect. Strings of the guitar were typically "choked" or "bent," and often a glass or metal "bottleneck" was slid across the strings in an eerie imitation of the sound of the human voice.

SELECTED PERFORMERS

Charlie Patton, Son House, Bukka White, Skip James, Mississippi John Hurt, Tony Johnson, Furry Lewis, Robert Johnson.

II. Texas Blues

The harsh, sparsely populated expanses of East Texas were dotted by small farms occupied by black share-croppers. Sugarcane fields stretched along the Brazos River, and Galveston's red-light district provided work for guitarists and barrelhouse blues pianists. In cities such as San Antonio and Dallas (where Blind Lemon Jefferson could be found signing on street corners and in the local bars), permanent field recording centers had been established during the mid-1920s.

CHARACTERISTICS

Versatile early performers (known as "songsters") created blues that drew from cowboy folk ballads, guitar rags, and country dance music, as well as from the rhythmic work songs of the chain gang. Often set off by high-pitched, wordless embellishments, Texas blues vocals were typically less harsh than those in the Delta style, and guitar accompaniments tended to function more independently of the vocals than in the Delta style.

The guitar style of the Texas blues is characterized by a rhythmic freedom; relaxed strummed accompaniments are combined with rapid, intricate single-string runs that fill the space between vocal statements. Although bottleneck or slide techniques are sometimes employed, they are not typical of most Texas guitarists.

SELECTED PERFORMERS

Blind Lemon Jefferson, Henry Thomas (Ragtime Henry), Little Hat Jones, Blind Willie Johnson, Texas Alexander, Leadbelly, Lightnin' Hopkins.

III. The Piedmont Blues

Stretching from Richmond, Virginia, down through North and South Carolina to Atlanta, Georgia, this region's diverse agriculture included rich tobacco farms that offered greater economic opportunities for its African-American inhabitants. The area was also more racially integrated and less culturally isolated (and repressive) than either the Delta or East Texas.

CHARACTERISTICS

The lighter, more flowing blues style of the area was influenced by black and white music from both commercial and folk sources. Atlanta-based performers devised a hybrid style that reflected the city's importance as a center for a wide range of popular entertainment. Atlanta was also an important blues (and hillbilly) recording center.

The guitar style that developed here was a refinement of the Delta bottleneck style. Less percussive and more elegant, the playing of performers like Blind Willie McTell (a twelve-string guitar master) maintained a complex yet relaxed interaction between vocals and instrumental responses.

PERFORMERS

Blind Boy Fuller, Rev. Gary Davis, Peg Leg Howell, Blind Willie McTell, Barbecue Bob.

IV. Memphis Blues

The city was the vital economic center for all of cotton country. With its river and rail links and wide open entertainment and recording activity, it was a lure for blues performers of all kinds. Legendary Beale Street was lined with cabarets, gambling joints, barrelhouse bars, and houses of prostitution, providing employment for a wide range of blues and jazz performers.

CHARACTERISTICS

The professional home of W. C. Handy (who led a famous brass band there), he also wrote two of his most famous songs about the city—"Memphis Blues" and "Beale Street Blues"—Memphis was also the center for a unique blues-based musical ensemble, the jug band.

Jug bands were comprised of guitars, banjos, harmonicas, and a range of homemade instruments (such as the kazoo and "washboard" bass), as well as the metal, glass, or ceramic jugs that provided the ensembles with their name. Jug bands played a mix of lively, improvised good-time music that was an important part of the Memphis scene during the 1920s and 1930s.

PERFORMERS

W. C. Handy, Memphis Jug Band, Gus Cannon Jug Stompers.

Most often, blues singers have discussed sexual themes through a technique known as the "double entendre," a French term that translates literally as "two meanings." By using this device, bluesmen (and blueswomen) created lyrics whose innocent-sounding surface disguised the song's distinctly sexual subtext. In country blues, which is grounded in the rural environment, sexual metaphors were often drawn from the animal world, but almost anything could be adapted for this suggestive purpose. And, in performance, singers could direct the audience's attention to their underlying intent with their facial expressions and body language, as well as through their insinuating vocal delivery. Be aware that in the world of the blues, "coffee grinders," "horseback riders," "deep sea divers," and "black snakes" may not always be what they seem.

The persona of the blues singer typically established in their songs is one of unbridled potency: the performer's exaggerated bragadoccio regarding his (or her) power—physical, supernatural, and especially sexual—had its origin in both the tradition of the American "tall tale" and the African-derived convention of self-praise known as "signifying." Set against the history of slavery, such declarations of empowerment are especially significant. But in the 1930s, when bluesman Peetie Wheatstraw billed himself as the "Devil's son-in-law and the High Sheriff from Hell," he not only reflected age-old folk traditions but established an image that would eventually find its way into R & B, rock, heavy metal, and rap.

Finally, although blues often has been referred to as "the devil's music"—for reasons that should be obvious from the discussion above—the blues also has been used as a vehicle for religious expression. Performers of "sacred blues" such as Blind Willie Johnson and Rev. Gary Davis adapted the themes of African-American spirituals to the blues form and saw themselves as singing ministers. Even Charley Patton, one of the most notorious bluesmen, occasionally sang religious blues under a pseudonym. Other blues singers continually struggled between the sacred and the profane. Some, such as bluesman Georgia Tom—who, after reverting to his given name, Thomas A. Dorsey, became the Father of Gospel Music—"crossed over" from one to the other often during the course of their careers.

FIGURE 2-7.   Blind Willie McTell infused the delicate nuances of the classic Piedmont blues into his own virtuosic guitar style. And, as Bob Dylan put it—in a song honoring the Atlanta-based performer—"no one can sing the blues like Blind Willie McTell." Archive photo. Frank Driggs Collection.

No One Can Sing the Blues Like Blind Willie McTell

When he arrived in Atlanta in the 1920s, the city was home to a lively music scene and the center of a distinctive twelve-string blues guitar tradition. Soon Blind Willie McTell was a significant contributor to both. His clear, high-pitched vocals and unique guitar style (blending intricate finger picking and fluid slide effects) brought the East Coast Piedmont tradition to its highest level of artistry.

Although he was an insatiable wanderer (despite his blindness), McTell's most famous song, "Statesboro Blues" (which became the basis of a blistering Allman Brothers cover version in the 1970s), is named for his beloved hometown.

53

FIGURE 2-8.   During the late 1920s, Jimmie Rodgers was the undisputed king of hillbilly music; but many of his biggest hits were recordings of original blues. One early reviewer even described Rodgers as "a white man gone black." Center for Southern Folklife. University of North Carolina at Chapel Hill.

Who Owns the Blues? Or Can a White Man Be a Bluesman?

Back in the 1920s, when America's folk music was first finding its way onto commercial recordings, blues was part of the repertoire of both black and white performers. In fact, one of the era's most adept bluesmen was a banjo player and singer named Frank Hutchinson who, despite his deep roots in the Anglo-American community of the West Virginia mountains, recorded craggy, hard-edged versions of "Cannon Ball Blues," "Worried Blues," and "K. C. Blues," to name just a few.

It shouldn't be a complete surprise, therefore, that when Jimmie Rodgers began to record, he achieved his initial fame largely on the strength of a series of songs he called "Blue Yodels," which grafted his unique falsetto vocal breaks onto about a dozen songs using the standard twelve-bar blues form. The first of these was a million-selling smash hit, best known as "T for Texas," recorded in 1927:

T for Texas, T for Tenn-e-sseeee . . .
T for Texas, T for Tenn-e-sseeee . . .
T for Thelma, that gal that made a wreck out of me.

On the basis of Rodgers's enormous influence, blues inflections and the blues form itself would become crucial elements in the sound of country music. By the 1960s, however, when scores of young white blues revivalists (such as Bob Dylan, Bonnie Raitt, and John Hammond) began appearing at folk festivals performing earnest recreations of Mississippi Delta classics and obscure jug band tunes, rights to the blues tradition had begun to emerge as yet another hot-button issue of this highly politicized decade. Since then, the question of who owns the blues (or more provocatively, "Can a white man be a bluesman?") has continued to be debated in blues journals and the mainstream media.

The Blues as Literature

Beginning in the 1920s, writers and intellectuals were already debating the literary significance of the blues. While most instantly rejected the idea that blues lyrics could have any intrinsic value, a few scholars like Howard W. Odum and Guy B. Johnson (who included a chapter on the genre in their 1926 book *Negro Workaday Songs*) did acknowledge their "quaint naiveté." About the same time, Harlem Renaissance writers such as Langston Hughes found in the folk poetry of the blues a source of inspiration for their own more ambitious works.

Unlike other twentieth-century literature, however, blues lyrics were created through a long oral tradition; its striking images can be traced back to spirituals, sermons, popular sayings, and old folk ballads. The best of these then coalesced into "floating or "wandering" verses, which became part of an enormous communal repository from which each blues musician could draw.

As Robert Palmer explains (in his book *Deep Blues*): "From a lyrical point of view, the art of 'writing' blues songs consists of combining phrases, lines and verses with compatible emotional resonances into associational clusters that reflect the singer's own experiences, feelings, and moods and those of his [or her] listeners. And more often than not, the result is truly original."

A BLUES SAMPLER

Now I met the blues this mornin' walkin' just like a man,
Now I met the blues this mornin' walkin' just like a man,
I said good mornin' blues, now give me your right hand.
(Edward "Son" House)

The big star fallin', mama, ain't long 'fore day,
The big star fallin', mama, ain't long 'fore day,
Need a little sunshine to drive the blues away.
(Blind Willie McTell)

Standin' at the crossroad, I tried to flag a ride,
Standin' at the crossroad, I tried to flag a ride,
Nobody seem to know me, everybody pass' me by.
(Robert Johnson)

You mistreated me, and drove me away from your door,
You mistreated me, and drove me away from your door,
But the Good Book says, "You gonna reap just what you sow."
(Alberta Hunter)

Judge gimme life this mornin' down on Parchman Farm,
Judge gimme life this mornin' down on Parchman Farm,
I wouldn't hate it so bad, but I left my wife and home.
(Bukka White)

While you're livin' in your mansion, you don't know what hard times mean,
While you're livin' in your mansion, you don't know what hard times mean,
Poor man's wife is starvin', your wife is livin' like a queen.
(Bessie Smith)

I believe I'll buy a graveyard of my own,
I believe I'll buy a graveyard of my own,
I'm gonna kill everybody that has done me wrong.
(Furry Lewis)

Layin' in bed this mornin' with my face turned to the wall,
Layin' in bed this mornin' with my face turned to the wall,
Tryin' to count these blues so I can sing them all.
(Gertrude "Ma" Rainey)

What blues performers and singers of religious music have always shared is a commitment to the expression of deep feelings through song. For this reason, the crossover phenomenon that originated in the blues era has been replicated time and again in every genre of pop music. It has touched the careers of performers from Little Richard to Whitney Houston and from Sam Cooke to Al Green. In fact, the secularization of religious music and the spiritualizing of profane music have consistently been one of the dominant energizing forces in American music throughout our history.

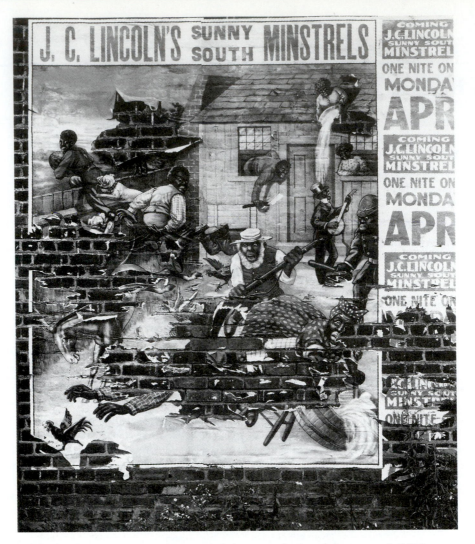

FIGURE 2-9.   Walker Evans photographed this tattered minstrel show poster in 1936. Although the minstrel show's demeaning stereotypes were difficult to dispel, some of the first black entertainers to overcome them were turn-of-the-century blues queens like Ma Rainey and Bessie Smith. Photo by Walker Evans. Courtesy of the Library of Congress.

The Minstrel Show: Blackface and the Blues

At the beginning of their careers, both Ma Rainey and Bessie Smith were featured performers in a Southern touring troupe known as the Rabbit Foot Minstrels. At the time it was just one of a score of all-black variety shows bringing dancers, musicians, comedians, and blues singers to towns both big and small.

In the mid-1800s, however, when minstrelsy first made its appearance in America, the only black faces one would have seen onstage were those of white entertainers who darkened their skin (with burnt cork and other "blackface" makeup) in order to amuse audiences with caricatures of African-American music, movement, and manners. For the next fifty years, the minstrel show reigned unchallenged as America's most popular form of entertainment.

At the end of the Civil War, talented African-Americans were suddenly presented with new opportunities to take their place on the stage. But while they may have been freed from bondage, the era's black performers weren't liberated from the symbolic chains imposed by the stereotypes of minstrelsy. At the beginning of the new century, however, blues divas such as Ma Rainey and Bessie Smith—who confidently strode the footlights dressed in beaded gowns and ostrich-feather headdresses—shattered the old stereotypes and provided their audience with its first positive public presentation of African-American culture.

THE CLASSIC BLUES:
WOMEN IN THE SPOTLIGHT

Although the blues may have been born on small-town street corners and in Delta juke joints, it made its first forays into the larger world of American popular music through the performances of the blues queens who starred in the traveling tent shows and minstrel shows that provided entertainment for rural black audience throughout the South.

Meanwhile, urban audiences could hear the blues performed from the stages of African-American vaudeville theaters. Some of the most famous of these formed a circuit that provided venues—from Dallas to New York—for black traveling shows. Although it was officially known as the Theater Owners Booking Association (and informally dubbed the "Tobi circuit"), the TOBA's itinerary was so grueling and the bus seats on which performers traveled so hard that they soon revised the meaning of the initials to "Tough on Black Asses."

Such shows usually consisted of comedians, musicians, and a chorus of long-legged dancers, but the highlight of every evening were the women who sang a style of blues that has come to be known as the *classic blues*. Dressed in beaded gowns, ostrich feathers, and rhinestone tiaras, performers such as Ma Rainey (often referred to as the "Mother of the Blues") and Bessie Smith (known as the "Empress of the Blues") were the embodiment of glamour and elegance.

No beat-up acoustic guitars or shrill harmonicas for these blues divas. The classic blues singers fronted full-sized bands comprised of the best musicians from New Orleans to New York. Clarinets wailed; trumpets, cornets, and trombones blared; piano and banjo pumped out rhythmic chords—and cutting through it all the majestic sound of women whose voices could reach the back of the audience at a time before the advent of electric microphones.

With the publication (in 1914) of W. C. Handy's "St. Louis Blues," a blues craze swept across the country. Over the next few years, dozens of songwriters—black and white—jumped on the blues bandwagon. In doing so, they bent the varied forms and uniquely personal styles of country bluesmen and classic blueswomen to the more rigid requirements of the New York music publishers of what was known colloquially as Tin Pan Alley.

Soon hundreds of hundreds of songs using the word "blues" (although not necessarily the blues form) were copyrighted by the New York publishing companies. With titles such as "Yankee Doodle Blues" and "Where Has My Hubby Gone? Blues" we can get an idea of just how far the blues had become absorbed into the mainstream of American entertainment. These "commercial blues songs" were absorbed into the repertoire of white female performers, and soon they could be heard in downtown vaudeville houses, theatrical revues, beer gardens, and, finally, on the (relatively) new medium of recordings. Meanwhile, authentic classic blues continued within the folk tradition and the segregated world of black popular entertainment.

It wasn't until August 10, 1920, that a vocal blues performed by an African-American singer was recorded. On that date, Mamie Smith, backed by a small jazz-style ensemble, recorded the song "Crazy Blues." Within the first month of its release by the Okeh Record Company, the song sold an astonishing 75,000 copies (at the not-insignificant price of $1.00). By the end of the year, it had sold over 200,000 copies!

Mamie Smith's "Crazy Blues" prompted thousands of African-Americans to buy their first phonograph (now that they had something to play on it), and its success encouraged other companies to begin recording more blues by African-American performers (now that they saw there was a market and profits to be made). This one song set off an avalanche of blues recordings specifically marketed to the black consumer (often through mail order ads in African-American newspapers). By the end of the 1920s, over two hundred black women singers had recorded the blues.

In addition to introducing songs written by the new breed of black professional songwriters such as W. C. Handy and Perry Bradford (composer of "Crazy Blues"), performers like Ma Rainey, Bessie Smith, and Alberta Hunter were recording their own songs. Like most blues songs, their lyrics focused on the heartbreak of love, but these women also documented the floods and other natural disasters of the era and generally bemoaned the troubles they'd seen. Often their songs were specifically addressed to the female members of their audience. And while

FIGURE 2-10. Author's collection.

Mamie Smith: First Woman of Blues Recording

On August 10, 1920, when Mamie Smith sang "Crazy Blues" in the New York studio of Okeh Records, she became the first African-American performer to record the blues. Ironically, Smith wasn't even supposed to have been there that day; but when a white vaudeville singer named Sophie Tucker (who had been scheduled to do the tune) backed out because of illness, Perry Bradford, the song's (black) composer arranged for Smith to step in. And the rest, as they say, is history.

they reveal enormous empathy for the plight of black women, just as often they offer images of empowerment. It was a message that was enhanced by the singer's own lifestyle, which was a potent blend of racial pride, glamour, and sexual independence.

RACE RECORDS

In 1920—when Perry Bradford finally cajoled Okeh's recording director, Ralph Peer, into approving the "Crazy Blues" session—the Okeh label was a relative newcomer to the rapidly expanding New York recording industry. The success of Mamie Smith's record, however, quickly catapulted the company into the forefront of a new musi-

Ma Rainey: The Mother of the Blues

FIGURE 2-11. Ma Rainey and her Georgia Jazz Hounds, c. 1923. As a young girl at the turn of the century, Gertrude Rainey began singing the blues in Southern minstrel shows. Rainey's pioneering status is reflected in her (self-proclaimed) title, "The Mother of the Blues." Archive photo. Frank Driggs Collection.

cal style directed at an enormous and previously untapped market. Soon Okeh had recruited a roster of young black women singers, including Sippie Wallace, Victoria Spivey, and Sara Martin, to record the classic blues.

In order to market Okeh's new series of blues recordings, Peer started a separate catalog, which he called the "Race" series, and Okeh began promoting its groundbreaking black classic blues records with the slogan, "The World's Greatest Race Artists on the World's Greatest Race Records." Soon the other labels that had joined Okeh in recording black performers also adopted the term for their own blues catalogs, and "Race records" became an established part of the industry.

Okeh's main rival was Chicago's Paramount label (a company totally unrelated to the famed movie studio of the same name). Founded in 1917, Paramount's first releases had been recordings of mainstream popular songs and dance music, but in 1921 it inaugurated its own "Race" catalog aimed at the enormous potential market in Chicago's black ghettos. Soon Paramount's pressing plant was turning out over 100,000 records a month and, by the mid-1920s, Okeh, Paramount, Columbia, Vocalion, Gennett, and Victor (and other Race labels) were producing—and selling—millions of recordings to a seemingly insatiable audience of blues fans.

In 1924, another new label entered the crowded blues record industry. With its very first advertisement, however, Black Swan proudly proclaimed its unique status. "The Only bonafide Racial company making talking machine records. All stockholders are colored, all artists are colored, all employees are colored," read one early ad.

Indeed, Black Swan was the first recording company owned by an African-American. Founded by Harry Pace, a successful songwriter and music publisher (who had been a partner of W. C. Handy in an earlier business venture), the company was named for the black opera star Elizabeth Taylor Greenfield, who was known as the

MA RAINEY (STERLING A. BROWN)

As a young instructor at Fiske University, the African-American poet Sterling Brown had the opportunity to see Ma Rainey perform. "Ma Rainey was a tremendous figure," he recalled years later. "She wouldn't have to sing any words; she would moan and the audience would moan with her. . . . Ma really *knew* these people; she was a person of the folk." It was just this close bond that Brown attempted to capture in his poem, "Ma Rainey."

I

1 When Ma Rainey
    Comes to town,
    Folks from anyplace
    Miles aroun',
5 From Cape Girardeau,

    Poplar Bluff,
    Flocks in to hear
    Ma do her stuff;
    Comes flivverin' in,
10 Or ridin' mules,
    Or packed in trains,
    Picknickin' fools. . . .
    That's what it's like,
    Fo' miles on down,
15 To New Orleans delta
    An' Mobile town,
    When Ma hits
    Anywheres aroun'.

II

    Dey comes to hear Ma Rainey from de little river settlements,
20 From blackbottom cornrows and from lumber camps;
    Dey stumble in de hall, jes a-laughin' an' a-cacklin',
    Cheerin' lak roarin' water, lak wind in river swamps.

    An' some jokers keeps deir laughs a-goin' in de crowded aisles,
    An' some folks sits dere waitin' wid deir aches an' miseries,
25 Till Ma comes out before dem, a-smilin' gold-toofed smiles
    An' Long Boy ripples minors on de black an' yellow keys.

III

    O Ma Rainey,
    Sing yo' song;
    Now you's back
30 Whah you belong,
    Git way inside us,
    Keep us strong. . . .
    O Ma Rainey,
    Li'l an' low;
35 Sing us 'bout de hard luck
    Roun' our do';
    Sing us 'bout de lonesome road
    We mus' go. . . .

IV

    I talked to a fellow, an' the fellow say,
40 "She jes' catch hold of us, somekindaway.
    She sang Backwater Blues one day:

      'It rained fo' days an' de skies was dark as night,
      Trouble taken place in de lowlands at night.

      'Thundered an' lightened an' the storm begin to roll
45   *Thousan's of people ain't got no place to go.*

      'Den I went an' stood upon some high ol' lonesome hill,
      An' looked down on the place where I used to live.'

    An' den de folks, dey natchally bowed dey heads an' cried,
    Bowed dey heavy heads, shet dey moufs up tight an' cried,
50 An' Ma lef' de stage, an' followed some de folks outside."

    Dere wasn't much more de fellow say:
    She jes' gits hold of us dataway.

"Black Swan". During the four years of its existence, Black Swan released recordings by such classic blues stars as Ethel Waters, Alberta Hunter, and Lucille Hegamin. But overexpansion and the recording industry's fiercely competitive environment soon drove the company into bankruptcy, and Black Swan was taken over by Paramount.

ENTER BESSIE AND MA: BLUES ROYALTY ON RECORD

The earliest classic blues recordings typically conformed to the general style Mamie Smith and her Jazz Hounds had established with "Crazy Blues." Smith's light, sweet, and clearly enunciated delivery—set to the syncopated beat of a small jazz ensemble—was consciously designed to appeal to a sophisticated urban audience and virtually all of the female pioneers of blues recording shared her refined vocal sound. Ironically, at this point, their rural sisters—who actually had originated the classic blues—were considered too coarse to appeal to the record-buying public.

For the Southern blues singers who had paid their dues in the traveling tent shows and on the TOBA circuit, the recording studios located in Chicago and New York were another world. Performers such as Ma Rainey and Bessie Smith had grown up singing under circus tents and from the backs of wagons. Their blues were deeper, rougher, and grittier than anything that had been recorded by Mamie Smith and the other vaudeville crooners—black or white.

Within a few years, however, as Race records began to filter down to the home of the blues (and as increasing numbers of recently migrated Southern workers began to find jobs and homes in Chicago, New York, Detroit, and other urban centers), a sizeable audience had developed, one which was now demanding more traditional songs by long-cherished queens of the blues such as Ma Rainey and Bessie Smith.

Bessie Smith got her first opportunity to record in 1923 at Columbia's New York studio. Her first release, "Down Hearted Blues," was a song that had already been recorded by its composer, Alberta Hunter. But Bessie's powerful version, backed by a simple piano accompaniment, was immediately embraced by an African-American audience eager for the down-home sound of the blues in all its poignant glory. The record quickly sold over three-quarters of a million copies and Bessie's phenomenal ten-year recording career was under way.

By the time of her death in an auto accident in 1937, Bessie Smith had recorded about 160 songs. Many of her records sold close to a million copies, proving beyond any doubt that the authentic blues queens could generate not only deep emotional responses from their audiences but impressive sales figures as well. Ultimately, Bessie Smith created a body of work that is recognized as one of the greatest artistic achievements in the history of American popular music.

A year after her own debut, Bessie's mentor, Ma Rainey—who had honed her rough-and-tumble style touring the South in shows such as the F. S. Walcott's Rabbit Foot Minstrels—got her chance to record. Rainey signed with Paramount, and between 1924 and 1928 she recorded about ninety songs, including traditional blues classics such as "Bo-Weevil Blues," "Moonshine Blues," "See See Rider Blues," and "Ma Rainey's Black Bottom." Later in her career, Rainey acknowledged the growing importance of blues recording by making her entrance through the huge doors of a giant wooden mock-up of an old-fashioned wind-up phonograph.

FIELD RECORDING: COUNTRY BLUES ON LOCATION

The sensitivity of recording companies to the demands of the marketplace finally led to the first records by a male country blues singer. This historic milestone took place in 1924, when Paramount issued "Lawdy Lawdy Blues" performed by Papa Charlie Jackson accompanying himself on his six-string banjo.

Charlie Jackson—like the first classic blues singers to record—was a seasoned vaudeville entertainer and a polished instrumentalist with a wide-ranging repertoire. And (again following the classic blues model) it was the popularity of his professionally slick records that encouraged Paramount to sign other more gritty country blues singers, including Southern street musicians and old-time songsters.

Swept up in the sudden surge of interest in country blues was the great Texas performer Blind Lemon Jefferson. Jefferson was born in 1897 on his family's farm in Couchman, Texas. Poor, uneducated, and blind from birth, Jefferson began singing as a teenager on the streets of Wortham, a small town six miles down the railroad tracks from his home. A few years later, however, he was earning his living playing in brothels and at house parties

FIGURE 2-12. Although Bessie Smith's designation as the "Empress of the Blues" may have been an early example of modern media hype, the title stuck and its appropriateness has only increased over the years. Southern Folklife Collection. University of North Carolina at Chapel Hill.

The Empress of the Blues

Having paid her dues touring the South in tent shows and on the TOBA circuit, by the early 1920s Bessie Smith was already a great artist and a beloved star to her audiences. Now, through the medium of recording, she became a national celebrity as well. In 1923, she made her first recording for Columbia, "Down Hearted Blues"; it was an instant hit. Over the next ten years, Bessie went on to cut about 160 songs for the label on which she was regularly accompanied by some of the greatest musicians of her day, including Fletcher Henderson, James P. Johnson, and Louis Armstrong.

In 1929, Bessie Smith set about conquering another form of popular entertainment: the "talking pictures." Movies with synchronized sound had become the new sensation and W. C. Handy had gotten backing to make a film adaptation of his popular composition, "St. Louis Blues." Although the film has its share of demeaning racial stereotypes, Bessie did emerge with her dignity intact, and the film offers the only opportunity to see this extraordinary artist in performance.

The Great Depression affected Bessie's career as it did every aspect of life in the United States, but during the early 1930s changes in musical taste also were making Bessie's style of music sound a little old-fashioned. She cut her last record for Columbia in 1933, and by the middle of the decade she could no longer command the star billing (and fees) in the top vaudeville shows as she had done a few years earlier.

In 1937, Bessie was touring the South with a traveling show when her car was hit by a truck. Although it is her artistry that has secured Bessie's place in the history of American music, in some ways it was the circumstances of her death that has become the most enduring aspect of Bessie Smith's legend. Early reports of the accident had included a charge that the seriously injured blues star had been refused admission at a nearby white emergency room and—forced to make the long trip to the closest "Negro" hospital—Bessie bled to death before she could be treated.

Although the accuracy of this story was challenged almost immediately, the account seemed consistent with the social realities of the era. And, in 1960, the story was revived once again with the publication of a one-act play—*The Death of Bessie Smith*—by the young American playwright Edward Albee. In fact, it was only with the publication of Chris Albertson's definitive biography—*Bessie,* in 1972—that this stubborn myth was finally laid to rest.

Meanwhile, ever since her death, Bessie Smith's body had lain in an unmarked grave. But in 1970, a small group of admirers finally gathered in a Philadelphia cemetery to erect a headstone on her final resting place. Among those who paid for the long-overdue marker was a new Columbia recording star—Janis Joplin—who often had cited Bessie as one of her inspirations. The words carved on the stone read:

The Greatest Blues Singer
in the World Will Never
Stop Singing
Bessie Smith
1894–1937

---

in Dallas, absorbing every song he heard, adapting and personalizing countless blues lines and guitar licks (as well as making up many of his own).

Nor did his blindness keep him from hitting the road. Jefferson traveled incessantly, and from 1926 on, Paramount's Chicago-area recording studio was a regular stop on his itinerary. Between 1926 and 1930, Blind Lemon Jefferson recorded some eighty songs, becoming the best-selling country bluesman of the decade and the first documented blues hero.

Naturally, Paramount's commercial success with Blind Lemon Jefferson inspired other companies to seek out and record other country blues performers. But unlike the classic blues singers who had emerged from the organized world of black show business, the bluesmen were often loners who carved out their own niches in the small towns and cities of South and whose deepest commitment was most often to the guitars slung across their shoulders.

By the mid-1920s, advances in recording technology led to a new system of recording that was particularly well suited to the personality and performance style of the country blues singers. With the more portable equipment that had recently become available, companies began to set up temporary "field" studios in order to record country blues singers on location. Typically, local talent scouts contracted by individual labels targeted specific prospects, but just as often companies would set up their equipment in a hotel room, banquet hall, roller rink, or empty storefront and post signs or take out ads in small-town newspapers. And it didn't take long before they had attracted a line of prospective recording stars that could stretch around the block.

In addition to the temporary field recording units set up for a few days in some tiny rural outpost, "permanent" field recording centers developed in cities such as Dallas, Memphis, and Atlanta, which attracted performers from all across the South. Virtually all labels eventually established their own field recording system, except (ironically) for Paramount, which continued to do the bulk of its recording in their home studios near Chicago.

FIGURE 2-13.   During the late 1930s, Albert Ammons and Meade Lux Lewis helped kick off a nationwide "Boogie Woogie" craze. In doing so, they brought a unique form of blues-based piano music—that had started in disreputable barrelhouse bars—to the stage of Carnegie Hall. Archive photo. The Frank Driggs Collection.

Boogie Woogie and Barrelhouse Blues

Away in the dark, there would always be an old broke-down piano and somebody playing the blues and singing. . .

from: Mister Jelly Roll (by Jelly Roll Morton)

Since much of their music was forged in a type of rough-and-tumble bar known as a "barrelhouse," that's also what they called the music they played. Often hired for little more than drinks and tips, it was the propulsive sound of barrelhouse pianists that typically provided the musical background for a night of drinking, gambling, and dancing.

It was not an environment that encouraged subtlety. Here pianists pounded out their blues with percussive eight-beats-to-the-bar bass patterns that could be heard over the din. Derived from a slang expression for sexual intercourse, the name "boogie woogie" would become permanently linked to the rocking rhythm when the phrase found its way into the title of a recording by Clarence (Pinetop) Smith, an Alabama pianist who had brought the style north and made it the music of choice at Chicago rent parties.

"Pinetop's Boogie Woogie," recorded in 1928, was the first in a long line of boogie woogie hits (by masters of the style such as Meade Lux Lewis, Jimmy Yancy, and Pete Johnson). That same year, however, Leroy Carr introduced a more sophisticated urban blues piano style with his enormous hit, "How Long-How Long Blues." Between 1928 and 1934, Carr's wearing-sounding, softly sung vocals and rippling piano lines were set against the complex, single-note fills of his guitar-playing partner, Scrapper Blackwell. Together, the pair created dozens of soulful and extremely successful recordings.

Throughout its evolution, the blues has been enhanced by pianists such as Roosevelt Sykes, Sunnyland Slim, Champion Jack Dupree, Little Brother Montgomery, Memphis Slim, Professor Longhair, and Charles Brown. And the echoes of their rhythms can be heard in the music of such piano-playing pioneers of R & B and rockabilly as Ray Charles, Little Richard, Fats Domino, and Jerry Lee Lewis. Meanwhile, blues and boogie woogie also have provided the foundation for the entire history of jazz piano from Jelly Roll Morton to Thelonious Monk.

BLUES IN THE 1930S: OUT WITH THE OLD, IN WITH THE NEW

The Great Depression had an even more devastating impact on the blues market than it did on the rest of the recording industry. Most of the field units that had first captured the sound of the country blues were abandoned and the Race catalogs of the major record companies were abruptly discontinued. In 1927, there had been over one hundred million records (of all kinds) sold in the United States; by 1932, the total sales figures were down to barely six million.

When the worst of the Depression did finally pass, the recording industry—and the nation's musical tastes—had changed dramatically. While many members of the African-American community continued to hold firmly to their cultural traditions, by the mid-1930s (when the economic recovery finally kicked in) the black population of the country was no longer as isolated from the mainstream of American society. It was during this transitional phase in blues history—when earlier folk styles were being subjected to the influence of rapid musical and technological innovation—that Robert Johnson recorded the twenty-nine songs that are now recognized as one of America's supreme artistic achievements.

Although he often drew on the rich repository of images that existed within the oral tradition (and on the recordings of his predecessors), Johnson also crafted highly original and haunting poetic conceits that have no earlier models. And he performed with such emotional intensity and instrumental virtuosity that the myths about how he'd sold his soul to the devil in exchange for his skill as a bluesman were easy to believe.

ROBERT JOHNSON: KING OF THE DELTA BLUES

In their attempts to describe the profound impact of Robert Johnson's music, even the most level-headed critics often seem to become enmeshed in the otherworldly ambiance evoked on his records. Writing about Johnson's place in blues history (in his book *Searching for Robert Johnson*), Peter Guralnick explains that for blues afficianados, "Robert Johnson became the personification of the existential blues singer, unencumbered by corporeality or history, a fiercely incandescent spirit who had escaped the bonds of tradition by the sheer thrust of his genius."

Yet, as analysis of Johnson's songs became more grounded in the specific musical aspects of his recorded performances, an understanding of his artistic accomplishment gradually formed. In his book *Deep Blues,* Robert Palmer aptly declares Robert Johnson "the Delta's first modern bluesman." While Palmer makes this claim in the context of Johnson's revolutionary guitar style ("He made the instrument sound uncannily like a full band, furnishing a heavy beat with his feet, chording innovative schuffle rhythms, and picking out a high, treble-sounding lead with his slider, all at the same time"), Guralnick finds his evidence for Johnson's greatness in his craft as songwriter ("Johnson intentionally developed themes in his songs; each song made a statement, both metaphorical and real").

In fact, as Guralnick goes on to make clear, it was actually the aesthetic interplay of thematic content, vocal delivery, and guitar accompaniment that set Robert Johnson apart not only from his contemporaries but from every other blues singer as well. For example, in his discussion of Johnson's "Come into My Kitchen" (a sensual song of seduction), Guralnick writes, "When Johnson asks, 'Can't you hear the wind howling?' in 'Come on in My Kitchen,' both guitar and voice moan with a sexual fall." He concludes that "unlike equally eloquent blues, this is not random folk art, hit or miss, but rather carefully selected honed detail, carefully considered and achieved effect."

Examined in the context of what little we know of Robert Johnson's brief and troubled life, his songs paint a dark portrait of a man haunted by demons and alienated from virtually all human society. In "Hellhound on My Trail" (which many consider his masterpiece), he conjures up the image of a demonic dog pursuing him through a world in which every aspect of nature is imbued with evil spirits ("I got to keep movin'/blues falling down like hail") and even the leaves "shiver" on the trees. Yet, in songs such as "Phonograph Blues" and "Terraplane Blues" (his biggest hit), Johnson also could create clever double-entendre songs that he delivered with strutting bravado.

FIGURE 2-14.   In 1936, at a three-day recording session in San Antonio's Gunter Hotel, the so-called King of the Delta Blues cut sixteen of the twenty-nine songs that comprise the total recorded output of his brief and turbulent life. Courtesy of Columbia Records.

Robert Johnson: King of the Delta Blues

Robert Johnson was born in the Mississippi Delta in about 1911. As a young man, he was drawn to the music (and the lifestyle) of the bluesman. But, according to the Delta blues pioneer Son House, Johnson's first attempts to perform at a local juke joint were so inept that he had to be forced to stop because he was driving the customers away. For about a year, Johnson disappeared from sight and when he returned, he was singing and playing guitar with a virtuosity unlike anything ever heard in the Delta. It didn't take long for the rumor to spread: Robert had gone down to the crossroads and sold his soul to the devil for the power to play the blues.

While references to supernatural rituals and magical potions are woven into the fabric of many of his songs, the true crossroads at which Johnson can be placed is the intersection between the ancient oral tradition and the modern world of commercial recording. Since he came of age in the 1930s, Robert was among the first generation of bluesmen to be exposed to a range of musical styles documented on the hundreds of blues recordings that had been released during the previous decade.

So, while Robert Johnson absorbed the regional hallmarks of the Delta blues firsthand (from bluesmen such as Son House and Tommy Johnson), he also was strongly influenced by modern urban blues singers (such as Lonnie Johnson and Leroy Carr) whom he heard on recordings. And rather than viewing his own music primarily as a vehicle for the spontaneous good times of a juke-joint-Saturday-night (as his predecessors had), Robert Johnson consciously crafted his songs in order to fit the constraints of a 78 r.p.m. record.

When the worst aftershocks of the Depression had finally subsided, the twenty-five-year-old Robert Johnson got his opportunity to set down on shellac the songs he had so carefully honed and polished. Between 1936 and 1937, Johnson recorded searing versions of twenty-nine original songs, including "Hellhound on My Trail," "Terraplane Blues," and "Cross Road Blues." Like some Ancient Mariner of the Delta, he seems to grab the listener by the lapels, singing and playing as if it might be his one chance to tell his story. In fact, within a year, Robert Johnson would be dead.

While rumors persisted that Johnson's soul had simply been claimed by Satan as payment "for services rendered," the facts were more mundane. In August of 1938, as his first records were being released, Robert was playing at a country dance near Greenwood, Mississippi. During the evening, he was passed a bottle of poisoned whisky by the boyfriend of a woman with whom he had taken up. Johnson was barely twenty-seven years old.

THE BLUEBIRD BEAT

During the late 1930s—as Robert Johnson was recording his country blues masterpieces in Southern field studios—a more sophisticated blues sound was evolving in Northern cities that seemed perfectly tailored to the self-image of newly urbanized black migrants desperate to shed the painful associations of their recent past.

While some of its elements can be traced back to the music of piano/guitar duos from the late 1920s (who played a form of novelty blues known as "hokum"), a decade later performers devised a modern blues style by drawing from a variety of mainstream genres including Tin Pan Alley pop songs and Big Band swing.

The current cadre of Chicago-based bluesmen (and women) adopted hokum's clever, double-entendre lyrics and performed them to similarly nimble pairings of piano and guitar. But soon, ensembles were supplemented by additional instruments (such as harmonica, saxophone, and clarinet), and performers infused their blues with a highly propulsive rhythmic drive.

Not only was this style ideally suited to the musical tastes of the urban black audience, it also was suited to the demands of their loud, fast-paced environment. And it sounded especially good on the jukeboxes that had become a major source of music for all of America during the 1930s. The one record company that would become most closely associated with this modern approach to the blues was "Bluebird"; in fact, the style of music became so identified with the label that it simply became known as "the Bluebird beat."

What also made Bluebird so distinctive—other than its colorful label design showing a pale bluebird streaking across a yellow sky—was that it established a permanent core of collaborative "house" musicians who were used to backing up virtually every artist on its roster. In this way, the label achieved a defining sound of its own and established a precedent that would be repeated in the 1950s and 1960s by Chess, Atlantic, and Motown Records (with similar beneficial results).

The list of artists who forged the Bluebird beat includes the bottleneck-guitar master and singer Tampa Red, Red's half-brother Washboard Sam, the harmonica virtuosos Jazz Gillum and Sonny Boy Williamson, the prolific songwriter and singer Big Bill Broonzy, and the powerful and charismatic blueswoman Memphis Minnie.

Memphis Minnie was one of the few blues singers to accompany herself on guitar. Born around the turn of the century in Algiers, Louisiana, as a young girl Lizzie Douglas (as she was then known) had been given a banjo by her father. While still a teenager, she switched to guitar and began to live the blues life. After traveling with a circus troupe for a few years, she ended up in Memphis (one of the great blues melting pots) where she found work and picked up her nickname.

FIGURE 2-15. Lizzie Douglas McCoy—better known as "Memphis Minnie"—has been hailed as one of the pioneers of the modern urban blues. Archive photo. Frank Driggs Collection.

Memphis Minnie: The Blueswoman Who "Played Like a Man"

After arriving in Chicago in the early 1930s, Memphis Minnie brought her potent blend of countrified soulfulness and urban swing to her long-running "Blue Monday" performances at Gatewoods Tavern. But it was at another local club that she would defeat the Bluebird Records star Big Bill Broonzy in what has become one of the legendary cutting contests in blues history.

Recounting the incident in his autobiography, Broonzy unabashedly describes the victorious blueswoman being carried around on the shoulders of the crowd until she was rescued by her jealous husband. In what we must take as the ultimate tribute to her skill as a blues guitarist, Broonzy proclaimed that Minnie "played like a man."

In 1929, Memphis Minnie was discovered playing in a barbershop on Beale Street (the notorious center of the city's black music scene) by a Columbia talent scout. But about a year later she adapted her intense vocals and virtuosic guitar playing to the standard Bluebird format and repertoire. Typically augmented by a second guitar or mandolin and occasionally by a clarinet and trumpet, her recordings include scores of national blues hits such as "Bumble Bee Blues," "Looking the World Over," and the double-entendre classic, "Me and My Chauffeur Blues."

MUDDY WATERS AND THE BIRTH OF THE BIG CITY BLUES

When Muddy Waters arrived in Chicago in 1943, he found himself in a very different world from the one he'd left behind in the Mississippi Delta. Chicago, site of this country's first skyscrapers, was second only to New York as America's great modern city. Millions of people crowded its streets and the elevated trains roared overhead. On the city's Southside, Muddy found a thriving black community that had been steadily growing since the turn of the century.

Most of those who preceded Muddy Waters north had already shed their country image as if it was a pair of dusty overalls. They were city people now, and the country blues that had once fit their daily lives so well was out of place in their new world. During the 1940s, Chicago—birthplace of the Bluebird beat a decade earlier—became the home of an even more radical blues style that echoed the pace, noise, and violence of the modern urban environment.

Bars and dingy nightclubs lined the Southside, and out of every door came music that could cut through the tumult of conversation, laughter, traffic, sirens, and even the roar of "the El"—for the latest incarnation of the blues was powered by electricity. Blues singers now fronted bands of amplified guitars, harmonicas, bass, drums, and even a saxophone or two. And instead of songs that sketched scenes of mules, plows, and lonely highway crossroads, now lyrics were filled with images of urban street life delivered with a new big-shouldered confidence. More than anyone else, Muddy Waters (born McKinley Morganfield) became the embodiment of the raucous Chicago branch of a style known as "electric blues" or "big city blues."

While Muddy had joined the Great Migration for the same reasons as the thousands of other African-Americans who fled the South during the 1930s and 1940s—a better lifestyle and freedom from the oppressive weight of segregation—by the late 1940s Chicago offered ambitious bluesmen another important reason for making the city their home: Chess Records.

Leonard Chess and his brother Phil had come to Chicago in 1928, not long after their arrival in the United States from Poland. They entered the entertainment business, and by the 1940s the Chess brothers owned two popular nightclubs on the city's Southside (the Macamba Lounge and the Cottage Grove) where they presented both the established stars of jazz and some of the pioneers of rhythm and blues.

Since the major record labels of the era seemed to be deaf to the new styles of postwar black music, the move from running a nightclub to making recordings seemed like the logical next step. Beginning with their Aristocrat label in 1947, the Chess brothers began to document the untapped talent that seemed to be all around them. But with only a small storefront studio and a "distribution network" (supplied from the trunk of their car) that consisted of local record stores, barbershops, and beauty parlors, the Chess brother's releases weren't exactly topping the charts.

Gradually, they began to focus their efforts on the new amplified blues sound that was emerging in the Southside clubs and bars. With a combination of great timing and an ear for talent, the brothers inaugurated a new label using their own family name; before long "Chess Records" had become synonymous with Chicago blues. The Chess brothers weren't just documenting a musical style, they were helping to create one.

The electronically amplified instruments and the heavy, insistent beat of the Chicago blues resulted in an entirely new approach to the whole recording process. The Chess brothers seemed willing to try anything to capture the style's raw power: They hung microphones in tile bathrooms and suspended long sections of sewer pipe from the ceiling of their studio to create a thickly textured ambiance you could cut with a knife. Much of the secret of the Chess brother's success, however, can be summed up in two words: Willie Dixon.

FIGURE 2-16.   Although the name on his birth certificate read McKinley Morganfield, to devoted blues fans around the world he was known simply as Muddy Waters. Photo by Lee Tanner.

Muddy Waters: Got His Mojo Workin'

Muddy Waters was already twenty-eight years old when he finally got hit with migration fever and left the Delta for Chicago. Back home, Muddy had sung the blues at a juke joint he operated on the outskirts of Stovall Plantation; once he had even recorded a few songs for Alan Lomax, who was traveling through Mississippi documenting the Delta blues for the Library of Congress.

Although Muddy's down-home blues might have been ideal for a Delta juke joint, up North he was considered crude and hopelessly out of date. Before too long, however, Muddy started to adapt to the modern urban blues style. And in keeping with Chicago's cutting-edge image, Muddy even got himself an electric guitar.

In 1948, he finally got the chance to cut his own record. But for his first commercial release (on the Aristocrat label), Waters reached back to his Delta roots for one of the songs he had recorded for Lomax back in Mississippi. This time, however, he infused the song with the power of electric amplification and energized it with a dose of big-city confidence and a thumping beat: When Muddy sang "I Can't Be Satisfied," you believed him.

Record buyers in the South—and on the Southside—certainly did. Backed with the nostalgic "I Feel Like Going Home," sales of the single took off. By this time, Aristocrat had changed its name to Chess Records, and Muddy had assembled his own working ensemble with Otis Spann on piano, Jimmie Rogers on guitar, and "Little Walter" Jacobs on harmonica. What followed was a string of national Top Ten rhythm and blues hits including "Louisiana Blues," "Long Distance Call," "Honey Bee," "She Moves Me," "I'm Ready," "Hoochie-Coochie Man"—and his signature song, "Got My Mojo Workin'"—that are now considered cornerstones of the modern blues.

With the advent of more sophisticated styles of R & B in the mid-1950s, Muddy Waters's generation of bluesmen suddenly found themselves with plenty of reason to sing the blues (but fewer and fewer fans to listen). It wasn't until the mid-1960s, when young, white blues revivalists on both sides of the Atlantic began covering their songs, that Muddy Waters and his peers reclaimed the attention of the public.

After the Rolling Stones, the Paul Butterfield Blues Band, Johnny Winter, Eric Clapton, and others proclaimed their debt to Muddy (by covering his songs and joining him on stage), he became a hero to an enormous new audience. Muddy Waters continued recording powerful music and performing to enthusiastic crowds virtually right up to the time of his death in 1983.

A huge, powerfully built man who cradled his stand-up bass with ease, Dixon served as a regular session musician and producer for Chess, but his genius was as an innovative blues songwriter who infused country-blues braggadoccio with contemporary urban pride. In songs such as "I'm Ready," "Big Boss Man," "I Ain't Superstitious," "Little Red Rooster," "The Seventh Son," and "You Shook Me," Willie Dixon helped define the image of the modern bluesman: a strutting sexual hero who, along with his own physical prowess, was often armed with both the appropriate artillery, and the power of hoodoo. (As a result, Willie Dixon can also claim credit—or accept the blame—for being one of the spiritual fathers of gangsta rap.)

In 1948, Muddy Waters brought his band into the Chess studio and recorded his aptly titled debut "I Can't Be Satisfied," the first of an enormous catalog of hits on what would become the definitive blues label of the postwar era. The sound Muddy's band generated—with his own electric slide pushing its way through the tightly packed ensemble of Jimmie Rogers's chorded rhythm guitar, the harsh wail of Little Walter's amplified harp, the rippling piano of Otis Spann, and the rock-steady beat of Elgin Evans's drums—metallic, industrial—was like an aural postcard of Chicago at the middle of the twentieth century.

Yet, despite his change of address—and the potent new sound it inspired—Muddy Waters's falsetto-tinged vocals and dynamic slide guitar style continued to reflect the folk traditions of the Mississippi Delta; and many of the songs he wrote for his early recordings—such as "Clouds in My Heart" (the story of a Delta flood)—also preserved the standard blues form and its evocative Southern imagery. In other instances, Muddy simply took a country blues classic such as "Catfish Blues," infused it with a dose of urban flair, and gave it a new name: in this case, "Rolling Stone" (a title that would eventually echo through rock history). In truth, a hefty portion of the macho persona that Muddy Waters would come to embody—what Robert Palmer described as "the steer-stud with down-home power and urban cool"—would be provided by none other than Willie Dixon.

In 1954, Waters recorded three Willie Dixon originals that not only quickly became huge hits on the R & B charts but also largely shaped Muddy's image for a couple of generations of blues fans. It proved to be one of the great collaborations in American music. Dixon's compositions (which put a modern spin on the badman sagas of the African-American ballad) also grafted elements of contemporary popular song forms onto the music's classic A-A-B lyric structure (Dixon's use of pop style choruses—not part of the blues tradition—were particularly effective). And Muddy's riveting vocals and swaggering stance—along with his band's gut-wrenching intensity—did the rest. Meanwhile, one didn't have to look much past their titles to get a sense of the macho themes with which Muddy would be forever associated: "I'm Your Hoochie Coochie Man," "Just Make Love to Me," and "I'm Ready."

Yet, as significant as Dixon's contributions were, the great songwriter has been quick to acknowledge that it was Muddy Waters's own stylistic innovations that had inspired him. "There was quite a few people around singin' the blues," Dixon told Robert Palmer, "but most of them were singin' all sad blues. Muddy was givin' his blues a little pep, and ever since . . . I began tryin' to think of things in a peppier form." And of course it was Muddy himself who, in 1957, wrote the song that would remain his personal anthem until his death in 1983. An unequivocal declaration of sexual potency (rooted in the ancient arts of hoodoo), "Got My Mojo Workin'" is both the supreme example of the big city blues and one of the essential components for the new blues-based genre—dubbed rock 'n' roll—that by the mid-1950s was beginning to marginalize the music of Muddy and his colleagues.

Although Muddy Waters would remain Chess Records' biggest star, the label attracted most of the best performers on Chicago's blues scene, and the Chess brothers signed others on their frequent Southern talent searches. The label's roster—Howlin' Wolf, Sonny Boy Williamson II, Arthur "Big Boy" Crudup, and Elmore James (to name just a few)—reads like a who's-who of the postwar blues.

PIONEERS OF ELECTRICITY

While Muddy Waters often is cited as the "Father of the Electric Blues," he was neither the first bluesman to plug in his guitar nor the only performer of his era to grope his way toward a more modern form of the music. By the late 1930s, for example, the guitarist Robert Nighthawk had already begun infusing his Bluebird sides with a rhythmic intensity that prefigured the mature Chicago sound.

At about the same time, John Lee "Sonny Boy" Williamson was in the process of transforming the "harp" into a dynamic solo instrument amplified by big city technology. With each new record, Sonny Boy's band (by the mid-1940s, it typically consisted of piano, bass, second guitar, and drums) pushed the blues closer to its modern sound, while Sonny Boy pushed the limits of the harmonica as a solo voice. Tragically, in 1948, Sonny Boy Williamson was stabbed to death outside Chicago's Plantation Club where he had been performing. His early hit—"Good Morning Little Schoolgirl"—has lived on to become one of the most enduring blues standards.

At about the same time, in such far-flung blues centers as Arkansas, Mississippi, and Detroit, other versions of the modern blues also were emerging; performers were joining together, plugging in, and—in a few cases—reaching a vast but unseen audience through another form of electronic technology: radio.

Without question, the single most significant example of this medium's impact on the blues world was a fifteen-minute, midday broadcast called "King Biscuit Time," in honor of the flour company that sponsored the broadcast. The live show was hosted by another harmonica virtuoso, Aleck "Rice" Miller (a.k.a. Sonny Boy Williamson II) and his partner, the guitarist Robert Jr. Lockwood. Heard by a loyal audience numbering in the tens of thousands, the program's powerful signal (and down-home ambiance) made the duo the blues world's first radio stars. (*Note:* At some point in his career, Miller had re-christened himself "Sonny Boy Williamson," thereby creating one of the most confusing situations in blues history. Although he always insisted that he was the original harmonica-playing "Sonny Boy," Rice Miller is usually identified as Sonny Boy Williamson II.)

Although he would become one of the architects of the modern blues, during his younger days Sonny Boy Williamson II had for a brief time actually traveled the Delta with the legendary Robert Johnson. At one point, they were joined by another guitarist who (after adopting Johnson's celebrated slide guitar technique) also went on to become an important blues innovator. By amplifying his guitar, Elmore James brought the master's style into the modern age. During the late 1930s, James also put together a high-powered ensemble that included sax and drums, and it was with just such a band that he recorded a version of the Robert Johnson classic "(I Believe I'll) Dust My Broom," now considered one of the masterpieces of big city blues.

By the time Elmore James made it up to Chicago in 1953, he was playing the loudest, meanest blues the city had heard. The recordings he made over the next decade are among the greatest modern blues recordings of the period. In the wake of the 1960s' blues revival, James became a hero for a whole generation of rock's guitar heroes. For example, in the middle of one of John Lennon's slide guitar solos (on the Beatles' album *Let It Be*), one can hear George Harrison call out encouragingly, "Elmore James got nothing on this fella!"

There were some important postwar blues singers who managed to establish recording careers without becoming part of the Chicago scene. John Lee Hooker, born in the Delta in 1917, carved out his niche in Detroit with dark, brooding monochromatic blues like his 1948 hit "Boogie Chillin'." Out on the West Coast, T-Bone Walker—a smooth jazz–oriented blues guitarist who was steeped in the Texas blues tradition of his birthplace—emerged as one of the most significant electric guitarists of all time (in addition to being one of the most sensa-

FIGURE 2-17. Harmonica virtuoso Aleck "Rice" Miller, better known as Sonny Boy Williamson II. As the host of his own daily radio show—"King Biscuit Time"—Sonny Boy became the medium's first blues star. Photo by Chris Strachwitz. Courtesy of Arhoolie Records.

King Biscuit Time!

Beginning in 1941, anyone within about a forty-mile radius of Helena, Arkansas, could turn his radio to KFFA at exactly 12:00 noon and hear an announcer's voice proclaim: "Pass the biscuits, 'cause it's 'King Biscuit Time'!" After breaking into their regular theme song (which sang the praises of their flour-company sponsor), Sonny Boy Williamson and his cohost, the singer/guitarist Robert Jr. Lockwood, would spend the next fifteen minutes playing requests and promoting their upcoming live shows.

By the late 1940s, Sonny Boy Williamson had settled in West Memphis, where he found a job on KWEM. A few years later, he finally made his first record—the classic "Eyesight to the Blind." Sonny Boy was now about fifty years old. After being signed by Chess Records, he produced a score of potent recordings that, a decade later, came to the attention of young British blues revivalists. Williamson even crossed the Atlantic for an extended tour that included a couple of recording sessions with rock groups such as the Animals and Eric Clapton's band, the Yardbirds.

tional showman in blues history). T-Bone's silky, single-note lead would also be an inspiration for a host of rock guitar players, including Jimi Hendrix and Eric Clapton.

The one bluesman who has always credited T-Bone Walker as the primary source of his own trademark guitar style was the Memphis-based performer, B. B. King. Born in 1925, in Indianola, Mississippi, King was another bluesman who came to fame through his own radio show. In 1949, B. B. King (the B. B. stood for "Blues

FIGURE 2-18.   Although he was born in the Mississippi Delta, it was in the thriving blues center of Memphis that Riley B. King established his reputation and picked up his nickname: "The Blues Boy from Beale Street." Before long the phrase was shortened to "Blues Boy" and then simply to "B. B."—King of the Blues. Photo by Lee Tanner.

B. B. King: King of the Blues

B. B. King began his career by serving the usual blues apprenticeship playing on Delta street corners and in local juke joints. But in 1946 Beale Street beckoned. Within a few years he was not only a fixture on the Memphis blues scene but a popular disk jockey on the city's historic African-American radio station, WDIA. He used the show to promote his live appearances, hone his guitar skills (he would often plug in and play along with records while on the air), and sing the praises of his sponsor, Pepticon (a high-octane "health" tonic).

In 1951, his recording "Three O'Clock Jump" went to number one on the national R & B chart, and B. B.'s career was on its way. A series of other hits followed that secured his place as one of the stars of black popular music. Even at the end of the decade—when most blues performers were struggling unsuccessfully against the tide of more modern R & B performers—B. B.'s blend of traditional blues and jazzy horn section riffs allowed him to maintain a large and devoted audience within the African-American community.

During the 1960s, King was discovered by the rock audience and suddenly he was appearing regularly at such hippie era enclaves as San Francisco's Fillmore Theater (home of the Greateful Dead and Jefferson Airplane). By holding on to his old fans as he garnered new ones—with hits such as "Paying the Cost to Be the Boss" and "The Thrill Is Gone"—the King of the Blues remains securely ensconced on his throne.

FIGURE 2-19.   In May 1965, the Rolling Stones made a pilgrimage to one of the holiest shrines of the blues, Chicago's Chess studio. It was there they recorded "Satisfaction," the song that launched their rock 'n' roll career. Author's collection.

Stonewashed Blues

Not only did the Rolling Stones get their name from the title of Muddy Waters's electrified adaptation ("Rolling Stone") of an old country blues song ("Catfish Blues"), but throughout their career the Stones also recorded classic songs by other blues heroes, including Robert Johnson ("Love in Vain"), Slim Harpo ("I'm a Kingbee"), Jimmy Reed ("Honest I Do"), Howlin' Wolf ("Little Red Rooster"), and, of course, Muddy Waters ("Mannish Boy").

Among the era's other rock bands that cut their teeth on the blues were the Animals, The Lovin' Spoonful (who got their name from Mississippi John Hurt's "Coffee Blues"), Cream, The Jimi Hendrix Experience, and Led Zeppelin, who had forged their early heavy metal sound from raw material provided by Willie Dixon ("You Shook Me") and Howlin' Wolf ("How Many More Times").

Selected Blues Songs and Their Classic Rock Covers

Blues Original	Rock Cover
"That's All Right" (Arthur Crudup)	Elvis Presley
"Crossroad Blues" (Robert Johnson)	Cream
"I'm So Glad" (Skip James)	Cream
"Spoonful Blues" (Willie Dixon)	Cream
"Boom Boom" (John Lee Hooker)	The Animals
"Love in Vain" (Robert Johnson)	Rolling Stones
"Stop Breakin' Down" (Robert Johnson)	Rolling Stones
"Statesboro Blues" (Blind Willie McTell)	Allman Brothers
"Ball and Chain" (Big Mama Thornton)	Janis Joplin
"Goin' up the Country" (Henry Thomas)	Canned Heat
"Back Door Man" (Willie Dixon)	The Doors
"Shake 'em on Down" (Bukka White)	Led Zeppelin
"Catfish Blues" (a.k.a. "Rolling Stone") Muddy Waters	Jimi Hendrix

FIGURE 2-20.   Lone Star native Stevie Ray Vaughn's passionate vocals and inspired guitar playing were deeply rooted in the Texas blues tradition. Courtesy of Sony Music Photo Archive.

Stevie Ray Vaughn: The Sky Is Crying

Stevie Ray Vaughn's 1983 debut album, *Texas Flood*, showcased the searing and soulful guitar style he had forged from the influence of such blues masters as Otis Rush, Lonnie Mack, Albert Collins, and the three "Kings" of the Blues (Freddie, Albert, and B. B.). But he also counted Jimi Hendrix as one of his personal guitar heroes, paying homage to the rock icon with cover versions of such classics as "Voodoo Chile" and "Little Wing."

When Stevie Ray emerged as a blues star in his own right, he not only continued to record heartfelt versions of his heroes' hits, but he also began sharing the stage with them at concerts around the world. In fact, it was just such an all-star jam that climaxed Ray's final concert on August 26, 1990.

After being joined on stage for an extended encore by Buddy Guy, Robert Cray, and Eric Clapton, Stevie boarded a helicopter for his next show. The following morning the news reported that Vaughn (along with the pilot and three other passengers) was killed in a crash shortly after takeoff. In 1991, the first in a string of posthumous albums was released; appropriately, it took its title from a classic Elmore James song that Vaughn had made his own: "The Sky Is Crying."

Boy") began playing his electric guitar along with the records he was broadcasting over WDIA, the Memphis station considered the first major radio outlet in the country with an "all-black" format. In 1951, King had his first number one hit on the R & B chart, "Three O'Clock Blues," recorded at the Memphis YMCA on a portable tape recorder. In the half-century since then, B. B. King has emerged as undisputed "King of the Blues."

Back in mid-century Chicago, of course, Muddy Waters still reigned supreme. But when Chester Burnett (better known as Howlin' Wolf) made his way to the Chess studio in 1952, he immediately became Muddy's fiercest rival. Although as a young man "the Wolf" had once crossed paths with Robert Johnson, his biggest influence was Charley Patton, the so-called Founder of the Delta Blues. In fact, one of Howlin' Wolf's early Chess recordings was a heavily syncopated, electric version of a Patton original, "Saddle My Pony." But it was Jimmie Rodgers, the so-called Father of Country Music, who was the inspiration for the sound that provided Burnett with his nickname. For one of Rodgers's trademarks had been his high, lonesome "blues yodel," and although he never managed to re-create its clear purity, Wolf was able to adapt Rodgers's soulful falsetto into his own unearthly "howl."

In the late 1940s, Howlin' Wolf was a familiar presence on the Arkansas and Mississippi blues circuit. In live shows and on his broadcasts over radio station KWEM, he was playing blues that blended his primitive country vocals and powerful harp with the amplified wail of electric guitars. In Chicago, he recorded a string of sensational hits for Chess. Accompanied by the thundering, riff-based beat of a band that included the guitarist Hubert Sumlin, Wolf's raspy, sandpaper vocals proved to be an ideal vehicle for Willie Dixon's most extravagently inflated lyrics. Among the Dixon classics Wolf turned into hits were "Smokestack Lightning," "Back Door Man," "Spoonful," "Wang Dang Doodle," and "The Red Rooster."

And while Waters was well known as a dynamic live performer, Wolf's stage show was positively frightening. He'd crawl out on stage in a feral crouch and stalk the wings singing and howling until the crowd was in a frenzy. All this made Howlin' Wolf a big favorite of the British rockers of the 1960s. The Rolling Stones (who'd had an early hit with their cover of "Little Red Rooster") occasionally used him as an opening act, and once got him a spot on a TV show they were doing. In the early 1970s, Chess brought Wolf to London to record an album of his hits with a band of his young white disciples that included Mick Jagger, Ringo Starr, Jeff Beck, Steve Winwood, and Eric Clapton, among others.

THE BLUES HAD A BABY AND
THEY NAMED IT ROCK 'N' ROLL

By the mid-1950s, something was happening in the world of popular music that would have a dramatic and disastrous impact on the bustling Chicago blues scene. According to some accounts, it all began in 1955 when Muddy Waters helped a young guitar player and singer get an audition with the Chess brothers. Unfortunately for Muddy and the other big city bluesmen, Chuck Berry turned out to be not just another challenger for the blues throne, but the founder of a whole new empire.

The release by Chess Records of Berry's "Maybelline" (and of Bo Diddley's debut single that same year) suddenly thrust the label into the uncharted territory of something called "rock 'n' roll." Soon this blend of blues, R&B, and country music would make Muddy and his generation seem like dinosaurs. While they didn't actually become extinct, however, the great postwar bluesmen soon found themselves relegated to the "Rhythm and Blues" ghetto and small-time radio outlets as a younger generation of black performers staked their claim to the pop charts and appeared on the Ed Sullivan show.

Although a second and third generation of Chicago bluesmen (like Buddy Guy, James Cotton, Otis Rush, Magic Sam, Son Seals, and others) would keep the tradition alive, it wasn't until the 1960s—when a young white audience discovered the blues—that the music and some of its authentic pioneers would be resurrected. Early in the decade, when a folk revival had swept college campuses, it brought to light some of the great country blues singers who had originally recorded back in the 1920s. Unearthed by folk-revival sleuths, Son House, Sleepy John Estes, and Mississippi John Hurt appeared at folk festivals around the country and re-recorded much of their old material, often with astonishingly undiminished powers.

FIGURE 2-21.   Corey Harris combines a scholar's knowledge of African-American folk music with the spontaneous authenticity of a born performer. By doing so, he has become one of the most exciting new voices in acoustic blues. Photo by Rick Oliver. Courtesy of Alligator Records.

Corey Harris: Latter-Day Songster

On the basis of his eclectic repertoire of badman ballads ("Frankie and Johnnie"), bottleneck Delta classics (Charley Patton's "Pony Blues"), ragtime numbers (Blind Blake's "Diddy Wah Diddly"), and traditional spirituals ("Just a Closer Walk with Thee"), Harris truly qualifies as a kind of latter-day "songster."

    After ceding the field to white blues revivalists during the 1960s, young African-American performers such as Corey Harris (Keb Mo and others) have, over the past decade, finally begun to reclaim the blues. As Harris explains, "Your past, your heritage is coming through you. I think it's my job to represent where I'm from through my music."

By the mid-1960s, white teenagers on both sides of the Atlantic began forming electric blues bands, and with tremendous enthusiasm—and varying degrees of skill—they attempted to re-create the classic sounds of Muddy Waters, Howlin' Wolf, Elmore James, and the other masters. Many of these groups took pains to acknowledge their debt to their spiritual fathers on their recordings and in their interviews with the media. And a few female performers—such as Janis Joplin and Bonnie Raitt—valiantly attempted to break through this old-boy network in order to call attention to Sippie Wallace, Victoria Spivey, Big Mama Thornton, and other matriarchs of the blues. In fact, only a few months before her own death, Joplin helped finance a headstone for Bessie Smith, the long-neglected "Empress of the Blues."

Before moving on to create their own original material and experiment with the latest advances in recording studio technology, the music of such 1960s rockers as the Rolling Stones, the Animals, Van Morrison, and the Yardbirds was largely comprised of blues covers drawn from the works of country blues pioneers such as Robert Johnson and more recent Chicago blues masters such as Muddy Waters. Indeed, throughout its history (from Bill Haley to Led Zeppelin and Nirvana), rock music has always been enriched by the blues in all its forms. For the simple truth is that—as a song title on one of Muddy Waters's last albums put it—"The Blues Had a Baby and They Called It Rock and Roll."

Since the 1960s, periodic blues revivals have gained strength and then faded. The music has been embraced by Hollywood (*The Blues Brothers*) and was the inspiration for a chain of theme restaurants (The House of Blues). Members of later generations of blues revivals have come and gone (Stevie Ray Vaughn), while Eric Clapton's 1994 Grammy Award–winning blues album *From the Cradle,* a tribute to his heroes, testified once again to the music's continuing vitality. Finally, young African-American performers (including Robert Cray, Keb Mo, and Corey Harris) have begun to carry on the tradition as well.

Through it all, the blues has endured not only as one of the most profound expressions of African-American identity but as one of the most significant influences on twentieth-century American culture. And while the blues itself forms an essential repository of American oral literature, it also has been the inspiration for many of our country's greatest writers and poets.

In August Wilson's powerful early play, *Ma Rainey's Black Bottom,* the "Mother of the Blues" thinks aloud about what the music means to her (and to her audience): "You don't sing to feel better," Ma explains; "You sing 'cause that's a way of understanding life. . . . The blues help you get out of bed in the morning. You get up knowing you ain't alone. There's something else in the world. Something's been added by that song. This be an empty world without the blues . . ."

Activities and Projects
Chapter 2: In the Beginning . . . There Was the Blues

1. Explain the influence of each of the following on the evolution of the blues form (music and lyrics):
   a. the work song
   b. the field holler
   c. the spiritual

2. Write a comparative study of performers representing different country/folk blues regions. Describe their unique characteristics (vocal quality, guitar style, imagery of songs) and explain the relationship of each to the history, geography, and culture of the region.

3. Using both recordings and anthologies of blues lyrics, explore the major themes of the country/folk blues. Identify their literary qualities, as well as the historical, cultural, and sociological insights they provide.

4. Based on an analysis of available recordings and sheet music, describe the actual blues content (harmony, lyric structure, use of blue notes, etc.) contained in the commercial blues songs associated with W. C. Handy and the other Tin Pan Alley composers of the 1920s.

5. Explore the repertoire of the Classic blues singers of the 1920s. Describe how their songs reflect the concerns, values, and attitudes of African-American women during this era.

6. Read August Wilson's play, *Ma Rainey's Black Bottom*. Relate the portrait of the main character to the actual facts of Ma Rainey's life and career and explain the insights the play provides into the world of the blues.

7. Research the minstrel show from its origins in the mid-nineteenth century to the era of the early "Blues Queens" of the 1920s.

8. Trace the evolution of the modern, urban blues during the 1930s and 1940s. Address both the changes reflected in the music (electric amplification, expanded ensembles, nontraditional song forms, etc.) and the changes in its imagery and themes.

9. Research the history of white blues performers from such hillbilly/country singers of the 1920s and 1930s as Jimmie Rodgers, Dock Boggs, Frank Hutchison, and the Allen Brothers up to modern blues revivalists such as John Hammond, Jr., Bonnie Raitt, Eric Clapton, Stevie Ray Vaughn, and Kenny Wayne Shepard. Explore the ongoing controversy regarding the "legitimacy" of white blues, and give your own opinion about this issue.

10. Develop a project that investigates the influence of the blues on one of the following:
    a. rock 'n' roll of the 1950s
    b. jazz (either early New Orleans style or hard bop)
    c. zydeco

11. Trace the history of blues piano styles such as barrelhouse and boogie woogie, as well as the contributions of piano-playing blues singers such as LeRoy Carr, Memphis Slim, and Charles Brown.

12. The blues has had a profound influence on writers and poets from the Harlem Renaissance to the present. Survey a variety of American literature that either uses the blues form, embodies the blues sensibility, or addresses the blues as a subject.

13. Explore the relationship between the blues (a.k.a. "the devil's music") and gospel (the music of the African-American church). Focus on this dynamic in the careers of performers such as Thomas A. Dorsey, Blind Willie Johnson, and Rev. Gary Davis.

14. Trace the influence of the blues on rock bands from the 1960s to the present. Discuss cover versions of blues songs, as well as the use of blues form and imagery in the groups' original material.

15. Write (and, if possible, perform) a selection of original blues songs.

3

Jazz: The Sound of a New Century

The history of jazz has become so shrouded in legend that the most difficult task for anyone looking back for the truth of the music's origin and evolution is simply to separate the reality from the myth. Among the more enduring jazz creation myths, for example, was the one offered by the colorful New Orleans pianist, Ferdinand "Jelly Roll" Morton, who boldly proclaimed that he had personally invented jazz in 1902. While Morton was indisputably one of the pioneers of the style—and its first great composer—he also was a notorious tale-spinner and self-promoter; yet his extravagant claim persisted for decades before it was completely debunked.

Today, most jazz historians concede only that the sound of a new and uniquely American genre of music first began to emerge at the turn of the twentieth century. An urban art, jazz drew its inspiration from the cultural, economic, and racial diversity of the city with its active social life and varied outlets for popular entertainment. And while a similar sociological and musical dynamic was operating in other population centers during this period, jazz (as we know it) is infused with a spirit that is peculiar to that multicultural melting pot known as the Crescent City.

NEW ORLEANS: BIRTHPLACE OF JAZZ

New Orleans was founded in 1718 as the gateway to the vast French land tracts in the New World. Although control of the city was briefly ceded to Spain, the entire territory would not become part of the United States until the Louisiana Purchase of 1803. And two centuries later, the city's French cultural heritage continues to affect every aspect of life in New Orleans—from its religion and language to its attitude toward race, art, sex, and death. Consider the following, each of which contributed in some way to establishing the ideal conditions for the creation of jazz.

Congo Square

Because of the fear that they would be used to foment slave revolts, drums had been banned throughout the South. But in New Orleans' Place Congo (or "Congo Square")—an open space near the center of the city—this vital aspect of African tradition thrived right up to the brink of the Civil War. Newspaper articles and journal entries dating back to the late eighteenth century describe Sunday afternoon rituals at Congo Square in which hundreds of black dancers circled to the sound of drums, rattles, and banjos. In fact, the gatherings became one of the city's most popular tourist attractions.

Creole Culture

In order to distinguish themselves from the "Americans" who took control of the city after 1803, the descendants of the original French (and Spanish) settlers zealously clung to their identity as "Creoles." One of the social conventions maintained by male members of New Orleans' Creole élite was the taking of mistresses (often selected from among the city's African-American population). Over time, these liaisons resulted in a class of Black Creoles (or "gens de couleur") who established their own tightly knit racial subculture.

Black Creole families established themselves as shopkeepers and craftsmen in their own French Quarter communities. In an attempt to establish their link to white Creole culture (and differentiate themselves from their dark-skinned African-American neighbors), many Black Creole families provided their children with a formal European-style education—which typically included the study of a musical instrument. In the more élite entertainment venues of New Orleans, creoles of color dominated the city's musical life for generations.

Religion

Rather than the austere Protestantism that was practiced in most of the United States, the religious life of New Orleans was characterized by the more elaborate rites and ceremonies of the Roman Catholic Church. As a result, many of the city's African-American inhabitants gradually forged their own religious synthesis by fusing images of Catholic saints and African deities. In doing so, they also began to place their own cultural (and musical) stamp on some of New Orleans' oldest traditions. Take that celebrated New Orleans ritual, "Mardi Gras," an annual outpouring of excess that precedes Lent. To this day, hundreds of thousands of tourists invade the city each year to witness parades accompanied by the sound of joyously swinging brass bands.

Code Noir (Black Code)

Throughout the eighteenth century (and the first half of the nineteenth), New Orleans' racial laws—known as the *Code Noir*—reflected the city's (somewhat) more tolerant attitudes. For example, one of the Code's provisions was for the "manumission" (legal freeing) of slaves on the basis of the owner's official consent. So even though African-Americans remained at the bottom of the city's social ladder—working the docks or as servants in the mansions of the upper-class Garden District—local statutes did allow the black residents of New Orleans greater opportunities for freedom than they had in other Southern cities.

Military Surplus Instruments

At the end of the Civil War, the musical instruments discarded by Union military bands (from among the troops that had occupied the city) began to circulate among the civilian population of New Orleans. As a result, many African-Americans had an opportunity to express their own musical conceptions through secondhand cornets, trombones, and clarinets. In 1898—when the first faint strains of jazz were beginning to emerge—another wave of military surplus band instruments hit the market. Since many of the troops returning from the Spanish-American War passed through the port of New Orleans, the city was again inundated with inexpensive brass and woodwinds.

The New Orleans Funeral

In New Orleans, death was marked by a unique rite of passage. Mourners would gather at the home of the deceased and—accompanied by the dirgelike music of a brass band hired for the occasion—they would make their way to one of the cemeteries located on the outskirts of the city. On the return trip, however, bands would break into joyous versions of popular spirituals that celebrated the glories of heaven to which the soul of the departed was no doubt bound.

Storyville

In 1897, a statute to control New Orleans' flourishing sin industry was introduced by a local politician named James Story. It designated a square mile of the old French Quarter as an official red-light district, which was immediately dubbed "Storyville." For the next two decades, the soundtrack for the hundreds of bars and brothels that dominated the area was provided by a sizeable contingent of local musicians ranging from highly trained ragtime piano "professors" to rough and tumble slow-drag blues bands.

THE NEW ORLEANS MUSIC SCENE, C. 1900

As a teenager, Ferdinand Joseph Lamothe escaped the shabby gentility of the Creole culture into which he had been born by becoming a pianist in one of the "sporting houses" of Storyville. Assuming the professional name Jelly Roll Morton, the young professor of the keyboard quickly established himself as one of the best pianists in the district—which was no small accomplishment. "New Orleans was the stomping ground for all the greatest pianists in the country," Jelly Roll recounted to Alan Lomax (in his oral autobiography, *Mister Jelly Roll*). "We had colored, we had white, we had Frenchmens, we had Americans, we had them from all parts of the world because there were more jobs for pianists than any other ten places in the world."

It was in the informal, fiercely competitive "cutting contests" that took place among these piano virtuosos that the transition from the more formal ragtime piano style to the freer improvisations of jazz probably took place. In one famous passage of his memoir, Morton attempted to explain the evolution between the two styles (while staking his claim to giving the new music its name).

"All these people played ragtime in a hot style," he began, "but man, you can play hot all you want to and you still won't be playing jazz. . . . Ragtime is a certain type of syncopation and only certain tunes can be played in that idea. But jazz is a style that can be applied to any type of tune. I started using the word in 1902 to show people the difference between ragtime and jazz." Finally, Morton declared, there was one other ingredient that was required to add the right spice to the new musical gumbo he claimed to have created. "If you can't manage to put tinges of Spanish in your tunes," he insisted, "you will never be able to get the right seasonings, I call it, for jazz."

But the recipe for the new Crescent City style wasn't exclusive to Morton and the other Storyville pianists. Back at the turn of the twentieth century, all of New Orleans was caught up in a nonstop swirl of musical activity. There were lawn parties, parades, picnics, and night dances held in elegant ballrooms and rented-out dairy barns. There were fish frys, riverboat excursions, amusement parks, and after-hour joints. There was music for every occasion and at every occasion a band to supply the appropriate musical accompaniment. The musicians themselves also represented an extraordinarily wide range of backgrounds and skills: from classically schooled Creole clarinetists to self-taught bluesmen (who worked the docks or drove coal wagons by day and blew cornet at night).

George "Pops" Foster, a pioneering bassist and author of one of the most detailed and engaging first-person accounts of this era, has described the New Orleans music scene in his autobiography, *Pops Foster: New Orleans Jazzman*. Along the way, he paints a multisensory portrait of the scene at one of the most popular venues for the Crescent City's party-loving residents—the nearby resort area of Lake Pontchartrain.

> After I turned professional, I spent a lot of time at Lake Pontchartrain. Sunday was your big day at the lake. Out at the lakefront and Milneberg [a resort community of small cottages on the shore] there'd be thirty-five or forty bands out there. The clubs would all have a picnic and have their own band or hire one. All day you would eat chicken, gumbo, red beans and rice, barbecue, and drink beer and claret wine. The people would dance to the bands, or just listen to them. . . . The musicians had just as much fun as the people you played for.

Foster's autobiography also reveals that while the complex network of clubs, fraternal organizations, and burial societies may have been dedicated to the same local motto—"Laissez les bon temps roulez" (Let the good times

FIGURE 3-1.   Published in 1899, Scott Joplin's "Maple Leaf Rag" set off a national ragtime craze. In New Orleans, the music's syncopations found their way into the improvisations of Storyville pianists and the cadences of the city's brass bands, making it a key ingredient in the musical gumbo called "jazz." Author's collection.

Ragtime: Ingredient in a Recipe for Jazz

Ragtime was a cross-cultural musical hybrid: From the European-derived march, ragtime took its multi-thematic form and its emphatic "on-the-beat" stride, while its syncopations and polyrhythms were a clear indication of its African sources (and it was these "ragged" rhythms that gave the music its name).

As written by such masters as Scott Joplin, ragtime was a complex, rigorously composed piano music that required great technical skills from the performer. The key to ragtime's appeal lay in the exhilarating tension that was created by the clash of strong, regular bass patterns (played by the left hand) and intentionally off-kilter accents (of the right hand); Joplin himself characterized this aspect of ragtime as its "weird and intoxicating effect."

In New Orleans, ragtime was liberated by rhythmically adventurous local performers and the music that emerged was perceived by everyone as something new and exciting. One of these pioneers, the Creole clarinetist Alphone Picou, recalled how, as a sixteen-year-old novice (just before the turn of the century), he was introduced to the mysteries of the Crescent City style: "I remember when we got a new piece of music we would get the music and play the tune with the music, then, after that we didn't need that music no more. We'd go 'out of the way' with it. That was ragtime." In fact—as we now know—it was jazz!

FIGURE 3-2.   At the turn of the twentieth century, groups such as the Onward Brass Band began infusing their marches with spontaneous improvisations and a syncopated beat; in doing so, such brass bands became crucibles of jazz. Courtesy of the Hogan Jazz Library. Tulane University.

The New Orleans Brass Band: Crucible of Jazz

As William J. Schafer explains in his illustrated history *Brass Bands and New Orleans Jazz,* "In New Orleans the brass band was a powerful influence on the new jazz music that developed around 1900. Brass bands gave jazz its instrumentation, its instrumental techniques, its basic repertoire. . . . To understand jazz, we must begin with its roots, and the taproot of the tradition is the nineteenth-century brass band."

In order to advertise their services, bands such as the Onward . . . Eagle . . . Excelsior . . . and Reliance brass bands would parade through the streets—or ride in open horse-drawn wagons—with banners and signs announcing their appearance at some picnic or dance. When they encountered each other, impromptu battles of the bands (known as "bucking" contests) would take place to the delight of the assembled crowds. In this way, innovation was encouraged and new techniques were unveiled, all in an atmosphere of unbridled and spontaneous creativity.

roll)—there was a long-established hierarchy based largely on skin color, cultural heritage, and the ability to read musical notation. "From about 1900 on," Foster recalled, "there were three types of bands around New Orleans. You had bands that played ragtime, and the ones that played sweet music, and the ones that played nothin' but blues."

So while the élite "society band" led by Creole bandleader John Robicheaux ("the best reading band in town," according to Foster) played arrangements of popular songs and Joplin rags for the "dicty" (upper-class) crowd, "It was a rule in New Orleans [that] if you didn't play any blues you didn't get any colored [African-American] jobs." By the turn of the century, however, the social stratification that resulted in the musical distinctions Foster describes was rapidly eroding.

In 1894, however, an amendment to the Black Code was passed that officially designated anyone who possessed any African ancestry a "Negro." Thus, the once-rigid distinctions that had separated New Orleans' Creole and African-American communities were effectively eliminated. Soon, blues-oriented improvisatory black performers and their lighter-skinned formally trained colleagues found themselves playing side by side. The interaction (and competition) that resulted from this social and musical integration brought about a merging of styles and influences that contributed to the creation of a wholly new form of musical expression.

Nor were white New Orleans musicians immune to the exciting new developments taking place at the beginning of the new century. No history of the early Crescent City scene would be complete without noting the role of the leader of the celebrated Reliance Band—Papa Jack Laine—who has been dubbed the "Father of White Jazz." Like his African-American counterparts, Laine described his musical method as "ragging the tunes"—that is, applying a loose syncopated element to improvised variations of popular melodies.

Laine organized his first brass band in about 1885, and before long he had at least three different aggregations all working under the "Reliance" banner. In fact, most of the white jazz musicians—who would go on to make the first jazz recordings—got their start with Papa Laine. Although it is not clear to what extent the musical and cultural fusions taking place in New Orleans actually breached the barrier between black and white performers, two of the most valued members of Laine's band were Achille Baquet and Dave Perkins—both light-skinned African-Americans. Although Laine is often portrayed as being ignorant of their racial identity, this seems unlikely, especially since Baquet's father and brother both played in the Excelsior brass band, one of New Orleans' oldest and most prestigious *black* bands.

BUDDY BOLDEN: FIRST MAN OF JAZZ

Certainly the dominant mythic figure in the creation of jazz was the cornetist Buddy Bolden—or "King Bolden," as everyone called him. Tragically, by the time the recording industry began to document the music that had been evolving in various subcultures of New Orleans, Bolden was an inmate in the insane asylum where he would spend the last twenty-four years of his life. But while the testimonies of his contemporaries are frequently contradictory, accounts of Bolden's performances (collected in the numerous oral histories of New Orleans) tend to agree about one thing: Back at the turn of the century, Buddy Bolden was doing something brand new.

The words of fellow cornet player Mutt Carey are typical: "When you come right down to it, the man who started the big noise in jazz was Buddy Bolden. . . . I guess he deserves credit for starting it all." Bunk Johnson, who claimed to have played second cornet in Bolden's band, told interviewers: "King Buddy Bolden was the first man that began playing jazz in the city of New Orleans, and his band had the whole of New Orleans real crazy and running wild behind it . . . that was between 1895 and 1896." Yet, it is with statements like these that the consensus ends. Some insist Bolden could read music, others claim that it was his very inability to read that was the motivation for his improvisatory style. There are those who describe him as a "ragtime" cornet player, while Pops Foster writes in his autobiography that Bolden "played nothing but blues."

Although he wasn't able to resolve all these conflicting issues, the jazz scholar Donald M. Marquis has painstakingly researched every available shred of evidence about Bolden's life, publishing the results in the definitive 1978 biography, *In Search of Buddy Bolden: First Man of Jazz.* Although Marquis does successfully refute many of the legends that have surrounded Bolden for most of the twentieth century, he doesn't challenge the cornet King's preeminent place in jazz history. Along the way, he also offers a succinct description of the new style Bolden seems to have forged. "Word was getting around that there was something new in the air":

> . . . and Buddy's audience continued to grow. Rags and blues had been played occasionally by the brass bands; now Bolden was playing them at smaller gatherings with his smaller band. His particular style of ragtime or blues did not occur by accident. What other bands had been doing in the street parades ('ragging the tunes' as indicated by Papa Jack Laine), Bolden began doing for a different audience—the dancers. . . . Buddy took musical bits from his background and environment and put them together in a way that utilized what he thought was best about the music, blending the parts with his own talent and personality.

So it was, around the turn of the twentieth century, that the characteristic march music of New Orleans brass bands along with the syncopations of ragtime and the gritty wail of the blues all filtered through the creative vision of an individual performer, thereby creating a new musical synthesis. And they called this new music "jazz."

FIGURE 3-3.   Buddy Bolden (standing, third from left, holding cornet) and his Ragtime Band, c. 1905. According to testimony of many of his contemporaries, Bolden was the first man to play jazz in the city of New Orleans. Courtesy of the Hogan Jazz Archive. Tulane University.

Charles (Buddy) Bolden: First Man of Jazz

At the turn of the twentieth century, Buddy Bolden was the leader of the band of choice for the city's serious party crowd. Old-timers have recalled that before every dance or picnic he played, New Orleans' first "Cornet King" would point his horn into the air saying, "I'm going to call my children home." And as if it was a royal summons, his subjects would appear.

But his hectic schedule of all-night dances and personal excesses ("He was crazy for wine and women," one contemporary recalled) finally took their toll. Suffering from delusions and violent outbursts, Bolden was arrested in 1906. A year later, at the age of twenty-six, he was committed to the insane asylum at Jackson, Louisiana, where he remained for the last twenty-four years of his life.

Or, at least, eventually they did. Pops Foster, for one, claims that he'd never even heard that word until sometime around 1917 when he was playing in one of the Mississippi riverboat bands operated by the Streckfus Company. "Captain Johnny Streckfus came up with a name for us—the Jazz Syncopators. That was the first time I heard the name jazz," Foster recalled. But in 1917 the word "jazz" (often spelled "jass") would burst into the public consciousness when it appeared on a record label for the very first time.

1917: JAZZ ON RECORD AND ON THE MOVE

Official histories of jazz often begin in 1917 in recognition of the music's debut on the medium that has become its primary form of documentation—recordings. And enshrined for all time as "The First Jazz Record" is a 78 r.p.m. disk by the Original Dixieland Jass Band. Consisting of two tunes—"Livery Stable Blues" and "Dixieland Jass Band One-Step"—the historic record was cut in a New York City studio by the Victor Company on February 26, 1917. It became an instant hit, quickly selling one million copies, and before long the sound of jazz filled the air—and the name of an evocative new musical style was on everyone's lips.

While it was fitting that the first band to introduce traditional style of New Orleans jazz (most often referred to as "Dixieland") to the nation's listening public were Crescent City natives, it is ironic that what has come to be recognized as an African-American art form was unveiled by an all-white band. So, while they may not (despite their name) have been the "Original" Dixieland Jazz Band—nor (as they often billed themselves, "The Creators of Jazz")—the ODJB were the first to introduce America and the rest of the world to the exhilarating music of their hometown.

To the uninitiated listener, the early New Orleans style—based on a technique known as "collective improvisation"—may seem random and chaotic. In fact, by the time jazz had found its way onto recordings, each instrument had developed a specific role within the ensemble. With a little careful attention, not only does the complex interplay (among the cornet, trombone, clarinet, and rhythm instruments) begin to become comprehensible, but in its purist form—as in the recordings of King Oliver's Creole Jazz Band of the mid-1920s—Dixieland's collective improvisation can be a thing of great joy and beauty.

Within the five- or six-piece New Orleans jazz band, the cornet (a close relative of the trumpet) traditionally assumes the dominant melodic role as it had in the larger New Orleans brass bands. At the same time, the clarinet begins to weave its own highly embellished obbligatos (scalar countermelodies) moving throughout its wide tonal palette from low "dirty" tones to piercing high notes. Meanwhile, at the lower end of the musical register, the trombone establishes a carefully harmonized bass pattern (often exploiting its potential for suggestive or humorous tonal effects). And, finally, a "rhythm section"—consisting of some combination of drums, piano, bass, tuba, and banjo—maintains a steady, unaccented $\frac{2}{4}$ beat. Ideally, this "collective" interaction was not only subtle and seamless but imaginatively and spontaneously "improvised."

In the case of the ODJB, however, this latter aspect (considered more than any other the defining element of jazz) was missing. After carefully analyzing the recorded output of the Original Dixieland Jass Band for his definitive musical study, *Early Jazz,* Gunther Schuller discovered that—despite their protestations to the contrary—"in truth their recordings show without exception exact repetitions of choruses and a great deal of memorization." His conclusion: "The ODJB thus did not actually improvise." By contrast, Schuller does give the group some credit. "The ODJB reduced New Orleans Negro music to a simplified formula," he explains. "It took a new idea, an innovation, and reduced it to the kind of compressed rigid format that could appeal to a mass audience."

Before long, the ODJB's odyssey would take them from the New York recording studio (where they made jazz history) across the Atlantic to Europe (where they became the first international jazz stars). The band's first stop after leaving home in 1916, however, had been Chicago. And in this respect, the Original Dixieland Jazz Band were again merely following a well-worn trail that had previously been traveled by black Crescent City musicians (as well as by tens of thousands of working men and women who made their way North in what is referred to as the Great Migration).

By 1900, not only had new river and rail links made Chicago the second largest city in the United States but also (following the historic fire in 1871) Chicago had emerged as the nation's most modern urban center. New engineering techniques employed in the rebuilding effort made Chicago the site of the world's first "skyscrapers." And with the passage of the Eighteenth Amendment (prohibiting the sale of alcoholic beverages), Chicago also quickly became the nation's first modern capitol of crime. Finally, the city's rapidly expanding industrial and commercial enterprises spurred a mass exodus of African-Americans from all over the South. During the first twenty years of the twentieth century, the black population of Chicago tripled. In 1920, there were over 100,000 black residents mostly crowded into the city's Southside streets.

FIGURE 3-4. In 1917, the Original Dixieland Jazz Band assured its (controversial) place in jazz history when it made the very first jazz recording, "Livery Stable Blues," a raucous novelty tune featuring instrumental barnyard effects. Author's collection.

"Livery Stable Blues" (The Original Dixieland Jazz Band)

The members of what would become the Original Dixieland Jazz Band grew up amid the spontaneous musical free-for-all that was New Orleans at the turn of the twentieth century. There was music everywhere and the sounds of marching bands and ragtime ensembles pulled through the streets on horse-drawn wagons didn't have much respect for geographical—or racial—boundaries.

The Original Dixieland Jazz Band was an authentic piece of the complex mosaic that was New Orleans jazz; but because they made the very first jazz record, were so extraordinarily successful, claimed credit for tunes that had emerged from the African-American tradition, and encouraged the idea that they had actually "invented jazz," the ODJB has, understandably, found itself the target of tremendous resentment. But what was even worse, say the band's detractors, they just didn't swing.

Postscript: "The Keppard Question"

In 1914, the African-American cornetist Freddie Keppard left New Orleans and began a five-year tour that took him across the entire country. In 1916, when he arrived in New York, the Victor label made Keppard an offer he seems to have had no trouble refusing. According to the New Orlean's clarinetist Buster Bailey, "He had a chance to make the first jazz records—before the Original Dixieland Jazz Band—but he was afraid people would steal his tunes and arrangements."

Too bad, since by all accounts Keppard was not only one of the greatest of the New Orleans "Cornet Kings" but, because after the ODJB's success, it would be five long years before an African-American jazz band would get another chance to record.

The energy generated by all these developments set the stage for the city to become the center of the jazz world at the dawn of what would soon be known as the "Jazz Age." Chicago's hundreds of saloons, night clubs, dance halls, and cabarets—from the raunchy to the resplendent—provided employment for musicians who could play the exciting new music that had begun to sweep the country. And who better to play it than the men who had invented it. Among the first of the New Orleans musicians who would soon flood Chicago was the veteran "Cornet King," Freddie Keppard.

"Freddie was the first guy to go North with a whole band and play," Pops Foster recalled in his autobiography. "Chicago paid more than New Orleans and those guys were doing great. Freddie and his Creole Band really opened up Chicago for the rest of the guys to go." And go they did. Soon most of the originators of jazz (including Joe "King" Oliver, Louis Armstrong, Jelly Roll Morton, and Foster himself) had abandoned the Crescent City for the Windy City.

While the availability of employment and a thriving recording industry were the primary forces in attracting performers north, in the music's mythology, accounts of the migration of jazz up the Mississippi often suggest a kind of classic inevitability. In 1917, the Department of the Navy (which operated a major base in New Orleans) became concerned that its image would be tarnished by the openly "immoral" ambiance of Storyville. Under pressure from the Navy, the district was officially closed. So, with much of New Orleans' gaudy nightlife abruptly dulled, scores of Crescent City jazz stars left town to add their brightness to Chicago's northern lights.

THE JAZZ AGE: PUTTING THE SIN IN SYNCOPATION

By 1917, the so-called New Orleans Diaspora had spread the sounds of jazz not only to Chicago but to Los Angeles, New York, and other cities large and small. And in the wake of the first recordings by the Original Dixieland Jazz Band, the entire country was won over by the music's irresistable rhythms. Nor was this overwhelming response a unique phenomenon in recent American history. In fact, over the preceding two decades, the country had periodically been swept up in other pop music crazes, ragtime being one recent example.

This time, however, what was truly revolutionary was not just the musical message but the medium that carried it. Unlike those earlier styles, here was music that couldn't be reduced to a page of sheet music or be cut into a paper piano roll. A spontaneous, improvised, ensemble style jazz existed only in actual performance—and the only way it could be preserved and marketed was on recordings.

Yet, while recordings might be the only medium that could capture the crowd-pleasing syncopations of the latest musical craze, many record companies were hesitant to jump on board the bandwagon. After all, it was only recently that the phonograph had gone from being a somewhat unsavory curiosity of amusement arcades to an accepted accoutrement of the middle-class home. And for many Americans there was still something uncomfortably intimate about bringing a record into the sanctity of the family parlor. For not only did a Victorian moral climate still reign over much of the country, so did an entrenched system of racial segregation.

Although there is historical evidence that back in 1916 the Victor label had offered the (light-skinned) Creole jazz cornetist and bandleader Freddie Keppard the chance to make what would have been the first jazz recording, Keppard had turned them down flat (claiming that it would have made it too easy for imitators to "steal his stuff"). Yet, it is also rather suspicious that in the four years following the Original Dixieland Jazz Band's debut no jazz band of color was given an opportunity to record.

In any event, while the Victor Company's publicity for that first ODJB record reflected the still unresolved issue of the new music's name ("Spell it Jass, Jas, Jaz, or Jazz—Nothing can spoil a jazz band," proclaimed one ad), they expressed less confusion about the nature of their product: "The Jass Band is the very latest thing in the development of music. It has sufficient power and penetration to inject new life into a mummy, and will keep ordinary human dancers on their feet till breakfast time." This effort to promote *jazz* (as its name was soon codified) as just good clean fun was aided by the ODJB's pink-cheeked, clean-cut image, and by the novelty aspects of their recording. In particular, "Livery Stable Blues," with its humorous barnyard sound effects, made a relatively unthreatening introduction to the revolutionary new style.

So, in 1922, when F. Scott Fitzgerald—a young writer who had recently been heralded as the spokesman for his generation—entitled his second book *Tales of the Jazz Age,* the name stuck. For Fitzgerald and his contemporaries, the recent world war had shattered the old moral verities and traditional aesthetic values. Fueled by a postwar economic boom (and hip flasks filled with bathtub gin), jazz now became the anthem of millions of young people who the expatriate literary guru Gertrude Stein dubbed the "Lost Generation."

Soon, however, the association of jazz with the rejection of traditional values and with the nighttime world of urban vice and corruption resulted in the music itself being targeted as the cause of the era's social upheavals. Suddenly jazz was being denounced (or derided) by the various guardians of the moral order. For example, an open letter from the head of the Chicago Musicians' Union, published in a 1921 issue of *Variety,* warned members against performing a musical style that made them sound "as if you had just escaped from your keeper in a sanitarium for the feeble minded." In popular periodicals, parents were warned about the dangers of jazz for their children, and one article in a 1921 issue of *Ladies Home Journal* bore the attention-grabbing headline, "Does Jazz Put the Sin in Syncopation?"

For many, the very word "jazz" became so invested with negative associations that one high-profile New York City bandleader, Meyer Davis, sponsored a contest to rename the music. Attracted by the socially redeeming nature of the competition (and by its $100 first prize), Davis received over seventy thousand entries. Contenders included: "Peppo," "Rhapsodoon," and "Hades Harmonies." The eventual winner was . . . "Syncopep!"

In fact, since so much of the small-group novelty records and anemic dance music that most of America thought of as "jazz" rarely deserved the name, perhaps that contest wasn't such a bad idea. But it was too late. Anything that even faintly echoed the syncopated rhythms, intricate intertwining melodies, and instrumental neighs and whinnies that the mass audience had come to associate with the new music was declared "jazz."

Meanwhile, African-American jazz bands long barred from recording studios and hotel ballrooms were flourishing in the speakeasies and cabarets of Chicago's Southside. Of the many black New Orleans bands that found work in that city's Prohibition-era night spots, the most significant was King Oliver's Creole Jazz Band. Oliver, who had inherited the New Orleans "Cornet King" crown first bestowed on Buddy Bolden, had arrived in Chicago in 1918 to play at the Royal Gardens. Despite their popularity, however, the Creole Jazz Band would not be heard on recording for another five years.

1923: FINALLY, MORE THAN THE DISK WAS BLACK

The first important step in breaking the record industry color line took place in 1920, when Mamie Smith became the first African-American performer to record the blues. The phenomenal success of her version of "Crazy Blues" took everyone by surprise, and it immediately opened the recording studio door for dozens of other African-American blues divas. In 1922, opportunity finally knocked for a black jazz musician when the New Orleans trombonist Kid Ory made a few records during a visit to Los Angeles. A year later, it was King Oliver's turn. Beginning in 1923, his Creole Jazz Band produced the first in an extended series of authentic jazz recordings.

By this point, Oliver's band was in the process of refining the traditional New Orleans style, eliminating its excesses, unifying the music's thematic content, and formalizing the role of each instrument in the ensemble as they carefully molded the polyphonic, collectively improvised New Orleans style to the confines of a three-minute shellac disk. The recordings of the Creole Jazz Band, however, also provide crucial evidence of an evolution in the fundamental nature of jazz.

For out of the band's more clearly defined instrumental lines (as well as their more blues-based, monothematic repertoire), a single voice began to emerge; what began simply as "breaks" (short individual statements amid the classic New Orleans polyphony) now begin to evolve into more sustained, individual melodic inventions that can be accurately described as "solos." Examples of such early solo improvisations can be heard in recordings such as "Dipper Mouth Blues" (1923), which showcases the band's gritty, rhythmically dynamic clarinetist, Johnny Dodds, as well as Oliver himself. But another Creole Jazz Band side cut that same year ("Chimes Blues") features the first recorded solo statement by a young New Orleans protégé of Oliver's who—through his improvisational genius and technical virtuosity—would elevate the solo to its preeminent status in jazz.

FIGURE 3-5. King Oliver's Creole Jazz Band: Featuring King Oliver (playing cornet, center rear), Louis Armstrong (kneeling front and center), the future Mrs. Armstrong, Lil Hardin (at the piano), and Johnny Dodds (playing clarinet). Courtesy of the Hogan Jazz Archive. Tulane University.

King Oliver's Creole Jazz Band

The King of all the musicians was Joe Oliver, the finest trumpter who ever played in New Orleans . . . That's why they call him "King," and he deserved the title.

(Louis Armstrong)

The series of recordings by the King Oliver Creole Jazz Band, released in 1923, provided the public with its real introduction to African-American jazz at the dawn of the Jazz Age. The records also introduced the world to the genius of Louis Armstrong, who had recently come to Chicago to join his mentor.

Both on disk and in their live appearances in the city's Southside clubs, the Creole Jazz Band's intricate collective improvisations and double cornet breaks (combining Oliver's lead lines and Louis's harmonized countermelodies) caused a sensation. Even today, one can feel something of the excitement those early Chicago fans must have experienced when they heard the duo's dynamic interplay on tunes such as "Snake Rag," "Where Did You Stay Last Night," and "Mabel's Dream."

Postscript: Lil Hardin Armstrong

Lillian Hardin Armstrong was more than just the "woman behind the great man." In addition to being an adept and reliable pianist, she was a talented songwriter and arranger who earned her place in jazz history as the only female member of the first significant African-American jazz band in recording history.

Hardin had already been working with King Oliver for two years when Louis Armstrong joined the band. Before long, the pair had developed a close professional and personal relationship, culminating in their marriage in 1924. It was at Lil's insistence that Louis accepted Fletcher Henderson's offer to come to New York as his featured soloist. A year later, when her husband returned to Chicago to make his immortal Hot Five recordings, Lil was at the piano. She is also credited as cowriter on a number of Louis's tunes, including "Struttin' with Some Barbecue," one of his most popular songs from this period.

Along with the new spotlight on the spontaneous improvisations of a single individual, these recordings also document a crucial change in the essential rhythmic conception of jazz—away from the more rigid, march and ragtime beat of early New Orleans music and toward a looser and more flexible time structure that would be known as "swing." And here, too, it was Oliver's recently arrived twenty-one-year-old disciple who would lead jazz into the future. For, as the recorded evidence of his relatively brief time with King Oliver's Creole Jazz Band makes clear, credit for both establishing the solo and the element of swing as the hallmarks of jazz belong to that towering figure in the music's history, Louis Armstrong.

From the moment he arrived in Chicago to join his mentor on second cornet, Armstrong's playing caused a sensation. The clarinetist Buster Bailey was one of the dozens of contemporary observers who have attempted to explain this extraordinary impact: "What made Louis upset Chicago so? His execution, for one thing, and his ideas, his drive. . . . They got crazy for his feeling." Before long, the recordings Armstrong made with Oliver's Creole Jazz Band would spread the excitement Chicago jazz fans had experienced through Louis's live performances. But Oliver's pianist, an astute and ambitious young woman named Lil Hardin, quickly recognized that Louis's development was being constrained by his secondary role in the Creole Jazz Band. So—after marrying Louis—she encouraged him to accept an invitation to join Fletcher Henderson's ten-piece band in New York, then considered the best in the country.

Louis's playing took New York by storm just as it had Chicago. While the recordings he made with Henderson were tightly arranged affairs and Louis's solo opportunities were limited, whenever they do appear, they shine through the ensemble passages like shafts of brilliant sunlight. While in New York, which had become the recording capital of the country, Louis was in constant demand. He had the opportunity to work in a variety of settings, including a number of recording sessions with blues queens such as Ma Rainey and Bessie Smith.

In addition to his own rapidly developing skills, the confidence he had achieved by playing with the cream of the New York music scene seemed to have had a liberating affect on Armstrong. In 1925, he returned to Chicago and initiated a series of recording sessions as a leader for the Okeh label. The sixty-five records he made over the next three years—billed as Louis Armstrong and either His Hot Five or His Hot Seven—reveal the full flowering of Armstrong's genius. Virtually every solo either extended the actual range of the instrument itself or revealed another example of what seemed to be an endless array of expressive slurs and vibrato effects. Each tune appeared to be propelled by another daring new rhythmic conception, and every note burst forth with an exuberant energy.

What's more, there seemed to be a new level of artistic consciousness to everything Armstrong played that went beyond his instrumental virtuosity; his improvisations reveal a masterful structural unity and thematic development while at the same time being totally natural and spontaneous. Virtually from the time they were first recorded, musicians and jazz scholars have meticulously transcribed into musical notation Louis's solo improvisations and subjected them to laborious analysis. Yet, decades later, they continue to reveal new aspects of his unique gifts. As Gunther Schuller put it in his book *Early Jazz:* "An Armstrong solo stands out like a mountain peak over its neighboring foothills."

Among these early masterpieces are "Muggles" (Louis's slang term for marijuana, which he used and promoted throughout his life), "Heebie Jeebies" (which introduced Louis's mastery of the wordless vocal style known as scat singing), "West End Blues" (which opens with a heroic, unaccompanied statement shaded by subtle rhythmic and tonal variations), and "Weatherbird" (a duet with pianist Earl Hines, marked by their seemingly intuitive interplay). A partial list of Armstrong's great performances from these years also includes "Potato Head Blues," "Cornet Chop Suey," "Muskrat Ramble," "Big Butter and Egg Man," and "Struttin' with Some Barbecue."

When we look beyond Louis Armstrong's mid-1920's masterpieces, however, one can find evidence of new musical conceptions in the work of other jazz performers who had recently found their way onto recordings. Foremost among these pioneering jazz soloists was Sidney Bechet, a Creole clarinet master, who had been playing in important New Orleans ensembles from the time he was in his teens. In 1919, Bechet had even been to Europe with Will Marion Cook's Southern Syncopated Orchestra. It was here that Cook's performances attracted the attention of a distinguished classical conductor, Ernest Ansermet, who wrote one of the first jazz reviews. While Ansermet praised the "astonishing perfection, the superb taste, and the fervor" of Cook's band, he singled out its "extraordinary clarinet virtuoso" for special attention. "I wish to set down the name of this artist of genius," the conductor wrote, "as for myself, I shall never forget it—it is Sidney Bechet."

FIGURE 3-6.   More than most pursuits, jazz has had its share of legendary figures; yet as one chronicler of the music's history has written, "Most legendary figures, being only human, fail to live up to their legend. . . . In Louis Armstrong's case, it was the other way around. The truth surpassed the legend." Courtesy of RCA Records. A Unit of BMG Entertainment.

Louis Armstrong: Pops Is Tops!

Louis Armstrong was born into a life of desperate poverty. The illegitimate son of a fifteen-year-old part-time prostitute and an absentee father, he had to fend for himself in the slums of New Orleans' notorious Third Ward. Although he got into the usual childhood scrapes with the law, along the way he was able to purchase a beat-up cornet from a local pawnshop and he began to teach himself to play.

At the age of twelve, Louis was sent to the Colored Waif's Home, a reform school, where he became lead cornetist in the brass band. When he left three years later, Louis formed his own jazz band and began working the picnics, riverboats, and dances around New Orleans. He also began to form a personal relationship with his musical hero, Joe "King" Oliver. Fifteen years older than Louis, Oliver became his lifelong mentor and spiritual father, and in 1918—when Oliver left for Chicago—Armstrong took his place in the great New Orleans' jazz band led by the trombonist Kid Ory.

Although Armstrong had previously refused other jobs that involved relocating to the North, in 1922 King Oliver sent for Louis to join his band in Chicago and Louis accepted. Louis's arrival caused an immediate stir among the city's Southside jazz enthusiasts. "I still remember the arrival of Louis Armstrong in Chicago. The news spread like wildfire among musicians who hurried that same evening to Lincoln Gardens," one Southside jazz enthusiast recalled. And although Oliver had been Chicago's reigning Cornet King, "Opposite the young Louis . . . Oliver's style rapidly appeared to us to date a little."

It was in Chicago, during his time with King Oliver's Creole Jazz Band, that Louis Armstrong (affectionately known as "Dippermouth," "Satchelmouth," "Satchmo," or, simply, "Pops") began his entry into the wider world of American popular music. And—following a brief sojourn in New York as a featured soloist of the Fletcher Henderson Orchestra—it was also in Chicago that he would make the series of recordings that are now ranked among the supreme masterpieces in jazz history.

But while these so-called Hot Five (and Hot Seven) recordings may be venerated by jazz afficionados, Armstrong's national reputation—as *the* American performer of his time—would be launched from the stage of a Broadway theater. For as the 1920s drew to a close, Armstrong returned to New York to star in a Fats Waller–written nightclub revue staged at Harlem's Connie's Inn, and it was the uptown success of Louis's version of Waller's "Ain't Misbehavin' " that led to the opportunity to sing it in the show's 1929 Broadway production.

Armstrong's recording of the song, released that same year, would become his first certified pop hit, initiating the final step in his transition from jazz star to national celebrity. In fact, over time, Armstrong's singing would become as significant (and as influential) as his cornet playing. In reality, one is simply an extension of the other; for in his vocal performances one encounters the same unique phrasing, the same swooping slurs and glissandos as those he created on his horn. Both Frank Sinatra and Billie Holiday have acknowledged their own debt to Armstrong, and as the title of one book on the history of American popular singers suggests, they're all *Louis' Children.*

Throughout the 1930s and 1940s, Armstrong toured with his own big band, had his own national radio show, and made appearances in numerous Hollywood films. When the Swing era ended, he launched a new small band, modeled on the original New Orleans ensembles of his youth. The personnel varied, but "Louis Armstrong and the All-Stars" became his regular working band for the rest of his life. His fourth (and last) wife, Lucille, finally managed to settle Louis into his first home, a modest brick house in Queens, New York, but he continued to tour at a grueling pace. After a quarter of a century, Armstrong was still the "King of Jazz," and in February of 1949 he appeared on the cover of *Time* magazine wearing a crown of trumpets.

During the 1950s, the new medium of television rapidly became the most powerful force in American culture, and Louis established himself as a popular guest on the most popular nationally broadcast variety shows. The 1960s, however, would become a disastrous decade for jazz, as the "British Invasion" swept across the country. Yet, in 1964, Louis's version of "Hello Dolly," the title song of a new Broadway musical, began climbing up the pop charts. In May, it took over the number one spot—replacing "Do You Want to Know a Secret" by the Beatles—thereby sparking a renewed round of TV guest appearances. When the film of *Hello Dolly* was released in 1969, Louis sang his hit as a duet with the movie's star, Barbra Streisand.

Not long after attending a gala seventieth birthday celebration given in his honor at the Newport Jazz Festival, Armstrong suffered a heart attack. He died on July 6, 1971. While there have been any number of attempts to do justice to the scope of Louis Armstrong's monumental contribution, in their stark simplicity perhaps the words of Duke Ellington can serve as his most eloquent epitaph: "I loved and respected Louis Armstrong. He was born poor, died rich, and never hurt anyone on the way."

FIGURE 3-7.   Although Jelly Roll Morton may not have been the "inventor of jazz"—as he claimed—the New Orleans pianist and bandleader is generally acknowledged as its first great composer. Courtesy of RCA Records. A Unit of BMG Entertainment.

Mister Jelly Roll

Ferdinand Lamothe (to use his birth name) was a member of New Orleans' musically oriented Creole community, and by the age of fourteen he was known as one of the best "junior pianists" in the Crescent City. By the time he was seventeen, he got his first job as a "professor" in one of the Storyville bordellos, and he'd begun competing in after-hours cutting sessions against the best pianists in the district.

By 1907, when Jelly Roll Morton left New Orleans for good, he had also written some of his most famous compositions (although most of them would not be published or recorded until ten or fifteen years later). Many of Morton's compositions—including "New Orleans Blues," "King Porter Stomp," "Wolverine Blues," "The Pearls," and "Alabama Bound"—have became jazz standards.

Unlike the other pioneers of jazz, Morton had his own carefully considered musical theories that he endeavored to infuse into each of his compositions and arrangements. His music reveals a precise structure in which complex thematic and rhythmic variations are set off by carefully planned solo breaks. Even supposedly "improvised" solos were shaped by Morton's input. After all, it was his music, and he wanted it played his way.

Throughout the second half of the 1920s, Jelly Roll Morton and His Red Hot Peppers was the Victor label's premier act. But the effects of the Depression hit Morton especially hard. By the late 1930s, Morton was working in obscurity as a solo act in a small Washington, D.C., nightspot. But he continued to retain his supreme confidence and absolute conviction about his proper place in the history of jazz.

At the invitation of Alan Lomax, director of the Library of Congress's Archive of American Folk Song, Morton spent the better part of a month sitting at a piano playing and talking about life in New Orleans at the turn of the century. An abridged version of the actual recorded conversations was soon issued and, in 1950, the text was published under the title *Mister Jelly Roll: The Fortunes of Jelly Roll Morton, New Orleans Creole and "Inventor of Jazz."*

Morton passed away in 1941, before these projects had come to fruition. Today, however, Morton's reputation is more secure than ever, and most jazz historians concede that—despite the hyperbole—there is some truth to his own assessment of his contribution to jazz: "Kansas City style, Chicago style, New Orleans style—hell," Morton once declared, "they're all Jelly Roll style."

It was on this same trip that Bechet had come across a soprano saxophone in a London music store. By mastering this instrument and investing his playing with a brilliant use of vibrato and other tonal effects, Sidney Bechet became not only one of the great early improvisors in jazz but music's first great saxophonist. An early example of his contributions to the development of the solo can be heard in the 1923 recording of "Wild Cat Blues," which Bechet made with the Clarence Williams Blue Five.

Now that the sound of authentic jazz had finally been recorded, the public's appreciation of the music progressed rapidly. And each new success prompted competing record companies to sign other African-American performers. Among the growing roster of jazzmen who got the opportunity to record during this period was the man who had always claimed to have invented the music in the first place: Jelly Roll Morton.

Not only was Jelly Roll Morton a brilliant pianist, but he was an innovative and prolific composer. So when he finally did get a chance to record, there was no shortage of material. Between 1923 and the end of the decade, he made over fifty solo piano recordings and about as many others using an ensemble he called the "Red Hot Peppers." In addition, he cut a number of piano rolls, accompanied a score of vocalists, and began publishing his vast storehouse of tunes. Although Morton's wanderlust had taken him from New Orleans to Los Angeles and back across the country to New York, like so many of his contemporaries, it was in Chicago that he found the warmest welcome—and produced much of his greatest work.

Among the other New Orleans émigrés who had found their way to the city—and taken up residence at the Friar's Inn (one of Al Capone's favorite nightspots)—were the New Orleans Rhythm Kings. In fact, the NORK had come to Chicago to fill the void for a hot white band that was created when the ODJB abandoned the Windy City for the Big Apple back in 1916.

Steeped in the traditional New Orleans style, the members of the Rhythm Kings had served their apprenticeships with "Papa" Jack Laine and the band's cornet-playing leader, Paul Mares, and its clarinetist, Leon Rappolo, could not only outplay their ODJB counterparts but also had benefited from closely studying the recent innovations of the great black bands on recordings (and in their Chicago club performances on the other side of town). Even in the NORK's earliest recordings—such as 1923's "Wolverine Blues"—one can hear the band's enhanced ability to swing and, in Rappolo's clarinet playing, an assured and expressive solo voice.

THE CHICAGOANS: FROM FAN CLUB TO THE BANDSTAND

Despite one multiracial musical collaboration (between Jelly Roll Morton and the New Orleans Rhythm Kings), the record industry was as segregated as the rest of 1920s America. It shouldn't be a surprise, therefore, that when young white jazz fans—inspired by the music they were hearing on recordings—decided to try their hand at playing it, they emulated those pioneering white New Orleans jazz bands with whom they could more easily identify.

One of the most revealing accounts of the transition from jazz fan to jazz performer comes from Jimmy McPartland, a white trumpet player who had grown up in a middle-class Chicago suburb during the 1920s. Looking back on this turning point in his life, McPartland recalled a day when he was hanging out with some friends after school at the local ice cream parlor, the Spoon and Straw:

> They had a Victrola there, and we used to sit around listening to records. . . . One day they had some new Gennett records on the table, and we put them on. They were by the New Orleans Rhythm Kings and I believe the first tune we played was "Farewell Blues." Boy when he heard that—I'll tell you we went out of our minds. Everybody flipped. . . .

McPartland remembers sitting there from three o'clock in the afternoon until eight that night playing the same few records again and again: "Right then and there we decided we would get a band and try to play like these guys."

McPartland and his friends, many of whom went to the same Chicago school, would eventually become known as the "Austin High Gang" or, simply, the "Chicagoans." Although they were initially inspired by the recordings of the white New Orleans bands, these aspiring Chicago-area musicians also visited the Southside clubs where they had the chance to listen to King Oliver, Louis Armstrong, Johnny Dodds, Sidney Bechet, and the other black jazz greats who had recently made their way to the city.

The first member of this generation of young white jazz aficionados to make the transition from fan to professional performer—and recording artist—was Leon "Bix" Beiderbecke. Beiderbecke, who was born in Davenport, Iowa, in 1903, had first encountered jazz as a young boy when the Mississippi riverboat bands docked along the shore of his hometown on one of their regular trips up from New Orleans. There is some speculation that he might have even heard Louis Armstrong, who was working on one of the riverboats during this time. But like so many others of his contemporaries, it was the first ODJB recordings that excited Beiderbecke enough to actually take up the cornet himself.

Although he had no formal instruction, by 1923 Beiderbecke was playing well enough to form his own band, the Wolverines, a name he lifted from the latest recording by the New Orleans Rhythm Kings ("Wolverine Blues"). In 1924, the band got its own chance to record for Gennett, and it is these disks that mark the debut of the performer who is now recognized as the first great white jazz musician in the music's history.

Although Bix's career was cut tragically short by the psychological and physical problems that resulted from his lifelong addiction to alcohol, the pure beauty of his tone, the sophistication of his harmonic ideas, and the elegance of his melodic solo improvisations made even Louis Armstrong an early admirer. "The first time I heard Bix," Louis remembered, "I said these words to myself: there's a man as serious about his music as I am. . . ." Not long after, when Beiderbecke was the featured soloist in the famous Paul Whiteman Orchestra, Armstrong heard Beiderbecke again. "They swung it all the way. . . ." Louis recalled, "and all of a sudden Bix stood up and took a solo . . . and I'm tellin' you those pretty notes went all through me. . . ."

Suddenly, it seemed the Chicago jazz scene was inundated with young ambitious white jazz musicians. In addition to Bix Beiderbecke, some of the other future jazz professionals who got their start in Chicago during this period were Jimmy McPartland and his brother Dick, Frank Teschemacher, Mezz Mezzrow, Bud Freeman, Gene Krupa, Dave Tough, Eddie Condon, Pee Wee Russell, Frankie Trumbauer, and Benny Goodman.

Meanwhile, following the recording breakthroughs of African-American jazz musicians such as King Oliver, Louis Armstrong, Jelly Roll Morton, and Sidney Bechet, the flow of young black musicians from across the country into the world of jazz also accelerated exponentially. And it seemed that every new record introduced another innovation, whether in the music's rhythmic conception, harmonic structure, instrumental techniques, or ensemble framework. By the end of the 1920s, jazz had traveled across all of America; it rode on rail, in buses, and on the grooves of shellac disks; now, as if by magic, it began traveling through the airwaves as well.

FIGURE 3-8.   Of all the young white fans who were inspired by those first recordings of New Orleans jazz to try their own hand at playing the exuberant new musical style, Bix Beiderbecke was one of the few to leave a lasting mark on jazz history. Author's collection.

Leon (Bix) Beiderbecke: Young Man with a Horn

Bix Beiderbecke was born in 1903 into a staid, upper-middle-class family in Davenport, Iowa. But, at fifteen, having heard the recently released recordings of the Original Dixieland Jazz Band, he got his hands on a cornet and began painstakingly reconstructing the performances of the ODJB's famed cornetist Nick LaRocca.

By the time he was nineteen, Bix was playing well enough to form his own jazz ensemble (the Wolverines) and begin recording for the local Gennett label. Almost immediately, he became one of the leading lights of Chicago's vibrant jazz scene. Although initially his playing lacked the buoyant rhythmic swing of King Oliver, Louis Armstrong, and the other pioneering African-American cornet kings, even these early recordings reveal Bix's burnished bell-like tone, shapely melodic lines, and harmonic inventiveness.

Unfortunately, as his reputation was rapidly rising, his personal life was heading precipitously downhill. By the time he was out of his teens, Bix was a confirmed alcoholic; it was a lifestyle that would lead to an untimely death at the age of just twenty-eight. Nevertheless, during his brief life he managed to make a number of recordings that have become jazz classics. Among these is his 1927 masterpiece, "Singing the Blues," a recording that provides an ideal example of Beiderbecke's improvisational mastery.

While the innovative brilliance and beauty of Bix Beiderbecke's music have earned him a place in jazz history, it was his troubled life and untimely death that made him one of the first "tragic heroes" of jazz mythology. Not long after his death, Dorothy Baker published a highly romanticized novel based on his life entitled *Young Man with a Horn,* and a 1949 film version starring Kirk Douglas brought Bix's legend to the silver screen.

JAZZ ON THE RADIO: INVISIBLE, BUT NOT COLORBLIND

The first attempts to use radio as a mass medium took place in 1920, and by 1923 regular radio programming was reaching 30 percent of American homes. Along with the introduction of instantaneous news reports, weather broadcasts, and the latest crop prices, radio brought hours of free music directly to a rapidly increasing listening audience. The result was a predicable and precipitous decline in record sales. In 1921 the recording industry had generated over $105 million; by 1925 that figure had plummeted to below $60 million. Of course, a few years later—in the aftermath of the 1929 stock market crash—total annual record sales would fall to just $6 million.

As radio penetrated more American homes, broadcast networks, corporate advertisers, and the federal government tightened their control of the airwaves. In a united front, both defenders of traditional moral values and profit-oriented media moguls declared that the sanctity of American homes would be protected against any threat from degenerate influences carried over the radio. Instead, the new medium would be a "civilizing" influence on the American masses—and a reliable source of profit for those who controlled it. Both of these imperatives encouraged a trend toward safe, bland, and inoffensive styles of music.

In addition, radio's status as the dominant medium for music resulted in a dramatic shift in the center of the jazz universe. As media historian Philip K. Eberly explained in his book *Music in the Air,* "New York was the place to be if you were a musician in the late 1920s. Network radio had created a demand for players of every musical inclination. As the Eastern hub of show business, New York was especially appealing to young instrumentalists like the Dorsey brothers, Benny Goodman, Jack Teagarden and Red Nichols." But, as Eberly goes on to explain a few sentences later, "There was only one catch—you had to be white. 'Blacks need not apply' was the unwritten rule."

As radio's racial policies relegated most African-American performers to the segregated world of ghetto nightspots and roadside taverns, a kind of anemic, syncopated pseudo-jazz came to dominate the major radio outlets. There were some exceptions to this race-based stratification, however. In fact, it was his radio broadcasts from New York dance halls that both established Fletcher Henderson's lofty reputation and enticed Louis Armstrong to leave Chicago to join him in the Big Apple.

The son of a high school principal, Fletcher Henderson had majored in chemistry at Atlanta University before he left to pursue his musical ambitions. Born in 1897, Henderson was just one member of a generation of educated middle-class African-Americans who entered the expanding entertainment industry during the 1920s. Henderson had a strong academic grounding in music, and before long he was engaged in a wide-ranging musical apprenticeship that included a few years as the house pianist for Black Swan records and a stint as a recording studio accompanist for Bessie Smith. Henderson formed his own band just in time to ride the crest of the "Charleston" craze, which—along with the hip flask and raccoon coat—has come to symbolize the decade.

But it was in 1922—when he was accompanying the cabaret singer Ethel Waters on tour for Black Swan—that Henderson made media history. During an appearance at New Orleans' Lyric Theater, the local radio station decided to broadcast one of their shows, and, according to Philip Eberly, "Tradition has it this was the first appearance of a Negro on radio." The trip to the Crescent City would prove to be historic for another reason; it was during Henderson's Lyric Theater engagement that he first heard Louis Armstrong. Henderson immediately sought to add Louis to the all-star band he was in the process of putting together, but it would take a call from his mentor, King Oliver, to persuade Armstrong to leave his beloved hometown. Henderson would just have to wait.

On returning to New York, Fletcher Henderson found plenty of work in the city's bustling ballrooms and nightclubs. And, in 1924, when he was booked into the Broadway-area cabaret, Club Alabam, Henderson again found himself "on the air." Although the broadcast studios and upscale hotels (from which the bulk of radio's music programming originated) were the exclusive domain of white bands, New York's WHN had installed wiring that allowed them to broadcast live from the Club Alabam, thereby providing New York's first radio outlet for black music. Before long, Henderson's band moved up to one of the city's premier dance venues, Roseland. Not only did Henderson suddenly find himself playing opposite some of the top white bands in the country, but the regular Roseland "remotes" (as the broadcasts from out-of-studio locations were known) brought his music to an even larger radio audience.

In order to play New York's huge dance halls, Henderson's orchestra expanded well beyond the five or six pieces of the standard New Orleans jazz band. And as his ensemble grew to nine—and then twelve—musicians, the informal "head" arrangements that had once served to provide a structure for jazz improvisations were no longer sufficient. Now more complex written arrangements were required, as were a corps of highly trained musicians who could play them.

Collaborating with his chief arranger, Don Redman, Henderson divided his band into separate "sections"—brass (trumpets and trombones), reeds (clarinet and sax), and a "rhythm" section (piano, bass, guitar/banjo, and drums)—which could be brought into creative interplay (or used to replicate the "call-and-response" structure that is such a fundamental element of African-American music). When these innovative *written* ensemble passages were then infused with the individual *improvised* solos of Henderson stars such as Coleman Hawkins (on tenor sax), Rex Stewart (on trumpet), and Buster Baily (on clarinet), an exciting new musical concept began to emerge.

In 1924, Louis Armstrong joined Henderson in New York and immediately propelled what was already the most sophisticated band in the country to a new level of creativity. For while Armstrong's virtuosic musical statements had already broken through the dense collective improvisation of King Oliver's Creole Jazz Band, Gunther Schuller contends that "Armstrong's, emergence as a soloist coincides with his joining the Fletcher Henderson band in New York." Although Louis Armstrong only remained with Henderson for about a year, his influence—on his fellow musicians (and on Henderson and Redman's arrangements)—was enormous.

But Louis Armstrong wasn't the only emerging jazz great to arrive in New York that year. Nor was Fletcher Henderson the only black bandleader to break radio's invisible color barrier. Not long after arriving in the Big Apple in 1924, Duke Ellington and his band began broadcasting from another New York nightspot. And it was on the basis of this national exposure that he began to carve out his unique niche in the American musical landscape. As Philip Eberly points out, Ellington's "five-year engagement at the Cotton Club, with its national radio wire, not only launched the career of one of America's leading musical originals, it also made possible the first important national propogation of popular music by a black group." At the time, however, there was only one band that occupied the pinnacle of the pop music pyramid and there was only one man who claimed for himself the title, "King of Jazz."

PAUL WHITEMAN: THE KING OF JAZZ?

By 1921, Paul Whiteman had established himself as the preeminent dance bandleader in the country. His recordings were selling millions of copies and he had attracted many talented musicians to his large orchestra. Among these were performers such as Bix Beiderbecke, Frank Trumbauer, Eddie Lang, and Joe Venuti, who had already absorbed the essential elements of jazz improvisation and rhythm.

And as America ventured further into the "Jazz Age," Whiteman and his stable of talented arrangers provided greater opportunities for these so-called get-off men to infuse hot solos into the ensemble's rather restrained style. In doing so, Whiteman created a curious musical hybrid. According to Gunther Schuller's generous assessment (in *Early Jazz*), "The Whiteman orchestra achieved much that was admirable, and there is no question that it was admired (and envied) by many musicians, both black and white. . . . It was not jazz, of course—or perhaps only intermittently so."

Alert to the changing musical tastes taking place during the era, however, Whiteman shrewdly dubbed himself "King of Jazz" and, in 1924, booked New York's Aeolian Hall to present his music to an audience of influential music world personalities. His express purpose was "to show these skeptical people the advances which had been made in popular music from the day of discordant early jazz to the melodious form of the present." As a nod to that past, Whiteman programmed an exaggerated novelty style re-creation of the ODJB's "Livery Stable Blues," but he quickly moved on to the lush symphonized syncopations that he was proposing as the new model for jazz.

The evening was climaxed by the première of George Gershwin's *Rhapsody in Blue,* which represented Whiteman's vision of a musical alchemy that would refine the base metal of jazz into the golden sounds of a new American music. Although it has gone on to take its place as one of the most cherished works in our nation's musical canon, initially the *Rhapsody* got a mixed critical reaction. It also shared another element with the rest of the

FIGURE 3-9.   After the 1924 première of George Gershwin's *Rhapsody in Blue,* the young composer was hailed as a hero of the "symphonic jazz" movement, which—as one critic put it—sought to redeem the "savage rhythm" of jazz by clothing it in "the classic garb of the concerto." Author's collection.

George Gershwin: "Rhapsody" and "Rhythm"

Whatever its virtues, most critics now agree that *Rhapsody in Blue* isn't jazz. In fact, Gershwin's real significance in jazz history isn't based on any of his "serious" compositions but on the popular songs he wrote for Tin Pan Alley, Broadway shows, and Hollywood musicals. While jazz musicians have continuously performed their own versions of these Gershwin tunes ever since they were first written, they have adopted one in particular as their own.

Composed in 1932, "I Got Rhythm" is probably the most frequently performed tune in the history of jazz. Although scores of jazz greats (including Benny Goodman, Art Tatum, Louis Armstrong, Don Byas, Glenn Miller, and Oscar Peterson) have recorded the song itself, countless new jazz tunes have been created using the tune's appealing harmonic structure (or "chord changes"). In fact, it's such a jam-session favorite that any time performers get together to engage in informal improvisation, someone's bound to announce that it's time to play some " 'Rhythm' changes."

An exceedingly abbreviated anthology of jazz tunes constructed on the harmonic foundation of "I Got Rhythm" includes: "Cotton Tail" (Duke Ellington), "Lester Leaps In" (Count Basie/Lester Young), "Anthropology," "Shaw 'Nuff," "Red Cross," and "Moose the Mooche" (all by Charlie Parker and/or Dizzy Gillespie), "Apple Honey" (Woody Herman), "Chippie" (Ornette Coleman), "Hesitation" (Wynton Marsalis), and "Tuskegee Strutter's Ball" (Don Byron).

pieces on the evening's program; for while Gershwin's brilliant composition assimilated some jazz tonalities and rhythms into a classically oriented impressionistic pastiche—it wasn't jazz.

In her musical/social history of the 1920s, *The Jazz Revolution,* Kathy Ogren explains the motivation of those figures who were attempting to "rescue" jazz and establish its cultural legitimacy: "In a sense, Whiteman and others like him were trying to have it both ways," she writes. "They wanted to disassociate jazz from its Afro-American traditions, but to preserve the excitement of the music. . . . The musicians would play (even with some bursts of carefully controlled improvisation), but there would be little of the spontaneity and none of the challenge to conventional morality that the cabaret and rent party posed."

So, as we've seen, despite the vastly different conceptions of "jazz" they embodied, Fletcher Henderson, Duke Ellington, and Paul Whiteman had all found a home for their music in the same city. For, by the mid-1920s, not only was New York the capitol of the theater world (Broadway) and the center of music publishing (Tin Pan Alley) but—with the rise of network radio—it also had become the national headquarters of the new electronic media. The increasingly important dance band booking agencies and the burgeoning movie industry also called New York their home. But there was one other factor in establishing the city as the epicenter of jazz activity at this point in its history—Harlem.

TAKE ME TO HARLEM

During the first two decades of the twentieth century, a huge influx of migrants from the South resulted in a doubling of New York City's African-American population. And as the city's real estate market adapted to this demographic pressure, one venerable neighborhood of stately brownstones and bleak tenements—known as Harlem—was transformed into New York's dominant African-American enclave.

Attracted by the same opportunities that had made Manhattan a magnet for their white counterparts, black musicians, artists, and writers also gravitated to the city, and a dynamic African-American creative community began to form "Uptown." But the fact that distinguished intellectuals (such as W. E. B. Dubois and E. Franklin Frazier), writers (such as Langston Hughes and Zora Neale Hurston), and musicians (such as Duke Ellington and Fats Waller) all walked the same Uptown streets doesn't mean they all shared the same vision for the cultural renaissance that was taking shape in Harlem.

In fact, for most of arbitors of African-American art, jazz was an embarrassment. As the historian Nathan Irvin Huggins explains in his book *Harlem Renaissance,* "While many Harlem intellectuals enjoyed the music of the cabarets, none were prepared to give someone like Jelly Roll Morton the serious attention he deserved. Jazz was entertainment and not an ingredient of high civilization."

Of course, for white New Yorkers, debates concerning the cultural status of the African-American jazz musician were absurd; for, while some Downtown visitors were attracted to Harlem's exotic nightspots by the exciting music, many others simply came for the illicit thrill of observing the "primitive rites of the darker races." And Harlem's clubs, cabarets, and dance halls offered such explorers everything from the funkiest cellar speakeasy to the "whites-only," celebrity-studded sophistication of the Cotton Club (the gangster-operated nightspot where Duke Ellington's five-year engagement—and live radio broadcasts—would bring him to the attention of the nation).

While Harlem's own residents may have been excluded from the Cotton Club, they found a warmer welcome at such favorite local haunts as Small's Paradise, the Alhambra Ballroom, the Lenox Club, and—the legendary "home of happy feet"—the Savoy Ballroom. Here anyone could enjoy an affordable night out dancing to swinging jazz bands such as those led by Fletcher Henderson, Elmer Snowden, Teddy Hill, and Fess Williams, among dozens of others. Along such major thoroughfares as Seventh Avenue and Lenox Avenue there also were theaters, musician's hangouts, and after-hours clubs where Harlem's jazz scene flourished. Finally, there was the more intimate world of the Harlem "rent party," where pianists provided the entertainment for an apartment full of guests who had kicked in some spare change to help a needy neighbor avoid eviction.

It was an intensely creative musical environment filled with colorful characters who were in the process of forging a new conception of jazz piano and who, through their dazzling techniques, were helping to raise the level of jazz performance in general. Born in the last years of the nineteenth century, the pioneers of the Harlem piano

FIGURE 3-10.   Weighing in at over three hundred pounds, he wasn't called "Fats" for nothing. But Thomas ("Fats") Waller—an awesome pianist, prolific composer, and engaging vocalist—was not just physically big, he was also one of the biggest (and highest paid) jazz stars of his time. Courtesy of RCA Records. A Unit of BMG Entertainment.

Fats!

Born in 1904, Fats Waller began to play piano as a child and soon he was accompanying silent films on the organ at one of uptown New York's famous movie palaces; but his real musical studies began when James P. Johnson—the acknowledged master of the Harlem Stride piano style—took him on as a pupil. Before long, Fats was a regular on the local circuit of rent parties, jam sessions, and cutting contests.

While still a teenager, he also had found a niche in New York's burgeoning music industry, making piano rolls and writing songs. Some of these songs—especially those he wrote with the lyricist Andy Razaf—have become American pop classics. Then Fats began to record definitive versions of his songs (including "Honeysuckle Rose," "Keepin' out of Mischief Now," "The Joint Is Jumpin'," and "Ain't Misbehavin' ") in his own inimitable style.

On the basis of his musical skills, as well as his enormous personal appeal, Waller quickly became a familiar figure on both big-time radio and the silver screen. The classic Fats Waller image was captured in his scene-stealing performance in the 1943 Hollywood film *Stormy Weather:* Derby hat planted just so, his ever-mobile eyebrows seeming to put quotes around each line he sang, Fats combined comic mugging with a seemingly effortless instrumental virtuosity.

But his partying wasn't only limited to the stage or screen. His life became one long, nonstop jam session fueled by huge quantities of food and alcohol. And then suddenly the party ended. Fats Waller died on a train bound for New York from Hollywood shortly after filming *Stormy Weather.* He was just thirty-nine years old.

concept—such as Luckeyth (Luckey) Roberts (b. 1895), James P. Johnson (b. 1891), and Willie (the Lion) Smith (b. 1897)—had started out during the ragtime era. But, after abandoning the formal syncopations of Joplin (and the other ragtime composers), they began infusing their improvisations with a rhythmic freedom and propulsive swing that qualified as jazz.

The Harlem "ticklers" (as they were called) evolved a rich chordal piano style built on steady, heavily percussive left-hand patterns that sounded like the confident "stride" of a urban dandy. And that's exactly what the keyboard wizards who invented the so-called Harlem Stride piano style were. Each affected his own sartorial trademarks—like spats or a bowler hat—and zealously guarded his repertoire of trademark pianistic devices. And they moved like royalty through their own private realm of rent parties and insider's hangouts (where a shifting hierarchy was established based on the outcome of the most recent "cutting contest"). Through their influence on younger pianists such as Fats Waller, Teddy Wilson, and Ellington himself, Harlem Stride became a foundation for the entire twentieth-century jazz piano tradition.

GOIN' TO KANSAS CITY: THE STORY OF SOUTHWESTERN SWING

While histories of jazz used to present the music's evolution as a mythic journey up the Mississippi River from New Orleans to Chicago and eastward to New York City, it has long been recognized that jazz had taken root in many cities large and small during the early twentieth century. And like the diversification that occurs when a species of plant is grown in different environments, regional variations soon began to flower across America.

One locale that nurtured a particularly hearty strain of jazz was the "Southwest." In this case, the reference is not to the painted deserts and mesas of New Mexico and Arizona but to the area *south* and *west* of Illinois that runs from Missouri down through Arkansas, Oklahoma, and into northern Texas. The entry point to this vast geographical expanse was Kansas City.

Back during the great westward expansion of the early 1800s, Kansas City had been the starting point for adventurous emigrants heading out on the Santa Fe and Oregon Trails. But from the end of the Civil War into the first decades of the twentieth century, Kansas City itself became the destination of choice for thousands who sought opportunities in what had become the region's urban and commercial center. Yet Kansas City retained its frontier ambiance, and as it was also a cattle and railroad hub, there was always a demand for unskilled labor. Among those who flocked to "Kaycee" were black migrants escaping both the rigors of sharecropping and the ravages of the boll weevil that had destroyed the Southern cotton economy at the turn of the twentieth century. In addition, Kansas City already had a rich tradition of musical innovation.

With Sedalia, Missouri—the site of Scott Joplin's first triumphs—only a few miles way, Kansas City was right in the heart of ragtime country, and Joplin disciples such as James Scott continued to make the area their home well into the twentieth century. In addition, Kansas City had long been a magnet for blues singers who had followed their audience on each of their migrations out of the Deep South. Indeed, it seemed that African-American performers of all kinds could have joined in with the chorus of that Fifties' R & B classic, "Kansas City": "Goin' to Kansas City, Kansas City here I come. . . ."

Another element that contributed to the flowering of Kansas City jazz, however, was the compost of political corruption. As Mary Lou Williams (a pioneering Kansas City pianist and arranger) recalled many years later: "Now, at this time, which was still Prohibition, Kansas City was under Tom Pendergast's control. Most of the night spots were run by politicians and hoodlums, and the town was wide open for drinking, gambling and pretty much every form of vice. Naturally work was plentiful for musicians." By the mid-1920s, there were few places where jazz performers had greater opportunities for employment or where the music itself found a more appreciative audience.

While Kansas City was the epicenter of Southwestern jazz, within a two-hundred-mile radius dozens of so-called territory bands also had sprung up during this period to meet the needs of local dancers. Each of these mobile bands struggled to carve out a regional reputation, often by "carving" a rival band in regular "cutting contests." By defeating the competition in these battles of the bands, the victor could secure the best gigs the territory had to offer. Each band strove to be the first to assimilate the various innovations taking place in jazz while maintaining its distinctive regional accent. At first, area ensembles found it hard to shake off the remnants of the

FIGURE 3-11. In the 1930s, Mary Lou Williams was the pianist and arranger for Andy Kirk's Clouds of Joy, one of the best of the Kansas City swing bands. The skill and intensity she brought to both of these activities soon earned her the title "The Lady Who Swings the Band." Archive photo. Frank Driggs Collection.

Mary Lou Williams: The Lady Who Swung the Band

When the Swing Era began, the arranger became king—or in Mary Lou's case, queen. The "head arrangement"—a musical plan for a tune worked out through discussion—that had served the early New Orleans and Chicago bands was no longer sufficient now that jazz "orchestras" had grown to twelve or fourteen pieces. A more structured approach was required, a detailed *written* arrangement, like the score of a classical composition.

During her twelve years with Andy Kirk's band, and in those that followed—when she worked as a freelance arranger for Louis Armstrong, Benny Goodman, and Duke Ellington—Williams became one of the great practitioners of this underappreciated art. The only female member of the era's fraternity of innovative arrangers (that included Don Redman, Fletcher Henderson, Benny Carter, and Edgar Sampson), Mary Lou Williams helped make the Swing Era swing.

formal ragtime rhythm, but when they did, the Southwest jazz bands developed a rocking, bluesy, uninhibited sound that would soon be at the cutting edge of the music's evolution.

As territory bands from Oklahoma, Arkansas, and Texas also gravitated to Kansas City, the competition became even more fierce. The first to emerge out of this Darwinian struggle for survival—and gain wider recognition for the Southwestern style—was the Bennie Moten Band. Moten, a Kansas City native, had formed a six-piece ensemble in 1923 that had made some of the earliest records by a black jazz band. At that point, their music was a close approximation of the classic New Orleans style, but over the next few years—as the Moten band grew to eight and then ten pieces—their own distinctive sound began to take shape.

Rather than adopt the sophisticated, structurally complex arrangements Fletcher Henderson and Don Redman were creating for the newly expanded jazz orchestra back East, Moten constructed a more basic concept that was grounded in ensemble or section "riffs" set against strong solo passages. By structuring pieces around these short, imaginatively designed repeated patterns, Moten's band created a feeling of escalating intensity that must have thrilled the dancers who were their most important clients. And having attracted a core of highly skilled, blues-oriented improvisors, Moten provided them with every opportunity to solo.

Another reason for Kansas City's more free-wheeling style of jazz was the fact that for the most part it had originated in the seemingly nonstop "jam sessions" for which the city would become so (in)famous. Sammy Price, one of the era's most versatile pianists, has provided us with one of the best descriptions of a typical Kansas City jam. "I remember once at the Subway Club, on Eighteenth Street," he recalled decades later, "I came by a session at about ten o'clock and then went home to clean up and change my clothes. I came back a little after one o'clock and they were still playing the same song." With so much of Kansas City jazz developing in these marathon sessions of informal music making, it was no wonder that the ensemble riff and the competition-honed solo gradually emerged as the key elements of the classic Kansas City style.

Legend has it that the only time Benny Moten's band was ever "cut," it was at the hands of Walter Page's Blue Devils, another ambitious territory band that had recently come to Kansas City from Oklahoma. Having gradually built a roster of exciting soloists (such as alto saxophonist Buster Smith, trumpeter "Hot Lips Page," trombone/guitarist/arranger Eddie Durham, blues shouter Jimmy Rushing, and William Basie—who had not been dubbed "Count"—on piano), by the late 1920s, the Blue Devils had vanquished most of the regional competition.

But while Page may have won his battle with Benny Moten, it was Moten who won the war. He immediately "raided" Page's band and took over all his great soloists. Something else he took from the Blue Devils was a new rhythmic concept that Walter Page—the first great string bass player in jazz—is created with originating. For, rather than the strongly accented two-to-the-bar rhythmic patterns that had characterized jazz since it emerged out of the marching bands of New Orleans, Page used his bass as the foundation of a smoother, evenly accented yet propulsive four-to-the-bar beat.

As the Twenties drew to a close, other territory bands such as the Alphonso Trent Band and Andy Kirk's Twelve Clouds began to attract attention with their own versions of the Southwest style. Propelled by a steady, driving $\frac{4}{4}$ beat, a repertoire of infectious riffs and a bevy of blues-inflected soloists, it was the gritty, Kansas City jazz bands—as much as their big city cousins back East—that would swing America into a new musical era.

THE SWING ERA: SETTING THE STAGE

Over the lush backdrop of some slickly arranged theme song, the announcer's smooth, syrupy voice intones an introduction that has become one of the cliches of 1930s popular culture: "From high atop the elegant 'Hotel Xanadu' in New York City, we bring you the scintillating sounds of the 'Rus Washburn Orchestra'. . ." And in homes all around the country millions of Americans gathered each night in the soft glow of their radio dial—listening.

By the mid-1930s, radio linked all of America together with an immediacy and thoroughness that had never existed before and, more than any other single factor during this decade, it was radio that established itself as the most potent force shaping the musical taste of the country. While some local stations might offer a particular regional style—like the dozens of Southern stations transmitting country music—for the most part national networks dominated the airwaves, and bland dance music and the latest Tin Pan Alley songs were overwhelmingly their music of choice.

Both the major radio networks (the National Broadcasting Corporation and the Columbia Broadcasting System), as well as the less powerful Mutual network, adhered to a "live music" policy. Even the few nonnetwork radio shows that did feature recordings (like the famous "Make Believe Ballroom") attempted to replicate the ambiance of a live broadcast. Programming was usually organized in fifteen-minute or half-hour blocks that were financed in their entirety by a single national brand sponsor. As for the music itself—whether it originated in some New York studio or was a "remote broadcast" from a hotel ballroom or nightclub—it was, for the most part, little more than a sweet salve that seemed carefully formulated to sooth the raw wounds of a Depression-scarred nation.

The 1929 stock market crash had sent its shockwaves across the entire economy. Although much of the record business was devastated, the segment of the industry marketed to the African-American community simply shattered like one of the fragile shellac disks it had once sold in the millions. Many of the era's black recording artists—including jazz stars like Jelly Roll Morton, King Oliver, and Sidney Bechet—lost their contracts, and the entire Race catalogs of major labels were abruptly discontinued. Unfortunately, opportunities for live performances were also drastically reduced during this period—and not only by of the absence of the discretionary income that could finance a night out at a club or speakeasy.

In 1927, the first commercially successful sound film was released. Entitled *The Jazz Singer*, it was really just a sentimental melodrama built around the blackface minstrel act of vaudeville star Al Jolson. But the novelty of the new medium—as well as the escapist fantasies it projected onto the screen—quickly thrust the new medium into the forefront of popular entertainment. The "talkies" became one more factor in the disappearance of authentic jazz from the mainstream of American popular culture during the early 1930s.

One other factor that played a significant role in the decade's musical environment was the repeal of Prohibition in 1933. Part of the appeal of the venues that had first featured jazz was their illicit, forbidden aspect. With the legalization of alcohol, much of that mystique vanished. Of course, another reality of American society—racial segregation—remained as entrenched as ever. So, while adventurous whites might make nocturnal forays into Harlem to hear black jazz, notoriously timid radio executives and corporate advertisers (as well as the ever-present guardians of public morality) combined to ensure that it would not sully the purity of the American home.

As black jazz bands provided propulsive, swinging accompaniment for a profusion of complex and acrobatic new dance styles in African-American enclaves across the country, white jazz bands filled the airwaves with the soothing, "sweet" dance music that radio programmers demanded. That's certainly what Benny Goodman did when he arrived in New York just as the bottom fell out of the stock market.

BENNY GOODMAN: KING OF SWING

Benny Goodman was born in Chicago in 1909. One of a dozen children, he began studying the clarinet at the age of ten at a local Jewish settlement house and, by the time he was twelve, he had already started down the path to a career as a professional musician. It was also during these formative years that Goodman first heard recordings that exposed him to the early New Orleans jazz clarinetists.

In 1924, Goodman's technical virtuosity and jazz skills had so advanced that he was hired to be the featured soloist in a nationally known band led by Ben Pollack (the former drummer of the New Orleans Rhythm Kings, the pioneering white jazz band that had been one of young Benny's favorites). And although he was barely into his teens, Goodman had already developed the unique musical personality—combining a searingly hot surface intensity with a core of cool detachment—that he would maintain throughout his long career.

Unlike many of the other young white jazz performers of his generation who had come to the music as "true believers" (for whom authenticity was the supreme quest), Goodman's criteria were those of the "true professional" (whose values were instrumental mastery, absolute reliability, and musical adaptability). Although this pragmatic philosophy may have been rooted in Goodman's own economically deprived childhood, the result was

FIGURE 3-12. Benny Goodman and longtime drummer Gene Krupa. According to most jazz histories, the Swing Era officially began on August 21, 1935, when the Benny Goodman Orchestra's performance at Los Angeles' Palomar Ballroom sent young fans into a dancing frenzy. Goodman was immediately dubbed the "King of Swing," and the entire nation was swept up in a propulsive style of jazz that had been the music of choice in African-American communities for at least five years. Courtesy of the RCA Records Label. A Unit of BMG Entertain-

Benny Goodman: King of Swing

A clarinet virtuoso, imaginative improviser, and compulsive perfectionist, Benny Goodman made the cross-country jaunt that culminated in his Palomar breakthrough as the leader of a young, aggressive, and finely honed ensemble studded with superior soloists. And unlike the era's other white bandleaders, who were churning out some variation of the "sweet" dance music concocted to soothe a Depression-ravaged America, Goodman had committed himself to a style of swinging "hot" jazz pioneered by black bands led by Chick Webb, Benny Moten, and Fletcher Henderson.

The enthusiastic embrace of Goodman's exuberant sound and infectious arrangements signaled a profound shift in the musical landscape. As the musicologist and Swing Era historian Gunther Schuller has pointed out, "Here was a happy and rare coincidence: a large segment of the public seemed to prefer the best and most advanced arrangements the band had to offer, not, for once, the worst. Incredibly, jazz—at least one kind of jazz—had reached a potentially huge audience." And with an astonishing rapidity made possible by the (relatively) new medium of radio, the bespectacled twenty-five-year-old clarinetist became the most successful jazz performer in the music's history.

a personal aesthetic that served him well as the effects of the Depression forced him to depend on anonymous session work in New York recording studios and temp jobs in network radio dance bands.

After arriving in New York in 1928, Benny Goodman put in countless hours churning out bland commercial dance music, eventually appearing on over six hundred recordings. But he also started playing on sessions with some of the greatest soloists in jazz, both white and black. He made a brief appearance on Bessie Smith's last records and was featured on Billie Holiday's first. Meanwhile, Benny was assembling a dance band of his own and was beginning to get work as a leader. But just when it seemed he was on the verge of being permanently typecast as an all-purpose pop-music pro, Benny Goodman emerged as the first musical superstar of the electronic mass media.

CORONATION IN CALIFORNIA

When the three-hour weekly radio show "Let's Dance" went on the air late in 1934, Goodman's recently formed band was hired to close the program. The live-from-New-York studio broadcast began at 10:30 on Saturday night, with half-hour blocks devoted to different bands, each playing their own variation on the standard commercial musical fare. Since his segment didn't go on the air until about 1:00 A.M., the show's producer and wary advertisers weren't too concerned that Goodman was pushing the outer edge of the musical envelope (at least within the context of network radio). For, especially when contrasted with the syrupy sound of the show's other bands, Goodman's up-tempo, sharply honed ensemble actually swung.

The real importance of radio for any band wasn't its pay scale (which was relatively modest), but its promotional power (which proved awesome). Network exposure meant better gigs and higher fees when a band toured. So, soon after Goodman's "Let's Dance" contract was up, he hit the road with a book of "hot" arrangements and an obsessively rehearsed band. But rather than generating the kind of excitement their music was designed to inspire, they were greeted apathetically at best and, more often, with open hostility.

Although by the summer of 1935, the most devastating affects of the Depression were beginning to recede, audiences still didn't seem ready to give up their security blanket of soothing "sweet bands." The tour was a disaster and by the time they got to California, a thoroughly disappointed (but ever-adaptable) Goodman was ready to pack it in and give audiences what they wanted. But when he got to the Palomar Ballroom in Hollywood that August he found a mob of teenagers that stretched around the block, and what they wanted Benny to do was swing! What had happened? Well, the explanation reveals a great deal both about the power of the media and the influence of a youth culture that was about to assume its role as the arbiter of popular music in America.

As it turned out, Goodman's "Let's Dance" slot was simply broadcast too late for the East Coast teenagers and twenty-somethings who might have responded to his soaring, fast-paced rhythms. But, their West Coast cousins (benefiting from the three-hour time difference) had turned his live radio performances into the soundtrack for their own prime-time Saturday night dance parties. So, as soon as the posters went up advertising Benny's upcoming Hollywood appearance, the youthful crowds started to form. Goodman had found his audience, and after months of frustration, the band became an overnight sensation. They stayed at the Palomar for eight months and, by the time they left, both Benny and Big Band Swing had taken over the country.

Back in the 1920s, a generation of young white rebels formed a "Jazz Age" vanguard. But, in fact, these record-collecting hipsters were a numerically small subculture drawn from narrow geographical and demographic groups. The "Swing Era" audience, by contrast, was drawn from a much broader demographic base of adolescents and this generation of fans coalesced around a style of music that was disseminated by a potent, national mass medium. By forging a group identity not only through a particular style of music, but through styles of dance, dress, and speech, these swing kids represent both a cultural phenomenon unlike any that had previously existed and provide an archetype for every pop music revolution that would follow.

A QUESTION OF COLOR

In supplying the musical inspiration for the Swing Era, however, Benny Goodman not only can be credited with establishing a pattern for pop music success, but he can be viewed as personifying a troubling trend that also would be replicated throughout the second half of the twentieth century. For the bulk of the brilliant arrangements that Goodman had been performing on his "Let's Dance" broadcasts—and that, through his Palomar triumph, had ignited the Swing Era—happened to be the creation of the black big band leader, Fletcher Henderson.

As we have seen, it was Henderson, as much as anyone else, who evolved the basic techniques that moved jazz away from the collective, polyphonic, small-group concept of the New Orleans era. In its place, he (and his coarranger, Don Redman) created the blueprint for the modern big band sound that balanced a swinging ensemble performing written arrangements along with solo improvisations. So in 1934, when economic difficulties caused the breakup of his band (despite an array of brilliant musicians like Red Allen, Benny Morten, and Coleman Hawkins, among others), not only did Goodman jump at the chance to buy Henderson's "book" (repertoire of unique arrangements), but he hired Fletcher himself to write new material for his weekly radio broadcasts.

Goodman was a consummate musician, as well as a skilled and creative improviser. During an era of strict racial segregation, he made it a point to hire the hardest-swinging white musicians on the scene (including Bunny Berigan, Harry James, Jess Stacey, and Gene Krupa), and he honed them into a tight and exciting jazz band. Yet, the degree to which Benny Goodman's phenomenal commercial success was predicated on the creative contributions of a marginalized African-American musician has continued to cloud Goodman's reputation in many minds. Yet as others have pointed out, however, once Goodman secured his royal title—and the power that went with it—he devoted himself to the risky job of breaking down the racial barriers that continued to prevent musical integration both on the radio and on stage.

In the anonymity of the recording studio Benny had long played in integrated esembles, but after achieving national prominence, he became the first bandleader to perform in public with a racially "mixed" group. The Benny Goodman Trio—featuring the African-American pianist Teddy Wilson—debuted in Chicago in 1936. On the basis of Goodman's commercial clout, the band played from the bandstands of the nation's most élite hotels and the stages of its most prestigious concert halls. Over the next few years, Goodman would expand his small group to a quintet with the addition of two other extraordinary black musicians, the vibraphonist Lionel Hampton and the pioneering electric guitarist Charlie Christian. While the recordings he made with these small groups had little commercial impact at the time, today they are generally acknowledged to be Goodman's greatest artistic achievement.

Although Goodman's big band (on which his reputation and income were primarily based) remained all white for another few years, when Goodman gave a historic jazz concert at Carnegie Hall in 1938, one of the evening's highlights was an integrated jam session featuring members of both the Count Basie and Duke Ellington bands, including Buck Clayton, Lester Young, Johnny Hodges, and Freddie Green.

Benny Goodman's career, therefore, not only reflects the racial dilemmas of American culture, but it also reveals the difficulty of perserving one's artistic integrity in the face of the marketplace. To his credit, Goodman continually struggled to reconcile his strong jazz instincts (as preserved in his small group masterpieces and such big band jazz classics as "King Porter Stomp," "Devil and the Deep Blue Sea," and "Wrappin' It Up" among others) with his innate drive for commercial success. Yet, for most of the other big-name white orchestras that came to symbolize the "Big Band Era," such conflicts rarely arose.

While the actual jazz content of their styles varied, white bands—like those led by Jimmy Dorsey, Glenn Miller, and Harry James—usually adhered to the same basic formula of showcasing one or two "hot" soloists within a context of slick (but rather tame) arrangements of contemporary popular songs. And as the market became glutted with new bands, the music became less important than either the "image" a band projected or the "personality" of its leader; increasingly bands relied on corny gimmicks, novelty tunes, and—most importantly—the appeal of their featured vocalists in order to claim their share of the Swing Era audience.

Meanwhile, Black America had been swinging for years. Scores of extraordinary black bands had been making the most dynamic music of the decade in relative obscurity—or, at best, on the commercial margins of the national music scene. In Kansas City, Count Basie's band was bursting with bluesy riffs and searing soloists, while at

FIGURE 3-13.   Although this publicity photo was artfully staged to create an aura of romantic glamour, in fact during its heyday (in the early 1940s), the Glenn Miller Orchestra was regularly playing its glossy, jazz-tinged dance music in swank hotel ballrooms and upscale resorts. It was a rarified—and financially rewarding—world that few other Swing Era bands could even dream of attaining. Courtesy of the RCA Records label. A Unit of BMG Entertainment.

Glenn Miller: Putting America "In the Mood"

During the late 1920s and early 1930s, Glenn Miller was performing in assorted dance bands and playing his trombone on hundreds of miscellaneous recording sessions; gradually, he also was garnering a considerable reputation as an arranger for bands led by Red Nichols, Ray Noble, and the Dorsey brothers. In 1937, he decided it was time to reap the rewards of his varied talents for himself.

By 1939, the Glenn Miller Orchestra's live appearances were breaking attendance records in every dance hall and theater he played, and his nationally broadcast show was one of the highest rated on the radio. Of the hundreds of recordings the band made, some, such as "In the Mood" (an elegant and cleverly arranged riff-based number) and "Chattanooga Choo Choo" (featuring the vocal harmony group, the Modernaires) are counted among the biggest sellers of the entire pre-rock era.

Then in 1942, along with a number of other Swing Era veterans, Glenn Miller went to war. After enlisting, he formed a large orchestra to entertain the troops overseas. Two years later, while flying across the English Channel, his small plane disappeared and his body was never located.

Harlem's Savoy Ballroom, drummer Chick Webb had taken up long-term residence with his powerful orchestra. Other bands led by Earl Hines, Jimmie Lunceford, and Cab Calloway were also keeping the dance floors filled. And, while black America may not have had a "King" (of Swing), it did have its "Duke."

DUKE ELLINGTON: IT DON'T MEAN A THING IF IT AIN'T GOT THAT SWING

Back in 1932—some three years before Benny Goodman was crowned the "King of Swing"—Duke Ellington had already recorded the song that would serve as the era's anthem: "It Don't Mean a Thing if It Ain't Got That Swing." At this point, the Ellington band was completing the historic five-year engagement at New York's Cotton Club that had elevated Duke to a unique status in black music. He had assembled a band of stellar musicians (many of whom would remain with him for their entire professional lives) and he had begun to amass a body of work that would entitle him to be numbered as one of the greatest composers of the twentieth century.

Despite its exclusive, celebrity-studded ambiance, however, the Cotton Club didn't exactly provide the most suitable environment for Ellington's unerring artistry or his personal dignity. Owned by the Prohibition-era gangster Owney Madden, the Cotton Club's interior design was constructed around pseudo-African images and its admission policy excluded black patrons. Stage shows featured light-skinned chorus girls and exotic dancers set against a stereotypical "jungle" motif. Yet, as he would throughout his career, Ellington miraculously transcended the demeaning context he found himself in to create transcendent music.

One of the most famous and apt descriptions of Ellington the musician is that—although he played the piano—his real instrument was his band. Unlike most leaders, Ellington didn't simply write or arrange his tunes for an instrument but, rather, each arrangement was tailored for the unique qualities of a specific musician. Ellington used each of the fourteen members of his band the way a painter might use a particular color on his or her palette.

And Duke had some extraordinary colors to work with: from the earthy richness of Harry Carney's baritone sax to the expressive warmth of Johnny Hodges's alto and from the magisterially lyrical trombonist Lawrence Brown to the high-note pyrotechnics of trumpeter Cootie Williams. Each player contributed another tonal quality or stylistic voice and Duke found ways to combine them in brilliant, harmonically rich, impressionistic masterpieces.

After composing such Cotton Club–era hits as "Mood Indigo," "Creole Love Call," and "Rockin' in Rhythm," Ellington began to create extended works that broke the three-minute barrier (which was the outer limit of what could fit on one side of a 78 r.p.m. record). The first of these, "Reminiscing in Tempo" (recorded in 1935), was a beautifully developed composition almost thirteen minutes in length that filled both sides of two ten-inch 78s.

During this period, Ellington also began to compose his great musical "landscapes," pieces such as "Daybreak Express" (that brilliantly evoked a train ride), or "Caravan" (a collaboration with his trombonist Juan Tizol, which suggested exotic images of a Middle Eastern journey). In his composition "Harlem Airshaft," Ellington used the same techniques to capture the rich life of one Uptown tenement. Throughout his career, Duke also tried his hand at musical "portraits" of cherished black performers such as the singers Ella Fitzgerald and Florence Mills and the multitalented vaudeville entertainer Bert Williams.

It was on his band's first visit to England in 1933 that Ellington began to receive serious validation for these efforts; in Europe, he was treated as an artist. But America seemed unable to reconcile its prejudices (both musical and racial), so—as big band swing became the popular music of America—Ellington continually had to struggle against constricting stereotypes. Yet, just as he had once transcended the demeaning stereotypes of the Cotton Club, Ellington was now able to gain unprecedented access both to radio and film without being subjected to the standard racial caricatures. Through a rare combination of personal dignity and musical genius, Duke Ellington established his own unique and permanent niche in American culture.

FIGURE 3-14. As a young man, Edward Kennedy Ellington was dubbed the "Duke" on the basis of his sartorial elegance and courtly demeanor. But, in fact, America's greatest jazz composer/bandleader earned his royal title over the course of a fifty-year career unrivaled for its breadth, variety, and sophistication. *Courtesy of the RCA Records Label. A Unit of BMG Entertainment.*

Duke Ellington: The Maestro

America's love affair with Duke Ellington began in 1927, when his brilliant young orchestra began its regular radio broadcasts from Harlem's legendary Cotton Club; it was during this same period that Ellington began recording his first classic compositions such as "The Mooch," "Creole Love Call," "Rockin' in Rhythm," and "Mood Indigo."

As his ambition and skill grew, Ellington became the first jazz composer to break out of the constraints of the standard three-minute record. On his 1935 recording "Reminiscing in Tempo," he created a unified piece that occupied both sides of two disks (with a total playing time of thirteen minutes). Duke continued to turn out classic jazz instrumentals and traditional popular songs, but over the next decade, he increasingly turned his creative energy to his so-called extended works. Among these masterpieces was the fifty-minute suite, "Black Brown and Beige" (described by its composer as "a tone parallel to the history of the American Negro"), which he premiered in 1943 at Carnegie Hall.

Among the long list of musicians who attained their place in jazz history as "Ellingtonians" were the alto saxophonist Johnny Hodges, tenor saxophonists Ben Webster and Paul Gonsalves, the baritone saxophonist Harry Carney, trumpeters Cootie Williams and Ray Nance, the clarinetist Barney Bigard, trombonists Lawrence Brown, Joe "Tricky Sam" Nanton, and Juan Tizol, the drummer Sonny Greer, and the bassist Jimmy Blanton (to name just a few). Unquestionably, however, the one person who stands as Duke Ellington's closest collaborator was his fellow composer/arranger and alter ego, Billy Strayhorn.

Beginning in 1939, when Strayhorn first brought Duke a couple of his compositions (including the now-classic ballad "Lush Life"), the two men forged a personal and working relationship that was so intimate that often neither one could identify what elements of a particular work belonged to whom. The other "Ellington" hits that are actually credited to Billy Strayhorn include "Satin Doll," "Chelsea Bridge," and Duke's world-famous theme song, "Take the A Train."

While any attempt to neatly summarize a career spanning more than half a century and encompassing over two thousand works would be foolhardy, the writer Albert Murray places Ellington's achievement alongside the literary accomplishments of "Emerson, Melville, Whitman, Twain, Hemingway, and Faulkner." "In any case," Murray concludes, "the Ellington canon, which consists mainly of three-minute dance pieces, is by far the most comprehensive orchestration of the actual sound and beat of life in the United States ever accomplished by an American composer."

COUNT BASIE: LAST OF THE BLUE DEVILS

Although the men who ran the music business in the 1930s were not exactly known for their philosophical inclinations, here's a metaphysical riddle, they might have entertained: "If a band swings in Kansas City, does it make a sound?"

Of course, for musicians criss-crossing the country on their endless one-nighters, K. C. was a musical mecca famous for the nonstop jam sessions that have become a part of jazz legend. But for record company executives, radio network programmers, band booking agents, and song pluggers, it was just "the sticks." As far as they were concerned, if it wasn't happening in New York, it just wasn't happening.

So where did that leave Bill Basie and the incredible band he had put together in 1935 with the cream of several defunct Kansas City ensembles, including the remnants of Walter Page's Blue Devils (with whom Basie had played at the end of the 1920s)? Perhaps stuck in Kansas City's sleazy Reno Club forever. That is, until fate intervened in the unassuming guise of the only New York music industry insider who was not only able to recognize the Basie band's greatness but who also had the clout to help them get a crack at the big time.

Freelance talent scout and record producer John Hammond was only twenty-five years old, but he had already been responsible for producing the last sessions of Bessie Smith and the first sessions of Billie Holiday, in addition to having had a crucial role in the skyrocketing career of Benny Goodman. In fact, it was while he was in Chicago with Goodman that Hammond turned on his car radio and happened to catch a late-night broadcast all the way from Kansas City.

"The nightly broadcast by the Count Basie band from the Reno Club was just beginning," Hammond wrote in his autobiography. "I couldn't believe my ears. . . . After that I went to my car every night to listen to Basie. . . . Once I even dragged Benny out to listen with me in that cold, cold car. . . . There I was in the parking lot of the Congress [Hotel], telling him that a nine-piece group in Kansas City was the best I ever heard. . . ." Through Hammond's connections, Basie was able to expand his band to fourteen pieces and get a record contract and a gig at Roseland Ballroom in midtown Manhattan.

Now that they were in the big city, the Basie band wondered what kind of reception they would get from an audience accustomed to the complex arrangements and professional sheen of the top East Coast orchestras. They needn't have worried. "When we first came to New York," Basie drummer Jo Jones recalled, "we tried to experiment. We tried to play some of the so-called modern arrangements of that era. Basie was of the opinion that the things we were playing were old hat. So after about a week of experimenting we found out that there was nothing old hat about what we had been doing." Before long, Basie's urgent, Southwestern swing (and impassioned, blues-based soloists) completely won over the New York audience.

With the media platform New York provided, Basie and his musicians began to attract national attention, and have a profound impact on the era's musical direction. After Basie's breakthrough, everyone had to swing a little harder just to keep up. Now the jazz world added a "Count" to its roster of musical royalty.

FIGURE 3-15.   Although "Count" Basie's royal title may have been somewhat less exalted than the Swing Era's "King" (Benny Goodman), most critics agree that, more than any other ensemble of the period, the band Basie led in the late 1930s embodied the very essence of the elusive—but essential—element of jazz that gave the decade its name. Archive photo. Frank Driggs Collection.

William ("Count") Basie: Swingin' the Blues

By the late 1920s, Bill Basie had found his way to Kansas City, Missouri, where a flourishing jazz scene was developing amid a frontier atmosphere of raucous bars, nightclubs, and brothels. After working as a sideman in two of the best of the Southwestern "territory bands," Basie put together his own nine-piece outfit with the cream of the region's talent. Unlike the jazz being made in the Big Apple, the "Kaycee" style was rough-edged and drenched in the blues. And rather than conform to complex written arrangements infused with sophisticated harmonies (as they did back East), Basie relied on a storehouse of spontaneously devised rhythmic patterns (known as "riffs") to provide the foundation for the improvisations of his incredible soloists.

While the band did boast a roster of stellar soloists such as Lester Young and his tenor sax compatriot, Herschel Evans, the trumpeters Buck Clayton and Harry "Sweets" Edison, and the trombonists Dicky Wells and Benny Morton (to name just a few), much of the credit for the unique Basie sound can be attributed to the almost telepathic connection achieved by the band's "rhythm section," which in addition to the Count's piano consisted of the guitarist Freddie Green, the bassist Walter Page, and the drummer Jo Jones. Hailed as the "All American Rhythm Section," they were the engine that both powered the Basie band and made it swing. This brings us to the inevitable question: What is swing? Judging from the responses of both jazz critics and performers it's a question whose answer is as much metaphysical as it is musical.

For example, in his two-volume study of the first fifty years of jazz history, the musicologist Gunther Schuller grapples with a definition of swing in several extended passages. Here is one of the most concise and focused of his conclusions (presented in his book *Early Jazz*): " 'Swing' is a force in music that maintains the perfect equilibrium between the horizontal and vertical relationships of musical sounds; that is a condition that pertains when both the verticality [the harmonic, or chordal, aspects of a musical structure] and horizontality [the melodic, or linear aspects of a musical structure] of any given musical moment are represented in perfect equivalence and oneness." By contrast, the great Basie drummer, Jo Jones—who should know a thing or two about the subject—rejects even the possibility of defining this fundamental aspect of jazz: "It's a real simple thing, but there are things you can't describe, some things that never been described. And swinging is one of them."

For further elucidation on the subject of swing, therefore, one might best be served by engaging in a little primary research within the Basie discography itself. For beginning in 1936, when they arrived in New York, the Basie band (and its small group spin-offs) recorded such essential examples of this essential element of jazz as "One O'Clock Jump" (Basie's famous theme song), "Every Tub," and "Swingin' the Blues" (with written charts by Eddie Durham, who led the band's evolution away from informal head arrangements), "Goin' to Chicago" (featuring the vocals of the band's great blues shouter, Jimmy Rushing), and Swing Era classics such as "Taxi War Dance," "Lester Leaps In," and "Jumpin' at the Woodside."

And, with the recording opportunities that were available in the city, many members of the Basie band had the chance to record as sidemen in a variety of contexts, including accompanying singers in small group settings. In fact, early in 1937—not long after the Kansas City band had established itself in New York—a couple of Basieites cut their first sides with the era's greatest singer, Billie Holiday.

LADY DAY

What Basie's sidemen—and the other musicians who accompanied her—quickly realized was that Billie Holiday was one of them. She was not just a vocalist but a jazz singer. She put her own personal stamp on everything she sang, subtly reshaping the melody of songs, playing with their rhythmic structure, and always interacting with the other members of the band. As Billie herself described it: "I don't think I'm singing. I feel like I playing a horn. I try to improvise like Les Young, like Louis Armstrong, or someone else I admire. What comes out is what I feel. I hate straight singing. I have to change a tune to my own way of doing it. That's all I know."

Although the 1930s was a golden age in the history of the American popular song, at first Billie had to work with second-rate material by third-rate songwriters. Song pluggers would save their best stuff for more prominent vocalists and, besides, they didn't approve of the "liberties" Holiday took with those songs she was given. But no matter how trite the material, Billie was always able to infuse it with meaning, or at least make it swing. And, throughout her career, Billie continually returned to the roots of jazz itself by singing the blues with heartbreaking authenticity.

Gradually her expanding popularity and reputation opened new opportunities for Billie to perform songs that matched her artistry. Over the next few years, Billie got a chance to record the best work of masters such as Cole Porter, Jerome Kern, Irving Berlin, Hoagy Charmichael, and the Gershwins. She also began to work with a corps of sympathetic sidemen that included such Basie band luminaries as the guitarist Freedy Greene, the trumpeter Buck Clayton, and the great tenor saxophonist Lester Young.

Although there is no evidence of a romantic connection between them, Billie's personal and musical bond with Young evolved into the most significant relationship in her life; it also proved to be one of the most creative and sympathetic partnerships in the history of jazz. She called him "Prez"—the President of the Tenor Sax—and he dubbed her "Lady Day." They may not have been lovers, but they made beautiful music together.

While Holiday conceived of herself as "playing a horn," she once said of Young that he "sings with his horn; you listen to him and can almost hear the words." During the late 1930s, Billie and Lester created a score of classic recordings (including "All of Me," "The Man I Love," "When You're Smiling," "I Must Have That Man," and

FIGURE 3-16.   After honing his skills in one of the best of Oklahoma's regional dance bands (the Blue Devils), Rushing made the move to Kansas City. It was here that he joined Count Basie's celebrated band as its first vocalist. Rushing remained with the Count for over twenty years. Along the way, he recorded such blues classics as "Good Morning Blues," "Sent for You Yesterday," and "Goin' to Chicago." On the basis of these recordings, many critics agree with the assessment of Will Friedwald (historian of the American singing tradition), who called Rushing "our all-time greatest male blues singer." Photo by Lee Tanner.

Excerpt from: "Remembering Jimmy" (Ralph Ellison)

In the old days the voice was high and clear and poignantly lyrical. Steel-bright in its upper range and, at its best, silky smooth, it was possessed of a purity somehow impervious to both the stress of singing above a twelve-piece band and the urgency of Rushing's own blazing fervor. On dance nights, when you stood on the rise of the school grounds two blocks to the east, you could hear it jetting from the dance hall like a blue flame in the dark; now soaring high above the trumpets and trombones, now skimming the froth of reeds and rhythm as it called some woman's anguished name—or demanded in a high, thin, passionately lyrical line, "Baaaaay-bay, Bay-aaaay-bay! Tell me what's the matter now!"—above the shouting of the swinging band.

 Nor was there need for the by now famous signature line: "If anybody asks you who sang this song/ Tell 'em/ it was little Jimmy Rushing/ he's been here and gone"—for everyone on Oklahoma City's "East Side" knew that sweet, high-floating sound. "Deep Second" was our fond nickname for the block in which Rushing worked and lived, and where most Negro business and entertainment were found, and before he went to cheer a wider world his voice evoked the festive spirit of the place. Indeed, he was the natural herald of its blues-romance, his song the singing essence of its joy. For Jimmy Rushing was not simply a local entertainer, he expressed a value, an attitude about the world for which our lives afforded no other definition. We had a Negro church and a segregated school, a few lodges and fraternal organizations, and beyond these there was all the great white world. We were pushed off to what seemed to be the least desirable side of the city (but which some years later was found to contain one of the state's richest pools of oil), and our system of justice was based upon Texas law, yet there was an optimism within the Negro community and a sense of possibility which, despite our awareness of limitation (dramatized so brutally in the Tulsa riot of 1921), transcended all of this; and it was this rock-bottom sense of reality, coupled with our sense of the possibility of rising above it, which sounded in Rushing's voice.

FIGURE 3-17.   "Mom and Pop were just a couple of kids when they got married," Billie Holiday tells us in the opening line of her 1956 autobiography, *Lady Sings the Blues.* "He was eighteen, she was sixteen, and I was three." Photo by Don Hunstein. Courtesy of Columbia Records.

Lady Sings the Blues

Although some of the factual details in Billie's book may be subject to question, the trauma and abuse she describes were only too real. Her childhood in Baltimore began with her abandonment by her father (Clarence Holiday, a jazz guitarist) and ended with her rape at the age of ten (by a forty-year-old neighbor).

While her mother worked as a domestic, Billie began earning her own income by scubbing the white stoops of the local rowhouses (for a nickel apiece) and by running errands for the girls at the corner whorehouse. This is where she first heard recordings by Bessie Smith and Louis Armstrong, the two performers who would become her greatest influences.

Although Billie joined her mother in the great migration north, things weren't any easier in New York than they had been back home. She turned to prostitution to survive, was arrested, and, after her release, began to make the rounds of Harlem speakeasies. In 1933, the eighteen-year-old Billie was singing at Monette's Supper Club when John Hammond heard her for the first time. Within a year, Hammond (who had already earned a considerable reputation on the New York music scene as a talent scout, record producer, and critic) arranged for her to make a record with Benny Goodman.

Her first vocal was on a corny, up-tempo number called "Your Mother's Son-in Law." She was paid $35. A few months later she sang one more number with a Goodman-led ensemble; but with the recording industry still suffering from the chilling effects of the Depression, Holiday wouldn't get the chance to make another record for almost two years. Finally, in 1935, John Hammond put together a small band (led by the pianist Teddy Wilson) to accompany Billie on a series of loose, jam-session style recordings for the expanding jukebox market. Over the next two years she recorded about one hundred songs that have become the basis of her musical reputation.

Billie continued to record into the early 1950s, often backed by large studio orchestras and occasionally by lush string arrangements. Although the sheer beauty of her voice had become ravaged by time, drugs, and alcohol, many of these songs possess their own haunting grandeur. In an essay on her later recordings, jazz critic Martin Williams referred to this period as "the triumphant decline of Billie Holiday." In July of 1959, following months of isolation and illness, she died in a New York City hospital.

The twentieth-century American poet Frank O'Hara documented his reaction to the news of Holiday's passing in one his most famous works, "The Day Lady Died." The poem captures how our preoccupation with the events of our daily lives can suddenly seem petty and inconsequential when confronted with the tragic death of a great artist.

"The Day Lady Died" (Frank O'Hara)

It is 12:20 in New York a Friday
three days after Bastille Day, yes
it is 1959 and I go get a shoeshine
because I will get off the 4:19 in Easthampton
at 7:15 and then go straight to dinner
and I don't know the people who will feed me

I walk up the muggy street beginning to sun
and have a hamburger and a malted and buy
an ugly NEW WORLD WRITING to see what the poets
in Ghana are doing these days
                       I go on to the bank
and Miss Stillwagon (first name Linda I once heard)
doesn't even look up my balance for once in her life
and in the GOLDEN GRIFFIN I get a little Verlaine
for Patsy with drawings by Bonnard although I do
think of Hesiod, trans. Richmond Lattimore or
Brendan Behan's new play or *Le Balcon* or *Les Negrès*
of Genet, but I don't, I stick with Verlaine
after practically going to sleep with quandariness

and for Mike I just stroll into the PARK LANE
Liquor Store and ask for a bottle of Strega and
then I go back where I came from to 6th Avenue
and the tobacconist in the Ziegfeld Theatre and
casually ask for a carton of Gauloises and a carton
of Picayunes, and a NEW YORK POST with her face on it

and I am sweating a lot by now and thinking of
leaning on the john door in the FIVE SPOT
while she whispered a song along the keyboard
to Mal Waldron and everyone and I stopped breathing

"Laughing at Life" to name just a few) that are a testament to their musical and personal bond. Over the course of the next two decades, the two soulmates occasionally reunited in live concerts and they appeared together one final time in a historic 1957 TV show, *The Sound of Jazz*. When Billie died only four months after Lester (in 1959), it prompted John Hammond to observe, "The relationship between Billie and Lester was deep and long-lasting. . . . When he died the last vital spark from her followed him."

Although her brilliant small-group recordings had brought Billie to the attention of the public, during the Swing Era, the big band was where the real action was. So late in 1937, Billie officially became the "girl singer" with the Count Basie orchestra. The rigors of the road—and Billie's own personal problems—cut short her tenure with Basie and after only a few months she left the band. Although she was immediately hired by bandleader Artie Shaw, this new foray into the big band mainstream proved just as short-lived, and for even more troubling reasons.

Artie Shaw was a young clarinetist who was not only attempting to experiment with new musical conceptions (at one point he added a string section to the standard big band instrumentation), but he was committed to social innovations as well. Although Benny Goodman had already made some progress in this area, a rigid color barrier still barred integrated bands from most live venues and virtually all network radio shows. So—bolstered by the phenomenal success of his recent hit recording of Cole Porter's "Begin the Beguine" (one of the biggest sellers of the Swing Era)—Shaw hired Billie Holiday as the vocalist of his all-white orchestra.

The problems started right away. During their first tour, Billie often couldn't sit on stage with the rest of the band and on some radio broadcasts her spots were canceled altogether. When the band was booked into the Lincoln Hotel in New York City, Billie was forced to use the freight elevator. While the exposure (and income) that working with a big name white band offered was tempting, the continual harrassment quickly wore her down. Billie's departure from Artie Shaw's band was one of the most bitter experiences of her life.

Billie's encounters with racism continued to take their toll. So when a new nightclub named Cafe Society opened in Greenwich Village in 1938 with the express purpose of presenting the best in contemporary music to an integrated audience, it was appropriate that Billie became one of its first performers. It also was fitting that the one explicitly racial song in Holiday's repertoire was introduced at Cafe Society. "Strange Fruit," with its chilling description of a Southern lynching, became the biggest selling record of her career.

The other song most closely associated with Billy Holiday was one she wrote herself. "God Bless the Child," a heartbreaking existential lament, was supposedly prompted by an actual incident in which her mother had refused to loan Billie money during the depths of the singer's heroin addiction. Throughout her life, Billie suffered personal tragedies and professional humiliation, but she also used those experiences to create a body of work touched by genius. And, in the process, she transformed popular singing for all time.

In 1958, a year before her death (from the effects of her heroin addition), Frank Sinatra spoke for many popular singers when he acknowledged that "Billie Holiday was, and remains the greatest single musical influence on me." Then, expanding his statement, he declared, "Lady Day is unquestionably the most important influence on American popular singing in the last twenty years." The decades since her death have only served to confirm the validity of Sinatra's assessment.

CLAP HANDS, HERE COMES ELLA

Of all the "girl singers" who rose to prominence during the Swing Era, a performer who actually did begin her big band career as a girl turned out to be one of the handful of truly great jazz singers in the music's history.

The account of the discovery of sixteen-year-old Ella Fitzgerald at a Harlem amateur night contest has become one of the classic Cinderella stories in jazz. Actually, it was a member of Chick Webb's acclaimed jazz band who had first heard Ella at that Apollo Theater performance, but, after a brief audition, Webb did hire the teenager and, not long after, she joined the band during their regular Savoy Ballroom showcase.

Although he is generally recognized as one of the most dynamic drummers of the Swing Era, Chick Webb had tuberculosis of the spine that stunted his growth (he was under five feet tall) and twisted his spine (he had an extreme hunchback). But at "The Track"—the nickname for Harlem's famous Savoy Ballroom—Webb's orchestra sent thousands of hardcore dancers into a frenzy. He also sent away the big-name bands who'd come to challenge him, licking their wounds. Benny Goodman's drummer, Gene Krupa recounted the night he faced Webb in their 1937 "Battle of the Bands": "I'll never forget that night, the night when Benny's band battled Chick at the Savoy— he just cut me to ribbons—made me feel awfully small. . . . When he felt like it, he could cut down any of us."

Yet Webb had never been able to translate his great music into commercial success—until Ella came along, that is. In 1938—a few years after she joined Webb—she recorded a novelty song with the band called "A Tisket, A Tasket," which became one of the biggest hits of the decade. Tragically, Chick Webb was only able to enjoy his newfound success for a short time. His always precarious health had suddenly deteriorated and a flare-up of his tuberculosis brought his life to an end in 1939. He was just thirty years old.

It was ironic that it was Ella's buoyant ditty and not the band's earlier powerhouse sides (such as "Stompin' at the Savoy" or "Clap Hands! Here Comes Charlie") that finally brought Webb to the attention of the listening public. But the public knew what it was doing. Ella's offhand virtuosity, enormous vocal range, endearing personality, and soaring flights of wordless improvisation (known as "scat" singing), earned her a place in the pantheon of jazz immortals.

Ella Fitzgerald went on to a long career as perhaps the most brilliant and beloved jazz singer in history (along with Louis Armstrong, of course, with whom she made a few classic duet albums). Ella eventually transcended all the limitations that typically constrain the careers of jazz performers. In a series of "Songbook" albums she began recording in the 1950s, she offered her unique interpretations of the works of Tin Pan Alley's greatest songwriters (including Harold Arlen, Rodgers and Hart, Jerome Kern, George and Ira Gershwin, and Cole Porter). Later in her life she was embraced by a huge mainstream audience that honored her with the title of America's "First Lady of Song."

BIG BANDS BEGIN TO SHRINK

Among the black and white images from the 1940s that have become implanted in America's collective memory is the "big band dance scene" that seemed to find its way into so many World War II era movies. There they are, the Swing Era heroes in crisp dress uniforms entertaining the troops on the front lines or performing at some serviceman's hangout on the home front. Although—like most Hollywood versions of reality—these images may be hopelessly romanticized, the fact is that many bandleaders and musicians did become an important part of the war effort.

In 1942, along with scores of less notable figures, Artie Shaw enlisted in the Navy and Glenn Miller (the most successful bandleader in the country) was commissioned as a captain in the Air Force. And as scores of big band sidemen were drafted into the armed forces, the drain of talent resulted in a sharp decline in the quality of the bands that were left. In addition, wartime gas rationing made it hard for bands to maintain their usual schedule of one-nighters and for their audiences to drive to some roadside dance hall to enjoy them. Finally, a wartime federal amusement tax also cut into the profits that were needed to meet those steep big band payrolls.

But while global politics and harsh economic realities were weakening the structure on which the big bands were built, there were other internal factors moving popular music and jazz into new directions. For example, during the course of the Swing Era, arrangements had become increasingly ponderous or gimmicky as each orchestra struggled to create a unique and marketable "sound." Individual creativity expressed through the improvised solo—which had once been the essence of jazz—had become almost completely subordinated to the vision of the arranger, the constraints of radio programmers or the matinee idol image of the big band vocalists.

During the 1920s, the progress of jazz often was described in geographical terms—moving from New Orleans to Chicago to New York. By the 1940s, however, the evolution of jazz wasn't geographical but numerical; jazz was moving away from the big band and back to the small group.

Among the early archetypes of this process were the trios, quartets, quintets, and sextets led by Benny Goodman. Freed from the rigidity of the big band format, Benny (accompanied by Lionel Hampton, Teddy Wilson, and the electric guitarist Charlie Christian), developed a refined version of the spontaneous interplay that had once characterized the small band jazz that had emerged from the New Orleans tradition.

Another early example of this trend were the groups that the pianist Teddy Wilson formed to back Billie Holiday on the recordings she began making during the mid-1930s. Even though Billie's accompanists were drawn primarily from the Basie big band (which had provided more solo opportunities than most swing orchestras), these six- and seven-piece units gave Lester Young, Buck Clayton, and the others a chance to communicate in a more intimate and interactive context.

52ND STREET

It wasn't only on recordings that "small-group swing" (as it came to be known) found an outlet during the 1930s. For example, with the advent of Prohibition, the basement apartments on a block of Manhattan brownstones had gradually been converted into speakeasies. After the repeal of the Eighteenth Amendment in 1933—when bars were again able to operate openly—many of these Midtown establishments added live music as a way of drawing customers. Soon Fifty-second Street was lined with clubs such as the Onyx, Kelly's Stables, the Three Duces, and the Famous Door, each of which began featuring ad hoc ensembles made up of two or three horns and a rhythm section (which is about all that could be squeezed onto the tiny bandstands).

These small bands—now freed from the need to adhere to rigid arrangements—turned into laboratories of spontaneous improvisation. According to one observer of the scene, the atmosphere that existed in these settings

FIGURE 3-18. Coleman Hawkins, Lester Young, and Ben Webster (left to right). Together, these three tenor saxophonists were responsible for establishing their instrument as one of the dominant voices in jazz. In its ability to shout, cry, sing, and preach, the saxophone recalls the expressiveness of the human voice. Photo by Don Hunstein. Courtesy of Columbia Records.

The Three Tenors

Coleman Hawkins

"Hawk" (or "Bean" as he was also known) was born in Missouri in 1904. By the time he was seventeen, he was playing saxophone in Mamie Smith's Jazz Hounds (accompanying the singer whose record "Crazy Blues" had kicked off the blues craze of the 1920s). In 1923, Hawkins arrived in New York to join the Fletcher Henderson Orchestra, and it was during his years with Henderson that he began to stake his claim to the title "The Father of the Tenor Sax."

Majestic and sensual, Hawkin's sound seems to envelop the listener, his wide vibrato like waves rolling off some bottomless sea. It was more than just a new style; it was as if Hawkins had invented a new instrument. And after they heard him play it, everybody wanted one. Almost single-handedly, Hawkins had transformed the saxophone into the great solo instrument of jazz.

But it wasn't only the enthralling voice that he projected through his horn, but what he said with it that made Coleman Hawkins one of the great musicians in jazz. As an improviser, Hawkins looked much more deeply than most other performers into the harmonic structure of a composition. Rather than simply embellish a melody, he worked out his own new melodies by extending the chords that formed the basic construction of the original tune and by substituting related chords in order to rearrange its very foundation.

This approach reached its pinnacle in Hawkins's immortal version of "Body and Soul," considered by most jazz critics to be one of the greatest recordings in the music's history. Made with a small ensemble in 1939, only a few months after Bean's return from a five-year European sojourn, the record was an artistic triumph that had a profound influence on the evolution of jazz—and a commercial hit.

By the mid-1930s, there was an entire generation of saxophonists who can be considered graduates of the "Hawkins School"—including Herschel Evans, Chu Berry, and Ben Webster—who filled the ranks of the era's big bands. Indeed, for a while it seemed there was only one way to play the tenor saxophone; that is, until Lester Young came along.

Lester Young

While Coleman Hawkins stood like some colossus, feet firmly planted on the earth, Lester Young seemed always to float just above it. And while Hawkins's solos sounded like imperial proclamations issued to the multitudes, Lester seemed to whisper elegantly phrased confidences in your ear. Suddenly there were two ways to play the saxophone.

Lester Young began his musical career in his father's carnival band as it barnstormed across the South and Midwest. At first he played drums, but when he was thirteen he switched to alto sax. He didn't start playing tenor until he was about twenty years old, and the sound of the alto—higher pitched than the tenor and without that instrument's brawny sound—remained the basis for Young's unique tone.

When he was eighteen, Young went off to pursue his own career. After working in various Southwestern "territory bands," he gravitated to Kansas City, where he became a star soloist with Count Basie. Because of his unusual sound and the deceptive simplicity of his improvisations, Lester's intensity sneaks up on the listener. But he was one of the key ingredients in the Basie band's potent swing.

Although it took a little while for him to emerge from behind the massive shadow Hawkins cast over the jazz saxophone landscape, gradually, Young (or "Prez" as he was dubbed by Billie Holiday) began to attract his own disciples. By the mid-1940s, there were at least a dozen Lester Young clones and his style continues to echo across the world of jazz to this day. Young's breathy vibratoless sound, characteristic behind-the-beat phrasing, and melodic improvisational excursions have been the primary influences on generations of saxophone masters including Lee Konitz, Dexter Gordon, Paul Desmond, Charlie Parker, and Stan Getz.

One person who had immediately recognized Lester's unique genius was Billie Holiday. "For my money," she wrote in her autobiography, "Lester was the world's greatest. I loved his music, and some of my favorite recordings are the ones with Lester's pretty solos." Because they shared not only a musical conception but a spiritual bond ("their sounds a single voice split in two," wrote jazz critic Whitney Balliet), the music that Billie and Lester made together carries a powerful emotional impact that has rarely been rivaled.

Ben Webster

Born in 1909—the same year as Lester Young—Ben Webster's early career path eerily shadowed that of his more famous contemporary. In the late 1920s, Webster encountered Prez for the first time when he got a job playing in Lester's father's band. Then, a few years later, when Young bailed out of the Fletcher Henderson Orchestra (where he had taken over Coleman Hawkins's place), it was Webster who stepped in to replace Young. In the mid-1930s, it was Ben Webster who took the lead when he became the tenor saxophonist on Billie Holiday's first recordings, a role Lester would go on to claim as his own.

And just as Lester Young had initially made his reputation as a soloist in the Count Basie Orchestra, Ben Webster established his place in jazz history as the featured tenor saxophonist with Duke Ellington, the other preeminent band of the Swing Era. From the moment Webster officially joined the band, in 1940, Ellington began tailoring arrangements to suit the unique strengths of his new saxophonist. Taking advantage of Webster's gutsy, rough-edged sound and impassioned, blues-based style, Duke provided him with opportunities to solo on the band's up-tempo numbers—including "Perdido," "Main Stem," and (most famously) "Cotton Tail"—and Webster made many of them his own. Yet, on ballads such as "What Am I Here For?," Webster (affectionately known as "Frog") could rein in his extroverted bluster and transform his gutteral, vibrato-heavy "fuzz tone" into a breathy whisper that is one of the most romantic sounds in jazz.

After leaving Ellington in 1943, Ben Webster fronted a succession of small swing bands on New York's Fifty-second Street that allowed him to give free rein to his enormous expressive range. Increasingly, however, it was the heart-stopping beauty of Webster's ballads (and the richly melodic quality of his improvisation) that attracted both legions of listeners and an army of imitators (from Paul Gonsalves to Archie Shepp).

In fact, as the tenor saxophone became the dominant voice in the creative cocophony of mid-twentieth-century jazz, major innovators on the instrument such as Sonny Rollins and John Coltrane (as well as Eric Dolphy, Albert Ayler, and a score of others) all grounded their radical new styles on the strong foundation laid by the tenor titans pictured here. And today, as dynamic young tenor saxophonists—such as Branford Marsalis, Joshua Redman, Joe Lovano, and James Carter—help shape the future of jazz, they do so by standing on the shoulders of these giants of the past.

encouraged creativity and collaboration: "At that time everybody used to sit in. Like Ben Webster and Roy Eldridge had a band at one club, and Erroll Garner would come in from across the street and sit in. It happened all the time. The feeling was so wonderful. Any time you came into a joint, they'd ask you to join them."

A related (and even less formal) version of this phenomenon was taking place Uptown at the permanent floating jam sessions occurring at Harlem's after-hours joints and private apartments. Often the music wouldn't start until 3:00 A.M. (when the performers finished their regular gigs on Fifty-second Street). They'd head to Minton's up on 118th Street, where they'd play until nine or ten the next morning, before walking out into the sunlight.

As musicians from different big bands (and different musical generations) began to interact in these intimate settings, new conceptions of jazz gradually began to emerge. At the time, however, powerful commercial forces—led by the major record labels and radio networks—provided a supportive infrastructure that allowed the big bands to dominate the mainstream of American popular music until well into the 1940s.

THE END OF AN ERA

The end of a musical era can never be precisely dated, but in his exhaustive historical survey, *The Big Bands,* George T. Simon suggests December 1946 as "the official end of the big band era." That was the month that the eight prominent orchestras led by Woody Herman, Benny Goodman, Harry James, Les Brown, Jack Teagarden, Benny Carter, Ina Ray Hutton, and Tommy Dorsey all announced that they were disbanding. "All gone at once," Simon exclaims. And after considering his list of fallen heroes, he asks the rhetorical question, "What was left?" Then supplies his own bleak answer, "Not much."

Although even they had a few shaky years, only Count Basie and Duke Ellington managed to maintain their Swing Era big bands following the demise of the Swing Era itself. And—despite the racial inequities and commercial intrusions—it truly had been a remarkable era. For ten straight years, a jazz-based style had been the dominant form of popular music in America. In addition, the success of the Swing Era orchestras had transformed the image of jazz, made it available to a diverse national audience, and initiated the first breaches in a color line that was still drawn sharply across American society.

Just as there was no single cause for the collapse of big band jazz, no one genre immediately emerged to replace it. While this fragmentation may have dissipated the enormous popular impact of jazz in American society, the music's creative energy did not vanish. In fact, jazz was about to enter one of the most explosively inventive periods in its history.

THE BEBOP REVOLUTION

While one faction of the fragmented post–Swing Era jazz scene embraced a nostalgic New Orleans Revival that looked back to the music's past, another was in the process of charting its future. And although both of these subcultures can be seen as reactions against the overcommercialization of the Swing Era, the members of the jazz vanguard also were motivated by a deepening sense of frustration over the separate, and unequal, opportunities that had been the lot of African-American musicians for too long.

Many of the young musicians who gathered at the after-hours jams at Harlem's Minton's Playhouse had become increasingly resentful about what they saw as the exploitation of black music by the hugely successful white Swing Era orchestras. For example, while Count Basie did manage to considerably improve on the $18 per week he had been earning at Kansas City's Reno Club, there certainly weren't any black bands pulling down the $100,000 per month (just from recording royalties) that the Glenn Miller Orchestra was earning during the early 1940s.

During this period, the pianist/arranger Mary Lou Williams (who had paid her dues in some of Kaycee's most notorious joints) became a mentor to the young New York musicians who were forging modern jazz. As she explains it, "bebop," as the style became known, originated (at least in part) as a response to these socioeconomic facts of Swing Era life:

> Now, I want to tell you what I know about how and why bop got started. Thelonious Monk and some of the cleverist of the young musicians used to complain, "We'll never get credit for what we're doing." . . . Anyway, Monk said, "We're going to get a band started. We're going to create something that *they* can't steal because *they* can't play it." So the boppers worked out a music that was hard to steal.

By embracing this "for us, by us" attitude, the beboppers added yet another layer to the factionalism that had already been set in motion by the New Orleans revivalists. Looking back at the avalanche of jazz books, magazine articles, and newsletters published during the early 1940s reveals the passionate partisan debates that existed among the increasingly fragmented jazz audience. Each faction united behind its own version of jazz history, worshiped its own jazz deities, and scathingly condemned all others as false gods.

ROOTS OF THE MODERN

It wasn't the musicians who began calling their adventurous new music "bebop." In fact, while there are a couple of theories about the origin of the name, it was first employed as a term of derision: an absurd name for a ridiculous music.

The pioneers of the new style—trumpeter John Birks ("Dizzy") Gillespie, pianist Thelonious Monk, drummer Kenny Clarke, alto saxophonist Charlie Parker, guitarist Charlie Christian—just called what they were doing "modern." ("If Charlie had lived, he would have been real modern," Clarke commented after Christian's untimely death in 1942.) For better or worse, however, the name stuck and bebop (or simply bop) transformed jazz more dramatically than anything since Louis Armstrong's innovations twenty years before.

During this transitional period, the beboppers were still serving traditional jazz apprenticeships in various swing style big bands. Meanwhile, they would gather informally to exchange musical ideas that they would unveil at Minton's (a popular musicians' hangout) after finishing their regular gigs. As Dizzy Gillespie remembers it, this process began to shape the nature of their musical experiments:

> On afternoons before a session, Thelonious Monk and I began to work out some complex variations on chords and the like, and we used them at night to scare away the no-talent guys. After a while, we got more and more interested in what we were doing as music, and as we began to explore more and more, our music evolved.

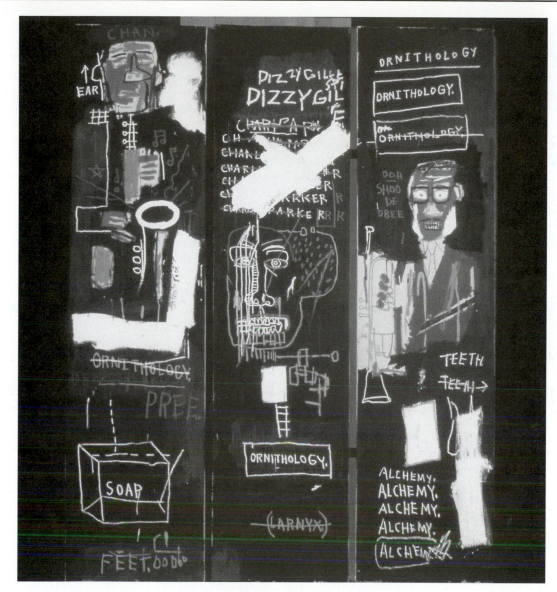

FIGURE 3-19. The young artist Jean-Michel Basquiat created this double portrait of Charlie Parker and Dizzy Gillespie using the graffiti-based style he had developed on the streets of New York. The painting, filled with scrawled references to the personal lives and musical careers of bebop's dynamic duo, attempts to capture on canvas the freedom and spontaneity of their sound. As prime architects of the angular, fast-paced brand of modern jazz—and the first to record it—Parker and Gillespie had achieved a unique rapport. When he was asked about the nature of their relationship, Dizzy described Bird as "the other half of my heartbeat." "Horn Players" (1983) by Jean-Michel Basquiat. Acrylic and mixed media on canvas (96″ × 75″). Courtesy of ARS (Artists Rights Society).

Bird and Diz: Bebop's Dynamic Duo

Along with other members of their generation, Charlie Parker and Dizzy Gillespie had begun their careers as sidemen in some of the big Swing Era bands that dominated the popular music scene of the 1930s. By the beginning of the following decade, however, a variety of social and economic factors were conspiring to wipe out these jazz orchestras. Now a score of small clubs lining New York's Fifty-second Street were featuring ensembles of four or five musicians playing more spontaneous styles of jazz, while an even more experimental scene was emerging further uptown in a musician's hangout called Minton's.

It was here that, along with a small contingent of their jazz contemporaries, Charlie Parker and Dizzy Gillespie had begun altering the accepted chord progressions that provided the harmonic foundation for improvisation and were finding ways of substituting chords with unexpected but related ones. While such techniques gave their music an exotic dissonant quality, their tendency to shift the accents of their furiously paced extended phrases (to the weaker offbeats) created unsettling rhythmic displacements that also would confound the jazz establishment.

Late in 1944, when Parker brought a band into one of the Fifty-second Street clubs, he provided the first opportunity for the general public to hear the radical new music. Although many members of the jazz community reacted with outrage or contempt, the response of drummer Stan Levey (who would later accompany Bird) was more typical of the younger players. "I'd never heard anything like it. I didn't really know what he was doing, but it made me feel good to listen to him."

Before long, Gillespie found his way to The Street—as musicians referred to the Midtown jazz mecca—and, together again, Bird and Diz showed increasingly receptive audiences what they were now calling *bebop* was all about. As Gary Giddens explains (in his book *Celebrating Bird*), "The responsiveness between Parker and Gillespie was unlike anything heard in jazz since the early twenties, when King Oliver and Louis Armstrong crossed trumpets at Chicago's Lincoln Gardens. Occasionally, they seemed to ad lib theme statements in perfect unison, and their reeling exchanges of four- and-eight-bar passages brought time to a stop and audiences to a roar."

BASQUIAT POSTSCRIPT

Tragically, as it had been for many of his contemporaries, Parker's heroin addiction may have been a model for Basquiat's own involvement with the drug. And, like his hero, the twenty-eight-year-old painter also fell victim to his habit, succumbing to an overdose in 1988.

Gillespie, who was still playing in Cab Calloway's big band, would even try to work some of the exotic-sounding chords and innovative rhythmic concepts into his solos on his regular gigs. But whenever he did, Calloway would invariably point his finger at Dizzy and take him to task for "playing that Chinese music in my band."

The drummer Kenny Clarke also had been moving through some of the important swing era orchestras during the late 1930s on his way to Minton's back room. Most recently he had played with Teddy Hill's band, but he too was beginning to change his style:

It was with Teddy Hill, when I really got the thing together that I wanted to play. I was trying to make the drums more musical instead of just being a dead beat. . . . Around this time, I began to play things with the band, with the drums as a real participating instrument with its own voice. I'd never heard anyone else do it before.

Meanwhile, Charlie Parker was playing Lester Young–influenced alto saxophone with a Kansas City big band led by Jay McShann when he arrived in New York. But he, too, was soon experimenting with bold new musical conceptions:

I'd been getting bored with the stereotyped [chord] changes that were being used all the time, and I kept thinking there's bound to be something else. I could hear it sometimes but I couldn't play it.

Parker's breakthrough—which he dates from late in 1939—occurred while he was improvising on a favorite jazz standard, "Cherokee." He began employing extensions of standard chords and substituting related chords for those in the usual progression. Suddenly Parker claims, "I could play the thing I'd been hearing." As he recounted later, it was the moment "I came alive."

Bebop and Beatniks

Inspired by the revolutionary music being concocted by Bird, Diz, Monk, and the others, Jack Kerouac (author of the classic beat novel *On the Road*) abandoned his traditional writing style and forged a new fast-paced, improvisatory method that his close friend (the poet Allen Ginsberg) dubbed, "spontaneous bop prosody."

In *Mexico City Blues*, Kerouac conceived of each of the 242 brief poems as a "musical chorus." The 239th of these is dedicated to that ultimate icon of modern jazz, Charlie Parker. Written shortly after the saxophonist's tragic death, the poem merges an appreciation of Bird's artistic significance with allusions to Kerouac's deeply held Buddhist beliefs.

"Charlie Parker" (by Jack Kerouac)

Charlie Parker looked like Buddha.
Charlie Parker who recently died laughing at a jug-
            gler on TV
after weeks of strain and sickness
was called the perfect musician
and his expression on his face
was as calm beautiful and profound
as the image of the Buddha
represented in the East—the lidded eyes
the expression that says: all is well.

This was what Charlie Parker said when he played:
            all is well.
You had the feeling of early-in-the-morning
like a hermit's joy
or like the perfect cry of some wild gang at a jam
            session
Wail! Whap!
Charlie burst his lungs to reach the speed of what
            the speedsters wanted
and what they wanted was his eternal slowdown.
A great musician
and a great creator of forms
that ultimately find expression
in mores and what-have-you.

Musically as important as Beethoven
yet not regarded as such at all
a genteel conductor of string orchestras
in front of which he stood proud and calm
like a leader of music in the great historic World-
            night
and wailed his little saxophone
the alto
with piercing, clear lament
in perfect tune and shining harmony
Toot!

As listeners reacted
without showing it
and began talking

and soon the whole joint is rocking and talking
and *everybody* talking—
and Charlie Parker
whistling them on to the brink of eternity
with his Irish St. Patrick Patootlestick.
And like the holy mists
we blop and we plop
in the waters of slaughter and white meat—
and die
one after one
in Time.

And how sweet a story it is
when you hear Charlie Parker tell it
either on records or at sessions
or at official bits in clubs
(shots in the arm for the wallet).
Gleefully he whistled the perfect horn
anyhow made no difference . . .

Charlie Parker forgive me.
Forgive me for not answering your eyes.
For not having made an indication
of that which you can devise.
Charlie Parker pray for me.
Pray for me and everybody.

In the Nirvanas of your brain
Where you hide—
indulgent and huge—
no longer Charlie Parker
but the secret unsayable Name
that carries with it
merit not-to-be-measured
from here to up down east or west.

Charlie Parker:
lay the bane off me
. . . . and everybody.

Unlike most of New York's other jazz visionaries, Charlie Parker (who was nicknamed "Yardbird" or, more familiarly, "Bird") had been jamming at another Harlem club, called Clarke Monroe's Uptown House. But soon the word about him began to spread. When Gillespie, Kenny Clarke, and Monk showed up to check him out, they quickly realized that Parker was developing some of the same harmonic and rhythmic ideas they were. Before long they joined forces, becoming the undisputed leaders of a modern jazz movement that is still being pursued today.

In hindsight, most jazz critics now recognize that the bebop revolution was really just another stage in a musical evolution that had been taking place in jazz for at least a decade. One of the factors that would make bebop seem such a shattering break with the past was simply the fact that it had been taking shape during a ban on recording (called by the musician's union in a dispute over royalties). So, when the larger jazz community finally did get to hear the new music on disk (in 1945), they did so without any exposure to the gradual process of development out of which it had emerged.

But perhaps another reason that bebop seemed to burst on the scene with such dramatic suddenness was the blistering speed at which it was played. While the rapid tempo of bebop might have been just one more element in Monk's strategy for a music "they" couldn't play, it also can be seen as an example of the music's connection to one of the defining characteristics of Modernism itself.

The astonishingly rapid technological progress that was evident in the years before and after World War II was reflected in many of the arts of the period. In fact, modern jazz had a lot in common with two other dynamic artistic movements that were also taking place in New York City during the mid-1940s. For both "abstract expressionist" painters such as Jackson Pollack and so-called beat generation writers such as Jack Kerouac shared with the creators of modern jazz an aesthetic based on spontaneity and velocity.

THE SOUND OF THE MODERN

Bebop's incendiary tempo contributed greatly to what was perceived as the style's jarring, angular sound. For example, in order to play with such rapidity, horn players were forced to even out their melody lines. Cascading streams of evenly divided eighth notes became the hallmark of bebop improvisations. To compensate for the reduced sense of syncopation that occurred during this acceleration, soloists introduced alterations in phrasing and shifted the placement of rhythmic accents.

In adapting to these changes, the role of each instrument in the rhythm section also had to evolve. Kenny Clarke led drummers away from the basic timekeeping role they had fulfilled in the Swing Era (when they pounded out four-beats-to-the-bar on their bass drums). Now Clarke began reserving the bass drum for percussive accents timed to add an explosive impact to a solo (a technique that became known as "dropping bombs"). Meanwhile, Clarke used the "ride" (top) cymbal to establish a steady sizzling beat, as well as to get more varied tonal effects.

With the drum now just another voice in the jostling interplay of the ensemble, the responsibility for establishing the ground beat fell on the bass player, who seemed to push the rest of the band with his subtly propulsive rhythmic figures, which in turn had an impact on the role of the pianist, who was able to move away from the responsibility of reinforcing the beat with each new chord in the composition. This allowed for a lighter, more open combination of fleeting melodic runs and occasional well-placed chords designed to provide soloists with a harmonic framework on which to hang their improvisations.

And a greatly expanded harmonic framework at that. Beboppers' use of chords that extended well beyond the narrow range of previous styles severely challenged the tolerance of both audiences and older musicians. For many listeners, they simply sounded "wrong." Or, as Cab Calloway had put it, like "Chinese music." According to one theory, bebop's most characteristic new harmonic interval—the "flatted fifth"—actually inspired the name of the new style, since as one musician sang this innovative interval to another, the verbal syllables they used seemed to echo the musical phrase: "Be-bop."

FIGURE 3-20. Although he wasn't the first guitarist to plug in, Charlie Christian is credited with transforming the instrument from a polite member of the rhythm section to an assertive solo voice. By infusing his blues-based style with sophisticated harmonies, Christian also helped forge the style of modern jazz known as bebop. Author's collection.

Charlie Christian: Blues to Bebop

Growing up Oklahoma City, Charlie Christian absorbed the traditional sounds of the blues and as a youngster he began playing guitar in his father's string band. By the 1930s, he had joined one of the swinging jazz bands that criss-crossed the Southwest.

It was during this period that Christian had two crucial encounters that would provide the inspiration for his own revolutionary musical direction. The first—with the tenor saxophonist Lester Young—provided a model for Christian's linear hornlike style (and highly melodic improvisational concepts); the second—with the progenitor of the jazz electric guitar, Eddie Durham—introduced him to the instrument on which he could give voice to these ideas.

In 1939 Christian was playing with a combo (for $2.50 a night) at an Oklahoma City club, when he was "discovered" by the talent scout/producer John Hammond. Hammond immediately flew the guitarist out to Los Angeles to audition for Benny Goodman, the reigning "King of Swing," and—virtually overnight—the obscure young guitarist became part of the most celebrated small group in jazz (at a starting salary of $150 per week).

Christian joined Teddy Wilson and Lionel Hampton as the third African-American sideman in what was now the Benny Goodman Sextet. Christian's bluesy, Southwestern riffs were first featured on the group's now classic recording "Flying Home," which (along with "7 Come 11" and "Air Mail Special") became his signature tune.

When his gigs with Benny were over for the evening, Christian joined a tight circle of collaborators—including Thelonious Monk, Charlie Parker, Dizzy Gillespie, and Kenny Clarke—who were exploring radical new musical concepts in informal after-hours jam sessions at Harlem's Minton's Playhouse. Before long Christian was one of the leading figures in the groundbreaking rhythmic and harmonic style of modern jazz that became known as "bebop."

But the frantic pace he was keeping finally took its toll. In 1941, the tuberculosis he'd had since childhood flared up again. Tragically, after being admitted to a New York City sanitarium, Christian caught pneumonia and died. He was just twenty-three years of age.

CHANGES ON THE STREET

BEBOP MOVES IN

By the mid-1940s, New York's Fifty-second Street had become a microcosm of jazz history. The tiny basement clubs that lined "The Street" (as it was known to the in-crowd) featured a range of jazz that encompassed the Dixieland jazz of New Orleans soprano saxophonist Sidney Bechet and the harmonically sophisticated swing of tenor saxophonist Coleman Hawkins who was enthralling the new legion of admirers he had amassed with his 1939 hit recording of "Body and Soul."

From nine in the evening to 3:30 the following morning, jazz fans, tourists, and off-duty servicemen moved from club to club. In September of 1944, Dizzy Gillespie was hired to lead a combo at the Three Deuces, a typical Fifty-second Street dive (with a seating capacity of about 125 people). Standing side by side with Charlie Parker on the tiny "Deuces" stage, the pair began to perform some of the original material they had been developing at Minton's; now bebop also took up permanent residence on The Street.

With bebop finally out in the open, jazz musicians and fans were forced to take a position on the new music. A few members of the older generation of musicians spoke up in support of the modernists. Coleman Hawkins, for one, quickly voiced his approval ("They say what Monk and Dizzy and Bird were doing was so different. Well whatever they were doing they did great, and whatever they did I liked . . ."). In fact, the Hawk even played with the beboppers and was the first to record some of their tunes.

But most members of the jazz establishment were harshly critical ("Bebop has set music back twenty years," said the famous Swing Era bandleader Tommy Dorsey). While Louis Armstrong—who had come under attack from the modernists for what they saw as his overly ingratiating persona—dismissed the controversial new style out of hand ("First people get curious about it just because it's new, but soon they get tired of it because it's really no good and you got no melody to remember and no beat to dance to"). Many others shared the belief the music was simply a bad joke.

The initial rejection of their music only added to the bebopper's sense of alienation and defensiveness. And while audiences (and other musicians) gradually did come to accept the new musical concepts of bebop, the new attitude projected by the beboppers proved to be a tougher nut to crack. Having rejected the stereotypes associated with the role of "entertainer," some beboppers (literally) turned their back on the audience or walked off the stage after they soloed; they refused to announce the names of compositions or engage in the usual between-tune patter or indulge the audience with current Tin Pan Alley hits or recognizable standards. They demanded to be accepted as "artists" (a notion that required a difficult adjustment for audiences accustomed to a particular relationship with jazz performers—especially black jazz performers).

But for some fans, the modernist's musical innovations and the image of artistic integrity they projected created a powerful attraction. A subculture of aspiring converts and admiring aficionados began to develop. Young musicians began to absorb the new musical theories and fans began to affect the bebop fashions and slang. The cult of the modern "hipster" was born.

In his 1963 book about African-American music, *Blues People,* the poet and essayist, Le Roi Jones made an effort to place this aspect of the bebop phenomenon in its cultural context:

> In a sense the term *cultists* for the adherents of early modern jazz was correct. The music, bebop, defined the term of a deeply felt nonconformity among many young Americans, black and white. And for many young Negroes the irony of being thought "weird" or "deep" by white Americans was as satisfying as it was amusing. It also put on a more intellectually and psychologically satisfying level the traditional separation and isolation of the black man from America. It was a cult of protection as well as rebellion.

As Jones (who changed his name to Amiri Baraka in the late 1960s) goes on to point out, however, the self-conscious isolation of the beboppers was not only expressed in the unapologetic modernism of their music or in their costumes and accessories (goatees, berets, and shades) or in their coded figures of speech ("That cat at the Deuces was a gas, you dig?"). Tragically, the ultimate symbol of their separation from the "square" world became heroin.

Charlie Parker—the supreme hero of bebop—had been a junkie ever since he was about seventeen years old. So while every young jazz musician aspired to Parker's creative genius and personal charisma (which were unattainable), anyone could shoot up and "be like Bird." And drug addiction became the ultimate occupational hazard of modern jazz.

In 1945, the major recording companies were ignoring bebop just as they had ignored the resurgence of traditional Dixieland jazz, and this gap was soon filled in a similar way: small, newly formed independent labels now found it economically viable to record specialized music for a specific audience.

Dizzy got a record deal with Guild, and beginning in May of 1945, he recorded with Bird the fruits of their recent collaborations. Most of the tunes—"Groovin High," "Shaw 'Nuff," "Salt Peanuts," "Dizzy Atmosphere"—were Gillespie and Parker originals that have become modern jazz classics. Because they weren't able to use their drummer of choice (Max Roach), however, some critics feel that a crucial component of a bebop style was missing on their bebop debut. This was rectified a few months later when Parker entered the Savoy studio to make his first records as a leader.

With a band that included Roach, the brilliant bebop drummer, and a nineteen-year-old trumpet player named Miles Davis (who had come to New York to study at the Juilliard School), Parker made what are generally considered the first "pure" bebop masterpieces. (Because he was signed exclusively to another label, Dizzy appears on these sides without official credit.) Parker used the opportunity to record his composition "Ko-Ko," which had been the outgrowth of his original harmonic breakthrough on the chord changes of "Cherokee." As Gary Giddens has written (in his book *Celebrating Bird*): "Ko-Ko was the seminal point of departure for jazz in the postwar era. Its effect paralleled that of Armstrong's 'West End Blues' in 1928."

Like "Ko-Ko," many bebop tunes were "composed" according to a process that, while not new to jazz, had been extended to another level by the modernists. In Hawkin's "Body and Soul," for example, after a brief and subtle statement of the original melody, Hawkins begins an extended improvisation based entirely on the harmony or "chord changes" of the song. Now, bebop compositions typically dispensed with the song's melodic theme entirely. Performers began to create their own new melody line based on the composition's harmonic framework and simply supplied their own new title.

Looking at the tunes that made up these first bebop sessions, we can see excellent examples of this method. Dizzy's composition, "Shaw 'Nuff," for example, was based on Gershwin's "I Got Rhythm" (a song whose interesting chord structure would make it the source of dozens of bebop compositions). And as we've seen, "Ko-Ko"'s convoluted whirlwind melody had been constructed on the harmonic skeleton of the Swing Era hit "Cherokee."

The other ongoing source of material for the beboppers—which also linked them to the music's past—was the blues. Parker, who came from Kansas City, was, like all Southwest jazzmen, steeped in the blues tradition. "Now's the Time," like many Parker compositions, is simply a modern version of the classic blues form. In the words of trumpeter Howard McGhee: "Bird could make more tunes out of the blues than any musician who ever lived."

FIGURE 3-21. For much of his career, Thelonious Monk's true genius was obscured behind a seemingly impenetrable cloud of cliches and misconceptions. Gradually, however, jazz critics and fans were able to get past the "Mad Monk" facade that had been conjured up in the media (out of little more than a pair of dark glasses, a beret, and a smattering of dissonant chords). In doing so, they discovered not only a brilliant musician, but a composer now ranked with Ellington as the greatest in jazz history. Photo by Don Hunstein. Courtesy of Columbia Records.

Thelonious Monk: Straight, No Chaser

Along with a corps of like-minded young performers—spearheaded by Dizzy Gillespie, Charlie Parker, the guitarist Charlie Christian, and the drummer Kenny Clark—Thelonious Monk is credited with evolving the rhythmic and harmonic innovations that became the basis of bebop. But, as his collaborators began getting recognition and recording contracts, Monk remained virtually invisible and—as far as the jazz public was concerned—silent.

In fact, when Coleman Hawkins did hire Monk for a series of live appearances at a Fifty-second Street club, the great tenor saxophonist faced a barrage of complaints. "I used to get it every night," Hawkins recalled, " 'Why don't you get a piano player? And 'What's that stuff he's playing?' " But Monk's spare, percussive, abstract piano style, filled with "weird" chords and "wrong" notes, was, in fact, simply another aspect of his all-embracing artistic vision (in which, as the musicologist Gunther Schuller has written, "the components composer-pianist are as inseparable as the elements of an alloy").

Finally, in the late 1940s, Thelonious Monk began to document on recordings a wealth of original compositions including "Round Midnight," "Ruby My Dear," "Well You Needn't," "In Walked Bud" (his tribute to close friend Bud Powell), "Epistrophy," "Straight No Chaser," "Misterioso," "Criss Cross," and "Monk's Mood," all of which are now considered jazz standards. While these recordings did give Monk the opportunity to present his music to the broader jazz audience, they had little impact outside of a small coterie of fans (and awed fellow musicians).

In 1956, however, Monk released another new album of original material, *Brilliant Corners,* which turned out to be a critically acclaimed hit; soon he had kicked off what would be a historic, six-month stint at New York's Five Spot Café, and suddenly—or so it seemed at the time—Monk's name was appearing at the top of jazz popularity polls and major popular music labels were courting the once-scorned pianist.

In 1962, he signed with Columbia Records (the most commercially potent of the majors) and, two years later, *Time* magazine placed Monk on its cover as the personification of the modern jazz musician. Asked to talk about his contribution to jazz history, he declared, "Maybe I'm a major influence. I don't know. Anyway my music is my music. . . . That's a criterion for something." And, in a statement that could stand as his epitaph, Monk concluded, "Jazz is my adventure."

There has also existed in jazz a more formal compositional tradition that is usually traced back to Jelly Roll Morton. Among all of the modern jazz pioneers, no one else embodies this role more than Thelonious Sphere Monk, whom the critic Martin Williams had called "the first major composer in jazz since Duke Ellington."

Musically, Monk was a creative visionary; physically, he was tall and powerfully built; intellectually, he was brilliant. Yet, he also was possessed of an emotional or psychological fragility that periodically caused him to withdraw into a reclusive silence. In addition, his piano style was as idiosyncratic as his personality. His phrasing, harmonic substitutions, and erratic rhythmic accents were so unique that even in the context of the bebop revolution Monk's music was "difficult"—both for listeners and for other musicians.

So, after helping to give birth to bebop at Minton's, Monk watched as others brought the modern musical concepts into the Fifty-second Street clubs and onto recordings. While he did work briefly as the pianist in a small group Coleman Hawkins assembled in 1944, when the rest of the beboppers emerged as leaders on The Street, Monk was conspicuously absent.

Although a few of his tunes had been recorded by other performers during bebop's formative years, Monk didn't get a chance to document his own music until 1947 when he made his first recordings for the Blue Note label. Always ahead of his time, Monk suddenly began to find an audience in the late 1950s and early 1960s and, like Armstrong before him, Monk even achieved that rare distinction for a jazz musician: In 1964 he made the cover of *Time* magazine.

In the fifty years since they were written, Monk's complex and surprisingly lyrical compositions (" 'Round Midnight," "Ruby My Dear," "Well, You Needn't," "Straight No Chaser" and "In Walked Bud," to name just a few) are considered among the most enduring classics in the jazz canon and form a significant part of the repertoire of every jazz performer.

THE TRIUMPH OF BEBOP

Within a few short years, bebop had outgrown its status as a stylistic curiosity or a subject for debate; it had become quite simply the way jazz was played. Bird, Dizzy, Max, and Miles—working together and in their own ensembles—had recorded the style's great anthems such as "Anthropology," "A Night in Tunisia," "Confirmation," "Yardbird Suite," "Hot House," and "Milestones," among others. Bebop spread from Fifty-second Street out to California. And it was carried over the airwaves live from the stages of the New York City jazz clubs by the hipster's DJ, "Symphony Sid."

It seemed that every couple of weeks another important musician would add his voice to the bebop chorus. Trumpeters Howard McGhee, Clifford Brown, and Fats Navarro; saxophonists Sonny Stitt, Dexter Gordon, and Stan Getz; pianists Bud Powell and Tadd Dameron (who also had significant impact as a composer and arranger); bassists Oscar Pettiford and Charles Mingus; trombonist J. J. Johnson; guitarist Barney Kessel—on every instrument, older musicians adapted to the new style and younger ones cut their teeth on it. In every jazz magazine popularity poll, modernists dominated the top spots.

And by the end of the 1940s, when the Fifty-second Street clubs began to close their doors (because of local economic and political pressures), larger and more upscale nightclubs opened up a block away on New York's famed entertainment thoroughfare, Broadway. Many of them proudly proclaimed their bebop allegience in their names and slogans: "Bop City" . . . "The Royal Roost: The House That Bop Built" (alternately: "The Metropolitan Bopera House"). But the most lavish of all the new jazz nightspots paid tribute to bebop's greatest hero: "Birdland"—"the Jazz Corner of the World"!

In 1949, Bird brought bebop to Europe. Appearing at the Paris International Jazz Festival, Parker was a sensation. He also was the recipient of the overwhelming adulation and reverence that Europeans have always accorded American jazz musicians from the time of Sidney Bechet's first tour back in 1918. Kenny Clarke—who was living in Paris's expatriate community along with a number of other American jazz musicians—urged Bird to stay ("Over here you'll be appreciated as an artist," Clarke told him). Bird was tempted, but ultimately he was drawn home. He had been signed to a major label and a series of sessions with strings was in the works.

But the triumph of modern jazz also began to exact its price. By the end of the decade, it has been estimated that between one-half to three-quarters of the modern musicians were at least part-time users of heroin, and that as many as 25 percent were hardcore addicts. On his first trip out to the West Coast in 1946, Bird had been busted and sentenced to six months in a rehabilitation program at Carmarillo State Hospital. Although during his stay he was weaned from his addiction, the withdrawal was only temporary. He remained an addict until he died of complications from his drug habit at the age of thirty-five. Too many other brilliant careers were cut short by jail terms and overdoses to name them all.

Luckily the other designated cocreator of modern jazz, Dizzy Gillespie, never became mired in the pervasive drug scene that destroyed so many of his bebop cohorts. While his antics on various bandstands during his apprenticeship have become legendary (they didn't call him "Dizzy" for nothing), Gillespie had become the model of professional responsibility.

But that didn't mean that Gillespie's exuberant personality or irrepressible sense of showmanship had been stifled. In addition to his technical virtuosity on the trumpet and sophisticated use of harmony, Dizzy (more than any of the other beboppers) maintained the connection to a tradition of black entertainment that can be traced back to turn-of-the-century vaudeville shows, as well as to the extroverted mugging of Louis Armstrong and the Swing Era hepcat posturings of Cab Calloway.

By applying a contemporary layer of irony to this tradition, however, Gillespie also was able to transform the negative associations that had accrued to these images for so long. Dizzy was so hip that if anyone thought he was still just "playing the clown," the joke was on them. It's unclear what percentage of his audience appreciated these subtleties, but his personality, musicianship, and newfound sense of professionalism made Gillespie the most marketable of the modernists.

So it was that about a year after his 1945 recording debut with a bebop combo, Dizzy got financial backing to front his own big band. Despite the accelerating collapse of the Swing Era orchestras, Dizzy was able to keep his bebop big band together for the rest of the decade. Yet, in taking this direction, Dizzy seemed to be violating the very ethos of modern jazz. Bebop was the quintessential small band style, giving absolute priority and unlimited freedom to the soloist. Big bands were all about arrangements and form. While imaginative orchestrations and creative soloists might be able to resolve this paradox, another contradiction was more problematic.

The music of the big band era had always been associated with hotel ballrooms, nightclubs, and dance palaces, where the music fulfilled a distinctly functional role. But because of the complexities of modern jazz and its atmosphere of cool hipness, the bebop audience had entered into a more passive relationship with the music.

In order for his big band to succeed, Dizzy knew that the innovative elements of modern jazz needed to be energized by a potent rhythmic infusion. He didn't have to look very far to find the perfect source.

CUBOP: BEBOP WITH A SPANISH TINGE

There was already one big band on the New York scene band that was generating a kind of ecstatic fervor on dance floors during this period. It was a fiery Latin band called Machito and His Afro-Cuban Orchestra. "Machito" (the nickname of Cuban musician Frank Grillo), had devised a formula that fused the complex (African-derived) layers of Cuban rhythms with the harmonic richness and power of the best American swing bands. The chief architect of this sound was the extraordinary composer/arranger (and multi-instrumentalist) Mario Bauza. Coincidentally, in the late 1930s, Bauza and Gillespie had shared a music stand (as well as musical ideas) when they sat alongside each other in the trumpet section of Cab Calloway's band.

While the synthesis of Latin music and jazz wasn't exactly a new idea (it can be traced back at least to ragtime and turn-of-the-century New Orleans jazz), the cultural cross-pollinations taking place in New York during the 1940s amounted to the most fertile blending of Afro-Caribbean rhythms and American popular music in a long time. But it was the collaborations that began taking place in New York between the beboppers (especially Gillespie) and Cuban musicians (including Bauza, Machito, and Chico O'Farrill) that would create some of the most interesting, and profound, music of the period. They called it "Cubop."

Shortly after Dizzy formed his big band, a whirlwind of Afro-Cuban rhythm blew into New York direct from Havana in the person of Luciano Pozo y Gozales. Better known as Chano Pozo, this composer and master of the conga drum added the deep rhythms associated with Cuba's religious cults (one of the purist remnants of Africa in the New World) to the sophisticated harmonies of Dizzy's bebop big band.

Chano Pozo became the rhythmic centerpiece around which Dizzy arranged harmonically advanced ensemble sections along with his own stratospheric trumpet solos. Pozo joined the band officially at a Town Hall performance in the winter of 1947. During the concert, he took a staggering thirty-minute solo—his hands a blur and his voice calling out an ancient Yoruba chant—that brought down the house. No one had heard anything like it. Teddy Stewart, the drummer in Dizzy's band, had to admit afterward, "Man, that Chano was way ahead of us all."

Cubop tunes became an important part of the Gillespie band's repertoire. In addition to compositions such as "Afro-Cuban Suite," "Tin-Tin Deo," "Manteca," and a double-sided disk titled "Cubana Be/Cubana Bop," the band also re-recorded a Latin-tinged version of one of Dizzy's early bebop compositions ("Woody 'n You"), featuring Chano Pozo on congas. Then in 1948, Chano Pozo—who seemed to live his life offstage with the same degree of reckless abandon as he always put into his performances—was shot to death in a Harlem bar.

Not even the tragedy of Chano Pozo's death, however, could stop the momentum of the Latin tidal wave that was sweeping across the New York jazz scene. After Machito's Afro-Cuban Band with Mario Bauza took up residence at the Palladium dance hall (located in the same building as Birdland), even Charlie Parker got into the act. In 1948, Bird recorded the tune "Mango Mangue" with the Afro-Cubans and also performed as a featured soloist on Machito's most ambitious Latin jazz fusion—a multipart, extended work (seventeen plus minutes long)— entitled "Afro-Cuban Jazz Suite"—written by the Cuban composer/arranger Chico O'Farrill.

Parker continued to explore Cubop and other "South of the Border" styles for the rest of his career. And like everything that Bird did, his involvement directly inspired other musicians to join the Afro-Cuban movement. The New York DJ "Symphony Sid" became heavily involved in producing both live shows and radio broadcasts highlighting the latest Latin-Jazz collaborations. Although the momentum of this particular fusion finally dissipated by the mid-1950s, new blends of jazz and Latin-based styles have continued to ignite the American music scene in every decade.

FIGURE 3-22.   Born in the slums of Havana in 1915, Chano Pozo was a dedicated member of the Abakwa cult, a Nigerian religion that had been preserved by the Cuban descendents of African slaves. In 1947, he came to America and introduced the rhythms of his homeland into Dizzy Gillespie's new bebop big band. When he was asked how—despite the language barriers—he and Dizzy could collaborate so easily, Chano replied, "Diz no speak Spanish. I no speak English. But we both speak Africa." BMI Archives.

Chano Pozo's Talking Drums

During the brief time he was with Gillespie's band, Chano Pozo wrote a handful of compositions that represented a dynamic Latin-jazz fusion, and he brought audiences to their feet with his long, ecstatic drum solos. After just a few months, however, Pozo's drums were stolen and he left Gillespie's tour to return to New York. He was planning a trip back to his homeland to buy new drum skins when he was shot to death in a Harlem bar. According to one account, the jukebox was playing his biggest hit, "Manteca," when the bullets were fired and his body hit the floor.

In assessing Chano Pozo's significance, Latin music scholar John Storm Roberts has written, "Perhaps most important of all, his work was a major factor in breaking down the old stereotype of Latin music as something agreeable, but essentially light. Whatever else Pozo's music was, it certainly wasn't light."

"I See Chano Pozo" (Jayne Cortez)

In her poem, "I See Chano Pozo," Jayne Cortez attempts to capture—through the rhythmic repetition of her words—the incantatory power of Pozo's drums. Along the way, she invokes the names of his sacred deities and conjures her own images of ancient Abakwa rites.

A very fine conga of sweat
a very fine stomp of the right foot
a very fine platform of sticks
a very fine tube of frictional groan
a very fine can of belligerent growl
a very fine hoop of cubano yells
very fine   very fine

Is there anyone finer today   ole   okay
Oye   I say
I see Chano Pozo
Chano Pozo from Havana Cuba
                              You're the one
You're the one who made Atamo into
a tattooed motivator of revolutionary spirits

You're the one who made Mpebi into
an activated slasher of lies

You're the one who made Donno into
an armpit of inflammable explosives

You're the one who made Obonu into
a circle of signifying snakes

You're the one who made Atumpan's head strike
against
the head of a bird   everynight   everyday
in your crisscrossing chant
in your cross river mouth
                              You're the one
Oye   I say
Chano
what made you roar like a big brazos flood
what made you yodel like a migrating frog
what made you shake like atomic heat
what made you jell into a ritual pose
Chano   Chano   Chano
what made your technology of thumps so new so
mean
I say
is there anyone meaner than Chano Pozo
                              from Havana Cuba

Oye
I'm in the presence of ancestor
                              Chano Pozo
Chano connector of two worlds
You go and celebrate again with
the *compañeros* in Santiago
   and tell us about it

You go to the spirit house of Antonio Marceo
and tell us about it
You go to Angola
and tell us about it
You go to Calabar
and tell us about it
You go see the slave castles
you go see the massacres
you go see the afflictions
you go see the battlefields
you go see the warriors
you go as a healer
you go conjurate
you go mediate
you go to the cemetary of drums
return and tell us about it

Lucumi   Abakwa   Lucumi   Abakwa

Olé   okay
Is there anyone finer today
Oye   I say
did you hear
Mpintintoa smoking in the palm of his hands
did you hear
Ilya Ilu booming through the cup of his clap
did you hear
Ntenga sanding on the rim of his rasp
did you hear
Siky Akkua stuttering like a goat sucking hawk
did you hear
Bata crying in a nago tongue
did you hear
Fontomfrom speaking through the skull of a dog
did you hear it   did you hear it   did you hear it

A very fine tree stump of drones
a very fine shuffle of shrines
a very fine turn of the head
a very fine tissue of skin
a very fine smack of the lips
a very fine pulse
a very fine *encuentro*
very fine   very fine   very fine
Is there anyone finer than
Chano Pozo from Havana Cuba
Oye   I say
I see Chano Pozo

THE POST-BOP ERA: BACK TO BASICS

The powerful connection between popular music and dance—from which bebop had seemed to turn away—also reasserted itself as a potent force in popular music of the Forties through an exciting new hybrid known as rhythm and blues. While it drew from a variety of musical sources, R & B's jazz roots provided one of the most distinctive elements in its unique character.

By excavating the complexities of modern jazz to unearth the music's deepest roots, rhythm and blues—a blend of the funky riffs of Southwestern swing with the sly double entendres of the big-city blues and the ecstatic fervor of gospel music—emerged as a populist alternative that restored music's traditional social function. Marketed on an assortment of scruffy independent labels, R & B rapidly filled the niche for a modern black style of popular music played by black musicians specifically for a black audience.

For Charlie Parker—whose music was so rooted in the blues—the idea of needing to reconcile the modernist concepts of bebop with earthier impulses of rhythm and blues was never an issue. In 1949, saxophone honker Paul Williams eagerly grabbed the riff Bird had created in his early bebop classic, "Now's the Time" for his funky R & B hit, "The Hucklebuck." A few years later, Parker explicitly expressed his own affinity for the new style of black popular music. Making reference to an R & B vocal harmony group then on the charts, Bird told one young musician, "If you want to understand my music, listen to the Clovers."

This ability to absorb diverse sources was one of the most remarkable aspects of Bird's transcendant musical vision. By the early 1950s, Parker was also introducing into his music elements from the twentieth-century European classic composers to whom he had become increasingly drawn. Bird made it no secret that he was engaged in a serious personal exploration of contemporary masters from Debussy and Ravel to Prokofiev and Stravinsky. At one point, he even approached the French experimental composer Edgar Varèse (who was living in New York at the time) about becoming his student. No music seemed beyond his ability or outside his scope. Certainly few of his colleagues could understand his appreciation for country and western music; Bird's only explanation was, "Just listen to the stories!"

Meanwhile, Parker also had initiated a series of recordings of American popular songs accompanied by a chamber orchestra made up of oboe, harp, and English horn—along with a small string section. His version of the standard "Just Friends" (with this ensemble) quickly became Bird's biggest selling record, and his interpretations of other classic songs by George Gerswhin, Cole Porter, and Jerome Kern earned him an unprecedented level of popular success. On one mid-December appearance at Birdland (which was captured on a live broadcast recording), Parker acceded to a telephone request for "White Christmas" from a home listener. Bird was even able to transform this sugar-coated seasonal confection by infusing it with an earthy elegance and soul.

But Parker's all-encompassing musical vision and blues-based populist instincts were as unique as every other aspect of his genius. Most of the other young musicians who had become bebop converts rigidly adhered to the orthodox modernist line in both their music and their attitudes. For example, the pianist Walter Bishop, Jr. (who often played with Bird) later recalled how difficult it had been for him to transcend the negative associations of the blues: "I didn't even want to know about the blues because to me, the generation of the blues was representative of the subservient black. We'd graduated from that."

By the middle of the decade, however, as rhythm and blues strengthened its grip on the black community, young beboppers such as Bishop allowed themselves the freedom to get back in touch with the blues tradition. In Bishop's words, "I had to reach a certain level of confidence, of being secure in my power to know that it wasn't a drag to play the blues. Then I could let that go and relax enough to absorb some of the roots."

By the mid-1950s, bebop's alienating abstract veneer was gradually peeled away and modern jazz was brought down to earth. By re-rooting bebop innovations in the fertile soil of the blues (and by infusing it with the joyously ecstatic spirit of gospel), the participatory origins and populist spirit of jazz were restored. Jazz historians have labeled this music *hard bop* (although it also has been referred to as "funky jazz" or "soul jazz"). Among the bands that epitomized this more accessible mid-century style of jazz were Art Blakey's Jazz Messengers, the post-bop quintet led by Clifford Brown and Max Roach, and the various ensembles fronted by the pianist/composer Horace Silver.

Tragically, the person who had been most responsible for the fundamental transformation of jazz wouldn't survive to see—and help shape—its continued evolution. By the mid-1950s, Charlie Parker's personal life was in shambles. He was not only still struggling with his heroin addiction but was drinking more and more heavily during periods when he tried to kick. He was devastated emotionally by the death of his young adopted daughter, and frustrated professionally by his inability to expand his musical horizons. He was on a downward spiral, characterized by erratic playing and missed gigs; and for two years the loss of his cabaret card prevented him from playing New York nightclubs. Then, in late 1954, there was a well-publicized suicide attempt.

In the months that followed, his horn often in hock, Bird wandered the streets spending the night with a friend and then moving on. On March 9, 1955, he found himself at the apartment of the wealthy jazz patroness, Nica de Koeningwater. But now he was too ill to move on. Three days later he was dead. The death certificate cited lobar pneumonia as the cause and the doctor's estimate of Parker's age as fifty-three. In reality, Bird was only thirty-five. Within days, as the shocking news spread through the New York jazz world, the first appearance of what became Parker's most enduring epitaph began to show up scrawled on tenement walls and abandoned storefronts: "Bird Lives!"

JAZZ AT MID-CENTURY: DIVERSITY AND DIVISIVENESS

THE COOL SCHOOL

Partially in reaction to the constraints placed on soloists in the Swing Era big bands, absolute improvisational freedom became the central pillar of bebop's musical philosophy. Yet the limits of this credo soon became apparent. While the heroic efforts—and liberating example—of bebop's founders did initiate an outpouring of inspiring music, even for the most creative soloist, reserves of spontaneous inspiration eventually become depleted.

By the late 1940s, a small circle of like-minded, conservatory-trained young collaborators began exploring ways to integrate the creative breakthroughs of bebop with the unifying structure that could be provided by the shaping vision of a sensitive arranger. And since the scorching intensity of bebop seemed to be consuming so many of its practioners (even Bird burned out!), perhaps what the music needed was a little cooling off. Using the basement apartment of pianist/arranger Gil Evans as their headquarters, the group—which included Gerry Mulligan, John Carisi, and John Lewis—became the founding members of a postbop spin-off that would become known as *cool jazz.*

Soon, Miles Davis—who had been the trumpeter on Charlie Parker's bebop recording debut—became a convert to the cool jazz ideology. In 1948, he introduced the more subdued and formally structured style performances at Fifty-second Street's Royal Roost. Fronting a nine-piece ensemble, employing French horn, tuba, and trombone (in addition to the typical small-group instrumentation), Davis played a selection of original compositions characterized by their impressionistic colors and reflective mood. For many listeners, the lush, pastel arrangements, set off by brief chiseled solos from Miles and other members of the ensemble, provided a soothing respite from bebop's heated intensity.

In 1949, a series of studio recordings was released that documented the new sound. Employing a corps of sympathetic sidemen (including Lee Konitz on alto sax, Gerry Mulligan on baritone sax, and John Lewis on piano), the Davis nonet's versions of cool school classics such as "Boplicity" and "Israel" would later be collected on an LP whose title—*The Birth of the Cool*—aptly reflects the abrupt change in the emotional temperature of jazz that the album helped bring about.

The postbop era, however, was neither serenely harmonious nor entirely cool. In fact, for most of the decade, the jazz scene seemed to split into two distinct (and often devisive) factions—hard bop and cool jazz. Efforts to define the essence of the two branches of mid-century jazz usually result in a litany of opposites: the geographical (and recording) center of hard bop was the East Coast, while members of the cool school gravitated to the West Coast; hard bop was a return to the African-derived roots of jazz, while cool jazz drew its inspiration from

European concepts; hard bop was rhythmically oriented, while cool jazz was concerned with harmonies; hard bop musicians were black, while members of the cool school were white.

While the broad outlines of this dichotomy may be accurate, there are significant exceptions to each of these defining characteristics. For example, two of the primary architects of the birth of the cool—Miles Davis and John Lewis—were black (as was the arranger Tadd Dameron, whose harmonic innovations had a crucial influence on the movement). Finally, in recognition of his harmonically advanced improvisations, dulcet tone, and cool-cat persona, the movement's patron saint was none other than the tenor saxophone master, Lester Young.

Nor were the barriers between the two styles absolute. For example, in the mid-1950s, when Miles returned to the scene (after an extended hiatus during which he freed himself from his heroin addiction), he organized a small band that adapted the funky, soulful flavor of hard bop to his own spare, elliptical style. And, in a way, it was the fundamental tension between hard bop and cool jazz that actually provided the creative spark for a group John Lewis began leading at this time.

The Modern Jazz Quartet paired Lewis's mastery of form and pianistic restraint with the passionate, blues-based virtuosity of vibraphone master Milt Jackson (who had often performed with both Charlie Parker and Dizzy Gillespie). Joined by drummer Connie Kay and bassist Percy Heath, the MJQ symbolized the ability of jazz to resolve all its stylistic contradictions, and over the next quarter of a century the group became a jazz institution, making refined art that swung. During this time, the Modern Jazz Quartet was also in the forefront of another synthesis—between jazz and classical music—that was dubbed (by Gunter Schuller, its most committed proponent) *third stream*.

PLAYING THE CHANGES: A NEW MEDIUM AND A NEW MESSAGE

During the 1950s, two new ways of presenting jazz to the public were introduced. The first was the result of a technological revolution in the field of sound recording. In 1948, Columbia unveiled its 33⅓ r.p.m. "long playing" disk. The LP was the first significant advance in the recording industry since the mid-1920s (when the "electrical recording" process had been developed). The new format increased the number of potential minutes of music from about three per side (on a 78 r.p.m. disk) to as much as twenty-five per side (on the new LP). It also resulted in profound changes in how jazz was performed, marketed, and perceived (both by the audience and by the musicians themselves).

The other important innovation also was a result of the changing perception of jazz in the postbop era. For, gradually, a segment of the jazz audience had come to view the music as more than merely an accompaniment for a night of lindy hopping or the bizarre soundtrack for some beatnik cult. This encouraged promoters to put jazz on the stages of concert halls and eventually to establish regularly scheduled jazz festivals.

Beginning in the mid-1940s, a series of concerts at the Los Angeles Philharmonic Hall billed as "Jazz at the Philharmonic" brought Swing Era soloists (such as Lester Young) and bebop pioneers (such as Charlie Parker) together on the same stage in spontaneous jam-session style shows. The concerts were a huge success and, over the next decade, JATP (as it became known) toured concert halls around the country and generated a series of popular live recordings released on the new LP format.

In 1954, the first Newport Jazz Festival debuted. The annual summer event became one of the most significant and influential settings for jazz, garnering enormous publicity and becoming the model for every subsequent outdoor celebration of popular music that followed (including "Woodstock"). Right from the start, a sizeable segment of the audience that showed up at Newport was college students, for whom jazz had become a badge of intellectual sophistication. And with the unprecedented boom in university enrollment during the 1950s, the college campus itself emerged as an important venue for jazz concerts.

A regular college circuit quickly became established that—in keeping with the racial demographics of most institutions of higher education during the era—served primarily as venues for such (white) West Coast, cool school alumni as Stan Getz, Gerry Mulligan, Chet Baker, and George Shearing. And, based on their collegiate appeal, the quartet led by pianist Dave Brubeck quickly became the most commercially successful band in jazz.

Meanwhile, a host of young African-American performers—such as Horace Silver, Art Blakey, Julian "Cannonball" Adderley, and Lee Morgan—who were closely identified with the hard bop (or "soul jazz") movement—

FIGURE 3-23.   Beginning in the early 1950s, the Dave Brubeck Quartet could be heard on college campuses across the country, as well as on hi-fis throughout suburbia. Courtesy of Sony Records.

Take Five with the Dave Brubeck Quartet

In the wake of the birth of the cool, Dave Brubeck—a San Francisco–based pianist who had studied briefly with the contemporary classical composer, Darius Milhaud—teamed up with the lyrical Lester Young–influenced alto saxophonist Paul Desmond. Along with the contributions of drummer Joe Morello and bassist Eugene Wright, the pair forged an innovative style that often set their intricate interplay to a variety of adventurous time signatures. For example, the composition "Take Five" (an infectious Desmond tune from their million-selling 1960 album *Time Out*) was written in $\frac{5}{4}$; among their other experiments in exotic meters were "Blue Rondo a la Turk" ($\frac{9}{8}$) and "Unsquare Dance" ($\frac{7}{4}$).

Although by the time they disbanded in 1967 the quartet had become one of the most popular (and financially successful) in jazz history, some critics have suggested that the ensemble's music can best be appreciated as a reflection of the era's so-called third-stream movement (whose adherents sought to blend elements of classical music and jazz).

were establishing their muscular, blues-based music as the dominant jazz style within the black community. Although they had pared away many of the excesses of bebop (and turned away from its overly abstract qualities), what the new generation of performers did inherit from the modernists of the previous decade was a strong sense of pride—in both their racial heritage and their identity as artists.

Inevitably, the vast economic gulf between the mostly white musicians who toured the college circuit and the virtually all black hard bop bands who played a considerably less remunerative circuit of inner-city clubs began generating considerable hostility. The jazz writer Nat Hentoff quotes one black musician from the 1950s who expressed a commonly held perspective on this issue: "I was on the same bill with Brubeck, and his combo got nearly all the attention even though they were playing nothing. It's like people took it for granted that we could swing because we were Negroes, but thought it was something to make a fuss about when whites do it."

Along with the era's economic disparities, African-American jazz musicians also addressed the prevailing racial issues of the 1950s. For example, while many members of the soul jazz contingent were reconnecting jazz to its blues and gospel roots, others were directing their gaze back even further—to the music's African origins. The quintessential hard bop drummer Art Blakey even went to live in Africa for two years. While other performers—such as Max Roach (who went to Haiti to study native drumming techniques)—drew on African-influenced Caribbean traditions, a number of jazz musicians (such as the pianist Ahmad Jamal) expressed their black consciousness by converting to Islam and adopting Muslim names.

Meanwhile, the gathering momentum of the Civil Rights movement—marked by the Supreme Court decision in *Brown v. Topeka* and the Montgomery bus boycott—served as the inspiration for a new assertiveness of black jazz. By the late 1950s and early 1960s, a number of jazz performers began confronting racial issues directly in their music. For example, the composer and bassist Charles Mingus, who began leading his own experimental ensembles during this period (after playing as a sideman with bebop masters like Charlie Parker and Bud Powell), responded to Arkansas Governor Orville Faubus's notorious segregationist stance with his searing composition "Fables of Faubus."

In addition to its collection of Afrocentric experimentors, funky hardboppers, and elegant practitioners of cool, the diversity of the mid-century jazz scene was enriched by a couple of important voices of the past that had returned to the fore with renewed vigor.

For example, the Dixieland revival had provided Louis Armstrong the opportunity to work again in the small New Orleans–style setting that was his forte. And after a triumphant appearance at the 1956 Newport Festival, the Duke Ellington Orchestra resumed its place at the top of the jazz pyramid (after five years of wandering in the post-Swing wilderness). Meanwhile, as the decade drew to a close, perhaps the most distinctive and innovative jazz was being played by bands led by two of bebop's greatest heroes.

It wasn't until late in the decade (ten years after the unveiling of the modernist style he helped create) that bebop guru Thelonious Monk's genius was finally recognized by both the jazz public and the mainstream media. The idiosyncratic nature of the man and his music were part of the reason for the delay, as was the revocation of Monk's "cabaret card" in 1951. For years, Monk was legally prohibited from playing in any New York jazz club. But in 1957—after legal efforts to restore his card were successful—Monk was booked into the Five Spot Café. He filled the place for months, playing six nights a week to a euphoric audience of fans and fellow musicians.

As the jazz critic Nat Hentoff remembered it, "the first question a New York musician in Los Angeles or London was likely to be asked by the resident faithful was, 'Have you heard Monk lately? What's he doing?' " Through his live appearances and bold new recordings, Thelonious Monk not only solidified his own place in jazz history but also helped propel the careers of numerous younger performers (including future tenor saxophone giants Sonny Rollins and John Coltrane) who accompanied him during this period. Not-so-coincidentally, both Rollins and Coltrane also were involved in important collaborations with Miles Davis, who had already earned his place in jazz history through his early collaborations with Charlie Parker as well as his role in the birth of the cool.

Then in 1954, when he reappeared in the jazz spotlight (after a four-year hiatus), Miles Davis immediately began to reestablish his reputation as one of music's dominant bandleaders, stylistic innovators, and talent scouts. As if making up for lost time, Miles immediately initiated a frantic recording schedule, and with each album he seemed to strike another blow in his crusade to propel jazz into the future.

MILES AHEAD

On the basis of his critically acclaimed performance at the 1955 Newport Jazz Festival, Miles Davis suddenly found himself riding the crest of a jazz resurgence. Fueled by revenues it was generating from the astonishingly successful LP format, Columbia Records began seriously courting Davis (who was then signed to Prestige, a struggling independent jazz label). "After my Newport appearance," Miles recalled in his autobiography, "things began to happen for me. . . . [They] were talking about money, *real* money, so stuff was starting to look good."

Miles's initial contract with Columbia included a $4,000 advance for his first record and guarantees of as much as $300,000 per year. These were unprecedented figures for a jazz musician in the 1950s (or even in the 1990s, for that matter); as a result, Miles achieved sufficient economic security to maintain a permanent band for the first time. The ensemble that he put together in 1955 performed and recorded intensively for over two years, and in the process became one of the great small groups in jazz history. Often referred to as Miles's "classic quintet," the personnel consisted of the pianist Red Garland, the bassist Paul Chambers, the drummer Philly Jo Jones, and the tenor saxophonist John Coltrane.

It wasn't only his music that was responsible for Miles's unprecedented celebrity and financial success, it was the Miles mystique. He drove a Ferrari, appeared on GQ's best-dressed list, and seemed to cultivate a defiant public personna that only intensified the adulation of his audience. Miles was the dark prince of jazz—sullen, brooding, explosive. But as Davis was quick to point out, "I didn't get recognition based only on my rebel image. I was playing my horn and leading the baddest band in the business, a band that was creative, imaginative, supremely tight, and artistic. And to me that was why we got the recognition."

By playing together constantly, the band established a secure foundation for Davis to experiment with bold new concepts. According to Miles, "If any group was going to change the concept of music and take it to someplace altogether different, a new place, forward and fresh, then I felt this group was it." On his 1958 composition "Milestones," the new sound that Miles had been evolving first emerged. As an outgrowth of his interest in stripping away the complex chord changes and maze of harmonic extensions that had proliferated with the bebop revolution, Miles turned to an alternate approach for his improvisations. Rather than use chord changes to supply the structure of a composition, he used "modes" (harmonic structures that actually predate major and minor scales).

The modal system provided tremendous freedom for improvisation and also gave the music, in Davis's words, a "more African or Eastern, and less Western sound." A year later, after making a few personnel changes—primarily the addition of the blues-based alto sax of Cannonball Adderley and the haunting, harmonically advanced pianist Bill Evans—the band recorded the album that many critics consider the greatest album in jazz history, *Kind of Blue*. A moody masterpiece of the new modal style, the compositions were based largely on scale patterns that Davis sketched out (with Evans) immediately prior to recording. Yet again, Miles would have a major role in turning jazz in a new direction and as always his motivation was liberation of the musician from any constraints on his freedom.

Ironically, while this creative freedom became the vehicle for the musical success the group achieved, it also planted the seeds for the inevitable breakup of the band itself. Cannonball Adderley, whose gutsy, accessible playing had made him an extremely popular performer, was able to form his own successful group. In addition, both Bill Evans and John Coltrane also decided to leave the band to pursue their own personal musical visions. Evans's departure, however, was complicated by the tense racial climate of the period.

Although Miles has often been perceived as overtly hostile on issues of race, his priority was always the music. In fact, throughout his career, Davis had initiated important collaborations with white musicians including Gerry Mulligan, Gil Evans, and Lee Konitz. "I have always just wanted the best players in my group and I don't care about whether they're black, white, blue, red or yellow," Davis always insisted. Nevertheless, hostility directed at Evans from militant factions within the black jazz community certainly had its effect on the sensitive pianist, who soon left to form his own trio. Over the next two decades, Bill Evans created a body of work that has established him as one of the most influential jazz pianists of the modern era.

Meanwhile, John Coltrane—who had been making huge creative strides during his years with Davis—started taking some of his own giant steps toward an innovative new approach to jazz. Not only had Trane added Miles's new modal approach to his formidable stylistic repertoire, but he also had greatly expanded his technical

FIGURE 3-24.   This photo of Miles Davis was taken during the recording sessions for the historic LP *Kind of Blue*. Since its release in 1959, the record has been cherished by generations of jazz critics and fans as their favorite album of all time. Photo by Don Hunstein. Courtesy of Columbia Records.

Prince of Darkness

Miles Davis had come to New York in 1944 to study as the Juilliard School of Music, but within a few weeks of his arrival, the eighteen-year-old trumpeter was sitting in with Charlie Parker on Fifty-second Street. One year later, when Bird entered the Savoy studio to record his classic bebop compositions—including "Ko Ko," "Billie's Bounce," and "Now's the Time"—it was Miles who was holding down the trumpet spot in the quintet. And in 1947, after Dizzy Gillespie went off to form a new band, Miles found himself a full-time member of the era's most important jazz ensemble.

Unlike Gillespie and other bebop trumpet players such as Clifford Brown and Fats Novarro, Miles Davis was not a technical virtuoso, ripping off spectacular stratospheric runs at blistering speed. Instead, he played with a deliberate simplicity, etching brief, middle-register phrases whose evocative power came from the placement of each note within the silence that surrounds it. In keeping with his minimalist aesthetic, Miles affected a spare, often muted sound shaded by a variety of subtle tonal effects. While Gillespie and the rest traced their brilliant, extroverted style back to a long line of "Trumpet Kings," the aura of romantic mystery Miles created earned him the title "Prince of Darkness."

Once Miles began leading his own bands, he consistently hired the music's most promising young performers (including John Coltrane, Bill Evans, Tony Williams, Wayne Shorter, and Keith Jarrett) to collaborate with him in his restless quest for new avenues of expression. In every decade, Miles ventured into some new uncharted musical terrain—from the cool jazz sounds of the Forties to the modal masterpieces of the Sixties to his experiments with jazz-rock fusions in the Seventies; in the process, he also became the most commercially successful jazz musician of his time.

When he died in 1991, Miles Davis had been in the vanguard of every significant phase in the evolution of jazz for virtually the entire second half of the twentieth century. As the century came to a close, the acclaimed jazz vocalist Cassandra Wilson issued a CD of her interpretations of tunes associated with the trumpeter, entitled *Traveling Miles*. Speaking for many of her contemporaries, Wilson told an interviewer, "Miles Davis is more than a man for me now; he's a metaphor of exploration, movement [and] creativity."

prowess. He became famous for his marathon practice sessions; even after playing three sets with Davis, Coltrane was known to return to his hotel to work out ideas on his horn.

In 1957, Coltrane briefly left Miles's band to work with Thelonious Monk during his extended engagement at the Five Spot. Trane made the most of this rare opportunity to learn from someone he considered "a musical architect of the highest order." When he rejoined Davis to record *Kind of Blue,* Coltrane claimed that he had experienced a "spiritual awakening" during this period. "He had always been serious about his music," Miles recalled in his autobiography, "but now it was almost like he was on a mission."

CHASIN' THE TRANE

The fruits of the harmonic explorations and instrumental advances Coltrane had made as a sideman were immediately apparent on his first albums as the leader of his own band. In fact, just before he left Miles for good in 1959, Coltrane recorded an album whose title—*Giant Steps*—perfectly captures both his conceptual leap forward as well as the confident, muscular stride of his playing.

By tearing his way through dense sequences of scales, Trane constructed a radical new style that the jazz critic Ira Gitler has described as "sheets of sound." "His multinote improvisations were so thick and complex they were almost flowing out of the horn by themselves," Gitler explained. "It was almost superhuman, and the amount of energy he was using could have powered a spaceship."

It wasn't only the intensity and freedom of his playing but the sheer length of his solos that began to attract attention. When he was still playing with Miles Davis, Coltrane's tumultuous, extended solos would sometimes go on for fifteen or twenty minutes. According to one famous anecdote, Miles is supposed to have asked his saxophonist why he played so long. Trane responded that sometimes he got so absorbed in the music that he didn't know how to stop, to which Miles is alleged to have snapped, "Just take the horn out of your damn mouth." After he left Miles, Coltrane's solos got longer. One tune might stretch out over an entire live set or fill the whole side of an LP.

Coltrane also was experimenting with a new instrument, the soprano saxophone. Notoriously difficult to master, the only major jazz musician to be identified with the instrument had been the New Orleans pioneer Sidney Bechet. It was on this instrument, however, that Trane had his breakthrough with the jazz public. In 1960, he made a recording with the musicians who would, for the most part, remain his permanent band for the bulk of his career (McCoy Tyner on piano, Elvin Jones on drums, and Jimmy Garrison on bass). The album's title track—which featured Coltrane's soprano sax—was a hypnotic version of the Broadway show tune "My Favorite Things" played as a jazz waltz. The recording quickly sold over fifty thousand copies (about ten times the average sales of a "successful" jazz album). Although many critics and fans had initially found Coltrane's music chaotic and even painful in its intensity, gradually there was growing recognition of the validity of his musical concepts.

But Coltrane wasn't the only musician who was attempting to either rearrange the basic vocabulary of the jazz tradition or to develop a new voice for his instrument. In fact, Coltrane hadn't even been Miles Davis's first choice when he was looking for a tenor saxophonist to fill out his "classic quintet." If Miles had his way, that job would have gone to a young player named Sonny Rollins, who in the early 1950s was being touted as the dominant saxophonist of his generation.

SONNY ROLLINS: SAXOPHONE COLOSSUS

Even while he was still in high school, Sonny Rollins's reputation had began to spread through the upper reaches of the New York jazz scene. He was part of a circle of talented young musicians who all lived in the same Harlem neighborhood. A few—including the alto saxophonist Jackie McLean and the bassist Art Taylor—also would become important jazz musicians in their own right.

At first Sonny was drawn to the rhythm and blues scene that was flourishing throughout black America at the beginning of the 1950s, but soon he was being introduced to the intriguing complexities of bebop by two neighbors—Thelonious Monk and Bud Powell—who just happened to be among the movement's leading

FIGURE 3-25.   This evocative photo of John Coltrane captures the serene and reflective quality that always seemed to lie just behind the passionate intensity of his music. By including the shadowy figure of Miles Davis in the background, it also serves a visual metaphor for Trane's emergence from the trumpeter's "Classic Quintet" to his role as leader of his own celebrated band. Photo by Don Hunstein. Courtesy of Columbia Records.

Man on a Mission

In 1959—when John Coltrane made the first recordings under his own name—the tenor saxophonist was approaching his mid-thirties, an age when most major jazz artists had already been fronting their own bands for at least a decade. Miles Davis, who was born the same year as Trane, had released his debut recordings as a leader back in 1949. Over the next eight years (until his untimely death from liver cancer), however, Coltrane made up for lost time, adopting and discarding new creative approaches in a frantic quest for some ultimate form of self-expression. Along the way, he made some of the most beautiful, profound and challenging music of the twentieth century.

Coltrane pursued his musical vision with single-minded dedication. Commenting on his saxophonist's famous work ethic, Miles Davis recalled that "while [Coltrane] had always been serious about music and always practiced a lot," by the late 1950s "it was almost like he was on some kind of mission." In fact, not only did the saxophonist's family tree have deep religious roots (both his grandfathers were ministers), but Coltrane also alluded to a religious awakening he had experienced during this period that transformed him personally and musically.

Among the many compositions and album titles that reflect Coltrane's ongoing spiritual quest are "The Father and the Son and the Holy Ghost," *Ascension,* "Selflessness," "Spiritual," "Psalm," "Dear Lord," "Amen," "Offering," *Om,* and *A Love Supreme* (whose liner notes include a Coltrane-penned prayer and the dedication, "This album is a humble offering to Him").

In 1966, when he visited Japan, an interviewer asked Coltrane where he wanted to be ten years in the future. Coltrane responded, "I would like to be a saint." Coltrane died less than a year later, and for many jazz fans around the world that is exactly what he has become.

Jazz musicians have attracted the attention of a wide range of contemporary poets who see in the spontaneous creativity of these performers a model for their own artistic endeavors. Meanwhile, African-American poets—recognizing the jazz musician's vital role in black history—often have celebrated the jazz musician as a culture hero.

In the poem below, the African-American poet Michael S. Harper begins by establishing Coltrane's role as an artist ("a tenor blossoming, which would paint suffering a clear color") and ends by linking him to such twentieth-century martyrs as Martin Luther King, Jr., and Malcolm X. Along the way, Harper makes a number of allusions to Trane's life and career, including the titles of both his most acclaimed album, *A Love Supreme,* and his enduring 1963 composition, "Alabama" (written in memory of the four young black girls killed in the racially motivated bombing of a Birmingham church).

"Here Where Coltrane Is" (Michael S. Harper)

Soul and race
are private dominions,
memories and modal
songs, a tenor blossoming,
which would paint suffering
a clear color but is not in
this Victorian house
without oil in zero degree
weather and a forty-mile-an-hour
  wind;
it is all a well-knit family:
a love supreme.

Oak leaves pile up on walkway
and steps, catholic as apples
in a special mist of clear white
children who love my children.
I play "Alabama"
on a warped record player
skipping the scratches
on your faces over the fibrous
conical hairs of plastic
under the wooden floors.

Dreaming on a train from New York
to Philly, you hand out six
notes which become an anthem
to our memories of you:
oak, birch, maple,
apple, cocoa, rubber.
For this reason Martin is dead;
for this reason Malcolm is dead;
for this reason Coltrane is dead;
in the eyes of my first son are the browns
of these men and their music.

From: *History Is Your Own Heartbeat* © 1971 by Michael S. Harper. Used with the permission of the author and of the University of Illinois Press.

practitioners. And while Rollins came under the powerful spell of Charlie Parker (as did every other young jazz saxophonist of his generation), he also was inspired by another local celebrity, the "Father of the Tenor Sax," Coleman Hawkins.

Rollins quickly began to synthesize his diverse influences into a personal style to which he brought both an awesome technical virtuosity and a profoundly rich harmonic conception. By 1949, when he was just nineteen years old, he began recording with Bud Powell, Fats Navarro, and other bebop heavyweights. Virtually overnight, Rollins had become one of the most sought-after sidemen in jazz. Even on these early recordings, his sound seems to explode out of his horn with a majestic authority, and even at the most torrid tempos, there is a coherent structure to his improvisations. He also was beginning to write compositions that seamlessly fused the entire range of his musical heritage—from the blues and gospel roots of R & B to the formal abstractions of bebop to the sultry rhythms of the Caribbean (which he had heard at home as a child).

In 1954, Rollins made important contributions to Miles Davis's album *Oleo,* through both his dynamic solos and his assured and varied compositions. In addition to the album's now classic title track, Rollins was responsible for writing two other tunes on the session that also have become jazz standards, "Doxy" and "Airegin." "Sonny Rollins was something else," Miles recalled in his autobiography. "Brilliant. He was interested in Africa, so he turned Nigeria backwards and called that tune 'Airegin' for that date . . . as a matter of fact, he brought the tunes in and rewrote them right in the studio." Miles desperately wanted Sonny as a member of the permanent band he was about to form, but suddenly Rollins had dropped out of sight. Another victim of the heroin plague that had so devastated the jazz world during the decade, the saxophonist had gone off to free himself of his addiction.

When he returned to the scene a few months later, Rollins was invited to join the prestigous Clifford Brown–Max Roach Quintet. For about a year, Rollins flourished as a member of a band many critics consider one of the best in the music's history. But, tragically, in June of 1956, "Brownie" was killed in an auto accident at the age of twenty-six. The loss of this brilliant young trumpeter, a model of pure musicianship (dedicated and drug-free) was a profound one for the jazz community; and it had an enormous effect on Rollins. When he entered the studio as a leader later that year, he did so with a heightened sense of commitment to his music. The title of the resulting album—*Saxophone Colossus*—perfectly captured the overwhelming force of Rollins's playing, and the favorable critical response it received was equally monumental. It was with this recording, wrote the jazz historian David Rosenthal, that "Rollins established a reputation as the most original and compelling saxophonist since Charlie Parker."

Just as Rollins had fused diverse elements from jazz history in his playing, his playing on *Saxophone Colossus* was deemed (by at least one critic) also to have resolved the eternal jazz conflict between compositional structure and improvisational freedom. According to jazz scholar Gunther Schuller, Rollins's performance on his own composition, "Blue 7," marked the introduction of a new creative conception (in which spontaneously improvised solos achieved a level of structural cohesiveness that extended throughout the entire performance); Schuller dubbed this technique "thematic improvisation." Writing in the magazine *The Jazz Review*, he contended that "with Rollins thematic and structural unity have at last achieved the importance in *pure* improvisation that elements such as swing, melodic conception and originality of expression have already enjoyed for years."

While Rollins may have sparked the adulation of jazz fans, influenced generations of saxophonists, and inspired writers to new heights of hyperbole, he was his own harshest critic. His quest for even deeper musical insights (and personal self-awareness) periodically led him to withdraw from the jazz scene. His most famous "sabbatical" occurred in 1959, when he was at the peak of his popular and critical success. For almost two years, he immersed himself in the study of harmony and composition, adopted a regimen of physical fitness and nutrition, and practiced. One of the most enduring and romantic images in jazz is of Rollins playing his horn late at night in the middle of the Williamsburg Bridge (that spans New York's East River). In fact, when he returned to the music scene in 1961, he titled his now classic comeback album *The Bridge* as an acknowledgment of these late-night explorations.

THE AVANT GARDE: OUT OF THE MAINSTREAM

Inherent in the nature of jazz as a music of improvisation is the challenge faced by every performer "to make it new." From the very beginning, however, most performers have channeled their creativity within the context of a recognized tradition.

In an effort to bring a historical perspective to this phenomenon, the critic Stanley Dance created the term "mainstream jazz," which he defined as "the jazz idiom which developed between the heyday of King Oliver and Jelly Roll Morton on the one hand and that of Charlie Parker and Dizzy Gillespie on the other." Dance asserted that this tradition reflected a dominant or "central" current "emphasizing the twin virtues of communicable emotional expression and swing."

Periodically, however, great leaps forward have occurred that seemed to propel jazz out of its fixed orbit and into a completely new musical dimension. For example, when bebop first emerged in the late 1940s, it generally was perceived to be a fundamental alteration in the course of jazz history. But, as we've seen, once listeners absorbed the harmonic and rhythmic innovations of Parker and Co., the modernists also became an accepted part of the jazz tradition.

FIGURE 3-26.   Charles Mingus was more than just the preeminent bassist of his generation; he was an overpowering creative force who secured his lofty reputation as a prolific
composer, innovative bandleader, social activist, and author. Photo by Don Hunstein. Courtesy of Columbia Records.

Charles Mingus: Better Get Hit in Your Soul

Growing up in Watts (Los Angeles' black enclave), Charles Mingus heard the blues on recordings and the
sound of gospel music in the Holiness Church he attended with his stepmother. One of the most indelible
musical experiences of his childhood was hearing the Duke Ellington Orchestra perform live at a local concert hall. Eventually, Mingus would—like "the Maestro"—transform the rich legacy of African-American
music into his own unique form of expression.

After emerging as a leader during the mid-1950s, Mingus set about exploding the accumulated cliches
and stereotypes that he felt had come to constrain free and spontaneous expression in jazz. He explored new
methods of composition (combining written passages, traditional solos, and collective improvisation), established a collaborative "workshop" approach to performance, and struggled against the exploitive business practices he had come to despise.

Charles Mingus composed approximately 150 works during his career covering a stylistic range from
hard bop and funk to Ellingtonian impressionism and free jazz (often all in the same piece). Among those
that have gone on to become jazz classics are "Better Get Hit in Your Soul" (an ecstatic re-creation of a gospel
service), "Goodbye Pork Pie Hat" (a haunting elegy for Lester Young), "Ysabel's Table Dance" (a Spanish-
tinged workout replete with castinet rhythms), "An Open Letter to Duke" (one of his tributes to the Master),
and "Fables of Faubus" (a scathing indictment of racism created at the height of the civil rights movement).

Gradually, "mainstream jazz" proved itself to be an expanding universe capable of encompassing not only Bird's startling flights of imagination, but also each succeeding stylistic spin-off. So, with the passage of time, Lennie Tristano's excursions into abstract realms of melodic formalism, Horace Silver's funky exoticisms, Charles Mingus's experiments in primitive modernism, Dave Brubeck's fractured time signatures, Miles's modal meanderings, and even Coltrane's raging sheet of sound were all eventually absorbed into the jazz mainstream.

As the new decade approached, however, a number of performers appeared on the horizon who would surpass even Miles, Mingus, and Coltrane in their assault not only on the jazz mainstream but on such fundamental musical principles as formal meter, standard key signatures, and the basic rules of Western harmony. As if mirroring the explosive social ferment of the early 1960s, the cry of many jazz musicians also seemed to be "Freedom Now!"

One group of performers—best represented by the pianist Cecil Taylor—drew inspiration not only from the pioneers of modern jazz, but from the cutting-edge twentieth-century classical composers who had been part of the revolutionary movement in all the arts known as the "avant garde." Taylor used his prodigious technique and conservatory training to expand jazz traditions with dissonance—crashing blocks of notes and random shifts in meter that seemed to owe more to contemporary heroes of European modernism like Stravinsky and Stockhausen than to anyone in the jazz pantheon.

When Taylor got his first significant gig—at New York's Five Spot Café in 1957—he precipitated a dramatic rift in the jazz world. Both fans and other performers reacted to his music with hostility that far exceeded anything the beboppers had to contend with. While virtually everyone agreed his playing fell well outside the boundaries of "mainstream jazz," many questioned whether it was jazz at all; still others contended that it wasn't even music.

Naturally, all the controversy only served to fuel an intense curiosity and Taylor filled the club for weeks. In the process he also began to win some converts on the basis of both his obvious artistic commitment and the overwhelming physical power of his playing. He also attracted a core of musicians who shared his interest in breaking out of the standard jazz forms and harmonic principles. Along with drummers Sunny Murray and Andrew Cyrille, soprano saxophonist Steve Lacy, alto saxophonist Jimmy Lyons, bassist Buell Neidlinger, and others, Taylor steadfastly held to his avant-garde musical vision. "It is important, wholly important, to fulfill yourself," Taylor has maintained. "It is your life. If you are doing that then you are doing something for someone else, even if it's for only one someone else."

Although he has never achieved popular or commercial success, over the last half of the twentieth century Taylor has garnered a cult of faithful fans (especially in Europe) and established a secure reputation among fellow musicians and critics. Along the way, his links to the jazz mainstream have become increasingly apparent as well. Early in his career, Taylor wrote, "Everything I've lived, I am. I'm not afraid of European influences. The point is to use them—as Ellington did—as part of my life as an American Negro." Today, critics identify the highly percussive nature of his piano playing with jazz's African roots, while others have recognized the influences of a long line of jazz pianists—including Ellington, Monk, and Horace Silver—on Taylor's own style. In the mid-1970s, the great Swing Era pianist/arranger Mary Lou Williams gave Taylor her own coveted seal of approval by appearing with him in a series of duo-piano concerts.

ORNETTE COLEMAN: THE SHAPE OF JAZZ TO COME

In 1959, when the alto saxophonist Ornette Coleman first appeared with his band at New York's Five Spot Café, the storm of controversy he generated made the furor that had greeted Cecil Taylor's debut two years earlier seem like a tempest in a teapot.

As Ornette recalled in an interview years later, "Every night the club would be jammed, with some people hating what I was doing and calling me a charlatan, and other people loving it and declaring me a genius." One well-known drummer expressed his disapproval by physically attacking Coleman in the club's bathroom. Miles Davis offered his reaction in the form of this unsolicited diagnosis: "If you're talking psychologically, the man is all screwed up inside." By contrast, Leonard Bernstein spoke for a number of important critics and musicians when—after hearing Ornette—he announced, "This is the greatest thing that has ever happened to jazz!"

Volatile reactions to his music were nothing new to Ornette Coleman. A self-taught musician who had been born in Fort Worth, Texas, in 1930, Ornette began his career playing tenor sax in R & B bands throughout the South and Southwest. In 1950, after getting fired from a succession of jobs, he wound up in Los Angeles, which had both a flourishing R & B and a modern jazz scene. After being exposed to Charlie Parker's early bebop recordings, Ornette switched to alto sax and began making his first appearances in L.A.'s Central Avenue jazz clubs. Reactions were immediate and intense. Dexter Gordon, the premier jazz saxophonist on the West Coast, literally kicked him off the stage, and when Coleman walked in the door at local jam sessions, musicians started packing up their instruments so they wouldn't have to play with him.

Although his wild hair, beard, and exotic style of dress didn't help, the hostility Ornette Coleman provoked was based primarily on his rejection of what had always been considered the essential organizing principles of jazz. For Coleman rejected both the use of chord changes as the basis of his improvisations and abandoned any adherence to traditional rhythmic structures. Yet, even more than the perceived formlessness of his music, listeners were appalled by his very "sound." His tone—shrill, out-of-tune, and overlaid with honks and squeals—seemed like an insult to many listeners and musicians. While Cecil Taylor had the credibility of his conservatory training, European classical models, and technical virtuosity, the conventional wisdom was that not only didn't Ornette understand the basic elements of jazz, but he simply couldn't play the saxophone.

But Ornette had an answer for every criticism. To charges that he didn't know the fundamentals of jazz harmony, Ornette responded, "If I'm going to follow a preset chord sequence, I may as well write out my solos." To attacks on his intonation, he offered an alternate theory of pitch: "You can play sharp in tune and you can play flat in tune." Nor was his sound the product of ineptitude. He insisted that "there are some intervals that carry the *human* quality if you play them in the right pitch. You can reach the sound of a human voice on your horn." In place of a formal, hierarchical ensemble structure, Ornette offered his musicians freedom and a collaborative adventure. "Each player is free to contribute what he feels in the music at any given moment," he explained. "I don't tell the members of my group what to do. I want them to play what they hear in the piece themselves."

Ornette soon began to attract a circle of young jazz musicians (including the bassist Charlie Haden and trumpeter Don Cherry) who, drawn by the creative freedom his music offered, became members of his working band. During the late 1950s, Coleman began documenting his music on a series of recordings whose titles clearly proclaim their revolutionary intentions: *Something Else!!!, Tomorrow Is the Question, The Shape of Jazz to Come,* and *Change of the Century.* But it was another album—released a little while after his sensational Five Spot debut—that actually provided the name of the whole movement he helped initiate. It was comprised of a single thirty-six-minute piece of collective improvisation entitled *Free Jazz.*

An even more radical extension of the avant-garde experiments of Coltrane, Rollins, and Mingus, the so-called Free Jazz movement suddenly seemed like the ideal soundtrack to the cultural upheavals of the 1960s. In fact, among those attracted to the startling new sounds were the very same jazz innovators who had been supplanted at jazz's cutting edge by the advances wrought by Cecil Taylor and Ornette Coleman. Although Miles made no secret of his disdain for what he heard at Ornette's Five Spot performances, Coltrane had a very different reaction. "'Trane was there a lot more than I was," Davis wrote in his autobiography, "watching and listening." Coltrane, who had been liberating himself from many constraints traditionally imposed on jazz, was inspired by Ornette's example to take even bolder musical strides.

In albums such as *Impressions* (recorded in 1961), Trane can be heard exploring the new uncharted territory opened by the Free Jazz pioneers. A few years later—after expanding his quartet with some musicians associated with Ornette Coleman—Coltrane recorded *Ascension,* his most ambitious statement of free-form principles, along with his own version of Coleman's shrieking microtonal saxophone style. In 1962, Sonny Rollins also went through a Free Jazz phase, actually hiring Ornette Coleman's main musical cohort, Don Cherry, as his own sideman.

In its chaotic and confrontational style, a great deal of the music made by such Free Jazz journeymen—as bassist Charlie Haden and drummer Ed Blackwell (who were members of Ornette's quartet); saxophonists Eric Dolphy, Archie Shepp, and Pharoah Sanders; trombonist Roswell Rudd; and pianist/composer/bandleader Sun Ra—did seem to directly reflect the spirit of its time. Some performers formed "collectives" to create and market their music (and to escape from what they saw as the corporate stranglehold on jazz). Many turned to Africa (and

FIGURE 3-27.   When Ornette Coleman burst onto the New York jazz scene in the fall of 1958, he made the hard-won innovations of avant-grade saxophonists like Sonny Rollins and John Coltrane suddenly seem obsolete. Archive photo. Frank Driggs Collection.

Ornette: Looking Forward through a Rearview Mirror

Although the musical revolution Ornette Coleman initiated came to be known as Free Jazz, the anarchic quality that repelled so many early listeners wasn't nearly as chaotic—or as "free"—as it first sounded. While it's true that he did jettison the harmonic foundation (or chord changes) that had long provided the basis for solo improvisation in jazz and abandon the use of strict rhythmic structures, there was, in reality, more than a little method to his madness. For example, after acknowledging his music's lack of "metric time," Ornette Coleman insisted, "It has time, but not in the sense that you can time it. It's more like breathing, a natural freer time."

As open-minded listeners grew more familiar with his music, the alto saxophonist's links to jazz tradition became more apparent. In addition to the inevitable influence of Charlie Parker, there was, in his rhythmically angular compositions, an obvious debt to Thelonious Monk. In fact, in many respects, Coleman seemed to be looking into the future through a rearview mirror. For in the plaintive keening wail of his horn one can hear the echoes of the most primitive country blues, while in his embrace of collective improvisation we are taken back to the dense ensemble sound of New Orleans jazz at the turn of the twentieth century.

As jazz makes its way into the twenty-first century, Ornette Coleman remains a controversial figure; but after almost half a century (and over thirty albums of original music for jazz combo, string quartet, and symphony orchestra) he also has taken his place as one of the great visionaries in the history of the music.

other developing world cultures for musical inspiration), using their music to promote an Afrocentric identity or to create anthems of black nationalism.

Although much of the music that was recorded in the 1960s still seems to fall outside anyone's definition of the "jazz mainstream," some of what sounded so abrasive and incomprehensible then doesn't sound nearly so extreme today. In the case of Ornette's first albums, it's even hard to hear what all the fuss was about. Indeed, with the passage of time, Free Jazz's connections to the music's past begin to seem increasingly obvious.

As a Texas-born saxophonist who served a rigorous rhythm and blues apprenticeship, Ornette's playing echoes the characteristic wail of the blues, while his collaborative ensemble concepts can be linked to the "collective improvisation" of the very first New Orleans jazz bands. And not only did he arrive on the scene playing the same kind of white plastic saxophone Charlie Parker used late in his career, but Ornette can often be heard "quoting" actual excerpts from Bird's solos on some of his own improvisations.

Similar connections can be established for other cutting-edge performers. For example, when the multi-reed modernist Eric Dolphy participated in a jazz festival in Washington, D.C., he had the opportunity to hear the Eureka Jazz Band, one of the most authentic surviving New Orleans brass bands. "I stood right in the middle of those old men," Nat Hentoff quotes Dolphy as recalling, "and I couldn't see much difference from what I'm doing. . . . You know something? They were the first freedom players."

While the confrontational attitudes and harsh dissonance of the decade's avant garde did alienate a large segment of the audience, jazz itself was about to be seriously marginalized by a potent new sound that had taken the American music scene by storm. On February 7, 1964, the Beatles landed in New York, where they were greeted by thousands of hysterical teenage fans. One inadvertent consequence of the so-called British Invasion—and the musical and social revolution it heralded—was a profound depression that cut across the entire jazz scene. Jazz clubs closed by the dozens (or converted to a rock format), scores of bands lost their recording contracts, and even successful performers were forced to scuffle for anonymous session work or a gig in the pit band of a Broadway musical.

Yet, even during the darkest days of the mid-1960s, jazz did have its bright spots. Tenor saxophonist Stan Getz's Top Ten pop hit, "The Girl from Ipanema," kicked off a "bossa nova" craze by blending jazz and Brazilian samba rhythms. Veteran performers such as Cannonball Adderley and the guitarist Wes Montgomery also scored commercial successes with their accessible and soulful styles. In 1964, Miles Davis formed a *second* "classic quartet" with dynamic young musicians (Wayne Shorter, Herbie Hancock, Ron Carter, and Tony Williams) that became almost as venerated as the band he'd led with John Coltrane at the end of the previous decade; in fact, even Coltrane had a hit (at least in jazz terms) when his inspirational 1965 album, *A Love Supreme,* sold a quarter of a million copies.

FUSION: JAZZ PLUGS IN

By the early 1970s, rock music not only was producing unprecedented profits for America's media conglomerates, but it was generating an extraordinary outpouring of experimentation (enhanced by innovations in electronics and recording technology) that was pushing rock in new and exciting directions. Now, a handful of jazz performers—already pushed to the margins by the rock revolution—were poised to challenge rock on its own terms.

Among the first to begin incorporating rock elements into jazz was the band Dreams (featuring drummer Billy Cobham along with saxophonist Michael Brecker and Randy Brecker on trumpet). Other early proponents of the jazz-rock fusion included vibraphonist Gary Burton (who teamed up with the electric guitarist Larry Coryell in 1967) and Jeremy Steig, whose electrically amplified flute was finding its way into various ensembles at about the same time.

The jazz musician who responded most boldly to rock dominance, however, was the creatively restless veteran innovator Miles Davis. Miles first took his own tentative steps toward a union of rock and jazz elements in 1968; he added an electric keyboard (played by a young musician named Chick Corea) to his ensemble and began emphasizing funky rhythmic figures against which he etched spare melodic lines with his horn.

While some have questioned his motives, Miles Davis always insisted that the new style was simply a reflection of his own evolving musical tastes during this period. As he recalled years later, "The music I was really listening to in 1968 was James Brown, the great guitar player Jimi Hendrix, and a new group who had just come out with a hit record, 'Dance to the Music,' Sly and the Family Stone." It was also about this time that Davis abandoned his stylish continental suits in favor of a wardrobe of custom-made bell bottoms and leather fringe jackets.

In 1969, he committed himself completely to a powerful new electric style of jazz. Since various members of Miles's second classic quartet had already expressed an interest in leaving to form their own bands, Miles began replacing them with performers who shared a common interest in exploring the potential for a new, improvised, electric musical hybrid. A few months after recording a transitional album called *In a Silent Way* (1969) with a new band that—in addition to saxophonist Wayne Shorter and drummer Tony Williams (from his previous quintet)—also included the electric bassist Dave Holland, the electric keyboards of Joe Zawinul and Chick Corea, and the cutting-edge electric guitar of John McLaughlin, Miles returned to the studio. The result was the first fully realized recording of the jazz-rock synthesis that came to be called "Fusion."

Entitled *Bitches Brew,* the double album (combining funky vamps and a broad palatte of tonal colors) sold 500,000 copies in its first year, becoming the biggest-selling jazz record in history. Suddenly Miles was playing sold-out shows at rock auditoriums on the same bill as the Grateful Dead, Santana, and Crosby, Stills, Nash, and Young. While traditional jazz fans felt betrayed by what they saw as Miles's abandonment of his musical values, the trumpet player vehemently denied that he had "sold out" to rock for commercial success or because of pressure from his record label: "I was going for it for myself, for what I needed in my own music. I wanted to change course for me to continue to believe in and love what I was playing."

Soon there were dozens of Fusion bands exploring their own blends of jazz and rock. And among the most significant of these were the groups led by a contingent of Miles's former sidemen. Drummer Tony Williams and guitarist John McLaughlin formed a high-powered ensemble called Lifetime, pianist Herbie Hancock led a self-titled sextet that exploited the new electronic keyboard technologies, and Wayne Shorter joined forces with Joe Zawinul to create a band named Weather Report. Each band formulated its own recipe for success by carefully proportioning precise elements from each genre to create its own unique synthesis. For instance, Herbie Hancock's Sextet emphasized a funky dance beat, while on Weather Report's first albums electronic gimmicks took a back seat to inventive compositions and strong improvisation. And when Chick Corea and electric bassist Stanley Clarke forged a collaboration called Return to Forever, a Latin tinge often was added to the mix.

It seemed everybody had "plugged in." Acoustic instruments were pushed into the closet, and jazz bands— surrounded by towers of enormous speakers—became a regular part of the programming at rock venues like the Fillmore (East and West) and at festivals from Newport to England's Isle of Wight. While electric pianos, organs, and the newly developed synthesizers made important contributions to the Fusion sound, the primary focus in many bands was an electrically amplified instrument that had been a mainstay of jazz bands since the 1930s: the guitar.

In jazz, the electric guitar had first been used as a rhythm instrument whose amplified sound allowed it to cut through the din of Swing Era big bands. In the mid-1940s, the single note, hornlike style pioneered by Charlie Christian became an important element in mainstream jazz combos. In the years that followed, improvised jazz played on the electric guitar became an established tradition in a variety of contexts from bebop quartets to soulful organ-guitar combos.

But during the 1960s, rock had so completely coopted the electric guitar that the instrument was enshrined as the music's ultimate symbol. Building on a basic blues vocabulary, rock guitar heroes such as Eric Clapton, Peter Townshend, Jeff Beck, and Jimi Hendrix forged a new guitar aesthetic that exploited extreme volume— along with some technologically derived sonic enhancements—as a vehicle for an exciting new sound textured with feedback, distortion, and reverb.

So, in 1969, when he began working on Miles's breakthrough electric jazz albums, the British guitarist John McLaughlin turned away from the polite tonalities and restrained improvisations of the jazz tradition. By combining the virtuoso technique and sophisticated harmonic foundation of his jazz training with the extroverted showmanship and overpowering volume levels of rock, McLaughlin found himself in the forefront of a generation of innovative electric guitarists such as Larry Coyell, Jerry Hahn, Al DiMeola, and Pat Metheney.

For the next ten years, Fusion became the dominant style of jazz. During this period, jazz achieved a level of commercial success it had not seen since the end of the Swing Era over a quarter of a century earlier. Second-, third-, and fourth-generation electric jazz bands carried the Fusion movement into the 1980s and 1990s, often

FIGURE 3-28.   Formed in 1971 by alumni of Miles Davis's pioneering electric band, Weather Report soon established itself as the most creative practitioners of that (often-denigrated) synthesis of rock and jazz known as "Fusion." Courtesy of Sony Records.

Time for a Weather Report

After working with Miles Davis on such groundbreaking late-1960s experiments in amplification as *In a Silent Way* and *Bitches Brew,* tenor saxophonist Wayne Shorter and keyboard player Joe Zawinul initiated their own jazz-rock fusion. Over the next decade and a half, their band, Weather Report, would go on to make some twenty recordings charting the outer limits of the Fusion frontier from atmospheric minimalism to funk grooves and from improvisational jams to arena rock pyrotechnics.

Although Shorter and Zawinul retained their status as co-leaders, Weather Report's other personnel changed extensively from one album to the next. Among the band's numerous sidemen, the performer who had the single greatest impact on Weather Report's music was the brilliant electric bassist Jaco Pastorious, who joined the band in 1976. Considered by many to be the most influential bass player of the last quarter century, Pastorious's technical virtuosity, energy, and improvisational genius inspired his bandmates to new heights. During his tenure, the band issued its most critically acclaimed (and best-selling album), *Heavy Weather* (featuring the Zawinul-written hit, "Birdland").

serving as a point of entry for listeners into more traditional genres of jazz. In addition, some rock performers (such as Steely Dan) periodically began drawing inspiration (and occasional sidemen) from the world of electric jazz to create their own rock-jazz hybrids.

Despite its commercial success, however, most jazz critics continued to raise serious questions about the artistic validity of the whole Fusion movement. And by the end of the 1970s, many of the original Fusion pioneers also began to sense that they had exhausted the creative possibilities of the new style, feeling increasingly trapped by its static riffs and technological pyrotechnics. Although Miles Davis continued to explore fusions of jazz, rock, pop, and funk employing the full array of electronic paraphernalia, most of his former sidemen began to unplug.

FIGURE 3-29. When Wynton Marsalis's debut album as a leader was released in 1982, the twenty-one-year-old trumpeter was heralded as a musical savior and guru of the decade's jazz renaissance. In the mid-1990s, he became the first jazz composer to win the Pulitzer Prize. Photo by William Coupon. Courtesy of Columbia Records.

Wynton Marsalis and the Jazz Renaissance

Born in New Orleans (birthplace of jazz), second son of Ellis Marsalis (a respected jazz pianist), student at New York's Juilliard School of Music (as Miles Davis had been forty years before), and graduate of Art Blakey's Jazz Messengers (perhaps the music's premier "finishing school"), Wynton Marsalis's bio seems like it was scripted by a public relations genius. So it was no wonder that his arrival was greeted with such fanfare. Besides, after a decade of stagnation had renewed fears about "the death of jazz," he could be cast as the mythic hero destined to breathe new life into America's greatest art form.

By 1983, Marsalis had received his first Grammy award, for the album *Think of One*. Sparked by Wynton's dazzling technical virtuosity, the ensemble (featuring his brother Branford on sax, Kenny Kirkland on piano, and Jeff "Tain" Watts on drums) brought a high-gloss sheen to the album's bebop-oriented originals. For many disheartened jazz fans, the recording recalled nothing less than the glory days of Miles Davis's "classic quintet" of the mid-1960s. But that had been two decades earlier—and therein lay the problem for many critics for whom the rallying cry of jazz was "make it new."

Yet even those who criticized Wynton's "neo-mainstream" orthodoxy had to admit that that jazz had never had a more committed, articulate, and effective advocate. From the beginning, Marsalis had been a tireless spokesman for jazz education (giving lectures, workshops, and young people's concerts across the country); and when he was appointed the artistic director of jazz at Lincoln Center—a newly created component of the formidable cultural institution—he expanded his efforts exponentially.

But by the mid-1990s, Wynton's musical ambitions required a larger canvas. Inspired by the later works of Duke Ellington, he began composing full-length pieces for the Lincoln Center Jazz Orchestra, a big band he led as part of his duties at JALC. In 1997, his three-and-a-half-hour oratorio exploring the horrors of (and eventual triumph over) slavery, *Blood on the Fields,* was awarded the Pulitzer Prize, something not even Marsalis's hero (Duke Ellington) had accomplished. Never one to rest on his laurels, Wynton Marsalis spent the remainder of the decade turning out new recordings, developing educational programs (such as the acclaimed PBS television series, *Marsalis on Music*), touring the world, and proselytizing for his conception of the jazz canon.

Although Fusion claimed the decade's jazz spotlight, other styles—from mainstream to avant garde—continued to be vigorously pursued throughout the 1970s by both veteran performers and newcomers. Between long periods of frustrated silence, both Cecil Taylor and Ornette Coleman expanded their explorations of jazz unfettered by chord changes and fixed meters and their Free Jazz concepts began attracting other musical visionaries. For example, some of the most dynamic and original music of the 1970s emerged from a Chicago-based organization known as the Association for the Advancement of Creative Musicians.

Formed by pianist-composer Muhal Richard Abrams, the AACM consisted of a coalition of musicians who shared a commitment to experimentation and a deep appreciation of jazz history. Along with Abrams, some of the association's other members (including trumpeter Lester Bowie, bassist Malachi Favors, multi-reedmen Joseph Jarman and Roscoe Mitchell, and percussionist Don Moye) formed a band known as the Art Ensemble of Chicago. Grounding much of their music on the principle of collective improvisation, the Art Ensemble also introduced African-derived elements into their performances (including tribal face paint and exotic percussion instruments). Another band associated with the AACM was a trio called Air (saxophonist Henry Threadgill, bassist Fred Hopkins, and drummer Steve McCall), which infused Free Jazz principles into the conversational, chamber jazz tradition.

At the beginning of the 1980s, these combined impulses of experimentation and preservation were most creatively embodied in the World Saxophone Quartet—an a cappella saxophone choir, consisting of David Murray, Hamiet Bluiett, Julius Hemphill, and Oliver Lake—which blended aspects of New Orleans brass bands, gospel vocal groups, and the soulful wail of R & B honkers with Ellingtonian harmonies and the microtonal excursions of Free Jazz heroes such as Ornette and Albert Ayler. In doing so, they created a unique sound that blended the best of the past, present, and future and managed to be both accessible and challenging at the same time.

Increasingly, jazz musicians sought to distance themselves from narrow labels and stylistic pigeonholes. So, Pat Methaney—a guitarist who initially attracted great attention for his technology-enhanced, high-voltage brand of Fusion—also made atmospheric albums with Brazilian musicians and collaborated with Ornette Coleman, Charlie Haden, and other Free Jazz pioneers on rigorous, avant-garde projects. Similarly, during the 1970s and 1980s, the pianist Keith Jarrett moved easily from Fusion to both highly personal acoustic solo improvisations and explorations of European classical music. The young pianist/composer Anthony Davis—who began his career on the fringes of the avant garde—went on to create ambitious large-scale works focusing on the intersection of jazz and classical music (including an opera based on the life of Malcolm X).

And while mainstream jazz found itself relegated to premature obsolescence during the Fusion era, a corps of veteran traditionalists stubbornly held their ground. The one band that did the most to keep the flame of tradition alive—and pass the torch to a new generation—was led by the indefatigable drummer Art Blakey. In 1954,

Blakey had cofounded a group called the Jazz Messengers with pianist Horace Silver. After Silver left to form his own band, Blakey assumed sole leadership, and for the next three decades, the Jazz Messengers became one of the foremost finishing schools in jazz history. The list of future greats who received their diploma from the "Blakey School of Music" includes Kenny Dorham, Bobby Timmons, Benny Golson, Jackie McLean, Lee Morgan, Wayne Shorter, Freddie Hubbard, and Donald Byrd, among many others.

During the 1970s and 1980s, however, most young musicians were no longer earning their jazz credentials through the venerable route of on-the-job apprenticeships, but they were the products of specialized music conservatories and college jazz programs. In fact, one of Art Blakey's most promising sidemen had enrolled in his band directly from the renowned Juilliard School of Music. But while the brilliant young trumpeter Wynton Marsalis represented jazz's newfound academic legitimacy, he also happened to embody its oldest traditions.

As the son of the New Orleans jazz pianist Ellis Marsalis, Wynton could trace his musical lineage to the fertile soil of the city in which jazz itself had first taken root. For Wynton, and his older brother Branford, who had attended the Berklee School of Music (the premier jazz conservatory in the country), Blakey's band provided the ideal transition from the world of jazz academia to the world of the jazz professional.

BACK TO THE FUTURE: WYNTON MARSALIS AND NEOMAINSTREAM JAZZ

By 1980, when Wynton Marsalis burst onto the scene, the jazz mainstream had been marginalized by rock's commercial supremacy and torn asunder by the creative ferment of the avant garde. No wonder the nineteen-year-old trumpeter was heralded as a savior by the multitude of beleaguered traditionalists. For two decades, the music they loved seemed to have been imprisoned in a desolate wilderness and suddenly the clarion call of his shining trumpet broke the awful spell.

At least that was how it was portrayed in the avalanche of news articles and feature stories celebrating Wynton's youth and astonishing virtuosity. And, to a considerable extent, Marsalis embraced the mythic role in which the media had cast him. "But you know why I've gotten all that publicity," Wynton asked the critic Francis Davis rhetorically. "Not just because I was so young when people first heard of me. This music has a long history of prodigies. . . . No, see, when I first came to New York in 1979, everybody was talking about fusion. Everybody was saying that jazz was dead. . . . So when people heard me, they knew it was time to start takin' care of business again. . . . at least I was playing some real music."

Having immediately won Grammys as both a classical and a jazz artist, Marsalis used his unprecedented media platform to launch scathing assaults on what he saw as the mediocrity of contemporary jazz, targeting Miles Davis's later work for special scorn. Leading a tight, highly disciplined quintet (which included his brother Branford on tenor and soprano saxophones), his own playing seemed to be bursting with youthful inventiveness and confidence. But it also teemed with respectful allusions to the past (and, ironically, reflected his deep debt to Miles). While Marsalis initially drew most of his musical inspiration from the bebop and hard bop eras, he gradually broadened his musical references (devoting much of his attention to Louis Armstrong and Duke Ellington). Yet, he continued to reject not only the entire Fusion movement but the innovations of the avant garde as well.

As a result of his creative and commercial success, articulate pronouncements, and high-profile appearances at jazz events around the country, Marsalis emerged as the guru of an entire generation of precocious, conservatory trained, neomainstream jazz performers the press quickly dubbed "the young lions." Although many were barely out of their teens, they played with a skill and assurance far beyond their years. And by reclaiming and reenergizing the music's traditional values, they transformed the jazz landscape. Over the next decade, major record labels—which had turned a deaf ear to a few generations of jazz masters—embraced youthful virtuosos such as Terence Blanchard, Roy Hargrove, Cyrus Chestnut, James Carter, Joshua Redmen, Christian McBride, Marvin "Smitty" Smith, and Brad Meldhau (to name just a few), and promoted their recordings with high-powered publicity campaigns.

While many critics celebrated the phenomenon, others expressed reservations about what they saw as the youth movement's conservative philosophy. After all, they asked, wasn't jazz supposed to be adventurous, challenging, "the music of surprise?"

FIGURE 3-30.   After releasing a series of highly acclaimed recordings during the 1990s, Cassandra Wilson was hailed as "the most original vocalist of her generation." She was in the forefront of a contingent of young jazz performers (that included the saxophonist Joshua Redman, vibraphonist Stephon Harris, pianist Brad Meldau, bassist Christian McBride, and drummer Leon Parker, among others) who were taking jazz into the new millennium. Photo by JoAnne Savio. Courtesy of Blue Note Records.

Cassandra Wilson: Taking Jazz into the New Millennium

After recording a couple of promising (but uneven) albums, Cassandra Wilson finally seemed to find her own voice in 1993 when her breakthrough CD, *Blue Light 'til Dawn,* garnered the vocalist both rave reviews and strong sales. Although critics were quick to note Wilson's debt to some of the greatest divas in jazz history (especially Billie Holiday, Abby Lincoln, and Betty Carter), it was the album's eclectic repertoire, unconventional instrumentation, and highly stylized arrangements that received the most attention. Set against an atmospheric wash of bluesy steel guitar riffs, wheezy accordion chords, and muted trumpet moans, Wilson delivered very personal renderings of vintage Mississippi Delta blues (Robert Johnson's "Come into My Kitchen"), singer-songwriter odes (Joni Mitchells's "Black Crow" and Van Morrison's "Tupelo Honey") and R & B ballads ("Charles Brown's "Tell Me You'll Wait for Me"). On a subsequent recording, *Rendezvous*—a collaboration with pianist Jackie Terrasson—Wilson established that she could shine in a more mainstream setting as well.

Meanwhile, Wynton continued to exploit his phenomenal success in the service of greater recognition for America's jazz legacy. This eventually led to his appointment as the artistic director of a newly created component of America's most prestigious musical institution. Under Marsalis's leadership, "Jazz at Lincoln Center" (as the organization became known) dedicated itself to the preservation of the jazz repertoire through an ongoing schedule of concerts, film programs, lecture series, and educational outreach. Using Ellington as his model, Marsalis also began devoting his creative energy to composing large-scale, extended works (such as the Pulitzer Prize–winning jazz oratorio, *Blood on the Fields,* and his massive millennial piece, "All Rise") for an all-star big band known as the Lincoln Center Jazz Orchestra.

Beginning in the 1980s, other institutions also began establishing jazz repertory programs. In addition, many record companies have initiated extensive re-issue programs that have made virtually the entire history of the music available on CD. Jazz courses have taken their place alongside the standard European classical music curriculum in colleges across the country and—throughout the rest of the world—jazz has been elevated to the pantheon of the greatest cultural achievements of the human race. Yet, America itself continues to be ambivalent about its only indigenous art form. Little more than the names of a few of the great creators of the past are known to the general population, and only a relative handful of contemporary jazz performers can make a comfortable living from their music. For the most part, jazz is still absent from our public schools, television sets, radios, movie screens, and concert stages.

Jazz emerged from the street parades and dance halls of New Orleans at the beginning of the previous century. Since then, its history has been intertwined with the history of our country. Jazz has embodied our racial and ethnic diversity while reflecting our struggles for national unity; it has consistently embraced and adapted to social and technological change, while at the same time remaining rooted in the values and traditions of the past.

So it was that as jazz approached its second century, Wynton Marsalis was interviewed by *American Heritage* magazine about the significance of this uniquely American art. Looking back to the style's formative period in his home city of New Orleans, the distinguished trumpeter/composer neatly transformed one of the music's most enduring features into a metaphor for our national identity: "Collective improvisation [places] maximum emphasis on personal expression within a voluntary group format," he explained. "The group encourages and nourishes individual development." And—as Marsalis reminds us—"That's America!"

Activities and Projects
Chapter 3: Jazz: The Sound of a New Century

1. Based on the autobiographies and oral histories of early New Orleans jazz musicians, write a report on the city's unique musical and cultural environment at the turn of the twentieth century.

2. Research the life and music of one of the following and explain his role in establishing a foundation for the development of jazz: Scott Joplin or James Reese Europe.

3. Explore the varied sources of jazz's Spanish tinge. Identify the contributions of New Orleans' Creole musicians (of Spanish descent), as well as the influence of the so-called Mexican band and traditional Cuban dance rhythms.

4. Research the early history of jazz recording (c. 1917–22). Include a discussion of significant performers and ensembles, as well as their repertoires and musical techniques.

5. Trace the evolution of the improvised solo from the "breaks" used in the collective improvisation of early New Orleans jazz ensembles to the fully formed solos of Louis Armstrong and Sidney Bechet.

6. Research the varied responses to jazz during the 1920s. Discuss the reactions both of the American cultural mainstream and of the African-American intelligentsia (as represented by the Harlem Renaissance).

7. The concept of "swing" is one of the most vital and elusive elements of jazz. Using musical notation, recorded examples, the analysis of musicologists, and testimony of jazz musicians, create your own definition of swing (and illustrate with recorded examples).

8. Trace the evolution of the jazz piano tradition from ragtime and barrelhouse blues to stride, boogie woogie, and later styles.

9. Highlight any aspect of Louis Armstrong's enormous influence on jazz and American music in general (e.g., the improvised solo, the rhythm conception of jazz, or styles of popular singing).

10. Explore the Chicago jazz scene of the 1920s and describe the contributions of the "Austin High Gang" and the era's other white jazz performers.

11. Describe the impact of jazz on America during the Swing Era. Include a discussion of its place in the mass media (radio and film) and its connection to the social dances of the period.

12. Compare any of the Swing Era's white big bands (Benny Goodman, Tommy Dorsey, Glenn Miller, etc.) with any of its African-American counterparts (Fletcher Henderson, Count Basie, Chick Webb, etc.) Analyze the musical qualities of each, as well as their status in the musical environment of the period.

13. Describe the Kansas City jazz scene and the unique characteristic of Southwestern Swing (comment on its rhythmic qualities, blues influences, arrangements, and improvisation).

14. Survey one of the following aspects of Duke Ellington's music and career: his "jungle period," his musical portraits (people or places), his extended works, his popular songs.

15. Research the role of the arranger during the Swing Era. Illustrate your discussion with reference to any of the following: Don Redman, Fletcher Henderson, Eddie Durham, Mary Lou Williams, Glenn Miller, Eddie Sauter.

16. Create a survey of significant women in jazz history (include instrumentalists, vocalists, bandleaders, composers, and arrangers).

17. Bebop: evolution or revolution? Describe how the modern jazz movement of the 1940s can be linked to earlier styles of jazz and highlight its innovative aspects.

18. Use the career of Miles Davis to survey the evolution of jazz during the second half of the twentieth century. Include in your discussion his association with each of the following: bebop, cool jazz, hard bop, Sixties mainstream, and fusion.

19. Explore the relationship of jazz to the social and political environment of the 1960s (e.g., civil rights, black power, and Afrocentrism).

20. Write a paper on the links between literature and jazz during one of the following periods: the 1920s (focusing on the works of the Harlem Renaissance), the 1940s and 1950s (using the works of the beat generation), the 1960s (based on the works of the so-called Black Arts Movement). Other literary figures associated with jazz include James Baldwin, Amiri Baraka (a.k.a. LeRoi Jones), Ralph Ellison, Jayne Cortez, Michael S. Harper, Ishmael Reed, Al Young Ntozake Shange, and Albert Murray.

21. Survey the history of jazz in the movies. Focus on any of the following: the use of jazz soundtracks, jazz biopics, fiction films with jazz themes, and documentaries.

22.   The Fusion Debate. Explore the conflicting perspectives on the jazz-rock movement of the 1970s and beyond. Offer your own opinion and support your point of view with references from jazz historians, critics, and musicians (illustrate with recorded examples).

23.   The Jazz Canon: A Debate. Research the current conflicts over the jazz canon (that is, the music's essential creators and accepted body of great works). Summarize the competing perspectives on this issue and explain your own opinion.

24.   Analyze the current state of the jazz nation. Consider the place of jazz in contemporary culture, in the university, in clubs and concert halls, and on the charts.

25.   Survey the status of jazz in other countries. Include in your discussion the impact of and opportunities for American performers, and assess the state of the international jazz scene. You also can research the contributions of non-American musicians (and musical styles) on the history of jazz.

4

R & B, Rockabilly, Rock 'n' Roll, and Rock

HAIL, HAIL ROCK 'N' ROLL

It's been called the Fabulous Fifties—Rock 'n' Roll's Golden Age. It's an era that's become familiar to most young people through the happy daze of Hollywood: a Technicolor world of slicked-back hair and sock hops, hot rods, and malt shops, where a pony-tailed fifteen-year-old screams her way through an Elvis concert while Mom and Dad shake their heads and ask each other: "Kids, what's wrong with these kids today?"

Although it is impossible to sum up a decade in a few images, it is also impossible to understand rock 'n' roll without some understanding of the historical reality surrounding its creation. So, let's look back at some (generic) news stories of the 1950s . . .

"TEENAGERS": NEWEST SOCIAL CLASS

Experts report that, for the first time, Americans between thirteen and nineteen years of age can be considered a significant new social class. The economic prosperity of the early 1950s is making it less necessary for this age group to take up their adult responsibilities. This generation of adolescents—or "teenagers"—has already begun to create its identity through its own style of clothes, slang, and music.

SOUTHERN NEGROES ORGANIZE TO END SEGREGATION

Using a strategy of boycotts and court challenges, Southern Negroes are increasingly demanding the right of equal access to schools, public transportation, and the voting booth. Under the leadership of a young minister, the Rev. Martin Luther King, a Montgomery, Alabama, boycott has resulted in the integration of that city's buses. Along with the recent Supreme Court decision (*Brown v. Topeka*, 1954) overturning "separate but equal" statutes, a new era for the Negro in American society has begun.

JUVENILE DELINQUENTS TERRORIZE
COMMUNITIES ACROSS AMERICA
RESPONSE TO "CONFORMITY," SAYS EXPERT

Identified by their slicked-back hair, denim jeans, and black leather jackets, gangs of young hoodlums have disturbed the peace in large and small cities across the United States. Asked for his explanation of this phenomenon, Dr. John Smith, a sociologist who has studied this new trend says: "These teenagers are exhibiting a response to

FIGURE 4-1. The Rock and Roll Hall of Fame and Museum—a $92 million, I. M. Pei–designed exhibition space located in Cleveland, Ohio—opened its doors to the public in 1995. According to the museum's promotional material, it is "the world's first museum dedicated to the living heritage of rock and roll music." Photo by Hal Stata. Courtesy of the Rock and Roll Hall of Fame and Museum.

Museum of . . . Rock and Roll?!

Of course, the very idea of a museum dedicated to rock 'n' roll would certainly have seemed more than a little bizarre to anyone present during the music's first turbulent years. For when Elvis, Chuck Berry, and Little Richard began shattering America's placid mid-century calm, spokesmen for the country's political and cultural establishment lined up to condemn the strange new sound.

the pressure of 'conformity.' Today's society expects people to all be the same, to follow the prescribed codes of dress, employment, living styles. These so-called Juvenile Delinquents are merely rejecting these values in an extreme way."

TELEVISION ENTERS MOST OF NATION'S HOMES

Recent statistics reveal that, as of 1952, television now has a prominent place in twenty-seven million American homes (five years ago this figure was only one million). This new method of mass communication and entertainment is having a profound effect on American society. Any product or performer appearing on TV today has an instant impact on the entire nation.

As these news stories indicate, America in the 1950s was changing in very significant ways, but when we look back at the era's popular music, we find that much of it was stuck in the same bland "moon-june-spoon" rut it had been in since the end of Tin Pan Alley's "Golden Age" (c. 1940). Too often, songwriters simply concocted their songs as if they were following a familiar family recipe; every week another batch would be written, recorded, and shipped out to radio stations, jukebox outlets, and record stores.

Neat and pleasantly smooth vocalists dominated the airwaves and filled the trade magazine record charts. They were also featured on the *Hit Parade,* a weekly TV show that broadcast their pink-cheeked smiles across the country. For Mom and Dad, this may have been just fine, but for Junior and Sis, "It was like Dullsville."

Although, at first, mainstream America seemed deaf to the incredible changes that were in the air, by the middle of the decade, musical, cultural, and technological forces had all aligned to create the conditions for the evolution of a new species of popular music. The advent of rock 'n' roll is a story filled with greed and generosity, racism and brotherhood, fear and courage; and—once the new music took off—it all happened with the speed of one of those experimental jet planes that also were breaking sound barriers during the era.

TWO AMERICAS

While the days of legal segregation were fast drawing to a close, the existence of "Two Americas"—one white, one black—seemed an unshakeable fact of life during the early 1950s. Certainly this clear racial separation was reflected in the world of popular entertainment.

For the most part, there was no music by black performers played on the major network radio stations, no records by black performers issued by the major labels, and virtually no black performers appearing on television. This was at a time when African-American music was experiencing one of the most vital and creative periods in its history.

In New York's basement jazz clubs and late-night jam sessions, a startling new form of modern jazz, known as bebop (which had emerged in the late 1940s) was attracting a cult of dedicated fans. Meanwhile, rhythm and blues—an exciting blend of jazz, blues, and gospel with a beat that wouldn't quit and lyrics that promised "good rockin' tonight"—had become the popular music of black America. Yet, it all seemed to exist in a kind of parallel universe that was outside the radar of mainstream America. Because of the exclusionary policies of the era's major media outlets, virtually all African-American music was recorded and transmitted through alternate channels of communication.

For example, as advances in technology made professional-quality recording equipment more affordable, dozens of small, independent labels had emerged in cities such as Los Angeles, New York, Chicago, Cincinnati, and Memphis to record local African-American performers. With shoestring budgets and a distribution system that was usually operated from the trunk of someone's car, companies such as Chess, King, Atlantic, and Specialty had begun to record scores of R & B singles destined for the jukeboxes that were a fixture in every bar, café, and Dew-Drop Inn in the black community.

At the same time, a loosening of Federal Communications Commission (FCC) regulations had begun to reduce the dominance of the national radio networks, thus opening the door to dozens of new radio stations targeted to African-American listeners. By the mid-1950s, there were approximately six hundred local stations clustered on the edges of the radio dial, broadcasting the entire spectrum of black popular music. The first of these stations—WDIA, located in Memphis, Tennessee—went on the air in 1949 beaming black music to the region's black residents . . . as well as to at least one thirteen-year-old white boy who had just come to the city from Tupelo, Mississippi. Soon it would become apparent that the young Elvis Presley wasn't the only outsider listening in.

For, late at night, with their doors closed, increasing numbers of white teens were beginning to tune in their radios to these same obscure corners of the AM band (although it existed as a technological reality, FM was not commercially a factor at the time). In doing so, they discovered a style of music that seemed to speak directly to a new generation of young people hungry for music that could match their restless energy. And if their parents and teachers were horrified at the idea of this "degenerate, jungle music"—as it was openly characterized—corrupting their purity and innocence, so much the better.

FIGURE 4-2.   Beginning in the early 1940s, Louis Jordan unleashed a string of irresistible jukebox hits that earned him the title "The Father of Rhythm and Blues." Archive photo. Frank Driggs Collection.

Rhythm and Blues: The Roots of Rock 'n' Roll

After playing alto sax and singing novelty numbers with the Chick Webb Orchestra, a dynamic Swing Era jazz band, Louis Jordan formed his own small combo in 1939. Billed as Louis Jordan and His Tympany Five (although it usually had seven or eight pieces), he fashioned a blend of wailing horns and bluesy riffs that took black America by storm; but it was Louis Jordan's wit and charisma, as much as his musical talents, that accounted for his tremendous popularity.

When it came to pure showmanship, Louis Jordan didn't take a back seat to anybody. Decked out in slick suits and spouting the latest hipster slang, Louis Jordan sold millions of copies of records—like "Choo-Choo Ch'Boogie," "Saturday Night Fish Fry," "Is You Is or Is You Ain't Ma' Baby?" and "Caldonia (What Makes Your Big Head So Hard?)"—that set hilarious down-home vignettes to an infectious jump-blues beat. More than any other single performer, it was Louis Jordan who put rhythm and blues onto the national stage, making him a key transitional figure in the birth of rock 'n' roll. But he wasn't the only one.

Take Big Joe Turner. One of the greatest of the Kansas City blues shouters, Turner was first propelled into the spotlight back in the late 1930s when he teamed up with the pianist Pete Johnson, a master of the rollicking eight-to-the-bar piano style known as "boogie woogie." But it wasn't until 1954, when Big Joe Turner released his classic recording of "Shake, Rattle, and Roll," that he created one of the biggest hits in R & B history, and—through Bill Haley's cover version—assisted in the birth of rock 'n' roll.

By the early 1950s, a new generation of gospel-influenced vocal harmony groups—including the Dominoes ("Sixty-Minute Man") and the Chords ("Sh-Boom"), among others—had not only come to dominate the national rhythm and blues charts but were regularly "crossing over" onto the pop charts as well.

Any list of "The Legends of Rhythm and Blues" would surely include the following: T-Bone Walker, Roy Milton, LaVerne Baker, Wynonie Harris, Big Mama Thornton, Ruth Brown, Ray Charles, the Dominoes, Fats Domino, Joe Liggins, the Ravens, Bill Doggett, Charles Brown, the Coasters, Little Willie John, Johnny Ace, Johnny Otis, and (the mythical) "Johnny B. Goode."

ROCK 'N' ROLL: WHAT'S IN A NAME

It wasn't long before the existence of this secret audience was recognized by a few of the more adventurous mainstream radio stations around the country. Among the white disc jockeys who began squeezing R & B segments in between their pop programming was an ambitious young DJ who would soon become one of rock 'n' roll's mythic figures (and tragic heroes)—Alan Freed.

Freed had been doing a nightly semiclassical and popular music show at Cleveland's WJW when he was approached by the owner of the city's largest record store with an idea for a new show. Leo Mintz had noticed a phenomenon that also was taking place in other cities: More and more white teenagers were coming into his Record Rendezvous store asking for the latest rhythm and blues single. So it was that, in 1951, Alan Freed adopted an on-air persona he dubbed the "Moondog" and began spinning the latest R & B records for the new teen audience. Rasping out the intros and song titles with a fever-pitched, slang-filled hipster delivery—and sometimes banging along with the beat on a phone book—Freed seemed to embody the excitement of the new sound. He is also credited with giving it a new name.

Numerous variations on the phrase "rock and roll" had been around for a long time. It can be heard at least as early as the 1920s on blues records, and by the late Forties it had become a common catchphrase in dozens of R & B songs. Over time, its meaning had taken on a spectrum of good-time connotations that ranged from "dance" or "party" to "sexual intercourse." By adopting this bit of exotic, double-entendre jargon, Freed hoped to liberate a marginalized music from its racial stigma, thereby making it a little more acceptable to skittish radio station managers and advertisers. Soon, Alan Freed had changed the name of his radio program to "The Moondog Rock and Roll House Party," and the rest, as they say is history.

Of course, it didn't fool everyone. When Fats Domino was asked by an interviewer how he would define this new sound called "rock 'n' roll" that was sweeping America, he told the interviewer: "Oh, that ain't nothin' but rhythm and blues. I've been singing it for years down in New Orleans."

Meanwhile, Freed had begun producing live shows featuring black R & B acts to sold-out crowds of (mostly) white teenagers and, in 1954, he brought both his radio show and live concerts to New York City. Now that he was broadcasting on WINS—probably the most commercially successful radio station in the country's most important market—Freed would become a key figure in the national breakthrough of the musical style he referred to as "the Big Beat."

BILL HALEY LOSES HIS COWBOY BOOTS

The musical tastes of America at the beginning of the 1950s weren't segregated along only racial lines but along regional ones as well. Across the rural South and in urban enclaves (like Bakersfield, California) populated by Southerners who had left the farm by the thousands to seek employment during the previous decade, country and western was the music of choice.

C & W shared with R & B both its marginalized status and the scorn of the New York–based popular music industry. Unlike rhythm and blues, however, major record labels had been recording country music for years in the studios they had established in Nashville, Tennessee. Although they had always been willing to profit from it, those who ran the mainstream music business had from the very beginning derided the music itself. Up until 1949 they were still referring to it (in record catalogs, ads, and radio schedules) as "Hillbilly." And while it had also carved out a secure niche on the radio, here, too, it was relegated to its own electronic ghetto.

If the popular music industry of the 1950s, embodied by such easy-listening singers as Patti Page, Perry Como, and Eddie Fisher, seemed obsessively safe and bland, when compared to the country music establishment symbolized by the Grand Ole Opry (a Nashville-based country music variety show broadcast live every Saturday night since 1925), pop seemed positively adventurous. Country music had produced its own roster of beloved stars, whose long and stable careers were an outgrowth of the powerful bond they established with their loyal audiences. Yet, the same upheavals taking place in American popular music were beginning to shake up even the placid landscape of country music.

FIGURE 4-3.   By the time this publicity photo of Bill Haley was taken, he had already traded in his cowboy boots and shaved off his sideburns. Although he created the first hit of the rock 'n' roll era, Haley had begun his career as the leader of a band called the Four Aces of Western Swing. Southern Folklife Center. Universty of North Carolina at Chapel Hill.

Rock around the Clock

By the early 1950s, the former country singer had a new group—Bill Haley and the Comets—and a new sound. After covering a couple of rhythm and blues songs (like Jackie Brenston's "Rocket 88" and Joe Turner's "Shake, Rattle, and Roll"), Haley's electrifying version of "Rock around the Clock" was used for the title sequence of the 1955 movie *Blackboard Jungle*. The single immediately skyrocketed to the number one spot on the national pop charts. Nobody knew if rock 'n' roll was here to stay, but it was here!

Although he was raised in Pennsylvania, Bill Haley's first love was country music. After turning professional at the age of fifteen, Haley donned a snap-button Western shirt, string tie, and cowboy boots and performed in succession of groups with names like the Down Homers, the Saddlemen, and the Four Aces of Western Swing. And at first, Haley's country music career followed a well-worn path: he appeared on the WLS "National Barn Dance," a hugely popular radio show broadcast from Chicago, and he even got the chance to perform on the Grand Ole Opry itself. Among his biggest thrills was the time he shared the stage with the country music legend they called the "Hillbilly Shakespeare," Hank Williams.

As he was touring the country-music circuit, however, Haley increasingly found himself drawn to the sounds of black rhythm and blues that were just finding their way onto the radio. In 1953, he recorded his own version of Jackie Brenston's hard-driving hit "Rocket 88," which had been number one on the rhythm and blues charts two years earlier. Gradually, the two distinct styles also began to blend together in his stage act. Years later, Haley remembered his decision as being tinged with an attitude of youthful rebellion: "It was unheard of in those days. . . . I didn't see anything wrong in mixing things up. I liked to sing rhythm and blues tunes and I sang them."

The commercial success of his follow-up single, "We're Gonna Rock This Joint Tonight" (1954), would show that his instincts were correct. "The people didn't know what we were playing," Haley recalled, "it wasn't rhythm and blues and it wasn't country and western." But, he continued, "Soon we got rid of the cowboy boots and shaved off the sideburns."

By this point, the mix of black and white musical sources had acquired its own name, and with his next song Haley would create its first anthem. It wasn't until a year after its 1954 release, however—when "Rock around the Clock" was selected for the soundtrack of a gritty black and white film about violent urban teens—that the song became an unprecedented national hit and rock 'n' roll itself became linked to the image of wild rebellion that it still carries to this day.

In an effort to take advantage of the tabloid headlines reporting on the perceived national crisis of juvenile delinquency, Hollywood studios began turning out a succession of films focusing on stories of "troubled teenagers." In 1953, *The Wild One* projected the image of a black-leather-jacket-wearing Marlon Brando onto America's movie screens. Asked by a local resident into whose town he had ridden as a member of a notorious motorcycle gang, "What are you rebelling against?," Brando mumbled the movie's classic catchphrase: "Whattaya got." One year later, in *Rebel without a Cause,* a more sensitive portrait of the troubled teen was captured in James Dean's performance of a young man alienated from the constricting pressures of the mid-1950s status quo.

But it was 1955's *Blackboard Jungle* that first fused the story of rebellious teenagers with the pounding beat of rock 'n' roll. When the film's opening credits appeared, and the first exuberant chords of "Rock around the Clock" blasted from the movie-theater speakers, young viewers across the country went into a frenzy. They also propelled the movie's theme song to the top of the record industry sales surveys. In June, "Rock around the Clock" became the first rock 'n' roll record to reach the number one position on the popular music charts.

What had begun as a slowly evolving process taking place on the margins of society had become a national phenomenon. And having been magnified to larger-than-lifesize dimensions on movie screens across the country, "rock 'n' roll" suddenly became headline news.

CHUCK BERRY: A NEW KIND OF CROSSOVER

During the same year that Bill Haley and the Comets' "Rock around the Clock" broke through as the nation's number one pop hit, another song based on the same basic rock 'n' roll recipe made its way up the charts. Chuck Berry's "Maybellene" was the first of his rapid-fire teen sagas to bring together the powerful combination of hot rods and teenage romance. And like "Rock around the Clock," Berry's song was a blend of black and white music that couldn't be fit into any previously existing category.

Chuck Berry had come to Chicago during the early 1950s determined to break into the music business. In Chicago, black music meant the blues, and blues in Chicago meant Chess Records, the independent label that recorded the great Muddy Waters, as well as most of the other giants of the powerfully amplified big city blues. In fact, it was Muddy who got Berry his audition with Chess. But the truth was, Chuck Berry really wasn't a bluesman.

FIGURE 4-4.   The answer to the question: "What's a two-word definition of rock 'n' roll?" Archive photo. Frank Driggs Collection.

Chuck Berry

Although he had been brought to Chess Records by Muddy Waters, the first single Chuck Berry recorded for the legendary Chicago blues label was an R & B adaptation of a country music classic, originally named "Ida Red" (or "Ida May"). Released in 1955, Berry's souped-up version—quickly retitled "Maybellene"—became one of the first salvos in the rock 'n' roll revolution.

In addition to virtually inventing the image of the guitar-wielding rock 'n' roll hero and writing some of the genre's greatest anthems (including "Roll over Beethoven," "School Days," "Sweet Little Sixteen," and "Johnny B. Goode"), Berry's patented riffs have been coopted by everyone from the Beatles to the Beach Boys and from Bob Dylan to Bruce Springsteen.

Although Berry had been working in a St. Louis R & B trio, the singer also was a big country music fan. In fact, Berry's breakthrough song was actually a souped-up remake of a traditional country tune known as "Ida Red." Chuck transformed the song into the story of a high-speed car chase between the singer's V-8 Ford and a dream girl who passes him "in a Coup de Ville." At the suggestion of his record label, Berry also changed the girl's name—and the song's title—from "Ida Red" to "Maybellene." By doing so, Berry (and the Chess brothers) could copyright it as a new song and collect the writer's royalties that accrued. And with the addition of Alan Freed's name to the writing credits (a venerable music business ploy by which the record could get the airplay it needed), Berry wound up with his own Top Ten hit.

There was nothing unusual about "Maybellene" making its way to the number one spot in the rhythm and blues charts. That's where a fast-paced, exuberant record by a black performer released on the independent Chess label belonged. But by 1955, music wasn't staying where it "belonged." Two weeks after it reached the top of the R & B list, "Maybellene" climbed to the number five position of *Billboard* magazine's national popular music chart. Before long, "Maybellene" had raced its way toward the top of the country and western chart as well! It was a phenomenon that seemed to violate all the fundamental rules of America's racial, cultural, and commercial segregation. Chuck Berry had "crossed over" big time.

In music industry jargon, a "crossover" is a record that makes the transition from its niche on one of the genre-specific sales charts (like country and western or rhythm and blues) directly onto the list devoted to another musical style (ideally to the coveted pop chart, where mainstream hits brought in the big bucks). "Maybellene" was hardly the first record to make this leap; in the 1930s and 1940s, records by black vocal harmony groups such as the Mills Brothers and the Ink Spots occasionally crossed over to the white market. But, by the early 1950s, the speed and frequency of crossovers had intensified to the point where the fundamental nature of this once-rigid system of classification was called into question.

For example, in 1951 a raucous, sexually suggestive record titled "Sixty Minute Man" ("I rock 'em and roll 'em all night long" was one line from the song) by the Dominoes, a popular rhythm and blues number, not only became a huge number one R and B hit but (two months later) also crossed over into the popular music chart as well. That same year, an impassioned, gospel-tinged record, "Cry," by a new white singer named Johnnie Ray, crossed over from the number one position on the popular music chart to the number one spot on the R and B chart. And in the fuss over Bill Haley scoring a number one pop hit, not many people noticed that "Rock around the Clock" had climbed into the number three spot on the R and B charts as well.

Meanwhile, Chuck Berry was not only in the process of establishing his own personal crossover connection, but he was almost single-handedly inventing the concept of the rock 'n' roll hero. Although he was almost thirty years old at the time, Berry seemed to have a special genius for describing teen life—school, soda shops, and sweet little sixteens—from the inside. Through a series of crossover hits filled with fast cars, pretty girls, and a spirit of rebelliousness, Berry became the very personification of rock 'n' roll; he fronted his own band, wrote his own songs (with what Bruce Springsteen has described as the "natural poetry of everyday speech"), and played his own lead guitar—and he did it all with riveting showmanship and a strutting duckwalk.

Gradually, rock 'n' roll had begun to symbolize a musical "Promised Land" of racial unity and brotherhood. For the first time in its history, the pop charts became a checkerboard of black and white performers: from Bill Haley ("Rock around the Clock") to Chuck Berry ("Maybellene"), from Gene Vincent ("Be-Bop-a-Lula") to Little Richard ("Tutti Frutti"), and from Carl Perkins ("Blue Suede Shoes") to Fats Domino ("Ain't That a Shame").

And at the live "Rock 'n' Roll Revues" that were touring the country, the same diverse roster of black and white performers all appeared on the same stage in front of racially mixed audiences (this only one year after the Supreme Court offcially declared racial segregation unconstitutional). But, while everyone from record company executives to radio DJ's liked to say that the only color they cared about was "green," the music business remained far from color blind.

UNDER THE COVERS

While the sudden surge of mid-1950s "crossovers" may have suggested the demise of color-coded musical categories, a new onslaught of "covers" during this period dispelled any such optimistic notions.

FIGURE 4-5.   After he'd joined the other pioneers of Fifties rock 'n' roll on the pop charts, Antoine "Fats" Domino was asked to define the new sound that was sweeping the country. "Oh, that ain't nothin' but rhythm and blues," he explained. "I've been singing it for years down in New Orleans." Archive photo. Frank Driggs Collection.

Fats Domino and New Orleans Rhythm and Blues

Although New Orleans is most famous as the birthplace of jazz, the city also boasted its own distinctive brand of R & B, a gumbo of blues and West Indian carnival rhythms. During the 1950s, the pianist Fats Domino combined these ingredients—along with his laid-back, Creole-accented vocals—to create such early rock era classics as "Ain't That a Shame," "I'm in Love Again," and "Whole Lotta Lovin'." With total sales of approximately sixty-five million records, Domino is considered second only to Elvis himself in a list of the decade's greatest hitmakers.

Like other rhythm and blues centers, New Orleans had not only its own unique regional style of R & B but its own celebrated recording studios (like Cosimo Matassa's J & M Studio), creative producers (like Dave Bartholomew), and community of gifted session musicians (like Earl Palmer, the premier drummer of Fifties rock).

In music business jargon, "to cover" a record simply means to create a new version of a song that had already been recorded by someone else. Covers were nothing new. In fact, multiple versions of popular songs had always been the norm. During the early decades of recording, a good song could be counted on to attract a number of different singers. Each version would have its own musical style and arrangement, and each version would compete to attract the listener's favor or to conform to the aethetics of a particular genre.

For example, one of the biggest pop recordings of 1951, Patti Page's "The Tennessee Waltz," had originally been a hit for Pee Wee King on the so-called hillbilly chart. And while Page's record quickly sold over two million copies, the other *nine* versions of the song released that year didn't do too badly either. By the mid-1950s, however, the cover version had taken on disturbing racial overtones.

Because of their restrictive policies the huge, nationally distributed "majors" (RCA, Columbia, Capitol, Mercury, and Decca) that had for decades supplied America with its musical entertainment found themselves looking on from the sidelines as the records that fueled the rock 'n' roll revolution were released by tiny independent rhythm and blues labels (such as Atlantic, Sun, Savoy, Vee-Jay, Chess, and Imperial). The degree to which the avalanche of rock records dramatically transformed the balance of power in the music industry becomes clear with a glance at *Billboard*'s annual sales chart.

In 1954, the major record companies continued to retain their domination of the mainstream market, as only eight of the year's Top Fifty pop records were released on an independent label. Just one year later, that figure had jumped to nineteen. Startled by the dramatic inroads the R & B indies were making into the free-spending teen audience, the major labels immediately reacted to preserve their economic base. They confronted the situation head on by converting the "cover version" into a weapon of mass (media) destruction.

Take "Sh-boom," a catchy song by the Chords, a black vocal harmony group, that was released on Cat Records (an R & B label owned by Atlantic) in 1954. Barely one week after it had begun to show signs of being a hit with both the traditional (black) rhythm and blues audience and the new (white) teen market, Mercury released a cover version of the song by the Crew Cuts, which came close to being an exact copy of the original record in every detail—except for the skin color of the singers. As a major, Mercury had the muscle to out-advertise and out-distribute the original, and by the time the dust settled, the Crew Cuts' cover stood at number one on the charts, while the Chords' recording quickly disappeared from sight. And so the pattern became established.

One year later, the original indie recording was titled "Tweedle Dee," by a soulful R & B singer named LaVerne Baker also released on Atlantic. This time Mercury didn't just set about to craft its own cover, but to create a virtual *copy*. They hired the same arranger and many of the same musicians. Then they simply plugged in a white pop singer, Georgia Gibbs, who mimicked as best she could Baker's vocal style. Needless to say, Mercury took advantage of their financial resources (and their ability to pressure DJ's into playing its version), and Baker's original was effectively sabotaged.

The "King of the Covers," however, was unquestionably Pat Boone, a wholesome young singer sporting white buck shoes and a boy-next-door smile. In 1955 and 1956, Boone had three successive number one pop hits with cover versions of recently released R & B songs by Fats Domino, Ivory Joe Hunter, and Little Richard. Boone was aided by sympathetic DJ's and television hosts who were eager for an engaging performer who would smooth out the rough edges and wildness of the originals.

Based on the enormous media exposure they received, Boone's covers dominated the charts. Only Fats Domino, with his irresistible, laid-back New Orlean's groove was able to transcend Boone's assault. As Little Richard recalled years later with understandable resentment, "Pat Boone started covering my tunes while they were still hot, and the pop stations would play his version and kill mine from ever having the chance of crossing over. You'd go into the record shops and there would be his version but not mine."

Ironically, many black performers had initially welcomed the pop world's sudden interest, since it brought their own recordings to the attention of the huge popular music market. Later in his life, even Little Richard was willing to acknowledge the up-side of the phenomenon: "At the time I didn't like what was happening because he [Boone] was cutting off my sales," Richard recalled. "Now, when I look back on it, it really was a blessing and a lesson because he opened the doors for us by making white kids more aware of me. From then on, it was always my version they wanted."

Eventually, a small but influential group of DJ's—led by Alan Freed—began to take a stand against cover versions, vowing to only play originals. As their power grew and as the rock 'n' roll audience became more sophisticated, covers gradually lost their effectiveness, and the real thing began to prevail. By 1956, it was the independent labels that dominated the pop market, claiming thirty-four slots on *Billboard*'s annual Top Fifty.

ELVIS PRESLEY: ENTER THE KING

In 1956, Elvis Aron Presley, ex-truck driver, went into an RCA Victor studio, recorded "Heartbreak Hotel" and emerged the god of rock 'n' roll.

The Rockin' 50's (Arnold Shaw)

At least, that's how one pop music historian describes this defining moment in rock history. But no matter what the particular version, the legend of how Elvis Presley was transformed from a $1.25-per-hour truck driver from Tupelo, Mississippi, into rock 'n' roll's archetypal hero is one of the central myths of American popular culture.

Elvis was the only surviving child in a family deeply rooted in the fundamentalist faith. He had grown up listening to (and singing) gospel music as a member of the fervent Pentecostal First Assembly of God Church. Like almost everyone in the South, he was also a devoted fan of the Saturday night broadcasts of the Grand Ole Opry, the venerable radio barn dance show that had been bringing the sounds of country music to millions of loyal listeners for over a quarter of a century. And, like most of America, Elvis also had a fondness for Dean Martin and the other pop crooners of the period.

Unlike many of those who shared his social, geographic, and racial background, however, Elvis was powerfully drawn to the music of African-American blues singers such as Big Bill Broonzy, Arthur (Big Boy) Crudup, and Lonnie Johnson, as well as to the energetic new R & B singers and vocal harmony groups. And as he listened in to these sounds on Memphis' pioneering black radio station, WDIA, Elvis dreamed of hearing his own records coming out of the speaker of the family radio.

A MOMENT IN THE SUN

At the time, the only place in Memphis for a boy with Elvis's dream to go was Sam Phillips's storefront studio at 706 Union Avenue. In 1950, Phillips had formed the Memphis Recording Service to provide local performers—especially blues singers and R & B bands—with a place to make a record. Of course, since it was just a recording facility, anything of commercial potential would have to be released and distributed by someone else.

This had been the case when a band fronted by a singer named Jackie Brenston cut a song called "Rocket 88" at Phillips's studio shortly after it opened. Cited by some rock historians as "The First Rock 'n' Roll Record," it wound up on Chicago's Chess label, becoming a number one R & B hit and inspiring Bill Haley to create his own cover version.

So, two years later, realizing that he was missing out on a rapidly expanding new market, Phillips decided to expand his operation into what would soon become one of the most significant independent labels in rock history—Sun Records. Sam Phillips began signing his own acts and releasing his own records on a label whose logo featured a crowing rooster crowned by halo of sunbeams. The success of records by Sun rhythm and blues performers such as Rufus Thomas and Junior Parker made the studio an especially powerful magnet for Presley, and, in late 1953, he could no longer resist its attraction.

When Elvis finally did show up at Sun's front office, he claimed he just wanted to record a couple of songs as a birthday present for his mother. But hearing something special in the two songs Elvis cut that day, Phillip's assistant Marion Keisker brought the shy but polite eighteen-year-old to the attention of her boss. Having sparked Phillips's interest, Elvis was brought back to try out a couple of tunes with a some of Sun's regular studio musicians. After a few failed experiments, Elvis's dream to make a record finally came true.

When she had asked him at their initial meeting who he sounded like, Elvis had told Keisker that he "didn't sound like nobody." Elvis's first single made it clear that he wasn't lying. Recorded in July, 1954, the record's A-side was a cover of an Arthur Crudup blues song, "That's All Right," and on the B-side was a version of Bill

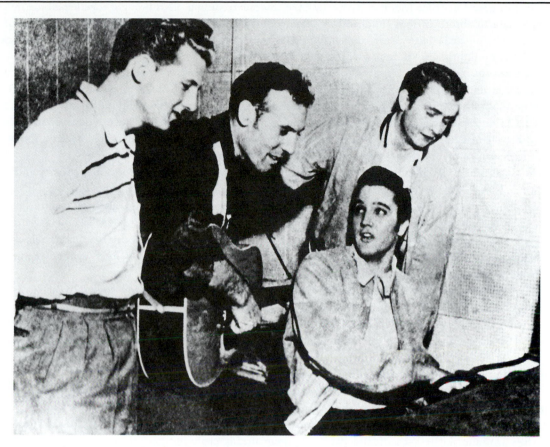

FIGURE 4-6.   On December 4, 1956, Jerry Lee Lewis, Carl Perkins, and Johnny Cash welcomed back Sun Records' original rockabilly rebel for a brief visit. Southern Folklife Center. University of North Carolina at Chapel Hill.

Rockabilly Rebels

Not long after his contract was purchased by RCA, Elvis Presley returned to Sun's studio to join his former labelmates in an impromptu songfest of country, R & B, and gospel favorites. Based on the phenomenal impact their recordings were having on the national pop charts, a local Memphis newspaper reporter who covered the session immediately dubbed the foursome "The Million Dollar Quartet."

The music that Elvis and his young Memphis cohorts had concocted during the mid-1950s was at the cutting edge of an innovative stylistic synthesis that became known as "rockabilly" (a word that alluded to the style's blues-inflected "rock"-ing rhythm and revved-up hill-"billy" drive). Propelled by the slap-beat sound of a stand-up bass, the echo-enhanced twang of a lead guitar, and the tricked-up vocals of a hip-shakin' country boy, rockabilly possessed a youthful exuberance and spirit of cocky rebelliousness that drove its teenage audience into a frenzy.

Nor was Memphis the only place where sideburned good-ol' boys were abandoning the traditional country music path and jumping on the rock 'n' roll bandwagon. Out in Lubbock, Texas, Buddy Holly was honing a Southwestern version of the classic rockabilly sound (in recordings such as "That'll Be the Day," and "Peggy Sue"), while elsewhere, performers—including Gene Vincent, Bill Haley, Roy Orbison, Eddie Cochran, and Johnny Burnette—were creating their own fusion of fuel-injected country and gritty rhythm and blues.

Monroe's bluegrass hit, "Blue Moon of Kentucky." On this one recording, Elvis brought together all the musical influences he had absorbed from childhood—gospel, country, blues, and pop—along with a heavy dose of his own spontaneous sexual energy. The result left Phillips excited, and a little confused. In this period before rock 'n' roll's national breakthrough, Phillips's concerns were understandable.

What was this new sound anyway? Was it country or blues? Black music or white? More to the point, what radio station would play it? And when he brought the record to a local disk jockey to get it on the air, listeners who lit up the station's switchboard with requests to hear it again seemed to share Phillips's excitement and his confusion. In order to clear up one aspect of the hometown singer's identity, the DJ made a point of announcing the fact that the new Sun sensation had been a student at Humes High School; in segregated Memphis, that was enough to reassure everyone that—despite the evidence of their ears—Elvis was white.

The single quickly sold twenty thousand copies, nudging its way to the top of Memphis' country and western chart and providing Presley with the opportunity to go out on the country music circuit. Although many traditional country music fans were appalled by what they heard—and saw—there was no question that he drove the kids wild. When Elvis got on stage he seemed to catch fire. All eyewitness reports from those first live performances tell the same story: with his heavily lidded eyes and swiveling hips, Elvis exploded the rigid racial and musical barriers of the early 1950s with a sound that echoed around the world. As John Lennon memorably described it a decade later, "Before Elvis, there was nothing."

Although all of the singles Elvis recorded for Sun were covers, they were not simply copies. In each case, Presley and his band—Bill Black on bass and Scotty Moore on guitar (and a little later, D. J. Fontana on drums)—tore apart the originals and remade them in Elvis's own image: the image of a nineteen-year-old boy in love with music and bursting with energy and ambition. On the basis of his slick, hipster wardrobe and eroticized stage persona, Elvis immediately picked up the nickname: the "Hillbilly Cat." And the sound he formulated, an energized hybrid of blues and bluegrass—rock and hillbilly—soon became known as "Rockabilly."

Although it reflected a similar fusion of black and white elements as those variants of rock 'n' roll emerging in other geographic areas, because of rockabilly's Southern setting (and association with the world of country music), its initial success had a more limited regional profile. For example, late in 1955—as Bill Haley, Chuck Berry, Fats Domino, Little Richard, and Pat Boone were already claiming their place on the nation's popular music charts—Elvis's first number one national hit (a cover of Junior Parker's R & B record "Mystery Train") was relegated to the country and western chart.

Years earlier, Sam Phillips had predicted "If I had a white man with the Negro sound and the Negro feel I could make a million dollars." As the hysteria generated by Elvis's live shows escalated and his records finally filtered into the mainstream market (a Cleveland DJ, Bob Randle, is credited with "breaking" Elvis to the pop audience), it seemed Phillips's prediction was about to come true. But there was already someone waiting in the wings to reap those rewards.

PRESLEYMANIA

About one year after his first Sun sessions, the man appeared who would take charge of Elvis's career for the rest of his life; he was an old-time C & W wheeler-dealer who called himself "Colonel" Tom Parker. Suddenly, Elvis found himself not only with a high-powered manager but with a new contract linking him to one of the oldest and most powerful of the major labels, RCA. In 1955, Sam Phillips accepted $35,000 for Presley's Sun Records contract, Elvis received a brand new Cadillac, and America was treated to its first taste of Presleymania.

On January 10, 1956, Elvis Presley recorded his first RCA single, "Heartbreak Hotel." By April, the song had sold over a million copies and was the number one pop hit in America. And that was only the beginning. In 1956 alone, nine of his singles made it into the pop, country, and R & B charts simultaneously. Fourteen records in a row racked up sales of at least one million copies as Presley provided RCA with almost half of the total income it made from popular music. No wonder they began to call him the "King."

But the incredible speed and phenomenal dimensions of Elvis's success would not have been possible without a medium that had only recently staked out its prominent place in living rooms across the country—television.

FIGURE 4-7. This publicity photo of Elvis was taken at a fateful moment of transition. Although it was only a few months after his Sun Records contract was purchased by RCA, his transformation from rockabilly rebel to pop icon was already well under way. Courtesy RCA Photo Archive.

Elvis on the Brink

In 1956, Elvis traded in the easy cameraderie of Sam Phillips's tiny Memphis studio for the high-powered efficiency of RCA's Nashville machine and gave up his slot on country radio's Louisiana Hayride for a series of guest appearances on Ed Sullivan's top-rated national television show. Within the next few months, Elvis would make his Las Vegas debut and begin shooting *Love Me Tender,* his first Hollywood film.

Elvis would be the first performer to fully exploit the power of TV's visual immediacy—and in the process help initiate the transformation of American culture.

Although Elvis had already appeared on a couple of popular television variety shows, Ed Sullivan—who hosted the nation's top-rated program—had simply refused to present the new pop sensation, declaring Presley's gyrations unfit for family viewing. But Elvis's success had a momentum that not even Sullivan could deny, and ultimately he signed Elvis to make three appearances for the unheard of fee of $50,000. On September 9, 1956, while a studio audience filled with thirteen-year-old girls shrieked, Presley rocked and rolled his way to the top of the entertainment pyramid.

The articles in Monday morning's newspapers, however, told a very different story. Virtually without exception, reviewers and columnists throughout the country labeled Elvis's performance "obscene." To *Life* magazine's reporter, he was simply "a howling hillbilly," while another clever critic compared Presley's movements to "the mating dance of an aborigine." Over the next two weeks, the hostility gathered momentum. By Elvis's final Sullivan performance, the strict orders to the cameramen were to shoot the singer only from the waist up.

As Elvis's image was projected into the American consciousness, the whole country seemed split: on one side, the hysterical fans and, on the other, the shocked and disapproving adults. But like a genie suddenly released from some ancient spell, the tiny black and white image of Elvis Presley that emerged from the nation's television sets possessed an astonishing potency. Elvis himself would soon move on to the larger than life Technicolor fantasies of Hollywood (and from there to the glitter and glitz of Las Vegas), but he had already transformed American popular music and the genie wasn't about to go back into the bottle.

THE RESPONSE: REVULSION AND RIDICULE

Although 1956 is typically celebrated as the dawn of "Presleymania," throughout the year, teen record buyers also propelled songs by Bill Haley and the Comets, Fats Domino, Frankie Lymon and the Teenagers, and Little Richard to the top of the once placid pop charts. It was also the year during which the negative response to the rock 'n' roll revolution reached a critical mass. The immediate reaction of parents, teachers, and other representatives of the social order was an avalanche of condemnation that matched their response to the other forces that were said to threaten the fabric of American society during the era: Communism and mutant alien invaders from outer space.

Like these, rock 'n' roll was viewed as an assault on our society's most basic values. While the edge of hysteria in their words may seem a little excessive today, the sentiments expressed by many public figures in the 1950s weren't that different from those that in the past had been directed at the pernicious influence of blues and jazz. Now the chorus of voices were raised up against rock 'n' roll, identifying it as the latest embodiment of the "devil's music."

Ironically, the first alarm against rock 'n' roll was sounded by the music industry itself. In 1955—before most Americans were aware of the growig menace, *Variety*—the so-called Bible of Show Business—began to publish articles decrying the immoral nature of the new music, along with descriptions of the violence that it had generated at some of the early rock 'n' roll shows. In fact, the entertainment journal was so concerned that an editorial was issued (focusing on the style's verbal content), titled "A Warning to the Music Business":

> The most casual look at the current crop of "lyrics" must tell even the most naive that dirty postcards have been translated into songs. . . . Music "leerics" are touching new lows and if the fast-buck songsmiths and music-makers are incapable of social responsibility and self-restraint the regulation—policing if you will—will have to come from more responsible sources. . . . What are we talking about? We're talking about "rock 'n' roll."

While most such exhortations also focused on rock 'n' roll's sexuality or antisocial attitude, some critics seemed obsessed by what they described as its "jungle beat." It soon became clear that this oft-repeated phrase was essentially a euphemism for rock's origins in African-American culture. During the 1950s, however, there were those willing to speak out about this trend in less veiled terms. "This rock 'n' roll music," announced one leader of a Southern white citizen's council, "is a way that the white youth can be brought down to the level of a nigger."

In addition to those who voiced their revulsion to rock 'n' roll on the basis of race, sexuality, or violence, there were others who took rock to task for its cultural deficiencies, and their weapon of choice was ridicule. For example, television personality Steve Allen (host of his own Sunday night variety show) would mockingly recite the lyrics of rock 'n' roll songs to the sound of a tinkling piano as a way of calling attention to what was perceived as their absurd simple-mindedness. And when (in an effort to boost his ratings) he booked Elvis as a guest, Allen's producers dressed the compliant young performer in formal attire and arranged for him to sing his latest hit—"Hound Dog"—to a live basset hound.

Meanwhile, local police and parent groups were less subtle in their attempt to stifle the music's evil influence; they simply banned rock 'n' roll shows from local theaters, pressured radio stations to stop playing it, and organized communal record-smashing events. But it soon became clear that these efforts to obliterate rock from radio stations, TV screens, and record store shelves was failing. Before long, opponents were reduced to reiterating the optimistic prediction that rock 'n' roll was just another passing fad and would disappear as suddenly as it had arrived.

Much to their chagrin, however, 1957 witnessed the ascent of a horde of new rock performers who emerged from every corner of the country, and a rapidly expanding teen audience propelled scores of diverse and exciting rock 'n' roll records directly to the top of the pop music charts.

1957: NEW HEROES, NEW SOUNDS

Following Elvis Presley's coronation as the "King of Rock 'n' Roll," Sam Phillips had a line of aspiring rockabilly royalty lined up in front of the door to his Sun studio. The first to walk out with a hit was a kid whose roots were in the same Southern, religious, working-class soil as Elvis himself. And it turned out that Jerry Lee Lewis had an act that made even Presley look tame.

Lewis released two frantic piano-pounding pop hits in 1957: "Whole Lotta Shakin' Goin' On" and "Great Balls of Fire." The music he unleashed was an explosive combination of country, gospel, and R & B, and Jerry Lee's riot-sparking live shows quickly made him one of the most infamous of the early rock 'n' rollers. If the sheer scope of Elvis's success was sufficient to qualify him for the title of "The King," it was Lewis's fiery abandon (at least one concert ended with his piano in actual flames) that had earned him the nickname "The Killer." Of course, not all the Southern rock heroes who emerged during the year were piano-burning good-ol' boys.

By 1957—when they hit the national pop charts with "Bye Bye Love"—the Everly Brothers had already been singing professionally on the country music circuit since they were about seven years old. And perhaps more than any of the other rock pioneers, their music retained the traditional elements of its hillbilly roots: from their high, close-harmony singing and acoustic guitars to the customized Western shirts and innocent sentimentality of their songs (written mostly by the Nashville-based husband and wife team of Felice and Boudleaux Bryant). Now sporting matching pompadours, Don and Phil suddenly became teen heartthrobs. After breaking through with "Bye Bye Love," the Everly's follow-up, "Wake up Little Susie," went to number one on the pop chart.

That same year also marked the first release of another rock 'n' roll original from the little town of Lubbock, Texas. In 1957, Buddy Holly and the Crickets plugged in at a tiny recording studio in Clovis, New Mexico, and came out with the first of a string of Holly-composed songs, "That'll Be the Day," built on a tight rockabilly beat. Buddy and the Crickets followed up a few months later with "Peggy Sue," another Holly song characterized by clever lyrics and a bare-boned, riff-filled melody.

African-American gospel music had been the foundation of many of the early performers who crossed over from rhythm and blues to the pop music charts. But when Sam Cooke left the Soul Stirrers (a legendary gospel quartet) for the world of secular music, he made the connections between the genres especially obvious. In Cooke's first R & B single under his own name, "You Send Me," he turned his soaring, passionate tenor from songs about spiritual love to one that celebrated a more secular variety. Released in 1957, the song went to number one on both the pop and rhythm and blues charts.

Meanwhile, the Coasters, a black vocal harmony group, had their first Top Ten pop single in 1957 with the double-sided Atlantic Records breakthrough "Searchin' "/"Young Blood." Having already scored a couple of R & B hits before joining the label (when they were known as the Robins), the quartet was one of dozens that—

because of their characteristic use of wordless, vocal sound effects—were dubbed "doo-wop" groups. A direct outgrowth of the call-and-response tradition of African-American gospel music, the doo-wop sound involved a creative blending of harmonized back-up vocals set against a soloist ("lead singer") who projected a combination of earthy passion and spiritual longing.

Not only were the Coasters masters of this secularized gospel style, but they were working with material crafted by a couple of rock 'n' roll geniuses: Jerry Leiber and Mike Stoller. This creative team went on to write and produce a string of hits for the Coasters that were filled with infectious good humor, as well as musical (and verbal) "hooks" that the teen audience couldn't seem to resist. (Although the Leiber and Stoller catalog—which included "Hound Dog," "Yakety-Yak," "On Broadway," and "Love Me Tender," among others—is a treasure-trove of rock classics, it is as "writer/producers" that they transformed the old Tin Pan Alley definition of pop songwriting. "We don't write songs," they once explained, "we write records.")

By the end of 1957, the words of one current hit—"Rock and Roll Will Never Die"—seemed to aptly proclaim rock's triumphant status. Early the very next year, however, an event occurred that in retrospect seems to foreshadow the fast-approaching end of the music's first Golden Age. That fall, headlines across the country reported that Little Richard—one of the rock's most flamboyant pioneers—was abandoning the devil's music to go to Bible college. "If you want to live for the Lord," Richard declared, "You can't rock and roll, too. God doesn't like it."

At the time, however, every day seemed to bring another new rock 'n' roll sensation to the rock-dominated pop charts and radio stations. The year 1957 also marked the network debut of a local Philadelphia television program that would probably have as great a role in permanently establishing the music of teenage America as any of the year's new performers. On August 5, *American Bandstand* had its national premier on ABC. Hosted by a boyish, ever-smiling master of ceremonies named Dick Clark, the daily afternoon program featured a studio full of high school kids who danced on camera to the latest rock 'n' roll records (or to lip-synching guest performers) and then "rated" the latest songs: "It's got a good beat and you can dance to it," became the show's standard assessment.

Broadcast on over one hundred stations around the country, *American Bandstand* reached an audience of over twenty million viewers every day and helped establish teen fashion and dance styles across the country. Yet, as television began to absorb rock 'n' roll into the mass media melting pot, radio—which had been the music's primary launching pad—was going through a painful identity crisis.

ON THE RADIO: PERSONALITY DJS, PLAYLISTS, AND PAYOLA

Ever since 1951, when Alan Freed began broadcasting "Moondog's Rock 'n' Roll House Party" over Cleveland's WJW, local AM radio stations across the country had been devoting a greater and greater percentage of their airtime to what Freed referred to as the Big Beat.

Men such as Bill Anson (KFWB/Los Angeles), Bill Randle (WERE/Cleveland), Bob Horn (WFIL/Philadelphia), and the rest of rock's original disk jockeys had seen themselves as pioneers leading their listeners through a dark and uncharted rock 'n' roll wilderness. Above all, they prided themselves on being able to "break" a record (DJ jargon for the art of discovering an unknown record and launching it as a national hit). Through a combination of instinct and tips from record store salesmen, these so-called "personality jocks" (who established their on-air identity with hipster slang and colorful catchphrases), claimed responsibility for developing their own playlists. And, as long as the "numbers" (both of ratings and ad revues) were up, stations were willing to let them work their magic.

"Exposure" had always been the key to a song's success. In the old Tin Pan Alley days, performances by vaudeville stars could generate the sale of millions of copies of sheet music, while during the Swing Era, a song added to the repertoire of a popular big band virtually guaranteed a hit. Because of the close relationship between airplay and the sales of any record, during the 1950s it was vital that companies get their recordings on the radio. This was the time when the unfettered hitmaking power of the personality jock was supreme.

The dependance of the record companies on radio DJs set the stage for a variety of unsavory practices that eventually ended in scandal. Before it was over, the federal government would intervene and a few careers (including Alan Freed's) would end in ruin. Meanwhile, however, the bidding wars between local radio stations to snag that one on-air personality who could bring in the most listeners escalated, and for a while, DJs became kings, commanding huge salaries and all the privileges of royalty.

TOP FORTY

But there was a flip side to the free-market philosophy espoused by the personality jock. Increasingly, there were those who believed that the best way for any radio station to be successful was to hold its audience in a viselike grip by programming an unbroken string of songs its listeners wanted to hear. This fundamental reality led to a new concept in radio programming known as "Top Forty."

Credited to Todd Storz, owner of a chain of radio stations in the South and Midwest, the Top Forty concept is a simple one: By strictly limiting a station's "playlist" to a tightly controlled handful of records with proven popularity, listeners would have no reason to change stations.

Now that the major labels had decided to join the independents by signing their own rock acts, the Big Beat had become Big Business. Unwilling to place their fate (and potential profits) in the hands of some renegade record spinner, record industry executives sought a more reliable (and controllable) outlet for their product. As Top Forty formats spread, listeners were increasingly subjected to the repetition of an ever-narrower range of music broadcast by a roster of ever-more bland and compliant disc jockeys.

Soon broadcasters would be provided with another powerful motivation to replace those high-salaried, independent-minded on-air hitmakers. For the stations that hadn't yet converted to the new Top Forty format, the final convincer would prove to be the "payola" scandals that began brewing in Washington, D.C., late in 1958.

PAYOLA

Payola. Although the word may have first been plastered across the front pages of the tabloid newspapers in the late 1950s, the idea behind it goes back to the earliest days of vaudeville theaters and Tin Pan Alley song pluggers.

Composers and song publishers had always been aware that even the greatest song needs to be heard before people will buy it. Often it didn't take more than a few dollars to convince a popular singer or bandleader to perform a particular tune at his or her next concert or radio appearance. After a while, the practice became so entrenched that some far-sighted music publishers even provided stars with an annual stipend, while other performers commanded (and received) partial writing credit for the songs they added to their repertoire (and thus a share of its income). Bribery? Well, let's just say a little "encouragement" could go a long way.

As radio airplay became the key to promoting a new record, it was the disc jockey who became the recipient of the record company's generosity. Methods of payments (and amounts) varied. A popular DJ might be offered a percentage of the local sales of a particular record in his listening area, or simply a flat fee of $50 or $100 for playing a new song for a specific time period. Other inducements ranged from free meals or trips to luxury gifts. And now it was the DJ who could demand the writing credit on a song, as Alan Freed had managed to do with "Maybellene." While this so-called pay for play policy had been standard practice throughout pop radio, its existence only became an issue for government agencies and the media when rock 'n' roll began to dominate the music business.

There were actually a number of factors that precipitated Congress's highly publicized payola investigations. Although the prime motivation may have been the corrupting influence of rock 'n' roll, in fact, the whole issue of corruption in the mass media had initially emerged in a very different context. Recently, national headlines had been filled with the shocking revelations that contestants on "Twenty-One," a network television quiz show, had been provided with the answers ahead of time.

Congressional hearings into the "Quiz Show Scandals" had turned out to be good publicity for a lot of government officials, and it would soon be an election year. What better image for a congressman running for re-election than to be seen as a protector of American youth against the depravity of rock 'n' roll? Payola became the vehicle for just such a crusade. Meanwhile, many of the leading figures in the music industry realized they could also benefit from anything that reigned in the rock-oriented independent labels that had carved out such a huge slice of the pop pie. The major labels wanted to reassert their control over popular music, and wiping the slate clean was a good way to start.

Although the activities of many disc jockeys were investigated—even Dick Clark narrowly escaped serious charges—it was Alan Freed who became the scandal's scapegoat. Gruff-voiced, street-tough, and champion of the music's R & B roots, Freed was never the most beloved figure of the mainstream forces that ran the music business. In November 1959, WABC (his then-current New York station) demanded that Freed sign the standard "I never took payola" statement that had quickly become a radio industry shield against charges of bribery. Freed refused. He said it was a question of principle. On November 21, he tearfully announced his resignation over the air. Freed went on to fight a five-year legal battle that broke his health and his bank account. That, and the affects of alcoholism, resulted in his death in 1964.

The federal investigations had a chilling effect that caused profound changes in the world of pop music. Many radio stations completely abandoned their rock 'n' roll format (since that seemed to be the target of the hearings). DJs were forced to sign pledges that they had never accepted payola (and even take lie detector tests to prove it) and Top Forty playlists were tightened even further in an effort to insulate stations against any possible charges of corruption.

TAKING CONTROL

Although scandals, congressional hearings, and restrictive Top Forty formats may have muffled the Big Beat, rock 'n' roll wasn't dealt the fatal blow for which many parents and civic leaders longed; but, as the Fifties drew to a close, a series of unrelated events did conspire to dull the music's cutting edge, while the pop music mainstream simply coopted rock's revolutionary spirit. Finally—beginning on that day in the fall of 1957 when Little Richard announced that he was abandoning the devil's music to serve God—a number of rock 'n' roll pioneers were, for various reasons, vanishing from the music scene they had helped create.

"Mrs. Lewis, I Presume . . ."

Late in 1958, reporters discovered that the quiet young woman who was accompanying Jerry Lee Lewis on his tour of England was his new bride. The only problem was that they also discovered that she was thirteen years old and his third (or fourth) cousin. The scandal forced Lewis to cut short his tour; he was welcomed back to America with shocked headlines, canceled concerts, and radio blacklists. His career as a rock star was over.

Pvt. Presley

That same year, an event of enormous significance had a nation of teenage girls in a state of high anxiety. Elvis Presley had been drafted into the army and would be spending the next two years in Germany. A new film (*King Creole*) was hastily scheduled to be released a few months after his induction, and a few singles and an album of "Golden Hits" was carefully timed to keep Elvis in the public eye during his absence. But the fact was that he would be three thousand miles away, and although he looked dashing in his crew cut and uniform, Elvis no longer exactly fit the image of the "King of Rock 'n' Roll."

Chuck Berry: Sweet Little . . . Fourteen

On June 2, 1958, Chuck Berry was arrested for violation of the Mann Act (which prohibited transporting underage persons across state lines for illicit purposes). Thus began two years of litigation. Needless to say, headlines such as " 'Rock & Roll Singer Lured Me to St. Louis,' Says 14-Year Old" didn't do wonders for Berry's career. Two separate trials (relating to two separate charges) eventually ended in Chuck Berry's conviction and a sentence of three years in a federal penitentiary.

FIGURE 4-8.   Beneath the mascara, six-inch pompadour, suggestive lyrics, and pounding keyboard riffs that made Little Richard one of the most flamboyant performers in rock history could be heard the echoes of African-American gospel music. Courtesy of Fantasy Records, Inc.

Awopbopaloobop Alopbamboom!

Long before he burst onto the pop charts with explosive hits such as "Tutti Frutti," "Long Tall Sally," "Lucille," and "Good Golly Miss Molly," Richard Penniman had been singing and playing piano in his local church. Even his trademark falsetto "whoops" were based on the vocal pyrotechnics of the great gospel diva Marion Williams. In fact, when "Bumps" Blackwell (his future producer at Specialty Records) first listened to the singer's demo tape, he immediately pegged Little Richard as "a gospel singer who could sing the blues."

FIGURE 4-9.   Fabian, the archetypal "teen idol," in all his slicked-back glory. When Bob Marucci signed the handsome sixteen-year-old to Chancellor Records (a Philadelphia indie label), he declared the singer "a natural"; he also admitted that Fabian did have one minor problem—"he couldn't sing." Archive photo.

Fabian and the Era of the Teen Idol

In an effort to reestablish their position in the post-Elvis pop music scene, record industry veterans unable to *discover* exciting performers who could appeal to the new rock 'n' roll market decided to *manufacture* them. The process was simple. Take one good-looking youngster, add a fashion consultant, songwriter, arranger, and PR person. Result: one teen idol.

Since many of rock's authentic pioneers were out of the picture for one reason or another, there was plenty of room on the charts for the likes of Fabian ("Turn Me Loose," "Tiger") and Frankie Avalon ("DeDe Dinah," "Venus"). Because their appeal was primarily visual (rather than vocal), teen idols found their most comfortable niche on television dance party shows such as *American Bandstand* and in teen films such as the Frankie Avalon classic, *Beach Blanket Bingo*.

The Day the Music Died

On February 3, 1959, a tragic plane crash took the lives of three of rock's newest and brightest stars. Buddy Holly, Richie Valens, and the "Big Bopper" (J. P. Richardson) were traveling to the next stop on their "Winter Dance Party" tour when the small plane in which they were flying crashed in bad weather. There was something about the extreme youth (Holly was twenty-two and Valens only eighteen), talent, and freshness of these performers that made the impact of their sudden loss seem especially profound, and somehow symbolic.

Valens's breakthrough record—"La Bamba"—released a few months earlier not only had introduced an exciting new rock 'n' roll performer, but it seemed to promise a significant expansion of rock's cultural base. After all, his real name was "Valenzuela," and his new hit happened to be a souped-up version of a traditional Spanish folk song. Richie Valens's story had all the ingredients of the ultimate Fifties fantasy. But within just a few short months, his dream of becoming rock 'n' roll's first Latino star was swept away in an Iowa snowstorm.

Over time, the tragic plane crash has been raised to mythic proportions. It's been dramatized in Hollywood bio-pics (*The Buddy Holly Story* and *La Bamba*) and a classic song ("American Pie" by Don McLean) in which the event is described as "the day the music died." In McLean's sng, the crash becomes a metaphor for the death of rock 'n' roll's first innocent Golden Age. For, when the "Winter Dance Party" resumed, the three performers who joined the tour as replacements for the fallen rock heroes were Paul Anka, Frankie Avalon, and Fabian: a triumvirate of "Teen Idols."

TEEN IDOLS

After the power (and profit) of rock 'n' roll finally became apparent to everyone, a kind of if-you-can't-beat-'em-join-'em attitude began to develop. Music industry professionals realized that with the right image—clothes, hairstyle, material, and promotion—one could take a good-looking and personable teen and magically transform him into a rock 'n' roll star. Anka, Avalon, and Fabian were prime examples of this new phenomenon. To varying degrees, they were essentially singing pompadours. But they also were the final revenge of those forces that had, from the beginning, conspired to tame the rebellious individuality of rock 'n' roll.

Whether because of scandal, tragic accident, tighter Top Forty radio playlists, or the advent of the so-called teen idol, as the Fifties drew to a close, rock 'n' roll experienced an undeniable loss of creative energy. To make things worse, an economic recession taking place in America was filtering down to the teen audience. The financial downturn took its toll on allowances and therefore on the available cash to purchase the latest record. In addition, because of the intensifying promotion of long-playing "albums," the excitement and immediacy of rushing out to buy the latest "45" also was gradually waning.

Meanwhile, Bobby Darin's finger-popping version of "Mack the Knife" (a song written by the experimental German theater composer, Kurt Weill, in the late 1920s) held the top spot on the charts for most of the last few months of the decade. The single was awarded the 1959 Grammy for Record of the Year and, in December, the twenty-two-year old Darin was appearing at the Copa Room of the Sands Hotel in Las Vegas.

Replacing Darin's record at the top of the pop chart during the last week of the year was Frankie Avalon's latest synthetic hit, "Why?" But an even better question for those fans who may have been wondering about the fate of the music they had come to embrace as their own was: "What next?"

THE DEATH OF ROCK 'N' ROLL: MYTH AND REALITY

In one of the more intriguing sections of their *Book of Rock Lists,* Dave Marsh and Kevin Stein itemize their top five "Discredited Rock Theories." The second of these is of particular interest to our discussion of rock 'n' roll at the end of its first decade. For, according to the authors, the conventional wisdom that "Rock 'died' between 1959 and 1964" is, in fact, just another of the music's myths ripe for discrediting.

They begin by summarizing the facts most often cited to justify the notion of rock 'n' roll's late Fifties demise: "This is thought to be true," they write, "because during that period Elvis was in the army, Buddy Holly died, Jerry Lee Lewis was banned, Chuck Berry went to prison, and Little Richard entered a seminary." Then they marshall the evidence for their rebuttal:

> Fact is, however, that from 1959 to 1964, the following not only had hits but had number one hits: Lloyd Price ("Stagger Lee"), Wilbert Harrison ("Kansas City"), the Drifters ("Save the Last Dance for Me"), Del Shannon ("Runaway"), Ernie K-Doe ("Mother-in-Law"), Roy Orbison ("Running Scared"), Gary "U.S." Bonds ("Quarter to Three"), Dion ("Runaround Sue"), Little Eva ("The Locomotion"), the Four Seasons ("Sherry," "Walk Like a Man," "Big Girls Don't Cry"), the Crystals ("He's a Rebel"), the Chiffons ("He's So Fine"), Stevie Wonder ("Fingertips—Pt. 2")—not to mention a batch of other girl groups, Chicago soul, Motown, and surf hits. And if that ain't rock and roll. . . .

So which was it? Did the early 1960s represent "the fallow years of rock and roll . . . tame, predictable, and dull," as one critic's version of the standard theory would have it, or was it in reality an extraordinarily fertile period offering a variety of exciting performers and exciting new styles as suggested above? Actually, it was both.

The truth is, even during its legendary "Golden Age," rock 'n' roll wasn't a paradise of creative purity. During the mid-1950s, when the Big Beat burst onto the popular music charts, it was represented by styles ranging from hardcore to easy-listening. And even as black music first made its presence felt in the world of mainstream pop, it did so not only through the hair-raising frenzy of Little Richard's "Tutti-Frutti" but with the perky innocence of Frankie Lymon and the Teenagers ("I'm Not a Juvenile Delinquent") and the laid-back smoothness of Fats Domino's Tin Pan Alley cover of "My Blue Heaven."

While the story that Fifties rock was suddenly stripped of its unbridled passion and authenticity may indeed be just another of the music's myths, both the abrupt departure of some of its early heroes and the assaults by the mainstream media did have a chilling effect on the music. By the end of the decade, however, there was also a shared acceptance of the fact that rock 'n' roll had unalterably transformed the pop music environment. Not only had the major labels gradually learned how to fit rock 'n' roll into their traditional production system, but the indies (which had once operated within narrow regional and stylistic confines) also began to figure out how to function as a part of the national pop music marketplace. In fact, the list of performers cited by Marsh and Stein provides an interesting example of these intersecting trends.

Both Lloyd Price and Roy Orbison each had successfully recorded for seminal independent labels during the early 1950s. Price had a couple of hits for the R & B label Specialty (including "Lawdy Miss Clawdy") in 1952, while Orbison had a rockabilly hit ("Ooby-Dooby") in 1956 for Sun Records. But, in fact, each performer's most significant work did take place during the period when rock 'n' roll had supposedly kicked the bucket.

In 1958, Price—who was now recording for the major label ABC-Paramount—scored a number one pop hit with "Stagger-Lee" (a modern version of a traditional ballad about an African-American badman/folk hero). A year later, his hit single "Personality" was number three in the annual *Billboard* list of the biggest records of 1959. It was with just such shrewdly conceived pop productions that the majors finally proved that they could make the adjustment to the new rock 'n' roll realities.

Meanwhile, in Nashville (where Elvis had been recording his string of increasingly mainstream number one hits for RCA), Roy Orbison found a home on a new independent label—Monument. Unlike the original indies that were founded by street-savvy hustlers or visionary music mavens, Monument was a calculated venture by the oldest and most prominent music publishing company in Nashville (Acuff-Rose), created specifically to tap the rock 'n' roll market. By setting Orbison's soaringly expressive vocals and well-crafted songs within elaborate productions that used the cream of the city's celebrated session musicians, the former rockabilly rebel released a series of singles (including "Only the Lonely," "Crying," and "Pretty Woman") that became instant pop-rock classics.

By this point, both the major labels and the indies began to revert to the kind of "factory system" that had its roots in the Tin Pan Alley era of the 1930s, when a record was the product of a collaboration among highly skilled specialists. This return to traditional music-industry practices imposed a new level of professionalism on a style of music that had previously been celebrated (or condemned) as the embodiment of individuality and rebellion. Finally, it also resulted in a dramatic shift in the balance of power away from the far-flung regional indies and back to what had always been the center of the music industry, New York City.

FIGURE 4-10.   When Sam Cooke's 1957 hit "You Send Me" ascended to the top of the national pop charts, it was more than just another example of the migration of African-American artists out of the R & B ghetto. It also represented the most dramatic (and influential) "crossover" in gospel music history. Courtesy of RCA Archive. A Unit of BMG Entertainment.

Sam Cooke Crosses Over

In 1950, Sam Cooke—the twenty-year-old son of a Baptist preacher—was selected to take over as the lead singer of the Soul Stirrers, one of the most respected quartets in the history of gospel music. Cooke's quietly passionate vocal style and extraordinary physical charms immediately electrified the gospel world.

For the next five years, Cooke was a gospel heartthrob. While the ethereal beauty of his lead vocals on such classics as "Touch the Hem of His Garment" and "Wonderful" won over the Soul Stirrers' traditional audience, the underlying sensuality of Cooke's voice and his matinee-star good looks inspired the younger generation to form "Sam Cooke Fan Clubs." But when Cooke decided to make the transition to secular music, many felt he had not only turned away from his gospel fans but turned his back on God.

With his first R & B record; however, Cooke guaranteed his place in pop music history. "You Send Me" quickly became a number one hit on both the rhythm and blues and the pop charts. Over the next few years, Cooke scored one pop hit after another, including: "Only Sixteen," "Everybody Likes to Cha Cha Cha," "Wonderful World," "Shake," and "Bringing It on Home to Me" (most of which he also wrote). Cooke also became one of the first R & B singers to make the move from a regional indie label (Keen) to a certified major (RCA).

Tragically, Sam Cooke was shot to death by a young female acquaintance under confusing (but unsavory) circumstances late in 1964, not long after he recorded the song that many consider his masterpiece, "A Change Is Gonna Come." Directly influenced by Bob Dylan's "Blowin' in the Wind," the song was an impassioned plea for justice and racial equality. In a final irony, Cooke had included the song on an album whose title—*Good News*—was the standard translation of the word "gospel"; so perhaps Cooke hadn't abandoned the style after all.

While it was apparent that even distinctive singers such as Lloyd Price and Roy Orbison could be successfully molded to fit rock 'n' roll's newly compartmentalized production style, vocal groups (rather than a solo singer) increasingly became the vehicle for the record producer's masterplan. As Charlie Gillett explained in his book *The Sound of the City: The Rise of Rock and Roll*, "Because a vocal group tended to have a less fixed vocal image than a solo singer, and so was more flexible and could more easily be shaped by a producer, a large number of New York productions [during the early 1960s] were with groups."

In fact, each of the most important centers of pop music to emerge during this period—New York's "Brill Building" (a complex of publishers and indie record labels) and Detroit's Motown empire—initially succeeded by implementing their own tightly structured musical assembly lines in which highly specialized professionals collaborated to produce records that were typically performed by young, compliant, vocal groups.

THE BRILL BUILDING: GIRL-GROUP HEAVEN

Late in 1960, all the elements of the classic "Brill Building" style came together for the first time with the release of "Will You Love Me Tomorrow" by the Shirelles. According to Alan Betrock, the author of the book, *Girl Groups: The Story of a Sound*, it was also the record that "made clear to many that the right song—with the right singer and the right arranger and the right producer—was the way to succeed."

Although its offices were actually across the street from the famous midtown Manhattan office building that gave the style its name, Aldon Music, an aggressive new company, was keeping alive the tradition of those venerable Tin Pan Alley music publishers, many of which had migrated to the Brill Building over the previous decades from the downtown neighborhoods that had been centers of the music business earlier in the century.

Now, in tiny, windowless cubicles furnished with little more than a couple of chairs and a beat-up piano, teams of young Aldon songwriters pounded out pop tunes for the teen market. In fact, though they had recently married, Carole King and Gerry Goffin (who wrote that first Shirelles' hit) were still teens themselves, as were the Shirelles. The four African-American high school girls from New Jersey had recently broken into the pop charts for the first time with "Tonight's the Night," written and produced by R & B veteran Luther Dixon. When Dixon heard the demo of Goffin and King's latest song, he knew it would be the perfect follow-up single for the group. It told the poignant story of a girl so in love with her boyfriend that she was willing to give herself to him *totally*, yet she couldn't help but wonder . . . would he still love her tomorrow?

Shirley Owens (the Shirelles' lead singer) performed the song's simple lyric with a mixture of yearning innocence and youthful passion, and Dixon's arrangement highlighted the song's dramatic theme (one that pushed the era's moral standards to the very edge of the envelope) with rhythmic tension and a soaring string section. It was a powerful combination. By the beginning of 1961, "Will You Love Me Tomorrow" had gone to the top of both the R & B and pop music charts where it remained for over four months.

FIGURE 4-11. The Shirelles became the definitive "girl group" of the early 1960s, producing a string of Top Ten pop hits such as "Dedicated to the One I Love," "Mama Said," "Will You Love Me Tomorrow," and "Soldier Boy." They were particular favorites of the Beatles, who covered two of the Shirelles' songs on their 1963 British debut album. Archive photo. Frank Driggs Collection.

The Shirelles and the Girl Group Era

By the early 1960s, the music industry's traditional modus operandi (and well-established prejudices) had finally begun to fall by the wayside. More than anywhere else, interracial and intergender collaborations became the hallmark of the so-called girl group era. In addition, many of style's songwriters (including Gerry Goffin, Carole King, Burt Bacharach, Ellie Greenwich, Barry Mann, and Cynthia Weill) and innovative producers (such as Phil Spector) weren't much older than teenagers themselves.

The genre not only unceremoniously overturned the testosterone-fueled world of Fifties rock but also its adventurous arrangements (especially the addition of Latin rhythms and string sections) and lyrics that pushed the edge of the typical teen-romance envelope (such as the Shirelles' own "Tonight's the Night" and "Will You Love Me Tomorrow") were obvious reflections of the accelerating social and musical upheavals of the period.

The first half of the new decade introduced a dozen tough-or-tender female trios and quartets that became fixtures on the pop music scene. In addition to the Shirelles, there were the Ronettes ("Be My Baby," "Baby I Love You," "Walkin' in the Rain"), the Crystals ("He's a Rebel," "Da Do Ron Ron"), the Chiffons ("One Fine Day," "He's So Fine"), the Shangri-Las ("Leader of the Pack," "Walkin' in the Sand"), and the Angels ("My Boyfriend's Back").

The Shirelles' enormous success prompted their record company, Scepter, to re-release the group's first effort on the label, a cover of a song by the male vocal group, the Five Royales, titled "Dedicated to the One I Love." Within weeks, that record also climbed its way up the charts and the Shirelles now had *two* of the Top Ten pop singles in the country. While most record buyers—responding to the Shirelles' thrilling sagas of teenage romance—were unaware of the incredible implications of their achievement, the group's feat was certainly not lost on music industry insiders.

After all, the Shirelles were the first *all-girl* group in the history of rock 'n' roll to have a number one record on the popular music chart. And as Alan Betrock describes it, "Once this fact sank in among record biz types, the rush was on. 'Gimme a girl group; gimme a love song; gimme a beat; gimme some strings—please, gimme a HIT!' "

Over the next few years, this Brill Building mantra resulted in an infusion of a new female presence in rock 'n' roll, as "girl groups" such as the Chiffons, the Crystals, the Cookies, and the Ronettes took turns at the top of the pop music charts. Songwriter partnerships associated with the style (such as Goffin and King, Cynthia Weill and Barry Mann, Jerome (Doc) Pomus and Mort Schuman, Ellie Greenwich and Jeff Barry) accounted for some of the most artistically—and commercially—successful records of the era. Certainly they were the most obsessively "crafted" of any in rock 'n' roll history.

While the distinctive sound of those early 1960s "Brill Building" acts has influenced every vocal harmony group (both black and white) ever since, it also has shown up in some rather unlikely places. In Liverpool, England, one young band seemed to have been paying especially close attention. The Beatles—who put at least as much emphasis on their vocal harmonies as they did on their instrumental sound—were clearly inspired by both the writing and the singing they heard on these records. In fact, at the beginning of the band's career, the Beatles covered several of the girl group songs (including "Baby, It's You" and "Boys" by the Shirelles and "Be My Baby" by the Ronettes).

PHIL SPECTOR: TOMORROW'S MUSIC TODAY

Many of the qualities that came to characterize the records associated with the Brill Building style had been established during the previous decade by Jerry Leiber and Mike Stoller. In addition to writing some of Elvis's early hits (including "Hound Dog" and "Jailhouse Rock"), this legendary songwriting and producing partnership also had crafted a string of classic R & B hits for the Coasters. Now they were bringing their innovative "we-write-records-not-songs" philosophy to their work with another vocal harmony group, the Drifters.

In early 1960s hits such as "There Goes My Baby," "This Magic Moment," and "Save the Last Dance for Me," the team produced records whose complex arrangements employed lush string sections and Latin-tinged rhythms that perfectly set off the emotive, gospel-based vocals by the Drifter's lead singer, Ben E. King. But when King left the group to forge a solo career, his first single—"Spanish Harlem"—was assigned to a twenty-year-old Leiber and Stoller protégé named Phil Spector, who had cowritten the song.

Over the next few years, Phil Spector created ever more lavish musical extravaganzas for girl groups such as the Crystals and Ronettes. Obsessed with producing the most innovative pop recordings of his time, when Spector started his own label—Phillies—he boldly printed the same motto on every disk he issued: "Tomorrow's Music Today." And by combining the roles of auteur and entrepreneur, Spector became (according to a 1964 New York *Herald-Tribune* article by Tom Wolfe), "The First Tycoon of Teen." Although Wolfe seemed more bemused than impressed with Spector's artistic accomplishments, his article actually provides an insightful description of Spector's (in)famous working method:

Spector had a system. The big record companies put out records like buckshot, 10, maybe 15 rock and roll records a month, and if one of them catches on, they can make money. Spector's system is to put them out one at a time and pour everything into each one. Spector does the whole thing. He writes the words and the music, scouts and signs up the talent. He takes them out to a recording studio in Los Angeles and runs the recording session himself. He puts them through hours and days of recording to get the two or three minutes he wants. Two or three minutes out of the whole struggle. He handles the control dials like an electronic maestro, turning various instruments or sounds up, down, out, every which way, using things like two pianos, a harpsichord and three guitars on one record; then re-recording the whole thing with esoteric dubbing and over-dubbing effects—re-inforcing instruments or voices—coming out with what is known throughout the industry as "the Spector Sound."

While Phil was busy constructing "the Spector Sound"—also known as the "Wall of Sound" because of its grandeur and aural intensity—other producers were crafting their own three-minute adolescent operas. George (Shadow) Morton, who created the melodramatic, "Leader of the Pack" for the white vocal group the Shangri-Las, used sound effects, recitation, and instrumental underscoring to record what one writer described as a "feature-length film crammed into two minutes and forty-eight seconds."

Whatever their stylistic differences, however, what united the new school of pop hitmakers was the shared conception of a record as the culmination of a painstaking process conducted among skilled professionals—a collaboration in the service of a single artistic vision. Actually, that's not a bad description of what was going on halfway across the country in the nation's Motor City—or "Mo'town," as it was referred to in the local slang.

THE MOTOWN EMPIRE: HITSVILLE, U.S.A.

By 1960, when he formed his first record label—Tamla—Berry Gordy Jr. had already been active on the Detroit music scene for a couple of years as a retailer, independent producer, and songwriter. But, according to the Motown myth, it was while working on the Ford assembly line that Gordy had the inspiration for his own hitmaking factory.

While he never quite achieved the economic status of Detroit's automotive giants, before long Berry Gordy had not only forged the most successful independent recording company in history, but had become the CEO of the largest black-owned corporation in America. While Gordy often used the metaphor of "the family" to describe the tightly knit bond that existed within Motown, the company's success can be traced to the highly structured production methods that were more characteristic of the auto industry Big Three.

Motown's assembly line also consisted of skilled professionals—songwriters, producers, arrangers, studio musicians—who put together pop music singles instead of four-door sedans. In fact, when he was asked about his own role in this process, Berry's answer often took the form of manufacturing metaphor: "Quality Control." In that capacity, Berry Gordy insisted on having final approval on every record released by Motown. And—in another connection to Detroit's main industry—Gordy would insist on listening to the finished product on a speaker that simulated the tinny sound of the typical car radio, which he knew was how most people would first encounter the records.

And, just as each member of the Detroit "car-tel" attempted to create its own automotive *look* (constructed out of tail fins and chrome), Gordy took pains to fashion a distinctive Motown *sound* that combined the emotional authenticity of gospel (along with its call-and-response structure and rattling tambourines) with the sophisticated sheen (and strings) of the recent Brill Building productions. In its rhythmically propulsive, finely honed, hook-filled hits, Motown's music also embodied the motto that appeared on the label of every one of its recordings: "The Sound of Young America."

In its conscious effort to transcend any race-based limitations (after all, its slogan wasn't The Sound of *Black* America), Motown was reflecting the pride, optimism, and confidence of a specific moment in American history. For 1960, the year Gordy formed his record label, was also the year John F. Kennedy was elected as the nation's youngest president. And, in his inaugural address, Kennedy ushered in an era of unlimited possibilities for the entire country when he proclaimed that the torch of leadership had been passed "to a new generation of Americans."

At the same time, across the South, Martin Luther King Jr. was leading a reinvigorated Civil Rights movement that seemed to be rapidly sweeping away the last strongholds of segregation. In 1963, when he gave his "I Have a Dream" speech at the historic March on Washington, D.C., King would announce that the time was at hand when black Americans would be judged by "the content of their character and not by the color of their skin." But Berry Gordy's success was not only a case of being the right man at the right time. Gordy was also the right man in the right place.

While Detroit had the fourth largest African-American population of any city in America (and many of these people had been attracted by the high-paying jobs in the auto industry), unlike other urban centers the city had never developed a successful independent R & B record company. The local nightclubs, amateur contests, and high school talent shows were bursting with talented young performers and Gordy had a field day. In fact, the very first group Berry signed was a vocal quintet whose members had met as students at the city's Northern High School. By 1961, the Miracles had produced the company's first million-seller, "Shop Around."

Not only did the Miracles provide Gordy with a solid act as the foundation for his new company, but in the person of William "Smokey" Robinson—the group's songwriter and lead singer—he acquired the person who would be one of the cornerstones of the entire Motown Sound. Over the next decade, Robinson created a series of soulful pop masterpieces (including "You've Really Got a Hold on Me," "I Second That Emotion," "Ooo Baby Baby," and "Tears of a Clown") in which he applied his achingly pure falsetto to the imaginatively conceived imagery of his own songs. (Early in his career, when Bob Dylan was asked to name his favorite poets, among those he cited was the beatnik bard Allen Ginsberg, the French symbolist Arthur Rimbaud, and Smokey Robinson.)

But Smokey Robinson's contribution wasn't limited to his work with the Miracles. Soon he was writing and producing hits for other Motown acts. The first to benefit from Smokey's creative touch was a local girl named Mary Wells who signed with Motown in 1961 when she was barely eighteen years old. A year later, Wells had her first Top Ten hit ("The One Who Really Loves You"), written and produced by Smokey Robinson. But in 1964, Smokey wrote and produced a single for Wells that became the very first Motown record to go to number one on the national pop music chart—the classic, "My Guy."

That same year, Robinson began collaborating with another vocal group that would become one of era's most popular acts and the epitome of the Motown Sound—the Temptations. Grounded by lead singer David Ruffin's resonant baritone and given flight by Eddie Kendricks's etherial falsetto, the "Tempts" brought their earthy call-and-response vocal harmonies (and their slick choreography) to a variety of material, eventually racking up forty-three Top Ten hits (including "The Way You Do the Things You Do," "My Girl," "Get Ready," and "Since I Lost My Baby").

Before signing with Gordy, the Temptations had been appearing in Detroit night spots as the Primes. In tribute to these local heroes, three young girls from the Brewster housing projects formed their own vocal "sister group." They called themselves the Primettes. After signing with Motown in 1961, however, the girls underwent a name change that turned out to be a prophetic one, since within the Motown pantheon, they would unquestionably be—the Supremes.

More than any other group, the Supremes were shaped by Berry Gordy (and the Motown machine) into international pop stars unlike any in the history of African-American music. Working with Brian and Eddie Holland and Lamont Dozier—a team of writer-producers who solidified and refined the early Motown style into its classic form—the Supremes became Motown's mainstream heroines. Fronted by Diana Ross's smooth, playfully seductive vocals and assembled with all the glitzy packaging that Motown designers and choreographers could muster, the Supremes sold tens of millions of records, racked up a dozen number one pop hits, made two dozen appearances on the Ed Sullivan show, and starred in an assortment of big-budget TV specials and Las Vegas nightclub spectacles.

On the basis of her own charismatic persona, as well as the special attention she received from Gordy (with whom she had a romantic relationship), Diana Ross launched a spectacular solo career in the early 1970s. And, having relocated to Hollywood with the rest of the company, Ross's film début as the tragic jazz singer Billie Holiday in Motown's first film production (*Lady Sings the Blues*) earned her an Academy Award nomination, thereby solidifying her status as the ultimate Motown diva.

Meanwhile, Motown accumulated an incredible roster of talent, both behind the "mike" and behind the scenes. While the label became home to a collection of creative and highly motivated writer/producers (such as Norman Whitfield, Barrett Strong, and the husband and wife team of Nick Ashford and Valerie Simpson), much of the distinctiveness of those classic Motown records can be attributed to a permanent "house band" that brought an expressive inventiveness and rhythmic precision to hit after hit.

Although they worked in virtual anonymity, leader-pianist Earl Van Dyke, guitarist Joe Messina, bassist James Jamerson, and drummer Benny Benjamin (collectively known as the Funk Brothers) are now celebrated as the unsung heroes of the Motown Sound. Meanwhile, the veteran dancer and choreographer Cholly Atkins is also

FIGURE 4-12.   The Supremes, c. 1964. Diana Ross, Mary Wilson, and Florence Ballard show off the results of their Motown makeover. Archive photo. Frank Driggs Collection.

The Supremes' Motown Makeover

The Supremes' ascent from Detroit's Brewster housing project to the top of the pop charts reads like yet another chapter in that never-ending saga known as the Great American Dream. In fact, back in 1961, when the three high school friends were signed by a local R & B label called Motown, it seemed their dreams had already come true. So, after being groomed, gowned, and choreographed within an inch of their lives, when their 1964 Motown release, "Where Did Our Love Go?" suddenly became the number one hit in the country, the Supremes were ready.

Having established the charismatic presence and sultry voice of Diana Ross as the group's focal point, Motown's premier songwriting/production team of Eddie and Brian Holland and Lamont Dozier (who had crafted their chart-topping breakthrough) helped turn the Supremes into the black-owned independent label's most potent hitmakers. Over the next two years, the Supremes released a string of number one singles—"Baby Love," "Stop in the Name of Love," "I Hear a Symphony," "You Can't Hurry Love" (among others)—that helped define the Motown Sound.

finally being credited for providing the slick moves that made performances by groups such as the Temptations such a dynamic visual, as well as aural, experience.

Throughout the 1960s, Motown dominated the pop charts in a way that no record company has before or since. The various Motown labels consistently found their way into the Top Ten through the raw and funky sound of the Contours ("Do You Love Me"), the classic girl-group style of the Marvelettes ("Please Mr. Postman," "Don't Mess with Bill") the hard-rocking exuberance of Martha and the Vandellas ("Heat Wave," "Dancing in the Street," "Nowhere to Run"), the monumental soulfulness of the Four Tops ("I Can't Help Myself," "Reach out I'll Be There," "Bernadette"), and the assured lead vocals and finally honed ensemble work of Gladys Knight and the Pips (as in their blistering original version of "I Heard It through the Grapevine").

A year after "Grapevine" made it to the number two spot on the pop charts, however, the song was covered by another Motown performer—the great Marvin Gaye. A gifted songwriter, musician, and producer and one of the most sensual singers of his generation, his brilliant version of "I Heard It through the Grapevine" became an enormous hit (selling over four million copies on its way to becoming the number one pop song in the country). Yet, as celebrated as he was for his solo efforts ("Pride and Joy," "Ain't That Peculiar," "What's Goin' On"), many listeners were even more drawn to Gaye's empathetic duets with Tammi Terrell (especially the towering, Spectoresque "Ain't No Mountain High Enough"); tragically their soulful partnership came to an end with Terrell's untimely death of a brain tumor in 1970.

Motown's amazing decade ended with the début of the Jackson Five ("ABC," "The Love You Save," "I'll Be There"), whose tightly knit vocals and dynamic footwork provided the setting for Michael's precocious star turns. But Michael Jackson wasn't Motown's first wunderkind. That honor belonged to a blind ten-year-old named Steveland Morris, who had walked into the Motown studio for an audition back in 1960 and, in front of Berry Gordy and the Supremes, proceeded to play every instrument in the room. By the time he was twelve (and rechristened "Little Stevie Wonder"), he'd had his first number one record—"Fingertips"—featuring his impassioned, gospel-based vocal and infectious harmonica riffs. Stevie Wonder quickly matured into one of Motown's most versatile and prolific performers. He also became one of the first to successfully challenge the Motown system.

Berry Gordy's fanatical control over his empire had not only been responsible for Motown's unprecedented success but, by the late 1960s, it also had engendered considerable frustration and resentment. A number of writers, producers, and performers began feeling trapped by Gordy's near-absolute authority over their careers (and income). This had already resulted in a number of lawsuits and bitter departures from the company. Then, in 1971 (as soon as he turned twenty-one), Stevie Wonder announced he was leaving Motown over the issue of creative control. Rather than lose the multitalented performer—just as he was about to fulfill his enormous artistic potential—Motown gave into his demands, which included the freedom to write and produce his own music and to share equally in the publishing rights to his songs. That same year, Marvin Gaye also won his long battle to chart his own creative course.

Unlike many of other acts who had abandoned Motown in order to assume more control over their careers and then floundered without the label's crack team of writers, producers, and studio musicians, both Stevie Wonder and Marvin Gaye went on to create their most ambitious, innovative—and commercially successful—work after establishing their artistic independence. Meanwhile Gordy was in the process of making his own ambitious move: out of the very city with which he had become so fundamentally identified.

In 1971, Motown moved its entire operation to Los Angeles; the company took over a glass-and-steel office tower on the Sunset Strip, and Berry bought himself a Bel Air mansion (not far from the one owned by *Playboy* magazine founder Hugh Hefner) and he began laying the groundwork for his first film venture. Taken together, these recent developments were not only symptoms of Gordy Berry's enormous ambition, but they were symbolic of a fundamental transformation that was taking place in the American mass media.

But, in creating Motown, Gordy had in many ways also replicated the experience of the founders of the Hollywood dream factories fifty years earlier, and in some ways his influence on American culture was just as profound. As the critic Elvis Mitchell wrote in his introduction to a four-CD collection, *Hitsville U.S.A.: Motown 1959–1971*:

Motown was as much a popular culture assimilation of the verve of rhythm and blues and gospel into the mainstream as can be found in the iron walls of the Jewish founders of the movie studios. This stoked brand of from-the-ground-up reinvention by savvy, ambitious outsiders that turns them from rag peddlers—or, in Berry's case, autoworker/tunes salesman—into dream merchants is at the heart of mass market entertainment. And their dreams led to a wholesale re-shaping of the culture.

While no one could question the success of Gordy's assimilation into the pop mainstream (between 1960 and 1970 an astonishing two-thirds of Motown's 535 singles became Top Twenty hits!), some did question the na-ture of this assimilation—including the Supremes' beehive wigs and Vegas-style nightclub routines. "Processed soul" some called it. One long-time participant in the Motown machine (voice coach Alan Silver) was even more frank in describing the secret of Berry Gordy's success: "He milked it down so it was acceptable to whites, Silver asserted. "That was Gordy's big trick." Many fans insisted that if you wanted R & B records that were the real thing, you had to go to Atlantic.

ATLANTIC RECORDS AND THE STORY OF SOUL

More than a decade before Motown fulfilled Berry Gordy's vision of a musical style that could appeal equally to all of "Young America," an unlikely pair of aspiring recording industry entrepreneurs had scraped together the money to start their own indie label. At the time, Ahmet Ertegun (the twenty-four-year-old son of the former Turkish ambassador to the United States) and his partner Herb Abramson (a Jewish dental student and jazz record collector), were pursuing a dream that was very different from Gordy's: "When we started Atlantic," Erte-gun later explained, "my aim was to record really good strong black blues music."

It was 1947, and the popular black music of the day was being made by vocal harmony groups and hard-driving jump blues bands. Although it was still classified as "Race" music in the *Billboard* magazine charts, soon that name would change to the more familiar (and more enlightened) "Rhythm and Blues." In fact, the staff writer who actually persuaded the influential trade journal to adopt the new designation—Jerry Wexler—was himself about to become one of the chief architects of the Atlantic sound.

When Jerry Wexler joined the young record company in the early 1950s, Atlantic was in the process of de-veloping a talented roster of rhythm and blues performers that included Ruth Brown, LaVerne Baker, the Clovers, and Big Joe Turner. It was also starting to make significant inroads into the national R & B charts by forging a soulful synthesis of a couple of different African-American musical styles. Ertegun described the label's defining sound as "urban black music with some blues feeling," while the music historian Peter Guralnick has referred to it as "a downhome sound with a sophisticated twist."

Although these early records were marketed specifically to the black audience, by 1954 something strange was starting to take place in the world of popular music. Virtually every record the company released was sud-denly being covered by a white performer. Radio disk jockeys had even come up with a new name for the music: "rock 'n' roll." In fact, that very year an Atlantic record—"Shake, Rattle, and Roll"—written by Jesse Stone, the label's chief arranger, and performed by veteran blues shouter Big Joe Turner, had been successfully covered by a young, country music rebel named Bill Haley.

Soon, however, Atlantic's R & B originals started to make their own appearance on the (previously all-white) popular music charts. The company had also just laid out $2,500 to purchase the contract of a laid-back, bluesy crooner and piano player that it hoped would become another profitable addition to the Atlantic roster.

While no one at the time could have foreseen the impact that Ray Charles would have (not only on the for-tunes of Atlantic Records but on the course of American music), it was a match made in heaven. As Peter Gural-nick later expressed it (in his book *Sweet Soul Music*), "Ray Charles and Atlantic Records—in history the two will be forever linked, seen as part of the same inevitable progression in which each was needed to complete the other's destiny. Ray Charles was the stylistic progenitor of soul music, Atlantic the colossus that bestrode its little world."

BROTHER RAY

In his autobiography, *Brother Ray*, Ray Charles modestly recounts the story of how he came to invent a new style of popular music: "Now I'd been singing spirituals since I was three and I'd been hearing the blues for just as long," he explained. "So what could be more natural than to combine them?" While it may have seemed natural to Ray, "the secularization of gospel" (as Jerry Wexler once defined soul music) was not a concept that was obvious to anyone else at the time, nor was it immediately acceptable to many.

After joining Atlantic in 1954, Ray Charles released a couple of singles based on the classic company formula: carefully rehearsed productions of tasteful arrangements, backed by veteran New York studio musicians—all recorded with the unrivaled skill of the label's chief engineer, Tom Dowd. Although Charles had a couple of modest early hits, it was apparent to everyone at the label that something was missing. So, when he suddenly called New York from Atlanta—where he was playing a one-nighter with his own recently assembled seven-piece band—to report that he had an exciting new tune he wanted to record right away, Jerry Wexler hopped on the first flight he could get.

"We met him at his hotel," Wexler recalled years later when asked to describe the moment when soul music was born. "He took us across the street to a nightclub called the Royal Peacock. . . . His band was sitting there all ready to play, just sitting there in their chairs, and he went to the piano and counted off and they hit into 'I Got a Woman,' and that was it."

If the musical structure and churning rhythms of "I Got a Woman" sounded familiar, there was a good reason. For a while now, Ray Charles had been playing around with an old gospel song that contained the line "I've Got a Saviour (Way over Jordan)." Although he kept the tune's ecstatic beat, Ray brazenly substituted a woman as the erotic object of what had previously been a joyous celebration of divine love. "If I was inventing something new, I wasn't aware of it," Ray recalled in his autobiography. "In my mind I was just bringing out more of me."

Wexler immediately recorded the song in the studios of an Atlanta radio station. With his band pumping out fast-paced riffs, Ray sang with an unrestrained passion that had been missing from his earlier efforts. He reached back to what he described as "the earliest part of my life on earth" and let loose with the rough-edged vocal cries and soaring falsetto embellishments that had long been characteristic of black gospel music. The record became Ray's first big hit; but it also provoked a storm of controversy in the African-American community.

"I got letters accusing me of bastardizing God's work," Ray remembered. "A big-time preacher in New York scolded me before his congregation. Many folks saw my music as sacrilegious." Even other African-American performers were offended by Ray's synthesis of the sacred and the profane. The blues singer Big Bill Broonzy protested, "He's crying sanctified. He's mixing the blues and spirituals. He should be singing in church." But Ray Charles has always claimed that such condemnation never bothered him: "I'd always thought that the blues and spirituals were close—close musically, close emotionally—and I was happy to hook 'em up. I was determined to go out and be natural. Everything else would spring from that."

Ray's next records expanded on his new sound. He delved even deeper into his gospel roots, recasting the religious imagery of its songs with an exuberant sensuality ("Hallelujah, I Love Her So"), and he supplemented his band with a trio of female vocalists (the Raeletts) to provide him with a secular choir with which to engage in the call-and-response exchanges that were a crucial aspect of African-American religious music. Ray Charles's appropriation of gospel's power to provoke a feeling of ecstatic release reached its climax in his 1959 release, "What I Say." Set against the incessant Latin-tinged rhythms of his band, each of Ray's cries and moans called forth an equally fevered response from his female choir. Their wordless interchanges mounted into an erotic crescendo that was so intense many radio stations banned the record. Nevertheless, it became Charles's first million seller.

A few months after his enormous success with "What I Say," Ray Charles's Atlantic contract expired and he was offered a deal with a major label (ABC-Paramount) that consisted of an extremely generous financial incentive and complete creative autonomy. Ray went on to create a body of work that—while it encompassed everything from R & B, jazz, and pop to country music and Pepsi commercials ("Uh-Huh!")—transcended all categories.

Not only had both black and white audiences come to accept both Ray's secular transformation of gospel music and his role as the unchallenged "High Priest of Soul" (or "Brother Ray," as he was affectionately known), but gradually he forged the most enduring and powerful bond between performer and audience in the history of African-American music. Years later, looking back at his extraordinary legacy, Ray remained modest about his

FIGURE 4-13. Of the various nicknames Ray Charles picked up during his long and remarkable career, one is particularly revealing. "Brother Ray" not only pays tribute to the unique place he holds in the African-American community but acknowledges the profoundly spiritual nature of his music. Courtesy of Atlantic Records.

Brother Ray

It was the late 1940s and among the biggest rhythm and blues stars of the period were a pair of smooth piano-playing vocalists: the sophisticated, jazz-oriented Nat "King" Cole, and the sultry voiced bluesman Charles Brown. So when Ray began singing on his own early R & B singles, he consciously emulated their suave and soulful styles. In fact, a few years later, when he released his breakthrough hit, "I Got a Woman," Charles claims he was less concerned about the furor provoked by his fusion of spirituals and the blues than he was about "whether Ray Charles as Ray Charles—not as Nat Cole or as Charles Brown—was going to work."

Well, needless to say, it worked very well indeed. The ecstatic brand of secular gospel Ray created—which came to be known as "soul"—would be one of the most potent forces in pop music during the second half of the twentieth century, while Ray Charles would take his rightful place as one of America's greatest natural wonders.

achievement: "Some people told me that I'd invented the sounds they called soul—but I can't take any credit. Soul is just the way black folk sing when they leave themselves alone."

Over the next decade, Atlantic dedicated itself to spreading the gospel of soul. In doing so, it was committing itself to a very different musical vision than the one being pursued by its famous Detroit rival. Although Motown's music drew from the same Southern musical roots, for Gordy, gospel was merely another raw material to be refined and shaped by his highly skilled production staff. In its drive for mass-market acceptance, Motown was reflecting the upwardly mobile values associated with the urban centers of the North.

Meanwhile, the folks at Atlantic were about to initiate a quest for the very source of soul, and it was with this in mind that they headed South.

STAX RECORDS: SOULSVILLE, U.S.A.

Like the old frame house in Detroit that served as the home of the Motown Sound, the abandoned Memphis movie theater that had been converted into the home of Stax Records also bore a sign with its company motto. While *Hitsville, U.S.A.* seemed the embodiment of Motown's mass-market, success-driven ideology, Stax's illuminated marquee bore a message that proclaimed a divergent (yet no less ambitious) corporate identity: *Soulsville, U.S.A.*

To a large extent, however, Stax not only represented the antithesis of the Motown philosophy (and its assembly line production methods), but its approach to record making also contrasted sharply with the self-conscious "professionalism" that had always been a secret source of pride at Atlantic. As described by music historian Robert Palmer in his essay "The Sound of Memphis" (published in the *Rolling Stone Illustrated History of Rock & Roll*), Stax was the embodiment of a unique geographical, cultural, and historical reality:

> The company's studio musicians were a mixed lot. Around half of them were black, while the others were whites from rural backgrounds. . . . The blend these musicians achieved together could only have happened in Memphis—which had been a Southern melting pot for generations—and perhaps only at a time, the mid-sixties, when racial integration still seemed to be a believable political goal. . . . Many of Stax's black musicians had grown up with country and western music. . . . The white musicians had lived in close proximity to blacks and had become steeped in the blues and R & B, and both whites and blacks had participated in or observed at close hand the same sort of fundamentalist church services which had furnished early training and stylistic models for most Stax singers.

Within a few years of its formation in 1960, Stax Records had already evolved its characteristic collaborative recording style, and it even produced a couple of its own hits. Local black vaudeville veteran and WDIA disk jockey Rufus Thomas's funky dance records (such as "Walkin' the Dog") had broken into the national R & B charts, while Thomas's seventeen-year-old daughter Carla's recording of an original tune ("Gee Whiz") made it into the Top Ten. Most significantly, an infectious instrumental ("Green Onions") by the nucleus of Stax's house band—working under the name Booker T. and the M. G.s—actually climbed to number three on the national pop chart.

Attracted by the tiny label's laid-back soulful sound, Atlantic entered into a distribution and promotion agreement with Stax. But it was the stunning debut of a twenty-one-year-old Stax vocalist from Macon, Georgia, that would inspire Atlantic producer Jerry Wexler to go one step further by bringing his own performers down from New York to record at the indie label's Memphis studios.

OTIS REDDING: THE NATURAL PRINCE OF SOUL

Even though it was Otis Redding's first solo record, "These Arms of Mine" (recorded in 1962) seemed to have been the product of a lifetime of experience, pain, desire, and courage. There was something regal about Redding. It was more than just his impressive physical stature, chiseled features, and majestic voice; in Jerry Wexler's words—"Otis was a natural prince."

FIGURE 4-14.   During its heyday in the late 1960s and early 1970s, Stax Records lived up to the proud billing on its famous marquee. Located in a defunct Memphis movie theater, Stax was the archetypal Mom and Pop indie label (except it was founded by a brother and sister, Jim Stewart and Estelle Axton). Courtesy of Fantasy Records.

Soulsville, U.S.A.

Memphis has a proud place in twentieth-century American music history: from the city's famous down-town entertainment district, Beale Street (home to bluesmen from W. C. Handy to B. B. King), to its leg-endary radio station, WDIA (the first in the nation dedicated to programming African-American music), to the Sun Records studio (where Elvis made his first rockabilly singles).

By the mid-1960s, the Stax studio had joined this pantheon by formulating its own unique synthesis of the city's racially diverse genres—a mix of blues, gospel, and country music—that was aptly dubbed the "Memphis Sound." Symbolized by the label's integrated studio band, Booker T. and the M.G.s, Stax assem-bled a multicultural family of session musicians, songwriters, producers, and performers that truly did transform their shabby downtown recording studio into "Soulsville, U.S.A."

He also wrote most of his own songs (often with his close friend, Stax house guitarist Steve Cropper), was a thrilling live performer, and became an astute businessman. In addition to following up his first record with a couple of equally heartwrenching ballads ("Pain in My Heart," "Mr. Pitiful," and "That's How Strong My Love Is"), he cut a couple of engaging duets with a young singer named Carla Thomas (listen to their sassy repartee on "Tramp," for example). In 1965, he had a major hit with an intense and emotionally charged recording of one of his own compositions, "Respect."

Then, a year later, Otis Redding covered the Rolling Stones' American breakthrough, "Satisfaction." The airplay the song received from white radio stations—attracted by the tune's connection to the world of rock—suddenly brought Otis to the attention of a whole new audience. Soon after, when he headlined a Stax tour of Europe, Otis was greeted as a star. On landing in England, he found a limo waiting, courtesy of the Beatles.

In 1967, Otis was added to the lineup of the first large-scale outdoor celebration of rock culture, the Monterey International Pop Festival. In a riveting performance (some of which was captured in the documentary film *Monterey Pop*), Redding won over the almost exclusively white crowd who had come to see Janis Joplin, the Jefferson Airplane, the Mamas and the Papas, the Who, and other bands that had emerged in the wake of the recent British Invasion.

Tragically, just as his enormous artistic potential was being realized—and with soul music entering its most creative and commercially successful period—Otis Redding was killed, along with four members of his band, when his private plane crashed on the way to a concert. He was twenty-six years old. A few months later, his final recording, the wistful "(Sitting On) The Dock of the Bay," became his only number one hit.

SOUL MEN

"It was different down there—a total departure from anything we'd known in New York," Jerry Wexler explained when asked about his decision to record the latest additions to Atlantic's soul roster in Stax's Memphis studio. "It veered away from formal written arrangements and back to head arrangements," Wexler went on. "It's Southern, very Southern," he concluded. "Which is to say extremely ad-lib."

The first hit Atlantic produced using Stax's ad-lib approach was Wilson Pickett's 1965 classic "In the Midnight Hour." The record was a perfect example of Stax's multiracial, collaborative method. The title of the song, by Stax's (Caucasian) studio guitarist Steve Cropper, had come from a throw-away line he noticed Pickett had used on a recent Atlantic live album. When the singer arrived in the Memphis studio, Cropper had already devised a funky little riff for the tune and Pickett and the Stax band worked out the rest of the song during the session. The song became the "Wicked Pickett's" first number one R & B hit.

Next, it was Sam and Dave's turn for the Stax treatment. When the two recently signed Atlantic singers came down to Memphis, they were matched up with Stax's newest songwriting team, Isaac Hayes and David Porter. Although it took a couple of sessions for the two teams to mesh, when they did, Sam (Moore) and Dave (Prater) unleashed a succession of soul masterpieces, including "You Don't Know Her Like I Know Her," "Hold on I'm Coming," and their classic anthem, "Soul Man" (which was covered by Jake and Elwood—the "Blues Brothers"—in the movie of the same name). Not only did Sam and Dave bring an ecstatic, gospel-based call-and-response fervor to their roster of hit recordings, but soul's dynamic duo were one of the most explosive live acts of the era.

As Peter Guralnick writes in his definitive history of the style, *Sweet Soul Music,* "Sam and Dave established Stax once and for all as pop contenders—and worlds apart from Motown, in intent as well as effect. They established themselves also as Stax's hottest act. And their success set a pattern for a wealth of hits, by a variety of different acts." By this time, however, Atlantic had already moved on, heading even further South, to what looked like greener pastures in Muscle Shoals.

FROM MEMPHIS TO MUSCLE SHOALS

Compared to Memphis, Muscle Shoals, Alabama, was just a country backwater. But amid the rolling hills and cotton fields, a couple of makeshift recording studios had sprung up, operated by a handful of good-ol' boys in love with rhythm and blues. And though it was a long way from New York, in 1965, when a twenty-five-year-old hospital worker named Percy Sledge came along with a righteous voice and a heartbreaking ballad entitled "When a Man Loves a Woman," local producer Rick Hall knew just who to call. After hearing the record, Atlantic immediately signed Sledge, and by the following spring the song he'd recorded in that nondescript Muscle Shoals studio had become the number one pop record in America.

Since tensions were beginning to escalate in its relationship with Stax, Atlantic decided to book Wilson Pickett on a plane to Muscle Shoals. "I looked down out of the plane and I see black folks pickin' cotton," Pickett remembered later with astonishment. He was even more incredulous when he landed and saw Rick Hall waiting to meet him. "How did I know Jerry Wexler would send me to some big Southern white cat?" But it didn't take long for Wilson to see the method in Wexler's madness: "Rick Hall made things grow down there. What happened was beautiful. But I never would have believed any of it before it happened."

Working out of producer Rick Hall's Fame Studio with a remarkable collection of white Muscle Shoals musicians (including pianist Spooner Oldham, guitarist Jimmy Johnson, and drummer Roger Hawkins) along with Memphis imports (such as bassist Tommy Cogbill and guitarist Chips Moman) and the interracial Memphis Horns, Pickett made classic examples of Southern soul such as "Land of 1000 Dances," "Mustang Sally," and "Funky Broadway." Once again, it seemed, Atlantic had discovered a Southern shangri-la of soul. Now Jerry Wexler was about to arrive with its queen.

ARETHA FRANKLIN: THE QUEEN OF SOUL

When Atlantic signed Aretha Franklin in 1967, she was hardly a novice. From the time she was fourteen, Aretha had been touring with her father, the Rev. C. L. Franklin, one of the most renowned preachers of his time, as a soloist in his choir. From the very beginning, young Aretha had been embraced as a gospel prodigy, and she seemed destined to become one of the great singers of African-American sacred music.

Then, in 1960, when she was eighteen, Aretha decided to follow in the footsteps of another former gospel legend—Sam Cooke—who had himself recently "crossed over" from the divine harmonies of the Soul Stirrers to pop fame with the sensual ballad "You Send Me." Although she had to contend with some of the same condemnation he had experienced for "abandoning the church," Aretha was signed (by veteran producer John Hammond) to a five-year contract with Columbia Records' popular music division.

From the moment he heard her first demo tape, Hammond—whose illustrious career had already included sessions with both Bessie Smith and Billie Holiday—declared Aretha "an untutored genius, the best voice I've heard since Billie Holiday." In fact, when he began to record her first album, Hammond reverted to some of the same concepts he had used with Lady Day back in the 1930s. He provided her with some blues and pop standards to sing, hired a small ensemble of jazz masters to accompany her, and kept things relatively loose and simple. Franklin's debut turned out to be a pleasant, mainstream record with flashes of gospel passion that included one modest R & B hit.

And things went downhill from there. Columbia, slow to pick up on the revolutionary changes in black music being generated most notably by Motown and Atlantic, smothered Aretha in strings and loaded her down with trite material that drained the last remaining vitality from her voice. By 1966, when her Columbia contract expired, it seemed so had her career. Instead, she signed with Atlantic, went down to Muscle Shoals, and emerged as the undisputed Queen of Soul.

Working with the same nucleus of white musicians Wexler had assembled for Wilson Pickett's recent Fame Studio sessions, Aretha's first Atlantic recording—"I Never Loved a Man (The Way I Love You)"—quickly fell into place. In the words of Peter Guralnick, it was "one of the most momentous takes in the history of rhythm and blues, in fact in the history of American vernacular music." Later, when he was asked the secret of his success with Aretha, Jerry Wexler said it was simple: "I took her to church, sat her down at the piano, and let her be herself."

Unfortunately, the same session that is often heralded as ushering in soul music's "Golden Age" can also be viewed, in retrospect, as foreshadowing its imminent demise. This is the "infamous" part of the story. It's an

FIGURE 4-15. When asked to explain his role in the coronation of Aretha Franklin as the "Queen of Soul," her producer at Atlantic Records, Jerry Wexler, responded simply: "I took her to church, sat her down at the piano, and let her be herself." Photo by Lee Tanner.

Aretha: Long Live the Queen

By bringing the unbridled passion and ecstatic call-and-response tradition of gospel music to secular songs addressing everything from love to racial and sexual empowerment, Aretha Franklin unleashed a string of soul classics—such as "I Never Loved a Man (The Way I Love You)," "Respect," "Chain of Fools," "Baby I Love You," and "Think"—that immediately became Top Ten pop hits.

Beginning in 1967, Aretha also won her first of seven Grammys in a row for Best R & B Performance by a Female Vocalist. At last count, she has placed over sixty singles on *Billboard* magazine's Hot 100 chart and is credited with generating more million-selling hits than any woman in recording history. She has gone on to amass a total of fifteen Grammys, including a well-deserved Lifetime Achievement Award.

episode that suggests that the recent reports about the discovery of a multicultural musical utopia in the American Southland had been greatly exaggerated.

According to Jerry Wexler, it was *supposed* to have been an integrated session: "I had asked Rick Hall to hire a certain horn section out of Memphis which was mostly black. And I wanted that section, because my whole rhythm section was white. . . . And Rick Hall just plain forgot." So, as the celebration in honor of the completion of Aretha Franklin's first Atlantic side moved into high gear, her husband (and manager) Ted White—who was already leery about Aretha working in a Southern studio with an all-white band—got into a confrontation with one of the musicians. Things soon escalated and, in the heat of the moment, a couple of the usual racial epithets were exchanged; some say a gun made a brief appearance. The session came to an abrupt, chaotic, and bitter end, and Aretha would never again return to Muscle Shoals.

But, in a way, Muscle Shoals would come to her. Wexler managed to lure the key members of the Fame Studio band (who *had* achieved a wonderful rapport with Aretha) to a New York session that also included the veteran R & B tenor saxophonist King Curtis. Soon, Atlantic not only had the B side for their single but enough material for what would be a historic debut album as well. Within a few weeks of its release, "I Never Loved a Man (The Way I Love You)" sold a million copies—Franklin's first single had gone gold. So did the next. And the next. And the one after that.

Each of Aretha's first six singles became Top Ten pop hits (and all but one went to number one on the R & B charts). When the year ended, she won the Grammy for the best R & B performance by a female artist. It was an award she would claim every year for the next seven years in a row. After a while, music industry insiders began to refer to the category as the "Aretha Award." Through her profound artistry—and soul—Aretha Franklin became a cultural icon who transcended every musical and racial boundary. Here's how Gerri Hershey describes Franklin's impact during this period in her book *Nowhere to Run:*

> She united pop and R & B audiences too. In black neighborhoods and white universities, in the clubs and on the charts, her hits came like cannonballs, blowing holes in the stylized bouffant and chiffon Motown sound, a strong new voice with a range that hit the heavens and a center of gravity very close to the earth. Here was a voice with a sexual payload that made the doo-wop era, the girl groups, and the Motown years seem like a pimply adolescence.

Remarkably, these qualities are perhaps most powerfully demonstrated on what was selected to be the very first song on her very first Atlantic album: "Respect." Not only was it a sign of Franklin's supreme self-confidence to take on a song that was so indelibly associated with the great Otis Redding, but by deconstructing the song and infusing it with her unbridled intensity (along with a chorus of "sock-it-to-me's"), she actually made the song her own. When Redding heard it, he turned to Jerry Wexler and said, "I just lost my song. That girl took it away from me."

Wexler couldn't disagree. "Aretha added another dimension to the song. This was almost a feminist clarion," he explains. "Whenever women heard the record, it was like a tidal wave of sororal unity. . . . It was a very interesting mix: an intuitive feminist outcry, a sexual statement, and an announcement of dignity . . . a minority person making a statement of pride without sloganeering." Although Aretha *was* able to infuse multiple layers of meaning into a single word, given the historical context, "Respect" does resonate with racial connotations that require little imagination to decode. And soul music's intimate connection to the black church provides a clear source for the metaphor that lies just below the surface of her version of Otis's song.

In the great African-American spirituals that evolved during slavery, images drawn from both the Old and New Testaments almost always had a double edge. While references to "making it to the Promised Land," for example, had an obvious religious significance, such allusions also clearly resonated with more immediate "political" intentions. While soul music was originally concerned with transposing gospel's ecstatic fervor from spiritual love to songs that sang the praises of more earthly passions, during the 1960s African-American performers increasingly began to introduce explicit social messages into their songs.

For example, on his 1964 R & B album *Good News* (which happens to be the standard definition of the word "gospel"), Sam Cooke recorded "A Change Is Gonna Come," which he had written specifically to address the contemporary racial struggle. And that same year, the great Chicago-based R & B group the Impressions released a song (by its main songwriter, Curtis Mayfield) with a similar optimistic theme—"Keep on Pushing."

By 1967, however—when Aretha's demand for "Respect" was blasting out of America's radios—the civil rights movement had escalated well beyond the previous generation's freedom marches and nonviolent Southern sit-ins. The bombing of black churches, the burning of urban ghettos, and the rise of Black Panther militancy (and Black Power rhetoric) had combined to traumatize the nation. Then, just one year later, in the wake of the assassination of Martin Luther King Jr., the flames of rage that engulfed cities across the country also would consume the feelings of optimism and brotherhood inherent in Sixties soul.

"That was the turning point," Booker T. (the black leader of Stax's integrated house band) admitted. "And it happened in Memphis," he added, acknowledging one of the many tragic ironies of the event. In fact, on the day of King's murder, black Stax staffers had to walk Steve Cropper and "Duck" Dunn (the two white members of the M.G.'s) to their cars through an angry Memphis mob. At King's funeral, a grief-stricken Aretha Franklin—who had known the slain civil rights leader since she was a child—sang his favorite gospel hymn, "Precious Lord."

Despite the chill that descended on the soul community that day in Memphis, over the next few years soul music itself not only continued to thrive but developed in creative new directions while becoming even more socially conscious. In fact, only a few months after the postassassination fires had cooled, a record was released that symbolized not only the radical transformation taking place in black popular music but also the empowering nature of its message. Unfortunately, the response to the record also reflects a deepening racial split that was once again about to divide the pop music audience.

JAMES BROWN: GODFATHER OF SOUL

Musically, James Brown's 1968 recording "Say It Loud—I'm Black and I'm Proud" was another example of the rhythmic revolution the performer had been expanding on ever since his 1965 breakthrough "Papa's Got a Brand New Bag." Lyrically, the new song was intended to be an uplifting anthem of racial pride at a moment of deep division and despair. In his autobiography, *James Brown: The Godfather of Soul,* Brown describes the song's motivation: "You shouldn't have to teach people [that] they should be proud," he wrote. "They should feel it from just living where they do. But it was necessary to teach pride then, and I think the song did a lot of good for a lot of people."

Not everyone, however, embraced Brown's soulful anthem to racial pride. "That song scared people too," Brown went on to explain. "The song cost me a lot of my crossover audience. The racial make-up at my concerts was mostly black after that." Although "Say It Loud" (already a number one R & B hit) did manage to climb into the pop Top Ten as well,—it was the last time James Brown would achieve this feat. A backlash was gathering momentum. "It got up to number ten on the pop chart," the singer recalled, "but a lot of people still didn't understand it. They thought I was saying kill the honky, and every time I did something else around the idea of black pride another top forty station quit playing my records." But looking back on the furor, Brown has no regrets: "No matter what people thought, I had to say what I believed needed saying and do what I believed needed doing."

In fact, from the very beginning of his career, Brown had always pursued his own uncompromising artistic vision. Through sheer force of will and a nonstop schedule of live shows characterized by a heart-stopping intensity that earned him another of his many professional nicknames—"The Hardest Working Man in Show Business"—James Brown became one of the most successful and innovative performers in the history of African-American popular music.

Back in 1956, when Brown was first "discovered" by Ralph Bass (a talent scout for the independent King label) in a tiny R & B club in Macon, Georgia, he had already begun to formulate a unique stripped-down style that made few concessions to mainstream taste. As is obvious from Bass's description, he was also well on his way to establishing his take no prisoners live act: "I [didn't] know James Brown from a hole in the ground, and I went to the club that night and saw him do his show, crawling on his stomach and saying 'Please, please, please'—he must have said *please* for about ten minutes."

Bass brought James Brown to Cinncinnati to record the song he had heard that night for Federal, a subsidiary of King Records, one of the oldest and most successful of the Midwestern indie labels. But when King's notoriously hard-nosed owner, Syd Nathan, heard Brown's recording of "Please, Please, Please" he was not impressed. "He said I was out of my mind to bring Brown from Macon to Cincinnati—and pay his fare," Bass recalled. "All he's saying is one word!" Nathan complained. Despite Syd Nathan's skepticism, "Please, Please, Please" became an R & B hit. Over the next couple of years, however, few of Brown's records made the charts, and those that did—like his 1958 number one song "Try Me"—reflected more traditional rhythm and blues styles.

Meanwhile, James Brown was touring nonstop, putting together a permanent working band, and honing a stage show that was attracting a devoted following. According to Robert Palmer's account of this phase, the performer's evolution (in the *Rolling Stone Illustrated History of Rock & Roll*): "His band was the toughest, loudest,

FIGURE 4-16. James Brown in action (c. 1965). They didn't call him "The Hardest Working Man in Show Business" for nothing. Archive photo. Frank Driggs Collection.

James Brown: Man of Many Titles

Over the course of his fifty-year career, James Brown acquired a long list of titles that attest to the powerful and pervasive impact of his music. During the 1960s, for example, there were few who would challenge his status as "Soul Brother Number One," while, in the 1970s, he emerged as the undisputed "Grand Minister of Funk." A decade later, a new generation of hip-hop pioneers (who built much of their music on samples from Brown's hits) acknowledged their debt by dubbing him the "Godfather of Rap."

and most together (as well it should have been, since fluffed notes were reportedly penalized by heavy fines). His clothes were the flashiest. . . . His dancing was the wildest, the most spectacularly acrobatic, the most perfectly controlled."

Although the participatory fervor of such shows can be viewed as secularized versions of the African-American church service at its most ecstatic, Brown's music was actually moving back in time past soul's gospel roots to the primal source of all black music: the rhythms of Africa. Robert Palmer's description of the dramatic changes taking place in Brown's style highlight this Afrocentric element:

> The change was probably determined at least in part by the structure of Brown's new songs. He continued to work in gospel and blues forms, but he also added another kind of composition: Brown would sing a semi-improvised, loosely organized melody that wandered while the band riffed rhythmically on a single chord, the horns tersely punctuating Brown's declamatory phrases. With no chord changes and precious little melodic variety to sustain listener interest, rhythm became everything. Brown and his musicians and arrangers began to treat every instrument and voice in the group as if each were a drum.

By 1963, James Brown's revolutionary sound was already familiar to attendees of the singer's live shows. In fact, it had already been documented on his 1963 album, *Live at the Apollo*. At a time when live recordings were rare (singles being the medium of choice for the R & B audience), this album would prove to be Brown's greatest commercial success—as well as one of his most significant artistic triumphs. It became a fixture on the pop music charts for over a year (climbing to briefly to the number two spot), earning Brown his first piece of the new crossover pie.

THE TAMI SHOW: CELLULOID TIME CAPSULE (IN BLACK AND WHITE)

While *Live at the Apollo* may have caught the aural component of James Brown in person, the visual drama, showmanship, and incendiary dance routines that made Brown's performances so legendary wouldn't be documented for a couple of years. Fortunately, however, the cameras were rolling at a 1965 concert that featured Brown at his most inspired. *The TAMI Show* (the initials stood for Teen Age Music International) was an all-star gathering of contemporary pop acts produced specifically for television. Although the undisputed highlight of the event is James Brown's over-the-edge rendition of "Please, Please, Please," the 1965 concert film figures prominently in pop histories of the Sixties for another reason.

With a cast that includes the Beach Boys, Chuck Berry, the Supremes, the Rolling Stones, the Barbarians, Marvin Gaye, and Jan and Dean, *The TAMI Show* has been celebrated for being a kind of a celluloid time-capsule capturing a rare interlude of pop music heterogeneity. For there have only been a few brief periods when such a racially and stylistically diverse collection of performers simultaneously shared the stage and the pop charts.

By 1965, Motown's strong presence in the TAMI film should come as no surprise. And, as we've seen, James Brown was riding the crest of his own crossover wave (his recently released single "Out of Sight" had become his biggest hit to date). By including the Barbarians, a Boston-based garage rock band that had just had a minor hit with "Are You a Boy or Are You a Girl?" (a song that poked fun at its members' prematurely fashionable long hair), the show even featured a representative of rock 'n' roll's long tradition of now-you-see-'em-now-you-don't novelty acts. The inclusion of Jan and Dean and the Beach Boys, however, requires a little more explanation.

SURF'S UP

As we've seen, the early 1960s was not exactly the teen-idol wasteland portrayed in so many rock 'n' roll histories. From one coast to the other, the music's creative energy had been harnessed by a new generation of ambitious entrepreneurs, and scores of talented young newcomers had taken over the charts. In New York, Brill Building writer/producers were crafting an extended series of "girl group" hits. In the Midwest, Berry Gordy's quality-con-

FIGURE 4-17.   During the early 1960s, the Beach Boys released a series of surf-sound singles (such as "Surfin' Safari," "Surfin' U.S.A.," and "Surfer Girl") that conjured up a mythical California dreamworld out of their ethereal close-harmony vocals and Chuck Berry–based riffs. Archive photos. Frank Driggs Collection.

The Beach Boys: Surf Sound Symphonies

By 1965, when they released "California Girls," Brian Wilson—the group's songwriter and producer—had transformed the surf sound into a multisection mini-symphony. A year later, the Beach Boys made what are generally recognized as their masterpieces: "Good Vibrations," a three-and-a-half-minute single on which Wilson lavished six months of obsessive attention (and almost $20,000 in studio costs), and the pioneering "concept album" *Pet Sounds* (which directly inspired the Beatles to conjure up their own experimental, multitrack magnum opus—*Sgt. Pepper's Lonely Hearts Club Band* in 1967).

trol techniques had turned Motown into a pop music powerhouse. Soon Memphis soul would bring the passions of black gospel into the musical mainstream. Meanwhile, on the West Coast, a fresh new sound was capturing the California dream of golden-haired youth and the quest for the perfect wave: They called it "surf music."

The surfer subculture that flourished on the beaches of Southern California had, by the beginning of the 1960s, evolved its own fashions and slang, as well as its own homegrown music. Records by Dick Dale and the Deltones—the first that specifically alluded to the surfer lifestyle—were propelled by Dale's twangy, reverberating guitar sound. In 1961, the band had a local hit with "Let's Go Trippin' " and Dale (who was himself a veteran of the Malibu beach scene) had become renowned as the "King of the Surf Guitar." (Although Dale didn't have much of an impact nationally at the time, his guitar sound had an enormous influence; in the 1990s, Dale's status as a cult figure was reinforced when his music was used by Quentin Tarrintino for the soundtrack of his film *Pulp Fiction*.)

Dick Dale has claimed that his distinctive guitar sound—filled with roiling, high-energy runs—was actually a re-creation of the strangely musical sound a surfer hears from inside the crest of a wave. Dale's guitar effects were adopted by a number of other Southern California bands, and soon a couple of their surfer-slang-titled instrumentals (including "Pipeline" by the Chantays and "Wipe Out" by the Safaris) began surfacing on the national pop charts. Perhaps the most significant aspect of the music at this point was that it seemed to revive (after a few years' absence) one of rock 'n' roll's most potent images—young white kids with guitars.

Although only one of the three Wilson brothers, who formed the core of the Beach Boys, actually participated in the sport itself, it was enough to give a veneer of authenticity to their odes to the surfer lifestyle; in 1961, the first of these—simply entitled "Surfin' "—became a regional hit. Written by Brian Wilson, like most of their early work the record grafted their smooth, complex harmonies (modeled on those of a mainstream vocal group from the early 1950s called the Four Freshmen) to a cruising rockabilly beat. After signing with the West Coast's only major label—Capitol—the Beach Boys' next series of singles ("Surfin' Safari," "Surfin' U.S.A.," and "Surfer Girl") introduced a fresh new pop sound to the national audience.

Inspired by the Beach Boys' surf sound, a Southern California duo called Jan and Dean took an unrecorded Brian Wilson song ("Surf City") to the very top of the pop charts in 1963. Although Jan and Dean had earned their place as performers (and hosts) of the TAMI show with a string of Top Twenty surf hits (such as "Honolulu Lulu," "Dead Man's Curve," and "The Little Old Lady from Pasadena"), a year after the concert was filmed, Jan was almost killed in a high-speed car crash and the group's career came to an abrupt end. The Beach Boys, by contrast, were just about to enter their most creative period.

By the time of their appearance on the TAMI show, the Beach Boys had become one of the biggest rock 'n' roll acts in the country. In "I Get Around," "Help Me Rhonda," and their tribute to the homestate beauties, "California Girls," Brian Wilson conjured up a mythic teen paradise; and as a result of the increasingly intricate and shimmering productions he devised, the Beach Boys' records took on an almost visual immediacy. Under the powerful influence of pop music maestro Phil Spector, Brian would soon begin work on his own obsessive, multi-layered studio creations (including the album *Pet Sounds* and the tour-de-force single "Good Vibrations").

The Beach Boys had clearly earned their place on the TAMI show lineup, and by sharing the stage with Chuck Berry, the more perceptive of their fans also were treated to a spontaneous lesson in rock history. To anyone who was paying attention, the Beach Boys' enormous debt to Chuck Berry would have been obvious. Following Berry's example, Brian Wilson crafted teen anthems whose lyrics were laced with keenly observed allusions to fast cars and pretty teenage girls. And—as should have been even more apparent—it was Berry's trademark guitar riffs that formed the backbone of the Beach Boys' own musical hooks. In fact, one of their early hits ("Surfin' U.S.A.") was virtually an exact copy of that Chuck Berry classic, "Sweet Little Sixteen." (Following a lawsuit, Berry would be awarded partial songwriting credit and a share of the royalties for "Surfin' U.S.A.")

Motown, soul, surf, and a novelty hit by a one-hit-wonder Boston garage band: The TAMI show was a model of diversity that harkened back to that brief period when Chuck, Elvis, Little Richard, and Jerry Lee had shared the stage at the dawn of the music's Golden Age. The final segment of the TV concert's line-up, however—a collection of bands that included Gerry and the Pacemakers and the Rolling Stones—offered the teenage audience something their older brothers and sisters had *never* encountered on a rock 'n' roll stage: Englishmen!

In 1963—only two years before the TAMI show was filmed—a final tally of the year's Top Ten hits would have revealed a reassuringly familiar demographic portrait: 106 singles made it into the *Billboard* pop chart and every one was by an American performer or band. But just one year later, it seemed the nature of reality had suddenly been transformed. Billboard's 1964 annual survey revealed that approximately one-third (31 out of 101) of the year's Top Ten records were by non-Americans. No, it wasn't the "Twilight Zone"; it was the "British Invasion."

THE BRITISH ARE COMING . . . .

For most Americans, "Beatlemania" seemed like just another of those weird media tempests that suddenly blow through the culture and just as suddenly disappear leaving behind a scattering of quaint artifacts (perhaps an "I Love Ringo" button) followed by the inevitable question: "Whatever happened to . . . ?"

FIGURE 4-18.   The Beatles at the Cavern Club, c. 1961. Mathews. Author's collection.

Meet the Beatles

At the time this photo was taken, the Beatles' repertoire consisted of an assortment of rock, pop, and R & B cover songs that included Chuck Berry's "Roll over Beethoven," the recent Broadway show tune "Till There Was You," Fats Waller's "Your Feets Too Big," and the Shirelles' "Baby It's You." But a year later, when the band went into the Abbey Road studios, George Martin (their new producer) selected two Beatles originals—"Love Me Do"/"P.S. I Love you"—for their first single.

   By playing their own instruments and writing their own songs, the Beatles helped reestablish the primacy of the performer that had existed during rock 'n' roll's "Golden Age."

There's no disputing that when the Beatles made their appearance, they had all the necessary attributes to qualify for flash-in-the-pan novelty status: a silly love song, peculiar accents, funny haircuts, and shrieking hordes of teenage girls. "An English rock 'n' roll group? What'll they think of next?"

   But whatever one thought about their significance or potential longevity, at least one had to give them credit for the blinding speed and staggering scale of their success. On December 26, 1963, Capitol Records finally agreed to release a Beatles single (having passed on earlier records by the group for all the obvious reasons cited above). Ten days later, the record went gold, and by the middle of January "I Want to Hold Your Hand" was the number one single in America.

By February 7, 1964, when the Beatles landed at Kennedy International Airport to a welcoming throng of four thousand screaming fans, they had five singles and three albums racing up the charts. Two days later when they appeared on the *Ed Sullivan Show,* an estimated audience of seventy million home viewers (the most in television history) tuned in to see what all the fuss was about. By March, industry estimates indicated that Beatles' records were then accounting for 60 percent of all singles sold in the United States. That same month, their first LP, *Meet the Beatles,* became the best-selling album in history; on April 4, the Beatles held each of the top five slots on the Billboard singles chart.

There was more to "Beatlemania," however, than just the mania, and it's to this part of their story that one must turn for an understanding of the group's profound musical and cultural impact.

IN THE BEGINNING . . . THERE WAS LIVERPOOL

In Liverpool, England, during the mid-1950s, even youthful fantasies of rock 'n' roll success rarely extended beyond the banks of the Mersey River. The damp gray seaport itself had little of the romantic aura that it would later assume in the official myth of the Beatles. To working-class teenagers in Liverpool, not only did the America of Elvis, Little Richard, Buddy Holly, and the Everly Brothers seem a distant musical Oz, but even the London of Lonnie Donnegan seemed very far away indeed.

In 1956, Lonnie Donnegan had become the reigning king of British pop. Donnegan's repertoire consisted of an eclectic assortment of blues and traditional American folk songs that his band performed on the kind of homemade instruments that had been characteristic of African-American jug bands of the 1920s (washboards, comb kazoos, a broomstick and washtub bass, and acoustic guitar). This style—which also was known as "skiffle"—was simple, good-time music with a jaunty dance beat. And since it was inexpensive to reproduce (only the acoustic guitar or banjo was store-bought) and easy to play (three of four basic chords would do), hundreds of British teens suddenly began to form their own skiffle bands.

The skiffle craze was pushed into high gear when Lonnie Donnegan achieved the British version of the Impossible Dream: In 1956, his single, "Rock Island Line"—a song he learned from a recording by the celebrated folk-blues singer Leadbelly—crossed the Atlantic and became a Top Ten American pop hit. Among the dozens of amateur skiffle groups that immediately added the song to their own repertoire was one whose leader, a fifteen-year-old named John Lennon, had named the "Quarry Men" (after Liverpool's Quarry Bank School that he and his bandmates attended).

In 1957, the Quarry Men made a significant change in its personnel. Paul McCartney, a Liverpool lad (who attended another local school) had recently acquired an inexpensive guitar and had painstakingly figured out the basic skiffle chords. Soon after Paul joined the group, he also began writing some songs with John and it was during these sessions that they discovered a mutual passion: American rock 'n' roll. Lonnie Donnegan's quaint folk tunes were all well and good, but what they really wanted was to cut loose "like Elvis" (John) or "like Little Richard" (Paul).

Gradually, the skiffle craze began to peter out; rock 'n' roll records from "the States" became increasingly accessible, and some of the American performers whose popularity had begun to fade back home found an enthusiastic audience waiting at every stop on their British tours. At this point, a slightly younger (but quietly serious) Liverpool guitar player named George Harrison joined the Quarry Men. Soon a change in the band's name signaled a change in its musical direction. After a brief stint as "Johnny and the Moondogs," and the "Silver Beatles," they finally settled on the "Beatles" (a homage to another of their rock 'n' roll idols, Buddy Holly, whose band—the Crickets—provided the insect inspiration.)

So, at a time when the chilling effects of payola hearings and Top Forty radio were reining in the original wild men of rock 'n' roll (and pop music was increasingly being shaped by Brill Building pros or being passed through Motown quality-control checklists), Liverpool teens had begun picking up electric guitars and bashing out enthusiastic approximations of mid-1950s classic rock.

In his book *Shout: The Beatles in Their Generation,* Philip Norman offers a portrait of the city circa 1957 that helps explain how this dank gray seaport became the birthplace of the British invasion:

> Liverpool stood closer to America than any other place in Britain. There was still, in 1957, a transatlantic passenger route, plied by ships returning weekly to tie up behind the Dock Road's grim castle walls. With them came young Liverpublian deckhands and stewards whom the neighbors called the "Cunard Yanks" because of their flashy New York clothes. As well as Times Square trinkets for their girlfriends and panoramic lampshades of the Manhattan skyline for their mother's front room, the Cunard Yanks brought home records not available in Britain. Rhythm and blues, the genesis of rock 'n' roll, sung by still obscure names such as Chuck Berry and Ike Turner, pounded through the terraced back streets each Saturday night as the newly returned mariners got ready to hit the town.

Inflamed by the raw power of American rock 'n' roll, the Beatles and their Liverpool compatriots established a thriving local music scene that gradually began to evolve its own distinctive sound. Named for the murky river that flowed through the city, it became known as the "Mersey beat"—or just "beat music."

As Charlie Gillett defines it in his book *The Sound of the City,* "Beat music . . . was always conceived as popular music, essentially as a local dance club alternative to the national forms of pop music distributed by the music industry and played by the BBC." Other writers recognized in its steady pounding beat and in the exuberant freedom of its vocals the back-to-basics musical philosophy that has always been the defining characteristic of the typical rock 'n' roll "garage band" (a phenomenon that would later be repeated in other musical microcosms—from CBGBs to Seattle).

By 1960, the Beatles and other Liverpool bands were also beginning to export the new Mersey beat. The initial target of this preliminary British invasion was Hamburg, Germany. The bars and strip joints that lined Hamburg's tawdry entertainment district, the Reeperbahn, were hungry for American rock 'n' roll—even if it *was* played by British bands. And the Hamburg experience turned out to be a crucial one for the group as it struggled to hone the disparate influences it had been absorbing (Elvis, Little Richard, Chuck Berry, Buddy Holly, girl groups, and doo-wop) into a coherent style. Here's how the critic Lester Bangs described the significance of the band's baptism under fire:

> Hamburg was a crucible, a proving ground, a place where groups were required to play loud and fast and raw all night, hour after hour, using stimulants to maintain the pace, forcing members of the band who thought they could not sing to take the mike when the leader's lungs gave out. Things got wild, and the sound took on a mania that became a crucial factor in the coming assault on the United States.

When they returned to Liverpool, the Beatles joined the dozens of other beat groups like Cass and the Cassanovas, Ian and the Zodiacs, the Searchers, Gerry and the Pacemakers, and Rory Storm and the Hurricanes (whose drummer, "Ringo Starr," would soon be making a major career move) that were filling the city's run-down ballrooms, concert halls, and ice rinks with hordes of passionate teenage fans. But not even the worst of these venues was quite so pungently seedy as the underground chamber called the Cavern Club that would soon become the Beatles' home turf, as well as the site of their imminent discovery.

In 1961, a homegrown "fanzine," simply called *Mersey Beat,* had been inaugurated to keep track of Liverpool's fast-paced pop music scene. One of the local businesses that began distributing the paper was a furniture store with a well-stocked record department operated by Brian Epstein, the owner's twenty-seven-year-old son. When a brief item in the second issue of *Mersey Beat* happened to mention the existence of a Beatles single (actually it was an anonymous back-up session they had made in Hamburg), the group's fans began showing up asking for the record. Epstein was intrigued enough to venture down the stone steps, past the packs of dancing teens, into the dank recesses of the Cavern Club to see what all the fuss was about.

That was November 1961. Before the year was out, Brian Epstein had become the Beatles' manager and, using his record-industry contacts, he'd secured the band an audition with Decca Records. Although the London-based label decided to pass on the group (preferring instead to sign a London-based band, Brian and the Tremeloes), by the spring of the next year EMI agreed to give the Beatles a shot. In June, George Martin, an executive with EMI's Parlophone label, supervised the Beatles' audition, and in July he sent word to Epstein that he wanted to sign the group.

The Beatles who walked into EMI's Abbey Road studios in September 1962 to cut their first record was a very different band from the one Brian Epstein had seen up on the Cavern stage less than a year before. For one thing, Brian had entirely "re-imaged" the group for optimum pop appeal: Gone were the greasy waterfall pompadours, scruffy jeans, and black leather jackets, and, in their place, the distinctive bowl-shaped "Beatle" hairstyles and matching velvet-collared suits that soon would be famous around the world. Under pressure from George Martin, Epstein had also deftly replaced their current drummer, Pete Best, with Ringo Starr, a rock-steady veteran of the Liverpool scene.

Although the band had an extensive repertoire of covers (everything from Chuck Berry's "Memphis" to the recent Broadway showtune "Till There Was You," to a 1930s Fats Waller novelty song, "Your Feets Too Big"), George Martin chose two of John and Paul's own songs for the Beatles' début single. The record—"Love Me Do"/"P.S. I Love You"—was released on October 4, 1962. It gradually moved up the British pop chart (assisted by an order of ten thousand copies from Epstein's own record department), and by the end of the year it quietly broke into the Top Twenty. Meanwhile, the Beatles had returned to the studio to cut a follow-up single. After the band's first take of "Please Please Me," George Martin pressed the button to the studio intercom and announced, "Gentlemen, you have just made your first Number One."

The record was released in January 1963 and by March it had, as Martin promised, become the number one song in the country, as did their next single ("From Me to You")—and their next ("She Loves You"), whose chorus of "Yeah, Yeah, Yeah" 's became an early Beatle trademark. In addition, each song was a "Lennon-McCartney" original. So, while their live shows and early LPs continued to pay homage to American mentors such as Chuck Berry ("Roll over Beethoven"), the Isley Brothers ("Twist and Shout"), the Shirelles ("Baby It's You"), and Motown ("Money—That's What I Want"), one of the most significant aspects of the Beatles' success was the fact that they were a "band" whose members played their own instruments and sang their own songs.

As Charlie Gillett has written (in *The Sound of the City*), "The Beatles re-established the singer's autonomy in the studio. They were able to do so because they played their own instruments, and were therefore less subject to their producer than a studio group would have been. They came to their recording sessions with their own songs, many of which they had tried before live audiences on their tours."

Meanwhile, the so-called Fab Four was breaking into the British mainstream by appearing on the pop music shows that the BBC had recently begun scheduling on radio and TV. Not only did these appearances provide promotional support for the band's records, but they also exposed the Beatles' rapidly expanding audience to their refreshingly witty and charming personalities. Both their skyrocketing success and their celebrated charm were magnified to extraordinary proportions when they were invited to appear at London's prestigious Albert Hall as part of the Royal Command Performance.

An annual event hosted by the British monarch, it was typically a staid affair offering a variety of popular entertainment to its refined, upper-class audience, all in support of some suitably worthwhile charity. But the day after 1963's Royal Command Performance, every newspaper headline proclaimed its own version of the same remarkable story: "Beatles Rock the Royals," reported one tabloid, "Night of Triumph for Four Young Lads," read another, but the most memorable, was the one-word headline coined by the Daily Mirror: "Beatlemania!" Meanwhile, every newspaper's account of the band's triumphant performance gave special attention to the "cheeky" introduction provided to the group's final song.

As the band prepared to play their usual show-closer, "Twist and Shout," an impish smile filled John's face as he walked up to the mike: "Will you people in the cheaper seats clap your hands, and the rest of you . . . if you'll just rattle your jewelry!" It was exactly this kind of irreverant humor that made the Beatles so appealing. They were just so infectiously good-humored, and the joy in their own success so palpable, that no one could resist. In fact, many commentators have suggested that it was just this spirit of joyous vitality that was most responsible for the Beatles' abrupt conquest of America. For at the end of 1963, there was not a lot of joy in America.

THE FOLK REVIVAL: MUSIC WITH A SOCIAL CONSCIENCE

About two weeks after the Beatles' Royal Command triumph and just as Brian Epstein was laying the groundwork for their U.S. début, President John F. Kennedy was assasinated and America was immediately plunged into a period of deep national mourning. Nor was it just the handsome, youthful, and charismatic president who died that day in Dallas; in retrospect, the event is symbolic of something even more profound: America's loss of innocence.

The optimism represented by Kennedy's "New Frontier"—embodying both the promise of uncharted horizons in space and the dream of racial equality at home—had suddenly turned to ashes. Two months later, the Beatles arrived in the United States. According to the rock critic Lester Bangs, this accident of timing may well have been a crucial element in the Beatlemania that swept the country during that fateful year: "America—perhaps young America in particular—had just lost a president who had seemed a godlike embodiment of national ideals. . . . We were down, we needed a shot of cultural speed, something high, fast, loud and superficial to fill the gap; we needed a fling after the wake."

Well, maybe. But, in fact, some of the fundamental national ideals that Kennedy personified were being sorely tested even before his assassination. During the course of his presidency, the country had endured an escalating pattern of protest and violence. Across the South, the civil rights movement's strategy of passive resistance increasingly was being met with violent responses. Nightly, on national TV news programs, Americans watched as firehoses and police dogs were turned on the ranks of peaceful black protesters. In August 1963, at the March on Washington, hundreds of thousands listened to Martin Luther King Jr.'s "I Have a Dream" speech. One month later, a church in Alabama was bombed, killing four young black girls.

While the national agenda was dominated by the specter of racial unrest, in the international arena, the Cold War suddenly seemed like it might get very hot indeed. Late in 1962, the Cuban missile crisis brought the superpowers to the brink of nuclear war. While the unthinkable was narrowly averted, the country had been left shaken by the experience. Meanwhile, on the other side of the world, events were being played out that would soon engulf the nation in another kind of war and even more wrenching civil unrest. In June 1963, there were news reports that a Buddhist monk had set himself on fire as an act of conscience in a place called Vietnam. Now Americans were told that the president was sending U.S. military advisors there to assist in the country's struggle against Communist rebels.

These unsettling events fueled what was already a growing network of civil rights and antiwar groups on college campuses across the country. Among those who filled the ranks of these organizations during the early 1960s were students who five years earlier had been innocently rocking and rolling to the music of Little Richard, Chuck Berry, and Elvis. But, as they had grown up, not only had rock 'n' roll changed, so had they. For this generation, the transition from "teen" to "college man" (and woman) was one that was often marked by a profound shift in musical taste. A new more mature status demanded a new more mature music. During this period, the music of choice on campus was either modern jazz or folk; often, this choice became a crucial element in establishing one's identity.

Among the favorites of the jazz crowd were the Dave Brubeck Quartet and the Modern Jazz Quartet, ensembles led by Stan Getz and Gerry Mulligan (especially the one that included the dashing young trumpeter Chet Baker), as well as the experimental big band of Stan Kenton. Although there were definite stylistic differences among them, what these particular jazz performers did share was a tendency toward musical complexity and an attitude of cool detachment that represented the epitome of sophistication for a sizeable segment of the collegiate audience. For their folk-music counterparts, however, these were among the very values from which they were trying to escape.

For these so-called folkies, it was the simplicity, authenticity, and engagement of their music that was most important. The current college folk boom had been initiated by the Kingston Trio. Against all odds, their 1958 recording of a traditional murder ballad, "Tom Dooley," had become a number one hit, inspiring a string of acoustic, guitar-strumming groups such as the Chad Mitchell Trio, the Limelighters, and Peter, Paul, and Mary. For the most part, these popular folk acts were made up of earnest, clean-cut, pleasant-sounding performers who

FIGURE 4-19. Their wholesome appearance, enthusiastic harmonies, and ringing acoustic guitar accompaniment helped propel the Kingston Trio's 1958 recording of a grisly nineteenth-century murder ballad to the top of the pop charts. Archive photo.

The Kingston Trio and the Folk Revival

The Kingston Trio's version of the ballad "Tom Dooley" has often been credited with launching the folk revival of the 1960s. In fact, the group's success was simply one more sign of the renewed interest in American folk music that had been taking place since the early 1950s. For example, Dave Guard, the group's banjo player, first took up the instrument after seeing Pete Seeger play one during a Weavers concert Guard had attended.

But the scale of the Kingston Trio's popularity and the impact of their folk-based songs on popular culture were unprecedented. According to one survey, sales of acoustic guitars doubled in each of the three years following the release of "Tom Dooley."

offered their audience a refreshingly simple, adult alternative to the perceived shallowness and commercialism of rock 'n' roll during the Brill Building era.

Before long, campuses across the country were holding regular "hootenannies" (the term for free-form songfests that had its origin in the folk revival of the 1940s), with their own workshirt-wearing balladeers and plaintive-voiced folk queens. This quest for authenticity also led to the rediscovery of old-time folk and blues performers who had been among the first generation to transfer songs from the oral tradition to recordings back in the 1920s. By the early 1960s, folk music's deeply rooted identification with political and social action also began to be reestablished, largely in connection to the civil rights movement. Depression-era folk heroes such as Woody

Guthrie and Leadbelly (along with singing union organizers such as Aunt Molly Jackson and McCarthy-era veterans such as Pete Seeger) became the models for a new dynasty of folkies. Then, in 1963, a song written by the recently crowned Prince of the Folk Revival suddenly became a Top Ten pop hit.

BOB DYLAN: THE TIMES THEY ARE A-CHANGIN'

In 1962, when Bob Dylan wrote "Blowin' in the Wind," he was already a well-known figure within the tightly circumscribed New York City folk community. But it was Peter, Paul, and Mary (then the most successful folk group in America) that first brought Dylan's song to the attention of the mainstream audience.

As the trio toured the country, they would preface every performance of "Blowin' in the Wind" with the same introduction: "Now we'd like to sing a song written by the most important folk artist in America today, Bob Dylan." Meanwhile, Joan Baez (then the reigning queen of the folk revival) was also doing her bit to bring Dylan to the attention of her audience. Not only did she begin adding his songs to her standard repertoire of traditional ballads, but she soon began bringing Dylan out during her concerts to sing his own songs.

By July 1963, Dylan's scheduled performance at the Newport Folk Festival had become the most eagerly anticipated event in what was the folk community's most prestigious gathering. Dylan dominated the festival. Naturally, Peter, Paul, and Mary made "Blowin' in the Wind" the centerpiece of their performance. As usual, Bob joined "Joannie" during Baez's set, and at Dylan's own solo appearance, she returned the favor by accompanying him during his own rendition of "Blowin' in the Wind." Here's how Anthony Scaduto describes the conclusion of this legendary evening in *Bob Dylan: An Intimate Biography*:

> All of those on stage rose from their chairs and celebrated his triumph with him: Seeger, Bikel, Peter, Paul, and Mary, and the Freedom Singers, harmonizing on Dylan's song. And the crowd shouted for more and the performers were all so affected by the ovation that they improvised a striking finale to the performance, all of them locking hands swaying from side to side, singing "We Shall Overcome."

A month later, Peter, Paul, and Mary would sing Dylan's song once again, this time in front of hundreds of thousands who gathered at the Lincoln Memorial during the historic March on Washington. Dylan himself chose to sing a new composition at the August 1963 rally, one that used the recent murder of the civil rights worker Medgar Evers to delve even more deeply into the insidious poison of racism. The song, "Only a Pawn in Their Game," would soon appear on Dylan's third album, *Times They Are a-Changin'* (which mixed a few reflective, personal songs with a series of scathing ballads focusing on contemporary political and social issues).

During the fall of 1963, major stories in *Time* magazine and a long profile in *The New Yorker* each celebrating Dylan as the youthful hero of the "Protest Song," Peter, Paul, and Mary had the top two best-selling albums in the country, and folk music seemed on the brink of even greater commercial success. Suddenly, Kennedy's assassination obliterated the optimism that had fueled the folk movement's momentum. A few months later, the Beatles—and the British invasion they spearheaded—took total possession of the American pop charts. For hardcore folk fans, the Beatles represented everything they detested about rock 'n' roll: they wrote infantile, shallow, songs with no redeeming social significance ("I Want to Hold Your Hand"?!), and they played *electric* guitars.

What these folkies who had deified Dylan never suspected at the time, however, was that their hero didn't share their scorn. Few knew that Dylan had once been a passionate rock and roller himself. Back in high school during the mid-1950s, he had organized his own rock band to play at local dances, and before he'd ever heard of Woody Guthrie, his greatest musical influence was Little Richard. "I had heard the Beatles in New York when they first hit," Dylan revealed to Anthony Scaduto years later. "But I just kept it to myself that I really dug them. Everybody else thought they were for the teenyboppers. . . . You see there was a lot of hypocrisy all around, people saying it had to be either folk or rock. But I knew it didn't have to be like that. I dug what the Beatles were doing, and I always kept it in mind from back then."

For their part, the Beatles—always quick to pick up on what was happening on the American music scene—had become big Dylan fans. As Paul McCartney acknowledged, "We were thrilled that he liked our music, because

FIGURE 4-20. Not long after the Prince of Protest shocked the folk community by "going electric," Bob Dylan began an extended collaboration with a quintet of anonymous back-up musicians who would later go on to form one of the most revered rock groups of the 1960s. Author's collection.

Going Electric: Bob Dylan and the Band

A few months after he unveiled his controversial new sound—and startling surrealistic lyrics—at the 1965 Newport Folk Festival, Bob Dylan launched an international tour with a heavily amplified rock band. At this stage of Dylan's career, he typically performed the first half of each show solo, singing his early acoustic folk ballads before returning with his back-up band to unleash blistering versions of his more recent folk-rock material. It was also in these groundbreaking compositions (such as "Ballad of a Thin Man," "Leopard-Skin Pillbox Hat," and "Desolation Row") that Bob Dylan revolutionized the rock song by fusing together allusive, image-laden modernist verse with the magic realism of traditional folk songs. In doing so, Dylan became—in Allen Ginsberg's memorable phrase—"the first poet of the jukebox."

Of course, by this time, Dylan's band had become "The Band," a group whose own series of brilliant roots-oriented albums (featuring their special brand of self-effacing instrumental virtuosity) earned them kudos from the critics and a kind of awed respect from their fellow musicians. After a decade and a half together, when the Band finally disbanded they were joined at a historic 1976 farewell concert by a star-studded lineup of well-wishers that included Muddy Waters, Van Morrison, Eric Clapton, Dr. John, Joni Mitchell, Ringo Starr, Neil Young, and, of course, Dylan himself. A film of the event by Martin Scorsese—titled *The Last Waltz*—is often cited as the greatest rock concert film of all time.

as far as we were concerned Dylan was our guru." In 1964, when Dylan toured England, the Beatles (as well as the Rolling Stones and other new English bands) had attended his sold-out London concert. After the show, Dylan and the Beatles spent the evening together, striking up a personal friendship and sharing musical ideas, as well as certain controlled substances (supposedly it was at this meeting that Dylan introduced the Beatles to marijuana).

FIGURE 4-21. The Byrds (from right: David Crosby, Roger McGuinn, Chris Hillman, Michael Clarke). It was their 1965 cover of Bob Dylan's "Mr. Tambourine Man" that is credited with launching the folk-rock era. Courtesy of Sony Music Photo Archives.

The Byrds: Folk-Rock Avatars

Although Bob Dylan had already recorded an acoustic version of "Tambourine Man," by adding a distinctive jangling twelve-string electric guitar along with a restrained rock beat the Byrds became the first to bring the "folk-rock" sound to the top of the charts. In 1966, the band scored another hit with an electrified adaptation of a folk-based original, Pete Seeger's "Turn! Turn! Turn!"

The Byrds went on to experiment with a new brand of highly produced "progressive rock" that resulted in their hit single "Eight Miles High." Although they consistently denied that the song contained any hidden meaning, the Byrds had the distinction of being the first band in the psychedelic era to have its record banned by radio stations for suspected drug-related messages.

Meanwhile, the platoons of British pop groups that followed the Beatles were quickly staking claim to the American pop music scene. For well over a year they came: the Dave Clark Five ("Glad All Over"), the Searchers ("Needles and Pins"), the Swinging Blue Jeans ("Hippie, Hippie Shake"), Gerry and the Pacemakers ("Don't Let the Sun Catch You Crying"), Freddie and the Dreamers ("I'm Telling You Now"), Herman's Hermits ("I'm into Something Good"), to name just a few. It got so bad that the only way an American group could get any airplay was to engage in the humiliating pretense that they, too, were perhaps just a little British themselves; at least that's what (the Texas-based) Sir Douglas Quintet and (San Francisco's) Beau Brummels let the public believe.

The situation for African-American music was even worse. When Ben E. King was interviewed for the video documentary *The History of Rock 'n' Roll* about his reaction to the Beatles' arrival in the United States, the great R & B singer claimed to have immediately recognized the disastrous affect it would have: "I said this is it; it's all over but the shouting. We had never seen kids fainting at concerts. We had never heard screams like that. We knew that there was a problem, and it had just landed." The statistics bear out King's prediction.

In 1963, thirty-seven of the year's Top 100 pop singles were by black performers. In 1964, that figure had plummeted to just twenty-one. Although the Motown Sound and Atlantic/Stax's brand of Southern soul would soon restore the power and passion of African-American music to the pop music charts, for the moment at least the headline in the pop press remained "Brits Rule."

And always one step ahead of all the competition were the Beatles themselves. Despite being swept up in the disorienting whirlwind of American Beatlemania, Lennon and McCartney were writing prolifically, and with each new recording the band seemed to take another creative stride. In addition, with the release of their first film, *A Hard Day's Night* (during the summer of 1964), the Beatles expanded their audience both quantitatively and qualitatively. As a result of the film's innovative visual style, as well as the close-up view it provided of their irresistable music and engaging personalities, the Beatles' audience immediately got both older and hipper.

That same summer, however, the initial wave of mop-topped British beat groups with feel-good lyrics and bouyant pop harmonies was followed by a second wave of British invasion bands to make their way across the Atlantic. Among them was one whose name provided a pretty good clue both to their image and their music: the Animals. The success of the group's first American single—"The House of the Rising Sun"—was surprising for a variety of reasons. For one thing, it had to overcome the enormous hype that accompanied the recent release of the Beatles' first film, and, unlike the sunny pop tunes on the Fab Four's soundtrack, the Animals' début was a dark descent into a world of fallen women and lost souls.

Based on traditional American folk sources, the "House of the Rising Sun" is a cautionary tale told by a young woman who describes her life as a prostitute in a New Orleans' brothel. A variant of the song ("Rising Sun Blues"), collected by the American folk music scholar Allen Lomax back in 1937, it had once been a favorite of the folk-blues singer known as Leadbelly. But it had come to the Animals' attention through a dramatic acoustic version that appeared on Bob Dylan's first album.

On the Animals' recording, lead singer Eric Burdon delivered the song's stark lyrics in a deep, haunted vocal that was colored by strong black inflections, while in the background Alan Price's surging, thickly textured electric organ accompaniment created a chillingly ominous mood. During his 1964 British tour, Dylan got a chance to hear the Animals' startling interpretation even before the record was released in the United States. According to Anthony Scaduto's biography, when Dylan returned from his trip, he told a friend: "My God, ya oughtta hear what's going down over there. Eric Burdon, the Animals, ya know. Well, he's doing "House of the Rising Sun" in rock. Rock!"

The idea of fusing the rigorous authenticity of folk with the excitement (and electricity) of rock 'n' roll soon created a popular new hybrid that would transform popular music. Although Bob Dylan would become its most visionary practitioner, the fact that the concept should have first surfaced in England is not surprising. British music fans had a long and obsessive interest in all forms of indigenous American music. In fact, the Animals' follow-up single—"Boom, Boom"—was a rhythmically intense cover of a song by the idiosyncratic African-American bluesman John Lee Hooker.

Inspired by the Animals' amplified adaptation of American blues and folk music, Bob Dylan began experimenting with his own folk-rock fusion. Having already moved from the political to the personal in his recent acoustic ballads, Dylan now put together his own band and enhanced his latest image-laden lyrics with a jolt of electricity. His 1965 album, *Bringing It All Back Home,* opened with "Subterranean Homesick Blues," a blistering, surrealistic fable that would inspire the beatnik bard, Allen Ginsberg, to dub Dylan the first "poet of the jukebox." Although the single version of the song managed to nudge its way into the Top Forty, a few months later the Byrds (a West Cost rock band with Greenwich Village roots) took another song from the album—"Mr. Tambourine Man"—to number one.

Before long, a score of Dylan-inspired "folk rock" groups—including the Mamas and the Papas, Buffalo Springfield, the Lovin' Spoonful—were making their way onto the pop charts with literate lyrics set to the ringing chords of electric guitars and a pounding rock beat.

FROM ROCK 'N' ROLL TO ROCK

So what were the Beatles doing in 1965 as America's homegrown folk-rockers were infusing mature new themes and socially conscious lyrics into the pop charts? Well, after playing to a sell-out crowd of 56,000 fans at New York's Shea Stadium (at the time the biggest rock 'n' roll concert in history), the Beatles returned to London to finish recording an album that would again confirm their status as the music's most innovative ensemble.

Not only did *Rubber Soul* offer exciting examples of the Beatles' own explorations of the off-beat, enigmatic lyric possibilities Bob Dylan had introduced to the standard pop song, but their album also introduced innovative musical textures and production techniques that would revolutionize the very nature of rock 'n' roll.

Virtually every aspect of *Rubber Soul* was to have an influence on the music and/or culture of the Sixties. In both the "heady" ambiguity of its lyrics and the album cover's bizzarely distorted photo and graphics, it reflected the influence of the drugs (first marijuana and, later, LSD) that would characterize the decade, while George Harrison's use of the exotic, multistring Indian sitar (on the song "Norwegian Wood") anticipated the profound Eastern influence (from fashion to philosophy) that would pervade the period. Finally, in their exploration of recording studio technology—and their conception of their new record "as an album" (rather than just a collection of potential singles)—the Beatles were in the vanguard of the transformation of rock 'n' roll into "rock."

With the active collaboration of their producer, George Martin, the Beatles moved away from the "live" approach to recording—in which the record is a simply a document of the band's performance—to a process (made possible by "multitrack" technology) in which the layering of individual elements creates a finished product that is only possible in the recording studio. So where their first LP (*Please Please Me*) was captured in one thirteen-hour session, *Rubber Soul* required weeks of complex assembly using layers of individually recorded vocal and instrumental tracks. Released late in 1965, *Rubber Soul* also was marketed as an *album* (there was no preliminary release of singles as had always been the industry practice); yet, within two weeks, it was the number one record in America.

The dramatic changes initiated by Bob Dylan (surrealistic drug-tinged imagery), as well as by groups such as the Rolling Stones (sexually charged white blues) and the Beatles (studio-produced eclecticism) would not have been possible unless there was a significant and receptive market. By the mid-1960s, cultural and demographic factors had, in fact, combined to create a huge and sympathetic audience that was very different from rock 'n' roll's first fan base. As Geoffrey Stokes explains in the "Sixties" section of *Rock of Ages*:

> For that first 1950's generation of teenagers, the assumption was that once you got a job/got married/graduated from high school, you would leave Little Richard behind and embrace Perry Como. Together, the Beatles and Dylan pushed that *terminus ad quem* so far into adulthood that it became meaningless. The rock audience was growing, not only thanks to the baby boom, but because comparatively fewer teenagers were dropping out of it in their twenties. The net effect was that the age at which the generation gap (measured by someone's shouting, or even wishing to shout, "Turn that radio down!") clicked in was being pushed upward and the number on the rock 'n' roll side of it was further swollen as the baby boomers hit adolescence.

Just as the creation of *rock 'n' roll* in the 1950s had been a consequence of social, cultural, and technological as well as musical factors, by 1965 the development of a rapidly expanding "youth culture," the introduction of an enhanced musical and lyric vocabulary, the creative potential of multitrack recording, and the advent of the album as the primary vehicle of expression resulted in a transition to a new style of popular music that would simply be called *rock*.

Two other vital components emerged at about this time that not only helped establish rock as a distinctive musical idiom but also helped define the music's role as a powerful cultural force. The first of these was a grass-roots fraternity of "rock critics" who began to discuss music with a combination of passionate enthusiasm and intellectual authority. The other was an expansion of what had been the primary medium of rock 'n' roll itself—radio.

ROCK ON, T. S. ELIOT

Just as some fans—inspired by the Beatles' exuberant experimentation or Dylan's scathing sarcasm—picked up an electric guitar and formed their own rock band, others picked up their typewriters. Having absorbed the basic critera of literary criticism in their college English classes, some students began writing about the Beatles' "Norwegian Wood" using the same basic approach as they brought to their assignments on T. S. Eliot's "The Waste Land." And since there wasn't an existing outlet for their writing, they created their own.

The first of these rock journals was *Crawdaddy: The Magazine of Rock* founded in 1964 by an eighteen-year-old college student, Paul Williams. Although, at first, the production values were modest—a bunch of mimeographed typewritten pages stapled together—both the attitude and writing were a world apart from the gushing teen periodicals that had previously kept track of the world of rock 'n' roll. For example, here's an excerpt from a *Crawdaddy* review of the title song from the Beatles' second movie, *Help!,* written by R. Meltzer, one of the most respected of that first generation of rock critics:

> They have noted the evolution of multitrack recording with "Help!", a single-tracked recording, at its pinnacle. In this work juxtaposed Greek-like lead and chorus seem separate in echoing each other, suggesting that the Beatles' self-restraint in limiting the song to a single track divided between George and Paul and John is a self-conscious comprehension of the effect of one being fully capable of echoing himself and yet refusing, a queer addendum to a movement continuously felt throughout rock 'n' roll history. Representing the evolution of rock made conscious of itself (just as Chardin asserts man to be the crown of the natural evolution of the universe, made conscious of itself), the Beatles have made ontologically important the concept of anachronism.

While not all the rock journalism published in the various fanzines that had begun appearing across the country were quite so impenetrable, they all embodied a very different attitude toward the music from the one expressed during the Golden Age of rock 'n' roll: "I like it; it's got a good beat and you can dance to it." In addition, the new rock magazines instilled in their readers an appreciation of rock as a distinct musical idiom, as well as an "art." They also provided the emerging youth culture with a sense of its own identity. But an even more powerful vehicle for expanding and consolidating the new rock audience was radio.

FM—NO STATIC AT ALL

At first, the various Top Forty style radio stations comfortably integrated the records of the Beatles and other British invasion bands into their own particular playlists. Gradually, however, as rock songs increasingly pushed the edge of the envelope in both their length and their content, radio stations were being overwhelmed by records that either obliterated their traditional two-minute-thirty-second ideal (Dylan's "Like a Rolling Stone" was over six minutes long) or generated controversy for their political, sexual, or drug-related content. It was just at this point that a policy change was announced by the Federal Communications Commission.

In 1966, an FCC regulation declared that anyone operating both an AM and FM radio station in the same market could not simply broadcast the same programming on both outlets. The ruling suddenly opened up the vast reservoir of previously insignificant air space on the FM band. Since FM listenership—and, therefore, advertising rates—were minimal, so was management scrutiny. Making the most of this attitude of benign neglect, a few hip young DJs began to create a new rock format that was known variously as "progressive," "underground," or "free-form" radio. The timing couldn't have been better.

Just as the new FM format spread across the country, the need for just such a flexible, album-oriented, uncensored, stereophonic medium was becoming more of a necessity than ever. During 1966, rock music was exploding old constraints and expanding creatively on every front. Simon and Garfunkel's folk-rock debut "I Am a Rock" brought a new level of poetic craft and literacy to popular music, while the Beach Boys' new single "Good Vibrations," the result of weeks of elaborate multitrack layering (and $20,000 in recording costs), set a new standard in studio production. At the same time, in songs such as "Mother's Little Helper," the Rolling Stones were continuing to challenge media watchdogs with ever-more brazen drug references.

ROLLING STONE

November 9, 1967
Vol. 1, No. 1

OUR PRICE:
TWENTY-FIVE CENTS

MFP

IN THIS ISSUE:

DONOVAN: An incredible Rolling Stone Interview, with this manchild of magic ....Page 14

GRATEFUL DEAD: A photographic look at a rock and roll group after a dope bust ....Page 8

BYRD IS FLIPPED: Jim McGuinn kicks out David Crosby ....Page 4

RALPH GLEASON: The color bar on American television ....Page 11

Tom Rounds Quits KFRC

Tom Rounds, KFRC Program Director, has resigned. No immediate date has been set for his departure from the station. Rounds quit to assume the direction of Charlatan Productions, an L.A. based film company experimenting in the contemporary pop film.

Rounds spent seven years as Program Director of KPOI in Hawaii before coming to San Francisco in 1966. He successfully effected the tight format which made KFRC the number one station in San Francisco.

Les Turpin, former program director of KGB in San Diego will replace Tom Rounds at KFRC. Turpin has spent the last year as a consultant in the Drake-Chenault programming service.

The new appointment could mean a tightening up of programming policies. Rounds liberalization of KFRC's play-list may well become more restricted.

Recognize Private Gripeweed? He's actually John Lennon in Richard Lester's new film, How I Won the War. An illustrated special preview of the movie begins on page 16.

THE HIGH COST OF MUSIC AND LOVE: WHERE'S THE MONEY FROM MONTEREY?

BY MICHAEL LYDON

A weekend of "music, love, and flowers" can be done for a song (plus cost) or can be done at a cost (plus songs). The Monterey International Pop Festival, a non-profit, charity event, was, despite its own protestations, of the second sort: a damn extravagant three days.

The Festival's net profit at the end of August, the last date of accounting, was $211,451. The costs of the weekend were $290,233. Had it not been for the profit from the sale of television rights to ABC-TV of $288,843, the whole operation would have ended up a neat $77,392 in the red.

The Festival planned to have all the artists, while in Monterey, submit ideas for use of the proceeds.

In the confusion the plan miscarried and the decision on where the profits should go has still not been finally made.

So far only $50,000 has definitely been been allocated to anyone: to a unit of the New York City Youth Board which will set up classes for many ghetto children to learn music on guitars donated by Fender. Paul Simon, a Festival governor, will personally over see the program.

Plans to give more money to the Negro College Fund for college scholarships is now being discussed; another idea is a sum between ten and twenty thousand for the Monterey Symphony.

However worthy these plans, they are considerably less daring and innovative than the projects mentioned in the spring: the Diggers, pop conferences, and any project which would "tend to further national interest in and knowledge and enjoyment of popular music." The present plans suggest that the Board of Governors, unable or unwilling to make their grandiose schemes reality, fell back on traditional charity.

The Board of Governors did decide that the money would be given out in a small number of large sums. This has meant, for instance, that the John Edwards Memorial Foundation, a folk music archive at the University of California at Los Angeles, had its small request overlooked.

In ironic fact, what happened at the Festival and its financial affairs looks in many ways like the traditional Charity Ball in hippie drag.

The overhead was high and the net was low. "For every dollar spent, there was a reason," says Derek Taylor, the Festival's PR man and one of its original officers.

Yet many of the Festival's expenses, however reasonable to Taylor, seem out of keeping with its announced spirit. The Festival management, with amateurish good will, lavished generosity on their friends.

• Producer Lou Adler was able to find a spot in the show for his own property, Johnny Rivers; Paul Simon for his friend, English folk singer Beverly; John Phillips for the Group Without A Name and Scott MacKenzie. None of them had the musical

Airplane high, but no new LP release

Jefferson Airplane has been recording more than a month to record their new album for RCA Victor. In a recording period of five weeks only five sides have been completed. No definite release date has been set.

Their usual recording schedule in Los Angeles begins at 11:00 p.m. in the evening and extends through six or seven in the morning. When they're not in the studios, they stay at a fabulous pink mansion which rents for $5,000 a month. The Beatles stayed at the house on their last American tour.

The house has two swimming pools and a variety of recreational facilities. It's a small small little paradise in the hills above Hollywood. Maybe suntans and guitars don't make it together.

status for an international pop music festival.

It is ironic that the Rivers and the rest appeared "free," but the money it cost the Festival to get them to Monterey and back, feed them, put them up (Beverly

—Continued on Page 7

FIGURE 4-22. *Rolling Stone* (Vol. I, No. 1). By November 9, 1967, when this first issue of rock's preeminent periodical hit the newsstands, the music—and lifestyle—it chronicled had suddenly become national news. Courtesy of Rolling Stone. Straight Arrow Publishing Company.

On the Cover of *Rolling Stone*

From the beginning, *Rolling Stone* had been a step up both in its journalistic standards and production values from the fanzines that had preceded it. Editor/publisher Jann Wenner assembled a young, talented staff who passionately documented the era's exciting new music (and unabashedly celebrated the intimate details of the lives of its creators).

Over the decades, the magazine has been accused of missing the boat (or worse) as challenging new genres—from punk to disco to rap—each appeared on the scene but, after thirty years, the ultimate symbol of "making it" in the world of popular music has remained the same: making it onto the cover of *Rolling Stone*.

In his 1966 double album *Blonde on Blonde,* Bob Dylan created the most expansive, word-drunk work of his career; one song, "Desolation Row" took up one whole side of the album. While in August, the new Beatles album *Revolver* proved to be their most lyrically ambitious and technologically complex to date; it was a collage of studio sound effects, string sections, instrumental overdubs, and backward tape loops through which their distorted vocals floated in an aural re-creation of the effects of the LSD with which they had begun to experiment.

Not only were the FM stations now in a position to offer a range of rock music in a static-free context (without program director playlists or screaming DJs), but some stations also began to serve their listeners as a kind of electronic "community center." It was no coincidence, therefore, that the city that more than any other pioneered the progressive FM format was also the city that became the Capital of the Counterculture.

SAN FRANCISCO: FROM COMMUNES TO COMMERCE

Unlike the cities that were associated with earlier eras in rock 'n' roll history (Memphis, New York, Detroit, and Los Angeles), San Francisco had never been a center of popular music. It did have a cherished reputation as a haven of tolerance for alternate lifestyles, however. A decade before, San Francisco had become headquarters for the Beat Generation, and now a neglected area of the city around the intersection of Haight and Ashbury Streets became a magnet for their spritual descendents. But, unlike their jazz-obsessed ancestors, the new bohemian subculture made rock their music of choice.

Under the direction of pop radio veteran Tom Donahue, the city's FM radio station KMPX instituted what most media histories identify as the first "progressive rock" format. And, as Phillip Ennis has noted in his book *The Seventh Stream,* the station had a particularly intimate relationship with its listeners: "The hippie community took over the place as one of their own. On air and off, the station was the conduit for Bay area music. Commercials were aired at a minimum, albums were played in part or in full, and the radio lore of forty years was given the heave-ho."

Throughout the Haight-Ashbury district, young people haphazardly stitched together a new alternate, anti-authoritarian "counterculture" through a combination of psychedelic drugs, Eastern philosophy, and rock music. By the mid-1960s, thousands of "hippies"—as they were dubbed by the media—had embraced an assortment of local bands who played at local dances promoted on their own local underground radio station. What came to be called the "San Francisco sound" had as much to do with the values of this unique subculture as it did with any particular musical characteristic.

For one thing, the Grateful Dead, Jefferson Airplane, Country Joe and the Fish, Big Brother and the Holding Company (to name just a few of the approximately one thousand bands in the Bay Area) had virtually all emerged from the folk music scene. Although they had traded in their banjos and Martin acoustic guitars for solid-body electric Fenders and drum kits (as they made the transition from blues-ballads, bluegrass, and jug bands to rock), what they did retain was a commitment to a "homemade" aesthetic that valued virtue over virtuosity. And, in keeping with the folkie ideal, they made every effort to efface the line between audience and performer.

While the Bay area bands may have held on to the folk tradition's populist ideology, they were less successful at retaining the music's political convictions. Ironically, just as San Francisco's counterculture was proclaiming its "Tune in, Turn on, Drop out" mantra, across the bridge in Berkeley, university students were in the process of forging what would be a national antiwar movement. Although rock music and Vietnam have become linked as two of the most potent symbols of the Sixties, in fact there was a deep and unresolved division over the role of politics in the counterculture. One of the few bands that did attempt to reconcile this breach was Country Joe and the Fish. In his essay "The Sound of San Francisco," Charles Perry describes Country Joe McDonald's evolution from "folkie" to "freak":

Joe McDonald was a folk singer with one foot in the grand old protest song tradition and the other in the good-time jug band scene. Six months after the first hippie dances in San Francisco he was running a rock band which established itself as *the* Berkeley acid group. They consciously explored LSD and strove to unite the hippies and the local radicals. Joe was famous for wearing protest buttons to hippie functions and flowers to the many political benefits he played.

Over the next three years, Country Joe and the Fish appeared at all the right places—from Montery to Woodstock—and their best-known song, "I Feel Like I'm Fixin' to Die Rag" (a rollicking old-timey number whose sing-along chorus offered a cheerily fatalistic attitude about Vietnam), made them a particular favorite at antiwar demonstrations and on college campuses across the country. The other San Francisco bands, however, seemed content to draw a tie-dyed curtain across the political landscape and retreat into a self-contained environment that embraced a more narrowly defined concept of community.

Within the hippie subculture, the rock "group" was seen as more than merely a musical aggregation; it was a new kind of extended family. Bands often lived together in the Haight's rambling old Victorian houses sharing not only a musical identity but a spiritual or political philosophy (as well as sexual partners). In this regard, the Grateful Dead was certainly the archetypal San Francisco band. And while they never achieved the kind of immediate, cross-over commercial success of some of their Bay Area colleagues, the Dead just kept on truckin' and— until his death in 1996—Jerry Garcia remained the ultimate musical (and spiritual) guru for generations of "Dead Heads."

Just as one of the models for the hippie lifestyle was the Hindu religious *ashram* (commune), the long, free-flowing melodic lines of many of these bands also had Indian sources. After attending a London concert by Ravi Shankar—a virtuoso on the sitar (an ancient multistringed Indian instrument)—George Harrison purchased his own sitar, began studying with Shankar, and the Beatles started incorporating some Indian spices into their own music. Soon, Shankar would become elevated to the status of hippie hero and the exotic sounds of the sitar would be heard at counterculture festivals from coast to coast.

Closer to home, San Francisco's rock vanguard also found in the Native American tradition an archetype for their own tribal lifestyle. And both "Indian" cultures made a contribution to the quintessential hippie fashion statement: headbands, sandals, beads, and feathers. Finally, there also was an attempt to connect the use of consciousness-expanding drugs to these same ancient cultural traditions. But, whatever its source, the central role chemical hallucinogens (primarily LSD) played in the lifestyle of these Bay Area bands resulted in their music (essentially a synthesis of their folk and blues roots with electronically amplified Eastern-tinged improvisation and a dance beat) being labeled "Psychedelic" or "Acid Rock."

By early 1967, San Francisco's underground network of light-show-illuminated dances held at Haight-Ashbury's abandoned Swing Era ballrooms came out into the open. In January, twenty thousand "freaks" (a self-imposed label) gathered in San Francisco's Golden Gate park for what was called a Human Be-In, a.k.a. "The Gathering of the Tribes" (with entertainment provided by the Quicksilver Messenger Service, the Grateful Dead, Jefferson Airplane, Country Joe and the Fish, among others). It was an event the national media—and major record labels—couldn't help but notice. There was even a hippie anthem cooked up by a Los Angeles pop producer on AM radio: Scott MacKensie's "San Francisco (Be Sure to Wear Some Flowers in Your Hair)."

Soon tour buses would be winding their way through the Haight as their occupants consulted glossaries of hippie slang ("What a drag that the groovy chick's bad trip was such a bummer"). Feature articles ran in every national magazine, "love beads" and incense went on sale at neighborhood variety stores across the country, and record company talent scouts were signing every long-haired band in sight. During the summer, a kind of official counterculture coming-out party was organized.

The Monterey International Pop Festival was the first of the major outdoor festivals that would become a staple of the rock era. Over the course of three days, fifty thousand fans showed up to see the members of the new rock pantheon, including the Grateful Dead, the Jefferson Airplane, the Byrds, Country Joe and the Fish, Otis Redding, the Mamas and the Papas, Big Brother and the Holding Company, the Who, and Jimi Hendrix, as well as honorary hippie, Ravi Shankar. One year later, millions more would see the documentary film made about the festival, *Monterey Pop*—which was another first of its kind.

For many of the San Francisco groups that appeared there, Monterey also signaled the transition from their identification with a communal, self-consciously pure subculture to a prominent place within the music industry mainstream. The Jefferson Airplane were the first of the "psychedelic" bands to be signed (for an advance of $20,000) to a major label recording contract (RCA, the oldest in the business), and it was the band's RCA debut album, *Surrealistic Pillow*, released in 1967 that introduced the San Francisco sound to the rest of America.

Unlike the Grateful Dead (and most of the other local bands), the Jefferson Airplane were able to tighten up the notoriously casual performance style that had evolved at the Haight's acid-drenched dances without losing

FIGURE 4-23.   The Jefferson Airplane were the first to bring the free-form psychedelia of the "San Francisco Sound" to the pop charts. Courtesy of RCA Records Photo Archive.

The Jefferson Airplane: The Counterculture Takes Off

Released in 1967, Jefferson Airplane's debut single "Don't You Want Somebody to Love?" introduced the nation to the new music emerging out of the Haight-Ashbury's hippie community. Their first RCA album, *Surrealistic Pillow,* is one of the icons of the flower-power ethos that bloomed in the Bay Area during the so-called Summer of Love (from its "trippy" cover art to the acid-drenched imagery of its hit single "White Rabbit").

their counterculture credibility. Many of their songs—which also perfectly captured the ethos of the era (equal parts communal love and anti-establishment rebellion)—were written by lead singer Grace Slick. While her hard-edged vocals added a dramatic intensity to the band's music, Slick was even more significant for embodying an outspoken, overtly sexual female image that was new to rock 'n' roll.

By the time they appeared at Monterey, the Jefferson Airplane also had become the first of the Bay bands to place singles on the national pop charts, first with "Somebody to Love" and then with "White Rabbit" (whose Alice-in-Wonderland allusions barely concealed the song's obvious drug references).

Meanwhile, it was her emotionally charged performance at Monterey that would launch the career of the era's dominant female performer, Janis Joplin. Before the festival was over, her band, Big Brother and the Holding Company, was signed to a Columbia Records' contract for more than ten times that which the Airplane had recently received. Finally, it was Jimi Hendrix's incendiary appearance—climaxed by the immolation and ritual destruction of his guitar—that first propelled the innovative guitarist into the front ranks of rock aristocracy.

Although Monterey may justly be famous for helping to break gender barriers and establish the reputations of a couple of 1960s superstars, it almost succeeded in destroying the career of one talented female performer before it had barely begun. For as soon as the New York singer-songwriter Laura Nyro walked on stage, dressed in a deconstructed, thrift-shop black gown, it was clear that she was seriously out of context amid the hordes of tie-dyed, West Coast counterculture celebrants. Nor did her intensely personal compositions and soul-inflected stage act go over any better. Reduced to tears by the hostile audience, neither Nyro nor her performing career ever completely recovered.

By contrast, at least a half-dozen of her songs became huge hits (for other artists ranging from Frank Sinatra and Barbra Streisand to the Fifth Dimension and Peter, Paul, and Mary). And, on the basis of some of her own critically acclaimed albums, Nyro did achieve a fiercely loyal cult following; by the time of her untimely death from cancer in 1997, she had influenced many women singer-songwriters.

Finally, the festival's only actual soul singer, Otis Redding, gave a typically dynamic performance that won over the huge, white, youth audience and in the process earned the singer a coveted place—which he shared with Aretha Franklin—as one of the few black artists to become a staple of progressive rock radio. In retrospect, however, it was precisely the festival's pallid racial complexion that has raised serious questions about the extent of the counterculture's sense of community.

As Geoffrey Stokes has written (in *Rock of Ages*), the exclusion of most black performers from the new rock mainstream made "a damning statement about that audience's shrinking openness—as well, perhaps, as about rock's increasing 'high art' pretensions." Stokes concludes that "[w]hile there was no doubt that the established media were infinitely more receptive both to rock and to certain countercultural values than they had ever been before, that acceptance—which threatened to resegregate the music—had exacted a terrible price."

HIGH ART/BIG BUSINESS

Considering the rock market's enormous potential, the sudden interest of the major labels and mainstream media was hardly surprising. Nor, unfortunately, was the de facto "resegregation" of rock cited in Geoffrey Stokes's Monterey postmortem. What *is* surprising about Stokes's critique, however, is his use of the words "rock" and "art" in the same sentence.

The fact is that by 1967, a music once villified as primitive and uncivilized was suddenly being taken seriously by members of America's cultural élite. For example, in April of that year, New York Philharmonic conductor Leonard Bernstein bestowed his seal of approval on the music in a laudatory television special entitled, *Inside Pop—The Rock Revolution*. But more than any other single event, it was the release of *Sgt. Pepper's Lonely Hearts Club Band* that would transform the perception of rock 'n' roll forever.

When it finally came out on June 2, 1967, after four months of intensive studio production and $100,000 in recording costs (as compared to one day and $2,000 for their first LP), the Beatles' new album not only generated an unprecedented outpouring of lavish praise, but—for better or worse—introduced a new notion of what a rock album could be. According to scores of college professors, critics, and other arbiters of high culture on both sides of the Atlantic who struggled to out-superlative each other, it could be "art."

Most of the praise was not devoted to any of the individual songs (although "A Day in the Life" was quickly dubbed a "masterpiece"); instead, the kudos were reserved for the way the Beatles had once again revolutionized the pop album, this time by presenting it as a total, creatively integrated *concept*. By adopting the fictional circus-band alter-egos of the record's title, the Beatles established a unified framework for songs that, in fact, exhibited an enormous variety of styles and influences: from the sitar-laced exoticism of "Within You Without You" to the cheery, music hall ambiance of "When I'm Sixty-Four" to the achingly sentimental "She's Leaving Home."

Meanwhile, the seven hundred hours of studio time that the Beatles and their producer, George Martin, had spent layering dozens of instrumental and vocal tracks (along with scraps of cut and randomly reassembled audiotape and a forty-one-piece orchestra) gave *Sgt. Pepper* a complexity that no pop album had ever approached. It was just this obsession with the artistic potential of the multitrack process (along with their own Beatlemania burn-out) that had motivated the band to stop playing live concerts the year before.

Although some mainstream reviewers (and radio programmers) found the new album's frequent drug allusions troubling (the acronym embedded in the title "Lucy in the Sky with Diamonds" was quickly decoded), *Sgt. Pepper's Lonely Hearts Club Band* was almost universally received as a cultural milestone. According to an article in the *New York Times* book review, the album marked "a new and golden Renaissance of Song." The classical composer (and critic) Ned Rorem, writing in the prestigious intellectual journal the *New York Review of Books,* analyzed the Beatles' music without apology: " 'She's Leaving Home,' while set to a less interesting verse, is a mazurka equal in melancholy and melodic distinction to those of Chopin."

Nor was the Beatles' album the only rock record to be elevated to the status of art during the summer of 1967. By using a very different approach, the Doors' début also achieved that lofty designation. Although their music was really just a basic—if well-played—blend of urban blues and jazz-tinged improvisation, Jim Morrison's lyrics earned the Doors the respectful attention of the critics. For, unlike most of the era's recent converts to rock, Morrison was neither a former folkie nor a pop music pro; instead, he identified himself as "a poet."

In 1967, when rock stars were suddenly being treated like poets, it seemed like the perfect opportunity for a poet to became a rock star. Of course, Morrison's sensual (somewhat androgynous) good looks and skin-tight leather jeans wouldn't hurt his chances to make that transition. It was a chance encounter on a Venice, California, beach that brought Morrison (who was then studying film at UCLA) together with the classically trained (blues-oriented) keyboard player Ray Manzarek. After hearing Morrison recite his poem "Moonlight Drive," Manzarek immediately recognized the possibilities: "I said, that's it . . . if we got a group together we could make a million dollars."

After adding guitarist Robby Krieger and drummer John Densmore, the band began honing a tight, often hypnotic sound that served as an ideal setting for Morrison's image-laden lyrics. In addition to their original material, their repertoire consisted of a hip mix of the blues (Willie Dixon's "Backdoor Man") and the esoteric (experimental German theater composers' Brecht and Weill's "Alabama Song"). For the band's name, Morrison turned to the title of a book about the spiritual potential of hallucinogenic drugs by Aldous Huxley, *The Doors of Perception* (which was itself originally a line from a poem by William Blake).

The first single from the Doors' self-titled début album was "Light My Fire." With its swirling, trancelike electric organ and sinuous guitar solo wrapping themselves around Morrison's passionate vocal, it was one of the few non-Beatles' records that managed to penetrate the summer of Sgt. Pepper. A different (original) composition on the album, however, would turn out to be the band's most emblematic—and notorious—song. Entitled "The End," it was an eleven-and-a-half-minute Oedipal melodrama climaxed by Morrison's orgasmic screams; it also served as proof of his infamous proclamation that the Doors weren't a band but "erotic politicians."

Although the Rolling Stones had long been the preeminent bad boys of rock (with busts for both drugs and public urination that had prevented the band for touring in the United States for three years), Jim Morrison seemed obsessed with becoming its first "tragic poet." For a while, the Doors managed to generate a series of sensual and successful singles ("People Are Strange," "Love Me Two Times," "Hello I Love You"), sell a lot of albums, and enthrall audiences with some mesmerizing live performances. But soon Doors concerts began degenerating into occasions for Morrison's alcohol-fueled obscenity and exhibitionism (the most notorious incident being the 1969 concert in Miami when he was arrested for "exposing his private parts" and "simulating masturbation and oral copulation"). It was this incident that signaled the rapid decline of the Doors, as concerts were canceled by nervous promoters and Morrison turned what remained of his creative energy to ambitious (but unfulfilled) poetry and film projects.

Interestingly, neither Morrison's Miami arrest nor the excesses of some other rock stars was arousing the ire of the kind of anti-rock coalitions that had been so effective during the 1950s. While it is true that the cultural upheavals of the intervening decade (assassinations, race riots, and Vietnam) had permanently transformed the country, the simple fact is that, unlike the early days of rock 'n' roll, rock was both high art and big business.

While that first generation of rock 'n' roll rebels had recorded primarily for small, regional independent labels that were vulnerable to both civic condemnation and commercial pressures, virtually all the new rock bands had been snatched up by the handful of major labels that were headquartered in New York or Los Angeles. Rock had become a rich man's game. In fact, by 1967, a number of events were taking place that nicely symbolize the dramatic transformation rock was having on the pop music industry.

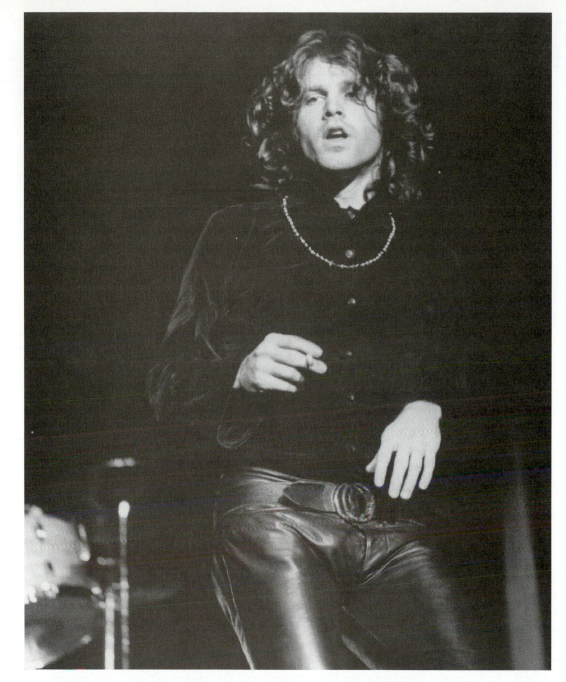

FIGURE 4-24.   Jim Morrison of the Doors—the rock star as "erotic politician." Courtesy of Elektra Entertainment.

The Doors: Break on through to the Other Side

Beginning with their 1967 début "Light My Fire," the Doors created a tightly honed blend of blues, jazz, and rock that provided the perfect backdrop for Jim Morrison's sexually suggestive lyrics and tragic-poet persona. By 1971, however, Morrison had fallen victim to his own myth.

Following an extended period of alcohol-fueled degeneration, Morrison left the Doors and moved to Paris. A few months later, he was found dead in his hotel bathtub. Yet, after more than a quarter of century, Morrison's grave in the historic Père Lachaise cemetery remains a place of pilgrimage, and thirty years after their initial release, classic albums by the Doors continue to sell to new generations of fans.

FIGURE 4-25. Janis Joplin was the only female performer to achieve equal status with such heroes of 1960s rock as Jim Morrison and Jimi Hendrix. And like them, she fell victim not only to the drugs and alcohol that took her life but to the rock 'n' roll myth she embodied. Photo by Lee Tanner.

Janis Joplin: Riding the Mystery Train

Born in Port Arthur, Texas, in 1943, Joplin left home at seventeen and began singing Leadbelly and Woody Guthrie songs for tips in Austin folk clubs. By 1965, she had moved on to San Francisco's Haight-Ashbury neighborhood, where a musical and cultural revolution was forming that soon would attract national attention.

Joplin's electrifying performance at the 1967 Monterey Pop Festival won her band, Big Brother and the Holding Company, a lucrative Columbia Records contract. A year later, their album, *Cheap Thrills*—featuring the distinctive artwork of San Francisco "underground cartoonist" R. Crumb—became one of the prime artifacts of the hippie era.

In 1970, Joplin died from an accidental overdose of heroin, just a few months before her first solo single, "Me and Bobby McGee," became her first number one hit. Under the circumstances, the song's chorus seemed to reverberate with added poignancy: "Freedom's just another word for nothing left to lose . . ."

"Mystery Train": Janis Joplin Leaves Port Arthur for Points West, 1964 (David Wojahn)

In his poem, " 'Mystery Train': Janis Joplin Leaves Port Arthur for Points West, 1964," David Wojahn takes us back to the beginning of the singer's doomed journey. The allusion to one of Elvis's first Sun singles contained in Wojahn's title helps link Joplin's quest to another figure who, after steeping himself in the blues, earned his own mythic place in American music and was eventually destroyed in the process.

Train she rides is sixteen coaches long,
 The long dark train that takes the girl away.
The silver wheels
    click and sing along

 The panhandle, the half-assed cattle towns,
All night until the misty break of day.
 Dark train,
    dark train, sixteen coaches long.

Girl's looked out her window all night long,
 Bad dreams:
    couldn't sleep her thoughts away.
The wheels click, mournful, dream along.

 Amarillo, Paradise,
    Albuquerque still a long
Night's ride. Scrub pine, cactus, fog all gray
 Around the dark train
    sixteen coaches long.

A cardboard suitcase and she's dressed all wrong.
 Got some cousin's address,
    no skills, no smarts, no money.
The wheels mock her as they click along.

A half-pint of Four Roses,
    then she hums a Woody song,
 "I Ain't Got No Home."
    The whistle brays.
The Mystery Train is sixteen coaches long.

 The whistle howls, the wheels click along.

In 1967:

- the archetypcal independent label, Atlantic Records, was sold to the giant media conglomerate, Warner Brothers
- after their Monterey performances, Janis Joplin's Big Brother and the Holding Company and Jimi Hendrix each received contracts worth approximately a quarter million dollars
- following *Sgt. Pepper*'s example, the production costs for many rock albums sky-rocketed to six figures
- propelled by rock's phenomenal success, annual revenues for all U.S. record sales topped $1 billion for the first time (with albums generating more money than singles—another first).

Finally, 1967 was also the year that all these events (as well as the latest backstage gossip about rock groups and their "groupies") began being chronicled in a groundbreaking new magazine. Based in San Francisco, *Rolling Stone* was in many respects a reflection of its hometown's countercultural ambiance. Yet, in keeping with rock's new status as a significant cultural and commercial force, the monthly magazine also tried to balance fanzine ardor with trade industry professionalism. Founded by an ambitious Berkeley College freelance writer, Jann Wenner, and San Francisco's veteran jazz critic (and early advocate for the city's acid-rockers), Ralph J. Gleason, *Rolling Stone* attracted a roster of talented writers and quickly became the premier journal of the new rock culture. Meanwhile rock also had begun entering the mainstream media in other ways.

Inspired by the Beatles' fast-paced, tuneful adventures in *A Hard Day's Night* a year earlier, American television decided to assemble its own rock band. With the help of studio sidemen and Brill Building songwriters, a quartet of lip-synching actors—transformed into the Monkees—began to make their weekly appearance in American living rooms. Over the next two years, this Fab(ricated) Foursome put six singles on the top of the charts. Meanwhile, rock in its new artistically enhanced and culturally evolved guise began infiltrating the world of both Hollywood and Broadway.

In 1968, Paul Simon and Art Garfunkel created a soundtrack for one of the defining films of the decade. Their songs for *The Graduate* received as much critical acclaim as Dustin Hoffman did for his début as the movie's alienated young antihero. Meanwhile, *Hair* (billed as an "American Tribal Love-Rock Musical") promoted itself as the first, genuine counterculture creation to find its way to the Broadway stage.

As a result of this mainstream embrace, rock performers were faced with a challenge to their deepest counterculture values. The prevailing anti-establishment idealism of the Sixties—which included a strong belief in communal creativity (and free concerts)—was difficult to maintain as the pace of artistic ambition and big-budget deals gained momentum. By 1968, the symptoms of this inner conflict were everywhere, as groups fragmented and merged in ever more egocentric and star-studded configurations.

For example, there was the L.A.-based band, Buffalo Springfield (featuring Neil Young, Stephen Stills, and Richie Furay). A year after releasing their 1967 hit single, "For What It's Worth" (an anthem of youth culture empowerment), Buffalo Springfield had disintegrated. Stephen Stills quickly decided to join forces with David Crosby (formerly of the Byrds) and Graham Nash (singer and songwriter of the Hollies, a successful British invasion band) to inaugurate the first of what would be a series of major rock-star mergers.

If the name "Buffalo Springfield" was intended to conjure up a folksy, Old West image, then the new band—"Crosby, Stills, and Nash"—sounded more like a high-powered law firm. Familiarly known as CS&N (and after being joined by Neil Young, CSN&Y), they became the prototype for what many viewed as a problematic trend in late 1960s rock, the "Supergroup." It was a syndrome that could be identified throughout the entire pop music scene, both in England and America, and among groups both black and white.

So intense was the pressure to exploit the vast commercial potential of the rock market that even the Motown "family" wasn't immune. In 1967, Berry Gordy began preparing the way for Diana Ross's transition—*from* the group she had joined as a teenager *to* what would eventually be a phenomenally successful solo career. First, he fired Florence Ballard (one of the original Supremes, whose strong vocal presence was now viewed as a distraction). Then he unveiled the newly redesigned trio along with the newly revised billing, "Diana Ross and the Supremes."

Meanwhile, one of San Francisco's pioneering bands was also about to succumb to a loss of faith in the counterculture's own version of "family" values. In 1968—a year after their Monterey breakthrough (and record-breaking Columbia contract)–Big Brother and the Holding Company released their album, *Cheap Thrills*. Everything about it seemed designed to reinforce the band's "hippie" image. With a cover created by San Francisco's celebrated underground cartoonist, R. Crumb, the album featured a collection of blues covers and original songs that were all performed with the band's notoriously sloppy good-time vibe and shot through with the ecstatic intensity of Janis Joplin's singing. Yet, by the time it came out, the record already seemed like an artifact of a bygone era.

Joplin quickly became a rock icon and the foremost female star in the male-dominated rock pantheon. So—critics and music industry executives began asking—what was she doing in a third-rate band? Before long, Janis Joplin turned her back on what had once been the rock's counterculture fundamental symbol: the band. Abruptly abandoning Big Brother and the Holding Company, she embarked on what would turn out to be a tragically abbreviated solo career.

The critic Ellen Willis used the issue of Joplin's departure from Big Brother to explore this failure of the communal ideology of the Sixties. Willis saw Sixties rock's growing obsession with "technical accomplishment" (musicianship) as "a sign that the tenuous alliance between mass culture and bohemianism . . . the fantasy of stardom and the fantasy of cultural revolution—was breaking down." For, as she explained:

> The elitist concept of "good musicianship" was alien to the holistic, egalitarian spirit of rock and roll as the act of leaving one's group the better to pursue one's individual ambition was alien to the holistic, egalitarian pretensions of the

cultural revolutionaries. If Joplin's decision to go it alone was influenced by all the obvious professional/commerical pressures, it also reflected a conflict of values within the counterculture itself—a conflict that foreshadowed its imminent disintegration.

SUPERGROUPS AND GUITAR HEROES

Conflicts concerning issues of musicianship, communal creativity, and individual artistic expression had long been central to the career of a performer who had become the embodiment of one of the era's most potent symbols, the "guitar hero." By 1966, when Eric Clapton formed Cream (the group with which he achieved international stardom), he had already become so celebrated as a master of the rock guitar that the graffiti—"Clapton is God"—had become almost as familiar a part of the London environment as its Cadbury chocolate signs.

Like many of his contemporaries, Clapton had started out by serving an apprenticeship in a couple of R & B–style bands, one of which—the Yardbirds—suddenly broke into the charts with a Top Ten pop hit ("For Your Love") in the months following the Beatles' invasion of America. As a dedicated member of the English blues revival, however, this unexpected pop success prompted Clapton's first crisis of conscience. He immediately quit the group (to be replaced first by Jeff Beck and then Jimmy Page) and took refuge in England's most respected blues band, John Mayall's Bluesbreakers. It was during the year-and-a-half that Clapton spent playing straight Chicago blues with Mayall that he refined his skill and attracted the adulation of British blues aficionados.

But immediately following his first album with the Bluesbreakers, Eric Clapton decided to form a band that would provide the opportunity for more creative freedom. Along with drummer Ginger Baker and bassist Jack Bruce, Clapton founded rock's breakthrough power trio, Cream. Although the band aspired to the counterculture's values of communal music making (and equal solo time), according to Charlie Gillett, Cream actually became the personification of that new rock phenomenon—the supergroup.

"Cream represented a new concept in pop music," Gillett explains in *The Sound of the City,* "an all-star line up of poll-winning musicians from different groups who came together to display their virtuosity and pursue a policy of musical adventure and exploration together." As we've seen, this inherent conflict between technical prowess and rock's "egalitarian spirit" was one that a number of musicians were struggling to resolve during this period (and to his credit, Clapton kept trying).

With Cream, however, Clapton dedicated himself to exploring the outer limits of virtuosity—and volume—in rock. And while the power trio concept that the band pioneered may have been an example of numerical minimalism, in every other way Cream was the epitome of excess. Huge banks of amplifiers blasted out a barrage of sound as Bruce, Baker, and Clapton each attempted to shoulder their way out of the ensemble's jumble of textures to claim the solo spotlight; and, once claimed, it was not something that would be easily relinquished. In concert, solos seemed to go on forever (although often it turned out to be a case of an expanding investment with diminishing returns). At its most inspired, however, Cream was able to achieve a rare combination of intuitive, ensemble interplay along with moments of individual, improvisational brilliance.

By 1968, Cream had achieved both extraordinary commercial success (their double album *Wheels of Fire* was number one on the American charts) and influence (inspiring, as Dave Marsh put it, "a seemingly infinite array of imitators—boogie bands, power trios, heavy metal groups"). The album also was significant because it contained a supercharged cover version of Mississippi Delta bluesman Robert Johnson's 1936 masterpiece "Cross Road Blues," thereby alerting the mainstream rock audience to the ultimate hero of so many of the Sixties guitar players.

Yet, once again, Clapton was ready to move on. As he explained after Cream's breakup, the band's succession of American triumphs had sent each member of the group on "a huge ego trip." Therefore, Clapton conceived of his next (equally short-lived) band, "Blind Faith" (a collaboration with Ginger Baker and Traffic's Steve Winwood) as an antisupergroup in which each member's ego would be submerged; but, after one lackluster album, it was the band itself that sank.

Over the next few years, heightened audience expectations (as well as a loss of blind faith in the egalitarian spirit of rock) led to an era of "supergroups" and "session men" (as the anonymous, highly skilled instrumentalists who brought a professional polish to recordings were known). But, while Eric Clapton may have served as the

FIGURE 4-26.   Cream (from left: drummer Ginger Baker, guitarist Eric Clapton, bassist Jack Bruce). The short-lived British band blended blues, rock, and jazz into a high-powered fusion; in the process, Cream became the era's first "supergroup." Author's collection.

Cream of the Crop

Having come together from a couple of prominent British bands in 1966, Cream played its farewell concert on November 26, 1968. In just two years, however, the band sold some fifteen million albums and became one of the most successful live acts in rock history.

At its best, Cream's extended forays into psychedelia and jazz-oriented improvisation were grounded by Eric Clapton's deep reverence for the blues (best exhibited in the band's covers of such blues classics as Skip James's "I'm So Glad" and Robert Johnson's masterpiece "Cross Road Blues"). But Cream also was capable of crafting radio-friendly singles such as "Sunshine of Your Love" and pop classics such as "Badge."

prototype of the "guitar hero" (a role later assumed by Jeff Beck, Jimmy Page, and Eddie Van Halen, among others), the one rock guitarist of the era whose claim to that coveted title has only become more secure with each passing year is Jimi Hendrix.

JIMI HENDRIX: COSMIC BLUESMAN

It was at the 1967 Monterey International Pop Festival that Jimi Hendrix first stunned the rock audience with a combination of instrumental pyrotechnics and showmanship. The tall, slender black man crowned by a halo of frizzy hair and draped in ruffles and silk presented the mostly white rock fans with an intriguing and paradoxical image. For, ironically, by this time the idea of a *black* "guitar hero" was quite a novelty.

In the beginning, of course, the guitar had been rock 'n' roll's archetypal instrument. But, while Chuck Berry may have been the music's first guitar hero (and Bo Diddley one of the genre's most original stylists), most of the guitar-playing idols of the 1950s who truly captured the imagination of that first generation of rock 'n' roll fans were white Southern rockabilly rebels such as Carl Perkins, Eddie Cochran, and Buddy Holly. And it was these same performers who had served as the primary inspiration for the Beatles and the other British pop bands who reinvented the music during the early 1960s.

Meanwhile, the folk revival taking place on both sides of the Atlantic was responsible for introducing the rich legacy of the blues to a new generation of white teenagers. A decade later, the guitar-playing refugees from this alternate subculture would reshape rock by reestablishing the music's blues roots. Drawing on the influence of African-American electric blues guitarists such as Albert King, Elmore James, Muddy Waters, and Hubert Sumlin, white blues revival performers such as Mike Bloomfield (of the Paul Butterfield Blues Band) and Danny Kalb (of the Blues Project)—along with their British counterparts such as Eric Clapton and Keith Richards—emerged as rock's first wave of guitar heroes.

Although Jimi Hendrix had served a long apprenticeship backing R & B acts (such as Little Richard, Sam Cooke, and the Ike Turner Revue) on the so-called chitlin' circuit of black nightclubs, it was while playing in a Greenwich Village club with John Hammond, Jr., one of the most dedicated of the blues revivalists (and son of the famous record producer), that Hendrix began to attract the attention of the cogniscenti. Mike Bloomfield—who was working with Paul Butterfield at a club across the street—told an interviewer from *Guitar Player* magazine about his first encounter with Hendrix:

I was the hot-shot guitarist on the block—I thought I was *it*. I went right across the street and saw him. Hendrix knew who I was, and that day in front of my eyes, he burned me to death. I didn't even get my guitar out. H-bombs were going off, guided missiles were flying—I can't tell you the sounds he was getting out of his instrument. . . . He just got right in my face with that ax, and I didn't even want to pick up a guitar for the next year.

But Hendrix's real transformation from blues sideman to rock superstar first took place in England where he'd been encouraged to move in order to take advantage of British blues fanaticism and the country's obsession with the myth of black potency. From the very beginning, the response to Hendrix was not based simply on his musical skills—as prodigious as they were—but on a complex of racial and sexual stereotypes that ultimately Hendrix both exploited and to which he would later fall victim. In any event, Hendrix immediately attracted a cult of awed fans that included most of England's major rock stars. In fact, it was on the insistence of Paul McCartney that Jimi was invited to perform at the Monterey Festival, thereby launching his career in his own country.

Although the novelty of a black rock star/guitar hero/cosmic bluesman soon wore off, most audiences continued to ignore Hendrix's truly revolutionary musical conceptions and instrumental virtuosity—seeming more impressed with stage tricks (like "playing" his guitar with his teeth) and sexual symbolism (like using his guitar as a phallic prop). But with the passage of time, Hendrix seems finally to have transcended both the demeaning superficiality of his initial image and the tragic sensationalism of his untimely death, in order to claim his place as one of the most significant musicians in rock history.

FIGURE 4-27.   Jimi Hendrix first established himself as a rock superstar at the 1967 Monterey Pop Festival when he dazzled the counterculture vanguard with his guitar-hero pyrotechnics. His career would reach its climax two years later when he took the stage at Woodstock, the movement's defining event. Archive photo.

Jimi Hendrix: Bombs Bursting in Air

Although Hendrix's sonic explorations are usually associated with the psychedelic spirit of the Sixties, the addition of the "Star Spangled Banner" to his repertoire has been interpreted as his response to the era's political turmoil. In his Woodstock performance of the song, Hendrix uses his guitar—not to commemorate the bombs bursting over some dimly remembered nineteenth-century battlefield—but to evoke the shattering sound of rockets that at that very moment were raining down on the jungles of Vietnam.

Vietnam: The Rock 'n' Roll War

While much has been written about the links between Sixties rock and the antiwar movement, the decade's musical revolution had as profound an impact among the soldiers on the front lines as it did among the protesters on the home front. Nowhere was this captured more clearly than in *Dispatches,* Michael Herr's acclaimed account of what one reviewer referred to as "our first rock-and-roll war." In the excerpt below, Herr describes a mission "up country" where, pinned down in a rice paddy by enemy fire, he hears Jimi Hendrix for the very first time.

One day I went out with the ARVN on an operation in the rice paddies above Vinh Long, forty terrified Vietnamese troops and five Americans, all packed into three Hueys that dropped us up to our hips in paddy muck. I had never been in a rice paddy before. We spread out and moved toward the marshy swale that led to the jungle. We were still twenty feet from the first cover, a low paddy wall, when we took fire from the treeline. It was probably the working half of a crossfire that had somehow gone wrong. It caught one of the ARVN in the head, and he dropped back into the water and disappeared. We made it to the wall with two casualties. There was no way of stopping their fire, no room to send in a flanking party, so gunships were called and we crouched behind the wall and waited. There was a lot of fire coming from the trees, but we were all right as long as we kept down. And I was thinking, Oh man, so this is a rice paddy, yes, wow! when I suddenly heard an electric guitar shooting right up in my ear and a mean, rapturous black voice singing, coaxing, "Now c'mon baby, stop actin' so crazy," and when I got it all together I turned to see a grinning black corporal hunched over a cassette recorder. "Might's well," he said. "We ain' goin' *no*where till them gunships come."

That's the story of the first time I ever heard Jimi Hendrix, but in a war where a lot of people talked about Aretha's "Satisfaction" the way other people speak of Brahms' Fourth, it was more than a story; it was Credentials. "Say, that Jimi Hendrix is my main man," someone would say. "He has *def*initely got his shit together!" Hendrix had once been in the 101st Airborne, and the Airborne in Vietnam was full of wiggy-brilliant spades like him, really mean and really good, guys who always took care of you when things got bad. That music meant a lot to them. I never once heard it played over the Armed Forces Radio Network.

While Hendrix modeled the style of his own power trio—the Jimi Hendrix Experience—on Cream's full-throttle, blues-based, improvisatory marathons, Hendrix's guitar playing was a far cry from Clapton's blues classicism. Jimi Hendrix revolutionized the electric guitar by bringing an array of innovative instrumental techniques and a mastery of the latest technological resources to the repertoire of musical influences he had accumulated throughout his R & B apprenticeship.

Hendrix had not only absorbed the entire history of the blues (from Robert Johnson to Muddy Waters and Buddy Guy), but—during his time in Greenwich Village—he had become aware of the experiments in jazz improvisation then being developed by performers such as Charles Mingus, John Coltrane, and Ornette Coleman (who were appearing at other area clubs). Finally, it was Hendrix who most aggressively expanded the guitar's sonic vocabulary by exploiting the potential of the latest high-powered amplifiers, fuzz boxes, and wah-wah pedals.

Yet, Jimi Hendrix's true genius was that, when he chose to, he could assemble these disparate elements into an extraordinarily original musical conception, both on stage and in the recording studio. As Geoffrey Stokes expressed it: "What set him apart from his contemporaries was his mastery of the instrument's—and the studio's—electronic (im)possibilities. Certainly there'd been other guitarists who had incorporated feedback in their solos, but Hendrix was the first—and, of his generation, probably the only—to tame it, make it fluid, flexible and melodic." And no matter how far his music expanded, it always remained firmly rooted in the blues.

B. B. King, one of the great blues guitarist of all time, recognized this kinship with Hendrix. "Jimi held his own with anybody," he once remarked. "To me, he was one of the great explorers of the so-called Delta blues."

FIGURE 4-28.   By combining two distinct communal traditions—that of the African-American church and the San Francisco counterculture—Sly and the Family Stone became crossover superstars and black culture heroes. Courtesy of Sony Music Photo Archive.

Sly and the Family Stone Take You Higher

Not only did their fusion of gospel music, R & B, and "psychedelic rock" generate an impressive string of 1960s rock classics ("Dance to the Music," "Everyday People," "I Want to Take You Higher," to name a few), but—along with James Brown—Sly and the Family Stone also became pioneers of Seventies funk. Finally, by providing hip-hop DJs with a treasure-trove of samples, the band has taken its rightful place (along with James Brown) as one of rap's most venerated ancestors.

But after unifying the almost half-million citizens of the Woodstock Nation at the famous 1969 festival, the musical and social utopia that Sly and the Family Stone symbolized began to come apart at the seams, and Sly's idealism was replaced by a darker vision. The band's last hit single, "Family Affair," was the one bright spot on their brilliant but bleak 1971 album, *There's a Riot Going On.*

Although the writer (and blues revivalist) Tony Glover concurred with King's assessment, his *Rolling Stone* article on the guitarist noted, "Hendrix plays Delta blues for sure—only the Delta may have been on Mars."

SLY AND THE FAMILY STONE: THE CHURCH OF PSYCHEDELIC SOUL

While Hendrix was being deified by a white audience that had been gradually sensitized to the African-American roots of rock through cover versions of blues classics offered by 1960s rock's blues-based bands (like the Rolling Stones and Cream), for most of the era's black community Jimi barely even existed.

Hendrix's embrace of (white) rock culture may have been responsible for alienating a segment of the more racially conscious black community, but in his book *The Death of Rhythm and Blues,* the African-American music

FIGURE 4-29.   Carlos Santana's ecstatic guitar solos—soaring out of dense layers of Latin polyrhythms—made the San Francisco band to which he lent his name an icon of Sixties rock. Thirty years later, his multiplatinum solo album, *Supernatural*, would earn the veteran rocker five Grammy awards, including Album of the Year. Courtesy of the Sony Music Photo Archive.

Viva Santana

Carlos Santana had come to the Bay Area from his native Mexico at the age of ten. For the most part, however, the distinctive Spanish tinge in his music can be traced to his love of *salsa,* a style of Cuban-jazz first cooked up in the dance clubs of New York City's barrios. And beginning with the hit single "Evil Ways" (written by salsa percussionist Willie Bobo), from Santana's 1969 self-titled début album, every one of their new LPs included at least one sizzling slice of Latin rock.

After leaving the band with which he created such enduring Top Forty hits as "Black Magic Woman" and "Soul Sacrifice," Carlos spent the Seventies and Eighties experimenting with a jazz-rock synthesis known as "Fusion." More recently, he paved the way for his triumphant pop comeback by contributing soulful Spanish guitar embellishments for the song, "To Zion" from the 1998 multiple Grammy Award–winning CD, *The Miseducation of Lauryn Hill.*

critic Nelson George suggests that, in fact, young black audiences rejected the famous guitar hero because he was . . . well, a guitar hero. "Unfortunately, Hendrix fatally damaged his connection with black audiences because of his innovative brilliance on the electric guitar, an instrument that, with the declining black interest in the blues, fell into disfavor." Not only did most African-Americans consider the blues (and therefore the guitar) a vestige of the past but, as George explains it, they had another problem with Hendrix's music: "You just couldn't dance to it."

That certainly wasn't a problem for Sly Stone—the other black performer to attract the adulation of 1960s rock fans. Although both Jimi and Sly drew from a variety of African-American musical sources, according to Nelson George, "Black America's reaction to each was different: Hendrix was rejected, while Sly was viewed . . . as a hero." To a great extent, Sly's unique role as both counterculture crossover superstar and black culture hero can be traced to a curious fusion of two distinct communal traditions.

Unlike Hendrix, who identified with the self-reliant image of the lone bluesman—and who emerged from the world of London's dueling guitars—Sly Stone (born Sylvester Stewart) had grown up as a member of a family gospel group, and he had begun his career in San Francisco just as that city's community of young people was forging a new collective consciousness. Even the name of his group—Sly and the Family Stone—alluded to the actual blood relationships among some of its members, as well as to the utopian ideal of "family" (as symbolized by the rock group) that was so central to the hippie philosophy.

By 1968, Sly had formed a tight, soulful seven-piece band that combined the ecstatic call-and-response fervor of gospel, the discipline of R & B, and the improvisatory flow and rhythmic drive of acid rock. At its best, Sly and the Family Stone seemed able to reconcile all of America's musical and cultural contradictions on the basis of their irresistible groove and the unifying idealism of their message. At a time when the country was being torn apart by political and racial tensions, Sly and the Family Stone became a metaphor for a visionary alternative: "Sly's sound was totally integrated," the writer Dave Marsh has pointed out, "not just musically, but sexually and racially—here was a band in which men and women, black and white, had not just one fixed role but many fluid ones. The women played, the men sang; the blacks freaked out, the whites got funky; everyone did something unexpected, which was the only thing the listener could expect."

Over the next three years, Sly and the Family Stone generated a remarkable string of hits, both on mainstream Top Forty AM stations and FM's hippest "progressive rock" outlets. Beginning with "Dance to the Music" (a celebration of the liberating power of that ancient art/ritual), every record the band issued seemed to be an anthem of reconciliation or collective empowerment: "Everyday People," "Stand!," "Life," "Everybody Is a Star," "You Can Make It if You Try," "I Want to Take You Higher."

During his heyday, Sly assembled one of rock's most passionate and diverse audiences and created a body of work that established him as one of the most influential performers of the era. Along with James Brown, it was Sly who would supply both the blueprints for the architects of Seventies funk and, a decade later, a treasure-trove of samples for hip-hop's aural collages. So back in 1969, when plans were being made for a mammoth rock festival—promoted with the slogan "Three Days of Peace and Music"—it would have been unthinkable not to have Sly and the Family Stone on the roster of performers.

WOODSTOCK NATION: THREE DAYS OF PEACE AND MUSIC

Ever since Monterey, the outdoor rock festival had become a familiar item on young America's summer calendar. But, as we've seen, in two short years the counterculture ideals that had infused the first "gatherings of the tribes" had already been considerably diluted by the music's phenomenal commercial success. Yet, as the decade drew to a close, it was Woodstock, more than any other single event, which would emerge as the most potent symbol of the communal ethos of "The Sixties."

What made Woodstock the watershed phenomenon of the era had as much to do with the idealistic principles (of "family," and "sharing") that were regularly invoked by the event's nervous organizers as with the music that emanated from its massive stage. Not that they didn't have good reason to be nervous. They had expected the weekend of August 15–17 to be a cozy gathering of about 150,000 rock fans (roughly what recent festivals had drawn in Atlantic City and Atlanta, Georgia). But when over four hundred thousand young people arrived, Max Yasgur's six-hundred-acre Catskill Mountain farm suddenly become the third-largest city in New York State.

With virtually no police supervision, and totally inadequate food, water, sanitary, and medical facilities, the entire event could easily have become a "disaster area," which New York's governor would eventually declare it. Instead—despite a series of storms whose torrential rains turned the farm into a field of mud—it turned out to be just what the organizers had promised: Three Days of Peace and Music. And while it may be the "Peace" that has become enshrined as Woodstock's most enduring legacy, a survey of the festival's "Music" (much of which has been preserved in the three-hour *Woodstock* film and its multidisk soundtrack album), also offers an intriguing portrait of the rock music scene at a crucial moment of transition.

Since the whole concept of outdoor, multiday music festivals had originated with the folkies (the Newport Folk Festival being the most prestigious example), it was only fitting that Woodstock include a choice selection of contemporary folk singers. Not only did they accompany themselves with their own acoustic guitars, but Richie Havens and Joan Baez (and an unplugged Country Joe) also introduced a political element to the proceedings by singing antiwar and freedom songs that offered a fitting link to the festival's folk-revival roots.

Despite recent political and social cataclysms (such as the assassinations of Robert Kennedy and Martin Luther King Jr., a string of violent urban uprisings, the Tet Offensive—one of Vietnam's most traumatic and bloody episodes), in the context of Woodstock's massive good vibe the earnest messages of these folkies seemed almost quaint. Meanwhile, throughout their restrained acoustic performances, the air above the vast audience was filled with a sound that had become indelibly associated with the war itself—"choppers." With access roads to the site blocked by abandoned cars, helicopters were flying in an army of rock stars.

Among these were an array of Monterey Pop veterans (including Janis Joplin, the Jefferson Airplane, the Grateful Dead, Country Joe and the Fish, and honorary hippie guru Ravi Shankar), who provided another of Woodstock's nods to tradition. The festival's counterculture credentials also were enhanced by the selection of "Chip" Mounk (one of the pioneer producers of the Haight-Ashbury's famous dance concerts) to be the event's MC. Finally, since the overwhelming crowds had made ticket collection impossible, Woodstock achieved another connection to more innocent times—it became a free concert.

Although neither the Beatles (who had stopped performing live two years before and who were on the verge of breaking up) nor the Stones (who had priced themselves out of the lineup) participated in the decade's epochal event, Woodstock's English imports comprised a cross-section of rock performers at a crossroads in rock history. There was a band of blues-revivalists (Ten Years After), as well as one of the new "progressive rock" bands (the Moody Blues), whose records (exemplified by their signature single, "Knights in White Satin") were awash in lush string orchestrations and misty, Romantic allusions.

There also was a new British band starring the latest "guitar hero" (the Jeff Beck Group) and a blue-eyed soulman on his first American tour (Joe Cocker), who invoked the absent Beatles with a soulful performance of *Sgt. Pepper's* "With a Little Help from My Friends." And, finally, there was the Who. Although up to this point they hadn't achieved the kind of success in America that the band's rigorous, tightly structured, aggressive recordings and dynamic live act deserved, it was the Who's Woodstock performance of a song ("See Me") from their recently released "rock opera" *Tommy* that not only provided one of the highpoints of the entire festival, but set the stage for the band's entry into the front ranks of rock stardom.

Among American bands, there was a similar range of familiar faces and new trends. In only their second live performance together, Crosby, Stills, and Nash introduced the concept of the "supergroup" to Woodstock. And while the appearance of a blues-revival band (Canned Heat) reflected Sixties rock's laid-back past, the debut of blues superstar Johnny Winter symbolized its high-stakes future. Only a few months before, Winter—a rail-thin albino bluesman—was working the local bar scene in Texas when a *Rolling Stone* article suddenly transformed him into a hot new guitar hero (with a freshly signed $300,000 Columbia recording contract in his back pocket). And it was their inspired performance at Woodstock that earned San Francisco's psychedelic Latin-rock band, Santana, a Columbia contract; a few months later, Santana would release an innovative (and commercially successful) début album shot through with Afro-Cuban rhythms and Carlos Santana's soulful guitar improvisations.

Despite Woodstock's reputation as the apotheosis of Sixties' rock counterculturalism, there were a couple of American bands that foreshadowed the "more is more" attitude that would soon become the prevailing philosophy of rock in the 1970s. Among these was a power trio in the Cream mold (Mountain), a big-band style

FIGURE 4-30.   The Who arrived on America's shores as part of the "British invasion." But unlike the warm reception accorded the Beatles, the Rolling Stones, the Dave Clark Five, the Animals, and Herman's Hermits, the country proved stubbornly resistant to The Who's unique charms. Trinifold. Courtesy of MCA Records.

The Who: My Generation

Although the band first broke into the British Top Ten in early 1965, it took another two years before they would accomplish a similar feat in the United States with "I Can See for Miles," their first and only American Top Ten single. In the meantime, the Who had already forged a highly original sound (comprised of Pete Townshend's windmill-power chords, Roger Daltry's emotive vocals, and the arachic virtuosity of Keith Moon's drumming) and a riveting stage act that typically concluded with a splintered guitar, an overturned drum kit, and a couple of wrecked (and howling) loudspeakers.

So it was more than a little ironic that the Who would become most identified with a ninety-minute rock opera. But *Tommy* remains the Who's most successful and enduring work. The band would go on to create another successful magnus opus, *Quadrophenia* (about the formative days of London's Mod subculture), as well as a brilliant, synthisizer-based album, *Who's Next;* but for many fans the definitive Who records remain their early go-for-broke three-minute singles: "I Can't Explain," "My Generation," "Substitute," "The Kids Are Alright," "Magic Bus," and "I Can See for Miles."

jazz-rock fusion group (Blood, Sweat, and Tears), a campy, golden-oldies act (Sha Na Na), and an organ-based, proto-heavy-metal band (Iron Butterfly), whose recent, best-selling LP, *In-a-Gadda-Da-Vida,* featured a seventeen-minute-long title track with perhaps the longest drum solo on record.

By contrast, there were two bands at the festival whose imminent success would be based on a back-to-basics approach that offered a bracing contrast to the forthcoming musical excesses of Seventies "art" and "arena" rock. Both the Creedence Clearwater Revival and the Band were neorevivalists who had each absorbed America's varied musical traditions and distilled them into their own distinctive home brews.

The Creedence Clearwater Revival had started as a high school garage band back when rock was still just rock 'n' roll. And since they first began to attract national attention at a time when rock itself was expanding into the heady realms of the "concept-album" and double-LP "opera," the group's tightly constructed singles blasted out of the radio like a breath of fresh air. Beginning with "Proud Mary" (released shortly before their Woodstock appearance), CCR embarked on a two-year string of Top Ten hits—including "Fortunate Son," "Who'll Stop the Rain," "Bad Moon Risin'," and "Lodi"—most of which were written by John Fogerty, who was also the group's singer, arranger, and lead guitarist. Creedence also established its connection with other musical styles and eras through its heartfelt covers of Motown soul ("I Heard It through the Grapevine"), rockabilly classics ("Susie Q"), and R & B weirdness ("I Put a Spell on You").

Creedence Clearwater Revival's rhythmically infectious music had an enormous appeal for a huge cross-section of rock's rapidly expanding (but increasingly fragmented) audience. The group's records became instant staples both on the rigidly programmed Top Forty AM stations and on the hippest, underground FM outlets—and they sounded great on both. While some listeners may have been attracted by the band's working-class persona, according to Ellen Willis, CCR's popularity was not only based on its "loyalty to rock's plebian roots" or its "populist instincts." According to Willis, the main reason for the band's popularity was considerably more simple: "Creedence was *the* white American dance band; no one even came close." Over the intervening years, Creedence Clearwater Revival has exerted a powerful influence on a host of proletarian roots-rockers from Bob Seeger and John Mellencamp to Bruce Springsteen and Dave Matthews.

Although they shared Creedence Clearwater Revival's flannel-shirted fundamentalism (as well as a similar allegiance to the primordial spirit of rock 'n' roll), the Band reached even further back to the deepest roots of American music in order to create a highly personal and much-revered style. And, unlike CCR—which had a special genius for putting together singles that were brilliant examples of that compact format—beginning with their first LP, *Music from Big Pink* (released about a year before Woodstock), the Band's richly textured songs seemed to require a larger canvas.

At a time when rock groups were straining to out-do each other with grandiose, multitrack masterpieces, an album by the Band was more like a subtly linked collection of classic American short stories. And if their lyrics (especially the early ones) also happened to sound a little "Dylan-esque," there was a good reason. Before they were the Band, the band had already garnered considerable acclaim for the contributions they made to Dylan's music during the earliest (and most exhilarating) phase of his folk-rock career.

For two years—beginning shortly after Dylan's "electric" debut at the 1965 Newport Folk Festival—the four Canadian musicians and their Arkansas drummer toured the world helping to create what critics at the time considered (and live bootleg albums confirm) were Bob Dylan's most powerful performances. In 1966, when a motorcycle accident consigned Dylan to an extended period of convalescence at his home in Woodstock, New York, his band settled nearby in a rented house they dubbed "Big Pink" for its unusual paint job. Although the Woodstock Festival was ultimately held about seventy-five miles away in Bethel, New York, it was Dylan's connection to Woodstock that had prompted the promoters to link their Music and Art Fair to that hallowed upstate village.

Now known officially as the Band (a name that can sound either modest or arrogant, depending on how you place the emphasis), they gradually began to assemble songs for their own debut album. Yet, in some ways, *Music from Big Pink* remained a collaboration with their legendary former front man. Dylan wrote or cowrote many of the album's songs—and also did the primitive/surrealistic watercolor painting that appeared on its cover. Ultimately, however, the Band established a musical voice that was uniquely their own. During an era of psychedelia and guitar heroics, the Band offered the deeper satisfactions of a kind of homespun versatility and a commitment to the ideal of communal creativity. Each member of the group was a skilled multi-instrumentalist, and often they would trade vocal chores back and forth a couple of times during the course of a single song.

By their second album—simply titled *The Band*—the group's brilliant lead guitarist Robbie Robertson ("The only mathematical guitar genius I've ever run into who does not offend my intestinal nervousness with his rear guard sound," as Dylan put it) also was writing almost all of their material. Drawing from a range of black and white musical traditions—from the traveling minstrel show and country string band to the rural jukejoint and rockabilly combo—the Band fashioned a sound as simple and sturdy as a nineteenth-century barn (although one decorated by the town eccentric).

After a couple of more albums studded with classic songs—and another fling backing up Dylan in 1976—the Band decided sixteen years together was long enough. Going out in style, their final concert (filmed by Martin Scorcese as *The Last Waltz*) was a sentimental celebration featuring guest appearances from a few friends come to pay their respects; these included Eric Clapton, Joni Mitchell, Van Morrison, Muddy Waters, Dr. John, the Staple Singers, Neil Young, and Bob Dylan, among others.

While the Band provided Woodstock with the spirit of community associated with small-town America (in the words of one writer, they were "the only band that could have warmed up the crowd for Abraham Lincoln"), the performance that captured the festival's more utopian communal aspirations turned out (not unexpectedly) to be the one by Sly and the Family Stone. And they did it by taking Woodstock to church. For example, their intensely funky version of "I Want to Take You Higher" included an audience-participation call-and-response section that turned the muddy upstate New York farm into one sanctified congregation. As the band locked into one of its patented grooves, Sly preached; "I Want to Take You Higher," he shouted, and 400,000 voices answered—"Higher!" throwing up their hands in the "peace sign" as Sly had requested.

Jimi Hendrix closed out the festival with a set that featured his now-famous deconstruction of the "Star Spangled Banner." Hendrix shredded the anthem with feedback, and the shriek of bursting rockets issuing forth from his guitar seemed to allude less to some long-forgotten battle in American history than to the unpopular war currently ranging in Vietnam (or to the civil unrest that was shattering the urban ghettos). In any event, since Hendrix didn't go on stage until early Monday morning, by which time much of the enormous audience had already left, his extraordinary performance turned out to be more of a coda than a climax.

Whatever the reality of that weekend may have been, Woodstock was immediately transformed into a pop culture myth. Throughout the country media commentators and newspaper editorials, confronted by the sheer dimensions of the event, reluctantly acknowledged that a "miracle" had taken place in upstate New York. Even *Time* magazine (considered by most in the counterculture as the house organ of the establishment) conceded that Woodstock "may well rank as one of the significant political and sociological events of the age." A few months later, Joni Mitchell's song "Woodstock" (covered most successfully by Crosby, Stills, Nash, and Young) immortalized the story of the festival as a ballad of communal pride.

It didn't take long, however, for Woodstock's beatific glow to be shadowed by an event that would also become enshrined in Sixties' pop history as a one-word metaphor; but "Altamont" was emblematic of the decade's darker forces. And appropriately it was brought to you . . . at Their Satanic Majesty's Request.

ALTAMONT: SYMPATHY FOR THE DEVIL

The Rolling Stones had always strongly identified with the traditional belief that the blues was "the devil's music" and, more than any other rock band of the era, it was the Stones who had consciously transposed the figure of the bluesman—that hard-drinkin', hard-lovin' social outcast of African-American mythology—into the image of the contemporary rock star. So, as the plans for Woodstock's idealistic celebration of "Peace and Music" were being finalized, the Rolling Stones were struggling to finish an album (*Let It Bleed*) charged with apocalyptic visions whose centerpiece was an epic tribute to the Prince of Darkness himself, appropriately entitled "Sympathy for the Devil."

Although each of the Rolling Stones had established his credibility as a rock rebel through occasional acts of public lewdness or drug-related misdemeanors, it was Brian Jones who most passionately embraced the band's decadent persona and who now became its victim. Tragically, as the decade drew to a close, Jones had became so mired in the "sex" and the "drugs" that he had all but abandoned the final element in that famous Sixties' trinity, "rock 'n' roll." Virtually absent from the *Let It Bleed* sessions (he was replaced by guitarist Mick Taylor, yet an-

FIGURE 4-31. The film *Gimme Shelter* was supposed to be a celebration of the Rolling Stones' 1969 U.S. tour. Instead, the murder of an eighteen-year-old fan at the band's Altamont Speedway free concert has made it a primary source for rock historians looking for the moment when "the Sixties" came to an end. Museum of Modern Art Film Stills Collection.

Altamont and the End of the Sixties

From the very beginning, the Stones' Dionysian persona (designed as an alternative to the Fab Four's good-natured irreverence) was a heady blend of the badman bravado the band had appropriated from American blues and a peculiarly British brand of crushed-velvet decadence. But when the Stones took the stage at Altamont, their carefully constructed fantasy was quickly shattered.

As they launched into "Sympathy for the Devil," the centerpiece of their latest album (*Let It Bleed*), a scuffle broke out near the stage. The platoon of Hells Angels, whom the Stones had hired as security, began randomly attacking overly zealous fans with pool cues. Then—as the film reveals in agonizing slow motion—there was the glimpse of a gun and then chaos as knife-wielding Angels closed in.

other graduate of John Mayall's Bluesbreakers), Brian finally agreed to announce his "retirement" from the band; within a month he was dead, having drowned in the swimming pool of his mansion in the English countryside.

Two days later, what had been planned as a free concert in London's Hyde Park to introduce the Stones' new lineup (and to kick off what would be their first U.S. tour in three years), became instead a wake for Brian Jones attended by 150,000 fans. As white doves were released into the air, Jagger, who was draped in flowing white garb, recited Shelly's "Adonais," a poem whose images of resurrection had been intended to dispel the reality of death itself. But when it came to fashioning his stage costume for the upcoming tour, Mick reverted to a more customary image; he selected a black latex shirt on which was emblazoned the Greek letter Omega—"the end." It was a symbol that would foreshadow events to come.

The Stones' next free concert would take place a few months later at the Altamont Speedway forty miles outside of San Francisco; it was supposed to have been a musical "thank you" from the Rolling Stones for what was the most spectacular (and most profitable) rock tour in history. It could also earn the Stones some coveted counterculture credibility and conveniently serve as a colorful climax to the documentary that was being filmed about the band (eventually released as *Gimme Shelter*).

After numerous venues were negotiated for and then suddenly canceled, finally just twenty-four hours before the day of the event, contracts for a free concert at Altamont were completed. But that didn't stop an estimated 300,000 fans from making their way to the bleak and litter-strewn abandoned Speedway. And no wonder, for in addition to the Stones themselves, the other scheduled acts included the Grateful Dead, Crosby, Stills, and Nash, Santana, and the Jefferson Airplane. But it quickly became apparent that this was not going to be—as the event had been hyped—the Woodstock of the West.

In the parlance of the period, the "vibes were bad" from the very start. The most obvious problem was turning out to be the members of a local Hells Angels chapter who had been hired as security for five-hundred dollars' worth of beer. Instructed to "protect the stage," they began by randomly pummeling overly enthusiastic fans and, when Marty Balin of the Jefferson Airplane tried to intervene, he was knocked unconscious by a blow from a pool cue.

By the time the Rolling Stones went on, darkness had fallen. Flanked by a horde of Hells Angels, Jagger launched into "Sympathy for the Devil." But the violent confrontation continued to flare up and the band ground to a halt. After entreating everybody to "cool out," Jagger tried to make a joke about the song's demonic effect: "We always have something very funny happening when we start that number." But when he tried to start the song a second time, another more serious scuffle broke out in front of the stage.

In the film, *Gimme Shelter,* the scene is replayed frame by frame: One minute the young fan was simply part of the vast crowd grooving to the music, then there is the glimpse of a gun, then chaos as knife-wielding Hells Angels close in. Although the next day's papers prominently featured the young man's obituary, the subsequent media postmortems made clear that something else had died that December day as the decade itself was about to draw its last gasp.

Not surprisingly, it was the local media that expressed the most profound sense of loss. After all, it was in San Francisco that the shining vision of a cohesive counterculture bound together by sex, drugs, and rock 'n' roll had been born. For *Rolling Stone* magazine, which had always had a special bond with the rock group with which it shared a name, Altamont represented the death of a dream. Now the magazine wrote its epitaph, declaring December 6, 1969, "rock and roll's all-time worst day." Ralph J. Gleason, the magazine's cofounder and San Francisco's most respected music critic (and a long-time champion of the city's youth culture), saw the event as the ultimate example of the decade's failed dreams: "Is this the new community? Is this what Woodstock promised? Gathered together *as* a tribe, what happened? Brutality, murder, despoliation."

In retrospect, all the collective post-Altamont doom and gloom seems more than a little overblown. Although the nature of the tragedy (as well as the date on the calendar) may have suggested at the time that "The Sixties" had come to an abrupt and traumatic end, much of what has come to represent that volatile decade was far from over.

In Vietnam, the war continued to escalate and, on college campuses across the country, so did the protests against it. (Crosby, Stills, Nash, and Young's "Ohio," released early in 1970, was a blistering account of the killing of four Kent State students protesting the escalation of the war into Cambodia by members of the National Guard.) In Washington, Nixon still occupied the White House, and his vice president, Spiro Agnew—the designated champion of the "Silent Majority"—continued his ongoing campaign against the pernicious influence of rock 'n' roll. Rock would not only survive, however, but—as it entered a new decade—it was on the brink of inaugurating a period of unprecedented growth.

Activities and Projects
Chapter 4: R & B, Rockabilly, Rock 'n' Roll, and Rock

1. Provide an overview of mainstream American popular music during the decade prior to rock 'n' roll's appearance on the national pop charts in June of 1955 (Bill Haley and the Comets' "Rock around the Clock" goes to number one).

2. Trace the evolution of the crossover phenomenon through a survey of the three main *Billboard* magazine charts (country and western, rhythm and blues, and popular music) between 1950 and 1957.

3. Research one of the important regional independent labels of the 1950s (i.e., King, Atlantic, Sun, Chess, Specialty). Discuss the company's musical style and identity and its role in the advent of rock 'n' roll.

4. Develop a project that explains the influence of one of the following on Fifties rock 'n' roll:
    a. gospel music
    b. blues and R & B
    c. country music

5. Describe the commercial radio scene during the 1950s. Discuss the role of "personality jocks" (black and white) and the transition to the Top Forty format. Relate what was taking place on the airwaves to the evolution of rock 'n' roll during the decade.

6. Survey the history of the "cover version" in popular music. Describe the changing concept of the cover version during the mid-1950s by citing specific examples. Discuss the positive and negative affect they had in the transition to rock 'n' roll.

7. Compare the recordings Elvis Presley made on the Sun label with his early RCA releases. Explain the changes in repertoire, instrumentation, arrangements, production, and performance style. Explore the insights this activity provided into the changing nature of rock 'n' roll during the second half of the 1950s.

8. Trace the evolution of the electric guitar. Cite the contributions of pioneers from various genres, including blues, jazz, and country music.

9. Analyze the response of mainstream institutions to the rock 'n' roll revolution. Include civic and political entities, the media, and the American Society of Composers, Authors, and Publishers (ASCAP) and other music industry organizations in your discussion.

10. Develop a project based on "Women's Voice in Rock 'n' Roll" (c. mid-1950s to mid-1960s). Include both performers and songwriters in your discussion.

11. By exploring the career of either Jerry Leiber and Mike Stoller or Phil Spector, describe the innovations that took place in rock 'n' roll recording during the late 1950s and early 1960s.

12. Analyze the Motown sound. Explain the role of the label's performers, songwriters, producers, and house band. Relate the label's musical and marketing philosophy to the social and racial climate of the 1960s.

13. Explain the meaning of Atlantic Records producer Jerry Wexler's definition of soul music as "secularized gospel." Support your explanation with specific examples of recordings by both gospel and soul performers from the 1950s and 1960s.

14. Describe the evolution of the folk revival of the 1960s and trace its impact on rock during the second half of the decade.

15. Research the impact of either of the following on Sixties rock:
    a. FM radio
    b. rock journalism

16. Explore the "guitar hero" in Sixties rock. Identify significant performers and describe their influences and approaches to the instrument.

17. Beginning in the 1960s, rock music had an enormous impact on art and popular culture. Provide an overview of "rock films" or Broadway "rock musicals" from this period.

18. Survey rock's response to the Vietnam War and the other social issues of the 1960s.

19. The so-called Spanish tinge influenced American popular music throughout the twentieth century. Trace the impact of Latin music on rock during the 1950s and 1960s.

20. "The Poetry of Rock": Explore the lyrics of Bob Dylan, Paul Simon, Jim Morrison, and other Sixties rock songwriters.

5

Rock: From the Me Decade to the Millennium

THE SEVENTIES: THE RISE OF CORPORATE ROCK

As America began to settle into the Seventies, there was no denying that enormous changes were taking place in both cultural politics and popular culture. One of the first to attempt an interpretation of the new decade was the journalist Tom Wolfe, whose witty chronicles of the 1960s had included such rock-related subjects as the life and times of the Brill Building producer Phil Spector, the arrival of the Beatles in America, and the advent of the San Francisco sound amid the electric kool-aid acid tests of Ken Kesey's Merry Pranksters.

In his 1976 *New York* magazine article, "The Me Decade and the Third Great Awakening," Tom Wolfe suggested that the incredible economic prosperity of the early 1970s had generated a wave of intense spiritual fervor across America, which was reflected in the sudden profusion of cults, self-help groups, and consciousness-raising seminars. Unlike the two previous religious revivals that had swept the country (during the eighteenth and nineteenth centuries), however, this "third Great Awakening" was not motivated by a quest for either earthly community or salvation in the hereafter.

Instead, the millions of Americans who had become adherents of Scientology, est, Arica, or the Primal Scream were motivated by something quite different. "The appeal was simple enough," Wolfe wrote. "It is summed up in the notion: 'Let's Talk about *Me.*'" For this reason, he identified the 1970s as "the greatest age of individualism in American history"—or, more succinctly, as "the Me Decade."

Although the article itself doesn't make any reference to the world of popular music, "The Me Decade" would be as good a title as any for a chapter on rock in the early 1970s. For, in just a few short years, the communal spirit of the 1960s counterculture—forever symbolized by Woodstock—had become as out of fashion as a tie-dyed T-shirt; and like the transformation taking place in popular culture, the changes that were occurring in rock also were traceable to the booming economy that was fueling the most dramatic period of growth in the history of popular music.

In 1967, the enormous record sales generated by the Beatles, Stones, and Doors, among others, had gradually pushed total annual revenues past the $1 billion mark for the first time. In less than five years, however, sales had doubled to $2 billion and, by 1978, they would double once more to $4 billion. Not surprisingly, a 1975 industry survey revealed that 80 percent of these sales were for rock recordings. But while the size of the rock pie was getting a lot bigger, by the mid-1970s, there were considerably fewer record companies to cut up the pieces.

A recent flurry of media mergers seemed to have taken the music industry back to the future, to a time before rock 'n' roll had propelled scores of regional independent record labels onto the national pop charts. But with the skyrocketing rock production costs—from signing a band to recording and promoting their albums—even the biggest of the independent labels were being priced out of the competition. Before long, the field was reduced to seven "majors" (most of which were themselves just one fragment of some giant corporate conglomerate consisting of movie studios, television production companies, banks, and parking lot chains). Unquestionably, the archetype of the new media colossus was Warner Communications, Inc.

Warner Brothers (which owned Reprise Records, a West Coast pop music company, as well as its own major record label) had been quick to jump on the Sixties-rock bandwagon. Having signed the Grateful Dead in the first heady days of the flower-power era, the company went on to add many of the era's major performers—from Jimi Hendrix to Joni Mitchell—to its rock roster. Then, in 1967, Warners significantly upped the ante when the company announced that it had bought Atlantic Records, the New York–based independent label that had been in the forefront of the transition from rhythm and blues to rock 'n' roll back in the late 1940s. For twenty years, Atlantic had shaped its own musical ideology, and in doing so had assembled a stable of great R & B, soul, and rock performers—from the Drifters, Ray Charles, and Aretha Franklin to the (Young) Rascals and Cream. But Warners didn't stop there.

In 1970, the voracious media giant swallowed up Elektra Records, an independent label that was home to a top-shelf assortment of folkies and progressive rock bands, including the Paul Butterfield Blues Band and the Doors. Elektra was not only one of rock's hippest companies but, more than its competitors, one that prided itself on its *musical* values (rather than its bottom line). Three years later, Warners set its sights on Asylum Records—which had been formed (by David Geffin) only three years earlier as a "boutique" label with a lineup of artists-in-residence such as Jackson Browne, Linda Ronstadt, and the Eagles.

Meanwhile, Columbia Records (and its sister label, Epic)—which had gotten into Sixties rock big time when it signed Janis Joplin for a quarter of a million dollars during the Monterey pop festival—continued to make liberal use of its checkbook. By 1970, its rock star roster included Bob Dylan, Paul Simon, Blood, Sweat, and Tears, Chicago, and Sly and the Family Stone. Between them, Columbia and Warners now claimed almost 40 percent of the rock market, just as that market was entering its most explosive period of growth.

So significant was this coopting of rock by these giant media empires that some writers began to refer to the main branch of the era's music simply as "corporate rock." As Paul Rothchild, a former Elektra Records executive and producer, described it (in Fred Goodman's study of the changing culture of the rock music industry *The Mansion on the Hill*): "This was the beginning of the end of the love groove in American music. . . . It used to be 'Let's make music, money is the by-product.' Then it became 'Let's make money, music is the by-product.' "

Yet, even if Woodstockian ideals had been able to survive the various assaults of the Sixties (from assassinations to Altamont), by the beginning of the new decade the sheer size of the pop music market inevitably would have resulted in a splintering of the audience into smaller, more insular subcultures. Record store "rock" sections became a kaleidoscope of distinct, specialized genres: There was Heavy Metal and Art Rock, Country Rock, L.A. Rock, Southern Rock, and Singer-Songwriters, while Soul music splintered into Funk and something called Urban Contemporary. The communal bonds that had made the rock band a metaphor for the Sixties counterculture gave way to an era of "supergroups" and "solo acts." And in an age of individualism, it seemed that even a group of four was too many.

If any single event can be cited as symbolizing "the end of the Sixties," it was the breakup of the Beatles. While the reasons may have been complex (personal, creative, and financial), the impact was simple and profound. Just as their arrival had coincided with our national loss of innocence in the wake of President Kennedy's assassination, now their own breakup seemed to embody the loss of belief in the musical and cultural revolution the Beatles had done so much to bring into being.

In the spring of 1970, Paul McCartney released his first solo album. Appropriately entitled *Paul McCartney,* he had written all the songs himself, recorded the album in his own private studio, and—using the multitrack techniques the Beatles helped to pioneer—played all the instruments as well. A few months later, John Lennon's first post-Beatles single was issued. Entitled, "Mother," the song was an outgrowth of Lennon's involvement with the Me Decade form of psychotherapy known as Primal Scream.

While the rock audience was still coming to terms with the metaphoric demise of the Beatles, the death that same year of two of rock's most potent personalities was only too real. In the fall of 1970, within weeks of each other, both Jimi Hendrix and Janis Joplin fell victim to what would become one of the decade's most familiar postmortems: "Cause of Death: Drug-Related." Less than a year later, Jim Morrison's name would be added to the list of fallen heroes. But while each death was a harsh reminder of the dangers of the rock star lifestyle, there were plenty of others to take up the mantle of those who had fallen by the wayside, and, after a moment of silence, the rock juggernaut resumed its meteoric ascent.

FIGURE 5-1. When they débuted in 1969, the Allman Brothers Band provided a powerful reminder of the South's vital contributions to rock 'n' roll. Archive photo. Frank Driggs Collection.

The Allman Brothers Band and the Sound of Southern Rock

Ironically, at the same time that such L.A.-based performers as the Byrds, Linda Ronstadt, and the Eagles were softening the rough edges of mainstream rock with soothing country harmonies, some of the hardest rocking music of the early 1970s was being played by a (racially integrated) band of young Southerners.

The Allman "brothers" consisted of Duane, a celebrated studio guitarist who had contributed his dazzling slide guitar parts to a score of soul records (as well as to the Eric Clapton classic "Layla"), and his gritty-voiced brother, Gregg. Propelled by a solid rhythm section—and the innovative addition of a second lead guitarist, Dicky Betts—their band quickly rose to national prominence by cranking out a no-nonsense brand of high-powered boogie that became known as Southern rock.

Like the Allman Brothers Band, regional compatriots such as Lynryd Skynyrd ("Sweet Home Alabama"), the Marshall Tucker Band, and the Charlie Daniels Band ("The South's Goin' Do It Again") pledged allegiance to their cultural roots. In doing so, they also found inspiration in some of the same country music heroes who had influenced Elvis, Jerry Lee Lewis, and the other rockabilly pioneers who had started it all back in the mid-1950s.

It was also during the 1970s that rock concerts outgrew the clubs and theaters that had been its main venues during the previous decade. In 1971, Bill Graham closed his famous Fillmore Theaters (East and West), as rock groups took over sports arenas and outdoor stadiums. As tours became carefully orchestrated operations, with private jets and corporate sponsors, even the illusion of counterculture idealism and anti-establishment authenticity become impossible to maintain. One immediate consequence of rock's new corporate status was a significant (if short-lived) nostalgia craze that swept the pop music and media landscape at the beginning of the decade.

In 1972, Don McLean's "American Pie"—an eight-minute elegy not only for rock's lost heroes but for its lost innocence—became a huge hit single. A year later, George Lucas's *American Graffitti*—a film whose disparate plot lines were brilliantly structured around an early rock soundtrack—achieved enormous success by looking back to a time *before* (assassinations, drugs, and Vietnam). Meanwhile, "oldies" concerts were selling out across the country and the 1950s-revival group Sha-Na-Na wound up with its own TV show.

In fact, by this time, a cynically contrived subgenre of ersatz rock innocence had already become institutionalized on AM radio. Although most of the so-called bubblegum bands cranking out these bouncy, hook-filled songs were directly inspired by the Monkees (who were mid-Sixties precursors of the genre), the style was essentially a sanitized recreation of late Fifties rock 'n' roll. Among the classics of early Seventies bubblegum are the 1910 Fruitgum Co.'s "1, 2, 3 I Love You," Ohio Express's "Chewy, Chewy," and the Archies's "Sugar, Sugar." Soon, bubblegum was not just something for the kids, it was also something by the kids (at least theoretically).

For it was during this period that made-for-television creations like the Partridge Family and the Osmonds became staples on both the small screen and the AM pop charts, while as hosts of their own TV show Sonny and Cher seemed to be experiencing a kind of second childhood of their own. Then there was the latest Motown phenomenon, the Jackson 5, fronted by a ten-year-old named Michael. After releasing a string of multimillion-selling kiddie-soul hits at the start of the Seventies, the talented young siblings were quickly transformed into a Saturday morning cartoon.

But while rock may have seemed like child's play on the tube and big business in corporate boardrooms, in huge arenas across America a new sound was being forged that would amplify Sixties rock's blues-based essence and guitar-hero posturing to a whole new level. In ways that transcended the slang of the period, things were about to get "heavy" indeed.

HEAVY METAL: THE DEVIL AND THE POWER CHORD

As prime architects of the sound that would become known as "heavy metal," Led Zeppelin was among the founding fathers of one of the most significant styles in rock history. Yet, like virtually all of this history, the story of heavy metal also begins with the blues. And like the blues—which was often referred to as "the devil's music"—heavy metal also would become closely associated with the kind of antisocial values that have been a source of concern to generations of parents and other traditional guardians of morality.

Prior to forming Led Zeppelin, Jimmy Page was one of the preeminent guitar heroes of the British blues revival. Along with Eric Clapton, Mick Taylor, and Jeff Beck, he had taken his turn as a lead guitarist in the seminal rock band, the Yardbirds. In 1968, when that group finally self-destructed, Page had developed a distinctive personal guitar style that was grounded in the blues, disciplined by years of session work (on albums by the Stones, the Kinks, and the Who), and liberated by the sonic innovations of Jimi Hendrix.

For his new band, Page began by recruiting bassist John Paul Jones (an old session buddy), then he added Robert Plant, a singer from the British industrial city of Birmingham. Although Plant was virtually unknown at the time, his passionate, gut-wrenching vocals (and stripped-to-the-waist sexuality) would soon become a key component of Led Zeppelin's world-famous image. It was also Plant who brought the explosive drummer John Bonham into the fold. Almost immediately, the band headed into the studio.

Led Zeppelin's 1969 début album, produced by Page, was the end-product of a marathon thirty-hour recording session. While it combined original songs with blistering blues covers (of classics by Willie Dixon and Howlin' Wolf), the sound the band created was completely their own. By the time the group released its second album (featuring the signature song, "Whole Lotta Love"), Led Zeppelin had emerged as prime candidate for the title of Most Popular Rock Band in the World.

The symbolic changing of the guard couldn't have been scripted more perfectly. It was the first month of the first year of a new decade when *Led Zeppelin II* wrested the number one spot on the charts from *Abbey Road,* by the recently disbanded Beatles. Then, in the fall of 1970, a poll by the British rock magazine *Melody Maker* seemed to make it all official: Led Zeppelin was voted the country's favorite band, a role the Beatles had filled for each of the eight previous years.

Although some critics felt that Led Zeppelin's style was as inflated as the gas-filled airships for which they were named, by their fourth album the band had become so successful that they could release a recording whose cover bore neither a title nor any trace of the group's identity. Instead, it simply set a series of mysterious "runes" (archaic pictographic symbols) into a vaguely mythological illustration. And just as the music on the record was a further extension of the band's synthesis of blues and traditional British folk music, its lyrics imaginatively fused references to African-American "hoodoo" with Celtic legends (along with the imagery of black magic).

The album's centerpiece, "Stairway to Heaven," offers an intriguing eight-minute amalgamation of all of Led Zeppelin's disparate influences. In his book *Running with the Devil: Power, Madness and Gender in Heavy Metal*, Robert Walser provides a detailed analysis of both the song's musical structure and what he describes as "the famously enigmatic lyrics." In his deconstruction of the instrumentation and vocals, for example, Walser identifies a "narrative juxtaposition of the sensitive (acoustic guitar, etc.) and the aggressive (distorted electric guitar, etc.)" that "has continued to show up in heavy metal, from Ozzy Osbourne to Metallica."

Turning his attention to the song's miscellaneous images, Walser suggests that "like the music, they [the song's themes] engage with the fantasies and anxieties of our time; they offer contact with social and metaphysical depth in a world of commodities and mass communication." Whatever its ultimate meaning may have been, however, "Stairway to Heaven" was an instant hit. And, after serving as a classic rock staple for over a quarter-century, it has long been cited as the most frequently played rock recording in radio history.

Meanwhile, other early Seventies British bands such as Deep Purple and Black Sabbath also were helping establish the sound of "heavy metal" during its formative period. As Robert Walser explains, the style's fundamental component was a musical chord that was more than merely the sum of its notes:

> If there is one feature that underpins the coherence of heavy metal as a genre, it is the power chord. Produced by playing the musical interval of a perfect fourth or fifth on a heavily amplified and distorted electric guitar. . . . It is at once the musical basis of heavy metal and an apt metaphor for it, for musical articulation of power is the most important single factor in the experience of heavy metal.

Not only did Deep Purple and Black Sabbath each employ the power chord to great effect, but they also helped forge the other weapons in the heavy metal arsenal, from the thunderous bass and drum sound to—in Walser's words—"a powerful vocal style that used screams and growls as signs of transgression and transcendence." While each band concocted its own special heavy metal formula (for Deep Purple, an onslaught of thickly textured, classically tinged guitar and organ, and for Black Sabbath, an aggressive, bluesy pseudo-Satanism), these proto–heavy metal bands also established the model for future metalists, all of whom had to contend with the universal rejection by rock radio. Their strategy: a combination of constant touring, increasingly elaborate stage spectacles, and a brisk recording schedule.

Meanwhile, back on this side of the Atlantic, a new generation of rock bands were evolving their own version of heavy metal. And like their British counterparts, they, too, achieved success without either the aid of rock critics (who mostly scorned them) or rock radio (which mostly ignored them). While the style's American roots can be traced back to such late Sixties hard-rock outfits as Blue Cheer, Vanilla Fudge, Iron Butterfly, and MC-5 (who had each mixed power chords, politics, and psychedelics in varying proportions to achieve their own loyal followings), it was another American band that is most often credited with providing the actual name of the genre itself.

Steppenwolf was a California band (by way of Canada) whose primitive, full-throttled, guitar-driven sound is best exemplified by their 1968 hit, "Born to Be Wild." An anthem to the joys of the biker lifestyle, its lyrics described the sound of a motorcycle roaring across the highway as "heavy metal thunder." It was the first time the soon-to-be-notorious phrase had appeared in a song. By the early 1970s, the phrase not only had its own peculiar musical connotations but there were millions of rabid fans pledging allegiance to the heavy metal flag.

Throughout the decade, succeeding generations of heavy metal bands firmly established the style's presence of the rock scene. Despite rock radio's continuing indifference, AC/DC, KISS, Judas Priest, Aerosmith, and Ted Nugent, among others, forged metal's basic vocabulary and solidified its commercial success. Well into the 1980s,

FIGURE 5-2.   Led Zeppelin inflated the blues-based guitar heroics that had been the hallmark of Sixties rock to an unprecedented level of virtuosity and sheer spectacle. Courtesy of Atlantic Records.

Led Zeppelin: Stairway to (Rock) Heaven

Led Zeppelin's self-titled 1969 début album featured imposing covers of Chicago blues classics by Willie Dixon ("You Shook Me," "I Can't Quit You Baby") and Howlin' Wolf ("How Many More Years"), but Jimmy Page's intensely amplified, thickly textured guitar chords, Robert Plant's harshly distorted vocals, John Bonham's massive beat, and John Paul Jones's impenetrable reverb-enhanced bass also prompted rock musicologist Robert Walser to credit the band with codifying "the sound that would become known as heavy metal."

Over time, Led Zeppelin balanced their thundering power chords with interludes of folky lyricism and tempered their egotism with a dose of ancient mysticism. The centerpiece of the band's third album was a song that, more than any other, embodied this creative tension and provided the band with its ticket to rock heaven; decades after it was issued, "Stairway to Heaven" remains not only the music's most analyzed song, but perhaps the most frequently played record in the history of rock radio.

metal bands consistently sold millions of albums (and sold out arena tours throughout the country) without the benefit of hit singles or Top Forty airplay.

Nor did most rock critics see fit to alter their initial disdain for the genre. For example, in his overview of post-1960s rock (in the book *Rock of Ages*), Ken Tucker relegates the style to little more than a curious (if profitable) psychosocial phenomenon: "Heavy metal was consumed by one generation of teenagers after another," he declared. "Heavy metal, with its deafening volume and proud hostility to cultural and aesthetic niceties, is the primary music of teenage rebellion and, almost by definition, something a listener outgrows." But, as he acknowledged, "a new set of teens is ever entering the marketplace."

In addition, heavy metal also began coming under assault from some of the same moral forces that had first targeted rock 'n' roll back in the 1950s. While the music may have been different, the charges against this latest incarnation of "the devil's music" had a familiar ring: sex, drugs, and violence. In fact, the only thing missing from the current criticism that had been a staple of the 1950s version was its thinly disguised racial hysteria. But—as we'll see in the next chapter—that was being saved for another rapidly expanding new genre: rap.

THE SINGER-SONGWRITER: POET LAUREATE OF THE ME DECADE

If the counterculture ideal of community that had infused 1960s rock did indeed fall victim to corporate hype, drugs, war-weariness, and the baby boomers' advancing adulthood, then the success of the so-called singer-songwriters of the 1970s was surely a sign of the times. In fact, from this perspective, the archetypal singer-songwriter was nothing less than the poet laureate of the Me Decade.

Although the individual performers identified with the singer-songwriter label actually embodied a range of musical styles and lyric concerns, for the most part they all shared a private, introspective point of view that was in sharp contrast to the more public (and political) pronouncements of the previous decade. And while rock bands of the 1970s often indulged in an orgy of inflated imagery, arena-stage spectacle, and technological overkill, here was a haven of radio-friendly, primarily acoustic songs that could appeal equally to both aging baby boomers and alienated adolescents.

The rock song had certainly experienced a profound transformation since the 1950s, when late-night TV's Steve Allen ridiculed recent hits such as "Be Bop a Lula" by reciting their lyrics with a scornful mock seriousness. Yet, some of the songs from rock 'n' roll's Golden Era—especially those that were connected to this style's blues or country roots—were, in fact, brilliant examples of folk poetry. Married to a driving beat, the lyrics of Chuck Berry, Willie Dixon, Leiber and Stoller, and Buddy Holly often had a directness, energy, and wit that had made them a refreshing antidote to the bland pop songs of contemporary Tin Pan Alley.

During the early days of the next decade, rock songs by young "Brill Building" writing teams such as Gerry Goffin and Carole King, Ellie Greenwich and Jeff Barry, and Barry Mann and Cynthia Weil brought an understated craftsmanship to the deceptively simple pop songs they created for the era's girl groups and vocal harmony quartets. By the mid-1960s, however, Bob Dylan had begun to fuse the imagery of traditional folk ballads with literary effects adopted from French surrealist poets and Beat Generation bards; in the process, he transformed the rock song forever.

As Richard Goldstein explained in the introduction to his 1969 anthology, *The Poetry of Rock,* Bob Dylan "demolished the narrow line and lean stanzas that once dominated pop, replacing them with a more flexible organic structure. . . . More important, he turned pop composers on to themselves." But after a series of increasingly intense electric albums, in which he pushed his lyrics to the limits of intelligeablity and challenged the endurance of his listeners (with individual songs that filled the entire side of an LP), Dylan staged a strategic retreat.

In 1968, he released *John Wesley Harding,* an album of short, narrative songs, filled with biblical references, on which he was backed by a spare, acoustic-based band. The following year's *Nashville Skyline* offered a selection of laid-back country songs. In 1970, Dylan's *New Morning* offered a collection of tightly constructed celebrations of the domestic life. But by retreating—from the inflated imagery and declamatory stance he had done so much to foster—once again, it seemed Dylan was leading the way.

In fact, most of the performers who were identified with the singer-songwriter label were really just Seventies-style folkies. While some, as loyal members of "Dylan's Army," combined their Guthrie (Woody) with a little Ginsberg (Allen), others were more comfortable with allusions to Eliot (T. S.) than they were to Elvis (Presley). There also were a couple who drew their inspiration from alternate traditions ranging from classic Brill Building pop to the soundtracks of classic Hollywood films. Despite the diversity of its membership, however, the new contingent of songwriters were declared "a movement"; and, in 1971, they even had their own cover boy.

Not only did James Taylor sing his poetic, obliquely confessional songs with a kind of haunted sensuality, but he even looked the part. It was no surprise, therefore, that *Time* magazine decided to feature Taylor on its cover in connection with a story about the new crop of singer-songwriters. As the article reported, not only had Taylor's 1970 breakthrough album, *Sweet Baby James,* been hovering near the top of the album charts for a few months, but two singles from the LP ("Fire and Rain" and the title song) were huge hits as well.

While his style was firmly grounded in traditional Anglo-American folk music (with a nod to the blues), what made Taylor's songs so representative of the new crop of singer-songwriters was their transparently autobiographical quality. Among his recent compositions, for example, were thinly veiled accounts of his brushes with heroin addiction ("Fire and Rain") and madness ("Knockin 'Round the Zoo"). But one of Taylor's biggest hits—"You've Got a Friend"—was actually written by the woman who was perhaps his most talented and certainly his most experienced colleague, Carole King.

Back in its early 1960s heyday, Carole King had been one of the foremost songwriters working at Aldon Music—the Brill Building song factory. Collaborating with her lyricist husband, Gerry Goffin, King had written such girl-group hits as "Will You Love Me Tomorrow" (for the Shirelles) and "Chains" (for the Cookies). Although initially she had a tough time making the transition from being a Tin Pan Alley pro to a pop music poet, when King finally did make it—she made it big time.

Anchored by her own piano playing and assisted by a tasteful ensemble that included most of James Taylor's own band (as well as Sweet Baby James himself), Carole King's 1971 album, *Tapestry,* featured a collection of originals old and new. In addition to generating a couple of hit singles ("It's Too Late," "So Far Away," and her own version of "You've Got a Friend"), the album itself went to number one—and stayed there. Eventually, *Tapestry* would sell over fourteen million copies, becoming one of the biggest-selling albums in rock history.

The King-Taylor connection was only one of a tangled web of collaborations, friendships, and romances that bound together the intimate (and often incestuous) world of Seventies singer-songwriters. Consider the following: It was James Taylor's volatile love affair with Joni Mitchell that had inspired many of the songs of her classic 1971 album, *Blue.* Mitchell, a Canadian folkie, had first established her reputation (for intensely personal songs filled with poetic allusions and exotic open guitar tunings) during the late 1960s, when an early Mitchell song, "Both Sides Now," had become a Top Ten hit for American folk music queen Judy Collins.

Soon, Joni's debut album—produced by ex-Byrd David Crosby and featuring guitar accompaniment by ex–Buffalo Springfield Steven Stills—introduced her own versions of her songs to the folk audience. Meanwhile, inspired by his romantic relationship with Judy Collins, Stills wrote a song ("Suite: Judy Blue Eyes") that would become the first hit for his new band, Crosby, Stills, and Nash. Before long, Nash and Joni Mitchell were having their own fling (out of which he wrote the song "Our House" and she wrote "Willy"). Then in 1972, James Taylor married Carly Simon, a singer-songwriter who had just released her own breakthrough hit ("You're So Vain"), which alluded to her own relationship with (either) Warren Beatty or Mick Jagger (who sang back-up on the record).

This is not to say that the whole singer-songwriter movement of the 1970s can simply be reduced to some kind of musical soap opera. But while certain writers did explore a spectrum of social issues and contemporary concerns, however, there's no question that private affairs (of home, hearth, and the human heart) began to replace public concerns (such as civil rights and Vietnam) as the focus of the era's original songs; and it was during the 1970s that the songwriter's pronoun-of-choice changed from "we" to "I." Among the few songs of the period to address political issues or explore the waning ideal of community was "Ohio," Neil Young's scathing account of the recent Kent State killings.

During the early 1970s, the ranks of folk poets performing their own self-referential songs had expanded to include both an old pro like Paul Simon and a recent refugee from the rarified ranks of the literary élite like Leonard Cohen. In contrast to Simon's formidable pop music career, which had begun in 1957 (with "Hey Schoolgirl," an Everly Brothers–style hit recorded with his boyhood chum Art Garfunkel), Leonard Cohen—a Canadian poet and novelist—was thirty-four years old when he released his 1968 debut album, *The Songs of Leonard Cohen.* Like his countryperson Joni Mitchell, Cohen initially had been discovered by Judy Collins, who had been the first to record his most famous song, "Suzanne." Unlike most of his folk-oriented counterparts, however, Cohen brought a rigorous literary quality and bitterly ironic point of view to his songs.

FIGURE 5-3.   This late Sixties portrait of Simon and Garfunkel captures the duo's aura of poetic sensitivity at the beginning of what would become one the most successful and critically acclaimed careers in rock history. Archive photo.

Simon and Garfunkel: From One-Hit Wonders to Poets of Pop

After "Hey Schoolgirl," a 1957 single they recorded under the name of Tom and Jerry made it into the Top Forty, Paul Simon and Art Garfunkel dutifully went off to college. By 1964, however, the old friends had reunited, this time as members of the Dylan-inspired folk revival. Signed (under their own names) by Columbia, they recorded an acoustic album of traditional folk ballads along with Simon's own poetic exploration of urban alienation, "Sounds of Silence." Unfortunately, sales of the LP did nothing to alter their one-hit-wonder status.

A year later, however, following one of Dylan's first folk-rock sessions, the producer Tom Wilson decided to overdub an amplified accompaniment onto an existing track by Simon and Garfunkel. Having relocated to England, where he was working the local folk club circuit, Paul Simon wasn't even aware of Wilson's experiment—until he got a call telling him that the new folk-rock version of "Sounds of Silence" was the number one pop single in the country.

Over the next few years, Simon and Garfunkel released an unprecedented string of best-selling albums and Top Ten singles. In such hits as "I Am a Rock," "Homeward Bound," and "Parsley, Sage, Rosemary, and Thyme," Simon crafted songs that reflected both his long musical apprenticeship and the influence of his college literature courses. Soon, hip high school English teachers had added Simon and Garfunkel songs to their curriculum.

In 1968, when the director Mike Nichols hired them to provide the songs for *The Graduate* (his contemporary coming-of-age film), Simon and Garfunkel not only transformed the nature of the movie soundtrack but created one of the seminal songs of the period, "Mrs. Robinson." Although their next release would be Simon and Garfunkel's most successful album, *Bridge over Troubled Water* also would be their last. In 1970, amid escalating tensions, Simon and Garfunkel ended their long and productive partnership.

Although his songs ultimately achieved more commercial success when they were covered by other performers (like Joe Cocker and Tim Hardin), it was Cohen's own plaintively intoned vocals and spare acoustic guitar accompaniments that most effectively communicated them. In fact, these were the very qualities that convinced the director Robert Altman to make prominent use of Cohen's songs in the soundtrack of his film *McCabe and Mrs. Miller,* a bleak, revisionist Western that was released in 1971.

It was the lush orchestrations of Hollywood's traditional film scores that actually provided an early inspiration for one of the era's most original and talented singer-songwriters, Randy Newman. Unlike his pop music peers, Randy had studied composition and orchestral scoring (at UCLA); he also had probably picked up a thing or two from his uncles (Lionel, Emil, and Alfred), who were all important members of musical Hollywood's old guard. What set Newman further apart from his singer-songwriter colleagues, however, was his rejection of their first-person, confessional stance. Not only were Newman's songs often laced with a subtle and perverse irony but most were sung from the point of view of one of his huge cast of fictional loners and misfits.

Although Randy Newman quickly attracted a small (but fanatical) cult of fans and garnered the awed praise of his fellow songwriters, except for a couple of novelty hits ("Short People" and "I Love L.A."), most of his commercial success came through cover versions by diverse performers such as Judy Collins, Ray Charles, Linda Ronstadt, Peggy Lee, Nina Simone, and Three Dog Night (whose 1970 single "Mamma Told Me Not to Come" became Randy's only number one hit). In addition to creating an extraordinary body of brilliant songs, by the mid-1970s, Randy followed the family tradition established by his uncles and became one of Hollywood's premier film composers (receiving Academy Award nominations for his scores to *Ragtime, Avalon,* and *The Natural,* among others).

Among the sizeable roster of the decade's folk-based singer-songwriters there were those who, like Newman, were more appreciated by their peers (and their own small cult of fans) than they were by the mass audience. Although John Prine, Steve Goodman, Loudin Wainwright III, Kate and Ann McGarrigle, and Richard Thompson (formerly of the respected British folk-rock band, Fairport Convention) did establish enduring (if commercially marginal) careers, typically their songs also became best known through cover versions by their more celebrated colleagues and disciples. For a while at least, it seemed that was going to be the fate of Van Morrison.

By 1970—when he briefly became identified with the evolving singer-songwriter movement—Morrison had already been a member of Them (a short-lived Irish rock band whose best-known song, "Gloria," was a Morrison original). Morrison went on to launch a one-hit solo career (his 1967 single "Brown-Eyed Girl" had made it into the American Top Ten), and make an album—1968's *Astral Weeks*—filled with impressionistic imagery and jazz textures that became an instant cult classic. But while the critics (and his peers) elevated Morrison to the pantheon of rock geniuses, it wasn't until 1970, when he released *Moondance* (an album whose more accessible lyrics were bolstered by Van's own tight R & B-style horn arrangements) that the rock audience also embraced him. *Moondance* proved to be a solid commercial success, generating such enduring mainstream radio hits as "Caravan" and the title song.

Over the next quarter-century, Van Morrison went on to become one of the most venerated figures in rock history. His visionary lyrics (blending the Celtic myths of his native Ireland and the primal imagery of the blues) and his impassioned blues-inflected vocals have had a profound influence on an array of performers on both sides of the Atlantic. Among those who have openly acknowledged Van's inspiration are Bono ("There's got to be a spiritual link between U2 and Van Morrison," he has confessed), Bruce Springsteen, Joan Armatrading, and Counting Crow's lead singer, Adam Duritz (who sounds like a virtual Morrison clone).

Like Morrison, many of the performers who were identified by the singer-songwriter label also established careers of remarkable longevity. For example, not only did Paul Simon and Joni Mitchell transcend the fashions of the pop-music scene, but the fierce loyalty of their fans gave them a chance to explore a variety of new stylistic tributaries: from doo-wop and South African *mbaganga* rhythms (Simon) to avant-garde jazz (Mitchell). Over the intervening decades, new performers have continually revived (and in some cases reconfigured) the singer-songwriter tradition. Some—such as Tracy Chapman, Suzanne Vega, and Jewel—fall safely within the folkie mainstream, while others—such as Alanis Morrisette, Beck, and Ani DiFranco—have pioneered their own cutting-edge hybrids.

In addition, the singer-songwriters of the early Seventies served as a link between the folk poets of the 1960s and a new generation of literate roots rockers who arrived on the scene during the middle of the decade. This entourage of rock revivalists (which included performers as diverse as Bruce Springsteen, John Mellancamp, Billy Joel, Elvis Costello, and Sting) were the beneficiaries of the singer-songwriter's efforts to expand the range of the rock song's style and subject matter. At times, it seemed all that separated them from their more introspective predecessors was either an inflated ego or a bigger beat.

Although the laid-back sound and domestic concerns of the singer-songwriters were clearly a retreat from the heavy political and cultural load that popular music had been expected to bear during the 1960s, during the early 1970s rock also was being pulled in another direction—toward theatrical spectacle and high art.

ART ROCK: NO LONGER
A CONTRADICTION IN TERMS

In many ways, the "art rock" phenomenon of the 1970s (a.k.a. "progressive rock") was a consequence of the newfound respect pop culture had acquired during the previous decade. After all, hadn't such high priests of high culture as Leonard Bernstein proclaimed the Beatles' *Sgt. Pepper's Lonely Hearts Club Band* "a work of art" just a few years earlier? So it shouldn't have come as a surprise that other rock groups aspiring to that coveted status began replacing the music's blues-based vitality—a blend of primal energy and folk poetry—with an ambitious combination of classical instrumentation and recording-studio experimentation.

Actually, the Beatles were already exploring the twin paths that would converge in the "art rock" movement of the 1970s well before *Sgt. Pepper*. For example, the haunting accompaniment for Paul McCartney's ballad of urban alienation, "Eleanor Rigby" (from their 1966 album *Revolver*), had been furnished by a small string ensemble; a few months later, the band had George Martin compose an ornate Baroque trumpet fanfare for their single, "Penny Lane." By the time they recorded *Sgt. Pepper*, there was a forty-piece orchestra on hand to enhance the final lingering chord of "A Day in the Life."

It also was during this period that the Beatles were diligently experimenting with the creative potential of avant-garde techniques such as multitrack recording, avant-garde tape collages, along with innovative electronic instrumentation. Back on *Revolver*, for example, they had played various prerecorded tapes backward to conjure up the appropriate ambiance for Lennon's Eastern-tinged acid saga "Tomorrow Never Knows." In order to achieve the hallucinatory effects the Beatles wanted on *Sgt. Pepper's* "For the Benefit of Mr. Kite," they recorded the sound of an old steam organ, cut the tape into pieces, and then randomly reassembled them.

By the early 1970s, a score of Beatles-inspired bands on both sides of the Atlantic were formulating an array of pop-classical hybrids and technology-driven modernism. Although there were a couple of significant American contributors to the genre (including the Mothers of Invention and Captain Beefheart's Magic Band), art rock proved to be primarily a British show (since that was where the Beatles' influence was strongest, where the European cultural heritage dominated, and where art colleges had long functioned as rock prep schools).

For example, early forays into pseudoclassical rock had already been undertaken by Procol Harum, whose 1967 hit single, "A Whiter Shade of Pale" was an adaptation of Bach's Suite No. 3 in D Major. A year later, the Moody Blues album *Days of Future Passed*—featuring the classic-rock staple "Knights in White Satin"—was recorded with the entire London Festival Orchestra, while Deep Purple's 1969 *Concerto for Group and Orchestra* featured the Royal Philharmonic. These art-rock pioneers also established the genre's lyric model by marrying their imposing musical statements to inflated images that conjured up either ancient mythical realms or fantastic, surrealistic dreamscapes (something else they borrowed from the Beatles).

Although Pink Floyd had initially come to prominence back in the mid-1960s for their light-show enhanced psychedelic pop, by 1973—when the band released their bleak concept-album, *Dark Side of the Moon*—they, too, had begun to concoct ambitious, multitrack high-art epics. The enduring popularity of this particular amalgamation of portentiousness and paranoia is attested to by the fact that in 1985 *Dark Side of the Moon* was still on the Billboard chart of the Top 200 albums—a record-breaking 566 weeks after it was first issued.

King Crimson's 1969 début, *In the Court of the Crimson King,* did manage to avoid the more ponderous excesses of their art-rock colleagues. But, a year later, when bandmember Greg Lake suddenly quit to form the first art-rock supergroup—Emerson, Lake, and Palmer—he made up for it by unleashing a string of particularly grandiose mock-classical "masterpieces." Not only did Emerson, Lake, and Palmer record their own arrangements of classical warhorses (from Mussorgsky's "Pictures at an Exhibition" to Bach's "Two-Part Invention in D Minor" to Aaron Copland's "Fanfare for the Common Man"), but they also introduced the rock audience to the most potent instrument yet divised by modern technology: the electronic synthesizer.

Developed in 1964 by Dr. Robert Moog, during the early 1970s the complex electronic device (which had the capability to artificially synthesize virtually any sound or musical instrument) moved out of the lab, into the recording studio, and, eventually, onto the stage. As the instrument improved—especially after it had achieved a "polyphonic" (that is, chordal) capacity—E, L, & P's classically trained keyboardist, Keith Emerson, took every opportunity to exploit the instrument's potential to produce exotic sounds and textures unlike any that had ever been heard before.

For sheer excess, however, it was hard to compete with the group Yes. Not only did this conservatory trained art-rock supergroup appropriate its share of the traditional classical repertoire (from Brahms's Fourth Symphony to Stravinsky's "Firebird Suite"), and arm itself with the entire arsenal of modern electronics (including Rick Wakeman's keyboard synthesizers and Steve Howe's guitar version), but they offered up it all up in huge helpings. Their 1971 live album, *Yessongs,* for example, sprawled over three LPs!

At the other end of the art-rock spectrum from the maximalism of Yes, Emerson, Lake, and Palmer, Renaissance, Genesis, and the Electric Light Orchestra were other groups exploring the creative potential of "minimalism." Just as the Beatles had been influenced in their use of tape-collages by the modernist classical composer Karlheinz Stockhausen, some Seventies art rockers used the new electric synthesizers and computerized keyboards to create spare, repetitive, trancelike music that took its cues from the experiments of an avant-garde underground that included Terry Riley, La Monte Young, Steve Reich, and Philip Glass. Perhaps the most innovative and influential of these art-rock minimalists was Brian Eno.

After providing elegant musical underpinnings for frontman Brian Ferry's self-consciously romantic posturings, Brian Eno left the British art-rock band, Roxy Music, to pursue his own more austere musical vision. Beginning in 1973, he initiated a series of projects involving synthesizers and tape-delay effects to create a multilayered atmospheric style he dubbed "ambient music" and began collaborating with like-minded instrumentalists such as Robert Fripp (the former guitarist for King Crimson). By the end of the decade, Eno and Fripp would bring their highly developed technical skills and aesthetic sensibility to New York's "downtown" arts scene where they produced records for new wave bands such as Blondie and Talking Heads that were in the vanguard of a leaner rock aesthetic.

In fact, as the ultimate symbol of Me Decade self-indulgence, the inflated experiments of the art-rock movement would soon inspire the scathing wrath—and assertive primitivism—of the punk-rock revolutionaries who were waiting in the wings. Later in the decade, art rock's technology-driven, producer-based formula also would be adapted (by the German synthesizer band Kraftwerk and the Euro-disco guru Giorgio Moroder, among others) to create slick new pop productions.

GLAM AND GLITTER: SEVENTIES ROCK TAKES A WALK ON THE WILD SIDE

Another pop music phenomenon of the early Seventies that also proved to be a precursor of the coming disco craze was "glam rock." Infusing their shows with elaborately staged spectacle, assuming gender-bending personas, donning a range of costumes (from campy to decadent), T-Rex, Elton John, David Bowie, and Alice Cooper and the New York Dolls introduced a glittery theatrical element to the hypermasculine world of rock.

Although manifestations of glam(orous) androgyny in rock go back at least as far as Little Richard, typically the rock star had always been one of the most potent symbols of male sexuality (with his guitar an amplified phallic prop). Although Mick Jagger occasionally may have teased fans with a glimpse of his feminine side—his cross-dressing role in Nicholas Roeg's 1970 film *Performance* is one infamous example—for the most part, Jagger (like other Sixties rock stars) never strayed far from the brand of heterosexual machismo he had adopted from the blues. Yet, by the early 1970s, not only was rock's once-unquestioned adherence to traditional sex roles being re-assessed but so was its standard denim and leather uniform. Gritty "authenticity" was out and campy artifice was in; and, once again, all eyes were on England.

Without getting too enmeshed in cultural stereotypes, or sociological speculation, the fact remains that there has always existed within the confines of the British music hall (their version of vaudeville) a long and honorable history of comedic cross-dressing and, within British society (at least when compared to the United States), a more open acceptance of homosexuality. It is within this context that the new glam rockers must be seen: as one part theatrical tradition and one part gay liberation. Among the first to explore the pop potential of this formula was Marc Bolan.

After an abbreviated career as both a male model and a pop singer (under the stage name Toby Tyler), in the late 1960s Marc Bolan formed Tyrannosaurus Rex, a folkish art-rock band whose songs fused ethereal music and Tolkienesque imagery. In 1970, however, Bolan abruptly transformed the band's image—and music. Not only did he re-christen the band with a punchy new name—T. Rex—to go along with their new hard-edged, guitar-driven sound, but Bolan also assumed a new persona as well. Costumed in spandex and platform shoes, his voice a sensual quiver, Marc Bolan became the embodiment of decadent glamour. Within a year, T. Rex had placed five singles on the British Top Ten and unleashed a wave of pop hysteria that the local tabloids dubbed "T. Rexstacy." This stardom proved short-lived, however; in 1977, after an aborted punk-inspired comeback, Bolan was killed in an auto accident.

Although they may not have inspired the kind of instant frenzy of T. Rex, the British band Queen steadily set about securing glam rock's largest and most loyal audience. After establishing a sizeable fan base at home with their dense, heavily overdubbed early releases, by 1975 Queen had even managed to conquer the United States with a Top Five album, *A Night at the Opera* (featuring their grandiose, quasi-classical hit, "Bohemian Rhapsody").

Fronted by the highly theatrical (and overtly gay) vocalist Freddie Mercury, Queen also were pioneers in formulating the elaborately costumed and choreographed live spectacles that became the hallmark of the genre. Perhaps the most ironic aspect of Queen's career was the fact that a band so notorious for its campy, androgynous image generated a song—"We Will Rock You"—that would become a staple at sports events across America. It was a couple of solo performers, however, who were most responsible for transplanting glam rock's exotic bouquets to the mainstream.

During the course of extraordinarily long, productive, and successful careers, David Bowie and Elton John drew on a kaleidoscopic array of popular music, which they each filtered through a series of ever-shifting, carefully devised personas. Although in their own unique ways both Elton John and David Bowie were brilliant (and versatile) songwriters and dynamic performers, it was this genius for continually reinventing themselves as pop culture icons that has been most responsible for their celebrity (and longevity).

Although Elton John had started his musical career in a mid-1960s British blues-revival band (Bluesology), it was as a member of the singer-songwriter movement of the early-1970s that he achieved his initial success. In 1970, Elton's self-titled solo début album produced a Top Ten ballad, "Your Song," that he'd written with his long-time lyricist, Bernie Taupin. It was the first of an unprecedented string of hits that included five number one singles and seven consecutive number one albums during the first half of the decade alone.

While Elton John's commercial success was certainly remarkable, it was the overall quality and range of his music that eventually convinced even the most skeptical critics of his status as a pop superstar. An avid fan of all forms of American popular music, as the years progressed, Elton proved himself a master of most of them: from 1950s rock 'n' roll ("Crocodile Rock") to 1960s rock ("Saturday Night's alright for Fighting"), from country music ("Country Comfort") to gospel ("Take Me to the Pilot"), from Tin Pan Alley sentiment ("Candle in the Wind") to Rolling Stones-ish swagger ("The Bitch Is Back").

Although he couldn't quite shake off his ambivalence completely, Robert Christgau spoke for all but the most recalcitrant rock critics when he offered this assessment of Elton's astonishing powers of musical alchemy: "The man's gift for the hook—made up whole or assembled from outside sources—was so universal that there was small likelihood that one wouldn't stick in your pleasure center. Or your craw. Or both."

Although the short, pudgy, balding Elton hardly fit the rock star stereotype, in concert, his vast repertoire of hits and his natural showmanship made him one of the most successful live acts in rock history. Each arena and stadium tour was more elaborate than the one before, the costumes changes more numerous, the platform shoes higher, the feather boas longer, and the stage shtick more outrageous. In 1975, however, the announcement of Elton's bisexual (later gay) orientation—and the intense public controversy that followed—precipitated an emotional crisis and extended creative decline.

Then in the late 1980s—it was Elton Redux! He reemerged with a string of new hits, became a fixture on MTV, and, in 1996, Sir Elton (now that he was officially dubbed a Knight of the British realm) won the Academy Award for his contributions to the soundtrack of Walt Disney's animated feature, *The Lion King*. A year later, following the death of Princess Diana, his revised remake of "Candle in the Wind" became the biggest selling single in rock history.

Unlike Elton John, David Bowie was never the consummate hitmaker or pop(ulist) superstar—nor did he want to be. Although he had his share of Top Ten songs and gold albums, Bowie aspired to a more rarified status. And while both Elton and Bowie built enduring careers based on a similar combination of fashion fantasies and solid songwriting, Bowie's influences (Jacques Brel, Kurt Weill, and Lou Reed among others) were both more élitist and more decadent. Although, for the most part, Bowie's debut album, *Man of Words, Man of Music* (1969) was a well-made pastiche of 1960s rock (from San Francisco psychedelia to Beatles-style tunefulness), it not only gave hints of the weirdness to come but generated his first hit single, "Space Oddity."

Over the course of the next two years, Bowie took a number of steps that established his status as one of glam rock's greatest heroes. He issued an album *(The Man Who Sold the World)* on whose original cover he appeared in drag, proceeded to publicly announce his bisexuality, and then wrote a provocative song that would be his personal anthem, "Changes." In 1972, he invented the first of his many alter egos, "Ziggy Stardust," the orange-haired, rail-thin, title character of Bowie's all-embracing concept album, *The Rise and Fall of Ziggy Stardust and the Spiders from Mars* (and of the elaborate live show that was built around it).

By this point Bowie held a unique niche in the pop pantheon—he was a "cult superstar." Each new album was accompanied by a tour featuring ever more costly theatrical staging infused with imagery he appropriated from sources as diverse as Japanese kabuki and Weimar-era cabarets. Bowie also branched out into such creative endeavors as record production and acting. As a producer, he actually did his best work with performers who had been major influences on his own style.

Bowie's work on Lou Reed's *Transformer* album—which included Reed's signature song (and transexual anthem) "Walk on the Wild Side"—helped establish the former Velvet Underground vocalist as an icon of glam rock decadence. Another of his forays into rock's darker recesses resulted in the Bowie-produced 1973 album, *Raw Power* by Iggy Pop and the Stooges. Iggy (a.k.a. James Osterberg) had formed his Detroit-based band in the late 1960s, and while his shirtless writhings and abrasive vocals had little impact at the time, Iggy is now cited as one of the seminal proto-punk heroes. In other cases, Bowie helped shape the image of rock newcomers such as Mott the Hoople, whose huge (Bowie-composed) hit "All the Young Dudes" transformed the mainstream hard rockers into glam rock pop stars.

Typically, just as Bowie seemed on the verge of being absorbed into the mainstream himself, he staged a strategic retreat by initiating a three-record series of cutting-edge collaborations with British rock's reclusive

FIGURE 5-4.   David Bowie in the guise of his early-1970s alter-ego, Ziggy Stardust. Over the years, Bowie has established one of rock's most enduring careers on a philosophy embodied in the title one of his first hits—"Changes." Courtesy of RCA Records Photo Archive.

Ch-Ch-Ch-Ch-Changes

By the 1990s, Bowie may have finally exhausted his vast repertoire of revolving (and gender-bending) personas, but he never lost his appetite for cutting-edge musical styles. Throughout the decade, he explored the strange worlds of "industrial," "techno," and "drum-and-bass." He also formed a new band (Tin Machine), fashioned a stark solo album (*Black Tie White Noise*), and, on one end-of-decade CD (*Outside*), renewed his experiments with his long-time collaborator, Brian Eno.

minimalist visionary, Brian Eno (who had taken up residence in Germany). Dubbed the "Berlin Trilogy," these late-1970s albums (*Low, Heroes,* and *Lodger*) set Bowie's images of world-weary alienation and shifting identities to the raw electronic noise and synthesized sound effects of which Eno was the acknowledged master.

The eclecticism and irony Bowie brought to his music throughout the 1970s even allowed him to escape the vitriolic end-of-the-decade assaults of the punks (unlike Elton John, whose emotionally direct songs and pop-oriented success made him one of their prime targets). Throughout the 1980s and 1990s, Bowie periodically experimented with each new fringe style that came along (from hard-edge industrial to dance-oriented techno-pop). But it was also during this period that Bowie's enormous influence on contemporary pop culture became increasingly apparent. He has been credited with stretching the boundaries of gender in rock and with introducing (on stage) the kind of surrealistic image-mongering that has become the basic formula of the music video.

Although America never proved to be fertile ground for Britain's glam rockers, the style's most successful practitioners invariably cited American performers as their primary inspirations. From this perspective, the founding fathers of rock decadence were unquestionably the Velvet Underground.

Formed in New York City at the height of the flower-power era, the Velvet Underground offered a dark and disturbing vision of hard drugs ("Heroin") and perversion ("Venus in Furs"). And at a time when rock's musical values were increasingly focused on virtuosity and professionalism, the Velvets were willfully crude. The band's lead singer and songwriter Lou Reed cultivated an abrasive (slightly off-key) vocal style, while their musical direction (conceived primarily by John Cale) turned away from rock's folk and blues sources to the dronelike minimalism of the classical avant garde.

After paying their dues in Greenwich Village's seamiest clubs, the Velvet Underground were "discovered" by pop art guru and entrepreneur Andy Warhol. Warhol adopted the band into his own self-consciously disfunctional circle of junkies and drag queens, introduced them to the blonde, beautiful but haunted-looking model Nico (who became the group's frontperson), and designed the cover of their first album (an engimatic but suggestive silkscreened banana). Although the band self-destructed even before the 1960s did, the Velvet Underground had a powerful influence not only on those decadent glam rockers, but on future punk rockers (who recognized in their unpretentious primitivism an antidote to the overblown art and arena rock of the era).

Drawing their inspiration from both the Velvet Underground's dark vision and David Bowie's more glittery (and commercially astute) variation on it was another marginal but influential American band, the New York Dolls. Affecting a cheap, androgynous image and performing a crude but enthusiastic brand of hard rock, the Dolls had acquired their own underground cult during the early 1970s. Among their most ardent admirers were a couple of local bar band veterans, the singer (and part-time public school teacher) Gene Simmons and guitarist Paul Stanley. "In the beginning," Simmons readily acknowledged, "we were extremely jealous of the New York Dolls and we were going to do them one better." The band they formed to achieve this goal was KISS.

By appropriating the black leather and red lipstick image of the Dolls and combining it with skilled musicianship, shrewd business instincts, and gallons of greasepaint, Simmons and Stanley transformed themselves into rock comic book characters. In the process, the duo also gave birth to one of the biggest bands of the decade. In 1974, when KISS made its dramatic debut, rock's young fans were ready for a music of their own, one that would be free of the taint of the 1960s, and yet provocative enough to rouse the ire of middle-class parents everywhere.

In addition to the carefully contrived malevolence of their face paint (without which they never appeared in public), the band's live show featured satanic flames, fake blood, and Simmons's own rather remarkable tongue. Before long, KISS had acquired its own "army" of loyal fans and had recorded a dozen multimillion selling albums. Through KISS, the androgynous decadence of the urban underground—at least a safe cartoon version of it—was embraced by a generation of suburban adolescents across America.

In many ways, this was the same tactic that had already propelled another band to national prominence. Founded in 1968 by Vicent Furnier, Alice Cooper—the name of both the band and Furnier's alter ego—soon emerged as one of most infamous acts in mainstream rock. After the two albums they recorded in L.A. (for Frank Zappa's Straight Records) went nowhere, Alice Cooper relocated to Detroit, where a song from from their 1971 album, *Love It to Death,* was picked up by a local radio station and turned into a nationwide hit.

Although the single ("I'm Eighteen") was a just another in a long line of rock anthems of adolescent rebellion (as was its even bigger follow-up, "School's Out"), it was the sexually suggestive grand guignol theatrics of the

FIGURE 5-5. Over twenty years after KISS released its first album, the band's legion of loyal fans still turned out in force to hear them play their trademark anthem—"Rock and Roll All Nite"—one more time. Photo by Michael Sexton. Courtesy of Mercury Records.

KISS: Rock 'n' Roll All Nite (and Beyond)

From the very beginning, most critics reviled KISS and its "anonymous heavy-metal thud-rock" (as *Rolling Stone's Encyclopedia of Rock & Roll* put it). By inflating glam-rock's decadence and theatricality to comic book proportions, however, KISS became one of the most successful groups in the music's history. In fact, in the late 1970s, the Marvel company actually published a couple of issues of a KISS action comic; according to one rumor, the red ink used in the drawings was spiked with a drop of each bandmember's blood.

band's live show—which included a live python, decapitated mannequins, and Furnier in blood-stained drag—that really made Alice Cooper so notorious, and enormously successful.

In fact, by the mid-1970s, the combined success of all of rock's various subgenres (from corporate to art to glam) had expanded the pop music market to undreamed-of proportions. In doing so, rock was transformed from its 1960s status as a kind of communal village green into an assortment of separate, carefully cultivated gardens, some of which—as we've seen—featured displays of particularly exotic blossoms.

BLACK MUSIC IN THE SEVENTIES: MANY NATIONS UNDER A GROOVE

During the 1960s, it was soul music that fueled black America's sense of community much the way rock music did for the white youth culture that had come together at Woodstock. But as we've just seen, the enormous growth of rock during the early 1970s resulted in a fragmentation of that audience and stripped the music of its social relevance. When black music entered the "Me Decade," it confronted many of these same forces, and—like rock—it was transformed in the process.

After making major inroads into the rock mainstream during the 1960s (through the efforts of performers such as Aretha Franklin, Otis Redding, Sly and the Family Stone, Jimi Hendrix, and the members of the Motown dynasty), during the early 1970s, black popular music seemed to lose its center. For the most part, contemporary R & B either adopted the uncompromising rhythmic rigor of funk or else it embraced an unrestrained crossover vision that would eventually lead down the slippery slope to disco. Meanwhile, the huge commercial breakthroughs of Motown and soul had transformed the way that black popular music had been created and marketed since at least the 1940s.

For better or worse, the age of quickly produced singles issued by mom-and-pop indie labels and targeted to black radio stations was over. By the end of the 1960s, even Motown's performers had begun to achieve artistic control of their music and break out of the constraints of the three-minute single (just as their white counterparts had done). Although it took a protracted legal battle in each case, Stevie Wonder and Marvin Gaye both managed to negotiate new contracts that gave them the opportunity to make elaborately produced concept albums, using the kind of state-of-the-art studio technology and multitrack techniques that the Beatles and other rock groups had pioneered.

SEVENTIES SOUL: SOCIAL CONSCIOUSNESS AND CREATIVE CONTROL

In 1971, Marvin Gaye produced a brilliant and achingly beautiful concept album entitled *What's Goin' On* that explored the fractured social and political landscape of black America in songs about drugs, racism, Vietnam, and the breakup of the family. A year later, (no longer "Little") Stevie Wonder released the first of his breakthrough albums, *Talking Book,* which contained his first number one pop hits in almost ten years ("Superstition" and "You Are the Sunshine of My Life"). With each succeeding album, Wonder's records became as ambitious in conception and technological sophistication as any art-rock masterpiece—and they were a lot more soulful.

Like his Seventies rock colleagues, Stevie Wonder began exploring the exciting potential of the new electronic synsthesizers, quickly becoming one of the most creative exponents of the instrument. And rather than being constrained by the traditional R & B timetable that demanded a new single every couple of weeks, Wonder retreated into the studio for months (then years) in order to perfect and polish his increasingly complex productions. Not that it wasn't worth the wait. For example, a year after *Talking Book,* Stevie released *Innervisions,* featuring the seven-minute musical pseudo-documentary "Livin' for the City," a minutely observed nightmare vision of urban America.

FIGURE 5-6.   As the dominant voice of reggae, Bob Marley became the first developing world performer to make a significant impact on the rock mainstream. After his tragic death by cancer in 1981, Marley attained the status of culture hero and secular saint. Archive photo.

Bob Marley: Rock's First Third World Hero

Employing reggae's heady blend of American R & B and indigenous Caribbean rhythms, Bob Marley gave voice to a spirit of righteousness and redemption that formed the basis of his Rastafarian religious beliefs. While many rock fans tended to focus on his odes in praise of "ganga" (marijuana), a Rastafarian sacrament, the bulk of his songs were expressions of either his messianic religious fervor ("Rastaman Vibration," "Redemption Song") or his revolutionary political vision ("Slave Driver," "War"). He also wrote both haunting love songs ("No Woman, No Cry") and sensual slow-dance grooves ("Stir It Up").

For the most part, however, the American mainstream audience was content to get its reggae second-hand. For example, in 1971, Paul Simon had a Top Ten single with a reggae-ish original, "Mother and Child Reunion," while Eric Clapton's 1974 cover of Bob Marley's "I Shot the Sheriff" went straight to number one. In 1980, Blondie also topped the charts with a reggae-tinged single, "The Tide Is High." And while Stevie Wonder concocted a couple of soulful reggae compositions of his own (such as "Boogie on Reggae Woman"), the African-American audience never really embraced the music of their Jamaican brothers and sisters.

Although Bob Marley gained posthumous entry into the Western pop pantheon, his utopian vision of postcolonial unity and empowerment made him a figure of veneration not only in his homeland but throughout Africa and Latin America. Reggae lost considerable momentum in the wake of Marley's death, but the style has continued to exert a powerful influence on the music of the developing world. In addition, two members of the Wailers—Peter Tosh and Bunny (Wailer) Livingston—carried on the performer's legacy in separate solo careers, and some of Bob's sons (most prominently Ziggy Marley) have followed in their father's footsteps.

Stevie Wonder never degenerated into bitterness or pessimism for long, however. In fact, it was Wonder's positive vision and profound idealism—as well as his infectious groove—that made him one of the most successful performers of the period. By mid-decade, Wonder had earned ten Grammys and signed a $13 million contract with Motown (recognized at the time as the most generous in pop music history). But even more than its financial aspects, his new agreement with Motown was significant because it provided the budding musical auteur with complete artistic control over his increasingly ambitious productions.

Across the entire spectrum of black popular music, other performers also were beginning to stretch the boundaries of rhythm and blues conventions. For example, at the start of the decade, a former gospel singer, Donny Hathaway, released a debut single, "The Ghetto." In contrast to the typical R & B formula of the 1950s and 1960s, this was a six-minute forty-seven-second, highly produced narrative of inner-city reality that layered Latin rhythms over a moody jazz organ. And it was a hit. About this same time, R & B veteran Curtis Mayfield also was expanding his own soulful songs of social consciousness (such as his mid-1960s classics "Keep on Pushin'" and "People Get Ready").

In 1972, Curtis Mayfield created a subtle, sonically complex, and highly danceable soundtrack for the "blaxploitation" film, *Superfly.* The album featured both a hit title song and an anti-drug anthem, "The Pusher," that he had written specifically to deglamorize the image of this romanticized figure as portrayed in the film itself. With their new producer, Norman Whitfield, even the Temptations began crafting a new socially conscious brand of "psychedelic soul" during the 1970s (in songs such as "Ball of Confusion," "Papa Was a Rolling Stone," and "Psychedelic Shack").

One of the era's most innovative R & B albums came from Stax Records, that bastion of traditional Southern soul, whose multiracial creative team had once produced the classic works of Otis Redding, Booker T & the MGs, Wilson Pickett, and Sam and Dave. After their utopian vision had fallen victim to the racial turmoil set off by the assassination of Martin Luther King Jr., Stax also found itself a victim of the new economic realities. Like the even older and more prestigious independent R & B label, Atlantic (which had been sold to Warner Bros. in 1967), Stax was absorbed by a giant media conglomerate, Gulf & Western. Among the first releases of the new regime was an album that seemed to defy every element of the classic Stax formula. Yet, true to Seventies form, Isaac Hayes's *Hot Buttered Soul* quickly became the biggest selling album in the label's history.

During Stax's Sixties heyday, Isaac Hayes had been a member of the label's celebrated house band, as well as a producer and composer (with his partner David Porter) of some of its biggest hits (most notably Sam and Dave's "Soul Man" and "Hold on I'm Comin' "). But while those records were tightly compressed, rhythmically charged three-minute explosions of soul, the album Hayes produced for himself (on the cusp of the new decade) was a meandering, lushly arranged work whose centerpiece was an eighteen-minute-plus version of a contemporary country song. Hayes's cover of "By the Time I Get to Phoenix" (which had recently been a number one hit for Glen Campbell) not only featured an expansive string ensemble, but it contained an extended, spoken rap. Two years later, Hayes used many of these same effects in the Academy Award–winning soundtrack he created for the hard-boiled black detective film, *Shaft.*

While some black performers of the early 1970s, such as Memphis' own Al Green, did keep faith with soul music's gospel roots (and communal vision), the majority began gravitating to the new decade's slicker styles. Among the slickest—and most commercially successful—of these was the one whipped up by Barry White, a Los Angeles–based producer-arranger, who assembled a forty-piece ensemble (he dubbed the Love Unlimited Orchestra), which served up massive portions of syrupy confections over which White poured his suggestive basso-voiced raps. In hits like "Walkin' in the Rain with the One I Love" (1972) and "Can't Get Enough of Your Love, Babe" (1974), Barry White re-vamped a time-honored R & B image—the "love man"—as an upscale sexual fantasy figure.

And just as Motown had become the dominant label in African-American music during the 1960s by forging its own distinctive sound out of assorted elements of black popular music—and then institutionalizing it through a stable of house writers, arrangers, and studio musicians—during the new decade another black-owned independent label applied a similar creative (and entrepreneurial) formula in order to create one of the dominant styles of Seventies soul.

TSOP: THE SOUND OF PHILADELPHIA
(THE MESSAGE IN THE MUSIC)

Until the advent of Motown, Detroit had never been a significant center of the rhythm and blues business. By the time Philadelphia International Records began its reign as the preeminent R & B label of the 1970s, however, the City of Brotherly Love had long been famous for a local pop music scene that was dominated by the varied enterprises of Dick Clark (who had begun hosting a teen dance show on local TV in 1952).

Five years later, Clark's *American Bandstand* had become a daily fixture on national television and the city had become home to at least a half-dozen successful independent record labels. Along the way, Philly was the launching pad for many of the era's "teen idols" and for that massive, Chubby Checker–inspired dance craze of the early 1960s, the Twist. Along with scores of musicians, songwriters, and arrangers who were eking out a living in the city were the lyricist Kenny Gamble and his partner, the pianist-arranger Leon Huff.

After paying their dues playing on local sessions, as well as writing and producing some modest R & B hits, Gamble and Huff finally produced a record that crossed over into the upper reaches of the national pop charts. Their 1967 single "Expressway to Your Heart" (recorded by the "blue-eyed" Soul Survivors) was a tightly arranged, propulsive dance record cleverly interwoven with the sound of car horns and highway traffic. Soon Kenny Gamble and Leon Huff had earned a reputation for creating fresh, danceable R & B with a carefully honed veneer of urbane sophistication. Having assembled a core of local session musicians who would, as the band, MFSB, record their own instrumental hits (including "TSOP," the future label's anthem and the theme song of TV's *Soul Train*), the duo set up shop in Philadelphia's Sigma Studio, which quickly became one of the meccas of Seventies soul.

Gamble and Huff began by working their magic for R & B veterans such as Jerry Butler and Wilson Pickett. Soon they had a growing stable of solid, mostly male vocal groups and solo acts. In 1971—with financial backing from CBS Records—they were finally able to realize a long-held dream. They founded their own independent label, Philadelphia International Records.

Even in the overheated commercial climate of the early 1970s, the success of PIR was immediate and extraordinary. Beginning with the O'Jay's first hit, "Backstabbers," in 1972, Gamble and Huff wrote, arranged, and produced a string of contemporary R & B classics. In addition to the O'Jay's and the label's other major act, Harold Melvin and the Bluenotes (whose lead singer Teddy Pendergrass would also have a prominent PIR solo career), they produced a series of successful singles for Jerry Butler and one for the one-hit wonder Billy Paul (who scored with a sultry cheating ballad, "Me and Mrs. Jones"). By the middle of the decade, PIR was bringing in close to $30 million a year in revenues and was second only to Motown itself as the most profitable black-owned business in America.

Just as Motown had its slogan ("The Sound of Young America") printed on its record label, Philadelphia International had its own motto ("The Message in the Music") printed on every album. Although PRI's "message"—of African-American unity and self-determination—was often promoted in the lyrics of their songs, in a way that Gamble and Huff may not have intended, PIR's message literally was *in the music* itself. It was in the lavish orchestrations, the slick arrangements, the throbbing bass, the scintillating strings, and the Latin rhythmic accents. It was, in fact, PRI's glossy production values that more than anything else came to define the Sound of Philadelphia. And to a great extent, it was its upscale aesthetic that provided the foundation for the disco craze that would dominate pop music during the second half of the decade.

Just as Motown had often been castigated for its carefully crafted, assembly-line style—especially when compared to Atlantic Records' gritty brand of urban and Southern soul—PIR came under attack for its high-gloss brand of polyester pop soul; if you really wanted to get down with the real deal, its critics suggested, it was time to bring on the funk.

MAKE IT FUNKY!

Funk: a strong smell or stink (1623: '. . . Betwixt deck there can hardlie a man fetch his breath by reason there ariseth such a funke in the night . . .')

The Oxford English Dictionary

"If it makes you shake your rump, it's the Funk."

George Clinton

By the time "Soul Brother Number One" re-christened himself the "Grand Minister of Funk," James Brown had become the spiritual leader of a sizeable congregation of disciples who had converted to the rhythmic revolt he had initiated in the mid-1960s.

By stripping his music to its most visceral, rough-edged, down-and-dirty essence, Brown created a visionary new form of black music that drew directly from the deepest wellsprings of African-American culture. In doing so, he pointed the way for (among others) the syncopated communal celebrations of Sly and the Family Stone; the state of the art Seventies soul of Stevie Wonder; the groove-based spirituality of Earth, Wind, and Fire; the raucous good-time vibe of Kool and the Gang; the Jherri-curled raunch of Rick James; and the surreal tribal pyrotechnics of George Clinton. For, despite the superficial distinctions that existed among them, what united all these performers was their devotion to a primal component of black music known as "funk."

Although it has defied most attempts at precise definition (see quotes above), the musical roots of funk in America can be traced back to the dank and pungent dance halls of New Orleans at the turn of the twentieth century, when the legendary cornetist Buddy Bolden ruled New Orleans' rough-and-tumble Uptown district with the power of his horn.

Some people have claimed that you could hear his horn from twenty miles away! And many insist that "King Bolden"—as he was known throughout the Crescent City—was the leader of the first jazz band in history. In about 1902, Buddy composed what became his band's theme song, "Buddy Bolden's Blues." Although he never recorded the song (or anything else for that matter), there is ample testimony not only about what it sounded like but about the nature of its suggestive lyrics as well: "I thought I heard Buddy Bolden say, Funky Butt, Funky Butt, take it away."

As jazz historian Donald M. Marquis wrote in his book, *In Search of Buddy Bolden: First Man of Jazz,* "The crowd loved the song. . . . And because Bolden was also identified with the Union Sons Hall [a notorious site for local dances], before long the sporting crowd that frequented the hall renamed it 'Funky Butt Hall' in honor of the Bolden band." Not all New Orleans jazz fans recognized Bolden as their king, however—nor did everyone join his loyal court in their celebration of funk.

According to jazz pioneer Bunk Johnson, who claimed to have played with Bolden, the local white and up-scale Creole audience (comprised of the mixed-race descendents of New Orleans original French and Spanish settlers) tended to favor a band led by John Robechaux that played more refined, "sweet" dance tunes. But, as Johnson recalls, "Amongst the Negroes, Buddy Bolden could close a Robechaux dance up by 10:30 at night. . . . Old King Bolden played the music the *Negro* public liked." So it was that, in addition to retaining its olfactory associations—that combination of sweat and sexuality—1970s funk shared both the same aesthetic as its New Orleans ancestor (an earthy eroticism and polyrhythmic texture) and the same audience. For while many styles of black music have comfortably crossed over to the white mainstream during the twentieth century, a few have not.

For example, writing about James Brown's first forays into funk, the critic Robert Palmer hypothesized that the divergent reactions to the performer's percussive new style may indeed have had a cultural component. "Where the European listener may hear monotonous beating," he begins, "the African distinguishes subtle polyrhythmic interplay, tonal distinctions among the various drums, the virtuosity of the master drummer, and so on." The effect on Brown's career, according to Palmer, is that "White Americans have rarely bought his records in large numbers. In fact, he has never had a number one pop hit." By contrast, Brown's quintessential 1970s funk singles—like "Make It Funky"—regularly made their way to the top of the soul/R & B charts.

Like most of Brown's hits from this period, "Make It Funky" (released in 1971) was, as its title suggests, a textbook example of the genre's fundamental nature. By jettisoning virtually all melodic and harmonic content, Brown assembled layer on layer of interlocking rhythms into a single overarching, hypnotic "vamp" (repeated chord pattern or rhythmic figure): there was the percolating pulse of the bass, a drummer kicking out a syncopated groove, the guitar's metallic choked-string "chanka-chank," a chorus of horns uniting around a single brassy riff—even Brown's endlessly reiterated vocal exhortation ("Make it funky!") was conceived as just one more rhythmic element.

In his exploration of mid-1950s jazz—a time when another generation of African-American performers was also embracing the music's rhythmic roots—the writer Frank Kofsky argued that, once again, "making it funky" was a culturally specific concept. In his book, *Black Nationalism and the Revolution in Music,* Kofsky maintains that "to call a composition or a [musical] passage or a player 'funky,' was not only to offer praise in general, but a means of lauding the object of praise for its specifically black qualities."

Although these mid-century jazz performers neither declared themselves a movement (nor gave their style of music a specific name), in 1954, when veteran jazz vibraharpist Milt Jackson recorded an album that featured this impassioned, soulful sound, he titled it *Opus de Funk.* And just as James Brown's own brand of Seventies funk coincided with the rise of the "Black Power" movement, the earthy, blues-based style formulated by jazz artists a decade or two before also had been associated with a pivotal era in our country's racial history. For it was just as the modern civil rights movement was beginning to mount its most concerted effort both in the courts (*Brown v. Topeka Board of Education*) and in the streets (Montgomery bus boycott) that Milt Jackson, Art Blakey, and Horace Silver, among others, embraced funk as a fundamental expression of black culture.

Although the centrality of its rhythmic component (and the cultural consciousness of its practitioners) may have limited funk's mainstream appeal, as the 1960s drew to a close, one unique expression of multicultural funk did cross over briefly to the rock audience. By grafting the jagged rhythmic juxtapositions of James Brown onto the free-form jams of the San Francisco sound, Sly and the Family Stone came up with a potent brand of psychedelic funk (which Sly used to accompany his messages of utopian brotherhood). Not only did they sell a ton of records, chart a string of Top Ten pop hits, and galvanize the half-million (mostly white) citizens of the Woodstock Nation, but Sly and the Family Stone got as much airplay on the powerful "progressive rock" radio stations as Cream and the Rolling Stones.

Unfortunately, by the middle of the 1970s, when the new generation of funk bands began constructing its own variations on the rhythmically insistent, horn-punctuated form, the genre again was confined to its traditional audience—especially within the ever more restrictive world of radio. With a tightly programmed brand of AOR (Album Oriented Rock) now dominating rock radio, the Seventies funk of Kool and the Gang ("Jungle Boogie," "Funky Stuff"), Rich James ("Superfreak"), Earth, Wind, and Fire ("Serpentine Fire," "Shining Star"), and the Ohio Players ("Funk Worm," "Skin Tight") became relegated to the contemporary urban media's equivalent of Buddy Bolden's Funky Butt Hall.

And when George Clinton attempted to reassemble Sly and the Family Stone's multicultural constituency with his various P-Funk enterprises, he proved too funky for these mainstream rock stations. Ironically—as the era's black radio stations began assuming an increasingly upwardly mobile veneer—Clinton proved too strange for the rapidly evolving "urban contemporary" format as well.

Early in his career, George Clinton had been a member of the Parliaments, a classic Motown-style vocal group that had scored a Top Ten R & B hit in 1967 with the gospel-tinged single "I Just Want to Testify." Inspired by the late 1960s revolution in black popular music (including Sly's psychedelic funk and Jimi Hendrix's instrumental pyrotechnics), Clinton soon began assembling a band with the suggestive name, Funkadelic (a.k.a. Parliament-Funkadelic, a.k.a. P-Funk). After adorning the band in shiny jumpsuits (and himself in a blond wig), "Dr. Funkenstein" (Clinton's nom de funk) issued the first musical statement of his new dynasty, an album simply called *Funkadelic.* Over the next few years, Clinton constructed his own futuristic funk mythology, and the titles of later albums—*Free Your Ass and Your Mind Will Follow, Cosmic Slop, America Eats Its Young, Maggot Brain,* and *Mothership Connection*—began to take on a baroque weirdness.

Although Clinton's imagery owed a debt to ancestors of musical eccentricity such as Frank Zappa and jazz keyboardist/bandleader Sun Ra, his primary musical sources remained Sly Stone, Jimi Hendrix, and James Brown (many of whose disgruntled former sidemen—such as innovative bassist Bootsy Collins and sax legend Maceo

Parker—found their way into Clinton's ever-expanding aggregations). Not only did the size of Clinton's band continue to swell during this period, but his stage shows soon became as elaborate and costly as any glam or art rock supergroup's. By mid-decade his stage set—which included a gleaming full-scale flying saucer—had a price tag of over a quarter-million dollars.

Ironically, by 1978, when Clinton released the album whose title more than any other summed up his vision of universal funkhood—*One Nation under a Groove*—most of America's pop audience was, in fact, already united. The groove under which the nation would had come together, however, turned out to be the sanitized rhythms of disco. But while funk may have once again been relegated to margins of American culture, its pungent aroma would continue to waft through more recent musical styles.

Beginning in the late 1970s, for example, rappers locked onto James Brown's funkiest beats, making them the samples of choice for an entire generation of hip-hop DJs. And in the mid-1980s, when Talking Heads wanted to enrich their new wave minimalism with the earthy rhythmic textures of African-American music, the new wave minimalists turned to former Clinton keyboardist Bernie Worrell, whose contributions are documented on the band's funky live album (and concert film), *Stop Making Sense*. Finally, in 1996, George Clinton's own extraordinary (and ongoing) contributions to the history of funk were officially recognized when he was voted into the Rock and Roll Hall of Fame.

ROCK AT MID-DECADE: FROM THE MAINSTREAM TO THE MARGINS

BLOCKBUSTERS AND BRUCE

As we have seen, the big bang that occurred in the rock universe during the first half of the 1970s resulted in an explosive period of growth and fragmentation. But, having passed the decade's midpoint, the pop music cosmos began to coalesce into a handful of fixed galaxies while continuing to expand in both scope and sales.

By the mid-1970s, many bands and solo performers seemed to share the same characteristics as the media conglomerates for which they recorded: professional, predictable, and profitable. In 1976, for example, the Eagles released their Grammy Award–winning L.A.-rock masterpiece, *Hotel California*. Worldwide sales of the album soared to an astonishing eleven million copies. That same year, when Peter Frampton—former singer and lead guitarist of a second-tier British pop group (Humble Pie)—released a live solo album, the two-record, hook-filled package (*Frampton Comes Alive!*) sold twelve million copies. A year later, sales of Fleetwood Mac's beautifully crafted and tuneful LP, *Rumors*, topped fifteen million copies. Based on such megahits, the record industry as a whole had grown into a $3 billion a year behemoth.

It was in this context of rock's expanding revenues (and shrinking cultural significance) that a review in the May 22, 1974, issue of a Boston-based alternative weekly, *The Real Paper*, heralded the appearance of a rock 'n' roll redeemer. In what would become perhaps the most quoted review in rock history, the respected critic Jon Landau described his reaction to a young singer's performance at the Harvard Square theater: "I saw my rock 'n' roll past flash before my eyes," Landau wrote. "And I saw something else: I saw rock 'n' roll's future and its name is Bruce Springsteen."

Whatever one thought of Landau's hyberbolic prediction, no one could dispute the authenticity of Springsteen's rock credentials. After playing in local New Jersey shore bands since he was about fourteen years old, Bruce had become a seasoned and relentless performer who had attracted an intensely loyal cult following based largely on his exhilarating three-hour concerts. It was his songwriting talent, however, that initially prompted Columbia Records to sign Springsteen. Both his debut album (*Greetings from Asbury Park*) and his 1974 follow-up (*The Wild, the Innocent, and the E Street Shuffle*) drew from a rich repertoire of original songs characterized by their long lines of densely packed images. In fact, before Landau's review dubbed him the future of rock 'n' roll, Springsteen had been touted as "the next Bob Dylan."

Actually, the Dylan comparison happens to work on a number of levels. For while Bruce Springsteen's music reflected a thorough knowledge of the whole history of rock 'n' roll (from Elvis's and Jerry Lee Lewis's earliest Sun sessions to Phil Spector's Brill Building masterpieces to the Rolling Stones' barbed-wire riffs), in his earliest songs Springsteen was clearly following in the footsteps of Bob Dylan's lyric revolution. The evidence was there for anybody to hear; in addition to the sheer length of the tunes (a Dylan trademark), there was the Dylanesque surrealism of Springsteen's urban ballads, and his tendency to generate endless bumper-to-bumper rhymes.

Nor was Bruce shy about directly acknowledging his debt to, and admiration for, Dylan's music. "It's the greatest music even written," he told one interviewer. "The man says it all, exactly the right way. Incredibly powerful. You don't get no more intense." Never much of a reader as a youngster (although he would become omnivorous in adulthood), by the time he was out of his teens one of the only books Springsteen claimed to have actually read was a biography of Bob Dylan written by Anthony Scaduto. In it he surely must have been intrigued by the scene in which Dylan was signed to his first Columbia recording contract by the legendary producer/talent scout John Hammond. Ten years later, it would be Hammond himself who signed Bruce to the same label.

And as with Dylan, Springsteen also was viewed as something more than just another rock 'n' roller. As Fred Goodman put it in his book *Mansion of the Hill,* "Springsteen was being heralded as the keeper of the promise that rock—despite surrendering its ties to an anticorporate counterculture—was still about something more than acquiring the trappings of success. It proved a powerful mystique." Yet ironically, as Goodman goes on to document, Bruce was also about to become the beneficiary of one of the most costly and effective promotional campaigns in rock history. For just two months after John Landau's portentious pronouncement, Columbia (then the undisputed record industry giant) initiated a $50,000 ad campaign for Springsteen around the famous "rock 'n' roll's future" quote.

As the hype built during the long wait for Bruce's next record (with Landau himself on board as coproducer), Columbia orchestrated a PR blitz that included a series of showcase performances Springsteen gave for critics and industry insiders at the hippest clubs in New York and L.A. By the time *Born to Run* was released in the fall of 1975, the critical buzz had reached a crescendo, culminating in what would be an unprecedented media coup: Bruce Springsteen's face on the cover of both *Time* and *Newsweek* during the same week.

While Springsteen's artistic ambitions and blue-collar persona helped insulate him from the taint of "commercialism," for some fans, the difference between Springsteen's brand of "roots-rock" and the music of any of the era's other hyphenated rockers (art-, glam- arena-) was really rather negligible. They scorned the elaborate studio productions that took months and hundreds of thousands of dollars in time and high-tech wizardry. They had contempt for the corporate-sponsored tours mounted like military operations. They ridiculed the media hype and rock-star ego trips. For them, rock 'n' roll wasn't about either instrumental virtuosity or commercial viability—it was about energy, noise, and rebellion.

PUNK: UP FROM THE UNDERGROUND

By the mid-1970s, signs of a growing reaction against mainstream rock with its massive stadium tours and months-in-the-making multiplatinum albums were emerging on both sides of the Atlantic. In New York, the so-called downtown art scene had acquired its own musical wing (descendants of proto-punk bands such as the Velvet Underground and the New York Dolls) and combined a decadent, self-consciously ironic stance with an intentionally primitive musical style. Their home base—a skid-row storefront known as CBGB—soon became the headquarters for New York's new rock underground.

Although the club's initials actually stood for "Country Blue Grass and Blues," these forms of traditional American folk music were a far cry from anything being made on CBGB's tiny stage. Instead, there was Patti Smith shrieking the words of her latest poem to the angular guitar accompaniment of rock-critic-turned-sideman Lenny Kaye. Among other regular performers at the club during this formative period were innovative bands such as Television, Richard Hell and the Voidoids, Talking Heads, and Blondie, each of whom had formulated its own personal recipe out of the basic ingredients of the new sound: a sledge hammer beat, a handful of abrasive, rapid-fire guitar chords, and a vocal rant that (when it could be heard over the chaotic din) most often proved to be an ode to sex, drugs, rock 'n' roll, or ennui.

Having already recorded what is generally recognized as the first punk single in history—"Hey Joe" b/w "Piss Factory" (1974)—Patti Smith became the first of her compatriots to sign with a major label. And her 1975 Arista

FIGURE 5-7.   With the release of their self-titled 1976 debut album, the Ramones helped define the punk aesthetic by recapturing the heady abandon of 1950s rock 'n' roll. Archive photo.

The Ramones and the Aesthetics of Punk

After a decade of flower-power fashions, interminable guitar heroics, multitrack concept albums, and rock operas, the Ramones' black leather motorcycle jackets and pedal-to-the-metal two-minute, three-chord songs helped initiate a punk rock revolution. Initially, however, the band rejected the punk label, preferring to describe their repertoire of original tunes—such as "I Don't Want to Go Down to the Basement," "Beat on the Brat (With a Baseball Bat)," and their classic, "I Wanna Be Sedated"—as "sick bubblegum music."

It was the Ramones' whirlwind tour of England in 1976 that is credited with transforming a loose affliation of British bands—united by their primitive sound and nihilistic stance—into a mass movement. Yet, on this side of the Atlantic, neither the Ramones nor punk rock itself ever really achieved a significant audience.

debut album, *Horses,* produced by Velvet Underground founder John Cale, brilliantly captured Smith's stark, anarchic power. Soon, she was joined in the record store's "New Releases" section by the Ramones (whose thirteen-song, thirty-minute album on Sire Records contained such CBGB-tested hits as "Beat on the Brat" and "I Want to Sniff Some Glue"), Television (whose Elektra LP *Marquee Moon* blended Sixties psychedelia and avant-garde jazz influences), and Talking Heads (whose aptly titled Sire album *'77* contained David Byrne's signature composition "Psycho Killer," along with other examples of the band's well-honed punk minimalism).

While New York was unquestionably the capital of America's underground rock movement, by this time regional outposts were springing up across the country. For example, there was the obsessively quirky, Boston-based singer-songwriter Jonathan Richman whose 1976 debut, *Modern Lovers,* was a collection of material he had recorded with his band earlier in the decade (and assembled with assistance from the ubiquitous John Cale). Not only were songs such as "Roadrunner" classic examples of the rock underground's back-to-basics philosophy, but—in an age of major-label media conglomerates—the LP was released on Beserkley Records, a tiny independent label.

As a matter of fact, just as Bruce Springsteen emerged as "the future of rock 'n' roll" by mining the music's entire history, the underground rockers of the mid-1970s also were reviving elements from the past on their way to rock's cutting edge. In addition to the 1950s style fundamentalism of their music, these bands typically signed with low-budget, regional independent labels and were promoted by a network of self-produced "fanzines." By the end of the decade, reenergized local scenes had sprung up in the Midwest (with Cleveland's Pere Ubu and Akron's Devo) and in San Francisco (with the Dead Kennedys), L.A. (with Germs and X), and Atlanta (with the B-52s). There was only one problem with this outpouring of exciting new popular music: For the most part, it just wasn't popular.

Even when bands secured major label contracts, they went against the grain of everything that mainstream rock had become. This was music that was, by design, antivirtuosic, anticorporate, and antisocial. And with Album Oriented Rock stations mired in mainstream rock's version of "easy listening," their provocative, intentionally abrasive style could hardly be considered radio-friendly (which more than anything helped to seal its commercial fate). Not that the rock press (a.k.a. *Rolling Stone*), with its dependence on Big Rock ad money, was much more receptive.

Meanwhile, the mainstream media's response to the onslaught of punk rock wasn't much different from the reception accorded rock 'n' roll at its inception two decades earlier. At best, it was seen as a bad joke that would soon fade away; at worst, it was degenerate, dangerous, and a threat to all traditional musical and social values. But while punk rock was relegated to cult status in America, in England it was being embraced by a bitterly disaffected youth culture; fueled by a sensation-hungry tabloid press, punk quickly became a cultural phenomenon.

BRITISH PUNK: SEX PISTOLS AND SAFETY PINS

In the fall of 1975 (while the Bruce Springsteen cover issues of *Time* and *Newsweek* were still on the newsstands), the Sex Pistols made their first public appearance at London's St. Martin's College of Art. Although the school's administration stopped the show midway through the performance in the name of public safety and good taste, the point had been made: British punk had arrived.

Within a year, the Sex Pistols were signed to a major British label (EMI); two months later they released their first single (the infamous "Anarchy in the U.K."), and by the end of 1976—after an obscenity-laced appearance on an afternoon talk show scandalized the country—they were immediately and very publicly "freed" from their record contract. All in all, it was everything Malcolm McLaren could have hoped for.

Often described as the "Svengali" of British punk, McLaren was the owner of a London bondage-wear boutique and a self-proclaimed social revolutionary. Having recently returned to England after (mis)managing the New York Dolls during the final stages of their career, McLaren saw in the increasingly restive youth culture of his recession-plagued country an opportunity for both a musical insurrection and a quick financial score.

Although the Sex Pistols were, as rock historian Ken Tucker has provocatively put it, "as manufactured a rock band as the Monkees had been," from their inception, they had been formulated not to charm but to shock. From the very first line of their first single ("I am the Anti-Christ") to their savagely spiked haircuts, saftey pin accessories, and technical ineptitude, the band engaged in an assault on the prevailing musical and political establishments. As the critic Greil Marcus wrote in an article on British punk in *The Rolling Stone Illustrated History of Rock & Roll*:

> [T]he Sex Pistols damned rock and roll as a rotting corpse—as a monster of moneyed reaction, a sentimentalized corruption that no longer served as more than a mechanism of glamorized oppression, self-exploitation and false consciousness—and yet, because they had no other weapons and because they were fans in spite of themselves, the Sex Pistols played rock and roll, stripping the music down to essentials of speed, noise, fury and manic glee no one else had been able to touch before. They used rock and roll as a weapon against itself.

FIGURE 5-8.   Sex Pistols frontman Johnny Rotten and (in the background) a shirtless Sid Vicious. Museum of Modern Art Film Stills Collection.

The Sex Pistols Burn Out (Before They Fade Away)

After one number one British album and an abortive American tour, the Sex Pistols self-destructed. Despite their brief tenure, however, the band paved the way for a punk rock revolt on both sides of the Atlantic. Over the next few years, bands from L.A.'s X to London's Clash would refine the punk aesthetic and help establish an enduring alternative indie-rock scene that continues to this day.

Among those who saw the Sex Pistols as the embodiment of rock 'n' roll's essential ethos was Neil Young, whose song, "My My, Hey Hey (Out of the Blue)" links the band to another of the music's mythic heroes. "The King is gone but he's not forgotten/This is the story of Johnny Rotten." And as Young's song goes on to remind us—in the world of rock 'n' roll—"It's better to burn out than to fade away."

What followed was a fascinating existential drama in which all the players performed their roles as if they had been scripted. After being dropped by EMI in the spring of 1977, the Sex Pistols signed with an American label (A & M Records) and cut their second single, "God Save the Queen," a blistering diatribe directed at Britain's most sacred symbol. Predictably, A & M broke the band's contract rather than issue the record. When Virgin Records, an ambitious new London-based label, stepped in to release the single (timing it to coincide with Queen Elizabeth's Silver Jubilee), the powers-that-be responded by banning the record from the airwaves. Much to McLaren's delight—it was publicity no money could buy—by the summer "God Save the Queen" had zoomed to number one on the British charts (although in most publications editors refused even to print the title, substituting a blank space instead).

Over the next few months, six more of the band's singles made their way into the U.K. Top Ten and their first (and only) album, *Never Mind the Bollocks, Here's the Sex Pistols*, went to number one. Early the next year, however—in the middle of their ill-conceived first (and only) American tour—lead singer Johnny Rotten quit the band and the Sex Pistols self-destructed. By this time, however, punk had swept the British music scene. Scores of new bands were performing in small clubs throughout London, and hundreds of hastily recorded singles were being issued on a welter of independent labels. It was the soundtrack for a cultural revolution that encompassed not only music, but hairstyles, fashion, and graphic design.

Although Joe Strummer was directly inspired to form the Clash after seeing an early Sex Pistols show, it was the Clash who would actually harness the anarchic power of punk and focus its political nihilism in order to create the genre's most potent music. Well versed in such varied styles as rockabilly, R & B, and reggae (which it absorbed by way of England's large Jamaican community), the band was also more technically assured than most of its punk comrades. From their self-titled 1977 debut album, the Clash brought a thoughtful, ideological slant to songs that addressed everything from American cultural imperialism ("I'm So Bored with the U.S.A.") to England's own chronically circumscribed employment possibilities ("Career Opportunities").

Just before the close of the decade, the Clash recorded its masterpiece, the double album *London Calling*. Not only did it attract extravagant praise from the American rock press, but also it achieved—as no other British punk album had—a fair share of commercial success in the United States eventually breaking into the Top Thirty on the album charts. In the band's final days, the Clash even managed to chart an American Top Ten single, "Rock the Casbah." But for the most part, America proved immune to punk rock in either its domestic or its imported varities. Instead, a very different style of music was emerging from the underground that was about to take over the American pop charts and revive what had come to seem like a lost art . . . dancing.

DISCO FEVER

Beginning at the turn of the twentieth century with the ragtime era's cakewalk craze and on to the Charlestown phenomenon of the jazz age, the lindy hop of the Swing Era, and the sock hops of rock 'n' roll's Golden Age, and on to the twist fad of the early Sixties, popular music and dance have been inseparable. Even during the height of the psychedelic rock movement, colorfully costumed "freaks" lost themselves in a myriad of free-form dance styles amid the pulsing strobe lights of Haight-Ashbury ballrooms.

During the 1970s, massive arenas had become the standard venue for elaborately staged spectacles in which the rock audience was relegated to the role of passive (if awed) observer. While their reasons varied, over the past decade, the once-innocent pastime of dancing had become anathema not only to arena rockers but to art rockers, punk rockers, roots rockers, and heavy metalists as well. It turned out, however, that not all segments of the audience shared this elitist, and essentially puritanical, attitude. In urban centers across the country, dance—and the music that propelled it—was flourishing in the elegant (or at least pseudoelegant) night spots familiarly known as "discos."

Originally, "discotheque"—a variation on the French word "bibliotheque" (library)—referred to underground World War II–era clubs where jazz fans listened to "discs" forbidden by the Nazi forces that had occupied Western Europe. During the early 1960s, however, the word was revived in London and Paris as a name for the swank nightclubs in which sophisticated "jet-setters" danced to rock 'n' roll records played by a hip young disk jockey. The fad quickly spread to major American cities. It was in New York discos such as the Peppermint Lounge, for example, that the twist became the dance of choice for the aging in-crowd.

During the early 1970s, however, the disco had evolved into the pleasure palace for a collection of urban subcultures increasingly alienated from rock's macho ambiance or for those who simply couldn't afford the rapidly inflating price of live concert tickets. So it was that a gay male vanguard and inner-city youth (a euphemism for blacks and Latinos) initiated the decade's disco craze and together defined its sensibility; that is, along with the club DJ. Employing two turntables, electronic equalizers, and various switching devices, it was the disk jockey who was most responsible for orchestrating the evening's ecstasies by smoothly segueing from one record to another in order to achieve a kind of mass sexual climax that left a room full of dancers spent but satisfied.

During this period, discotheque competed to "break" the latest hot single (as their radio namesakes had done in the 1950s) and mined the past for the most obscure oldies, all in an effort to assemble their own unique dance-inducing soundtracks. Soon, savvy record producers—recognizing the potential of the disco market—began to issue recordings specifically designed for danceability. In an effort to aid the DJ in programming his selections, producers even began listing the number of beats per minute on their labels (a bpm of between 125 and 160 was considered the optimum range to construct the ultimate disco experience).

In 1975 (the same year of Springsteen's news magazine double header and the Sex Pistols' début), an unknown group named K.C. and the Sunshine Band released an archetypal dance-floor single, "Get Down Tonight," that actually crossed over to the top of *Billboard's* pop and R & B charts. An early example of the music that came to be called "disco," the record was the brainchild of Harry Wayne Casey and Richard Finch, a pair of white songwriter/producers, working with a nine-piece band made up of South Florida's top black session musicians. "Get Down Tonight" proved that by reining in funk's pungent rhythmic punch, one could not only get people onto the dance floor but get records onto the radio.

The propulsive, Latin-tinged style Casey and Finch created (which became known as the "Miami Sound") quickly resulted in at least a half-dozen more hip-shaking hits for K.C. and the Sunshine Band (including "That's the Way (I Like It)," "(Shake, Shake, Shake) Your Booty," and "I'm Your Boogie Man"). At this point, not only did veteran soul music writer-producer Van McCoy's own 1975 single, "The Hustle," emerge as one of disco's biggest early hits, but McCoy's infectious instrumental also inspired the first of disco-era's slickly choreographed dance crazes. Before long, disco devotees across the country were doing the New York Hustle, the Latin Hustle, and the California Hustle. Unfortunately, the funky rhythms of these early disco pioneers were about to give way to a highly polished, high-tech formula in which much of the music's rhythmic dynamism would be lost.

For most of the mainstream audience, the first record that clearly signaled the existence of a strange new entity in the pop music universe was Donna Summer's 1976 blockbuster, "Love to Love You Baby." While a number of recent dance-oriented singles such as "Rock Your Baby," "Up for the Downstroke," and "That's the Way I Like It" had titilated listeners with their coy, double-entendre lyrics, it was this song that brought the highly sexualized aspect of the disco experience to the radio airwaves. Set to a pulsating synthesized beat (concoted by Munich-based producer Georgio Morodor), by the end of the record, Summer's sensual repetition of the song's title gave way to the unmistakeable sound of her orgasmic moans.

While the record's enormous success may have been generated by its brazen sexuality, "Love to Love You" proved to be a trendsetter in a number of respects. For example, although the hit single—designed for radio airplay—was about four minutes long, Morodor also assembled a multisectioned, seventeen-minute extended-play version specifically for the disco market. To do so, he used a new record format, the so-called twelve-inch single. With one song per side, these album-sized discs quickly became the genre's standard.

Along with other European producers (such as Cerrone and Alex Costandinos), Morodor also can be credited (or blamed) for concocting the producer-dominated, synthesizer-driven sound—known as "Eurodisco"—that would ultimately dehumanize disco. Finally, by plugging Summer's emotive vocals (and sensual image) into the mix, "Love to Love You" also inaugurated the phenomenon of the Disco Queen, a role later incarnated in Gloria Gaynor ("I Will Survive") and Grace Jones, among others.

Unquestionably, however, the spark that truly ignited the era's disco fever was the 1977 film *Saturday Night Fever.* Not only did the movie transform John Travolta into a superstar, but his portrayal of a straight, white, working-class dance floor hunk made the disco itself safe for Middle America (and sent the sale of white polyester suits through the roof). Meanwhile, the movie's double album soundtrack—featuring the music of the Trammps ("Disco Inferno"), K.C. and the Sunshine Band ("Boogie Shoes"), and, of course, the Bee Gee's disco anthem, "Stayin' Alive"—became one of the biggest selling records of all time.

In addition to Travolta, it was the Bee Gees who would benefit most from the *Saturday Night Fever* phenomenon. Although they began their career as one of the more adept late-1960s Beatles clones, with the success of 1975's "Jive Talkin'" the Bee Gees transformed themselves into a hot dance-music act. Now they emerged as disco's blue-eyed superstars. By the end of the disco era, the brothers Gibb would become (with the exception of Elvis and the Beatles) the best-selling recording group in pop music history. Following the release of *Saturday Night Fever,* hundreds of radio stations switched to a disco format, an estimated 20,000 discos (including prefabricated, nationally franchised chains) opened in cities large and small; by the end of the decade, disco records accounted for 20 percent of *Billboard's* Top 100 hits of the year.

Virtually anything could be given the disco treatment—and almost everything was. There were disco versions of Motown classics (Gloria Gaynor's "Reach out, I'll Be There") and Beethoven classics (Walter Murphy's "A

FIGURE 5-9.   Museum of Modern Art Film Stills Collection.

Making Disco Safe for the Mainstream

This promotional photo for Saturday Night Fever brings together the movie's two main attractions: The Bee Gees—whose music provided the bulk of the dance-oriented soundtrack—and John Travolta—whose charismatic performance as a working-class disco stud helped make the underground music of urban minorities safe for mainstream America.

During its initial run, *Saturday Night Fever* grossed $130 million, but the soundtrack album did even better; along the way, it launched a slew of Top Ten singles for the Bee Gees ("How Deep Is Your Love," "Stayin' Alive," and "Night Fever"), as well as for Yvonne Elliman ("If I Can't Have You"), the Trammps ("Disco Inferno"), and Tavares ("More Than a Woman").

Fifth of Beethoven"); there was even a disco "Hava Nagila." Before long, mainstream rockers jumped on the disco bandwagon. Rod Stewart produced a couple of disco hits (including "Do Ya Think I'm Sexy"), and in 1978 the Rolling Stones issued an extended-play disco remix of "Miss You," employing all the state of the art technology available to the modern record producer.

In this overheated climate, it would have been strange if someone didn't fabricate a disco novelty act, and French producer Jacques Marali came up with one of pop music's all-time greats—the Village People. Costumed as cartoon versions of a half-dozen gay stereotypes, the Village People scored Top Ten hits with camp classics such as "Macho Man" and "Y.M.C.A" and between 1977 and 1979 they were the best-selling act in the country. For many observers, however, the entire disco phenomenon had become nothing less than the ultimate embodiment of "Me Decade" self-indulgence first defined in Tom Wolfe's famous essay.

By the end of the 1970s, the disco's gold chain and velvet rope values were incarnated in élite discos such as New York's Studio 54, with its celebrity-studded clientele and cocaine-fueled ambiance. And in 1978, chances are that the record most likely to be on the Studio 54's turntable was an upscale ode to the hedonistic disco lifestyle, the aptly titled "Good Times" by the aptly named ensemble, Chic.

Chic was the brainchild of veteran studio musician/producers Bernard Edwards (bass) and Nile Rodgers (guitar), each of whom had participated in such early disco hits as Carl Douglas's "Kung Fu Fighting" and Walter Murphy's "A Fifth of Beethoven." Now, they brought their considerable instrumental skills and studio genius to their own designer band. Crafting their music out of highly polished funk riffs and cunningly devised pop hooks, Chic offered a sophisticated brand of dance music and a visual image of cool elegance.

Take their 1978 smash single, "Le Freak." Set into an irresistible rhythmic groove, the song's repeated catch phrase—"Le freak, c'est chic"—not only combined contemporary black slang and French, but it included a punning plug for the band itself: "It's Chic!" No wonder that during the 1980s, Rodgers and Edwards became the producers of choice for a host of performers—including Duran Duran, David Bowie, Mick Jagger, and Madonna—who wanted to project a stylish dance-oriented pop image.

Ironically, Chic also provided an essential ingredient in what was emerging as one of the grittiest styles in the history of American popular music—rap. For the first recording to document the new genre (and the one that actually helped establish its name)—the Sugarhill Gang's 1979 breakthrough, "Rapper's Delight"—unabashedly appropriated the basic riff of Chic's recent hit, "Good Times," as the rhythmic backdrop for its rough-hewn rhymes. Two years later, Grandmaster Flash would put the same "Good Times" riff (along with a variation from Queen's "Another One Bites the Dust") to good use on his own old-school masterpiece, "The Adventures of Grandmaster Flash on the Wheels of Steel."

During its heyday, disco even had the power to do what many thought impossible—it propelled a punk band onto the top of the American pop charts. On the basis of its heavily synthesized, dance-oriented production (and Debbie Harry's sex-kitten persona), Blondie's 1979 "Heart of Glass" surprised fans from the band's CBGB days by becoming a disco-era crossover hit. By now, however, it also was becoming increasingly apparent that not everyone was thrilled by America's disco fever.

As the ultimate symbol of contemporary music's *pop* sensibility, disco—with its glossy veneer and its brazen commercial aspirations—was a natural target for the mainstream rock audience. Nor were the record divisions of the mammoth media conglomerates (that relied on rock revenues) thrilled to see a huge chunk of their annual album sales being lost to the "single"-minded profits of the small independent labels (such as Casablanca, T.K. Records, R.S.O, and Salsoul) that were home to most of the disco hitmakers. Similarly, the once powerful rock radio stations resented the market share they had lost to dance-oriented media outlets that had jumped onto the disco bandwagon. And as the antidisco movement gathered momentum, an ugly (but familiar) subtext began to surface.

Back in the 1950s, when rock 'n' roll first began to challenge the dominance of the American popular music tradition, a similar tension had arisen as entrenched and ponderous major labels (and major market AM stations) were left in the dust by tiny, fast-paced "indies' (and their radio equivalents) who had their finger on the pulse of the new teen market. Soon a coalition of anti–rock 'n' roll forces were rallying against the pernicious effect of the Big Beat. And, in keeping with the prevailing social attitudes of the 1950s, they often did little to disguise the underlying racism of their efforts.

Two decades later, the leaders of the "Disco Sucks" movement may have been more sophisticated in their campaign, but many observers recognized in their rhetoric a similar racial bias (along with a newfangled tinge of homophobia). So, on July 12, 1979, when Steve Dahl, a prominent Chicago disk jockey on one of the country's most powerful Album Oriented Rock stations, organized an antidisco rally at a White Sox baseball game—setting fire to a pile of records bearing the distinctive taint of black dance rhythms—a chilling feeling of deja vu was unavoidable. Then—more abruptly than most musical movements—the momentum of the disco era seemed to run out of steam just as the 1970s came to an end.

THE EIGHTIES AND THE TRIUMPH OF POP

Fueled by the disco craze of the late 1970s, music industry profits had skyrocketed; by 1978, sales of recorded music reached an all-time high of $4.13 billion. Then, just a year later, when the disco bubble burst through overexposure and the corporate-rock backlash (symbolized by the "Disco Sucks" movement), annual sales figures suddenly plummeted to $3.69 billion, a one-year decline of over 11 percent. All across the country, thousands of strobe-lit discos suddenly went dark, an assortment of independent disco record labels folded, and major media conglomerates were forced to jettison thousands of employees.

By contrast, those who may have gloated about what they perceived as the well-deserved demise of disco were having their own problems. For by the end of the 1970s, the promise of punk also was rapidly fading. While punk rock's self-proclaimed revolution (against bloated arena rock and pretentious art rock) had never generated much momentum in America anyway, even in Britain (where it had created a sizeable subculture), it didn't last much longer than disco. In a 1978 interview conducted not long after the Sex Pistols disbanded, Johnny Rotten (true to his anarchist ethos) proudly proclaimed: "The Pistols finished rock and roll. That was the last rock and roll band. It's all over now." The death of punk was just one more factor in the music industry's end-of-decade depression.

In music (as in life) where there is death, however, there can be rebirth. So it was that by the early 1980s, out of the compost heap of twelve-inch dance mixes and safety pins, synthesized beats and three-minute singles, makeup and minimalism, androgyny and angst, new musical hybrids began to flower. Although some of the varieties of 1980s *popular* music ("synth-pop," "electro-pop," "pop soul," and "pop metal") actually incorporated that word into their names, the *rock*-based style known as "new wave" bore the unmistakeable hallmarks of pop as well. As Johnny Rotten might have put it: Rock is dead . . . Long live Pop.

What's in a name? Well, looking back at this intriguing period of transition in her essay "McRock: Pop as a Commodity" (collected in *Facing the Music,* edited by Simon Frith), the British music critic Mary Harron proposes an answer to the fundamental question of "what pop and rock really mean." She prefaces her analysis by suggesting that, since labels like "pop" and "rock" can be used to describe an array of musical styles, "it's easier to assess them in terms of the values they represent."

According to Harron, "Pop stands for mutability and glitter. . . . Its value is measured by record sales and the charts. Pop is about dreams and escapism. . . . It believes in cliches and its philosophy is 'give the people what they want.' " In contrast, she suggests, "Rock is about the search for permanence. . . . It is about tradition (blues, country and folk roots). . . . Rock wants deep emotion and catharsis and truth. . . . Rock believes in originality and self-expression in defiance of crass commercialism." Finally, Harron offers two contemporary figures who she believes best represent each side in this musical dichotomy: "Rock in the 1980s is exemplified by Bruce Springsteen . . . pop by Madonna."

For other popular music pundits the demise of rock values during the decade was symbolized by the sudden tragic death of one of the music's most revered symbols. On December 8, 1980, just as he was about to enter his New York City residence, John Lennon was gunned down by an erstwhile fan obsessed with the notion that the former Beatle had "sold out." Talk about irony.

So it is that the story of the 1980s gets it title. But "the triumph of pop" is not only represented by Madonna and Michael Jackson (who would eventually anoint himself "The King of Pop"), but by bands such as the Police ("I don't think pop music is a pejorative term," Sting confessed), as well as by scores of so-called New Pop acts on both sides of Atlantic, including Duran Duran, Cyndi Lauper, Culture Club, and the Eurythmics. Even Prince (who could rock as hard as anyone) went both ways. In fact, by the end of the next decade, pop values were so

FIGURE 5-10.   While Elvis Costello may have shared punk rock's attitude of nihilistic rage, he never embraced its aesthetic of ineptitude. In fact, during the course of his twenty-five-year career, he has proven himself to be one of rock's most meticulous craftsmen. *Courtesy of the Sony Music Photo Archive.*

Elvis Costello: From Punk Rocker to Pop Poet

After releasing a stunning series of hard-edged albums *(My Aim Is True, This Year's Model, Trust)* featuring his own acerbic, tightly constructed compositions (and the potent precision of his band, the Attractions), Elvis Costello began exploring other avenues of expression.

During the 1990s, he turned his attention to that last bastion of traditional pop—the so-called Brill Building era of the early 1960s. After collaborating with veteran songwriter Burt Bacharach (one of the originators of the Brill Building style) on the song "God Give Me Strength" for the soundtrack of *Grace of My Heart* (a feature film about the glory days of 1960s pop), the pair went on to cowrite an entire album *(Painted from Memory)* that fused Costello's hard-edged lyrics with Bacharach's haunting melodies and lush orchestrations.

pervasive that a band that had been among the 1980s' foremost exponents of traditional rock values—U2—would record an album paying homage to the new orthodoxy; its title *Pop,* seemed to say it all.

At the beginning of the 1980s, the rapidly assembling forces of pop took advantage of a powerful weapon that would be the decisive factor in their ultimate victory: highly charged beams of electronic particles that could penetrate into virtually every living room, bedroom, or den across the entire globe. It was called "MusicTelevision" or more familiarly, MTV.

VIDEO KILLED THE RADIO STAR

When it premiered on August 1, 1981, as the first twenty-four-hour-a-day, all-music television network, MTV announced its arrival by airing a video that proclaimed the station's status as the medium of the moment, by a new pop band that perfectly represented the new medium's preferred musical style. For the Buggles' frothy, tongue-in-cheek production, "Video Killed the Radio Star" was pure pop. And like so many of the bands MTV relied on during those formative days, the Buggles heralded from the kingdom of New Pop: England.

While America's rock tradition was being maintained on mainstream AOR radio stations and in arenas across the country, concepts such as "catharsis," "truth," and "defiance of crass commercialism" (outlined by Mary Harron) proved antithetical to the new mass medium. According to Andrew Goodman, author of a scholarly study of music television and popular culture (*Dancing in the Distraction Factory*), what the New Pop offered MTV was "music whose stress on style and artifice perfectly suited marketing through video, and whose production practices perfectly suited the promotional techniques of the music video." Or as he writes elsewhere in his book, "The New Pop openly acknowledged pop performance as a visual medium with a sound track." In his exploration of this video revolution, Goodman also notes that the performers who dominated MTV's first era amounted to a virtual "Second British Invasion."

In fact, as we have seen, during the 1970s England had already been home to a couple of hyphenated-rock genres (like glam-rock and art-rock), whose emphasis on artifice and visual imagery was at least as important as its musical concerns. Over the previous decade, for example, David Bowie had made a career of chameleon-like transformations of his persona often involving elaborate costumes, makeup, and extravagant stage sets. In 1975, the glam-rock band Queen had already created a groundbreaking six-minute video to accompany their hit recording of "Bohemian Rhapsody" that is often cited as "the first music video."

By the early 1980s, advances in technology made it easier than ever for ambitious, attractive, English art-school alumnae to become pop stars. Synthesizers, drum machines, sequencers, and sampling devices could be programmed relatively easily in order to create what amounted to a "virtual band." As Andrew Goodman explains, "It was becoming commonplace for producers to store all the appropriate sounds in a computer, which could then be programmed to an astonishing degree of sophistication—thus obviating the need for the musicians to play at all. Often they did not even have to be present." But they did have to be *seen.*

The role call of technologically enhanced British New Pop acts (classified variously as "Electro-Pop," "New Romantics," "Synth-Pop," and "Haircut Bands") that were introduced to the American audience via their music videos include: Duran Duran, the Human League, Ultravox, Gary Numan, ABC, the Thompson Twins, Thomas Dolby, Frankie Goes to Hollywood, Wham!, Soft Cell, and Depeche Mode. Each band assembled its own peculiar brand of New Pop, either by adding a dose of Motown-style soul (Culture Club, the Eurythmics) or a glossy veneer of synthesizer-generated effects (Human League, Soft Cell) to their prefabricated disco beat and airy pop background vocals.

It was a time when an act's fashion consultant and hair stylist were as important as its sound. Some "groups" (they could no longer very well be called "bands") actually prided themselves on their instrumental ineptitude. For example, Neil Tennant, lead singer of the Pet Shop Boys, later bragged to a *Rolling Stone* interviewer about his group's lack of musical prowess: "It's kinda macho nowadays to prove that you can cut it live. I quite like proving we can't cut it live." We're a pop group," he asserted, "not a rock group." So, as Andrew Goodman has written, "It was thus through video clips that the New Pop acts established themselves as 'performers,' often miming to music they did not actually play."

FIGURE 5-11.   The Police came together in the wake of the British punk movement of the 1970s; before long, they had become one of the emblematic bands of the 1980s. Courtesy of A & M Records.

The Police: From Punk Rockers to Pop Stars

The Police polished punk's minimalist approach with a combination of melodic hooks and instrumental virtuosity, while coloring its monochromatic rhythms with exotic tinges of jazz and reggae. In fact, when the band's early singles—such as "Don't Stand So Close to Me" and "Roxanne"—began to make their way up the charts, critics dubbed their music "white reggae" (a description the band itself seemed to embrace when they entitled their second LP *Regatta du Blanc,* a French translation of the phrase).

In keeping with their role as pioneers of 1980s pop, the band's image was as carefully crafted as their music. And while multiplantinum albums such as *Ghost in the Machine* (1981) and *Synchronicity* (1983) catapulted the Police into stadiums around the world (their sell-out concert at New York City's Shea Stadium was the first since the Beatles), the band also made particularly effective use of the new medium of the music video. By the middle of the decade, however, tensions within the group resulted in the Police going permanently off duty.

And MTV was there, twenty-four hours a day, seven days a week, 365 (and 1/4) days a year to provide them with a forum to do just that. It was the ultimate symbiotic relationship: the New Pop bands needed a *visual* outlet for their music and MTV needed videos to satisfy its insatiable appetite. It didn't take long before both the new medium and the new music began to make their mark.

At a time when most of America's radio stations and rock arenas were still featuring the same array of mainstream rock bands (such as Foreigner, the J. Geils Band, REO Speedwagon, and Journey), in those particular areas of the country where MTV was offering up its New Pop menu chartwatchers began to notice a startling and dramatic shift in record sale statistics. By 1982, British electro-pop groups such as Duran Duran and Human League—whose videos had been placed on the station's "heavy rotation" schedule of three to four plays per day—soon found themselves with Top Ten hits.

Although, initially, some record labels had been reluctant to just hand over their expensively produced videos free of charge, soon all the major record companies recognized the enormous promotional clout of MTV and did just that. And as the station rapidly began to penetrate more and more geographical markets, MTV became the dominant force in a resurgent multibillion-dollar music industry. Video may not have killed the radio star but seemingly overnight it did make (M)TV stars out of a host of photogenic New Pop acts. Before long, members of the rock élite joined their upstart heirs in demanding, "I want my MTV." Increasingly, as the buzz about the latest hit song spread, the familiar question "Did you hear that new record" was being fundamentally transformed into "Did you see that new video." Not everyone was thrilled, however, about what they saw.

While some media pundits and cultural critics made esoteric pronouncements about the inevitable power of a visual context to overwhelm its musical content (the "imperialism of the image," as one writer expressed it), others worried that the new medium's fast-paced format and rapid-fire cutting techniques would create an entire generation afflicted with mass attention deficit disorder. Meanwhile, guardians of traditional morality once again found ample evidence in rock 'n' roll's latest manifestation of those same old bugaboos: sex and violence.

This time around, however, many of these familiar accusations were being echoed by feminists, who noted that, for the most part, the role of women on MTV was limited to scantily clad bimbos frolicking in the background of some male teenage fantasy. Still other social critics saw in the narcissistic materialism of the New Pop videos a clear reflection of the greed-is-good philosophy of President Ronald Reagan's era. Finally, there was another even more serious charge leveled against MTV during its formative years: racism.

MICHAEL JACKSON: I WANT MY MTV

By 1983, MTV had not only begun to establish its pivotal place in the popular culture, but it had already proven its hitmaking power by propelling the New Pop acts it promoted onto the top of the charts. And now that Los Angeles and New York City, the country's most densely populated and media-savvy metropolises, were finally wired for cable, not only did MTV's power increase exponentially but so did the scrutiny to which it was subjected. So when an end-of-year survey conducted by *Rolling Stone* revealed that "Of the 750 videos shown by MTV during the channel's first eighteen months, fewer than two dozen featured black artists . . ." there was considerable consternation in some quarters.

Speaking in the station's defense, MTV founder and executive vice president Robert Pittman resorted to the standard disclaimer. Like radio station programmers who once faced similar charges, Pittman explained that MTV's exclusionary policy was not based on racial grounds, but was simply an innocent consequence of its chosen format. That black performers were not represented on its airwaves was not a consequence of their skin color, but rather, Pittman explained, of the fact that what they played simply "was not rock and roll." While such de facto segregation may have been tolerable in the medium of radio (where the number of available stations assured that black music had at least some outlets), since MTV was effectively the only *video* game in town, such restrictions amounted to virtual censorship.

Meanwhile, Michael Jackson, former kiddie-soul star and frontman for the 1970s Motown brother act the Jackson 5, was all grown up and he had begun making his own astonishing solo records. Not only was Jackson's 1979 release *Off the Wall* one of the year's biggest albums (selling upward of nine million copies), but, as Nelson George points out in his book, *The Death of Rhythm and Blues,* "[it] was a masterpiece, and it was a natural

FIGURE 5-12.   In the early 1990s, when Michael Jackson crowned himself "King of Pop," he was simply engaging in a desperate attempt to revive a flagging career (beset by scandal and overshadowed by the dominance of rap). In fact, his true coronation as a member of pop music royalty had occurred almost a decade earlier. Archive photo.

Michael Jackson: King of Pop

It was May 16, 1983, when viewers tuning in to watch the broadcast of "Motown 25," a televised celebration of the label's silver anniversary, were treated to one of the most spectacular performances in the medium's history. Overnight, Michael Jackson's explosive live version of "Billie Jean"—highlighted by his mesmerizing "moonwalk"—propelled the performer to the pinnacle of pop superstardom. MTV immediately reconsidered its (race-based) reluctance to air Jackson's brilliantly produced, big-budget videos, and based in large part their inclusion in the station's heavy rotation, Jackson's album, *Thriller,* went on to sell over forty million copies—a record industry record.

crossover." In fact, as George goes on to explain, "top-forty radio, CBS [parent company of Jackson's new label] and Michael Jackson himself began describing the singer as a 'universal' artist, a 'pop' performer. . . ." According to Nelson George, "Jackson's sales were so remarkable that he'd never have to cross over again." Unfortunately, however, it seemed no one had informed MTV of this fact.

Late in 1982, Columbia Records released Jackson's much-anticipated new album, *Thriller,* and despite the fact that its sales quickly exceeded everyone's most optimistic expectations, MTV adamantly declined to air any of the ambitious and hugely expensive videos that had been made to promote the record. At this point, Columbia—perhaps the era's dominant label—is said to have made MTV an offer it couldn't refuse: either air Michael Jackson's videos or the company would impose a total embargo of all its other artists. Motivated by the potential loss of a significant percentage of its "product" and unable to resist the Jackson juggernaut (especially after Michael's galvanizing star turn at the nationally broadcast Motown's twenty-fifth anniversary TV special), MTV quietly acquiesced.

In retrospect, it seems inevitable that the extraordinary dimensions of Jackson's appeal would have made it impossible for MTV to hold out against the tide of "Michaelmania," yet the unprecedented success of *Thriller* is also hard to imagine without the unrelenting visual exposure MTV provided. Of course, there was the music itself. Often overlooked amid all the racial politics and video veneration was the fact that Jackson (and his producer, Quincy Jones) had crafted an irresistible contemporary pop/R & B classic. Exploiting every technological device and sonic nuance the state-of-the-art studio had to offer, the album was by turns airily melodic, pungently funky, infectiously danceable . . . and very smart.

For while *Thriller* was unquestionably a masterwork of musical ingenuity, as a battleplan for cross-over conquest it was pure genius. In a strategic move to soften up the opposition, Jackson began by forging an alliance with a certified (white) pop legend, Paul McCartney. After launching their innocuous duet ("The Girl Is Mine") as the album's first single, Jackson proceeded to advance his cause with a now-legendary televised performance of "Billie Jean" (during which he unveiled his patented "moonwalk"). Then Jackson brought in the heavy artillery; his third single ("Beat It") not only provided MTV with a song set to a pounding rock beat, but he reinforced its appeal by including an incendiary guitar solo by the emerging heavy-metal superstar, Eddie Van Halen.

Once MTV began airing Jackson's videos, *Thriller* began generating sales of one million copies every four days! Eventually, seven of the record's ten songs made it into the pop Top Ten, and its worldwide total of over forty million copies made it what it still remains: the biggest selling album in history.

POP'S PRINCE

Although Michael Jackson is often (and justifiably) credited with "breaking the MTV color line," a year before Jackson's video debut, another African-American performer had already crossed over into the pop mainstream by crafting his own cunning hybrid of rock and pop soul—and by creating a video-enhanced image that was as naughty as Michael's was nice.

For while Michael Jackson was carefully shaping an image of childlike innocence (after all, his California playland was named "Neverland"), tinged with apolitical social activism (he did spearhead the "We Are the World" hunger-relief effort), Prince was staking out a more perverse persona. From such subtly suggestive titles as "Soft and Wet" (from his 1978 debut, *For You*), he quickly advanced (some would say "degenerated") to more blatant expressions of sexuality that included songs about incest ("Sister"), oral sex ("Head"), and mènages a trois ("When You Were Mine"), all from the aptly named third album, *Dirty Mind*.

In fact, it was the references to masturbation in his song "Darling Nikki" (from his *Purple Rain* soundtrack) that supposedly provided the motivation for Tipper Gore to form the Parents' Music Resource Center. Although the 1985 Senate hearings initiated by the PMRC attracted anti-censorship testimony from diverse freedom of speech advocates such as Frank Zappa, John Denver, and Twisted Sister frontman Dee Snider, the influential organization was eventually successful in pushing through a labeling agreement warning potential record buyers of explicit lyrics.

While Prince was never a child star like his celebrated contemporary (he and Michael were born two months apart), he was something of a wunderkind himself. In 1976, at the precocious age of eighteen, he had signed a record contract with Warner Brothers that gave him virtually unprecedented "creative control" of his music. And from his very first album he left little doubt that it was *his* music—since Prince wrote the songs, sang the vocals, played most of the instruments, and produced the recording. And in 1982, when his video for "Little Red Corvette' (from his LP *1999*) beat Jackson's "Beat It" onto MTV, Prince become the station's first African-American video hero.

Just as Chuck Berry had done thirty years before when he crossed over with his own automotive ode, "Maybellene," Prince's "Little Red Corvette" video breakthrough, combining black and white musical sources into a brilliant pop synthesis, arrived. And with every new album (he released at least one every other year), Prince revealed his debt to other black crossover pioneers who had preceded him: a Stevie Wonderesque vocal here, a Hendrix-style guitar riff there, along with some funky Sly and the Family Stone grooves, all highlighted with a dash of Little Richard's mascara and a live act that owed more than a little to George Clinton's notorious P-Funk roadshow.

Yet, somehow, Prince was able to filter these and other influences through his own sensibility to create something truly original. In fact, Prince's music seemed to obliterate the very categories (rock, soul, pop, R & B) that his predecessors had struggled to cross over. And, unlike so many of his musical mentors, Prince was both a shrewd businessman and hugely ambitious. For example, Prince's next foray was into the world of Hollywood, and once again Prince asserted total creative control in yet another medium.

When the credits of his film *Purple Rain* scrolled across theater screens in 1984, Prince's name appeared as producer, author of the film's (semi-autobiographical) screenplay, composer of its (Academy Award–winning) score, as well as its star. Not only did *Purple Rain* become one of the biggest-grossing films of the year, but the soundtrack album dominated the pop charts for almost six months, generating five Top Ten singles, including two number one hits ("When Doves Cry" and the title song). Eventually, the album would sell over seventeen million copies, and—within a few months of its release—an impressive 500,000 copies of the *Purple Rain* videotape had also found their way into home VCRs.

Although Prince may have flouted the prevailing moral conservatism of the Reagan era, he was certainly in tune with its work ethic and economic agenda. Propelled by the enormous success of *Purple Rain,* Prince quickly established himself as a one-man conglomerate. He built an elaborate multimillion-dollar multimedia headquarters in Minneapolis (dubbed Paisly Park) and began unleashing an avalanche of albums. By the end of the decade, these included *Around the World in a Day* (1985), *Parade* (the 1986 soundtrack for his disappointing second screen venture, *Under the Cherry Moon*), the double LP *Sign O' The Times* (1987), and *Lovesexy* (1988).

Prince also released an elaborate soundtrack album from the original *Batman* movie in 1989, and somehow found time to create material and serve as producer for a stable of his own proteges (including Sheila E., Apolonia, and Sheena Easton). There was even enough left over to fuel other artists' rise to the top of the charts; after all, it was a Prince song—"Nothing Compares 2 U"—that was the vehicle for Sinead O'Connor's riveting breakthrough.

As Prince moved into the new decade, he not only maintained the prolific pace of his recording schedule but he continued to push the edge of the sexual envelope with each new release. But while some fans and critics continued to remain fiercely loyal to a performer they viewed as one of the most original and dynamic in the music's history, many others began to drift away. By the early 1990s, not only had the burgeoning gangsta rap movement come to dominate the black music scene, but Prince's ungovernable creative drive had all but overwhelmed all but his most rabid supporters. Although Warner Brothers re-signed him to an enormously lucrative contract in 1992, Prince (as always obssessed with his artistic freedom) began to chaf at their attempts to restrain and shape his output.

Then, in an effort to create a persona separate from his corporate identity (and to highlight his pansexual self-image), Prince renounced his name and replaced it with a pictographic symbol based on a synthesis of the traditional symbols for male and female. As his cold war with Warners intensified, "The Artist Formerly Known as Prince" (or TAFKAP for short) began appearing in public with the word "slave" scrawled across his cheek. As he explained to *Rolling Stone* in 1996, "If I can't do what I want to, what am I? When you stop a man from dreaming, he becomes a slave." Later that year, he finally extricated himself from the company he had come to perceive as a little more than a slavemaster and he formed his own record label (NPG). His first order of business: the release of a sprawling three-CD set of new material aptly titled *Emancipation.*

FIGURE 5-13. Back in 1984—when he made his cinematic debut with *Purple Rain*—The Artist Formerly Known As Prince was still known as Prince. Museum of Modern Art Film Stills Dept.

The Prince of Retronuevo Pop

Prince may have succeeded in becoming one of the biggest pop stars of his time by being his own man, but his music paid homage to a roster of the great creators from the recent past, including Little Richard, James Brown, Jimi Hendrix, Sly Stone, and George Clinton, to name just a few.

The Artist shared this "retronuevo" tendency (as music critic Nelson George had dubbed it) with the era's other African-American pop music hero, Michael Jackson. As George explains in his book, *The Death of Rhythm and Blues,* "This dynamic duo proved to be the decade's finest music historians, consistently using techniques that echoed the past as the base for their superstardom."

MADONNA: FROM MATERIAL GIRL TO MEDIA MOGUL

Prince was not the only one-name superstar whose instinct for self-promotion and sexual controversy, multimedia image mongering, racial gamesmanship, and unquenchable ambition resulted in a spot at the top of the 1980s pop pyramid. In fact, along with Michael Jackson himself, the one performer who perhaps best symbolized both the decade's pop values and video-driven culture was the material girl herself—Madonna.

Although she seemed to become an instant icon of the Video Era, Madonna began her career as the Last of the Disco Divas. By the time she arrived in New York (just another girl from the Midwest with dreams of stardom), the music industry was already confronting the first troubling symptoms of post–Saturday Night Fever depression. Despite the premature rumors of its demise, however, disco wasn't dead; the synthesized beat of dance music was, in fact, alive and well in the electro-pop of the British haircut bands that MTV beamed into millions of suburban homes, as well as in the so-called new wave pop-rock of Blondie. Disco itself receded back into the hip underground New York dance clubs where the craze had begun in the first place. And it was here—amid the black, Latino, and gay urban subcultures—that Madonna found her initial audience.

In 1983, after signing with Warner Brothers (yet another link with Prince), Madonna's self-titled debut album produced a couple of hook-filled dance hits ("Holiday," "Borderline," "Lucky Star") that propelled her out of the underground into the pop mainstream—and onto MTV. Unlike Prince (and Michael Jackson), each of whom had generated a *musical* identity independent of his video image, it was almost entirely through the visual magic of MusicTeleVision (and the movies) that Madonna would establish her career and craft a procession of ever-shifting personas. Among the first of these were the Lolitaesque street slut in thrift-shop chic of her early MTV hits, and the Marilyn Monroe–inspired blonde bombshell of what proved to be her signature song.

Despite Madonna's later attempts to distance herself from its mercenary values, the message of the "Material Girl" video fit neatly into the 1980s materialistic mindset. And while Madonna's overt sexuality stirred the fantasies of millions of teenage boys, her image also motivated millions of their prepubescent sisters (henceforth known as "Madonna wannabes") to adopt the singer's see-through blouses, black lace bras, and "Boy Toy" belt buckle.

Meanwhile, feminists, cultural studies professors, and media pundits had a field day deconstructing Madonna's social significance, just at a time when issues of gender politics and charges of music video sexism were being hotly debated in the editorial pages of newspapers across the country. And naturally, the more the era's PMRC watchdogs clucked their tongues, the more records Madonna sold.

By 1987, Madonna had amassed two number one albums (*Like a Virgin* and *True Blue*) and produced a dozen Top Ten singles. Then, one year after the film *Purple Rain* had projected Prince onto movie screens (and into the pop culture pantheon), Madonna's own cinematic debut, in the hip, low-budget independent film *Desperately Seeking Susan,* helped establish her as a multimedia icon. Although most of her subsequent films fizzled at the box office, Madonna's paparazzi-plagued marriage to the actor Sean Penn and her increasingly provocative videos blending religious symbolism and sexuality ("Like a Prayer") or celebrating her unique brand of highly stylized perversion ("Justify My Love"), generated sufficient notoriety to maintain her momentum.

But while she made some missteps along the way, Madonna survived the 1980s, and as she made her way into the new decade, she added single mom (of a daughter, Lourdes Maria), author/model (of the soft-core coffee table book *Sex*), and media mogul (of her own record label, Maverick) to her list of credits. By the mid-1990s, not only had Madonna become perhaps the wealthiest and most powerful female pop star in history, but she even restored some of the former luster of her acting career with her popular and critically acclaimed performance in the 1996 film *Evita.*

By this point, even the rock press, which had reviled her early dance-oriented music (echoing some of the same coded language they had used at the height of the "Disco Sucks" campaign), grudgingly began to acknowledge Madonna's legitimacy, making special note of her songwriting talents. And in 1998, she finally achieved her quest for pop legitimacy when her CD, *Ray of Light,* won the Grammy for Pop Album of the Year.

FIGURE 5-14.   As the millennium drew to a close, Madonna released *Ray of Light,* a CD celebrating the peace and enlightenment that the former Material Girl had obtained through her embrace of Eastern spirituality. Photo by Mario Testino. Courtesy of Warner Bros. Records, Inc.

Madonna Gets Respect

Madonna's mutation from materialism (and celebrity mongering) to mysticism (and humility) was rewarded with new respect from pop music critics—and, in 1998, with the Grammy Award for the Pop Album of the Year. By setting her philosophical musings to the cutting-edge synthesized soundscapes provided by her producer (the English electronica pioneer, Willian Orbit), however, she also kept faith with her disco roots—and picked up the Grammy for the year's Best Dance Record as well.

G I R L S   J U S T   W A N T   T O   H A V E   F U N

Madonna may have benefited most from MTV's unwavering focus on pop music's visual component but, to the surprise of many, the new medium turned out to be a boon to a number of women performers. Yet while physical beauty and sexual allure have often been the route to a show biz career, contemporary women entertainers had to find a way to exploit the old stereotypes without being exploited by them.

From the very beginning of her career, in fact, Madonna was taken to task for perpetuating obsolete female images. From the very beginning, however, she also insisted that she knew just what she was doing. "I may be dressing like the typical bimbo," she told Ted Koppel on a 1990 *Nightline* appearance, "but I'm in charge. . . . And isn't that what feminism is all about? Aren't I in charge of my life, doing the things I want to do, making my own decisions?" Although most female commentators initially denounced the material girl's politically incorrect incarnations, others (including feminist pundit Camille Paglia) championed Madonna as a modern pop-culture heroine.

But not all the decade's debates about gender roles focused on Madonna. Throughout the 1980s, other female performers also confronted these issues and constructed their own personas over the MTV airwaves. Among the first of these was Annie Lennox, one half (along with synthesizer maestro/producer Dave Stewart) of the 1980s British techno-pop duo the Eurythmics. Beginning with their 1983 American breakthrough—the number one single "Sweet Dreams (Are Made of This)"—Lennox used her videos to subvert traditional sexual stereotypes. "I didn't want to be seen as a 'girlie singer' wearing pretty dresses," she wrote in her autobiography. "I want to sidestep them, and to confound people a little bit with something fresher and less cliched."

Initially, Lennox challenged such cliches by adopting an androgynous image, appearing in the "Sweet Dreams" surrealistic concept video with an orange buzz-cut, dressed in a beautifully tailored men's suit. Not only did the Eurythmics go on to create a string of hit singles (as well as some of the most imaginative videos in MTV's early history), but Lennox branched out on her own with a couple of high-profile collaborations, including a 1985 duet with Aretha Franklin (aptly titled, "Sisters Are Doin' It for Themselves") in which she voiced a clear feminist message to go along with her liberated image.

Despite the fact that the Eurythmics had always been an equal partnership—Lennox shared the bulk of the songwriting responsibilities and provided a soulful voice (along with her high-cheeked beauty)—there were always those who gave Stewart the bulk of the credit for the group's creative direction. After the duo permanently parted ways at the end of the decade, however, Lennox launched a solo career that left little doubt about her own creative powers. Her 1992 début, *Diva,* not only confirmed her vocal attributes (one reviewer called her "the best white soul singer alive"), but the liner notes also revealed that she had written eight of the platinum album's compositions (and had cowritten two others).

Another early 1980s performer who used her videos to create a unique female persona was Cyndi Lauper, whose breakthrough single—"Girls Just Want to Have Fun"—was an anthem to "girl power" that preceded the Spice Girls' artifical seasonings by over a decade. The song was the first of five Top Forty singles to emerge from her 1982 quadruple-platinum album debut *She's So Unusual* (a title designed to highlight the singer's New Yawk-flavored little-girl voice and quirky costumes). Although, like Lennox, Lauper also cowrote most of her own songs, she was dismissed by many as just another ditzy bonde; it was an image she found difficult to break out of, and by the middle of the decade her career had gone into a steep decline.

GIRLS WITH GUITARS AND POP DIVAS

One of the major barriers women performers faced throughout rock 'n' roll history was an enduring bias against women musicians. Although there had been a number of female rock bands that had gotten some attention during the 1970s, most were either hopelessly mired in the underground (such as British punk rockers the Slits and Siouxsie and the Banshees) or they were written off as simply a novelty act (such as Joan Jett's teenage hard-rock outfit, the Runaways).

This also began to change considerably during the 1980s. There were successful mixed-gender bands such as Talking Heads (with bassist Tina Wymouth) and Sonic Youth (with bassist/songwriter, Kim Gordon), female-dominated bands such as the Pretenders (fronted by rock-icon Chryssie Hynde) and Heart (founded by Ann and Nancy Wilson), as well as all-female bands such as the Go-Gos (Belinda Carlisle's presolo band) and the Bangles (who went to number one with the single "Walk Like an Egyptian"). During the 1980s, however, women rockers gradually began breaking down these barriers, thereby paving the way for a new generation of guitar-based female rock bands that took place a decade later.

But while girls-with-guitars did begin to infiltrate the pop charts and MTV airwaves, the most successful women performers of the 1980s were those who put a contemporary spin on the traditional role of the pop music "diva." Although originally this word may have been used to describe the stereotypical prima donna of the oper- atic stage, American popular music has had its own lineage of larger than life pop divas, as well—from Bessie Smith to Barbra Streisand and from Patsy Cline to Diana Ross (not to mention the flurry of "Disco Divas" such as Gloria Gaynor and Donna Summer). In 1985, Whitney Houston became the newest member of this select sorority when a self-titled debut album heralded the beginning of her spectacular career.

Whitney Houston not only had all the physical and vocal attributes required for pop superstardom, but she had the right genealogical background as well; her mother, Cissy Houston, was the leader of one the preeminent female R & B/soul backup groups of the 1960s and 1970s (the Sweet Inspirations), and her cousin Dionne War- wick had become an international star on the basis of her sophisticated and sensual singing style. Whitney had been honing her own singing technique from the time she was a child singing in her church choir, and by the time she was fifteen, she was already recording backup vocals for performers such as Lou Rawls. While she did re- tain some of her early gospel influences in her mature pop style (and used them to good effect in the film *The Preacher's Wife*), for the most part Houston placed her extraordinary voice in the service of safe, middle-of-the- road material enhanced by the glossiest of production values. The result: a series of multiplatinum albums, num- ber one singles, Grammy awards, and a big-time movie career.

The next female pop megastar of the 1980s had some fairly significant family connections of her own. Janet Jackson had followed her famous siblings into the business, and with the release of her third album, *Control* in 1986, she finally stepped out from behind their media shadow (especially the daunting one cast by brother Michael). Not only did the title of her breakthrough album symbolize Janet's newfound independence, but by cowriting most of the record's (semi-autobiographical) songs and taking a hand in the arrangements and produc- tion (along with contemporary black dance music's hottest producers Jimmy "Jam" Harris and Teddy Lewis), she could claim considerable credit for its phenomenal success. *Control* generated five hit singles on its way to becom- ing the number one album in the country, while its sale of eight million copies also helped shatter the music in- dustry's stereotypes about the commercial potential of women performers.

Janet Jackson's 1989 follow-up album, *Rhythm Nation 1814*, proved that she wasn't a one-hit wonder; the album, which looked beyond her own life to address social issues such as racism and homelessness, sold some seven million copies and generated seven hit singles (largely on the basis of her state-of-the-art, elaborately chore- ographed videos). In 1991, Jackson signed a record-breaking $32 million contract with Virgin records (at the time the most lucrative in pop music history). Future sales of her 1990s' releases such as *Janet* and *The Velvet Rope*, however, would eventually make the deal seem like a bargain.

While Janet Jackson's musical evolution can be seen as a metaphor for the stuggle of young women to assert their personal autonomy (and sexuality), the career of another pop diva who began her mainstream career during the 1980s symbolized the quest for another form of self-assertion. More than any other contemporary singer, it was Gloria Estafan who succeeded in breaking out of the cultural ghetto to which Spanish-language performers had always been relegated. Born Gloria Fajardo in Havana, Cuba, she had emigrated to Miami in 1959 at the age of two, and by the time she was a teenager, Gloria was fronting the city's premier Latin dance band, the Miami Sound Machine, and had married its leader, Emilio Estefan.

After producing a string of Spanish-language dance hits on regional independent labels, Gloria Estafan and the Miami Sound Machine were signed by Columbia Records' Hispanic division, Discos CBS, and more hit al- bums—primarily for the Latin American market—followed. Then in 1984, the band issued its first English- language album, *Eyes of Innocence,* and Estafan had her first taste of crossover success. Over the next couple of years, albums such as *Let It Loose* and *Cuts Both Ways* made it into the upper reaches of the pop charts; during the early 1990s, Gloria Estefan began to forge a solo career, writing her own material, moving at will between English and Spanish, and generating hits no matter what the language.

FIGURE 5-15.   When Gloria Estefan broke into the pop charts with a couple of mid-1980s hits (including "Dr. Beat" and "Conga!"), the Cuban-born performer helped break Latin music out of the cultural barrio to which it seemed permanently consigned. Over the course of the following decade, Estefan took her place as one of pop music's foremost divas, while continuing to move effortlessly between English-language albums (such as 1988's *Let It Loose*) and Spanish releases (such as 1993's *Mi Tierra*). Archive photo.

The Latin Explosion

Latin performers from Xavier Cugat and Carmen Miranda to Richie Valens and Carlos Santana have periodically infused Spanish tinges from across the hemisphere onto the American pop charts. Yet, despite their contributions (along with those by Prez Prado, Tito Puente, Chano Pozo, Freddy Fender, Los Lobos, and Selena), the kind of crossover success that Gloria Estefan has achieved is rare and, for the most part, it has always been accompanied by compromise.

While the exhilarating rhythmic complexity of their music has typically been simplified to appeal to American taste, the primary sacrifice that aspiring Latino pop stars have had to make in order to cross over is a linguistic one. Although a new wave of Spanish-speaking performers claimed the pop charts during the late 1990s, the (invisible) sign on the entrance to the Top Ten still read, "English Only." For example, after five years of solo success in Europe and Latin America, it was only when Ricky Martin released his first English-language (semi-Spanish-titled) single, "Livin' La Vida Loca," that he made it in America.

In the wake of the so-called Latin Explosion that followed Ricky Martin's breakthrough (as well as less spectacular crossovers by Jon Secada, Jennifer Lopez, and Marc Anthony), the old debate resurfaced: Would Latin music ever win acceptance on its own terms? Those who embraced the affirmative side of the question supported their optimistic point of view by citing both recent trends in pop music and certain demographic realities. For example, Oscar Llord, president of Sony Discos (Columbia Records' Latin division) told the *New York Times*, "Kids go for beats first, then they think about language." Meanwhile, the U.S. Census Bureau was predicting that by the year 2005, America's Latino population would surpass African-Americans as the nation's largest minority group.

While Gloria Estefan was breaking down barriers by infusing contemporary pop music with some of the infectious rhythms of her native Cuba, on the Texas-Mexican borders another young woman seemed poised for an even bigger crossover. Ironically, although she won the Tejano Music Award for best female vocalist, the fifteen-year-old Selena Quintanilla, from Lake Jackson, Texas, had to learn the Spanish lyrics to her songs phonetically. Soon, however, not only was Selena winning over Spanish-speaking audiences on both sides of the border by putting a contemporary spin on traditional Tejano's blend of Mexican folk styles and accordian-based German polkas (a synthesis that had first evolved during the 1930s and 1940s), but she was doing it with a provocative stage presence that had earned her the nickname the "Tex-Mex Madonna."

Having signed with a major U.S. label and won a Grammy Award for her 1993 release, *Selena Live,* the now twenty-three-year-old performer began the process of recording her first English-language album. The consensus within the music industry was that Selena was about to cross over as a mainstream pop megastar and perhaps give Madonna herself a run for her money. Tragically, before such predictions could become a reality, Selena was shot to death by the president of her own fan club in what seemed to be a lethal combination of jealousy and obsession.

Selena's unfinished album, *Dreaming of You,* which was released posthumously in 1995, immediately became the second-fastest selling record ever by a female artist (just behind *Janet,* the 1993 album by you-know-who). A major Hollywood film biography, *Selena* (starring the actress Jennifer Lopez), was also issued, and for many within the Mexican-American community the slain performer has become a kind of secular saint.

At the beginning of the next decade, another of the new generation's female pop divas took the stage when Mariah Carey released her debut album, *Vision of Love.* Like Whitney Houston, Carey not only possessed a precocious technical virtuosity and a five-octave vocal range, but she also infused her singing with a pronounced gospel inflection. Although she was marketed as a white pop performer, critics immediately recognized the influence of African-American spiritual music on Mariah Carey's style. As one *New York Times* reviewer expressed it, "Carey sounds as if she grew up singing in a Harlem church."

Nor was the singer (who was the product of an interracial marriage) reticent about acknowledging her debt to this tradition. In many of her early interviews, Mariah Carey described how—after tracing back the sources of her favorite soul singers to the church—she began exploring the world of gospel for herself. As she explained to the *Times,* "When I got older, I found out that Al Green and Aretha Franklin had recorded gospel records, and I went out and bought them. From there I discovered the Clark Sisters, Shirley Caesar, Mahalia Jackson, Vanessa Bell Armstrong and whoever. . . ."

Carey's début set a pattern for her later albums by crossing over into the top of both the pop and R & B charts on its way to sales of over six million copies. Although she would continue to infuse her pop ballads with a gospel flavor (and often used gospel choirs to enhance her live performances), in subsequent releases, Carey began to gravitate toward more dance-oriented styles, frequently collaborating with R & B and hip-hop performers. And despite all the upheavals that took place in the pop music industry during the 1990s (from gangsta rap to grunge), divas like Mariah Carey remained a staple of the pop scene.

In fact, the 1990s proved to be a particularly good decade for divas; there were classic divas like Celine Dion (whose impassioned ballads and histrionic delivery would not have been out of place on a 1950s hit parade), but there also were alternative divas like Tori Amos (who pushed the Joni Mitchell/Carole King/Laura Nyro singer-songwriter tradition to new heights with her provocative lyrics and charismatic persona). By the end of the decade there was a diva for every taste: there were country divas (teen sensation Leann Rimes), hip-hop divas (Mary J. Blige), New Age divas (Erykah Badu), Icelandic divas (Bjørk), and even a couple of R & B diva-ettes (Monica and Brandy).

EIGHTIES ROOTS ROCK MEN AND FOLK REVIVAL WOMEN

By the mid-1980s, the once preeminent mainstream rock establishment had become relatively resigned to the reality of the MTV-dominated pop landscape. Besides, despite all the divas and dance-oriented exoticism, they did have their own guitar-strumming, working-class hero: They called him "the Boss."

A decade had now passed since Bruce Springsteen was singled out as "rock 'n' roll's future," but it wasn't until the release of his 1984 masterpiece, *Born in the U.S.A.,* that the rock critics' predictions were validated by the record-buying public. The album steadily climbed the charts to the number one spot, generated five Top Ten singles, and eventually sold over eleven million copies, becoming one of the most successful records of the decade. Springsteen was even able to maintain his integrity as he made the transition into MTV's heavy rotation with video clips (such as "Glory Days"), in which he appeared both as performer and the narrative's main character.

By embodying such seemingly obsolete rock values as "authenticity" and "tradition," Springsteen heralded a return to the glory days of 1960s rock. His all-American, blue-collar image had even made him a coveted trophy of the 1984 presidential elections. It all began when Ronald Reagan, on a campaign trip to New Jersey (Bruce's home state), attempted to appropriate some of the singer's populist aura by quoting the title song of his patriotically titled new album. Springsteen, however, quickly stepped in to repudiate not only the candidate but also the conservative social policies he respresented.

In fact—having been deeply influenced by Joe Klein's 1980 biography of Woody Guthrie—Springsteen was increasingly focusing his creative attention on the lives of the homeless and unemployed, whom he saw as the victims of Reagan's economic revolution. He also embraced the social activism of the great Depression-era folk singer by performing at benefit concerts for striking miners and donating a percentage of his fees to local soup kitchens and relief organizations.

And while his music continued to draw its energy and inspiration from a roster of rock 'n' roll giants (from Chuck Berry and Roy Orbison to Bob Dylan and the Rolling Stones), during the 1980s Springsteen abandoned the grandiose, Phil Spectorish wall-of-sound production (of his 1975 *Born to Run* breakthrough) in favor of a more direct, uncluttered sound. And in keeping with his heightened social consciousness, he increasingly turned to folk music itself as a vehicle for his own gritty working-class ballads (first in *Nebraska* and later in his Grammy-winning acoustic album, *The Ghost of Tom Joad*). Nor was Bruce Springsteen the only performer of the decade to revive a distinctly Sixties sensibility by combining roots rock with folk music's social consciousness.

Among the other performers who staked a claim to the charts in the 1980s by reclaiming some of the musical values more closely associated with the 1960s, perhaps the most successful was John Mellencamp (a former glam rocker who had achieved some success in the 1970s under the pseudonym John Cougar). In songs such as "Small Town" (1982) and "Pink Houses" (from his Grammy-winning 1983 album of the same name), Mellencamp also brought a populist vision (and rock-historical sound) to his unsentimental portraits of Midwestern working-class life. And while the spirit of rock fundamentalism waned during the early 1990s (in the wake of the Nirvana-inspired "grunge" phenomenon), by mid-decade another generation of roots rockers—including Hootie and the Blowfish, the Dave Matthews Band, and the Wallflowers (whose frontman, Jakob Dylan, had a biological link to the style's spiritual father)—arrived on the scene to carry on the tradition.

Although both Springsteen and Mellencamp increasingly infused folk sources into their rock anthems, it was a new generation of women folkies who brought the sound of acoustic guitars to the top of the pop charts. In 1987, for example, a virtually unknown young female folk singer released a haunting single, titled "Luka." The song addressed the difficult subject of child abuse with a dispassionate first-person point of view and spare acoustic-based arrangement that only seemed to add to the song's emotional power. "Luka" quickly went to number three on the pop singles chart and its creator, Suzanne Vega, became folk music's newest heroine. Vega's album *Solitude Standing* also became a surprise hit (making it into the Top Twenty and selling a million copies); later

FIGURE 5-16. While Bruce Springsteen may very well have been "rock 'n' roll's future"—as he was dubbed in one prophetic review—Springsteen's music also embodied virtually the entire *history* of rock and roll from doo-wop to Dylan. Archive Photo.

The Boss

While Springsteen's 1973 debut album (*Greetings From Asbury Park*) fused hard-edged, horn-saturated rock with long lines of lyrics whose surrealistic imagery could only be described as "Dylanesque," longtime fans of his marathon concerts knew that he typically ended his shows with electrifying covers of classic songs by Roy Orbison, Chuck Berry, and his other 1950s rock heroes. In 1975 Springsteen added another layer to these disparate influences when he adopted a Phil Spectorish "wall of sound" production for his critically lauded 1975 album *Born to Run*.

Although Bruce had been a respected figure on the national rock scene for a decade, it wasn't until 1984 that he recorded an album that won him commercial success on a par with his critical acclaim. *Born in the U.S.A.* quickly went to number one, generated four Top Ten singles, and became one of the best-selling LPs of the year.

Ironically, the social commentary that infused the album's emotionally resonant new songs had come from Springsteen's immersion in the life and work of the great Dust Bowl balladeer, Woody Guthrie—who also had been the primary inspiration for Bob Dylan. It was a path Springsteen would go on to pursue in recordings such as *Nebraska* (a collection of bleak acoustic-based ballads) and his Grammy-winning contemporary folk album, *The Ghost of Tom Joad.*

another of the album's songs, "Tom's Diner," became an underground sensation when it was remixed by pioneering British techno wizards DNA.

In 1988, another young female folk singer scored a pop hit with her sensitive first-person account of the dead-end world of the economic underclass, set to the chords of an acoustic guitar. Tracy Chapman's song "Fast Car" not only made it into the Top Ten, but the following year Chapman also walked away with three Grammy Awards, including Best New Artist. After eight years of Washington-sponsored conservatism and Wall Street–sponsored materialism, it seemed the time was right for a return to folk music's simplicity and social consciousness. Other songs on Chapman's self-titled début, for example, explored domestic violence ("Behind the Wall") or warned about the possibility of class warfare ("Talkin' 'bout a Revolution"); and in keeping with folk music's activist traditions, Chapman also performed at the decade's numerous benefit concerts in support of the environment, Amnesty International, and Nelson Mandela.

As it turned out, what had first seemed like a couple of pop-chart abberations was, in fact, the beginning of a movement. By the mid-1990s, Suzanne Vega and Tracy Chapman were joined by a whole sisterhood of performers—including Michelle Shocked, Joan Osborne, Jewel, Sheryl Crow, Lucinda Williams, Nancy Griffith, and Ani DiFranco—who drew from both the socially conscious folk-revivalists of the 1960s and the more self-absorbed singer-songwriters of the 1970s. By the end of the 1990s, even Courtney Love was acknowledging her own debt to modern folk music's pioneers. In a 1997 interview (appearing in *Rolling Stone*'s special issue on "Women of Rock"), Love cited personal influences such as Joan Baez, Bob Dylan, Joni Mitchell, Loretta Lynn, and Leonard Cohen. "If you don't understand folk music," the Queen of Grunge stated flatly, "you can't understand rock & roll."

Meanwhile, during the second half of the 1980s, the spirit of tradition that had nourished American roots rock was also taking root across the Atlantic. In 1985, Dire Straits released a début album *Brothers in Arms,* which showcased Mark Knofler's carefully crafted songs, Dylanesque vocals, and virtuosic lead guitar. Not only would the group become a mainstay of AOR radio, but their anti-music-video anthem "Money for Nothing" (with its "I Want My MTV" chorus) was quickly adopted by the cable station as a testament to its own good-sport attitude. It was a band of Irish ex-punk-rockers, however, whose primal guitar-driven music, politically conscious lyrics, and declamatory vocals would make them—along with Springsteen himself—the decade's most potent exponents of rock integrity.

Beginning with their 1983 breakthrough album *War,* U2 released a succession of anthemic albums (brilliantly produced by Brian Eno and Daniel Lanois) that addressed social issues such as the enduring religious conflict in their homeland ("Sunday Bloody Sunday") and the racial turmoil in America ("Pride [In the Name of Love]"). At first, the band explicitly linked themselves to a more idealistic era than the one in which they lived. For example, after condemning the 1980s as a "barren era" for rock music, Bono (U2's lead singer and principal songwriter) allied himself with "the 1960s," identifying with its "great reservoir of talent, of high ideals, and of the will and desire to change things."

In 1985, *Rolling Stone* had christened U2 "The Band of the Eighties," and two years later they fulfilled that extravagant claim with the release of *The Joshua Tree.* Hailed by many critics as a masterpiece, the album was studded with such soon-to-be rock classics as "I Still Haven't Found What I'm Looking For" and "Where the Streets

Have No Name." It also quickly climbed to the top of the U.S. album charts, earned the band a *Time* magazine cover story, and a couple of Grammys (including Album of the Year). At the same time, U2 also maintained their social-consciousness credentials by performing at benefit concerts in support of Amnesty International, Nelson Mandela, and the Brazilian rainforest, while joining like-minded performers such as Bruce Springsteen, John Mellencamp, and Bob Dylan on a tribute album entitled *A Vision Shared* dedicated to the spiritual father of all socially conscious rock, Woody Guthrie.

As the decade drew to a close, however, U2's superstar status—and the quasi-religious fervor of their recent music and interviews—began to generate a critical backlash. Words like "pretentious" and "bombastic" began to appear regularly in reviews. For many of their original fans, the former punk rockers now seemed to embody some of the 1970s-style "art rock" values that the punks had set out to destroy forever. By the late 1980s, even the band was beginning to chafe at their own holier-than-thou public image. Bono now told interviewers that he "would hate to think that everybody was into U2 for 'deep' and 'meaningful' reasons." Instead, he proclaimed them just a "a noisy rock 'n' roll band."

In 1988, U2 released *Rattle and Hum,* a double album of live material and new songs in which they explored for the first time rock's African-American sources; the album included a collaboration with bluesman B. B. King ("When Love Comes to Town"), as well as a song inspired by jazz legend Billie Holiday ("Angel of Harlem"). Then—motivated by their desire to change their musical direction even more radically—U2 (along with producer Brian Eno) spent the next three years exploring the cutting edge of the cut-and-paste "industrial rock" style that had been sweeping through the European underground. The result, released late in 1991, was *Achtung Baby,* a densely textured sound collage that was a far cry from the pounding back beat and emotional intensity of their earlier music.

Although *Achtung Baby* further alienated many of their original fans, U2 continued to pursue its experimental direction with its follow-up release, *Zooropa.* Later in the decade they even delved into the brightly colored, disposable style that had dominated the decade's musical landscape, in an album they simply called *Pop.* By this time not only had U2 become masters the art of the music video, but their huge, elaborately conceived, multimedia-enhanced tours made the band one of the most successful live acts of the 1990s.

METAL HEALTH IN THE 1990S

By creating its own twenty-four-hour-a-day, seven-days-a-week electronic stage, MTV dramatically enhanced the importance of pop music's visual element. It should be no surprise, therefore, that the cable station proved to be the perfect medium for the genre of rock that had always placed as much emphasis on its exaggerated theatricality, outrageous costumes, and elaborate hairstyles as it did on its thundering power chords.

Although most of heavy metal's founding fathers (including Deep Purple, Black Sabbath, Judas Priest, KISS, and Aerosmith) were still active during the late 1970s, their impact had been considerably stifled by the pulsating rhythms of disco and angry rants of punk. But as the new decade got under way, a new battalion of heavy metal warriors donned their own leather or spandex uniforms; and for them, the arrival of the video as the music industry's primary form of promotion couldn't have come at a better time.

Across the Atlantic, early-1980s bands such as Iron Maiden, Motorhead, Sledgehammer, and Def Leppard were being hyped by record label promotion departments (and the rock journalists) as "The New Wave of British Heavy Metal." Meanwhile, in America, Van Halen and Motley Crüe were unveiling new homegrown versions of the genre to yet another generation of the young male audience that had always made up the bulk of the metal market. Then there was AC/DC, a band of Australian rockers and British ex-patriots whose 1981 LP, *For Those Who Are About to Rock We Salute You,* had climbed the top of the *Billboard* album chart despite the absence of the media saturation on which most pop groups relied. Suddenly, the signs of a restoration of metal health were everywhere.

From the very beginning, heavy metal had been ridiculed by mainstream journalists and by most of the rock press. It had been snubbed by radio progammers and by Grammy nominating committees (which didn't even institute an official Heavy Metal award until 1988). Despite this less-than-benign neglect, heavy metal bands had often sold massive amounts of records (and played sold-out arenas on their concert tours). Ironically, because they had succeeded in doing so without the pop music industry's standard promotional machinary, these bands were also freed of many of the industry's standard constraints. So what if their music was short on melody and long on guitar solos, or if their songs dispensed with the requisite pop hooks. In fact, much of the intense sense of community that had long characterized the heavy metal scene had been a direct result of its marginalized status.

LITE METAL

Compared to their more orthodox heavy metal ancestors, however, many members of the genre's new generation were considerably more "flexible" in their musical philosophy. For example, when asked about the roots of their own style, Def Leppard bassist Rick Savage not only acknowledged the inspiration of Led Zeppelin and Deep Purple, but he admitted that his band also had a keen awareness of "what was happening on the pop charts." As he told one interviewer, "We always want to have a commercial aspect that's pleasing on the ear, while the seventeen-year-olds can still get off on the power of it." In her book *Heavy Metal: A Cultural Sociology,* Deena Weinstein adopted the somewhat derisive term "lite metal" to describe the appealing new style that Def Leppard (and the other more pop-oriented heavy metal bands) were introducing.

Writing about this same period (in his classic study of the genre, *Running with the Devil*), Robert Walser detailed the various attributes of the new heavy metal bands that would help them make the transition into the pop mainstream and onto the MTV airwaves: "For the most part, the new wave of metal featured shorter, catchier songs, more sophisticated production techniques, and higher technical standards. All of these characteristics helped pave the way toward greater popular success." One of the first to forge these crucial elements into a successful pop metal synthesis was Van Halen, a Los Angeles–based band that had formed back in the mid-1970s.

Not only did Van Halen rein their music into tightly controlled arrangements (set off by concise guitar solos), but they tempered their traditional heavy metal assaults with a smoother more melodious sound (and even sweetened it with occasional harmonies). When David Lee Roth, the band's frontman, was asked to define the secret of their success, he came up with a formula that could have also served as a pretty good slogan for the entire pop metal movement: "Van Halen is entertainment delivered at maximum impact." While Roth provided the band's visceral vocals (along with a blend of macho swagger and raunchy humor), perhaps the most potent weapon Van Halen had in its quest for the mainstream was the unprecedented virtuosity of the band's lead guitarist (and namesake), Eddie Van Halen.

When Van Halen's first album was released, most critics were quick to herald the arrival of a guitarist who not only displayed impressive musical ability but who actually set a new standard for his instrument. Typical of these laudatory descriptions is the one that appears in *Running with the Devil:* "Eddie Van Halen revolutionized metal guitar technique with the release of Van Halen's debut album, fueling a renaissance in electric guitar study and experimentation unmatched since thousands of fans were inspired to learn to play by Eric Clapton's apotheosis in the late 1960s and Jimi Hendrix's death in 1970."

On the basis of his performance on that first album, readers of *Guitar Player* magazine elected Eddie Van Halen "Best New Talent," while in each of the following five years he was voted "Best Rock Guitarist." Employing a dazzling array of innovative techniques and blinding speed (which he used to weld together his extensive blues, rock, and classical vocabulary), Eddie Van Halen raised the bar of guitar virtuosity. Before long, however, he would be challenged by a virtual army of heavy metal guitar heroes including Randy Rhoads, Yngwie Malmsteen, Steve Vai, and Greg Howe, among others.

Meanwhile, just as the new pop metal bands were generating a guitar-rock revival, MTV was undergoing its first major reorganization. By 1983, just as the slick synthesizer-based sound of the New Pop acts (such as Duran Duran and the Eurythmics) was beginning to lose its novelty, the cable network was expanding its distribution both across the American heartland and into the vital communications centers of Los Angeles and New York. Hungry for something to replace the arty "concept videos" the cable station had been vigorously programming since its inception two years earlier, MTV turned to the video-friendly heavy metal bands that were conveniently waiting in the wings.

MTV WELCOMES YOU TO THE HEADBANGER'S BALL

When MTV decided to add a video from Def Leppard's 1983 release, *Pyromania,* to the station's heavy rotation, sales of the album quickly climbed to an astonishing nine million copies (on its way to becoming one of year's biggest hits). Before long an entire spectrum of heavy metal bands—British (Iron Maiden) and American (Motley Crüe), up-and-coming (Twisted Sister) and well-established (Ozzy Osbourne), macho (W.A.S.P.) and glam (Ratt)—followed Def Leppard on to MTV, and into the top of the charts. By the end of 1984, *Billboard* magazine's special feature on heavy metal reported that in just one year, the genre's share of the pop music market had surged from 8 percent to 20 percent!

Among that year's biggest hits was Van Halen's "Jump," a song that perfectly symbolized metal's new pop values: a tight arrangement, an infectious sing-along chorus, and just enough "attitude" to provide a thrill. Of course, the band's high-energy, eager-to-please video also proved irresistible, and when "Jump" was added to MTV's heavy rotation, it quickly became Van Halen's first number one single. Of course, the band had already benefited tremendously from MTV; after all, it was Eddie Van Halen's slashing solo on Michael Jackson's "Beat It" that had helped Michael make his own music video breakthrough two years earlier.

In 1986, the station introduced an extended block of all-heavy metal videos they called "Headbanger's Ball" (named for the rhythmic head-snapping movements that took the place of dancing at live metal concerts). It quickly became the station's highest rated show.

Another of those who benefited most from MTV's newfound attention was Bon Jovi, a band that both softened metal's sharp edges with a veneer of working-class rock "authenticity" and infused it with a heavy dose of pop music's "romantic sincerity." As Robert Walser explained, it was just this "fusion that enabled the band's mainstream success and helped spark the unprecedented entry of much heavy metal and metal-influenced music into the Top Forty of the late 1980s."

The astonishing sales racked up by Bon Jovi's 1986 album, *Slippery When Wet* (thirteen million copies, making it one of the biggest hits of the decade), couldn't have occurred without the support from fans who had, for the most part, been absent from the heavy metal audience: young women. According to Walser, "Bon Jovi's music . . . helped transform what had long been a mostly male subcultural genre into a much more popular style with a gender-balanced audience." By June 1987, the *Billboard* album chart confirmed heavy metal's dramatic inroads into the mainstream. Although the Irish rock band U2's breakthrough release *The Joshua Tree* occupied the number one position, each of the next five albums in the Top Ten—by Bon Jovi, Whitesnake, Motley Crüe, Poison, and Ozzy Osbourne—was by a heavy metal band.

During this period, Los Angeles became the heavy metal capital of America. And in August of 1987—just a few short weeks after the style's astonishing assault on the *Billboard* chart—another group emerged out of the L.A. scene, whose blend of heavy metal and hard rock quickly catapulted them to the very top of the Top Ten. The success of Guns 'n' Roses' début album, *Appetite for Destruction,* which quickly sold over ten million copies and produced three hit singles, was generated not only by unceasing support from MTV but also from the sudden interest of the mainstream rock press (i.e., *Rolling Stone*), who had once scorned metal for (what Ken Tucker had referred to as) its "proud hostility to cultural and aesthetic niceties."

As heavy metal's popularity continued to expand, however, so did the attacks against it. Although the genre had long been the focus of considerable public outrage, by the mid-1980s the assault on the music was not only more intense but better organized. While the criticism was directed at a range of evils supposedly promulgated by heavy metal bands, most fell under at least one of what might be called the genre's "Three S's:" Satanism (i.e., "The Number of the Beast" by Iron Maiden), Sex (i.e., "Animal [Fuck Like a Beast] by W.A.S.P.), or Suicide (i.e., "Suicide Solution" by Ozzy Osbourne).

Much of this heavy metal hysteria was played out in Washington, D.C., where the Parents Music Resource Center had managed to initiate Congressional hearings during the 1985 session that finally resulted in a system of "voluntary" album cover warning labels. Of course, as it always has in pop music history, such controversy simply generated even more sales. So, whether it was due to MTV or the PMRC, during the second half of the 1980s, heavy metal would experience its greatest upsurge in commercial success.

But while mid-1980s metal did retain essential elements of the genre—from perversity to power chords—for some fans, the style's newfound success seemed a violation of the very "outsider" status that had always been the basis of the special bond within the heavy metal community. According to this perspective, longtime fans felt that by adopting the aesthetic and commercial values of pop and rock, some bands had in fact sold their very souls. Before long, metal's mainstream status would provide the motivation for metal's new underground subgenres.

METAL FRAGMENTS

In her book, *Heavy Metal: A Cultural Sociology,* Deena Weinstein explains that what became known as "speed (or thrash) metal" "can be understood as an attempt to reclaim metal for youth and especially for males by creating a style that is completely unacceptable to the hegemonic [broad or dominant] culture. Speed metal represents a fundamentalist return to the standards of the heavy metal subculture."

Not only did Metallica, Slayer, Anthrax, and Megadeth attempt to recapture heavy metal's musical values—an intensity and abrasiveness unconstrained by melodic hooks—but they also sought to reclaim the style's I-did-it-my-way attitude. For, rather than joining the quest for major label contracts, MTV airplay, and front page articles in the slick, mass-market magazines (such as *Circus* or *Hit Parader*) that catered to the mainstream metal audience, speed/thrash bands embraced the purity of small independent labels, an underground club scene, and coverage in the smudged pages of xeroxed fanzines.

The archetypal thrash metal band was Metallica, which had formed in Los Angeles around 1981. By combining the instrumental virtuosity, thundering beat, and sheer volume of new wave British metal bands such as Iron Maiden and Motorhead with the headlong velocity and nihilistic stance of L.A.'s hardcore punk rockers such as the Dead Kennedys and Black Flag, Metallica forged a powerful new style. True to its principles, Metallica recorded its 1983 debut album, *Kill 'Em All,* for a small New Jersey independent label, Meagaforce.

But when the LP sold over 300,000 copies—largely on the basis of word-of-mouth within the hardcore heavy metal community—it became clear that Metallica had tapped into a deep hunger for an alternative to the eager-to-please lite metal style. By 1986, the band's (major label) breakthrough, *Master of Puppets,* quickly sold just under a million copies, climbing to number twenty-nine on the *Billboard* album chart. A few years later, when he was interviewed for a major article published in the *New York Times* Sunday magazine, Lars Ulrich (Metallica's Danish-born founder) outlined the tried-and-true heavy metal formula that his band had rejected: "It's gotten so safe," he declared. "You put on some makeup, you spike your hair, you go out and sing about sex, and driving fast cars and off you go, two million records."

Ironically, by this point, even those bands who consciously rejected this strategy for pop success were finding their own way to the top of the pop chart. During the second half of the 1980s, albums by thrash metal rebels including Anthrax and Megadeth (which had been formed by ex-Metallica guitarist Dave Mustaine) also made their way onto the best seller lists. In fact, Metallica's own 1988 album, *. . . And Justice for All,* not only became a Top Ten hit the following year—despite the band's continued absence from the radio and MTV airwaves—but a few months later, when the first Grammy Award exclusively devoted to heavy metal was presented, it was the members of Metallica who walked up to the stage to receive it.

By decade's end, the enormous expansion (and accompanying fragmentation) of heavy metal was reflected in the commercial success of bands from across the entire metal spectrum. In addition, some bands—particularly thrash metal rebels like Metallica—actually began to garner the respectful attention of the mainstream press and traditional rock critics. And, finally, new opportunities opened up for those who had previously been excluded from the heavy metal ranks. For example, in 1988, Lita Ford—one of the genre's only female singer/guitarists—had a Top Ten single ("Close My Eyes"), and Living Colour—the vanguard African-American metal band (led by guitar virtuoso Vernon Reid)—won a Grammy in 1989 for its hit single "Cult of Personality."

During the 1990s, however, heavy metal's energy seemed to wane as other marginalized subgenres (such as rap and alternative rock) began to assume a more significant share of the pop music market. In fact, rap's own mainstream breakthrough was the direct result of its acceptance by a substantial white, male, suburban audience. Teenagers whose older brothers had inspired fear and loathing in their parents' hearts by blasting Iron Maiden records in their bedrooms now turned to NWA's gangsta narratives in order to inspire a similar sense of parental trepidation.

FIGURE 5-17.   By fusing the intense volume, instrumental virtuosity, and thundering beat of the new wave of British heavy metal with the headlong velocity and nihilistic stance of L.A.'s hardcore punks, Metallica became the founding fathers of a new genre known as "speed metal" or "thrash." Photo by Ross Halfin. Courtesy of Elektra Entertainment.

Metallica: Banging Those Heads That Don't Bang

Metallica not only managed to stretch the definition of heavy metal but to earn the grudging respect of mainstream rock critics (who had always scorned the genre). At the end of the 1980s, when a Grammy category for heavy metal was finally established, Metallica won it each of the first three years it was offered.

During the 1990s, heavy metal once again splintered into sharp-edged fragments (such as black metal, new metal, death metal), but Metallica maintained its preeminent status. And they did it all without abandoning the band's original audience or deviating from its initial motto: "To Bang Those Heads That Don't Bang."

Meanwhile, the insatiable hunger for the "next-new-thing" had set in, and a now familiar pop ritual was about to be enacted once again. As the new decade began, an assortment of do-it-yourself, guitar-based rock bands—that had been hovering on the edge of music industry radar screens—was about to plucked out of its own cozy cocoon of regional indie labels, low-powered college radio stations, and crudely produced fanzines and thrust onto the cover of *Rolling Stone*.

ALTERNATIVE TO WHAT?

On September 24, 1991, Nirvana, an obscure Seattle rock band, released an album whose title—*Nevermind*—perfectly captured the offhand nihilism of both their music and their lifestyle. As the events of the next few weeks would make clear, however, the album's astonishing success not only signaled a kind of paradigm shift for the thriving underground scene out of which it had emerged, but ultimately for the multibillion-dollar music industry as well.

To begin with, unlike the band's 1989 début album *Bleach*—which had been recorded on Sub-Pop, a regional independent label (for the total cost of $606.17)—*Nevermind* was released on media mogul David Geffen's latest big-budget venture, DGC Records (home to such powerhouse pop acts as Guns 'n' Roses and Cher). And while Nirvana's promotion had previously been limited to word-of-mouth and airplay on KCMU (the University of Washington radio station), now MTV was running the artfully scruffy video for their single "Smells Like Teen Spirit" in its heavy rotation. A few weeks later, when the band made its appearance on *Saturday Night Live*, *Nevermind* was the number one album in America (having displaced Michael Jackson's *Dangerous*).

So, just as most of the country was discovering the very existence of an "alternative rock" scene, within this once self-consciously marginalized community, there was the recognition that *their* music had suddenly gone mainstream. And for a subculture whose motto—D.I.Y. ("Do It Yourself")—reflected its intense commitment to self-sufficiency, absolute musical integrity, and anti-corporate values, Nirvana's major-label, MTV-generated success produced a decidedly ambivalent reaction. It was one the group's leader, Kurt Cobain, clearly shared; the first time he appeared on the cover of *Rolling Stone*, for example, Cobain wore a T-shirt that read: "Corporate Magazines Still Suck."

In the wake of *Nevermind*'s massive sales (over ten million copies), the "Seattle sound" or "grunge" became the music industry's next next-new-thing. Before long, a couple of Nirvana's former Sub-Pop labelmates also found themselves in the somewhat uncomfortable position of being rock stars. Pearl Jam's recently released debut album, *Ten*, climbed steadily to the number two position on the Billboard chart (their 1992 follow-up, *Vs.*, would actually enter the chart at number one); Alice in Chains' current album *Dirt* also became an unexpected million-seller (and their 1993 follow-up, *Jar of Flies*, would go to number one as well). Meanwhile, Soundgarden—the first Seattle band to forsake Sub-Pop for the majors (A & M)—eventually found itself at the top the charts with their 1993 album, *Superunknown*.

It was the coming-of-age of a new generation of guitar-based rock bands. Although most of its members had grown up on the heavy metal of Black Sabbath and the hardcore punk of Black Flag, they also excavated 1970s punk rock (for guitar licks and attitude lessons from the Sex Pistols and the Ramones), while some of Nirvana's instinct for melodic hooks were clearly derivied from Kurt Cobain's boyhood obsession with the Beatles. In one way or another, each group in the great Northwest grunge alliance had formulated its own pastiche of the past—loud, distorted guitars, breakneck tempos, primal scream vocals—then filtered it through their own brand of contemporary alienation (the smell of teen spirit), and dressed it up in ripped jeans and a faded flannel shirt.

The "grunge" label, however, was not only applicable to the musicians' preferred sartorial style but to the sludgy, dirty sound of their records as well. According to Soundgarden's Kim Thrayil, however, what was most important about these bands was that they had—for the first time since the Woodstock generation—made rock really matter again. "They thought they had a monopoly on rock 'n' roll," Thrayil said disdainfully about the rapidly aging veterans of the 1960s, "and all of a sudden they realize they don't. It belongs to someone else now." Yet, even after the mainstream media officially announced the triumph of Nirvana and the other Seattle-based "alternative rock" bands, that still left one question unanswered: "Alternative" to what?

FIGURE 5-18.   Reuters/Lee Celano/Archive Photos.

Kurt Cobain and the Guitar-Rock Revival

By the time Nirvana's 1991 début single "Smells Like Teen Spirit" made its way to the top of the charts, Kurt Cobain was already being touted as the rock hero of the Nineties. Tragically, before the decade was even half over, Cobain was dead of a self-inflicted shotgun wound. But while he would later be relegated to the status of poster-boy for Gen-X's slacker values, Cobain's fusion of Beatlesque melodicism and punk abrasiveness almost single-handedly revived guitar-based rock—a concept that had been pushed to the margins during the MTV-generated electro pop explosion of the 1980s.

Well, a glance at the other albums that accompanied *Nevermind* on Billboard's 1991 annual Top Five might provide a partial answer to that question. At the top of the music industry's annual list of best-selling LPs was *Ropin' the Wind,* by hot new country superstar Garth Brooks; in the number two spot was *Gonna Make You Sweat,* C & C Music Factory's compilation of disco-ish dance grooves; following Nirvana's third-place finish was *Time, Love, and Tenderness,* Michael Bolton's latest offering of overwrought blue-eyed soul, and rounding out the list was *Unforgettable,* which (through the miracle of modern recording science) featured pop diva Natalie Cole's duets with her father, the legendary singer Nat "King" Cole, who had died in 1965. In the context of such safe, middle-of-the-road music, *Nevermind* did offer an exciting change of pace. But while millions may have heralded Nirvana as the avatars of alternative rock, the indie-underground out of which they emerged was at least a decade old.

INDIE ROCK: A BRIEF HISTORY

Back in 1981, when R.E.M. was first devising its unique blend of 1970s punk-rock and 1960s folk-rock down in Athens, Georgia, MTV had just gone the air with its New Pop playlist, a recent flurry of corporate mergers had made the handful of major labels that remained more conservative than ever, commercial radio had coalesced around a handful of middle-of-the-road formats all fighting over fragments of the market share, and Ronald Reagan was in the White House.

In this context, R.E.M.'s garage-rock fundamentalism, obscure lyrics and understated image (all of which amounted to a kind of anti-style), inevitably placed the band well outside the pop music mainstream. But as they—and the other ancestors of alternative rock would discover—that was where they could be most free. Since these bands recorded exclusively for small *independent* labels (where an album that sold a thousand copies was considered a hit) and received their only airplay on college radio stations (that were unfettered by commercial pressure), the music they made was typically dubbed "indie rock."

By 1983, when R.E.M. released their first full-length album, *Murmur* (for I.R.S., a prestigious indie label), they had for the most part already developed a signature sound based largely on Michael Stipes's sensually mumbled vocals and Peter Buck's jangly, Byrds-influenced guitar. And, as a result of their relentless touring—along with the airplay their previous singles and EP had received on college radio—R.E.M. were already attracting a sizeable underground following. Although *Murmur*'s sales of 150,000 copies would have made it little more than a blip on the annual sales report of one of the major labels, the record qualified as an indie-rock blockbuster. The band received even more attention when *Rolling Stone* magazine selected R.E.M.'s record as 1983's "Album of the Year" (over both Michael Jackson's *Thriller* and the Police's *Synchronicity*).

Another of indie-rock's most revered bands also emerged in 1981, but Sonic Youth was a product of the creative ferment of New York's avant-garde underground. When he reviewed their self-titled 1982 début EP, the *New York Times* music critic Jon Pareles had declared that Sonic Youth's heavily distorted sound "started out a few steps past the the taboo-busting of punk and heavy metal," as it enveloped its listeners with "barrages of noise."

Led by guitarist Thurston Moore and bassist Kim Gordon (who were not only bandmates but husband and wife), Sonic Youth had already become infamous for its experiments with dissonance and extreme dynamics, as well as for odd guitar tunings and unconventional song structures. Nor did Sonic Youth's lyrics and subject matter—a mixture of the perverse and the political—exactly fit the standard pop formulas.

But R.E.M. and Sonic Youth were only two members of what was a diverse and rapidly expanding indie-rock community. During the 1980s, while Seattle was nurturing such proto-grunge bands as Green River and Soundgarden, San Francisco and Los Angeles were home to abrasive, "hardcore" bands such as the Dead Kennedys and Black Flag (respectively); among the list of Minnesota's local heroes were the hyperdrive postpunk bands Husker Du and the Replacements; up in Amherst, Massachusetts, Dinosaur Jr. lumbered through the college-dense countryside. Boston gave birth to pop-punksters, the Lemonheads, and Washington, D.C., had Bad Brains. Although they all drew from varied sources and represented a broad spectrum of musical styles, most of the bands appeared on the same handful of indie labels (SST, Sub-Pop, I.R.S., Twin-Tone, etc.), and all shared a self-conscious pride in their "outsider" status.

INDIE ENTERS THE MAINSTREAM

R.E.M. was the first to face what would become indie rock's essential dilemma: how to retain the purity of one's underground values within the pop music mainstream. For, after releasing a series of increasingly successful albums on I.R.S. (culminating in *Document,* which steadily climbed its way into the Top Ten in 1987), R.E.M. was signed by a media giant (Warner Bros.) for what was reported to be an advance of $6 million. Yet, before the decade ended, R.E.M. had produced a major-label début album (*Green*) that managed to retain the band's idiosyncratic style while selling more than two million copies. The band even launched an extensive national tour that included some of the huge arenas and outdoor stadiums that were among the bête noirs of indie rock.

Meanwhile, after issuing a half-dozen uncompromising albums full of sound and fury for independent labels such as SST and Homestead, Sonic Youth also made the transition to the majors. In 1989, the band signed with DGC, David Geffen's latest corporate enterprise. When the album (*Goo*) came out a year later, however, longtime fans were reassured not only by the familiar sound of weirdly tuned guitars, harsh dissonances, and challenging lyrics, but by Sonic Youth's continued cross-genre experimentations; for example, the album's single, "Kool Thing," was a collaboration with Chuck D, of the rap group Public Enemy.

Although Sonic Youth's major-label début didn't generate any commercial breakthroughs (it sold fewer than 250,000 copies), the band did make its first arena tour, opening for veteran rocker (and "godfather of alternative," Neil Young). More important, Sonic Youth had preserved its reputation for absolute integrity. In fact, it was the band's presence on the DGC roster that was one of the main factors in Nirvana's imminent decision to sign with the label. By 1990, rock's underground had already made such inroads into the musical mainstream that the record industry bestowed its ultimate symbol of acceptance on the genre—its own Grammy award category.

The winner of that inaugural Grammy for "Best Alternative Music Performance" was Sinead O'Connor's *I Do Not Want What I Haven't Got.* The album was both a powerful exploration of personal and sexual politics and a musical fusion of Celtic folk, edgy synth-pop, punk, and jazz. And while it stayed true to the distinctive vision the Irish singer/songwriter had formulated on her 1987 début, *The Lion and the Cobra,* it was O'Connor's shaved head that became the focus of most of the media attention. Perhaps this was inevitable since most Americans had been introduced to O'Connor through a riveting video (for her single "Nothing Compares 2 U"), which consisted almost entirely of a headshot of the performer.

O'Connor's Grammy also served to highlight the conflict inherent in alternative music's new "insider" status. In what would be the first of numerous displays of ambivalence about her new role, O'Connor actually boycotted the ceremony that included her own award (and that served to generate a significant portion of her album's multiplatinum sales). Over the next few years, O'Connor continued to defiantly persue her own creative direction (losing much of her original audience along the way). She also precipitated a series of controversies over issues of sexism, racism, and freedom of speech. The most explosive of these was sparked when—while serving as host of *Saturday Night Live*—she held up a photo of the Pope and ripped it to shreds in front of the stunned TV audience.

Whatever one thought about her music (or her politics), however, O'Connor was a privotal figure, not only in alternative rock's transition into the mainstream but also in the rapidly evolving status of women within the male-dominated rock hierarchy. Although she cited Bob Marley, Van Morrison, and Bob Dylan as her strongest influences, feminist music critics also recognized in O'Connor's style the echoes of female rockers of the past—from the punk posturings of Patti Smith, Chryssie Hynde, and Siouxie (of the Banshees) to the political radicalism and banshee wail of Yoko Ono.

And when—by the end of the 1990s—women had become a powerful presence in every musical genre (including rock, rap, folk, R & B, and pop), O'Connor was able to hear echoes of her own style in the new generation of female performers. In a 1997 interview published in *Rolling Stone's* special "Women of Rock" issue, she memorably described Alanis Morrisette as, "Sinead O'Connor with hair," and when she reflected on the career of her countrywoman, Delores O'Riordan, O'Connor claimed that the Cranberries were nothing more than "a kind of well-behaved Sinead O'Connor."

Interviewed in the same *Rolling Stone* special issue, Sonic Youth's Kim Gordon suggested that it was indie rock's female contingent had actually been responsible for one of the style's most fundamental philosophical principles—embodied in the motto, "D.I.Y." (Do-It-Yourself). As Gordon explained it, "The whole do-it-yourself thing took a lot of ideas from feminism. But there are all different levels of it: women who are talking about the male [-dominated] society to girls who just want to have a band."

In their own way, one might even say that R.E.M. members were feminists. But not only did they speak out against sexism (in both their interviews and songs), they also declared their opposition to censorship, racism, pollution, the violation of animal rights, AIDS, and the Chinese occupation of Tibet. In 1991, the forum for R.E.M.'s progressive political views expanded dramatically when the band issued *Out of Time,* a subtle blend of melodic pop and folky authenticity that sold over four million copies on its way to becoming the number one album in the country. MTV bombarded viewers with their enigmatic (and beautifully produced) video for the single, "Losing My Religion," and the following spring, the album earned the band a Grammy for Best Alternative Performance of 1991.

Although R.E.M. may have won the Grammy, however, it was Nirvana (having released *Nevermind* the same year) that propelled rock's alternative subculture into the forefront of America's pop music consciousness. And while Michael Stipe would eventually become indie rock's most respected elder statesman, it was Kurt Cobain who would assume the mantle of cultural icon. Cobain's songs seemed to emerge unfiltered out of the depths of his own subconscious, yet no matter how personal—and emotionally painful—they might have been, they also seemed to tap directly into the disillusionment of a generation. The fact that Nirvana's music was as abrasive and raw as any that had ever made it into the pop charts only added to the cathartic sense of exhilaration they induced. So what if Cobain had gotten the title for his hit song from the name of an underarm deodorant marketed for young girls, through the alchemy of art, "Smells Like Teen Spirit" was transformed into a stirring Generation-X anthem. And their album just kept selling.

Unlike R.E.M.—which had made an incremental ascent into the mainstream over the course of ten years (and seven albums)—Nirvana was swept virually overnight into the pop music maelstrom. And not only was Cobain's charisma (and vulnerability) the real thing, so was his ambivalence about the whole starmaking machinery in which he had suddenly become enmeshed. As if to purge itself of any pop music pretensions, Nirvana's 1993 album *In Utero* was even more strident in its sound and deeper in its lyric subtexts. As one critic explained it, "Cobain set out to prove his noncorporate rocker status by making scabrous, abrasive music. To some extent he suceeded—and in the process he made the best record of 1993."

Gradually, however, it was Cobain's celebrity, rather than Nirvana's music that became the focus of media attention. There was his wedding to the notorious Courtney Love, leader of the aspiring Seattle alt-rock band Hole, and there also were numerous reports of drug abuse (heroin would prove to be as disastrous for alternative rock as it had been for jazz during the bebop movement of the 1940s and 1950s). Cobain's growing obsession with guns also began taking on a more ominous cast, and there were even rumors of a botched suicide attempt. Among the items of gossip that had filtered into the press preceding the release of *In Utero* was the story that Cobain had been planning to title the album *I Hate Myself and Want to Die.* Nevertheless, there was a profound sense of shock when, on April 8, 1994, Cobain's mangled body was discovered alongside a shotgun and a suicide note.

Within days of his tragic death, Kurt Cobain was being deified as the latest in a long line of rock 'n' roll martyrs. Nirvana's posthumous releases won virtually unanimous critical praise, and one of them—an album drawn from the band's "MTV Unplugged" appearance—won the 1995 Grammy for Best Alternative Performance. That same year, when *Spin* magazine issued an article on the most significant rock performers of the previous decade titled, "The Ten That Matter Most: 1985–95," they placed Nirvana at the very top of the list. A few others, however, took a more clear-eyed view of the performer's status. Looking back over Nirvana's brief career, one critic (from the *Chicago Tribune*) was particularly harsh in his assessment. "With *In Utero,* Nirvana have slid back into well-deserved obscurity. Kurt's star was waning near the end. He only became a 'spokeman for a generation' after he died."

In any event, by the mid-1990s, the floodgates that Nirvana opened had generated an alternative-rock tidal wave, sweeping a new generation of bands (including Pearl Jam and Smashing Pumpkins) into the mainstream of multiplatinum sales, marathon arena tours, and ambitious MTV videos. Understandably, this also provoked a crisis of conscious among longtime members of the indie-rock community (who saw such success as a betrayal of their outsider/alternative status). Cries of "sell-out," however, now seemed beside the point. An article in *Puncture* magazine titled, "Indie Rock: A Dying Breed or Just a Dead Issue," seemed to offer the most astute analysis of the situation when it suggested that most of these bands "[wouldn't] have gone in a radically different direction if

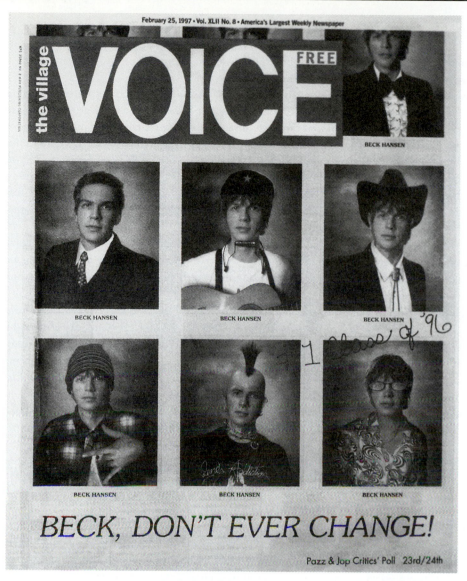

FIGURE 5-19.   After *Odelay* won the annual *Village Voice* critics' poll for the best album of 1996 (garnering twice as many votes as the second place Fugees), the newspaper came up with this clever front page layout. For Beck's multiple musical personalities—from folkie to funkster—could certainly fill the entire page of any high school yearbook. V.V. Publishing Corporation, reprinted by permission of *The Village Voice*.

Will the Real Beck Hansen Please Stand Up

Although his sample-laden, award-winning album earned Beck a reputation as a pop visionary charting the high-tech terrain of postmodern, premillennial electronic fusion, his connection to America's folk traditions seemed to inspire his deepest loyalties. Nor was this the first time that rock's cutting edge was honed by a young man whose irony-laced, surrealistic lyrics were wedded to music that echoed the unmistakable sounds of Woody Guthrie, Leadbelly, and Mississippi John Hurt. So it was no surprise when more than one critic immediately dubbed Beck (yet another) "new Dylan."

But while Bob Dylan's folk-rock revolution had seemed like a daring synthesis thirty years before, Beck's innovations required at least a half-dozen hyphens to summarize. And while Dylan's use of electric guitars had once been enough to generate consternation among traditionalists, Beck assembled his complex sonic collages using an array of electric beat boxes, samplers and synthesizers—along with "two turntables and a microphone."

they had stayed indie. Instead," as the author explained, "the mainstream moved towards them, to the point where their old indie styles are now standard hard rock."

In retrospect, therefore, the history of "alternative rock" can simply be seen as yet another round in rock 'n' roll's inevitable engagement with that great American institution known as the Popular Music Industry. Five years after Nirvana heralded the existence of a strange and unsettling alternative constellation, it had become a familiar part of the pop universe: R.E.M. signed a new Warner Bros. contract that was valued at $80 million; Smashing Pumpkins released a sprawling, elaborately produced double CD entitled *Mellon Collie and the Infinite Sadness* that would have made even the most ambitious art-rock band of the 1970s proud; even Pearl Jam (who continually struggled to maintain their alt-rock values), staked claim to a place in the rock canon by collaborating with counterculture heroes such as Neil Young and Bob Dylan—rebels who thirty years earlier also had emerged from the margins into the mainstream to create a musical revolution.

Meanwhile, the margins would remain a land of opportunity for those intent on charting new rock alternatives. As the decade (century and millennium) drew to a close, for example, a loose affliation of genre-busting visionaries began supplementing rock's guitar-based traditions with sampled hip-hop beats and turntable sound effects.

Although the dance-and/or-trance-oriented style known as "techno" (or "electronica") that fueled huge clandestine urban raves never made it into the American pop charts (as it did elsewhere), experimental DJs—such as Tricky, Moby, DJ Spooky, and others—did become underground heroes, while punk-rock–heavy-metal–hip-hop fusions by the likes of Limp Bizkit and Rage Against the Machine actually garnered considerable critical and popular success. And then there was Beck, who seemed to synthesize all of American popular music history. Perhaps more than any other contemporary performer, Beck worked the edges of the pop mainstream and the avant garde by cutting and pasting everything from traditional folk music and obscure blues to lounge music and Fusion jazz (along with radio-roulette noise and Balinese gamelon chimes) into funky sound collages.

ROCKIN' AT THE END OF THE MILLENNIUM

WOMEN ARE DOIN' IT FOR THEMSELVES

Anyone trying to fathom the state of rock 'n' roll at the dawn of the third millennium would have needed both a crystal ball and a rearview mirror. While pundits predicted a brave new world of plugged-in Internet explorers downloading cutting-edge cyborg rock by adventurous techno wizards, a quick glance at MTV or the latest issue of *Billboard* magazine revealed a more familiar vista.

As rock 'n' roll's own history passed the half-century mark, not only was the magic of digital sampling providing recording studio svengalis with the ability to instantly resurrect rock's past, but contemporary performers in every genre were perpetuating many of the music's most venerable traditions. Although rap's defiant beat and verbal barrages had begun to claim a sizeable share of the pop music market, the charts were still studded with classic rockers and R & B crooners, dance-music revelers and introspective singer-songwriters, young folkies, pop novelty acts, and one-hit wonders. What was new, however, was the fact that, by mid-decade, in virtually every one of these categories—women ruled.

Although a consortium of early-1990s female-dominated/feminist-oriented bands known as "riot grrrls" had never made it out of the underground, groups such as Bikini Kill, Bratmobile, and Huggy Bear were in the vanguard of an unprecedented explosion of women power that was shattering many of the sexual stereotypes that had dominated rock since its inception. As one riot-grrrl manifesto (appearing in an issue of a Bikini Kill 'zine) expressed it: "I believe with my wholeheartmindbody that girls constitute a revolutionary soul force that can, and will, change the world for real."

As the end of the millennium approached, a new generation of angry young women strapped on their electric guitars and invaded the mainstream. For the most part, these young female performers self-consciously identified themselves with rock's matriarchal heritage. For example, when Shirley Manson, the Scottish frontwoman of the late-1990s alt-rock band Garbage was asked what had drawn her to the world of rock, she immediately genderized her response. "The first *woman* who said something to me was Siouxsie Sioux," she replied citing one

FIGURE 5-20.   Alanis Morissette's 1995 début album, *Jagged Little Pill,* not only earned the twenty-one-year-old singer-songwriter glowing reviews but it went on to win four Grammys (including Album of the Year). By selling over seventeen million copies (in the United States alone)—the most ever by a female performer—she also shattered female rock's historic glass ceiling. Photo by Kevin Mazur. Courtesy of Maverick Recording Company.

Alanis Morissette Goes through the Glass Ceiling

In an era of ever-narrowing demographic niches and increasingly fragmented subgenres, Morissette appropriated elements of rock, pop, folk, and dance music in the service of her own idiosyncratic personal vision. Her scathing, word-drunk anthems and soul-baring confessions dispensed with contemporary pop's carefully constructed forms, just as her challenging in-your-face vocal style abandoned the pretense of pop accessibility.

Morissette's highly anticipated 1998 follow-up, *Supposed Former Infatuation Junkie,* further testified to her restless creativity as she pushed herself in new directions vocally, lyrically, and musically. While both the reviews (and sales) of the album fell short of the success of her record-shattering début, the CD did generate one sizeable hit, the Middle-Eastern-tinged "Uninvited" (which won Morrisette the Grammy for Rock Song of the Year.)

of Britain's 1970s punk rebels. And when pushed to talk about other musical inspirations, Manson insisted, "They've always been women," proceeding to rattle off a list that included Ella Fitzgerald, Peggy Lee, Patti Smith, Chryssie Hynde, and Tina Turner.

Other contemporary female rockers, however, asserted their right to tap into rock 'n' roll's deepest roots without regard to gender. So, in 1993, when she released her critically acclaimed début, *Exile in Guyville*, Liz Phair not only treated listeners to a provocative new take on rock's most primal theme—sex—but she made no secret of the fact that her album's primary inspiration had been the macho swagger of the Rolling Stones. When asked about the genesis of her new record, Phair explained, "I started listening to *Exile on Main Street* [the Stones' classic 1972 album] over and over again. . . . I kept thinking I've got answers to this."

Meanwhile, the English singer/songwriter/guitarist PJ Harvey (whose own début album, *Dry*, preceded Phair's by a couple of months) had evolved her own response to rock's entrenched stereotypes by grappling with the music of such legendary figures as Robert Johnson, Howlin' Wolf, Jimi Hendrix, and Bob Dylan. In addition to acknowledging her debt to these and other rock patriarchs, Harvey also staked her claim to an entire anthology of styles and subjects that had traditionally been reserved for male rockers. In the words of one reviewer, "*Dry* showcased the sex 'n' gender themes that Harvey has, time and again, made her own," yet, as he went on to note, "her songs comprise a visceral, living diary writ large of growing up female."

Throughout the 1990s, dozens of other women performers were shredding both rock's stereotypes and society's gender roles. There was Melissa Etheridge—whose brand of straight-ahead mainstream guitar-rock came to most people's attention with the 1993 release of the album *Yes I Am* (the title a not-so-subtle reference to her openly lesbian lifestyle). And there was singer-songwriter/bass player Me'Shell Ndegeocello, who was—in the words of an early *Rolling Stone* article—"Bald, black, bisexual, and so original that radio stations had no idea what to do with her." Or Ani DiFranco, who as a twenty-year-old, updated indie rock's "Do-It-Yourself" philosophy by launching her own label, Righteous Babe Records, on which she released a quick succession of self-produced albums fusing acoustic folk introspection with a contemporary punk attitude. Of course, that's not to mention the decade's sisterhood of pop divas—Madonna, Celine, Whitney, Janet, Mariah—who had become such music-industry powerhouses that they didn't even need last names.

Ironically, despite all these breakthroughs, in 1996, when Sarah McLachlan took a look at the proposed lineup of alternative rock's new summer concert tour—dubbed Lollapaloosa—she couldn't find a single female act in the bunch. McLachlan, a Canadian singer-songwriter who had begun to achieve considerable success with her 1994 album, *Fumbling towards Ecstasy* (a collection of songs that mixed the personal and political), decided to appropriate alt-rock's own D.I.Y. attitude and offer her own alternative.

A year later she launched Lilith Fair, a traveling festival that featured many of the new female artists—including the Cardigans, Joan Osborne, Fiona Apple, and Sheryl Crow—who had begun to take over the pop charts. Named for a feminist heroine of Jewish mythology (Lilith was supposedly Adam's first wife, expelled from Eden for her lack of subservience), the event became one of the surprise successes of the summer. The following year, Lilith Fair featured an even more diverse lineup including new hip-hop queen "Missy Misdemenor" Elliot, pop-folk heroine Jewel, and blues-rock matriarch Bonnie Raitt.

Although rock had always had its share of commercially successful women performers, the conventional wisdom within the music industry was that they just didn't sell records like the men did. Although Madonna, Janet Jackson, Whitney Houston, and Mariah Carey had already made a serious dent in such obsolete attitudes, now the stage was set for an honest-to-goodness female blockbuster. It was provided by another Canadian singer-songwriter named Alanis Morissette, whose hard-edged confessional songs (blending folk and contemporary rock styles) were delivered with full-throated angst.

When she released her 1995 American début, *Jagged Little Pill* (on Madonna's Maverick label), the album began selling and just didn't stop. In addition to producing a pair of massive MTV-fueled hit singles ("Ironic" and "You Ought to Know"), the album eventually generated sales of over seventeen million copies—making it the best-selling album ever by a female performer. Morissette also proved to be the big winner at the following year's Grammy ceremonies, taking home four awards, including the big one, Album of the Year.

In 1998, Morissette released her much-anticipated follow-up album, *Supposed Former Infatuation Junkie.* Although it proved to be an ambitious and adventurous exploration of Middle-Eastern melodies and personal soul-searching, it didn't achieve the sales of her earlier megahit. What the album—and her impassioned live performances—did promise, however, was the possibility of something even more difficult for modern pop stars to attain (no matter what their gender): a career.

STATE OF THE ROCK 'N' ROLL NATION

"Careers?" came the disdainful response of MTV executive, Brent Hanson. "Artists and acts shouldn't rely on that." Hanson's warning—quoted in an April 1998 cover story in *Music Business International*—was only one more gloomy pronouncement in a depressing survey of the state of the rock 'n' roll nation. The article, entitled "A Rocky Ride," had been prompted by a significant end-of-the-decade drop in the worldwide sales of rock records, but it also focused prominently on one of the music industry's most disturbing trends—"the trend whereby even those people buying into rock are no longer making a long-term commitment to a band."

Although most record industry big-wigs admitted they were "concerned by the speed with which bands come and go from album to album," there was little agreement on a cause. An executive at one major American record label pointed the finger at the media for not "supporting artists today. They're operating on a song-by-song basis which will prove negative in the long run." Someone else blamed the record companies themselves for cutting back on the financing for the concert tours that used to help an audience bond with a band, thereby ensuring the kind of long-term relationship that had existed in earlier decades; "Now," he explained, "money goes into making videos."

According to an Atlantic Records VP, both the slump in rock record sales and the "swing towards pop acts like the Spice Girls and the Backstreet Boys," were simply part of a demographic vicious cycle. "If there's more pop, that means there are younger people buying records," he pointed out. "In turn that means you need to sell more pop records in order to sell more records." (And with Christina Aguilera and Britney Spears waiting on the other side of the millennial divide, pop chart demographics seemed destined to continue their downward trend, just as pop vs. rock sales figures seemed more secure than ever.)

Others had their own theories. "Rock and roll has historically been about rebellion," hypothesized one industry insider, "but today's teenagers are choosing other ways to rebel, not least because they view rock as their parents' music." (And with rap—and its hardcore hybrids—about to precipitate a new wave of controversy and condemnation, there was certainly a potent alternative in place for rock's once [and future?] rebels.)

Yet another factor cited in the article was the glut of new media like cable, satellite TV, and the Internet, which "enable consumers to sample music or other forms of entertainment in bite-sized chunks that are as large as their shrinking attention span." (And with three hundred million households worldwide plugged into MTV and thirty thousand new albums per year issued in the United States alone, it's no wonder that "one-hit wonders"—rather than rock, R & B, or pop—had become the music industry's most successful format.)

Amid all the article's handwringing, however, a few observers were more optimistic about the future of a genre that had always managed to renew itself by drawing not only from its own history, but from the deep reservoirs of blues, folk, gospel, and country music out of which it had originally emerged. Those who adopted a more sweeping historical perspective recognized that once again rock was simply experiencing an inevitable dormant cycle in its continuing evolution. As one music industry executive put it, "In hindsight I think we'll find that rock is going through one of its temporary sleeping periods, but will emerge in another form."

When he was interviewed for the article, MTV chairman and CEO Tom Freston expressed this reassuring perspective even more succinctly: "No one can drive a stake through rock's heart." But perhaps the last word should be given to the man who had first given rock 'n' roll its name all those years ago, Alan Freed. "Let's face it," Freed said—at a time when the music was undergoing an assault on its very existence—"rock and roll is bigger than all of us."

Activities and Projects
Chapter 5: Rock: From the Me Decade to the Millennium

1. Analyze the various rock subgenres that emerged during the 1970s. Identify their characteristics and illustrate with recordings by performers associated with each style.

2. Trace the influence of classical music on art rock and heavy metal during the late 1960s and early 1970s.

3. Describe the first generation of electronic synthesizers (mellotron, Moog, etc.) introduced during the late 1960s and early 1970s and assess their impact on the music of the era.

4. Explore the transformation of gender roles in rock from the 1950s through the 1970s. Include in your discussion the changing images of both men and women.

5. Use the work of specific bands to compare British and American heavy metal of the 1970s.

6. Survey the evolution of the "guitar hero" in heavy metal. Highlight the style's significant performers and the innovations they introduced.

7. Trace the singer-songwriter tradition from the mid-1970s to the revival of personal, acoustic-based styles during the 1980s and 1990s.

8. Create an overview of African-American popular music during the 1970s. Provide descriptions of Seventies soul, funk, the Sound of Philadelphia, and disco.

9. Although Bruce Springsteen was hailed as "rock 'n' roll's future," his music has drawn from the entire history of rock. Identify the influences of Springsteen's music at various stages of his career.

10. Compare British and American punk rock. Describe the musical and cultural impact of each.

11. Trace the impact of reggae on British and American rock.

12. Assess the disco craze of the late 1970s. Provide an analysis of the music, as well as an evaluation of its impact on popular culture.

13. Explore the impact of MTV on the evolution of popular music during the 1980s. Compare the conflicting images and values embodied by "pop" and "rock" performers during this period.

14. Survey the impact of "World Music" on the pop scene during the 1980s and 1990s. Cite specific examples of pop/rock fusions with music from Africa, Latin America, and the Caribbean Islands, and address the issue of "cultural imperialism" they have generated.

15. During the mid-1990s, country music surpassed "popular music" and "rock" as America's best-selling musical genre. Assess this phenomenon in the context of the pop music scene of the 1990s.

16. "Pop Divas" and "Girls with Guitars": explore the role of women in rock during the 1980s and 1990s.

17. The bands that forged the "alternative rock" revolution of the 1990s drew their inspiration from a wide musical spectrum. Select one alternative or indie rock band and trace the performers and musical styles from which it drew.

18.   Explore any of the cross-genre fusions that evolved during the 1990s. Describe how elements of rock, rap, heavy metal, punk, and underground technology-based styles merged to generate new hybrids.

19.   Survey the role of the Internet in the marketing and distribution of popular music. Address the issues generated by this transformation of the recording industry.

20.   Trace the ongoing dynamic between "pop" and "rock" from the 1980s to the present.

6

Rap: Talking Drum of the Global Village

In 1979, when "Rapper's Delight" became the first rap record to break into the mainstream, hip-hop culture—and the music to which it gave birth—had already been evolving in Bronx, New York, schoolyards and Uptown dance clubs for five years. In fact, it was only after the surprising success of the Sugar Hill Gang's twelve-inch single (which went to number thirty-six on the *Billboard* pop chart) that the strange new musical style took on its now familiar name.

Set to the infectious groove of Chic's recent disco hit, "Good Times," the Sugar Hill Gang's stream of chanted rhymes went on for over fourteen minutes. After exhorting their listening audience to party, each of the "trecherous trio" of MCs (who named themselves after the New Jersey–based independent label for which they recorded) took turns extolling his wardrobe, sex appeal, and, most of all, his own verbal prowess (hence the title, "Rapper's Delight"). So it was that the newest species of urban dance music took for its name a word that has been associated with "oral expression" since at least the sixteenth century.

By the 1960s, the word *rap* had already secured a permanent place in the distinctive vernacular of black Americans, appearing in the *Dictionary of Afro-American Slang* as both a verb ("to hold conversation") and a noun ("a long impressive monologue"). In fact, one young civil rights leader of the era, H. "Rap" Brown, had earned his nickname on the basis of his highly charged political oratory. Any analysis that focuses exclusively on rap music's lyrical content, however, tells only half the etymological story.

For long before the word "rap" assumed its association with spoken language, it referred to pure sound—the sound of a quick, sharp blow. Therefore, through an intriguing quirk of linguistics (linking oral communication and percussive statement), a revolutionary form of contemporary popular music can be linked to one of the most ancient and significant elements in African-American culture: the talking drum.

Throughout the American South, and through painful experience, slaveowners learned of the ability of newly arrived Africans to communicate via the drum. As the black poet and musicologist Amiri Baraka (aka LeRoi Jones) explained: "They took the drum away. [The slaves] weren't just beating on that wood—they were actually communicating. . . . That's where the term 'rap' actually comes from. When they got through 'rapping' on that wood—then all kinds of things would happen: the storehouse might burn up, slaves would run off, somebody might get poisoned. So very quickly they had to take that drum away from the slaves." Yet, as Amiri Baraka notes, the beat went on. For even after the slaves had been deprived of the instrument itself, "all the music they made was percussive—without the drum."

A similar point has been expressed by Albert Murray, in his study of African-American music, *Stompin' the Blues*. Murray begins by pointing out that all the music made by black Americans throughout their history in the United States has been characterized by its "emphasis on percussive statement." He, too, traces this impulse to the Motherland, and again invokes the image of the talking drum: "[It is] the African-dervived disposition," he writes, "to use all instruments as if they were extentions of the talking drum—so the music is incanatory and percussive."

The origin and evolution of rap music—which was initially referred to as "break-beat music"—provides yet another link to this "African-derived disposition." The key to unlocking this connection depends on an understanding of the term "break" in the jargon of popular music. Traditionally, the "break" was (as the word itself suggests) a short respite or interlude within a musical performance. In a song, the break could refer to a brief instrumental section between the vocal passages, while in a jazz instrumental it usually described a short solo by one member of the ensemble. In the world of "break-beat music," however, the word specifically meant a *percussion* break.

TO THE HIP HOP

Looking back at this latest incarnation of the talking drum, Public Enemy producer and rap entrepreneur Bill Stephney stresses that for the music's inventors it was the "drum" and not the "talking" that was their prime concern. "The point wasn't rapping," he reminds us, "it was rhythm." As he goes on to describe the early hip-hop experience, we see not only how the innovative techniques of local disc jockeys turned neighborhood auditoriums into venues for modern versions of ancient African rites, but we are reminded once again that before there was the "word" there was the "beat."

"DJs cutting records left and right," is how Stephney remembers it, "taking the big drum break from Led Zeppelin's 'When the Levee Breaks,' mixing it together with 'Ring My Bell,' then with a Bob James Mardi Gras jazz record and some James Brown. You'd have two thousand kids in a community center in New York moving back and forth, back and forth, like some kind of tribal war dance. . . . It was the rapper's role to match this intensity rhythmically. No one knew what he was saying. He was just rocking the mike." Such was the role of the rapper in this pre–"Rapper's Delight" era.

During this formative period, the person "rocking the mike" was referred to as the Master of Ceremonies (a.k.a. Microphone Controller) or, more typically, "the MC." As one early participant points out, there is quite a difference between the modern rapper and the old-school MC of the mid-1970s: "The way rap is *now*—it isn't the way it was *then*," claims Lil Rodney Cee (who went on to become one-half of the duo Double Trouble). "Then it was just phrases; the MC would say little phrases like, 'To the Eastside, make money. To the Westside, make money, or 'To the rock, rock, rock, to the rock, rock, rock.'"

In fact, it was another of these free-form dance hall rhymes created by the old-school MCs to pump up their audiences that would provide the permanent label for the new street culture that was evolving in New York's minority communities. Appropriately, it was this very slogan that had found its way into the opening chorus of the Sugar Hill Gang's breakthrough record:

I said a hip hop
The hippie the hippie
To the hip hip hop, a you don't stop the rockit. . . .

By now, New York's indigenous "hip-hop" culture not only encompassed the DJ-generated dance music and the chanted exhortations of the MC, but the colorful iconography of the grafitti writers and the choreographic pyrotechnics of the breakdancers (as well as the creations of anonymous street-fashion trendsetters). Ironically, of all these forms of expressions, it was the music that initially got the least attention from the mainstream media. Although huge boom boxes blasting homemade cassettes did expose the sound of the new music to a dumbfounded (and, for the most part, repelled) general public, in the beginning, both breakdancing (or "b-boying" as it was also called) and graffiti writing attracted considerably more scrutiny.

At first, public officials, editorial writers, and TV commentators turned their attention to the "scourge of graffiti" that had suddenly turned New York subway cars into incomprehensible (anxiety-producing) mobile billboards. Before long, however, a few urban sociologists began heralding the magic-marker scrawls and spray-painted symbols as a positive affirmation of individuality and downtown galleries sponsored high-profile exhibits of "graffiti art." Soon, the novelist Norman Mailer would write a laudatory ode on the phenomenon which appeared as the introduction to *The Faith of Graffiti*, a glossy coffee table photo book. Finally, in 1983, the docudrama film, *Wild Style!*—whose title was a reference to a specific Brooklyn-based graffiti style—presented the first insightful (even celebratory) glimpse into the hip-hop scene in all its incarnations.

FIGURE 6-1. Museum of Modern Art Film Stills Collection.

Wild Style! and the Birth of Hip Hop

This image from the 1983 docudrama, *Wild Style!,* captures several key elements of the hip-hop culture that was emerging from New York's inner-city neighborhoods.

In the shadow of a graffiti-adorned wall, a couple of members of the celebrated Rock Steady Crew breakdance on a cardboard field as a boom-box blasts out beats from a homemade cassette. In just a few years, hip-hop's vibrant verbal component—known as rap—would become one of the most potent forces on the pop music market.

It was breakdancing, however, with its crowd-pleasing, acrobatic virtuosity that most successfully crossed over into the media mainstream. A year after the low-budget film *Wild Style!* documented the moves of such breakdance pioneers as the Rock Steady Crew, a major Hollywood feature film, *Flashdance,* incorporated hip-hop moves into the choreography supposedly created by its lead character (a hip New York dancer played by Jennifer Beals). Soon, photogenic young breakdancers had moved from street corner "throw-downs" (competitions) on fields of cardboard to featured spots in soft drink commercials and TV sitcoms.

While breakdancing may have been quickly appropriated by the media, the break-beats that accompanied its crowd-pleasing moves proved to be a harder sell. For, at the time, America was dancing to a different beat. In retrospect, however, it is clear that there was an intimate relationship between what was happening in Manhattan's glittery disco palaces and the revolutionary sonic explorations that was taking place on the gritty streets of the Bronx.

For example, both disco and break-beat music were fundamentally dance-oriented styles that relied on disc jockeys drawing from vast reservoirs of recordings as they segued from song to song looking for the perfect beat. According to David Toop (author of the definitive history, *Rap Attack*), the ultimate goal of the "less creative disco

DJs, was to slip-cue smoothly from the end of one record into the beginning of the next." The result was that "the disco records which emerged out of the influence of this type of mixing tended to feature long introductions, anthemic choruses and extended vamp sections, all creating a tension which was released by the break." In Toop's apt and appealing metaphor, however: "Break-beat music simply ate the cherry off the cake and threw the rest away."

Unlike their disco counterparts, the hip-hop DJs were all about discovering the best breaks and finding ways to extend them until they had an entire dance hall of "b-boys" and "b-girls" (as the denizens of the hip-hop scene were known) in an ecstatic spell. The pioneering break-beat disc jockey, Afrika Bambaattaa, recalled the technique of one of *his* heroes, the legendary Kool DJ Herc: "Now he took the music of like Mandrill, like 'Fencewalk,' certain disco records that had funky percussion breaks like . . . 'Apache' and he just kept that beat *going*. It might be that certain part of the record that everybody waits for—they just let their inner self go and get wild."

MASTERS OF RECORDS

In an effort to isolate and extend the break, hip-hop disc jockeys employed two turntables and two copies of the same record. In this way they could quickly cue up one disk just as the break on the other was coming to an end. A major milestone in the evolution of this technique occured when Grandmaster Flash (who, along with Grand Wizard Theodore, is recognized as the genre's most significant innovator) rigged up his turntables to a set of headphones so he could orchestrate these transitions with split-second accuracy. "I jumped for joy," Flash recalled years later, when he described the excitement he felt at that moment.

Originally, he explains, his "main objective was to take small parts of records and, at first, keep it on time, no tricks keep it on time. I'm talking about very short beats, maybe forty seconds, keeping it going for about five minutes." Later, Flash developed other techniques such as "punch phrasing" (cranking up the volume on one turntable to introduce a brief musical punctuation as the second copy of the record keeps spinning) and, of course, "scratching" (manually manipulating the record on the turntable in order to create a percussive rhythmic wash of sound).

Over time, therefore, hip-hop DJs actually transformed the turntable into a musical instrument. And, even more than other musicians, their appeal depended not only on how skillfully they "played," but also on the repertoire they chose. As David Toop explains, "A large part of the disc jockey's mystique and power is their resourcefulness in finding unknown or obscure records that can move a crowd" with what he describes as "non-stop collages of the b-boy style."

According to some of its creators, the music that emerged from such spontaneous assemblages was, in fact, a conscious reaction against the era's homogenized sound of disco. "The Bronx wasn't into radio music no more. It was like an anti-disco movement," Afrika Bambaataa remembers. "Like you had new wavers and other people coming out and saying, 'Disco sucks.' Well, the same thing with hip-hop [DJs] 'cos they was against the disco that was being played on the radio. Everybody wanted the funky style that Kool Herc was playing." In fact, it was after hearing Kool Herc's potent blends of reggae, disco, Latin music, and 70s funk that Bambaataa recalls thinking," "'Oh, I got records like that.' When I came on the scene after him I started getting a name for a *master of records*. Myself I used to play the weirdest stuff. . . . Everybody thought I was crazy."

A brief inventory of a typical Bambaataa mix makes clear just how schizophrenic the music of the early hip-hop scene really was. In addition to standard rhythm and blues–based cuts by the likes of James Brown, Sly and the Family Stone, Jimmy Castor, and George Clinton, he might throw in a riff from the Rolling Stones' "Honky Tonk Woman," a bass-and-drum segment off "Inside Looking Out" by Grand Funk Railroad, follow that with a couple of seconds of "Sergeant Pepper's Lonely Hearts Club Band," a snippet from the Monkees, a taste of the theme from the movie *The Pink Panther*, and a TV commercial.

There was, however, a method to Bambaataa's madness. "I used to like to catch people who'd say, 'I don't like rock. I don't like Latin.' he remembers. "I'd throw on Mick Jagger—you'd see the blacks and the Spanish just *throwing* down, dancing crazy. I'd say, 'I thought you said you don't like rock. . . . Well, you just danced to the Rolling Stones'." As David Toop expresses it in *Rap Attack:* "Hip hop was the new music by virtue of its finding a way to absorb all other music."

FIGURE 6-2. Hip-hop historians have dubbed Afrika Bambaataa (kneeling in foreground) the "Godfather of Rap." Photo by George DuBose. Courtesy of Tommy Boy Records.

Afrika Bambaataa: Making the Planet Rock

Along with Kool DJ Herc and Grandmaster Flash, Afrika Bambamaataa is credited with inventing the innovative "break-beat" style that became the foundation of a new musical and cultural movement. Celebrated as a "master of records," by the late 1970s Bambaataa was spontaneously cutting and pasting beats from his massive collection of rock, soul, and Latin albums into pulsating multicultural mixes.

In 1982, he introduced the new hip-hop dejaying style that he had perfected in Uptown schoolyards to white audiences at Downtown dance clubs. That same year, he assembled a new crew (the Soul Sonic Force) and—in the recording, "Planet Rock"—introduced a new high-tech style he called *electrofunk*. One of the most influential records of the past quarter-century, "Planet Rock" has become the inspiration for an ever-expanding family of synthesized dance styles from 1980s "house music" to 1990s "drum-and-bass."

From the very beginning, rap's nondenominational, multicultural mix reflected both New York's ethnic melting pot and the unfettered creative vision of those original "masters of records." One of these, the Bronx DJ Charlie Chase, was a founding member of the celebrated Cold Crush Brothers, who appeared prominently in the film *Wild Style!* Born Carlos Mandes, Chase—who traces his own roots back to Puerto Rican, French, and Jewish ancestry—made a conscious effort to introduce "the Latin point of view" into his hip-hop mixes. "It was great! I would sneak in Spanish records. Beats only, and if the bass line was funky enough, I would do that too," he explains. Like Bambaattaa (his African-American counterpart) he, too, was often way ahead of his audience: "They never knew it was a Spanish record. And if I told them that they'd get off the floor."

As in so many other styles of America's popular music, the vital Latin tinge in hip-hop has been largely ignored. As Juan Flores points out in his article "Puerto Rocks: New York Ricans Stake Their Claim," however, "Puerto Ricans are integral to the history of hip hop. . . . They helped make rap what it was to become, as they played a constituitive role in the stylistic definition of graffiti writing and breakdancing." Whether it was the Latin seasonings of Charlie Chase's mixes, the artful scrawls of Lee Quinones from the notorious Brooklyn graffiti squad, the Fabulous Five, or the patented head spins of Crazy Legs (Richie Colon) from the Rock Steady Crew, even a cursory glance at hip-hop's history attests to the validity of Flores's statement.

Nor was hip-hop's Spanish contigent the only one to add key ingredients to the style multicultural mix. In fact, the person who many consider rap music's primary progenitor—Kool DJ Herc—drew deeply from his own West Indian heritage. Born Clive Campbell on the island of Jamaica, Herc left Kingston for the Bronx in 1967. He brought with him two contemporary Jamaican musical traditions that would become twin pillars of the emerging hip-hop movement.

In Jamaica, enterprising freelance dance promoters had pioneered the use of mobile music units featuring powerful speakers, which were referred to locally as "sound systems." Often, rival operators would engage in competitions to determine who had the most powerful system, thereby claiming both bragging rights and customers for their own dances. When Herc came to New York, he constructed his own powerful sound system, wired it up to the nearest street light, and was soon attracting a loyal audience for his playground parties; in David Toop's words, "Herc murdered the Bronx opposition with his volume and shattering frequency range."

The other aspect of Jamaican popular music that Herc imported to America was "toasting," a peculiarly Jamaican form of verbal display. As their sound system pumped out the stripped-to-the-bones rhythm tracks (known as "dubs") drawn from recent ska and reggae records, early 1960s pioneers such as U Roy and Big Youth would celebrate themselves (or denegrate their rivals) in semi-improvised, boastful verses. By the mid-1970s, Herc also was in the process of creating his own synthesis of traditional Jamaican toasting with a new Bronx MC style. "He knew that a lot of American blacks were not getting into the reggae of his country," Afrika Bambaataa has stated. "He took the same thing that they was doing—toasting—and did it with American records, Latin or records with beats." By the early 1990s, many young rappers, looking back at the roots of their music, rediscovered the Jamaican toasting/dub tradition and began incorporating its flavas in their own productions.

US GIRLS CAN BOOGIE, TOO

Although many of hip-hop's founding fathers may have concurred with their patron saint, James Brown, that "It's a Man's World," as the lyrics of the Godfather of Soul's classic song make clear, "It wouldn't be nothin' without a woman or a girl." It should be no surprise, therefore, that behind the standard hip-hop history there lurks a hip-hop "herstory" as well.

In the realm of graffiti, for example, there were a number of women "writers" who were willing to brave the dangers of the train yards (as well as the contempt of their male counterparts) to make their mark on the traveling marquees of the NYC transit system. Although most of the creators of the elaborate subway car murals that flashed through New York in the 1970s have been forgotten, because of her featured role in *Wild Style!*, we know that Lady Pink (Sandra Fabara) was one of them. Not only did she evolve her own unique graffiti style—often using representations of women in her works—but Lady Pink also used her art to make political statements (including some with a distinctly feminist orientation): "War, Crime, Corruption, Poverty, Inflation, Pollution, Racism, Injustice . . . This Is a Man's World!"

There were even more women represented in hip-hop's breakdance scene. Some were involved in all-girl ensembles (such as the Dynamic Dolls); others such as Daisy Castro (a.k.a. Baby Love), one of the celebrated Rock Steady Crew, were valued members of mostly male groups. In an interview with Nancy Guevara for her article, "Women Writin' Rappin' Breakin' " (collected in William Eric Perkins's *Droppin' Science*), Castro explained that in order to differentiate themselves from the b-boys, she and the other b-girls consciously developed their own alternate style: "We'd do a more feminine style than the guys just to show that we're not girls trying to look like guys." Looking back, Castro regrets that she sometimes bowed out of the Rock Steady Crew's competitions against other all-male crews but is proud that others who followed her did take up the challenge. "There are girls that are dancing as good as the guys," she told Guevara. "And they're willing to take on anybody that comes their way."

In fact, it was its highly competitive nature that had encouraged the belief that hip-hop culture itself was inherently a man's world. As David Toop explains, this perception was especially true when it came to rap's verbal duels: "Since rapping has strong roots in the predominantly male activities of toasts and [the] dozens," he notes, "it is not surprising that men see it as the musical equivalent of a sport like baseball. They are prepared to accept that women can do it, but see the competitive element as the final deterrent." Yet, as Toop also found out—from a very reliable source—women rappers had been there from the very beginning.

"In the early days of hip-hop," Grandmaster Flash remembers, "there being more female crews than male." Among rap's roster of women pioneers were the Mercedes Ladies, Sweet-Tee, Sequence (who recorded the feminist-boast rap, "Funk You Up" for Sugar Hill Records back in 1979), and Us Girls (whose b-girl anthem, "Us Girls Can Boogie Too" was featured in the 1984 hip-hop film, *Beat Street*).

OUT OF THE UNDERGROUND

Now that all of the varied elements of a strikingly original new form of contemporary popular music were in place, what was needed was someone with the creativity and charisma to take it to the next level. As David Toop indicates, a Bronx crew—led by just such a figure—was about to do just that. It was none other than "Grandmaster Flash and the Furious Five," he explains in *Rap Attack,* who "embody the gradual move from underground to overground."

When Grandmaster Flash first started "cutting and mixing" records in neighborhood schoolyards, crowds would be so mesmerized by his technique that, as Flash remembers it, they "would stop dancing and just gather round as if it was a seminar." Therefore, in order to channel the audience's diverted energy, he decided to bring in an MC. Soon, Keith Wiggins (better known as Cowboy)—one of the genres' true pioneers—was working the crowd with rhymes that both entreated the crowd to party and paid homage to Flash's turntable skills. "He was the first MC to talk about the DJ," one old-school rapper asserted. "He would talk for Grandmaster Flash and say how great Flash is."

With as many as forty-five crates of LPs and twelve-inch singles behind his homemade DJ rig, Flash was a true "master of records," with a collection that ranged from the percussion heavy disco of Jamaica's Incredible Bongo Band to the jazz-funk of Donald Byrd to the 1960s street poetry of the Last Poets and the soul harmonies of the Delfonics. In addition, he also was one of the greatest showman in hip-hop history. Like blues guitar virtuosos (from Charlie Patton to Jimi Hendrix)—who would often wow the crowd by playing behind their backs or with their tongues—Flash sent his audiences into a frenzy by playing on his "wheels of steel" backward, as well as with his feet, nose, and other body parts. Before long, these skills had taken him from Bronx playgrounds and local high school auditoriums to Uptown clubs such as the Back Door. By 1976, Flash was performing at the famous Audubon Ballroom in front of more than three thousand b-boys and b-girls from across New York City and New Jersey!

"For three years things were going great," Flash told David Toop; "then all of a sudden you hear on the radio, 'To the hip-hop, hippety-hop, you don't stop.' " It was 1979, and the Sugar Hill Gang's "Rapper's Delight" had burst on an unsuspecting world. But Flash was not exactly delighted. "They got a record on the radio and that shit was haunting me," he told Toop. "I felt we should have been the first to do it. We were the first *group* to really do this—someone took our shot. Every night I would hear this fucking record on the radio. . . . I was hearing this shit in my dreams."

EVERYBODY'S RAPPING: FROM RHYTHM TO RHYME

The Sugar Hill Gang's 1979 début may have caused Grandmaster Flash a couple of sleepless nights when it became the record that introduced the hip-hop sound to a mainstream audience, but the success of "Rapper's Delight" also had the more fundamental effect of shifting hip-hop's traditional balance of power from its rhythms to its rhymes.

After five years of intense creative experimentation, break-beat DJs such as Flash had evolved a repertoire of revolutionary turntable techniques in order to cut and mix crateloads of vinyl into complex sonic assemblages. And while DJs did recruit a few fast-talking members of the hip-hop community to function as Masters of Ceremonies for their free-form dance parties, it was still the Masters of Records who were the main attraction. In the words of one old-school DJ (Grandmaster Caz), throughout this period, it was all about "who had the baddest beats."

When break-beat music moved from the streets and dance clubs into the recording studio, however, these turntable virtuosi found themselves replaced by professional musicians playing actual *musical instruments.* For example, when Sylvia and Joe Robinson (owners of Sugar Hill Records) decided to capture on disc the sound of the strange new style of music coming out of New York's underground, they did what they had always done when they cut a record—they hired a band. So, instead of hearing a DJ scratching out a sample from a *recording* of Chic's "Good Times" (as one element of a complex rhythmic collage), what one hears on "Rapper's Delight" is a couple of studio musicians simply re-creating Chic's hook endlessly throughout the fourteen-minute side.

Naturally, when they were set against such a simplified rhythmic foundation, the Sugar Hill Gang's lyrical blitz took on unprecedented significance. By the time the record ended, the nonstop series of slang-studded soliloquies by the three MCs totaled over 360 lines! No wonder the huge, new audience that discovered the world of hip-hop when they first heard "Rapper's Delight" immediately associated the style's name with its verbal component.

THE AFRICAN-AMERICAN ORAL TRADITION: FROM GRIOTS TO THE GODFATHER OF SOUL

Like its rhythmic foundation, rap's lyric component has deep roots in African-American culture. Nor was the talking drum the only ancient African tradition to find its way into the new genre. For example, some musicologists quickly established a direct connection between the hip-hop orators from the Bronx and the *griots* of the Senegambian region of Africa.

Variously defined as "praise singer" or "oral historian," the griot (a.k.a. *jali* or *finah*) has for many centuries had a significant role in various tribal societies of West Africa. In her book on the cultures of this area, *Mandigo Kingdoms of the Senegambia,* Charlote A. Quinn, explains that it is the griot's "profession . . . to collect bardic tales, songs, and poems which honor their patrons and vilify their sponsor's enemies." Whether they chanted verses passed down over generations recounting ancient tribal battles or performed newly improvised songs satirizing some stingy patron, the griot's verbal powers have made him a respected figure in tribal life right up to the present day.

So, although he may not have realized it, when Grandmaster Flash's first MC, Cowboy, picked up his mike to acclaim the break-beat master as "the pulsating, inflating, disco shaking, heartbreaking man on the turntable," he was just forging another link in an age-old oral tradition. In fact, this is just one of the numerous ways that rap can be related to the African-American affinity for the spoken word.

Take that traditional form of verbal jousting commonly known as "the dozens." Typically the province of adolescent males, the dozens is an informal contest involving an escalating exchange of personal and familial insult that has been played in America for countless generations. A related activity, "signifying," also involves a subtle form of linguistic self-aggrandisement and hyperbole. Although outsiders might be taken aback by what they perceive as unnecessarily extreme language or exaggerated imagery, within the culture there is the recognition that an individual is "just signifying."

Such inflated boasts, which have always provided one of rap's dominant themes, also draw their inspiration from early country blues recordings on which singers can be heard extolling their sexual magnetism, cleverness, and musical ability. A similar macho swagger often infused both the lyrics and the newly electrified musical accompaniment of post–World War II rhythm and blues. By the early 1950s, songs like the Dominoes' "Sixty Minute Man" (a thinly veiled ode to sexual stamina) and Bo Diddley's "Who Do You Love?" (in which the narrator brags, among other things, that he "wears a cobra snake for a necktie" and has a house with a chimney "made out of human skulls") had carried this tradition into the modern pop charts. In fact, even the new genre's most controversial branch—gangsta rap—has its roots in one of America's earliest form of popular music: the folk ballad.

From the very beginning of our country, these narrative songs were dominated by violence of every description. There are dozens of Anglo-American ballads such as "Omie Wise" and "Knoxville Girl" (both from the early 1800s) that recount the story of men who brutally murder their lovers, while scores of other ballads celebrate the exploits of outlaw heroes—from the Wild West gunslinger Billy the Kid to the Depression-era bankrobber Pretty Boy Floyd (who was the subject of a ballad by Woody Guthrie).

Gradually, elements of this Anglo-American tradition filtered into the songs of African-Americans, who—by the end of the nineteenth century—had created their own body of blues-style ballads. Often these feature so-called badmen such as Stagolee, Railroad Bill, and Jack Hardy, who are portrayed as remorsely reveling in their anti-social acts. As William Barlow explains in his book *Looking Up at Down: The Emergence of Blues Culture*, these African-American anti-heroes "who belligerently transgressed white society's legal and moral order," served as vehicles for vicarious rebellion for an oppressed people. And thus was the "gangsta" celebrated as a folk hero long before the advent of rap.

Nor was there much really new in hip-hop's colorful vernacular. Both rap's slang and its heavily rhymed couplets can be connected to an array of twentieth-century African-American musical and linguistic sources. Among these are the hipster jive introduced by popular entertainers such as Cab Calloway (who even published his own *Hepster's Dictionary* in order to aid the uninitiated), the style of jazz singing known as "vocaleeze" (in which slang-studded lyrics were adapted to fit the famous solo improvisations of bebop instrumentalists), and the distinctive rhymed patter of 1950s black radio disk jockeys (such as Dr. Daddy-O and Jocko Henderson).

Other rap antecedents not only include the age-old children's patting game, "Hambone" (which was typically accompanied by naughtly rhymes infused by Southern slang), but the powerful, intensely rhythmic rhetoric of the black preacher. More immediate sources of rap also can be found in the black poetry movement of the 1960s (as represented by LeRoi Jones and the Last Poets), in the clever couplets of Muhammad Ali, and in the so-called lover's raps of the 1970s (as intoned by Isaac Hayes, Millie Jackson, or Barry White). Many rappers also cite the work of Gil Scott-Heron, who (during the 1970s and 1980s) won considerable attention for his fusion of politically charged poetry and potent jazz and Latin-based rhythms.

Finally, rap embodies two of the oldest and most pervasive aspects of African-American culture. The first of these is ritual competition—whether it is in the arena of verbal wit (the dozens), musical vituosity (jam-session cutting contests), or dancing (either tap or break). The other is the *call-and-response* structure—between a soloist exchanging a series of brief musical statements with his band or a performer engaging in a similar forum with her audience.

Yet, if one had to choose the single source that most directly and profoundly influenced early rap (infusing every aspect of the music with its own essence), that source would be none other than the Godfather of Soul—and Grand Minister of Funk—James Brown. Not only did Brown's recordings provide break-beat DJs with much of their repertoire but, as David Toop explains, "Brown was the most direct connection between soulful testifying and Bronx poetry. Though he could sing the pants off the average vocalist . . . many of his best performances existed in a a unique vocal space somewhere between speech and scream. His position as a spokeman for black consciousness and minister of super-heavy funk might have been on the wane by the 70s, but for the b-boys he was still Soul Brother Number One."

RAP ON WAX: THE FIRST GENERATION

The first flurry of rap records all replicated the basic approach of "Rapper's Delight." Recorded as twelve-inch singles by tiny, independent labels (such as Sugar Hill, Enjoy, Tommy Boy, and Profile), they usually featured a three- or four-person "crew" of MCs who, in classic old-school style took turns declaiming their assorted boasts and party slogans, while a small studio band laid down a catchy riff (more than likely, yet another rip-off of Chic's "Good Times.")

One of the first to break this pattern was a former Harlem DJ turned rapper, Kurtis Blow, who released his first record—the seasonal novelty single, "Christmas Rapping"—late in 1979. In fact, from the very beginning of his career, Kurtis Blow had been breaking a number of already established rap precedents. Not only was Kurtis Blow a solo act (unlike virtually all of other early MCs on record), but he also pioneered the move away from the LP-sized single that had been the standard rap format; a year after his recorded début, he issued the first full-length rap album. Finally, as opposed to the other first-generation rappers, Kurtis wasn't signed to one of the up-start independent record companies, but to a major mainstream label—Mercury.

In 1980, "The Breaks," a single from Kurtis Blow's self-titled début album, earned the rapper the genre's first gold record. "The Breaks" was built around a taut, rhythmically propulsive groove that provided the perfect backdrop for Blow's humorous if-it-wasn't-for-bad-luck-I-wouldn't-have-no-luck-at-all plot line. He even helped establish rap's new visual image by appearing on the album cover shirtless, his pumped-up bare chest adorned only by a string of heavy gold chains. So it was no surprise that, later the same year, when the ABC-TV news magazine *20/20* wanted to do a story on pop music's latest fad, it was Kurtis Blow who was selected as the feature's main focus.

Of course, way before the mainstream media had picked up on the rap phenomenon (and even before it had found its way onto records), hip-hop culture in all its forms had infiltrated New York's hip Downtown dance scene. "Cassette tapes used to be our albums before anybody recorded what they call rap records," Afrika Bambaataa remembered. "People started hearing all this rapping coming out of boxes. When they heard the tapes down in the Village they wanted to know, 'Who's this black DJ who's playing all this rock and new wave up in the Bronx?' and," Bam boasted, "I was the only one playing all these different forms of music." Soon Bambaataa was spinning his mix of funk, rock, and experimental synthesizer records at traditionally white dance venues such as the Mudd Club, the Ritz, and ultimately (for as many as four thousand dancers) the Roxy.

Among those who encountered Bambaataa's innovative synthesis of hip-hop and new wave during this period was Blondie, one of the new wave's premier bands. In 1975, Blondie had been in the vanguard of the New York punk movement (along with Television, the Ramones, and the Talking Heads). The band had already proved themselves more "adaptable" than their colleagues, and before the decade ended they had even scored a number one pop hit (with a synthesizer-enhanced disco-oriented single "Heart of Glass"). Blondie's follow-up, a cover version of a reggae song, "The Tide Is High," also went to number one. In 1981, Blondie became the first to manage that same feat, by taking a rap-style single to the very top of the pop charts.

In the single—"Rapture"—Blondie's frontwoman, Debbie Harry, actually offers an ode to the Bronx-based street styles that had made their way Downtown. Set to a restrained rhythmic groove, Harry's rhymed couplets not only allude generally to various aspects of hip-hop culture, but they make specific references to some of its best-known figures. For example, according to the song's lyrics, "Fab Five Freddy" (a hip-hop promoter who eventually achieved fame as the host of "Yo, MTV Raps") tells the singer that everybody's "fly" (thereby introducing some up-to-the-minute b-boy slang). And when the lyrics go on to describe a "DJ spinnin' [records]" for a throng of happy dancers, Harry notes: "Flash is fast/Flash is cool;" of course, at this point, there's no mistaking to whom she's referring.

When we last left Grandmaster Flash, he was more than a little chagrined at the historic breakthrough of "Rapper's Delight." But Flash needn't have worried. Not long after the amazing success of the Sugar Hill Gang single, Grandmaster Flash and the Furious Five had the opportunity to cut their own rap record for Enjoy, an independent label (owned by R & B record producer, Bobby Robinson) that was trying to jump on the hip-hop bandwagon. Although the label's studio band gave "Superrappin' " a powerful rhythmic kick and the Furious Five were effective in transferring the free-wheeling, complex interplay of their live performances onto vinyl, Flash was disappointed both with the technical limitation of the record and with its lack of commercial success. "Bobby didn't really have the push to get us out there," Flash recalls. "We got kinda angry at him and we went to the Hill."

It was therefore as Sugar Hill artists that Grandmaster Flash and the Furious Five would make a record that for the first time truly reflected the radical innovations that had been devised by the first generation of hip-hop DJs. In David Toop's words, that single—"The Adventures of Grandmaster Flash on the Wheels of Steel" (released in 1981)—"was the first record really to show that rap was something other than an offshoot of disco. Where other releases *translated* hip-hop, 'Adventures' was as close as any record would ever come to being hip-hop." For, rather than simply relying on a band to provide the basic backing track for the Furious Five's rap, it was Grandmaster Flash's own turntables (his "wheels of steel") that took the record's audience on what would prove to be one of the greatest musical adventures in rap history.

Just as he had done for years at hip-hop dances (both Uptown and Downtown), Flash now used his formidable turntable technique to assemble a diverse assortment of records into a seamless sonic collage. Not only did he pay tribute to rap's first (and most overused) riff by spinning a couple of seconds of Chic's "Good Times," but he also mixed in the new variation of that song's distinctive hook, "Another One Bites the Dust," recorded by the British glam-rock band, Queen. Attentive listeners (and concerned copyright holders) also might have recognized bits and pieces of records by the Sugar Hill Gang ("8th Wonder"), Spoonie Gee ("Monster Jam"), the Furious Five ("Birthday Party"), and—in a final display of his wit and turntable mastery—the line "Flash is fast" (three times in quick succession), taken directly from Blondie's "Rapture."

THE SOUND AND THE FURY: "PLANET ROCK" AND "THE MESSAGE"

Meanwhile, Flash's old rival, Afrika Bambaataa, also was bringing some of the hip-hop DJ's former glory into the recording studio; in fact, he was in the process of charting rap music's most visionary new direction. Having signed with Tommy Boy Records (one of the most important of rap's independent labels), Bambaataa established a creative collaboration with Arthur Baker, a white record producer, who once again reinforced early rap's multicultural musical vision. Although their first record, "Jazzy Sensation," hinted at things to come, it was "Planet Rock," released in early 1982, that first introduced the revolutionary new musical concept that Bambaataa named *electrofunk*.

Ever the "master of records," Afrika Bambaataa had long been enamored of a particular style of synthesizer music that had developed as an offshoot of the Eurodisco sound created by producers such as Giorgio Morodor (best known for his work on Donna Summer's orgasmic hit, "Love to Love You Baby"). While Bambaataa collected recordings by experimental synthesizer-based bands such as Yellow Magic Orchestra and Gary Numan, his favorite electronic group was Kraftwerk, a German ensemble that had evolved a unique brand of atmospheric, minimalist dance music.

So when he set about assembling "Planet Rock," Bambaataa combined cut-up portions of Kraftwerk's thirteen-and-a-half-minute masterpiece "Trans-Europe Express" as the backdrop for the raps of his current crew of MCs, the Soul Sonic Force. He also infused his record's rhythm with the distinctive beats of another of the era's technological innovations, the Roland TR-808.

At the time, the TR-808 was the latest in a line of electronic "drum machines" that had first been employed by some of hip-hop's Seventies funk heroes (such as Sly and the Family Stone, Stevie Wonder, and Graham Central Station). Now, Bambaataa and Baker took the Roland's synthesized beats, combined them with Kraftwerk's "Trans-Europe Express" atmospherics and the Soul Sonic Force's old-school call-and-response raps, and created a complex and compulsively danceable hip-hop collage. An electrofunk masterpiece, "Planet Rock" not only earned Bambaataa a gold record (and reaffirmed his status as the "Godfather of Hip Hop"), but it also immediately made the drum machine (or "beat box" as it became known) one of the most important weapons in the hip-hop arsenal.

In retrospect, it is also apparent that what Afrika Bambaataa called electrofunk has become the forerunner of an ever-expanding family of synthesized dance (and trance) styles, including "house music," "drum-and-bass," "techno," "electronica," and "jungle" (among other permutations) that, during the 1980s and 1990s, would fuel dance parties and raves from Chicago to Tokyo, Detroit to Frankfurt, and Washington, D.C. to London, England.

But while "Planet Rock" marked a huge milestone in hip-hop's musical development, with the release of "The Message" (later that same year), rap also made a quantum leap in its narrative content. As a result, the performer who would become best known for advancing rap's lyrics was the very person whose initial claim to fame had been his mastery of its beats.

Although credited to Grandmaster Flash and the Furious Five, "The Message" (unlike Flash's "Adventures on Wheels of Steel"), places Flash's quintet of MCs at center stage. Set to a spare, slow electronic rhythm track, the song's graphic imagery paints an unsettling portrait of ghetto life as a nightmare world of crime, drugs, and random violence in which a failed school system and family dysfunction lead to a dead end of frustration and despair. Then—as if embodying a lifetime of pent-up rage—there was the song's chilling refrain—"Don't push me 'cause I'm close to the edge/I'm trying not to lose my head." It was a far cry from the party slogans and signifying that had dominated rap lyrics up to this point.

While its potent social commentary may have been new to rap, like so many elements of hip-hop culture, this aspect of "The Message" also can be traced back to earlier styles of African-American music. Within the blues tradition, for example, there are poignant accounts of the horrific living conditions Southern blacks endured at the beginning of the century, and—as Paul Oliver points out in his survey of blues lyrics, *The Meaning of the Blues*—there have been a small number of "socially conscious singers who . . . deliberately composed 'protest blues'." It was during the height of the civil rights movement of the 1960s and 1970s, however, that musical expressions of African-American social criticism were most prevalent.

As sit-ins, freedom marches, and boycotts spread across the South and into Northern cities, R & B performers such as Sam Cooke ("A Change Is Gonna Come"), the Impressions ("Keep on Pushin'"), Curtis Mayfield ("Freddie's Dead"), Aretha Franklin ("Think"), and James Brown ("Say It Loud, I'm Black and I'm Proud") all placed songs of political protest or racial pride onto the pop charts. In fact, in many respects, Stevie Wonder's own bleak narrative of urban despair, "Living for the City" (released in 1973), sounds eerily like a prequel to "The Message."

During the mid-1970s, another perspective on the politics of race began to make some inroads into American popular music from Jamaica, an island whose "sound systems" and "toasts" had already contributed significantly to the development of hip-hop. But it was the powerful influence of reggae—especially of Bob Marley and the Wailers ("I Shot the Sheriff," "Concrete Jungle")—that provided an important source of rap's budding social consciousness. Finally, it was also during this period that some politically oriented African-American writers—such as the Last Poets ("Niggers Are Scared of the Revolution") and Gil Scott-Heron ("The Revolution Will Not Be Televised")—began to supplement their militant messages with a beat. According to David Toop, "Both Gil Scott-Heron and the Last Poets are seen by most Bronx rappers as the godfathers of message rap."

Although "The Message" itself did have a significant impact within the hip-hop community, the newfound seriousness of the Furious Five's lyrics also inspired the respectful attention of another group who would be indispensible allies in rap's imminent transition into the pop mainstream—rock critics. Up to this point, most white pop music writers had dismissed rap as a kind of degenerate second cousin of disco (another music they hated). Now, as rap's focus shifted to songs of social significance (linked in critics' minds with the folk-rock protest music of "the Sixties"), they began to legitimize for their readers a style that they had previously denegrated as abrasive and unmusical.

Ironically, the rock critics' initial reaction to rap hadn't been much different from the response that a previous generation of popular music professionals had when they first heard rock 'n' roll. For example, back in the mid-1950s, Steve Allen (the original host of NBC's *Tonight Show*) used to amuse his mainstream audience by reciting the lyrics to recent rock hits such as "Be-Bop-a-Lula" to the accompaniment of a gently tinkling piano. Like these early rock 'n' roll songs—which subordinated traditional lyric artistry to an exhilarating beat—rap songs were at least as much about *how* the words were delivered as *what* they actually said. It would take a similar aesthetic adjustment for the unitiated to appreciate the way a great rapper uses his or her own carefully contrived delivery (or "flow")—along with the song's rhythmic structure—to establish the overall meaning of a performance.

In any event, based on the extraordinary impact of "The Message," a flurry of other message raps were immediately released; perhaps the most accomplished of these was "White Lines" by Melle Mel (a former member of the Furious Five), which graphically addressed the era's devastating cocaine crisis. But looking back at these milestones in hip-hop history, it's worth noting that, back in 1984, the vast majority of mainstream America was barely conscious of the rap phenomenon. That, however, was about to change.

HIP-HOP NATION: INTO THE MAINSTREAM

In less than a decade, hip-hop's musical innovations—first concocted at Bronx street parties—were beginning to make their way onto the pop music charts. Despite the limited geographical penetration (rap was still mostly a New York thing) and lack of media attention (it received only limited radio airplay), a couple of rap singles had even achieved gold-record status. Now, it was time for a second generation of rap artists and entrepreneurs to place the music firmly in the mainstream. The group that deserves most of the credit for doing just that is Run-DMC.

Unlike the genre's pioneers, Run-DMC (Darryl "DMC" McDaniels, Joseph "Run" Simmons, and Jason "Jam Master Jay" Mizell) were not inhabitants of any of the blighted inner-city neighborhoods that had given birth to hip-hop culture; instead, they were products of one of New York's middle-class suburban enclaves. Nevertheless, the group did have close links with some of rap's primary sources. For example, years before he became one-third of one of rap history's most successful acts, Joseph "Run" Simmons had served as a DJ for one of hip-hop's founding fathers (during this period of apprenticeship he was typically billed as "Kurtis Blow's Disco Son—DJ Run"). And like early hip-hop's "masters of records," Run-DMC also embraced a color-blind, genre-crossing philosophy when they constructed the rhythmic backdrops for their own rhymes.

As much as anything else, however, it was the group's commercial savvy that put them in the vanguard of the new generation of mainstream rappers. For Run-DMC's career is inevitably linked to the astonishing rise of rap's first corporate powerhouse (Def Jam Records), founded in 1984 by Rick Rubin and Russell Simmons (who just happened to be Run's older brother). The tale of how Rick Rubin (a white NYU film student and heavy-metal devotee turned rap record producer) joined forces with Russell "Rush" Simmons (a rap promoter and businessman extraordinaire) in order to parlay a combined $8,000 investment into a multimillion-dollar corporate empire has become one of the mythic sagas in rap history (see Def Jam's own 1985 docudrama *Krush Goove* for a fictionalized behind-the-scene's story).

From their very first recordings, Run-DMC's stripped-down beats and declamatory, overlapping old-school raps had an enormous appeal for fans both old and new. After cutting a couple of successful twelve-inch singles (including "Hard Times" that went to number eleven on the Black Singles chart), Run-DMC released the first in a series of LPs whose fusion of hip-hop and rock would propel rap music onto the pop charts and the airwaves. Although Run confessed that the group had "always rapped over rock records in the 70s," it wasn't until their 1984, self-titled debut album that Run-DMC put that musical synthesis onto a recording.

While "Rock Box" (the hit single from that album) was clearly an outgrowth of the group's own diverse musical tastes, it also reflected the heavy-metal predilections of their producer, Rick Rubin (who would soon bring his talents to the Beastie Boys' rap/rock fusions). Whatever its source, the idea of jolting "Rock Box" with the high-voltage virtuosity of session guitarist Eddie Martinez proved to be a stroke of tactical genius. After the song was turned into an engaging, low-budget video (starring the comedian, Prof. Irwin Corey), "Rock Box" became the first rap video MTV added to its regular programming.

A heavy dose of rock seasonings continued to infuse the funky hip-hop breakbeats of Run-DMC's 1985 follow-up album, *King of Rock,* but it was their third LP, *Raising Hell* (released a year later) that provided the group—and rap itself—with its greatest inroad yet into the pop mainstream. The album's first single, "My Adidas," used a lean, syncopated beat-box rhythm and some basic Bronx-style scatching to serve as the accompaniment for a celebration of the group's preferred brand of sneaker. In fact, unlike most of their immediate

FIGURE 6-3. Run-DMC (Darryl McDaniels, Joe Simmons, and Jason Mizell—a.k.a. Jam Master Jay) were in the vanguard of a new generation of rappers who propelled hip-hop onto the national stage. Courtesy of Profile Records.

Run-DMC: Taking Rap into the Mainstream

Although they had been raised in Hollis, Queens (a middle-class New York suburb), Run DMC were in close touch with the street culture out of which hip-hop had first emerged. And like those "masters of records" who had first created the style, they embraced a similar color-blind, genre-crossing musical philosophy.

In fact, it was Run-DMC's fusion of rock elements into their beats that initially attracted the attention of MTV. The rappers' 1986 collaboration with Aerosmith on a cover of the veteran rock group's eleven-year-old song "Walk This Way" was responsible for breaking down the last lingering resistance to rap's entry into the pop music mainstream.

predecessors (who had favored brightly colored leather and other disco-era fashions), it was Run-DMC who set the trend for the second-generation rappers with their basic street-style garb (warm-up jackets, untied sneakers, gold-braided "dookie" chains, and Kangol hats). The success of "My Adidas"—which included generous MTV airplay—further broadened the group's fan base. Then came "Walk This Way."

FIGURE 6-4. LL Cool J (an abbreviation of his motto, "Ladies Love Cool James") is one of the key figures in the mainstreaming of rap music. Photo by Wayne Maser. Courtesy of Def Jam Records.

LL Cool J and the Rise of the Rap Soloist

It was LL Cool J's impressive verbal skills that helped turn the spotlight on the individual rapper, as opposed to a crew of MCs. In his pioneering book *Rap Attack,* David Toop explains that "[t]he strength of his rapping was its precise articulation, the way in which he could deliver complex lines with such poise that it sounded like perfectly-structured, intimate conversation."

On the basis of such skills, LL Cool J's 1987 release "I Need Love" became the first rap record to make it to the top of *Billboard* magazine's Black Singles chart. In 1990, LL released *Mama Said Knock You Out.* The album quickly sold a couple of million copies and the title track has gone on to become a rap classic. Not only was it nominated for a Grammy award, but the dramatic, black-and-white video (featuring the pumped-up rapper as heavyweight contender) was one of the first rap clips heavily promoted on MTV.

According to rap historian David Toop, " 'Walk This Way' was one of the breakthrough records of rap, its metal guitar riffs, rock chorus, hard beats and raps fusing into an ultimate in rebel music that MTV and radio programmers, along with a lot of white rock fans, found impossible to resist." But Run-DMC's version of Aerosmith's 1977 hit didn't simply recycle the band's recording of the song; in a way, it actually recycled Aerosmith (at least, lead singer Steven Tyler and guitarist Joe Perry).

In suggesting that Run-DMC include the veteran rockers in the song's video, Rick Rubin was perhaps taking a cue from Michael Jackson, whose MTV coronation had been greatly abetted when he employed Eddie Van Halen to provide a prominent guitar solo to "Beat It" a few year earlier. Whatever the inspiration was, Run-DMC's "Walk This Way" video catapulted rap to new level of commercial success, earned Run-DMC a platinum record, and helped revive Aerosmith's own stalled career.

Meanwhile, a number of other second-generation rap acts were charting their own breakthroughs with new variations on rap traditions. LL Cool J (who, like Run-DMC, also hailed from a middle-class Queens, New York, neighborhood) introduced a mellower, "lover's rap" style on his 1985 debut album, *Radio*, and two years later his rap ballad, "I Need Love," went to number one on the Black Singles chart (becoming the first rap record to do so). Of course, LL's biggest hit, 1990's "Mama Said Knock You Out," would launch the virtuoso rapper (and future sit-com star) to even greater success.

In 1984, a Brooklyn aggregation, the Fat Boys, first introduced the concept of "comedy rap," with a self-titled single in which they indulged in a litany of good-natured jibes at their own rotund appearance. That same year, however, when UTFO, another Brooklyn rap group, released a record offering an early example of rap misogyny, little did they realize that they would be precipitating a fundamental alteration in the world of rap recording. "Roxanne, Roxanne," told the fictional story of a stuck-up girl who callously spurns the advances of each of UTFO's MCs. Within a few weeks of its release, the first in what would become an ongoing series of "answer records" by women rappers hit the streets.

The most potent of these responses came from a Queens teenager named Lolita Shante Gooden. Adopting the stage name Roxanne Shante, she replied to UTFO's sexist charges with her own street-tough rap, "Roxanne's Revenge," and over the next year, she recorded a series of feminist raps including "Queen of Rock" and "Shante's Turn." As rap began to claim an ever-larger piece of the pop music pie, female rappers such as Salt-N-Pepa, MC Lyte, Queen Latifa, and Lil' Kim would take their place among the style's most celebrated new practitioners.

Although rap had made enormous artistic and commercial strides by the mid-80s, its ascent into the upper reaches of the pop-music charts had always bumped into a seemingly impenetrable glass ceiling; that is, until the release of the Beastie Boys' 1986 Def Jam début album, *Licensed to Ill.* While many rap critics and long-time hip-hop fans praised the Beasties' thickly textured blend of breakbeats and rock riffs (as well as their verbal skills and the antic energy of their live shows), not everyone was thrilled that rap history's very first number one pop album—and single ("You Got to Fight for Your Right to Party")—were the creation of a couple of white punk rockers-turned MCs (in collaboration with the white producer Rick Rubin).

To some observers it smacked of "minstrelsey," the nineteenth-century entertainment in which white performers applied blackface makeup to create their own caricatures of African-American songs and dances. Others recalled the early days of rock 'n' roll, another form of popular music that drew a major share of its inspiration from black sources. Some even quoted the immortal words of Sam Phillips, owner of Sun Records, who before signing a young singer named Elvis Presley to his label had fantasized, "If I had a white man with the Negro sound and the Negro feel, I could make a million dollars."

While there can be little doubt that the Beastie Boys' racial identity made them more intriguing to the people who programmed mainstream radio and MTV, a majority of hip-hop fans (both old and new) cared more about the creative content of their grooves than the melanin content of their skin. And as we've already seen, hip-hop's founding fathers had embraced a distinctly multicultural philsophy from the very beginning. So, while Afrika Bambaataa may have forged his entire identity (including his name and Afrocentric attire) on the basis of the pride he took in his own racial heritage, as a "master of records" he also constructed his breakbeats from a hetero-genius assortment of R & B, reggae, rock, and Latin music. In fact, Bambaataa's greatest triumph, "Planet Rock"—the title itself is a metaphor for his all-embracing musical vision—was built around a record by Kraftwerk, a (blond-and-blue-eyed) German synthesizer band.

FIGURE 6-5.   The Beastie Boys: Adam Horovitz (a.k.a King Adrock), Michael Diamond (a.k.a. Mike D.), and Adam Yauch (a.k.a. MCA). Photo by Danny Clinch. Courtesy of Nasty Little Man.

The Beastie Boys: The Elvises of Rap?

Shortly after their 1986 album *Licensed to Ill* was released, Columbia Records announced that it had become the fastest-selling début in the entire history of that venerable label. Within a few weeks, both the LP and its hit single ("You've Got to Fight for Your Right to Party") went to number one on their respective sales charts—the first rap records to do so.

Although most of the rap community was gratified at the genre's newfound success, more than a few were chagrined that this milestone in hip-hop history would be attributed to a trio of *white* rappers. The Beastie Boys, however, were quick to place the troubling issue in its historical context. As Adam Yauch told a *Rolling Stone* interviewer, "Rock and roll was started by Chuck Berry, but it's Elvis who is called the King. So it's not surprising that it took the Beastie Boys to popularize rap. That's typical of America."

During the early 1990s, the Beasties were joined by a handful of other white rappers. Yet, unlike the 1950s—when Elvis and the rest of rock 'n' roll's first generation broke through with their energetic adaptation of R & B—rap has mostly resisted cooptation by white performers. Over the years, the "authenticity" of every new non-African-American MC has been carefully assessed by the hip-hop community; some—such as the Brooklyn-based group 3rd Bass and L.A's House of Pain—found considerable acceptance, while others—such as Vanilla Ice—have been brutally dismissed as "biters" (rip-off artists) or worse.

Although subsequent albums by the Beastie Boys (especially the underrated *Paul's Boutique* and their huge 1998 hit, *Hello Nasty*), further exposed the Beastie's fundamental allegience to their punk-rock roots (and genre-busting philosophy), they remained—until the appearance of rap megastar, Eminem—the only white rappers to have made a significant contribution to the genre. (For a fuller discussion of the issue of white rap, see Armond White's provocative essay, "Who Wants to See Ten Niggers Play Basketball?" collected in *Droppin' Science: Critical Essays on Rap and Hip Hop Culture,* ed. William Eric Perkins.)

Whatever the explanation, the Beastie Boys' 1986 breakthrough quickly sold in excess of four million copies. And *Licensed to Ill*'s unprecedented success made both the major record labels and the mainstream media immediately sit up and take notice. Soon, Def Jam had entered into a lucrative distribution deal with CBS Records, and Tommy Boy, one of hip-hop's pioneering independent labels, had been purchased by Time-Warner, the nation's most powerful communication conglomerate. By the end of the decade, "Yo! MTV Raps," a daily half-hour of rap videos, was one of the cable station's highest rated shows and approximately one-third of *Billboard* magazine's Top 100 black albums were by rap performers.

RAP ATTACKED: SAMPLING SUITS AND URBAN VIOLENCE

Not only did rap experience enormous advances in its commercial fortunes during this period but, as a result of innovations in recording technology, the sound of rap music itself was dramatically changing as well.

An outgrowth of the same digital revolution responsible for the invention of the gleaming, rainbow-streaked compact disk (that had recently come on the market), the sampling devices that found their way into major label recording studios during the early 1980s were making it possible to convert any musical source into numerical code (those familiar 0s and 1s). Once such a sample was obtained, it could be stored for later use on tape or a floppy disk. By the middle of the decade, the availability of affordable digital samplers such as the Akai S900 put this new technology into the hands of rap performers and producers.

Now, rather than cutting and mixing actual vinyl disks as hip-hop's first generation of turntable prodigies had done, recording studio wizards could, for example, simply "sample" a horn riff from Sly and the Family Stone, a drum break from Baby Huey and the Babysitters, and one of James Brown's patented shrieks, and then simply "loop" (repeat) the resulting rhythmic collage into a seamless backing track.

Not only could samples from hundreds of crates of records be contained on a single diskette, but sampling also provided producers with the ability to subtly alter any aspect of the source material. Sampling became an exciting new way of "composing" music. Rap producers soon began constructing layers of samples, along with an assortment of carefully constructed drum machine rhythms and some old-school "scratching" effects to create infinitely complex aural assemblages. Once upon a time, hip-hop DJs had transformed the turntable into a musical instrument; now rap producers were turning the entire recording studio into one.

Although sampling quickly resulted in some riveting musical compositions, the process also precipitated a series of high-profile court cases. So, while cultural critics were soon writing provocative essays linking the latest rap records to the "postmodernist" movement in the arts (and relating rap's "deconstruction" of American popular music history to the media-induced fragmentation of late-twentieth-century culture), copyright lawyers just started suing.

In fact, similar legal challenges can be traced back to the very first rap record, "Rapper's Delight," which had employed an obvious—and uncredited—studio re-creation of Chic's "Good Times." Chic's lawyer's had immediately instituted a suit against Sugar Hill Records and a settlement involving cash and copyright credit was eventually reached. Two years later, a veritable barrage of copyright-infringment cases was set off by the release of that cut-and-mix classic, "The Adventures of Grandmaster Flash on Wheels of Steel." And while the Beastie Boys'

Licensed to Ill may have been a prime example of rap's cacophanous new sound, their use of a couple of Led Zeppelin samples didn't exactly go unnoticed.

It wasn't rap's enormous technical and creative strides or even its legal entanglements that generated the bulk of the media coverage of the genre during this period, however; that continued to be focused almost exclusively on rap's growing association with urban violence.

In this respect, rap again seemed to be replicating rock 'n' roll's own early history. Headlines, like the one in the New York *Post* following a 1985 Madison Square Garden rap extravaganza—"Concert Violence Fells 5 at Garden"—were not only typical of the coverage of recent rap events, but could easily have served as the headline for newspaper accounts of the "riots" at one of Allen Freed's rock 'n' roll shows of the late 1950s. And as was the case three decades earlier (when Freed's shows brought black and white performers and audiences together for the first time), many in the hip-hop community believed the negative coverage of rap also had a racial dimension. In David Toop's words, the media still "blurred the distinction between the violence, whatever its cause, and the music."

Which is not to say that violence wasn't a reality both in the inner city and in the lives of some of those who documented that environment in their breakbeats and rhymes. Among the first to dramatize this aspect of ghetto life was Kris Parker (a.k.a. KRS-One) who, with his collaborator, DJ Scott La Rock, performed under the banner of Boogie Down Productions. After leaving home at thirteen years of age, Parker began living on the streets of the South Bronx just as the hip-hop culture was being born.

In songs such as "9mm"—from KRS-One's aptly titled 1987 début album, *Criminal Minded*—the rapper focused directly on the destructive aspects of the urban netherworld. In the process, he helped to forge the essential elements of the notorious subgenre that would become known as "gangsta rap." Using vivid, often brutal imagery, he created narratives that mirrored the escalating violence and gun culture that were a consequence of the crack epidemic that was ravaging America's minority communities.

At least that became the standard explanation offered when rappers were taken to task for the violent content of their songs. Whether rap was indeed just a reflection of reality, or nothing more than the aural equivalent of one of Hollywood's contemporary action films (which was an alternate rationalization), the more pressing problem was that, by the end of the decade, rap's hyperbolic "diss" wars and action-film story lines were becoming all too real. In fact, shortly after *Criminal Minded* was released, Boogie Down Production's cofounder, Scott La Rock (a former social worker and influential DJ) was gunned down in the Bronx when he was caught up in a confrontation between two warring rappers.

Although the cover of KRS-One's next album, *By All Means Necessary,* featured an image of the rapper peering through parted curtains while clutching an ominous-looking automatic weapon, a more sophisticated political analysis did begin to inform his lyrics. Nor did it escape notice that both the album's cover and title were obvious allusions to Malcolm X, or that the message of much of the music on the record within could be linked to the beliefs of the slain civil rights leader.

With the toll of inner-city anarchy mounting, however, KRS-One also began to address the issue of rap-related urban violence through his lyrics. While his song "Stop the Violence" is a plea for an end to the self-destructive behavior that he saw pervading the lives of young African-Americans, as Tricia Rose points out in her scholarly study, *Black Noise: Rap Music and Black Culture in Contemporary America,* it also drew "direct links between the media, the educational system, and the frustrations that contribute to street crime, especially as it relates to hip-hop."

Over the next few years, KRS-One continued to focus on more socially conscious raps in an attempt to forge a style that can best be summed up by the title of his fourth LP, *Edutainment.* By this point, KRS (an acronym for Knowledge Reigns Supreme) had become one of hip-hop culture's most respected figures and a popular speaker on college campuses across the country.

For those who preferred their sagas of urban violence unsullied by sociopolitical analysis, there was always Schoolly-D, a Philadelphia MC whose early singles, "Gangster Boogie" (1984) and "PSK—What Does It Mean?" (1985) get many hip-hop historians' vote as the first true examples of gangsta rap. Typically set against a thudding, reverberating beat slashed with turntable scratches, Schoolly-D's deep, resonant, and chillingly emotionless vocal delivery only added to the visceral effect of his grisly tales.

What's more, Schoolly-D didn't simply suggest that he was providing an eyewitness report on the violence of ghetto life but that he was part of it. It was this first-person point of view (whether it was based on reality or only used as a narrative device) that would be adopted by the West Coast rappers who were poised to bring gangsta rap to national prominence.

GANGSTA RAP: STREET JOURNALISM OR ACTION-FILM FANTASY?

Gradually, hip-hop culture had filtered across the country and taken root in many of California's black and Latino enclaves. Graffiti murals stretched for miles alongside Los Angeles freeways, and West Coast b-boys such as the Solomon Brothers were inventing innovative breakdance moves including the "electric boogaloo" (in which the dancer's kinetic gyrations pantomimed the effects of a thousand-volt charge). And, by the mid-1980s, an assortment of local MCs had become architects of a distinctive West Coast rap style.

Unfortunately, this was also a time when the gang violence endemic to many of California's minority communities was suddenly surging as a consequence of the influx of crack cocaine. The daily drama of drive-by shootings and police raids (accompanied by the ominous sound of helicopters) provided West Coast rappers with a ready-made subject. One of the first to make use of this material in his raps was Ice-T. A real-life graduate of the gangsta culture, his first album, *Rhyme Pays* (released in 1987 on Warner Brothers' Sire label) was a prototype of the emerging style.

Then, a year later, another Southern California rap group calling itself NWA (Niggas with Attitude) released *Straight outta Compton,* an album that unequivocally announced the arrival of a potent and disturbing rap sub-genre. Pounding, funk-heavy samples (often drawn from George Clinton's Parliament Funkadelic empire) provided the backdrop of intensely delivered, obscenity-studded raps whose explicit, richly cinematic depictions of violence and misogyny transcended anything that had come before. The album would prove to be one of the biggest (and most influential) hits in rap history.

NWA brought together an unlikely collection of characters including an innovative and ambitious producer who called himself Dr. Dre, a former drug dealer turned record company CEO known as Eazy-E, and a young college drop-out with a talent for writing sharply observed rap docudramas who used the pen name Ice Cube. With the release of *Straight outta Compton* (on Eazy-E's own Ruthless Records), the stakes were raised for any rapper who wanted to maintain his reputation for "keeping it real." Although their graphic images of gang violence, macho disdain for women and declarations of warfare against the police actually seem most inspired by traditional badman ballads and the overheated action fantasies of nearby Hollywood studios, NWA always stressed the "authenticity" of their nihilistic narratives. "We call ourselves underground street reporters," Ice Cube declared. "We just tell it how we see it, nothing more, nothing less."

On the basis of the intense controversy and media coverage provoked by the NWA album—particularly the single "Fuck the Police"—the album quickly sold a couple of million copies and put the phrase "gangsta rap" into the headlines (and editorial pages) of newspapers across the country; nor was their success lost on either the rap community or the record industry. Although their follow-up LP, *Niggaz4Life* (released in 1991), catapulted the group to the number one spot on *Billboard* magazine's pop chart, the group was already in the process of self-destructing. Dr. Dre launched his own record label, Death Row, dedicated to furthering the gangsta-rap cause and, toward that end, he released his own groundbreaking solo album entitled *The Chronic.* He also signed the rapper who would soon become the genre's next superstar, Snoop Doggy Dogg.

Meanwhile, Ice Cube—NWA's most prolific and talented writer—had already left the group, issued his own hit album (*AmeriKKKa's Most Wanted*), and was on the verge of establishing a successful acting career. Ironically, although he had been instrumental in formulating the hardcore West Coast style, when Ice Cube walked away from NWA to begin his solo career, he headed to New York, lured by the studio wizardry of a crew of producers who called themselves the "Bomb Squad."

FIGURE 6-6.   Ice Cube (born Oshea Jackson) won kudos from the critics when he made his feature film debut in John Singleton's 1991 hit, *Boyz in the Hood*. In fact, the title for the film had come from a rap about life in L.A.'s Compton neighborhood that Ice Cube had cowritten years earlier with future rap impressario Dr. Dre. Museum of Modern Art Film Stills Collection.

Ice Cube: Straight outta Compton

Ice Cube first came to prominence as a founding member of the controversial West Coast rap group, Niggas with Attitude. It was NWA's 1988 album *Straight outta Compton* that precipitated the gangsta rap craze, and NWA's principal writer Ice Cube had earned a reputation for creating highly cinematic street narratives (like "Dopeman") that combined action-film caricatures with a gritty dose of docudrama reality.

It was a technique he would go on to explore further when—after splitting from NWA—Ice Cube collaborated with the East Coast production team known as the "Bomb Squad" (who also were responsible for Public Enemy's dense collage of samples and sound effects). The result was Ice Cube's street-savvy, politically charged 1990 solo album, *AmeriKKKa's Most Wanted*.

PUBLIC ENEMY BRINGS THE NOISE

The Bomb Squad had established a reputation as rap music's most innovative producers when they collaborated on Public Enemy's 1987 album, *Yo! Bum Rush the Show* (Def Jam). Comprised of Bill Stephney, Hank and Keith Shocklee, and Eric "Vietnam" Sadler, the Bomb Squad were the first producers to fully exploit the creative potential of digital sampling technology.

Drawing from a private library of twenty thousand records, they layered endless samples—along with scratching, sound effects, and other recording studio manipulations—to create an almost impenetrable sonic labyrinth. Some critics compared the Bomb Squad's formula to the celebrated "wall of sound" constructed by the

1950s rock producer, Phil Spector, while *Village Voice* writer Greg Tate memorably dubbed the densely textured style, "artful noise."

However one describes it, the dissonant, anxiety-producing aural environment the Bomb Squad created (using as many as forty-eight tracks per song), proved to be the ideal setting for Public Enemy's free-wheeling, politically charged raps. For when Hank Schoklee, Bill Stephney, and Chuck D. (who would become PE's frontman) first came together on the campus of Long Island's Aldelphi University, it was with the specific idea of starting a rap group that could serve as a vehicle for promoting a nationalistic, Afrocentric political agenda.

Chuck D. recalled that, unlike the majority of rap groups whose anger "was always directed at other rappers—'I'm better than you' and so forth—when we came along, we decided to direct our anger at something real . . . the government and people who were responsible for what was happening in society." So, while they were often mistakenly linked with the gangsta rap movement, from their inception, Public Enemy infused their portraits of contemporary urban anarchy with what Tricia Rose has described as "a multilayered critique of the government, the police, the media, and the black bourgeoisie."

In their next album, *It Takes a Nation of Millions to Hold Us Back,* Public Enemy and the Bomb Squad pushed the cacophanous intensity of their production style and radical orientation of their politics to new levels. By this point, Public Enemy's confrontational style was not only embraced by the hardcore rap audience, but—after being actively promoted by rock critics (excited both by the group's avant-garde musical techniques and their socially conscious message)—PE began to draw a large, white, college audience as well.

Public Enemy's public image received another boost when the director, Spike Lee commissioned them to create the song ("Fight the Power") that would serve as a central element in his controversial 1989 film, *Do the Right Thing.* Lee knew exactly what kind of music was required in order to spark the film's explosive climax: "I wanted it to be defiant, I wanted it to be angry, I wanted it to be very rhythmic," he told a *Time* magazine reporter. "I thought right away of Public Enemy."

When they were taken to task by critics in the mainstream media for their aggressive stance, Public Enemy echoed the explanations offered by Ice Cube and other gangsta rappers (that they were simply functioning as inner-city reporters). As Chuck D. put it, rap was nothing less than "the CNN of young black America." Of course, not everyone was convinced about either PE's journalistic skills or the coherence of their sociopolitical analysis. Even Greg Tate, an African-American critic who had written approvingly of Public Enemy's musical experiments (as well as the skillfullness of their sloganeering), expressed reservations about some of "the whack retarded philosophy they espouse." As he pointed out in one article, "Since PE show sound reasoning when they focus on racism as a tool of the U.S. power structure, they should be intelligent enough to realize that dehumanizing gays, women, and Jews isn't going to set black people free."

What suddenly prompted the intense scrutiny of Public Enemy's message was a notorious interview given by Prof. Griff (PE's so-called Minister of Information) to the *Washington Times* shortly after the release of *Do the Right Thing.* Among various provocative assertions was Giff's claim that Jews were responsible "for the majority of the wickedness that goes on in the world." In the furor that ensued, Griff's association with the group was terminated; but that didn't mean that Public Enemy was turning its back on controversy. For example, after the Arizona state legislature voted against participating in the national observance of Martin Luther King's birthday, PE released a single—"By the Time I Get to Arizona"—that graphically described an armed assault on the Arizona statehouse ("I'm on the one mission/To get a politician," Chuck D. rapped).

The accompanying video—which simulated the assassination of Arizona politicians by an army of masked guerrilla soldiers—was narrated by a recent addition to the PE family, Sister Souljah. Soon she would have her own fifteen minutes of infamy when she became embroiled in an acrimonious debate with the 1992 Democratic Party candidate for president, Bill Clinton, over remarks she made following the post–Rodney King "uprising" in Los Angeles. Meanwhile, other battles in the rap war were being waged in record company boardrooms, newspaper editorials, and, ultimately, the courts.

FIGURE 6-7.   According to one critic, Public Enemy provided listeners with "a multilayered critique of the government, the police, the media, and the black bourgeoise." The group's spokesman, Chuck D., explained their mission more succinctly when he described PE as "the CNN of young black America." Courtesy of Def Jam Recordings.

Public Enemy Fight the Power

In albums like *Yo! Bum Rush the Show* (released in 1987) and 1988's *It Takes a Nation of Millions to Hold Us Back,* Public Enemy set their radical political raps against a revolutionary sonic backdrop that exploited the new technique of digital sampling. Working with a production team known as the Bomb Squad, Public Enemy created a dense wall of black noise that added its own defiant, anxiety-producing element to their militant message.

   During the early 1990s, Public Enemy continued their assault on the system in a series of controversial singles including "Fight the Power" (written for Spike Lee's incendiary film *Do the Right Thing*), "911 Is a Joke" (about the government's less-than-benign neglect of the African-American community), and "By the Time I Get to Arizona" (a response to the state's refusal to participate in the Martin Luther King national holiday).

RAP ATTACKED: TAKE TWO

While most of the furor over gangsta rap had focused on its explicit descriptions of violence, the genre's virulent sexism also was starting to attract criticism, even from those within the rap community. This controversy came to a head with the release of the 1989 album *As Nasty As They Wanna Be* by the Miami-based group, 2 Live Crew.

Offended by the LP's sexually explicit references, the Broward County sheriff's office decided to prosecute one record store owner for selling the album to minors. When the case found its way into the courts, a federal judge ruled the record obscene. Not only did this immediately unleash a stormy debate between feminists (concerned with the reality of domestic violence) and free-speech advocates (troubled by any form of censorship) but, not surprisingly, the accompanying publicity immediately made the album—as well as its salacious single, "Me So Horny"—among the biggest hits of the year.

One of those drawn into the escalating controversy was the distinguished scholar, Henry Louis Gates, Jr. A Harvard professor and prominent African-American intellectual, Gates wrote an op-ed piece in the New York *Times* in support of 2 Live Crew and, eventually, he was called to testify as a defense witness in their federal obscenity trial. Although his argument rested to a large extent on the issue of freedom of speech, Gates also took pains to place rap music's verbal excesses in the context of such cultural traditions as "signifying" and "the dozens." In fact, he ended his *Times* article by insisting that "the very large question of obscenity and the First Amendment cannot even be addressed until those who answer them become literate in the vernacular traditions of African-Americans."

Although 2 Live Crew's cartoonishly exaggerated sexism may have been intended (as Gates suggested in his trial testimony) "as a joke, a parody," many listeners found nothing remotely funny in their depictions of sexual abuse and rape. Nor did lectures on the concept of signifying in African-American culture do much to reassure citizens who were now being exposed to escalating levels of graphic violence in gangsta rap. Inevitably, as rappers pushed the edge of the rhetorical envelope and mainstream record labels became more deeply involved in producing and distributing hardcore rap, such conflicts only increased. Among the other recordings that prompted controversy during this period were the Geto Boy's, "Mind of a Lunatic" and Ice-T's notorious single, "Cop Killer."

In 1990—when an executive at Geffen Records first heard the litany of rape, murder, and necrophilia that the Houston-based Geto Boys had created for Rick Rubin's new Def American label—he pronounced it "the worst thing I ever heard" and refused to distribute the record (it was eventually issued on Giant Records, a hungry indie label). Two years later, "Cop Killer" not only added fuel to the gangsta rap debate but became the target of a well-organized anti-rap crusade.

According to Ice-T, his song was nothing more than a fictional revenge fantasy (based on the reality of police corruption). His own plot summary: "A black youth takes justice into own hands after his buddies are unjustly murdered by corrupt cops." Unconvinced, law-enforcement organizations from across the country—who viewed the song as a literal call to arms against the police—began exerting enormous pressure both on Warner Brothers Records (which distributed the song) and on its mammoth parent company, Time Warner, Inc.

By the time *Home Invasion* (the album that was scheduled to include "Cop Killer' was released), Ice-T had decided "voluntarily" to withdraw the song. In doing so, however, he simply provoked the wrath of many within the rap community who now saw the creator of "Cop Killer" as a cop out. Ice-T staunchly defended his decision: "In a war—and make no mistake, this is a war—sometimes you have to retreat and return with superior firepower."

In retrospect, what Ice-T found most ironic about gangsta rap's most notorious episode was that the record that sparked it wasn't even a rap song; it was actually one of Ice-T's collaborations with a black thrash-metal rock group named Body Count. In Ice-T's analysis, this fact was intentionally ignored in order to raise the emotional temperature of the situation: "Let's call it rap in the press to make it even more incendiary," he imagines his opponents conspiring. "Rap immediately conjures up scary images of Black Ghetto." He believed that identifying him as "Rapper Ice-T" was a key element in the strategy to demonize him.

Yet, as feminists, politicians, mainstream African-American civic groups, and religious leaders were mobilizing against the rising tide of gangsta rap violence and misogyny, scores of new hardcore performers were joining the battle-weary veterans. Among these were some performers who revived rap's multicultural identity. For example, Chicano rappers such as Kid Frost (Arturo Molina Jr.) and the members of Cypress Hill not only had their own tales of gang-banging, drive-bys, and police harassment to tell, but they delivered them in an accent that had been mostly absent from rap since its ascent onto the national stage.

In the song "La Raza" ("The People"), for example, Kid Frost created a nationalistic Chicano rap anthem using the unique bilingual dialect—known as Calo—that was spoken in the East Los Angeles barrio and California prison system. While many of the narratives on his 1990 album *Hispanic Causing Panic* conformed to contemporary gangsta-rap conventions, his style also showed the influence of the *corrido* (a centuries-old Mexican-American ballad tradition, which, like African-American folk ballads, had its share of badman sagas). And while the musical background of his raps drew from the usual storehouse of samples and beats, they occasionally incorporated some Tex-Mex saxophone riffs as well. Finally, just as some black rappers looked for inspiration to the ancient civilizations of Africa, Kid Frost identified himself with some of the great Meso-American cultures of the past ("It's in my blood to be/an Aztec Warrior," he declares in "La Raza").

Along with such classic gangsta rap scenarios as the antipolice diatribe, "Pigs," Cypress Hill contributed to the genre's multicultural tinge with "Latin Lingo," their own celebration of the expressiveness of that linguistic hyrid, Spanglish. And when they made marijuana the subject of a series of songs (including "Light Another" and "Stoned Is the Way of the Walk"), Cypress Hill discovered yet another way to arouse the ire of rap's critics—and to sell records.

Rap's ethnic diversity was expanded even further when the surviving siblings of a Samoan family from South L.A.'s Carson neighborhood united to form the Boo-Yaa T.R.I.B.E. Although two of the Devoux brothers had already been killed in gang-related violence, the remaining six had plenty of stories to tell. In their 1990 album, *New Funky Family*, the Boo-Yaas (the name was supposedly an attempt to imitate the sound of a shotgun blast) added a Pacific Rim spin to the notorious world of gangsta rap.

Meanwhile, Death Row Records, the label founded by former NWA member Dr. Dre (prior to the controversial reign of Marion "Suge" Knight) had emerged as the ultimate symbol of the West Coast's hardcore movement, an identity that was enhanced when it added Snoop Doggy Dogg and Tupac Shakur to its gangsta-rap roster. Snoop first appeared on Dr. Dre's own best-selling album, *The Chronic,* and the combination of his innovative laid-back rapping style and brutally misogynistic lyrics had an immediate and powerful impact on the rap audience. In 1993, when Snoop Dogg's solo album, *Doggy-style,* was released, it became the first album in history to enter the *Billboard* pop chart at number one.

Tupac Shakur not only brought a dynamic delivery and narrative drive to such best-selling albums as *2Pacalypse Now* and *Strictly 4 My N.I.G.G.Z.,* but his charismatic personality also led to one of rap's most critically acclaimed film careers (which would include a featured appearance in *Juice* and a costarring role opposite Janet Jackson in *Poetic Justice*). While Snoop Dogg's early life included just enough brushes with the law to establish the authenticity of his raps, Tupac's notorious life and tragic death would eventually bring the entire rap movement to the brink of its own demise.

Yet, for now, rap's controversies simply begot more publicity and the publicity begot more sales. So it was that throughout the 1990s, as gangsta rap became embroiled in one controversy after another, the sales of hardcore rap skyrocketed. With gangsta rap albums (by NWA, Cypress Hill, Snoop Dogg, and Dr. Dre among others) regularly climbing into the upper reaches of the pop music charts, it also became apparent to many observers that the genre had crossed over to a large white audience. At this point, music journalists and rap critics like William Eric Perkins began asking an intriguing question: "What makes gangsta rap so appealing to the middle-class white male market?"

While Perkins himself hypothesized that "hip hop speaks to youth's desire for identity, for a sense of self-definition and purpose no matter how lawless or pointless," others simply noted that the exciting, forbidden rhythms of black music—from Twenties jazz to Fifties rhythm and blues—had always held a fascination for white, mainstream America. Now, as Public Enemy producer, Hank Shocklee explained: "If you're a suburban, white kid and you want to find out what life is like for a black city teenager, you buy a record by NWA." For Shocklee gangsta rap offered its white audience a vicarious thrill: "It's like going to an amusement park and getting on a roller-coaster ride—records are safe, they're controlled fear, and you always have the choice of turning it off."

RAP GOES POP

While the gangsta rap hysteria being played out in newspaper editorials and on talk radio shows fueled the sales of the genre's most violent and sexist faction, it also tended to obscure the fact that some rappers had begun to concoct their own pop-rap hybrids while others were actually using the style to promote a positive vision. The first dramatic indication of rap's pop potential occurred in 1990 when a rap single hit the radio (and MTV) airwaves with a hook that proved to be self-fulfilling prophesy: "It's Hammer Time!"

The creator of the song—entitled "U Can't Touch This"—was Stanley Kirk Burrell, a former semi-pro baseball player and East Oakland local hero who went by the name MC Hammer. Much to the frustration of rap's hardcore community, the unprecedented success of Hammer's debut single and album (*Please Hammer Don't Hurt 'Em*) made the engaging performer the first international rap superstar.

Hammer's slickly produced video for "U Can't Touch This," featuring his exuberant dance moves and puffy, Arabian-knights pants helped propel his album to the top of the pop chart where it remained for an astonishing twenty-one weeks, while its grip on *Billboard*'s Black Album list would go on for an additional two months. Although he eked out a few more hits, Hammer's enormous popularity soon waned; but, by the time it did, he'd won three Grammy awards, provided the songs for a couple of feature films (including *Rocky V* and *The Addams Family*), been turned into a doll by the Mattel Toy Company and—as the animated character "Hammerman"—become the hero of an ABC television Saturday morning cartoon show.

Yet, even before Hammer's extraordinary breakthrough, there were those who had begun to chart rap's path into the world of pop. During the late 1980s, the Fat Boys set sagas of their gargantuan eating habits to the novelty sound effects of Darren "The Human Beat Box" Robinson and achieve considerable commercial success in the process. Tone-Loc (a bearlike, deep-voiced, and personable rapper) sampled a song by heavy metal heroes Van Halen to create rap's biggest crossover hit to date when his 1989 single, "Wild Thing" made it to the top of the pop chart. It was also about this time, that a rap performer emerged who would go on to become the genre's most enduring multimedia, mainstream success story—Will Smith.

Will Smith began his career as one half of one of rap's most popular duos, DJ Jazzy Jeff and the Fresh Prince. By 1988, the combination of Jazzy Jeff's virtuoso turntable technique and Smith's cleverly written and cleanly delivered raps, helped make the Philadelphia-based pair pop heroes. Their double album (a rap first) entitled, *He's the DJ, I'm the Rapper,* sold over 2.5 million units, while its good-natured single "Parents Just Don't Understand" also became one of the year's biggest hits. Not coincidentally, such successes would soon earn their creators the very first Grammy award ever given to a rap act—and in doing so provide the duo with their only brush with controversy.

In 1988, NARAS (the organization that awards the Grammys) was finally forced (by rap's ever-expanding share of the record market) to add a new category to its end-of-year ceremonies. When it was announced that the presentation of the first rap Grammy would not be held during the prime-time telecast, however, DJ Jazzy Jeff and the Fresh Prince, as well as the other nominees (who felt understandably "dissed" by the industry whose profit margins they were helping to swell), decided to boycott the event altogether.

While he may have missed out on one night in the TV spotlight, however, Will Smith soon found a regular home on network television when he became the featured character on the long-running sitcom *The Fresh Prince of Bel-Air.* A few years later, Smith made the transition to film, earning praise both for his sensitive performance in the highly acclaimed drama *Six Degrees of Separation* and for his convincing action-hero role in the 1997 blockbuster *Independence Day.* After a hiatus from his music career, Smith's theme song for his 1998 summer hit *Men in Black* marked his return to rap (and earned him another Grammy).

Another effort to cloak rap in a mantle of mainstream legitimacy during this period was undertaken by the legendary musician–record producer–entrepreneur, Quincy Jones. Unlike most members of his generation, Jones had immediately recognized the exciting potential of rap—which he astutely compared to the bebop movement in jazz (another revolutionary, rhythmically complex music with its own unique style of slang and dress). In his 1989 album, *Back on the Block,* Jones brought rappers like Ice-T, Melle Mel, and Kool Moe Dee together with a diverse collection of jazz, soul, and R & B performers (including Dizzy Gillespie, Ella Fitzgerald, Ray Charles, and Barry White) in an effort to connect hip-hop to its roots in African-American music. Unfortunately, like other such well-intentioned enterprises, *Back on the Block* was strained and artifical and, although it won Quincy Jones a few more Grammys, it had little real impact on rap's evolution.

Nevertheless, by the early 1990s, rap's rhythmic couplets had inspired a "spoken word" renaissance that was also reminiscent of the free-form poetry readings staged by members of the bebop-era Beat Generation back in the 1950s. And there were a couple of other grassroots jazz-rap experiments as well. Groups such as Gang Starr and A Tribe Called Quest incorporated jazz samples into their mixes and occasionally performed live with jazz musicians. In 1990, Gang Starr frontman Guru collaborated with the saxophonist Branford Marsalis on the single, "Jazz Music," which was later used in Spike Lee's film, *Mo' Better Blues.* In Britain, "acid-jazz" DJs also were fusing beat-box rhythms with sampled jazz riffs to create cutting-edge dance music. After receiving unlimited access to the back catalog of the famed jazz label Blue Note, the English collective US3 produced *Hands on the Torch,* one of the era's most promising hip-hop/jazz fusions.

POP RAP GOES CO-ED

One wing of rap's new pop-oriented vanguard not only helped make rap safe for prime time, but its members also introduced a strong female perspective that had long been absent from rap's macho narratives.

Although hip-hop's competitive nature—and hardcore tendencies—had turned rap into an exclusively male domain, as we have seen, during its formative period in the South Bronx, there were women graffiti artists, breakdancers, and MCs—some of whom had made significant contributions to hip-hop culture. Except for Roxanne Shante's 1984 underground hit, "Roxanne's Revenge," however, rap's recorded history was for the most part devoid of women's voices. All that changed with the release of *Hot Cool and Vicious,* the hugely successful 1986 debut of the female rap group Salt-N-Pepa.

Working with a female DJ (Spinderella), Salt-N-Pepa proved unequivocally that in rap, as in every other area of contemporary life, women were doing for themselves. According to David Toop, S-n-P not only devised a refreshingly-original pop/rap synthesis, but they offered an alternative to many of rap's female stereotypes: "On record they were witty and forthright, reacting against the prevailing trend of portraying women as dangerous sluts, 'skeezers', bitches, easy lays." As Toop goes on to explain, Salt-N-Pepa's singles " 'Push It' and 'Shake Your Thang' were both clever and successful pop records which mixed up break beats with go go [a style of supercharged dance music] in a smooth hip-hop style."

Salt-N-Pepa's second album, *A Salt with a Deadly Pepa* went gold and earned the group a 1988 Grammy nomination (another breakthrough for the gender); and in solidarity with their rap brothers, they, too, boycotted the event over lack of television coverage. During the early 1990s, Salt-N-Pepa expanded on their fusion of hip-hop roots and pop sensibility when they collaborated with the female R & B group En Vogue (resulting in the hit singles "Whatta Man" and "Shoop"). To a great extent, Salt-N-Pepa's mix of hip-hop attitude and pop/R & B production elements anticipated the direction rap would take later in the decade.

Among the other performers who began charting this new territory was TLC, three young women who also devised a clever pop-rap hybrid while projecting a positive (and video-friendly) image of female sexuality. Yet, as rap's female performers were prodding rap into a more pop-oriented territory, even they weren't immune to controversy.

Back in 1990, when Henry Louis Gates Jr. presented his defense of 2 Live Crew's obscenity-laced misogyny in the *New York Times,* he had also expressed the hope that rap's virulent sexism would soon be eliminated not by censorship but by women asserting their own freedom of speech. "Still, many of us look to the emergence of more female rappers to redress sexual stereotypes," he wrote in one optimistic passage. Yet, as feminists and social critics began to analyze the recordings and videos produced by women rappers—including Salt-N-Pepa, Mc Lyte (*Lyte As a Rock*), Yo-Yo (*Make Way for the Motherlode*), and Nikki D (*Daddy's Little Girl*)—many simply saw a mirror image of the diss-oriented posturing, sexual signifying, and materialism of their male counterparts.

Not long after Dr. Gates issued his call for a new feminist consciousness in rap, however, a new female rapper released a single that seemed to be just what the doctor ordered. In fact, according to rap scholar Tricia Rose, " 'Ladies First,' Queen Latifah's second release from her debut album *All Hail the Queen* is a landmark example of centralizing a strong black female public voice." Rose went on the praise Queen Latifah for making "a statement for black female unity, independence and power."

FIGURE 6-8.   With the 1989 release of their innovative album *3 Feet High and Rising,* De La Soul became pioneers of the kinder, gentler hip-hop style known as "alternative rap." Photo by Eric Johnson. Courtesy of Tommy Boy Records.

De La Soul and the Advent of Alternative Rap

Rather than wrapping hardcore scenarios in the usual hip-hop break-beats, De La Soul devised a laid-back, conversational style of MCing (they dubbed it "the new-speak") and assembled an eclectic mix of pop, rock, reggae, and soul samples to create a subtle impressionistic soundscape. And instead of the standard-issue home-boy street uniform, De La Soul's flowing, brightly colored attire harkened back to the flower-power era of the 1960s.

3 Feet High (along with its hit single "Me, Myself, and I") not only earned the group a couple of gold records but kudos from pop music critics who were attracted to the group's experimental concepts. Meanwhile, rap fans were intrigued by their enigmatic lyrics and complex layers of samples (as well as by the surrealistic comedy skits interspersed throughout the album).

By the beginning of the 1990s, other variations on De La Soul's "alternative rap" approach had found their way into the marketplace. Groups such as Arrested Development, A Tribe Called Quest, the Jungle Brothers, and others began to introduce Utopian and Afrocentric imagery into their lyrics and to infuse their music with jazz and other exotic flavorings.

In addition to the assertiveness of its title, the lyrics of "Ladies First" (a duet with the Afro-British rapper Monie Love), offered an unapologetically feminist message ("A women can bear you, break you, take you/ Now it's time to rhyme . . ."); and by employing images of Sojourner Truth, Harriet Tubman, Angela Davis, and Winnie Mandela in the video for their song, the rappers linked themselves to a long line of black women role models.

In addition to Queen Latifah's social consciousness and rhyming skills, her statuesque physical presence and African-inspired cloaks and headdressess brought a new image to hip-hop. And not only did she strike a chord with record buyers (her début LP sold over a million copies)—and with the record industry (it also was nominated for a Grammy in 1989)—but her charismatic persona also exerted a powerful attraction for casting directors. Before long, she had become a kind of Queen of All Media by appearing in movies (such as Spike Lee's *Jungle Fever* and James A. Brooks's *Living out Loud*), and on television (in the sitcom, *Living Single*). Queen Latifah won even more kudos from feminists when she took on the role of a businesswoman. In 1993, she started her own label (Flavor Unit Records) and began managing and producing other acts (including Naughty by Nature and Apache).

While Queen Latifah did bring a novel feminist slant to her subjects, neither her Afrocentrism nor her social consciousness were new to rap. From "The Message" to KRS-One's politically correct displays of "edutainment" and Public Enemy's radical proclamations, rappers have been "droppin' science" on the hip-hop audience in one way or another from virtually the beginning.

Earlier, Afrika Bambaataa had constructed his own Afrocentric mythology and gathered around him a legion of followers known as the Zulu Nation. Now, in the mid-1990s, the Wu-Tang Clan—a loose affiliation of rappers, DJs (and an extraordinarily innovative producer known as RZA or Rzarecta Prince Rakeem)—created their own blend of violence-riddled urban street imagery and ancient Shaolin philosophy. Their platinum debut, *Enter the Wu-Tang (36 Chambers)*, immediately became one of the most influential albums of the decade.

Despite gangsta rap's dominance of the genre during the early-to-mid-1990s, there were progressive rappers who continued to speak out against violence, sexism, and drugs and in favor of universal brotherhood and racial pride. Groups such as Arrested Development (*3 Years, 5 Months, and 2 Days in the Life Of . . .*), A Tribe Called Quest (*People's Instinctive Travels and the Paths of Rhythm*), De La Soul (*Three Feet High and Rising*), and The Disposable Heroes of Hiphoprisy (*Hypocrisy Is the Greatest Irony*), each introduced its own variation on what became known as "alternative rap." While they often won kudos from the critics, for the most part their uplifting messages (and inventive sonic experiments) were lost amid the din of bullets and braggadocio.

RAP AT THE MILLENNIUM: FUNERALS AND FRAGMENTATION

By 1996, rap had become a $1 billion industry. In addition to claiming a substantial portion of the annual pop chart, rap's slickly produced, million-dollar videos had become an indispensable component of MTV's heavy rotation, while rap's edgy rhythms had found their way into a score of Hollywood films (transforming a number of rappers into movie stars along the way). Finally, there appeared two glossy monthly magazines (*Vibe* and *The Source*) to chronicle every nuance of the style's astonishing success.

Yet, just a year later, a stark headline appeared in a national magazine devoted to African-American culture that speculated seriously about the genre's imminent demise. After raising the question "Does Rap Have a Future?" a second question posed by the article's subheading alluded to the reason for the sudden pessimism: "Will Gangsta Rap Sink Hip-Hop?" Writing in *Ebony's* June 1997 issue, reporter Joy Bennett Kinnon began by outlining the recent events that had so traumatized the rap community: "The recent violent deaths of rappers Tupac Shakur and the Notorious B.I.G., a.k.a Biggie Smalls, a.k.a Christopher Wallace, and thousands of children without big names or record contracts have led analysts, industry officials, and rappers to step back and as they say recognize."

What they were now forced to "recognize" was that gangsta rap's overheated rhetoric and macho signifying (fueled by the media-hyped rivalry between its East Coast and West Coast branches) had become deadly serious. With the recent murder of two of its most successful artists came the realization that gangsta rap's fundamental ethos—"Keep It Real"—might, in fact, become the genre's epitaph. Although investigations of both the drive-by

FIGURE 6-9.   The Fugees' 1996 hit, *The Score,* reconciled rap's seemingly irreconcilable differences. It balanced multicultural samples with acoustic guitars, progressive politics with pop hooks, and a street-real stance with a generous dose of hip-hop soul. The result: sales of seventeen million copies, a couple of Grammy awards, and a virtually unanimous chorus of critical praise. Marc Baptiste. Courtesy Ruff House/Columbia Records.

The Fugees Create the Mix Tape of Your Dreams

While *The Score*'s enormous sales were initially fueled by the sassy cover version of Roberta Flack's 1973 pop-soul ballad, "Killing Me Softly," it was the Fugees' kaleidoscopic originals that best revealed the group's inventiveness. Songs such as "Fu-Gee-La," "Cowboys," and "The Beast" fused reggae-tinged folk, doo-wop and hardcore hip-hop beats as a backdrop to express an optimistic, pan-African message of unity and pride. It was a sound that one reviewer described as "the mix tape of your dreams."

While fans waited for the group's follow-up, solo projects by Wyclef Jean (*The Carnival*) and Lauryn Hill (*The Miseducation of Lauryn Hill*) revealed new facets of both the Fugees' philosophy and their musical aesthetic. Hill's solo effort also confirmed her credentials as the reigning diva of hip-hop soul (as well as its leading feminist heroine).

shooting that took Tupac Shakur's life and the ambush of Nortorious B.I.G. a year later revealed a tangled web of personal enmity, gang rivalries, and record company irregularities, it was gangsta rap itself that came to bear the brunt of the blame.

In an editorial following the death of Shakur and Wallace, Quincy Jones—who had once been one of rap's most passionate mainstream champions—now decried the music's self-destructive turn: "The gangster lifestyle that is so often glorified and heralded in this music is not 'keeping it real;' it is fake, not even entertainment. A sad farce at best and a grim tragedy at worst." Although once again the latest round of violence accompanied by a wave of sensational publicity created an immediate upsurge in sales of the records of these martyred anti-heroes, other indicators were already beginning to reflect a growing disenchantment with hardcore rap.

Ironically, one of the primary forces behind the evolution away from gangsta rap's creative dead-end also happened to be the main man behind Notorious B.I.G.'s larger-than-life gangsta image. For while Sean "Puff Daddy" Combs had both discovered the Brooklyn-based rapper and produced his million-selling, hardcore album (prophetically titled) *Ready to Die,* his own roots were firmly in the music industry mainstream. While working as national A & R director for Andre Harrell's Uptown Records during the early 1990s, the twenty-year-old Combs had earned a reputation as a prodigy by guiding R & B acts such as Mary J. Blige and Jodeci to multiplatinum, crossover careers.

The commercial instincts he had developed during this period would serve him well when—as C.E.O. of his own label, Bad Boy Entertainment—Combs began producing rap records infused with traditional pop effects such as vocal choruses and melodic hooks. Take the single "I'll Be Missing You" that Combs created as a tribute to Notorious B.I.G. shortly after the rapper's murder. Not only did Puffy blend his own rap with some soulful singing by Faith Evans (B.I.G's widow), but he also appropriated the song's hook from a 1981 hit by the Police, "Every Breath You Take." And when Combs performed the song live at the annual MTV video awards, he was joined by none other than Sting himself. So, in addition to being a moving homage to the fallen rapper, the song can be seen as a symbol of Puff Daddy's own pop-rap revival.

Few were surprised, therefore, when *Billboard* magazine issued its year-end survey at the end of 1997 and the headline of the rap music column declared Combs "Rap's Man of the Year." Although the article went on to detail the many artistic and business accomplishments that qualified him as "the new king of hip-hop," the writer also alluded to the backlash Puff Daddy's pop-oriented style was provoking within the world of rap: "With success came the inevitable stabs. Folks took to attacking Puffy for being too commercial. They said his productions used too many sampled loops with the tags still showing."

While some of the heat he took from rap's advocates-for-authenticity was no doubt generated by jealousy, Combs was, in fact, simply pursuing a trend (albeit with a kind of single-minded ambition) that had been gathering momentum for a couple of years. In 1995, for example, rap's great success story was Coolio's "Gangsta's Paradise," which had been prominently featured in the big-budget Hollywood film *Desperate Measures.* It was no secret that both the song's title and its infectious chorus had been adapted from Stevie Wonder's mid-1970s composition, "Pastime Paradise"—especially not after Wonder himself joined Coolio on stage to perform it at the Academy Award show.

Then there were 1996's hip-hop heroes, the Fugees, whose breakthrough album, *The Score,* came along at the height of gangsta rap's turbulent reign. Both the album's sound (a fusion of hip-hop, R & B, folk, and reggae elements), as well as the life-affirming, socially conscious message of its lyrics were seen as offering a positive alternative to rap's violent nihilism. But what no doubt propelled the album to its eventual worldwide sales of over seventeen million copies was the appeal of its megahit single—a hip-hop cover of Roberta Flack's R & B ballad, "Killing Me Softly."

Subsequent solo projects by individual members of the Fugees continued both to push the genre further into the mainstream and to expand its multicultural identity. For example, Wyclef Jean's 1998 hit album, *Carnival,* combined a progressive political perspective with the street reality of his narratives, just as he combined the Haitian Creole dialect (of the island on which he spent his childhood) with the hip-hop slang he picked up on the streets of Brooklyn (where he came to live as a refugee). And by sampling from an astonishing array of world music (from recent hip-hop and salsa to vintage R & B and a Haitian dance style called *compas*), Wyclef created what one rap critic called "the first street-credible, global hip-hop album."

Meanwhile, in her 1998 solo album, *The Miseducation of Lauryn Hill,* the Fugee's frontwoman pursued the pop-rap synthesis that she had begun with her performance of "Killing Me Softly," while projecting a sassy feminist persona. In addition to covering the pop-shlock standard "Can't Take My Eyes off of You," Hill's album included collaborations with a couple of R & B stylists (Mary J. Blige and D'Angelo), as well as with a legendary rock guitar hero (Carlos Santana). The album not only sold over five million copies, generated a huge MTV-abetted hit single—"Doo Wop (That Thing)"—but it earned the talented singer-producer an unprecedented five Grammy awards (most ever by a female performer), including Album of the Year.

By this point, even Public Enemy (which had once been notorious for generating an impeneterable wall of black noise out of layer on layer of break-beat samples) were showing themselves to be as adept as anyone in the use of the melodic pop hook. In the title track they created for Spike Lee's 1998 film, *He Got Game,* PE buoyed their ominous rap with a chorus set off by one of the 1960s most identifiable guitar riffs, Steven Stills's brief but memorable intro to Buffalo Springfield's youth-power anthem, "For What It's Worth." Naturally, Stills also made a guest appearance on the video.

Puff Daddy also collaborated with one of rock's legendary guitar heroes, Jimmy Page, when he produced a hip-hop remix of the Led Zeppelin classic "Kashmir" for the soundtrack of 1998's summer blockbuster, *Godzilla.* That same year, a new rapper on the hardcore scene, Jay-Z, even hit it big by recycling a song from the Broadway musical, *Annie;* in the video for "Hard-Knock Life," the imposing rapper was accompanied by nothing more threatening than a posse of adorable street urchins.

Which is not to say that rap's hardcore had simply vanished. For, despite the recent death toll, gangsta rap itself was alive and well in the late 1990s and hip-hop's modern-day badman ballads continued to generate excitement, controversy—and sales. Although rap's bicoastal body count did diminish sharply following the murders of Tupac and Biggy Smalls, the overheated rhetoric continued unabated. For example, once the novelty of his racial identity wore off, it was Eminem's graphic tales of domestic violence (as in the song "Kim" from his megahit CD, *The Marshall Mathers LP*) that drew the ire of feminists, editorial writers, and outraged politicians.

In general, however, gangsta rap at the millennium seemed to turn away from depictions of bullet-riddled gang-banging to celebrations of the fruits of the gangsta lifestyle. And while hip-hop's materialism and misogyny may have escalated exponentially over the years (along with its sales figures), the debates the records provoked just seemed like deja vu.

By contrast, the advent of a new generation of alternative/progressive rappers was seen by many as a cause for optimism. Although it often seemed that their voices were struggling to be heard over the latest tales of luxuries and lust, positive points of view did find expression in the work of rappers such as Common, who spoke out against hip-hop's prevailing values. "A lot of my friends were getting turned off to hip-hop because we were growing up," the twenty-five-year-old Common explained following the release of his 1998 debut CD, *Retrospect for Life.* "We were coming out of that stage of drinking forties [malt liquor] and calling girls 'bitches'."

Those with even more of a historical perspective saw in the diversity of rap's late-1990s styles a replay of the fragmentation that had taken place in rock music two decades earlier (when it had first become a billion-dollar business). Just as the monolithic rock culture of the 1960s had splintered into a dozen subgenres (including heavy metal, progressive rock, glam rock, and punk rock among others), now rap seemed to headed in the same direction with "gangsta rap," "pop rap," "alternative rap," and other hybrids (including "gospel rap") being tailored to different factions—and generations—of the vast hip-hop audience.

As the decade drew to a close, potentially fertile new fusions between rap and rock began to be explored on a number of fronts. On his 1996 breakthrough, *Odelay,* for example, Beck—a latter-day "master of records"—seemed to weld together fragments from the entire history of American popular music. Although the self-conscious complexity of his musical pastiches made Beck difficult to categorize, the performer forthrightly pledged allegiance to his hip-hop roots; in the celebratory chorus of *Odelay*'s hit single, "Where It's At," Beck answered the question implied in the song's title with the modern-day rallying cry: "two turntables and a microphone."

Meanwhile, picking up on some earlier experimental collaborations—such as Chuck D.'s hardcore alliance with the heavy metal band, Anthrax (on a version of PE's "Bring on Tha Noise") or Ice-T's black thrash-metal outfit, Body Count (of "Cop Killer" infamy)—such late 1990s bands as Korn, Rage Against the Machine, 311, and Limp Bizkit began supplementing their own heavy metal and punk rock formulas with rapping and hip-hop beats.

In just twenty-five years, rap music had evolved from an underground South Bronx street culture to an international phenomenon. All around the world—and in dozens of different languages—there were rappers telling their stories (and dissing the competition), while DJs scatched and sampled classic American break-beats, along with exotic local rhythms. As the new millennium got under way, the echoes of the talking drum could be heard reverberating throughout the global village.

Activities and Projects
Chapter 6: Rap: Talking Drum for the Global Village

1. Trace elements of rap's distinctive lyric and rhythmic style to sources in both African and African-American music and culture.

2. Research the links between gangsta rap and badman ballads from the African-American folk tradition.

3. Research the links between "message rap" and the sociopolitical songs prevalent in rhythm and blues and soul music during the late 1960s and early 1970s.

4. Hip-hop's first "masters of records" prided themselves on the diversity of the music they used to generate their beats. Assemble an annotated discography of the songs that provided the raw materials of early rap music's aural collages.

5. Present an overview of New York's hip-hop culture c. 1979 including breakdancing, break-beat music, and graffiti, as well as slang and dress styles.

6. By referring to specific recordings from rap history, explore the ways that hip-hop DJs and producers have made creative use of each of the following: the turntable, the drum machine, and the digital sampler.

7. Provide an overview of the debates generated by the alleged obscenity, violence, and misogyny of rap lyrics. Explain your own point of view regarding these issues.

8. Explore the links between rap and jazz (suggested by Quincy Jones's 1989 album *Back on the Block*), as well as by the jazz/rap fusions of "acid jazz" DJs and rap groups such as Gang Starr and US3.

9. Create a "Hip-Hop Herstory." Survey the contributions of women rappers (from "Roxanne's Revenge" to the present). Explore various aspects of rap's female perspective.

10. As rap expanded into a billion-dollar industry during the 1990s, it went through a period of fragmentation similar to the one experienced by rock two decades earlier. Create a survey of contemporary rap subgenres or explore the fusions between rap and other styles of popular music.

Sound Sources

"I hear America singing, the varied carols I hear…"
(Walt Whitman)

Nothing can take the place of actually hearing those varied carols that comprise the history of America's popular music. By now, a century of sound has been preserved on recording, much of it readily available at one's local record store or via the Internet. Ultimately—once the legal and economic issues are resolved—most of these recordings will be accessible at the stroke of a computer key; but until that vast virtual archive opens to the public, there are a number of record companies whose catalogs offer compilations of special interest as well as more obscure items.

Sources

1. **Smithsonian Folkways:** 955 L'Enfant Plaza, Suite 7300, Washington, DC 20560-0953. Tel. (800) 410-9815. www.si.edu/folkways.

    In addition to a broad range of folk, blues, and early jazz recordings, the Folkways catalog contains excellent examples of regional, world, and ethnic music (including Native American material), field recordings (of work songs and spirituals), as well as spoken word and children's records. The label is perhaps best known for its classic Woody Guthrie material and for Harry Smith's celebrated *Anthology of American Folk Music.*

2. **Smithsonian Institution Books and Records:** Tel. (800) 863-9943. www.si.edu.youandsi/products.

    Along with authoritative anthologies of country music, popular songs, big band swing, and jazz vocalists, the label is most noted for the *Smithsonian Collection of Classic Jazz* (a ninety-five-selection history of the music from Scott Joplin to the World Saxophone Quartet).

3. **New World Records:** 701 Seventh Avenue, New York, NY 10036-1596. Tel. (212) 302-0460. www.musicmaker.com.

    Through its Recorded Anthology of American Music project, NWR currently offers 350 extremely thoughtful thematic collections of traditional and contemporary music, including many rare and obscure recordings of regional and ethnic music, blues, early jazz, and spirituals.

4. **Rounder Records:** One Camp Street, Cambridge, MA 02140. (800) 44-DISCS. www.rounder.com.

    The Rounder catalog assembles a wide-ranging selection of contemporary and traditional blues, bluegrass, folk, ethnic and world music, rock, and reggae both on its own label and from a dozen other speciality record companies.

5. **Arhoolie Records** (mail order from: Down Home Music Store, 10341 San Pablo Avenue, El Cerrito, CA. Tel 510-525-2129). www.arhoolie.com.

    One of best sources for classic recordings of country and urban blues, early jazz, Cajun, zydeco, and traditional Tex-Mex/Tejano music.

6. **Yazoo Records/Shanachie:** 177 Contiague Rock Road, Westbury, NY 11590.
    Tel. (516) 938-8080. www.yazoobluesmailorder.com.

    Most notable for its excellent collections of early folk blues and jug band recordings devoted to individual artists, specific instrumental techniques, or regional styles.

7. **County Records:** P.O. Box 19, Floyd, VA 20409.
    Tel. (703) 745-2001. www.countysales.com.

    Offers a comprehensive collection of country, bluegrass, and hillbilly-era music including many obscure recordings.

8. **Rhino Records:** P.O.Box 60008, Tampa, FL 33660-0008.
    Tel. (800) 546-3670. www.rhino.com.

    The Rhino catalog contains both reissues of classic out-of-print recordings as well as its own thoughtfully conceived anthologies of blues, jazz, country, ethnic, and regional music, show tunes, film scores, R & B, rock, and rap.

Bibliography

Albertson, Chris. *Bessie*. New York: Stein and Day, 1972.

Baker, Houston A. *Black Studies, Rap and the Academy*. University of Chicago Press, 1993.

————. *Blues Ideology and Afro-American Literature*. University of Chicago Press, 1986.

Balliett, Whitney. *American Musicians: 56 Portraits in Jazz*. Oxford University Press, 1990.

Bangs, Lester. *Psychotic Reactions and Carburetor Dung*. New York: Knopf, 1987.

Bean, Anne Marie, et. al. *Inside the Minstrel Mask: Readings in Nineteenth Century Blackface Minstrelsy*. University Press of New England, 1996.

Bechet, Sidney. *Treat It Gentle*. New York, 1960.

Bergreen, Laurence. *Louis Armstrong: An Extravagant Life*. New York, 1996.

Betrock, Alan. *Girl Groups: The Story of a Sound*. Delilah Books, 1982.

Blesh, Rudi and Harriet Janis. *They All Played Ragtime*. New York, 1971.

Bushell, Garvin and Mark Tucker. *Jazz from the Beginning*. New York. 1998.

Cantwell, Robert. *When We Were Good: The Folk Revival*. Harvard University Press, 1996.

Charters, Samuel B. and Leonard Kunstadt. *Jazz: A History of the New York Scene*. New York, 1984.

————. *The Country Blues*. New York: Rinehart, 1959.

Chase, Gilbert. *America's Music: From the Pilgrims to the Present*. University of Illinois Press, 1987.

Child Francis James. *The English and Scottish Popular Ballads*. New York: Dover, 1965.

Christgau, Robert. *Grown Up All Wrong: 75 Great Rock and Pop Artists From Vaudeville to Techno*. Harvard University Press, 1999.

Collier, James Lincoln. *Jazz: The American Theme Song*. New York. 1995.

Costello, Mark and David Foster Wallace. *Signifying Rappers: Rap and Race in the Urban Present*. Harper Collins, New York: 1997.

Covach, John and Graeme M. Boone. *Understanding Rock: Essays in Musical Analysis*. Oxford University Press, 1997.

Crenshaw, Marshall. *Hollywood Rock: A Guide to Rock'n'Roll in the Movies*. Harper Perennial, 1994.

Dahl, Linda. *Stormy Weather: The Music and Lives of a Century of Jazz Women*. New York, 1992.

Dannen, Fredric. *Hit Men: Power Brokers and Fast Money Inside the Music Business*. Vintage Books, 1991.

Davis Angela Y. *Blues Legacies and Black Feminism: Gertrude "Ma" Rainey, Bessie Smith and Billie Holiday*. New York: Random House, 1998.

Davis, Francis. *The History of the Blues: The Roots, the Music, the People: From Charlie Patton to Robert Cray*. New York, 1996.

Denisoff, Serge R. *Great Day Coming: Folk Music and the American Left*. University of Illinois Press, 1971.

————. *Solid Gold: The Popular Record Industry*. New Brunswick, NJ: Transaction Books, 1975.

Dettmar, Kevin J.H. and William Richey. *Reading Rock and Roll: Authenticity, Appropriation, Aesthetics*. Columbia University Press, 1999.

Deveaux, Scott. *The Birth of Bebop: A Social and Musical History*. Berkeley, 1997.

Dugaw, Dianne, ed. *The Anglo-American Ballad: A Folklore Casebook*. Garland Publishing, Inc., 1995.

Ellington, Edward Kennedy. *Music is My Mistress*. New York. 1975.

Emerson, Ken. *Doo-dah! Stephen Foster and the Rise of American Popular Culture*. New York, 1997.

Escott, Colin with Martin Hawkins. *Sun Records and the Birth of Rock'n'Roll*. New York: St. Martin's Press, 1991.

Ewen, David. *All the Years of American Popular Music*. Prentice Hall, 1977.

Feather, Leonard. *The Encyclopedia of Jazz*. New York: Horizon Press, 1959.

Filene, Benjamin. *Romancing the Folk: Public Memory and American Roots Music*. University of North Carolina Press, 2000.

Finkelstein, Sidney. *Jazz: A People's Music*. New York, 1948.

Foster, Pops, with Thomas Stoddard. *Pops Foster: The Autobiography of a New Orleans Jazzman*. Berkeley, 1971.

Friedlander, Paul. *A Social History of Rock and Roll*. Boulder, Colo., 1996.

Friedwald, Will. *Jazz Singing: America's Great Voices from Bessie Smith to Bebop and Beyond*. New York, 1996.

Garr, Gillian G. *She's A Rebel: The History of Women in Rock and Roll*. Seal Press, 1991

Gelatt, Roland. *The Fabulous Phonograph, 1877–1977*. New York: Macmillan, 1977.

George, Nelson. *Hip Hop America*. Viking Penguin, 1998.

Giddens, Gary. *Celebrating Bird: The Triumph of Charlie Parker.* New York, 1998.

———. *Satchmo.* Anchor Books, New York, 1988.

———. *Visions of Jazz: The First Century.* New York, 1998.

Gillett, Charlie. *The Sound of the City: The Rise of Rock and Roll.* New York: Pantheon, 1983.

Gitler, Ira. *Swing to Bop.* New York, 1985.

Goia, Ted. *The History of Jazz.* New York, 1997.

Goodman, Andrew. *Dancing in the Distraction Factory: Music Television and Popular Culture.* University of Minnesota, 1992.

Gottlieb, Robert, ed. *Reading Jazz: A Gathering of Autobiography, Reportage and Criticism from 1919 to Now.* New York, 1996.

Gourse, Leslie. *Madame Jazz: Contemporary Women Instrumentalists.* New York, 1995.

Greenway, Peter. *American Folksongs of Protest.* New York, 1970.

Gridley, Mark. *Jazz Styles: History and Analysis.* Prentice Hall, 2000.

Guralnick, Peter. *Careless Love: The Unmaking of Elvis Presley.* Little Brown & Co., 1998.

———. *Last Train to Memphis: The Rise of Elvis Presley.* Little Brown & Co., 1995.

———. *Searching for Robert Johnson.* New York: E.P. Dutton, 1989.

———. *Sweet Soul Music: Rhythm and Blues and the Southern Dream of Freedom.* Harper and Row, 1986.

Guthrie, Woody. *Bound for Glory.* New York: E.P. Dutton, 1976.

Hamm, Charles. *Yesterdays: Popular Music in America.* New York, 1983.

Hammond, John. *Hammond on Record: An Autobiography.* New York: Summit Books, 1981.

Harris, Michael. *Rise of Gospel Blues: The Music of Thomas Andrew Dorsey in the Urban Church.* Harvard University Press, 1997.

Heilbut, Anthony. *The Gospel Sound: Good News and Bad Times.* New York. 1971.

Hentoff, Nat. *The Jazz Life.* New York: Dial Press, 1975.

Herrera-Sobek, Maria. *The Mexican Corrido: A Feminist Analysis.* Indiana University Press, 1990.

Hirshey, Gerri. *Nowhere to Run: The Story of Soul Music.* New York: Times Books, 1984.

Holiday, Billie with William Duffy. *Lady Sings the Blues.* New York, 1965.

Jackson, Bruce. *Wake Up Dead Man: Afro-American Work Songs from The Texas Prisons.* Harvard University Press, 1972.

Jasen, David A. *Tin Pan Alley: The Composers, the Songs, the Performers and Their Times.* New York, 1988.

Jones, LeRoi. *Blues People: Negro Music in White America.* William Morrow, 1963.

———. *Black Music.* New York: William Morrow, 1968.

Keil, Charles. *Urban Blues.* University of Chicago Press, 1966.

Kenney, William Howard. *Chicago Jazz: A Cultural History, 1904–1930.* New York, 1993.

Klein, Joe. *Woody Guthrie: A Life.* New York: Alfred A. Knopf, 1980.

Leonard, Neil. *Jazz and the White Americans.* University of Chicago Press, 1962.

Lhamon, Jr., W.T. *Raising Cain: Blackface Performance from Jim Crow to Hip Hop.* Harvard University Press, 1997.

Light, Alan, ed. *The Vibe History of Hip Hop.* Random House. New York, 1999.

Litweiler, John. *The Freedom Principle: Jazz After 1958.* New York, 1984.

Lomax, Alan. *Land Where the Blues Began.* New York: Pantheon, 1993.

———. *The Folk Songs of North America.* Macmillan, 1947.

Lovell, John, Jr. *Black Song: The Forge and the Flame. The Story of How the Afro-American Spiritual Was Hammered Out.* New York, 1972.

Loza, Steven. *Barrio Rhythm: Mexican-American Music in Los Angeles.* University of Illinois Press, 1993.

Malone, Bill C. *Country Music, USA: A Fifty-Year History.* Austin: University of Texas Press, 1968.

Marcus, Greil. *Mystery Train: Images of America in Rock and Roll Music.* New York: E.P. Dutton, 1975.

Marquis, Donald M. *In Search of Buddy Bolden: First Man of Jazz.* Baton Rouge, 1978.

McDonnell, Evelyn and Ann Powers. *Rock She Wrote: Women Write About Rock, Pop And Rap,* 1999.

Millard, Andre. *America on Record: A History of Recorded Sound.* Cambridge University Press, 1995.

Miller, Jim, ed. *The Rolling Stone Illustrated History of Rock & Roll.* New York: Random House, 1980.

Mingus, Charles. *Beneath the Underdog.* New York: Knopf, 1971.

Murray, Albert. *Stomping the Blues.* New York: McGraw-Hill, 1976.

———. *The Hero and the Blues.* New York: Vintage Books, 1995.

Norman, Philip. *Shout! The Beatles in Their Generation.* New York: Fireside Books, Simon & Schuster, 1997.

Oakley, Giles. *The Devil's Music: A History of the Blues.* New York: Taplinger, 1977.

Ogren, Sarah J. *The Jazz Revolution: Twenties America and the Meaning of Jazz.* New York, 1989.

Oliver, Paul. *Blues Fell This Morning: The Meaning of the Blues.* New York: Horizon, 1960.

———. *Savannah Syncopators: African Retentions in the Blues.* Briarcliff Manor: Stein & Day, 1970.

Palmer, Robert. *Deep Blues.* New York: Viking Press, 1981.

Paredes, Americo. *A Texas Mexican Cancionero.* University of Texas Press, 1995.

———. *With His Pistol in His Hand*. University of Texas Press, 1986.

Perkins, William Eric, ed. *Droppin' Science: Critical Essays on Rap Music and Hip Hop Culture*, Temple University Press, 1996.

Piazza. Tom. *Blues Up and Down: Jazz in Our Time*. New York, 1997.

Placksin, Sally. *American Women in Jazz: 1900 to the Present*. New York, 1982.

Ramsey, Frederick, Jr. and Charles Edward Smith. *Jazzmen: The Story of Hot Jazz Told in the Lives of the Men Who Created It*. New York, 1939.

Reyes, David and Tom Waldman. *Land of a Thousand Dances: Chicano Rock 'n' Roll From Southern California*. University of New Mexico Press, 1998.

Roberts, John Storm. *Black Music of Two Worlds*. New York: Praeger, 1972.

———. *The Latin Tinge: The Impact of Latin American Music on the United States*. Oxford University Press, 1979.

Rose, Tricia. *Black Noise: Rap Music and Black Culture in Modern America*. Wesleyan University Press, 1994.

Russell, Ross. *Jazz Style in Kansas City and the Southwest*. New York, 1997.

Sanjek, Russell and David Sanjek. *American Popular Music and Its Business*. New York: Oxford University Press, 1991.

Savoy, Ann Allen. *Cajun Music: A Reflection of a People (vol.1)*. Bluebird Press, 1984.

Schafer, William John *Brass Bands and New Orleans Jazz*. Baton Rouge, 1977.

Schuller, Gunther. *Early Jazz: Its Roots and Musical Development*. Oxford University Press, 1986.

———. *The Swing Era*. Oxford University Press, 1989.

Sexton, Adam, ed. *Rap on Rap: Straight Up Talk on Hip Hop Culture*. New York: Del Publishing, 1995.

Shapiro, Nat and Nat Hentoff. *Hear Me Talkin' to Ya: The Story of Jazz as Told by the Men Who Made It*. New York, 1966.

Sharp Cecil. *English Folk Songs from the Southern Appalachians*. Oxford University Press, 1932.

Shaw, Arnold. *Honkers and Shouters*. New York: Macmillan, 1971.

Simon, George T. *The Big Bands*. New York: Schirmer Books, 1981.

Southern, Eileen. *The Music of Black Americans: A History*. New York: W.W. Norton, 1971.

Spellman, A.B. *Four Lives in the Bebop Business*. New York: Pantheon Books, 1966.

Spenser, John Michael. *Sacred Music of the Secular City: Blues to Rap*. Duke University Press, 1991.

Stearns, Marshall. *The Story of Jazz*. New York: Oxford University Press, 1970.

Stuessy, Joe and Scott D. Lipscomb. *Rock and Roll: Its History and Stylistic Development*. Prentice Hall, 1998.

Sudhalter, Richard M. *Lost Chords: White Musicians and Their Contributions to Jazz, 1915–1945*. New York, 1999.

Toll, Robert C. *Blacking Up: The Minstrel Show in Nineteenth Century America*. New York: University Press, 1974.

Toop, David. *Rap Attack*. Serpent's Tail Press, 1999.

Tosches, Nick. *Country: The Twisted Roots of Rock 'n' Roll*. Da Capo Press, 1996.

Waldo, Terry. *This is Ragtime*. New York. 1991.

Walser, Robert, ed. *Keeping Time: Readings in Jazz History*. New York, 1999.

———. *Running With the Devil: Power, Gender and Madness in Heavy Metal Music*. Wesleyan University Press, 1993.

Watkins, Mel. *On the Real Side: Laughing, Lying and Signifying*. New York, 1994.

Wells, Evelyn Kendick. *The Ballad Tree*. New York, 1950.

Whitburn, Joel. *Top Pop Records, 1955–1970: Facts About 9800 Recordings Listed in Billboard's "Hot 100" Charts, Grouped Under the Names of 2500 Recording Artists*. Detroit: Gale Research, 1972.

Williams, Martin. *The Jazz Tradition*. New York: Oxford University Press, 1970.

Wolfe, Charles and Kip Lornell. *The Life of Leadbelly*. New York, 1994.

Glossary

a cappella: vocal music without instrumental accompaniment.

arrangement: (a.k.a. "chart"): a written musical score for a jazz orchestra or band.

ballad: traditionally refers to a narrative folk song using a strophic structure; in the context of the popular music industry (and jazz) it describes a song with a slow tempo and lyrics related to love or romance.

beat box: the term—credited to the hip-hop DJ, Grandmaster Flash—refers to electronic percussion instruments that provide rhythmic accompaniment for rap recordings. Along the way, some MCs became adept at imitating these percussion sounds vocally, thereby earning the designation "human beat box."

blue note: the "flatted" (lowered) or "bent" notes occurring in the third, fifth, or seventh interval of major scales often employed by blues or jazz performers.

blues: an African-American song form that emerged at the turn of the twentieth century; among the defining elements of the blues are: a twelve-bar musical structure, three-line (AAB) lyric stanza, and a I–IV–I–V–I harmonic progression tinged with blue notes.

boogie-woogie: a jazz piano style emphasizing a repeated eight-beats-to-the-bar bass pattern (ostinato) set against free right-hand improvisations.

bottleneck (guitar style): see "slide guitar."

bridge: (a.k.a. "release") the eight-bar "B" section of a 32-bar (AABA) Tin Pan Alley popular song form characterized by a change in rhythm and key from the rest of the composition.

Brill Building: refers to the midtown Manhattan office building (1619 Broadway) that was the center of the pop music publishing industry (Tin Pan Alley) from the 1930s to the 1950s.

broadside ballad: originally referred to ballads printed on one side of a sheet of paper (often accompanied by a woodblock illustration); more recently, the term has been used to identify any topical folk song containing a political or social commentary.

brass section: the part of a jazz orchestra comprised of a combination of trumpets and trombones (and other brass instruments like cornet and tuba).

break: a short solo (usually two to four measures) placed between ensemble passages in a jazz performance. In early hip hop (a.k.a "break-beat" music), recorded percussion breaks provided the accompaniment for the raps of a crew of MCs.

call-and-response form: refers to musical structure in which a statement—"call"—by a soloist is answered by a "response" from an ensemble of chorus; an essential component of African-derived music perpetuated in America in work songs (and subsequently in gospel, blues, jazz, and R & B).

chord progression (chord changes, "changes"): any series of related chords; the series of chords that provide the harmonic foundation of a song (as well as the basis for jazz improvisation).

chorus: can refer to a few different (somewhat related) meanings:

a. the repeated refrain that occurs between the narrative verses of a folk-based song
b. one thirty-two-bar (AABA) section of a Tin Pan Alley pop song
c. the complete cycle of a song's chord progression (that forms the basis of a jazz improvisation).

collective improvisation: the style of simultaneous group improvisation that was characteristic of the original New Orleans jazz bands.

combo: the generic name for any small instrumental ensemble (usually ranging from a trio to a sextet or septet).

Country & Western: by the 1940s, the folk-based popular music known as "hillbilly" (see entry below) needed a name that reflected the style's new sound and legitimacy; the growing influence of cowboy imagery in the music and performers' clothing made this a natural choice; by the 1970s, the genre simply became known as Country.

cover version: any new version of a previously recorded song. In the early 1950s—during the transition to rock 'n 'roll—record companies would release cover versions by white performers of the latest R & B songs as a way of making inroads into the new teen market.

crossover: when a recording intended for a particular market (i.e., pop, R & B or Country) achieves such broad appeal with another segment of the market that it enters the sales chart devoted to a different genre.

cutting contest: informal jazz competitions during which individual performers (or bands) attempt to outplay—or "cut"—each other (as determined either by audience response or the general consensus of the musicians themselves).

doo-wop: during the late 1940s/early 1950s, male a cappella vocal groups often employed harmonized nonsense syllables to create a backdrop for their lead vocalists; it was one such set of syllables that gave this style of R & B its name.

drum machine: electronic instruments capable of generating drum sounds and programmable rhythm patterns; during the 1970s, funk performers such as Stevie Wonder and Sly and the Family Stone added the drum machine's mechanized beats to the more traditional contributions of their rhythm section (also see "beat box").

field holler (a.k.a. holler, shout, arhoolie): free-form vocalization (often employing melismas and falsetto effects) that were developed during slavery by field hands as a form of communication or personal expression; elements of the field holler can be identified in the traditional country blues that emerged at the turn of the twentieth century.

gospel music: generally refers to a style of American-American religious music (first developed in the late 1920s by Thomas A. Dorsey) that infused blues and popular song elements into traditional hymns and spirituals; the meaning of the genre's name—"good news"—is reflected in the style's optimistic, ecstatic quality. Beginning in the 1950s, many gospel performers (such as Sam Cooke, Dinah Washington, Aretha Franklin, and Lou Rawls) began to "cross over" to rhythm and blues.

Grand Ole Opry: name of the one of the oldest and most influential live radio "barn dance" shows; first broadcast on station WSM in Nashville in 1925, it brought—and continues to bring—the sounds of Country music to a large portion of the South.

griot (a.k.a. jail, finah): often referred to as "praise singers" or "oral historians," the griot has fulfilled a traditional role in West African tribal cultures for many centuries; they have often been identified as the spiritual ancestors of African-American bluesmen and modern-day rappers.

hardcore: general name for styles of rap that reflect a "gansta" sensibility (assertive, often profanity laced scenarios) set to aggressive, heavily percussive beats.

harmony: the simultaneous production of two or more tones (which can be combined to create chords).

harp (slang): harmonica, especially in a blues context. Among the genre's most-significant harp players are: Sonny Terry, Sonny Boy Williamson II (Rice Miller), Little Walter, and James Cotton.

head arrangement: an unwritten arrangement for a tune that is worked out informally by band members (memorized or maintained in their "head")

hillbilly music: the name given to the commercial recordings of string bands and ballad singers first issued during the 1920s; the demeaning name also reflected the stereotypical images embodied in the performers' costumes (tattered overalls, corncob pipes, and straw hats) and band names (The Skillet Lickers, Dixie Clodhoppers, Possum Hunters).

hootenanny: the term first emerged in the 1940s among New York City's politically progressive folk singing community (led by Woody Guthrie and Pete Seeger) to refer to their informal songfests; it was later adopted by members of the Sixties folk revival (led by Joan Baez and Bob Dylan).

honky tonk: the name of a rhythmically insistent brand of modern country music that originated during the late 1930s in the rural roadside taverns known as "honky tonks"; among the performers most closely identified with the style are Ernest Tubb, Floyd Tillman, Hank Thompson, and Hank Williams.

jam session: an informal gathering at which performers take turns improvising on familiar jazz tunes, popular standards, or the blues.

jitterbug: both the name of a Depression/Swing era dance (also known as the Lindy or Lindy Hop) done to up-tempo big band jazz—and of the young dancers who performed it.

jug band (a.k.a. spasm band, skiffle band): African-American folk ensembles comprised of such simple or homemade instruments as harmonica, kazoo, washboard (played with metal thimbles), guitar—and a jug that gave the style its name; blowing into the empty glass or ceramic jug would produce a deep, resonant sound that provided an effective bass part.

juke joint: name given to local establishments (often little more than a tiny shack or cabin) in the rural South where members of the African-American community could drink and party to the music of a blues singer or pianist.

key (tonality): name of the tonic (first and primary note) on which a tonal composition is based.

measure (bar): a musical unit containing an established number of beats (units of equal duration); in the standard blues tune, there are twelve measures (or bars) of music, each made up of four beats.

melisma: decorative vocal effects applied to a sustained note; often used by African-American gospel singers for their expressive and emotional quality, it was adopted as a technique by Sixties soul singers.

minstrel show: an extremely popular form of entertainment during the second half of the nineteenth century comprised of musical numbers and comedic skits based on caricatures of African-American culture performed by white entertainers in black-face make up. Around 1900, black entertainers in the South formed their own minstrel companies.

modal (scalar): music based on one of the twelve traditional modes; during the 1960s, musicians like Miles Davis and John Coltrane began using modal structures as a basis of their compositions and improvisations.

mode: a system of scales that developed in medieval times; limited to tones of the diatonic scale (that is, using only the white keys of the piano) and to one octave in range.

multitrack recording: during the 1960s, advances in audio technological provided the opportunity to add (overdub) separately taped components (tracks) onto the previously recorded vocal and instrumental material.

Negro spiritual: religious songs created by African-American slaves—based for the most part on Old Testament stories (i.e., "Go Down, Moses," "Didn't the Lord Deliver Daniel")—which expressed their hope for freedom and redemption. Beginning in 1877, performances by the Fisk Jubilee Singers brought these songs to the attention of enthusiastic audiences around the world. Later, traditional spirituals found their way into the repertoire of African-American concert performers like Marian Anderson and Paul Robeson.

novelty song: term used for both Tin Pan Alley or rock era popular songs and jazz tunes (especially from the 1920s and 1930s) designed around a comedic device (i.e., the Coaster's "Yakety Yak") or sound effects (i.e., the Original Dixieland Jazz Band's "Livery Stable Blues," which featured animal sounds played by the various instruments).

obbligato: an instrumental melody line played as an accompaniment to a vocal performance; in jazz history, the obbligato passages Louis Armstrong provided for Bessie Smith (in the 1920s) and those contributed by Lester Young for Billie Holiday (in the 1930s and 1940s) are especially noteworthy.

ostinato: a regularly repeated melodic phrase or rhythmic pattern (as in the left-hand part of a boogie-woogie piano piece).

payola: term given to the (widespread) practice wherein record companies provided cash or other inducements to radio disk jockeys for playing their recordings on the air.

pentatonic scale: a five-note scale (within the range of one octave); used in various traditional cultures around the world, such scales form the basis of most Anglo-American folk ballad melodies.

polyrhythm: two or more rhythmic patterns maintained simultaneously; a fundamental component of African music, polyrhythms became an essential element in jazz.

Race records: term adopted by the record industry in the early 1920s to market primarily African-American blues, jazz and religious music on specialized labels like Okeh, Vocalion and Black Swan.

rag: refers either to a ragtime composition (i.e., "Maple Leaf Rag" by Scott Joplin), or when used as a verb (to rag) to the act of improvising on a melody in a syncopated style.

ragtime: style of piano music that evolved during the turn of the twentieth century primarily in the Midwest; derived from African-American folk styles, it is characterized by a regularly-accented two-beat (march-like) rhythmic accompaniment set against a syncopated melody.

reed section: the part of a big band comprised of saxophones and clarinets (instruments whose sound is produced by the vibration of a reed inserted in the mouthpiece).

responsorial (singing): term given to style of performance in which a soloist alternates with a chorus; the fundamental technique of most American-American vocal music from work songs and gospel to R & B and Soul.

rhythm section: the group of instruments in a big band or combo that provide the music's rhythmic foundation; a rhythm section typically includes piano, guitar, bass and drum.

riff: a short, repeated rhythmic or melodic fragment.

sampling: the use of computer-based technology to appropriate, store, manipulate, and play any sound or musical excerpt; it has become a formidable creative technique in many genres of contemporary popular music, especially rap and techno.

scat singing: style of jazz singing (often credited to Louis Armstrong) that jettisons lyrics and substitutes spontaneously-improvised nonsense syllables.

sideman: term used to identify any member of a band or ensemble other than the group's leader.

slide guitar style (a.k.a. bottleneck style): technique in which the performer slides the blade of a knife or the neck of a glass bottle down the strings to create a whining, slithering sound.

strophic form: a song form in which every verse is set to the same melody; typical of traditional hymns and folk ballads.

swing: term used to describe the rhythmic quality peculiar to jazz that is generated by subtle inflections or alterations of the music's regular pulse; as Duke Ellington memorably expressed it, in the world of jazz, "It don't mean a thing if it ain't got that swing."

syncopation: shift in metrical accent to the weak or unaccented note; such displacements from the regular meter are characteristic of African-American music.

synthesizer: developed by the engineer Robert Moog in the mid-1960s, the synthesizer is an instrument capable of electronically replicating or generating virtually any sound; it was initially adopted the Beatles, Stevie Wonder, the Who, and other bands that were already experimenting with recording studio technology.

tempo: the speed at which a musical composition is performed.

Third Stream: a term credited to the musicologist and composer, Gunther Schuller, to identify styles of jazz that combine elements of jazz (i.e., improvisation and a swing feel) with aspects of classical music (i.e., instrumentation, extended or multi-section forms).

timbre: the unique sound or tonal color of an instrument or individual voice (the quality that allows one to distinguish one instrument from another or even one performer from another).

Tin Pan Alley: the name given to the popular song industry (comprised of music publishing companies, promoters and songwriters) that was centered in New York City during the first half of the twentieth century.

TOBA: the Theater Owners Booking Association was an organization that provided entertainment for a circuit of African-American theaters located across much of the South and Midwest during the vaudeville era (c. 1900–1930s). The working conditions on the T.O.B.A. were so rigorous that performers altered the meaning of its initials to: Tough on Black Artists (or "Asses").

twelve-bar blues: see "blues."

vaudeville: form of live popular entertainment offering a variety of acts—including dancers, comedians, vocalists, acrobats and jugglers—that flourished during the first few decades of the 20th century.

walking bass: used to describe a style of accompaniment played by the double bass (bass violin) in which plucked scale-like patterns of quarter notes create a relaxed, ambling effect.

work song: the songs used by workers primarily as a means of establishing the rhythm best suited to accomplish a particular task; in work songs created by African-American slaves, a statement by the work song leader would be answered by a group of workers using semi-improvised lyrics. These call-and-response verses have been identified as one of the essential sources of the blues.

zydeco: style of popular dance music created during the 1930s by members of the French-speaking, African-American ("Cajun") culture of Louisiana and West Texas; small ensembles consisting of accordion, violin, saxophone, and a rhythm section fused blues and indigenous folk styles to accompany lyrics sung in the distinctive local dialect.

Index

NOTE: *Italic page numbers indicate photographs.*

AACM. *See* Association for the
    Advancement of Creative Musicians
ABC (British New Pop group), 283
Abrams, Muhal Richard, 162
Abramson, Herb, 198
A cappella performances, 4
Accordions, 22
AC/DC, 254, 300
Ace, Johnny, 168
Acid-jazz DJs, 343
Adderley, Julian "Cannonball," 149, 150,
    161
"Adventures of Grandmaster Flash On the
    Wheels of Steel, The," 280, 327, 334
Aerosmith, 254, 330, 332
African-Americans. *See also under* Black;
    Racial division/segregation
  blues recording market of, 60
  blues themes, 48
  British Invasion and, 219–221
  call-and-response pattern, 45, 323
  on Ray Charles's soul music, 199, 201
  Congo Square, New Orleans, 81
  Free Jazz and, 159
  funk, 269–271
  girl groups, 191
  griots and songsters, 14
  heavy metal, 304
  on Hendrix, 240
  independent recording labels and, 167
  jazz bands, 90, 92
  migration to Chicago, 90
  migration to Kansas City, 108
  migration to New York, 105
  Motown, 194–195
  on MTV, 286
  narrative songs, 14–15, 17
  New Orleans' Creole culture and, 82, 86
  New York network radio and, 102, 111
  reggae and, 276
  rhythm and blues and, 145
  ritual competition, 323
  on Sly Stone, 240
  soul music, 1870s, 266–269
  spirituals of, 45, 207
  Swing Era and, 114
  talking drum and, 317
  U2's *Rattle and Hum,* 300
  vaudeville and, 58
African slaves
  blues, 52
  drums as communication for, 317
  work songs, 42

Afro-Cuban music, 144
Agnew, Spiro, 246
Aguilera, Christina, 313
"Ain't Misbehavin'" (Razaf/Waller), 96, 107
Air (trio), 162
Albee, Edward, 64
Albertson, Chris, 64
Aldon Music, 191, 257
Alexander, Texas, 51
Alhambra Ballroom, Harlem, 107
Ali, Muhammad, 323
Alice in Chains, 305
"All American Rhythm Section." *See* Basie,
    "Count"
Allen, Red, 114
Allen, Steve, 181, 256, 309
Allman Brothers Band, *251*
Almanac Singers, 30
Altamont Speedway, 245–246
Alternative rap, 343
Altman, Robert, 259
American Bandstand, 182, 188, 269
American Graffiti, 252
American Heritage, 162
"American Pie" (McLean), 252
Ammons, Albert, *64*
Amos, Tori, 296
AM radio, 253. *See also* Radio
A & M Records, 275
Angels, 193
Animals, 72, 77, 221–222
Anka, Paul, 186
Ansermet, Ernest, 98
Anson, Bill, 183
Answer records, rap, 332
Anthology of American Folk Music, The, 30,
    31
Anthony, Marc, 295
Anthrax, 304, 361
Anti-war movement, 217, 225, 246
AOR (Album Oriented Rock), 270, 274
Apolonia, 290
Apple, Fiona, 313
Archies, 253
Aristocrat (recording label), 71, 73
Arizona, Public Enemy on, 340
Armatrading, Joan, 260
Armstrong, Lillian Hardin, 92
Armstrong, Louis, 64, *94, 95,* 99, 110, 123
  and the All-Stars, 96
  on bebop, 136–137
  on Beiderbecke, 101
  Creole Jazz Band and, 92, 93, 94

  Dixieland revival and, 149
  Henderson's orchestra and, 102, 103
Armstrong, Lucille, 96
Arrested Development, 343
Art Ensemble of Chicago, The, 162
Art rock, 260–262
Ashford, Nick, 197
Ashley, Clarence, 32
Association for the Advancement of
    Creative Musicians, 162
Asylum Records, 250
Atkins, Cholly, 197
Atlantic Records, 71, 167, 198–199, 233,
    250
"Austin High Gang," 99
Avalon, Frankie, 186, 188
Avant garde jazz, 150, 152–155
Ayler, Albert, 162

B-52s, 274
Bachrach, Burt, 192, 277
"Back Door Man," 78
Bad Boy Entertainment, 343
Bad Brains, 308
Badu, Erykah, 296
Baez, Joan, 10, 30, 32, *33,* 37, 217, 241
Bailey, Buster, 90, 92, 102
Bajo sexto (twelve-string bass guitar), 18
Baker, Arthur, 327
Baker, Dorothy, 101
Baker, Ginger, *235,* 236
Baker, LaVerne, 168, 175–176, 198
Balin, Marty, 246
"Ballad of Gregorio Cortez, The," 19, 20,
    21
Ballad of Tradition, The (Gerould), 1–2, 14
Ballads. *See also* Folk ballads
  derivation of term, 1, 4
Ballad Tree, The (Wells), 7
Ballard, Florence, 234
Balliet, Whitney, 128
Bambaattaa, Afrika, 320, *321,* 322, 323,
    327
Band, The, 218
Bangles, 293
Bangs, Lester, 215
Baquet, Achille, 86
Baraka, Amiri, 317. *See also* Jones,
    LeRoi
"Barbara Allen," 4–5, 9
Barbarians, 210
Barbecue Bob, 52
Barlow, William, 323

Barrelhouse blues, 66, 67
Barry, Jeff, 193
Basie, "Count," 110, 115, *116*, 128, 129
    Hammond and, 118, 121
    (B.) Holiday and, 117
Basquiat, Jean-Michel, *127*, 128
Bass, Ralph, 208
Bauza, Mario, 141
B-boys/b-boying, 318, 320. *See also* B-girls
Beach Boys, 173, 208, *209*, 224
Beastie Boys, 332, *333*
Beatles, 49, 161, 173, 210–214, *211*,
    228
    American Tour, 214–215
    art rock and, 260
    breakup of, 250, 253
    as Dylan fans, 217
    early music, 212–213
    girl groups and, 193
    Harrison's sitar and, 225
    Royal Command Performance, Albert
        Hall, London, 214
    Rubber Soul and multitrack recording,
        221–222
    Sixties culture and, 223
Beat music, 215
Beat Street (film), 323
Bebop, 126–137
    on 52nd Street, 132–133
    compositions, 138
    recording, 137–138
    triumph of, 140–141
Bechet, Sidney, 94, 98, 99, 136
Beck, 260, *309*, 310, 361
Beck, Jeff, 78, 162, 242
Bee Gees, *279*, 280, 281
Beiderbecke, Leon "Bix," *99*, 101
Benjamin, Benny, 197
Berigan, Bunny, 114
Berlin, Irving, 122
Bernstein, Leonard, 158, 228
Berry, Chuck, 77, 171–173, *172*, 208
    Beach Boys and, 210
    Beatles and, 214
    Hawkins and, 128
    litigation against, 186
    lyrics of, 256
Beserkley Records, 274
Bessie (Albertson), 64
Best, Pete, 216
Betrock, Alan, 191, 193
Betts, Dicky, 251
B-girls, 320, 323. *See also* B-boys/b-boying
Bigard, Barney, 117
Big Bands, The (Simon), 126
"Big Bopper," 186
Big Brother and the Holding Company,
    225, 227, 232, 233, 234
Biggie Smalls, 343
Big Youth, 322
Bikini Kill, 312
Birth of Cool, The (Davis, et al.), 141
Bishop, Walter, Jr., 145

Bitches Brew (Davis, et al.), 156
Bjork, 296
Black, Bill, 178
Blackboard Jungle (film), 170, 171
Blackface make-up, 58
Black Flag, 304, 308
*Black Nationalism and the Revolution in
    Music* (Kofsky), 270
*Black Noise: Rap Music and Black Culture in
    Contemporary America* (Rose), 333
Black Sabbath, 254
Black Swan (recording label), 62, 102
Blackwell, "Bumps," 185
Blackwell, Ed, 159
Blackwell, Scrapper, 67
Blakey, Art, 146, 149, 162, 270
Blanchard, Terence, 162
Blanton, Jimmy, 117
Blige, Mary J., 296, 343, 348
Blind Blake, 82
Blondie, 261, 272, 276, 281, 290, 323–324
Blood, Sweat, and Tears, 242
Blood on the Fields (Marsalis), 162
Bloomfield, Mike, 237
Blow, Kurtis, 323
"Blowin' in the Wind," 35, 38, 218
Bluebird beat, 69, 71
Bluebird Records, 22, 69, 71
Blue Note (recording label), 138
Blue notes, 46
Blues
    of 1830s, 65–66
    big city, 71–72, 74–75
    birth of, 41–42
    Bluebird beat, 69
    Clapton and, 235, 236
    classic, 58
    classic rock covers, 78
    commercial, 58–59
    country blues, 44, 46–47
    electric, 75–76
    feeling and form, 45–46
    field recordings, 65
    geography of, 50–52
    heavy metal and, 253
    (R.) Johnson, 67–69
    as literature, 55
    lyrics and themes, 48, 52, 55–56
    race records, 61–62
    rock 'n' roll, 80, 82
    royalty, 62–64
    white performers of, 54, 55
Bluesbreakers, 236
"Blues Brothers," 204
Blues Project, 237
Bluiett, Hamiet, 162
Bob Dylan: An Intimate Biography
    (Scaduto), 219
"Body and Soul" (Hawkins), 127, 136, 138
Body Count, 341, 361
Bolan, Marc, 262
Bolden, Charles "King Buddy," 86–92, *87*,
    269

Bolton, Michael, 307
Bomb Squad, 338
Bonham, John, 252, 253
Bon Jovi, 302
Bono, 260, 299
Boogie Down Productions, 333
Boogie woogie, 67
Booker T. and the M. G.s, 203
Book of Rock Lists (Marsh and Stein), 187
Boone, Pat, 176
Boo-Yaa T.R.I.B.E., 341
Border corridos. *See* Corridos
Born in the U.S.A. (Springsteen), 296,
    298
Bossa nova, 161
Bound for Glory (Guthrie), 23, 26, 35
Bowie, David, 262, *263*, 264, 281
Bowie, Lester, 162
Boyz in the Hood (film), 337
Bradford, Perry, 59, 60, 61
Bragg, Billy, 25
Brandy, 296
Brass Bands and New Orleans Jazz (Schafer),
    85
Bratmobile, 312
Break, in music, 318. *See also* Collective
    improvisation
"Break-beat" music, 317–318, 319
Breakdancers, 318, 319, *319*
    West Coast, 333
    women, 322–323, 343
Brecker, Michael and Randy, 162
Brenston, Jackie, 171, 178
Bridge, The (Rollins), 155
Brill Building, New York, 191, 193, 256
British Invasion, 219–221. *See also* Beatles
    MTV, 283, 285
    Woodstock and, 242
Broadside (magazine), 39
Broadside ballads, 7–9, 10, 18
Brooks, Garth, 305
Broonzy, Big Bill, 70, 71, 199, 201
Brother Ray (Charles), 199
Brown, Charles, 67, 168, 201
Brown, Clifford, 140, 146, 155
Brown, James, 162, 206, *207*, 208,
    269–270, 323, 328
Brown, Lawrence, 116, 117
Brown, Les, 126
Brown, Ruth, 168, 198
Brown, Sterling, 60
Brubeck (Dave) Quartet, *143*, 144, 149
Bruce, Jack, 236
Brummels, Beau, 219
Bubblegum music, 253, 273
Buck, Peter, 307
"Bucking" contests, 85
Buffalo Springfield, 222, 234
Burdon, Eric, 222
Burnette, Johnny, 177
Burns, Robert, 2
Burton, Gary, 162
Butler, Jerry, 268

Butterfield (Paul) Blues Band, 74, 237
Byrd, Donald, 162
Byrds, *219,* 225
Byrne, David, 273

Cafe Society, New York City, 122, 124
Cale, John, 265, 273
"California Girls," 211, 212
Call-and-response pattern, 45, 323
Calloway, Cab, 116, 130, 136, 141, 323
Canned Heat, 242
Cannon (Gus) Jug Stompers, 52
Captain Beefheart's Magic Band, 261
Cardigans, 313
Carey, Mariah, 294, 296, 313
Carey, Mutt, 86
Carisi, John, 146
Carlisle, Belinda, 293
Carmichael, Hoagy, 122
Carney, Harry, 116, 117
Carr, Leroy, 67, 69
Carson, Fiddlin' John, 15
Carter, Benny, 126
Carter, James, 129, 162
Carter, Ron, 161
Carter, Rubin "Hurricane," 39
Carter Family, *11*
Casablanca (record label), 281
Casey, Harry Wayne, 280
Castro, Daisy, 323
Cat Records, 175
CBGB (New York club), 272
C & C Music Factory, 307
Celebrating Bird (Giddens), 131, 134,
    137–138
Chain gang, *42*
Chambers, Paul, 150
Chapin, Harry, 40
Chapman, Tracy, *38,* 259, 298
Charles, Ray, 67, 168, *199,* 259, 343
"Charlie Parker" (Kerouac), 129, 130
Chase, Charlie, 322
Checker, Chubby, 268
Cherry, Don, 159
Chess Records, 71–72, 74, 78, 167, 171,
    172–173
Chestnut, Cyrus, 162
Chic (disco group), 280
Chicago, 71–74, 90, 91, 99
"Chicagoans," 99
Chicano Pride, corridos and, 22
Chiffons, 193
Child, James Francis, 2
Chords (vocal harmony group), 168,
    175
Christgau, Robert, 263
Christian, Charlie, 114, 126, 130, *131,*
    131–132
Chuck D, 40, 308, 338, 361
Cisneros, Henry, 22
Clapton, Eric, 220, *234,* 246, 301
    electric guitar and, 162
    guitar playing of, 237

Hooker and, 77
Howlin' Wolf and, 78
reggae and, 276
Waters and, 74
Williamson and, 72
Clark, Dick, 182, 184, 268
Clarke, Kenny, 130, 132, 134, 136, 141
Clarke, Stanley, 162
Clark (Dave) Five, 219
Clash, 275, 278
Clayton, Buck, 114, 119, 122, 126
Cline, Patsy, 293
Clinton, George, 269, 270–271
Clovers, 145, 198
Coasters, 168, 182
Cobain, Kurt, 16, 304, *305,* 306, 308, 310
Cobham, Billy, 162
Cochran, Eddie, 177, 237
Cocker, Joe, 242
Cogbill, Tommy, 205
Cohen, Leonard, 40, 257, 259
Cold Crush Brothers, 322
Cole, Natalie, 307
Cole, Nat "King," 201
Coleman, Ornette, 152–153, *154,* 155
Collective improvisation, 88
Collectives, jazz, 159
College jazz programs, 162, 162
Collins, Albert, 80
Collins, Bootsy, 270
Collins, Judy, 39, 257, 259
Colon, Richie (Crazy Legs), 322
Coltrane, John, 129, *148,* 149, 156
    Davis and, 146, 147
    Free Jazz and, 154
    mainstream jazz and, 152
    Monk and, 145, 147
Columbia Records, 250
    Aretha and, 205
    Davis and, 150
    Hispanic Division, Discos CBS, 294
    LP (long playing) records, 147
    Monk and, 140
    MTV and, 286
    race records, 62
    Simon and Garfunkel, 258
    Springsteen and, 272
Combs, Sean "Puff Daddy," 343, 348
"Come Into My Kitchen" (Johnson), 67, 69
Common, 361
Como, Perry, 169
Condon, Eddie, 101
Congo Square, New Orleans, 81
Conjuntos (Mexican-American ensemble),
    22
Connie's Inn, Harlem, 96, 107
Contours, 197
Cook, Will Marion, 98
Cooke, Sam, 56, 182, *189,* 190, 207, 328
Cookies, 193
Coolio, 348
Cool jazz, 146, 147, 149
Cooper, Alice, 262, 265–266

Copyright-infringement lawsuits, 333
Corea, Chick, 162
Corporate rock, 249–253
"Corrido de Gregorio Cortez, El," 19, 20,
    21, 22
"Corrido de Kiansis, El," 18–19
Corridos, 17–19, 22, 23, 341
Cortez, Gregorio, *20,* 21. *See also* "Corrido
    de Gregorio Cortez, El"
Cortez, Jayne, 139
Coryell, Larry, 162
Costandinos, Alec, 280
Costello, Elvis, *282*
Cottage Grove, Chicago, 71
Cotton, James, 80
Cotton Club, Harlem, 103, 107, 118
Country and western, 169, 171, 173
Country blues, 44, 46–48, 65
Country Joe and the Fish, 225, 227
Country Music, U.S.A. (Malone), 13
Courlander, Harold, 15
Covers, 78, 173, 175–176
Cowboy (MC Keith Wiggins), 323
Cranberries, 309
Crawdaddy: The Magazine of Rock, 222
Cray, Robert, 80
"Crazy Blues" (Bradford/M. Smith), 59–60,
    62, 92
Crazy Legs (Richie Colon), 322
Cream, 77, 233, *234*
Creedence Clearwater Revival, 243
Creole culture, New Orleans', 82, 86
Creole Jazz Band, 88, 92, 93
"Creole Love Call" (Ellington), 116, 117
Crew Cuts, 175
Cropper, Steve, 203, 204, 207
Crosby, David, 257
Crosby, Stills, and Nash, 242, 246
Crosby, Stills, Nash, and Young, 162, 234
Crossovers
    Berry, 173
    (James) Brown, 210
    covers and, 175–176
    Estefan, 294, 295
    gangsta rap, 342
    (Michael) Jackson, 286
    Prince, 288, 290
"Cross Road Blues" (R. Johnson), 69, 236
Crow, Sheryl, 299, 313
Crudup, Arthur "Big Boy," 75
Crumb, R., 232, 234
Crystals, 193
Cubop, 137, 140
Cugat, Xavier, 295
Culture Club, 283, 285
Curtis, King, 207
"Cutting contests," Kansas City, 108
Cypress Hill, 341
Cyrille, Andrew, 156

Dahl, Steve, 282
Dale, Dick, and the Del-tones, 209–210
Dalhart, Vernon, 13

Daltry, Roger, 242
Dameron, Tadd, 140, 147
Dance, Stanley, 156
Dance music. *See* Disco
Dancing in the Distraction Factory
   (Goodman), 283
D'Angelo, 348
Daniels (Charlie) Band, 251
Darin, Bobby, 188
Davis, Anthony, 162
Davis, Francis, 162
Davis, (Rev.) Gary, 52, 55
Davis, Meyer, 91–92
Davis, Miles, 140, *146*, 150, 153, 157
   bebop and, 133, 136
   cool jazz and, 142, 143
   fusion and, 157
   mainstream jazz and, 151
   modal music and, 145
   resurgence of, 145–146
   second classic quintet, 156
"Day Lady Died, The" (O'Hara), 120
Dead Kennedys, 274, 304, 308
Death of Bessie Smith, The (Albee), 64
Death of Rhythm and Blues, The (George),
   240, 286, 289
Death Row Records, 337, 342
Decca Records, 30, 31
Deep Blues (Palmer), 56
Deep Purple, 254, 261
Def American label, 341
Def Jam Records, 309, 333
Def Leppard, 300, 301
De La Soul, *344*
Delta blues, 46. *See also* Mississippi Delta
   Blues
Denisoff, Serge, 30
Densmore, John, 232
Denver, John, 288
Depeche Mode, 285
Desmond, Paul, 128, 148
Devil's Music, 55
Devo, 274
DGC Records, 305, 308
Diddley, Bo, 82, 323
Difranco, Ani, 39, 260, 299, 312
Digital technology, sampling and, 333, 338
DiMeola, Al, 162
Dinosaur, Jr., 308
Dion, Celine, 296, 313
Dire Straits, 299
Disco, 277–281, 319–320, 327
Disco Queens, 280
Dispatches (Herr), 237
Disposable Heroes of Hiphoprisy, 343
Dixieland jazz, 88
Dixon, Luther, 191
Dixon, Willie, 74, 75, 78, 256
DJs (disc jockeys), 278, 319–320. *See also*
   MCs
Dr. Daddy-O, 323
Dr. Dre, 333, 337, 342
Dr. John, 220, 246

Dodds, Johnny, 92, 93–94, 99
Doggett, Bill, 168
Do-It-Yourself. *See* Indie-rock
Dolphy, Eric, 159, 161
Domino, Fats, 67, 168, 169, 173, *174,* 176
Dominoes (vocal harmony group), 168,
   173, 323
Donahue, Tom, 225
Donnegan, Lonnie, 214
Doors, 228, 232–233
Doo-wop groups, 182
Dorham, Kenny, 162
Dorsey, Jimmy, 115, 116
Dorsey, Thomas A., 55–56
Dorsey, Tommy, 115, 126, 136
Do the Right Thing (film), 338
Double-entendre, 15, 55
Douglas, Carl, 281
Douglas, Kirk, 101
"Down Hearted Blues" (Hunter/B.Smith),
   62, 64
(The) Dozens, rap and, 323, 340
Dozier, Lamont, 195, 197
"Dreadful Memories" (Gunning), 29
Dreams (fusion group), 162
"Drum-and-bass" music, 328
Drums, African slaves and, 317
"Dubs," Jamaican, 322
Dunn, "Duck," 207
Dupree, Champion Jack, 67
Duran Duran, 281, 283, 285
Durham, Eddie, 110, 120, 135
Duritz, Adam, 260
"Dust Storm, Cimaron County, Oklahoma"
   (Rothstein photo), *26*
Dylan, Bob, 10, 30, 32, 34–35, *36,*
   217–218, *218*
   Baez and, 32
   The Band and, 218
   Beck and, 309
   Berry covers by, 173
   circa 1861, *36*
   FM radio and, 224
   (W.) Guthrie and, 35, 38
   lyrics of, 255
   on McTell, 53
   PJ Harvey and, 312
   rock 'n' roll and, 217–218
   "See That My Grave is Kept Clean"
     (Jefferson), 50
   Smashing Pumpkins and, 311
   Springsteen and, 272–273
   Vision Shared, A (W. Guthrie tribute
     album), 25, 40, 299
Dylan, Jakob, 298
Dynamic Dolls (breakdancers), 323

Eagle Brass Band, 85
Eagles, 271
Early Jazz (Schuller), 88, 94, 103
Earth, Wind, and Fire, 269, 270
Easton, Sheena, 290
Eazy-E, 333

Eberly, Philip K., 102
Edison, Harry "Sweets," 119
Edwards, Bernard, 281
Eldridge, Roy, 126
Electric blues, 75–76
Electric Light Orchestra, 261
Electrofunk, 327–328
"Electronica," 328
Electro-Pop groups, 283
Elektra Records, 32, 250
Elliman, Yvonne, 280
Ellington, Duke, 105, 113, *114,* 115,
   129
   on Armstrong, 96
   at the Cotton Club, 103
   Goodman and, 114
   (W.) Marsalis and, 162
   Mingus and, 158
   resurgence of, 149
   Webster and, 128–129
   M. L. Williams and, 110
Elliot, "Missy Misdemeanor," 313
Ellison, Ralph, 121
Emerson, Keith, 261
Emerson, Lake, and Palmer, 261
Eminem, 361
EMI Records, 215–216, 274
English and Scottish Popular Ballads, The, 2,
   9
*English Folk Songs of the Southern
   Appalachians* (Sharp), 5, 6
Enjoy (rap record label), 327
Ennis, Phillip, 225
Eno, Brian, 261, 265, 299, 300
En Vogue, 343
Epstein, Brian, 215–216
Ertegun, Ahmet, 198, 199
Estefan, Emilio, 294
Estefan, Gloria, 293, *294*
Estes, Sleepy John, 44, 80
Etheridge, Melissa, 312
Eureka Jazz Band, 161
Eurodisco, 280
European ballads, 1–2
Eurythmics, 283, 285, 292–293
Evans, Bill, 150, 151, 152
Evans, Elgin, 74
Evans, Faith, 343
Evans, Gil, 146
Evans, Herschel, 119, 128
Evans, Walker, 56
Event songs, 13
Everly Brothers, 181–182
Evita (film), 292
Excelsior Brass Band, 85, 86

Fabara, Sandra, 323
Fabian, *186,* 187, 188
"Fables of Faubus" (Mingus), 149, 158
Fabulous Five (NY graffiti squad), 322
Faith of Graffiti, The (Mailer), 318
Fame Studio, Muscle Shoals, Alabama, 205,
   206–207

Fanzines, 274, 304
Fat Boys, 332, 342–343
Father of the Blues, The (Handy), 41, 44
Favors, Malachi, 162
Federal Communications Commission
    (FCC), 167
Ferry, Brian, 261
52nd Street jazz clubs, New York, 122–125,
    138, 140, 146
Fillmore Theater, San Francisco, 76, 251
Finch, Richard, 280
Fisher, Eddie, 169
Fitzgerald, Ella, 121, 122
Fitzgerald, F. Scott, 91
Five Royales, 191
Five Spot Café, 140
Flack, Roberta, 347, 348
Flash, Grandmaster, 281, 320, 321, 327
Flashdance, 319
Fleetwood Mac, 271
Flores, Juan, 322
FM radio, 222, 223. *See also* Radio
Fogerty, John, 242
Folk ballads, 1–42
    African-American narrative songs,
        14–15, 17
    America's border, 18–19
    authenticity movement, 31–32
    Baez and Dylan, 32, 34, 35
    broadsides, 7–9
    Chapman, 41
    collectors and scholars, 2, 5
    corridos in mainstream, 19, 22
    European, 1–2
    gangsta rap roots in, 323
    Guthrie followers, 35–36
    (W.) Guthrie's, 23–24
    hootenannies and hit parade, 30
    minstrels and, 6–7
    oral tradition and stories of, 5–6
    popular culture and, 10, 13–14
    protest and propaganda, 28–29
    Springsteen and the Guthrie tribute, 40
    U.S., 9–10
Folk music
    revival by women, 298–299
    roots rock and, 298
    Sixties, 217, 237, 241
Folk-rock, 221–222
Folkways Record Company, 32, 33
Fontana, D. J., 178
Ford, Lita, 304
Foreigner, 285
Foster, George "Pops," 83, 86, 88, 90
Four Tops, 197
Frampton, Peter, 271
"Frankie" (Hurt), 44
"Frankie and Albert," 15, 17
"Frankie and Johnnie" (Harris), 82
Frankie Goes to Hollywood, 285
Franklin, Aretha, 203–206, *204,* 293, 328
Franklin, C. L., 205
Freddie and the Dreamers, 219

Freed, Alan, 183, 184, 313
    Berry and, 173
    on covers *versus* originals, 176
    rock 'n' roll and, 169
Freedom Singers, 35
Free Jazz, 159
Freeman, Bud, 101
Fresh Prince of Bel Air, The, 342
Freston, Tom, 313
Friedwald, Will, 120
Fripp, Robert, 261
Fugees, *346,* 347
Fuller, Blind Boy, 52
Funk, 269–271
Funkadelics, 270
Funky jazz, 145
Furay, Richard, 234
Fusion, 155–156, 240

Gallo, Joey, 39
Gamble, Kenny, 268
Gangsta rap, 333. *See also* Hip-hop; Rap
    Chicano rap, 341
    crossovers, 342–343
    gang violence and, 333–334
    political critiques, 338, 340
    roots of, 13
    sexism, 340–341
Gang Starr, 343
Garage bands, 215
Garbage, 312
Garcia, Jerry, 225
Garland, Jim, 29
Garland, Red, 150
Garner, Erroll, 126
Garrison, Jimmy, 152
Gates, Henry Louis, Jr., 340, 343
Gatewoods Tavern, Chicago, 70
"Gathering of the Tribes, The," San
    Francisco, 226–227
Gaye, Marvin, 197, 198, 210, 266
Gaynor, Gloria, 280, 293
Geffen, David, 305
Geffen Records, 341
Genesis, 261
Gennett (recording label), 62, 101
George, Nelson, 240, 286, 289
Georgia Tom, 55–56
Germs, 274
Gerould, Gordon Hall, 1–2, 14
Gerry and the Pacemakers, 212, 215, 219
Gershwin, George, 101, *102,* 122
Gershwin, Ira, 122
Geto Boys, 341
Getz, Stan, 128, 140, 161
Giant Steps (Coltrane), 147
Gibbs, Georgia, 175
Giddens, Gary, 131, 134, 137–138
Gilbert, Ronnie, 30
Gillespie, Dizzy, 343
    bebop and, 126, 127, 136, 137
    Parker and, 127–128, 136
    Pozo and, 138, 139, 140

Gillett, Charlie, 191, 213, 214
Gillum, Jazz, 71
Gimme Shelter (film), *245*
Ginsberg, Allen, 222
Girl groups, 191–193
Girl Groups: The Story of a Sound (Betrock),
    191
Gitler, Ira, 152
Glam rock, 262–264
Glass, Philip, 261
Gleason, Ralph J., 233, 246
Glover, Tony, 240
Goffin, Gerry, 191, 192, 193, 257
Go-Gos, 293
Goldstein, Richard, 256
Golson, Benny, 162
Gonsalves, Paul, 117
Gooden, Lolita Shante, 332
Goodman, Andrew, 283, 285
Goodman, Benny, 101, 108, *109,* 110
    Christian and, 135
    disbands orchestra, 126
    Hammond and, 121
    (B.) Holiday and, 123
    "Let's Dance" radio show and, 110–111
    racial segregation and, 112, 114
    trios, quintets, etc., 126
    M. L. Williams and, 108
Goodman, Fred, 273
Goodman, Steve, 259
"Goodnight Irene," 16, 31
"Good Vibrations" (Beach Boys), 211, 224
Gordon, Dexter, 128, 140, 158
Gordon, Kim, 293, 307, 309
Gordy, Berry, Jr., 193, 194, 196, 201, 234.
    See also Motown
Gore, Tipper, 288
Gospel music, 55–56, 168, 199, 201
"Got My Mojo Workin'" (Waters), 74, 75
Graduate, The, 232, 258
Graffiti writers, 318, 323, 333, 343
Graham, Bill, 251
Grand Ole Opry, 169
Grapes of Wrath, The (Steinbeck), 40
Grateful Dead, 162, 225, 227, 246
Great Day Coming (Denisoff), 30
Great Depression, 111
Green, Al, 56, 267
Greenfield, Elizabeth Taylor, 62
Green, Freddie, 114, 119, 122
Green River, 308
Greenwich, Ellie, 192, 193
Greenwich Village, New York City, 32
Greer, Sonny, 117
Griffith, Nanci, 39, 299
Grillo, Frank. *See* Machito
Griots, *13,* 14
"Groovin' High" (Gillespie and Parker), 137
Grunge, 305
Guard, Dave, 218
Guevara, Nancy, 323
Guild (recording label), 137
Guitar heroes, 236–238, 240

Guitar Player (magazine), 301
Guitars
  acoustic, 40
  corridos accompaniment, 18
  electric, 39, 162
  sixties folk-revival and, 32
Gunning, Sarah Ogan, 29
Guns 'n' Roses, 302
Guralnick, Peter, 67, 69, 199, 204
Guru, 343
Guthrie, Arlo, 25, 40
Guthrie, Jeff, 23
Guthrie, Woody, 16, *23*, 24–26. *See also*
  Bound for Glory (Guthrie)
  Dylan and, 35
  hootenannies and, 30
  sampler, 27–28
  Sixties folk revival and, 217
  Springsteen and, 298
Guy, Buddy, 80

Haden, Charlie, 159, 162
Hahn, Jerry, 162
Hair (musical), 232
Haircut Bands, 283
Haley, Bill, 168, 169–171, *170*, 173, 177,
  199
Hall, Rick, 204, 205
"Hambone" game, 323
Hamburg, Germany, Beatles in, 215
Hammer, MC, 342
Hammond, John, 118, 121, 122, 123, 135
Hammond, John, Jr., 237
Hampton, Lionel, 114, 126, 135
Hancock, Herbie, 161, 162
Handy, W. C., 41–42, 46, 50, 52, 58, 60
Hanson, Brent, 313
Hard bop, 145, 146–147, 149
Hard Day's Night, A (film), 220, 232
Hardin, Lil, 92, 94
Hargrove, Roy, 162
Harlan County, Kentucky, 29
Harlem, jazz in, 105–107, 126, 136
Harlem Renaissance, 56
Harper, Michael S., 149
Harpo, Slim, 77
Harrell, Andre, 343
Harris, Corey, *78*, 79
Harris, Emmylou, 40
Harris, Jimmy "Jam," 294
Harris, Wynonie, 168
Harrison, George, 77, 214, 222, 225
Harron, Mary, 281–282
Harry, Debbie, 280, 323–327. *See also*
  Blondie
Harvey, PJ, 312
Hathaway, Donny, 267
Havens, Richie, 241
Hawkins, Coleman, 102, 114, *123*, 136,
  155
  Monk and, 138, 140
Hawkins, Roger, 205
Hayes, Isaac, 204, 267
Hayes, Lee, 30, *31*

Headbangers Ball, MTV, 302
Heart, 293
Heath, Percy, 147
Heavy metal, 252, 253–256, 300–305
  lite metal, 300–301
  Los Angeles and, 302, 304
  MTV, 301–302
Heavy Metal: A Cultural Sociology
  (Weinstein), 301, 302
Hegamin, Lucille, 62
Hell (Richard) and the Voidoids, 272
Hellerman, Fred, 30
Hell's Angels, 246
Hemphill, Julius, 162
Henderson, Fletcher, 64, 94, 96, 105, 107,
  127
  radio and, 102
  Swing Era and, 113, 114
Henderson, Jocko, 323
Hendrix, Jimi, 80, 162, 227, 235, *236*, 312
  death of, 240, 301
  Experience (trio), 77, 237
  guitar and, 162, 236–238, 240
  recording contracts, 233
  at Woodstock, 246, 246
Hentoff, Nat, 149, 161
Hepster's Dictionary (Calloway), 323
"Here Where Coltrane Is" (Harper), 149
Herman, Woody, 126
Herman's Hermits, 219
Herr, Michael, 237
Hershey, Gerri, 207
Hill, Joe, 29
Hill, Lauryn, *346*, 347
Hill, Teddy, 107, 130
"Hillbilly" music. *See* Country and western
"Hillbilly" recording industry, 13
Hines, Earl, 116
Hip-hop, 317. *See also* Gangsta rap; Rap
  break-beat music, 319–320
  drum and rhythm importance to, 318
  jazz singing ("vocalese") influence on,
    323
  roots, 13, 22, 322
  underground to overground, 323
  women and, 322–323
Hippie culture, 225–226
History of Rock 'n' Roll, The (documentary),
  219–220
"Hit Parade," 167
Hitsville U.S.A.: Motown 1859–1871
  (Mitchell), 198
Hodges, Johnny, 114, 116, 117
Hoffman, Dustin, 233
Hokum (novelty blues), 69
Holiday, Billie, 96, 113, 117, *119*, 120, 128
Holland, Brian and Eddie, 195, 197
Holland, Dave, 162
Holly, Buddy, 177, 182, 186, 237, 256
Hooker, John Lee, 77, 222
Hootenannies, 30, 217
Hootie and the Blowfish, 298
Hopkins, Fred, 162
Hopkins, Lightnin', 44, 49, 51

Horn, Bob, 183
"Horn Players" (Basquiat), *127*
Horovitz, Adam, *333*
Hot Five (and Hot Seven), Armstrong's, 94,
  96
House, Edward "Son," 51, 56, 68, 69
House music, 328
House of Pain (rap group), 333
"House of the Rising Sun" (Animals),
  221–222
Houston, Cissy, 293
Houston, Whitney, 56, 293–294, 313
Howe, Greg, 301
Howell, Peg Leg, 52
Howlin' Wolf, 75, 77, 78, 312
Hubbard, Freddie, 162
Huff, Leon, 268
Huggy Bear, 312
Hughes, Langston, 56
Human Be-in, 226–227
Human League, 283, 285
Hunter, Alberta, 56, 60–61, 62
Hunter, Ivory Joe, 176
Hurt, Mississippi John, 32, *43*, 44, 51, 80
Husker Du, 308
Hutchison, Frank, 55
Hutton, Ina Ray, 126
Hynde, Chrissie, 293, 309

Ian, Janis, 34
"I Can't Be Satisfied" (Waters), 73, 74
Ice Cube, 333, *337*, 338
Ice-T, 333, 341, 343, 361
Impressions, 328
Improvisation, bebop, 138
"I'm Ready," 74, 75
"I'm Your Hoochie Coochie Man," 74, 75
Indie-rock, 307–308
  mainstream, 308–311
Industrial rock, 300
Industrial Workers of the World (IWW), 29
In Search of Buddy Bolden: First Man of Jazz
  (Marquis), 86–92, 270
Inside Pop—The Rock Revolution (Bernstein
  TV special), 228
"In Walked Bud" (Monk), 138, 140
Iron Butterfly, 242
Iron Maiden, 300, 301, 304
I.R.S. (indie record label), 307, 308
"I See Chano Pozo" (Cortez), 139
Ives, Burl, 30
IWW Songs: To Fan the Flames of Discontent,
  29

J. Geils Band, 285
Jackson, Charlie, 65
Jackson, Janet, 293, 313
Jackson, Michael, 197, 253, 283, 285, *286*,
  287, 302
Jackson, Milt, 147, 270
Jackson, Molly, 29, 30, 217
Jackson Five, 197, 253
Jacobs, "Little Walter," 73, 74
Jagger, Mick, 78, 246, 257, 262, 281

Jamaica
   freelance dance promoters, 322
   reggae and, 328
Jamerson, James, 197
James, Elmore, 75, 77, 80, 126, 237
James, Harry, 114, 116
James, Rick, 269, 270
James, Skip, 51
James Brown: The Godfather of Soul
   (Brown), 208
Jan and Dean, 210, 212
Jarman, Joseph, 162
Jarrett, Keith, 151, 162
Jay-Z, 348
Jazz. *See also* Bebop; Swing Era
   African-Americans and, 92–101, 156,
      158
   avant garde, 156, 158–161
   Bolden, 86–92
   concerts and festivals, 147, 149
   cool jazz, 146–149
   Cubop, 141–145
   fusion, 161
   Gershwin, 104–105
   hard bop, 145, 146–147, 149
   Harlem, 105, 107
   Hendrix and, 237–238
   Jazz Age, 91–96
   Kansas City, 108, 110
   mainstream, 156
   neo-mainstrem, 162
   New Orleans, 81–90
   on radio, 102–103, 110–111
   rap and, 343
   on records, 88–95
   rhythm and blues, 145–146
   Whiteman, 103, 105
Jazz Age, 90
Jazz at Lincoln Center, 162
"Jazz at the (Los Angeles) Philharmonic,"
   147
Jazz Messengers, Blakey's, 146, 162
Jazz Review, The (magazine), 155
Jazz Revolution, The (Ogren), 105
Jazz Singer, The (film), 111
Jazz Syncopators, 88
Jazzy Jeff, 343
Jean, Wyclef, *346, 347*
Jefferson, Blind Lemon, 44, 46, *49*, 51, 65
Jefferson Airplane, 204, 225, *226*, 227, 246
Jenkins, Andrew, 13, 31
Jenkins, Gordon, 30
Jewel, 34, 260, 299, 313
Jimenez, Santiago, Jr., 22
Jive, hipster, 323
Jodeci, 343
John, Elton, 262–263
"John Hardy," 15, 17, 38
"John Henry," 15, 17
Johnson, Blind Willie, 51, 55
Johnson, Bunk, 269
Johnson, Guy B., 56
Johnson, J. J., 140
Johnson, James P., 64, 107

Johnson, Jimmy, 205
Johnson, Pete, 67, 168
Johnson, Robert, 48, 50, 51, 56, 65–67, 75,
   77, 312
Johnson, Tommy, 69
Johnson, Tony, 51
Jolson, Al, 111
Jones, Brian, 246
Jones, Elvin, 152
Jones, Grace, 280
Jones, Jo, 119, 120, 121
Jones, John Paul, 252, 253
Jones, LeRoi, 137, 246. *See also* Baraka,
   Amiri
Jones, Little Hat, 44, 51
Jones, Philly Jo, 150
Jones, Quincy, 286, 343
Joplin, Janis, 64, 80, 204, 227, *230*, 233,
   234, 250
Joplin, Scott, 84, 85, 108
Jordan, Louis, *168*
Journey, 285
Judas Priest, 254
Juilliard School of Music, 162
Jungle Brothers, 343
"Jungle" music, 328
Juvenile delinquents, in 1850s, 165–166,
   171

Kalb, Danny, 237
Kansas City jazz, 108, 121. *See also* Basie,
   "Count"
Karpeles, Maude, 6
Kay, Connie, 147
Kaye, Lenny, 272
Kazee, Buell, 13
K.C. and the Sunshine Band, 280, 281
Keb' Mo', 82
Keisker, Marion, 178
Kendricks, Eddie, 195
Kennedy, John F., 22, 195, 215
Keppard, Freddie, 89
Kern, Jerome, 122
Kerouac, Jack, 129, 132
Kessel, Barney, 140
Kid Frost, 341
Kincaid, Bradley, 13
King (recording label), 167
King, Albert, 80, 237
King, B. B., *74*, 78, 80, 238
King, Ben E., 193, 219–220
King, Carole, 191, 192, 193, 257
King, Freddie, 80
King, Martin Luther, Jr., 35, 37, 40, 165,
   195, 207, 217
King, Pee Wee, 175
King Adrock, *333*
King Biscuit Time, *73*
King Crimson, 260
King Oliver. *See* Oliver, Joe "King"
"King Porter Stomp" (Morton), 98, 116
Kingston Trio, 10, 31–32, *216*
Kinnon, Joy Bennett, 343
Kirk, Andy, 109, 110

Kirkland, Kenny, 162
KISS, 264, *265*
Klein, Joe, 23, 40, 298
Knight (Gladys) and the Pips, 197
Knofler, Mark, 299
Koenigswarter, Baroness Pannonica (Nica)
   de, 146
Kofsky, Frank, 270
"Ko-Ko" (Parker and Gillespie), 137–138
Konitz, Lee, 128, 146
Kool and the Gang, 269, 270
Kool DJ Herc, 320, 321, 322
Kool Moe Dee, 343
Koppel, Ted, 292
Kora (instrument), *13*
Korn, 361
Kraftwerk, 327–328, 333
Krieger, Robby, 232
KRS-One, 333
Krupa, Gene, 101, 114, 125
Krush Groove (docudrama), 309

Lacy, Steve, 156
Ladies Home Journal, 91
Lady Pink (graffiti writer), 323
Laine, Papa Jack, 86, 99
Lake, Greg, 261
Lake, Oliver, 162
Landau, Jon, 271
Lanois, Daniel, 299
LaRocca, Nick, 101
La Rock, DJ Scott, 333
Last Poets, 328
Last Waltz, The (film), 218, 244
Latin bands/performers, 295–296
   bebop, 142–144
   Chicano rap, 341
   hip hop, 322
   jazz, 141
   rock, 240
Latin Tinge, The (Roberts), 22, 23
Lauper, Cyndi, 283, 293
Leadbelly, *15*, 30, *51*, 217
Ledbetter, Huddie, 23. *See also* Leadbelly
Led Zeppelin, 16, 77, *254*, 333
Lee, Peggy, 259
Lee, Spike, 338, 343, 348
Leiber, Jerry, 182, 193, 256
Lemonheads, 308
Lennon, John, 178, 214, 250, 283
Lennox, Annie, 292–293
Lenox Club, Harlem, 107
"Let's Dance" (radio show), 113–114
Levey, Stan, 131, 134
Lewis, Furry, 15, 51, 56
Lewis, Jerry Lee, 67, *177*, 181, 184, 186
Lewis, John, 146, 147
Lewis, Meade Lux, *64, 67*
Lewis, Teddy, 294
Library of Congress, Archive of American
   Folk Song of, 9, 24
Lifetime (fusion group), 162
Liggins, Joe, 168
Lilith Fair, 313

Lil' Kim, 332
Lil Rodney Cee, 318
Limelighters, 217
Limp Bizkit, 311, 361
Lincoln Center Jazz Orchestra, 162
"Little Red Rooster," 74, 77, 78
Little Richard, 56, 67, 173, 176, 182, *185,* 219
Little Willie John, 168
Live at the Apollo (J. Brown), 208
"Livery Stable Blues," 88, 89–94, 91, 103
Living Colour, 304
Livingston, Bunny (Wailer), 276
LL Cool J, *331,* 332
Llord, Oscar, 296
Lollapaloosa, 313
Lomax, Alan, 9, 17
  Dylan and, 39
  Guthrie and, 23
  hootenannies and, 30
  (Molly) Jackson and, 29
  Jelly Roll and, 83, 98
  sixties folk-revival and, 32
  Waters and, 73
Lomax, John, 9
"Lonesome Death of Hattie Carroll, The" (Dylan), 37
Looking Up at Down: The Emergence of Blues Culture (Barlow), 323
Lopez, Jennifer, 293, 295
Los Pinguinos Del Norte, 20
"Lost Generation," 91
Louis' Children (Gourse), 96
Lovano, Joe, 129
Love, Courtney, 299, 309
Love Me Tender (film), 179
Lovers' raps, 323, 332
Lovin' Spoonful, 77, 222
LP (long playing) records, 147
Lucas, George, 252
Lunceford, Jimmie, 116
Lymon, Frankie, 191
Lynryd Skynryd, 251
Lyons, Jimmy, 156

Macamba Lounge, Chicago, 71
Machito and his Afro-Cuban Orchestra, 141, 144
Mack, Lonnie, 80
Madonna, 281, 283, 290, *291,* 292, 313
Magic Sam, 80
Mailer, Norman, 318
Mainstream music
  corridos, 19, 22
  indie-rock, 308–311
  jazz, 156
  rap, 309
Malcolm X, 333
Malmsteen, Yngwie, 301
Malone, Bill, 13
Mamas and the Papas, 204, 222, 227
Mandigo Kingdoms of Senegambia (Quinn), 323

Mann, Barry, 192, 193
Mansion on the Hill (Goodman), 273
Manson, Shirley, 312
Manzarek, Ray, 228
"Ma Rainey" (Brown), 60
"Ma Rainey's Black Bottom" (Rainey), 61, 79
Marali, Jacques, 281
March on Washington (1863), 37, 217, 219
Marcus, Greil, 274–275
Mares, Paul, 99
Marley, Bob, *267*
Marquis, Donald M., 86–91, 270
Marsalis, Branford, 129, 162, 343
Marsalis, Ellis, 162
Marsalis, Wynton, *158,* 159, 160
Marsh, Dave, 187, 236, 241
Marshall Tucker Band, 251
Martha and the Vandellas, 197
Martin, George, 215–216, 222–223, 228, 260
Martin, Ricky, 294
Martin, Sara, 62
Martinez, Eddie, 309
Martinez, Lupe, 22
Marucci, Bob, 187
Marvelettes, 197
Masters of Records, 320, 323
Matthews (Dave) Band, 298
Maverick (record label), 292
Mayall, John, 236
"Maybelline" (Berry), 77, 171, 184
Mayfield, Curtis, 267, 328
McBride, Christian, 162
McCall, Steve, 162
McCarthy-era blacklists, 30
McCartney, Paul, 214, 219, 237, 250, 260, 286
McCoy, Van, 280
McDaniels, Darryl (DMC), 309, *330*
McDonald, Joe. *See* Country Joe and the Fish
McGarrigle, Kate and Anna, 259
McGhee, Howard, 138, 140
McLachlan, Sarah, 313
McLaren, Malcolm, 274, 275, 278
McLaughlin, John, 162
McLean, Don, 252
McLean, Jackie, 162
MC Lyte, 332, 343
McPartland, Dick, 101
McPartland, Jimmy, 99, 101
"McRock: Pop as a Commodity" (Harron), 282–283
MCs (Master of Ceremonies or "Microphone Controller"), 318, 323, 333, 343
McShann, Jay, 130
McTell, Blind Willy, 46, 48, 52, *53,* 54, 56
Megaforce (record label), 304
Meaning of the Blues, The (Oliver), 328
Me Decade, 249
Megadeth, 304

Meldhau, Brad, 162
Melle Mel, 309, 343
Mellencamp, John, 25, 298, 299
Melody Maker, 253
Meltzer, R., 223–224
Melvin (Harold) and the Bluenotes, 268
Memphis blues, 52
"Memphis Blues" (Handy), 44, 52
Memphis Horns, 205
Memphis Jug Band, 52
Memphis Minnie, *68,* 69
Memphis Recording Service, 176, 178
Memphis Slim, 67
Mercedes Ladies, 323
Mercury, Freddie, 262
Mercury Records, 175–176, 323
Mermaid Avenue (Bragg), 25
Mersey Beat, 213
"Message, The" (Flash and Furious Five), 328
Message raps, 309
Messina, Joe, 197
Metallica, 302, *303*
Metheny, Pat, 162
Mexico, corridos of, 17–18
Mezzrow, Mezz, 101
MFSB, 268
Miami Sound, 280
Miami Sound Machine, 294
Mike D., *333*
Miller, Aleck "Rice," 75
Miller, Glenn, 112, 125
  Orchestra, *112,* 116, 129
Mills, Florence, 118
Milton, Roy, 168
Mingus, Charles, 140, 149, *151,* 153
Minstrels, 6–7
Minstrel shows, 57
  poster (1836), *56*
Minton's Playhouse, Harlem, 126, 136
Miracles, 195
Miranda, Carmen, 295
Mississippi Delta Blues, 50–51
Mister Jelly Roll: The Fortunes of Jelly Roll Morton, New Orleans Creole and "Inventor of Jazz" (Morton), 83, 98
Mitchell, Joni, 40, 220, 246, *246,* 257, 260
Mitchell, Roscoe, 162
Mitchell (Chad) Trio, 217
Mizell, Jason "Jam Master Jay," 309, *330*
Modernaires, 115
Modern Jazz Quartet, 147
Modes, 4
Molina, Arturo, Jr., 341
Moman, Chips, 205
Monica, 296
Monk, Thelonious, 133, *134,* 144, 149, 155
  bebop and, 125–126
  boogie woogie and, 67
  Coltrane and, 152
  Parker and, 126
Monkees, 233, 253

Monterey International Pop Festival, 204, 227, 236–237
Monterey Pop (film), 227
Montgomery, Little Brother, 67
Montgomery, Wes, 161
Monument (recording label), 190–191
"Mood Indigo" (Ellington), 116, 117
Moody Blues, 261
Moog, Robert, 261
"Moondog Rock and Roll House Party, The," Freed's, 169
Moore, Sam, 204
Moore, Scotty, 178
Moore, Thurston, 307
Morgan, Lee, 149, 162
Morissette, Alanis, 260, 309, *311,* 312
Morodor, Georgio, 280, 327
Morrison, Jim, 228, *229,* 232–233, 250
Morrison, Van, 220, 246, 259–260
Moten, Bennie, 114
    Band, 108, 110, 113
Morton, Benny, 119
Morton, George (Shadow), 194
Morton, Jelly Roll, 67, 81, 83, 90, *96,* 97
Mothers of Invention, 261
Motley Crue, 300, 301, 302
Motorhead, 304
Motown, 71, 194–198, 216, 266, 267, 281
Mott the Hoople, 266
Mounk, "Chip," 242
Mountain, 242
Moye, Don, 162
MTV (MusicTelevision), 283, 285, 287, 289
    heavy metal, 300–301
    Madonna, 290, 292
    Nirvana, 304
    "Yo! MTV Raps," 333
Mulligan, Gerry, 146
Multitrack recording, 222–223, 260
Murphy, Walter, 281
Murray, Albert, 118, 317
Murray, David, 162
Murray, Sunny, 156
Muscle Shoals, Alabama, 204
Music conservatories, jazz, 162
Music From Big Pink (The Band), 245
Music in the Air (Eberly), 102
Mustaine, Dave, 304
"'Mystery Train': Janis Joplin Leaves Port Arthur for Points West, 1864" (Wojahn), 231

Nance, Ray, 117
Nanton, Joe "Tricky Sam," 117
Nashville, country and western recording industry in, 169
Nathan, Syd, 208
Native Americans, San Francisco rock culture and, 226
Navarro, Fats, 140, 155
Ndegeocello, Me'Shell, 312
Nebraska (Springsteen), 40

Negro Folk Music, U.S.A. (Courlander), 15
Negro Workday Songs (Odum and Johnson), 56
Neidlinger, Buell, 156
Nelson, Willy, 40
Neo-mainstream jazz, 162
Newman, Randy, 259
New Masses, 29
New Orleans, 81–87
    Armstrong's life in, 95–96
    Black Codes, 82, 86
    Bolden and jazz in, 86–92
    Fats Domino and rhythm and blues, 174–175
    funerals, 82, 83
    jazz bands, 88, 90–95
    military surplus instruments, 82
    Morton on, 97–98
    music scene circa 1800, 83, 86
    religion in, 82
New Orleans Rhythm Kings, 99
New Pop, 283, 285
Newport Folk Festival, 32, 219
Newport Jazz Festival, 147
New Romantic groups, 283
New York. *See also* 52nd Street jazz clubs, New York
    Brill Building, 191, 193
    Harlem jazz, 105–107, 126, 136
    Henderson gigs in, 102–103
    hip-hop dances, 323
New York Dolls, 262, 265, 274
Nichols, Mike, 259
Nichols, Red, 115
Nikki D, 343
1810 Fruitgum Co., 253
Nirvana, 304, 306, 309, 310
Noble, Ray, 115
NORK. *See* New Orleans Rhythm Kings
Norman, Philip, 214
Notorious B.I.G., 343
Nowhere to Run (Hershey), 207
Nugent, Ted, 254
Numan, Gary, 283, 327
NWA (Niggas With Attitude), 333, 337
Nyro, Laura, 227

Ochs, Phil, 39
O'Connor, Sinead, 290, 308
Odetta, 39
ODJB. *See* Original Dixieland Jazz Band
Odum, Howard W., 56
O'Farrill, Chico, 144
Ogren, Kathy, 105
O'Hara, Frank, 120
Ohio Express, 253
Ohio Players, 270
O'Jays, 268
Okeh (recording label), 22, 59–60, 61–62, 94
Oldham, Spooner, 205
Oliver, Joe "King," 88, 90, *92,* 93, 96, 99
Oliver, Paul, 328

Ono, Yoko, 309
Onward Brass Band, 85
Oral traditions, 5–6, 56. *See also* Rap
Orbison, Roy, 177, 190–191
Orbit, William, 291
Original Dixieland Jazz Band, *89,* 91, 99
O'Riordan, Delores, 309
Ory, Kid, 92, 96
Osborne, Joan, 299, 313
Osbourne, Ozzy, 301, 302
Otis, Johnny, 168
Outlaw ballads, 15, 17
Owens, Shirley, 191
Owens, William, 19

Pace, Harry, 62
Page, Jimmy, 252, 253, 348
Page, Patti, 169, 175
Page, Walter, 110, 119
Palmer, Robert, 56, 74, 203, 210, 269
Paramount (recording label), 62, 65
Paredes, Americo, 17, 18, 19, 20, 22
Pareles, Jon, 307
Parents' Music Resource Center (PMRC), 288, 292, 302
Parker, Charlie "Bird"
    bebop and, 126, *127,* 128, 129–130
    Cubop and, 140
    Davis and, 146
    death of, 142
    Gillespie and, 136, 137–138
    rhythm and blues and, 145
    Rollins and, 155
    Young and, 128
Parker, Junior, 178
Parker, Kris, 333
Parker, Maceo, 270–271
Parker, Tom, 180
Parliaments, 270
Pastorious, Jaco, 162
Patton, Charley, 46, *47,* 48, 51, 55, 78
Paul, Billy, 268
Paxton, Tom, 39
Payola scandals, 183–184
Pearl Jam, 305, 311
Peer, Ralph, 11, 61, 62
Pendergrass, Teddy, 268
Penn, Sean, 292
Pentatonic scales, 4
Peppermint Lounge, New York, 278
Pere Ubu, 274
Perkins, Carl, 49, 173, 237
Perkins, Dave, 86
Perkins, William Eric, 342
Perry, Charles, 225
Peter, Paul, and Mary, 30, 35, 37, 217, 218
Pet Shop Boys, 285
Pettiford, Oscar, 140
Phair, Liz, 312
Philadelphia International Records, 268
Phillies (record label), 193–194
Phillips, Sam, 176, 178, 180, 181, 333
Pickett, Wilson, 204, 205, 268

Picou, Alphonse, 85
Piedmont blues, 46, 48, 51–52
Pink Floyd, 261
Pittman, Robert, 286
"Planet Rock," 322, 327–328, 333
Plant, Robert, 252
Play-party songs, Leadbelly's, 16
Poetry of Rock, The (Goldstein), 256
Poison, 302
Police (band), 283, *284,* 285
Pollack, Ben, 111
Pollack, Jackson, 134
Pomus, Jerome (Doc), 193
"Pony Blues" (Patton), 48, 82
Pop music, 282–283
Pop, Iggy (James Osterberg), 263, 265
Pops Foster: New Orleans Jazzman (Foster), 83, 86
Porter, Cole, 122
Porter, David, 204, 267
Powell, Bud, 140, 155
Pozo, Chano, *138,* 139–140
Prater, Dave, 204
Prendergast, Tom, 108
Presley, Elvis, 167, 176–180, *177, 179,* 186
Pretenders, 293
"Pretty Boy Floyd" (W. Guthrie), 27–28, 323
Price, Alan, 222
Price, Lloyd, 190, 191
Price, Sammy, 110
Prince, 283, 288, *289*
Prine, John, 259
Procol Harum, 261
Professional "folk song" writers, 13
Professor Longhair, 67
Progressive rock, 225, 241. *See also* Art rock
Protest and propaganda songs, 28–29
Psychedelic bands, 227
Psychedelic soul, 267
Public Enemy, 40, 308, 338, *339,* 340, 348
"Puerto Rico Rocks: New York Ricans Stake Their Claim" (Flores), 322
Puff Daddy, 343, 348
Punch phrasing, in rap music, 320
Punk rock, 262, 273–275, 282
  British, 275–276, 279
  women, 292

Queen, 261
Queen Latifa, 332, 343
Quinn, Charlotte A., 323
Quinones, Lee, 322
Quintanilla, Selena, 295

Rabbit Foot Minstrels, 58, 64
Race records, 61–62, 111. *See also* Rhythm and blues
Racial division/segregation. *See also* Covers; Crossovers
  civil rights movement and, 207–208, 217
  (Miles) Davis quintet and, 150
  Goodman and, 114

hard bop and cool jazz, 149
Hendrix uses, 237
Monterey International Pop Festival, 227–228
MTV, 285, 286, 288
in New Orleans, 82, 86
on radio, 102–103
rhythm and blues and, 167
Shaw's band with Billie and, 122
Sly Stone and, 240–241
Southern Negroes organize to end, 165
Radio
  AM bubblegum bands, 253
  AOR (Album Oriented Rock), 270, 274
  bebop on, 140
  disco format, 281, 282
  FM stations, 224
  "Let's Dance," 113–114
  payola scandals, 183–184
  progressive rock format, 225
  racial policies, 102–103, 167
  Swing Era and, 110–111
  television and, 182–183
  "Top Forty" playlists, 183
  "Urban Contemporary" format, 270
Rage Against the Machine, 311, 361
Ragtime, 83, 84–86, 107
Rainey, Gertrude "Ma," 41, 42, 56, 58, *59,* 60, 64
Raitt, Bonnie, 80, 313
Ramones, *274*
Randle, Bob, 180, 183
Rap, 40. *See also* Gangsta rap; Hip-hop
  alternative rap, 343
  answer records, 332
  Beastie Boys, 332–333
  Chic and, 281
  fragmentation, 343–361
  jazz and, 343
  in mainstream music, 333
  Masters of Records, 320, 323
  origin/derivation of term, 317–318
  "Planet Rock," 327–328
  pop rap, 342–343
  Public Enemy, 338–340
  records, 323–327
  rock critics on, 328
  roots of, 13, 15, 323
  sampling suits, 333
  "The Message," 328
  urban violence, 333
  verbal duels, 323
  white, suburban males and, 304
  women pop rappers, 343
Rap Attack (Toop), 13, 319–320
"Rapper's Delight" (Sugar Hill Gang), 317, 323, 333
Rappolo, Leon, 99
"Rapture" (rap-style single), 323–324
Ratt, 301
Ravens, 168
Raves, 328
Ray, Johnnie, 173

Razaf, Andy, 107
RCA Records, 180
Reagan, Ronald, 296
Real Paper, The (Boston weekly), 271
Rebel Without a Cause (film), 171
Record sales, 233, 271, 282
  drop in rock records, 313
  heavy metal, 302
  Janet Jackson, 294
  media mergers and, 249–250
  Michael Jackson, 286, 288
Redding, Otis, 200, 202, 227
Red Hot Peppers, 98, 99
Redman, Don, 103, 114
Redman, Joshua, 129, 162
Reece, Florence, 29
Reed, Jimmy, 77
Reed, Lou, 263, 265
Refrains, in ballads, 4
Reggae, 276, 328
Reich, Steve, 261
Reid, Vernon, 304
Reliance Brass Band, 85, 86
R.E.M., 307, 308, 309, 311
"Remembering Jimmy" (Ellison essay), 121
"Reminiscing in Tempo" (Ellington), 116, 117
Renaissance, 261
REO Speedwagon, 285
Replacements, 308
"Respect," 204, 207
Return to Forever, 162
Rhapsody in Blue (Gershwin), 101–103
Rhimes, Leann, 296
Rhoads, Randy, 301
Rhythm and blues, 145–146, 167, 168, 169, 174–175. *See also* Race records
  Atlantic Records, 198–201, 204–208
  Brown (James), *207,* 209
  Jordan's jukebox hits, 168
Richards, Keith, 237
Richman, Jonathan, 274
Riddles, Leslie, 11
Righteous Babe Records, 312
Riley, Terry, 261
Riot grrrls, 312
Ritual competition, African-American, 323
Roach, Max, 137, 140, 146, 149, 155
Robichaux, John, 85, 269
Roberts, John Storm, 22–23, 143
Roberts, Luckeyth (Luckey), 107
Robertson, Robbie, 245
Robin Hood ballads, 7, 15, 17, 19
Robinson, Bobby, 327
Robinson, Carson, 13
Robinson, Darren "The Human Beat Box," 342–343
Robinson, Sylvia and Joe, 323
Robinson, William "Smokey," 195
Rocha, Pedro, 22
Rock. *See also* MTV (MusicTelevision)
  African American soul music, 266–271
  alternative, 305–307

art rock, 260–262
   blockbusters, 271–272
   corporate, 249–253
   demise of, 282–283
   disco and, 278–282
   glam rock, 262–266
   heavy metal, 253–256, 300–305
   indie-label, 307–311
   Prince, 288–290
   punk, 272–275, 278
   reggae, 276
   roots rock, 296–300
   singer-songwriters, 256–260
   women performers, 290–296, 298–299,
      312–313
Rockabilly, 177, 178
Rock and Roll Hall of Fame and Museum,
   166
"Rock Around the Clock" (Haley/Comets),
   170, 171, 173
"Rock Box" (rap record and video), 309
Rock concerts, 251–252
Rock critics, 254, 256, 328, 338. *See also*
   Rolling Stone
"Rocket 84" (Brenston/Haley), 171, 178
Rock festivals, 227
"Rockin' in Rhythm" (Ellington), 116, 117
Rock 'n' roll, 80, 82. *See also* Rhythm and
      blues
   album as integrated concept, 228
   Altamont, 246
   art of, 228–234
   Beatles, 212–216
   Berry and, 171–173
   covers, 175–176
   crossovers, 173, 175
   fallow years, 188, 190–191
   FM radio, 224
   folk revival, 216–221
   folk-rock, 221–222
   Freed's radio show, 169
   girl groups, 191–193
   Haley, 169–171
   Hendrix, 236–238, 240, 245–246
   Motown, 194–198
   negative response to, 180
   1850s news stories, 165–167
   payola (bribery) scandals, 183–184
   Presley, 176–180
   proliferation after Presley, 181–182
   rock journals, 223–224
   San Francisco, 224–228
   setbacks in, 184, 186
   Sly Stone, 239, 240–241
   Spector and, 193–194
   Stax Records, 201–204
   supergroups, 234, 236
   surf music, 210–212
   teen idols, 186, 187, 188
   white teenagers and black music, 167
   Woodstock, 241–242, 244, 246
Rock of Ages (Stokes), 223, 227–228
Rock Steady Crew, *319*, 322, 323

Rodgers, Jimmy, *54*, 55
Rodgers, Nile, 281
Rogers, Jimmie, 73, 74, 78
Rolling Stone, 223
   Cobain and, 305
   Illustrated History of Rock & Roll, The,
      274–275
   on MTV, 286
   on R.E.M., 307
   on U2, 299
   underground rock and, 274
Rolling Stones, 74, *75*, 78, 210, 212, 233,
   245, 281
   at Altamont Speedway, 245–246
   Sixties culture and, 223, 224
Rollins, Sonny, 129, 147, 149, 150
Ronettes, 193
Ronstadt, Linda, 259
Roots rock, 296, 298
Rorem, Ned, 228
Rose, Tricia, 333, 338, 343
Rosenthal, David, 155
Ross, Diana, *195*, 234, 293
Roth, David Lee, 301
Rothchild, Paul, 250
Rothstein, Arthur, 26
Rotten, Johnny, *276*, 278, 282
" 'Round Midnight," 138, 140
R.S.O. (record label), 281
Rubber Soul (Beatles), 221–222
Rubin, Rick, 309, 332, 341
"Ruby My Dear" (Monk), 138, 140
Rudd, Roswell, 159
Ruffin, David, 195
Run-DMC, *330, 332*
*Running With the Devil: Power, Madness and
      Gender in Heavy Metal* (Walser), 254,
   301
Rush, Otis, 80
Rushing, Jimmy, *118*
Russell, Pee Wee, 101
Ruthless Records, 333

Sacred blues, 55
Sadler, Eric "Vietnam," 338
"St. Louis Blues" (Handy), 58, 64
St. Marie, Buffy, 39
Salsoul (record label), 281
Salt-N-Pepa, 332, 343
Sam and Dave, 204
Sampling, rap, 333, 338
Sanders, Pharoah, 159
San Francisco, 224–228, 226–227, 246
Santana, Carlos, 162, *239*, 240, 242, 246,
   295, 348
"Satisfaction," 77, 204
Saturday Night Fever, 280–281
   poster, *279*
Saturday Night Live, 305, 308
Savage, Rick, 300–301
Savoy Ballroom, Harlem, 107
Saxophone Colossus (Rollins), 155
Scaduto, Anthony, 35, 219, 272

Scepter Records, 191
Schafer, William J., 85
Schooly-D, 333
Schuller, Gunther, 88, 94, 103, 113,
      119–120, 140, 147, 155
Schuman, Mort, 193
Scorsese, Martin, 218
Scott, James, 108
Scott-Heron, Gil, 323, 328
Scratching, in rap music, 320
Seals, Arthur "Baby," 44
Seals, Son, 80
Searchers, 219
Searching for Robert Johnson (Guralnick), 67
Seattle sound, 305, 308
Secada, Jon, 295
Seeger, Charles, 30
Seeger, Pete, 29, 30, 32, 35, 39, 217
Selena, 294
Sequence, 323
Sgt. Pepper's Lonely Hearts Club Band, 228,
   259
Seventh Stream, The (Ennis), 225
Sexism, of gangsta rap, 340–341
Sex Pistols, 275–276, *276*, 278
Sexual themes, of the blues, 52, 55
"Shake, Rattle, and Roll," 168, 170, 199
Shakur, Tupac, 342, 343
Sha Na Na, 242, 252
Shangri-Las, 193, 194
Shankar, Ravi, *225*, 227
Shante, Roxanne, 332, 343
Sharp, Cecil James, 5, *6*
Shaw, Artie, *122*, 125
"Shaw Nuff" (Gillespie and Parker), 137,
   138
Sheila E., 290
Shepp, Archie, 159
Shirelles, *191*, 192, 193, 216
Shocked, Michele, 39, 299
Shocklee, Hank, 338, 342
Shocklee, Keith, 338
Shorter, Wayne, 151, 161, 162
Shout: The Beatles in Their Generation
      (Norman), 214–215
"Signifying," rap and, 323, 340, 341
Silver, Horace, 146, 149, 156, 162, 270
Simmons, Gene, 265
Simmons, Joseph "Run," 309, *330*
Simmons, Russell "Rush," 309
Simon, Carly, 257
Simon, George T., 126, 129
Simon, Paul, 257, 260, 276
Simon and Garfunkel, 224, 232, *257, 258*
Simone, Nina, 259
Simpson, Valerie, 197
Sinatra, Frank, 32, 96, 124
Singer-songwriters, 227, 256–260. *See also*
      Songwriters
Singleton, John, 337
Sing Out!, 32
Siouxsie and the Banshees, 309, 312
Sir Douglas Quintet, 219

Sister Souljah, 340
Sixties youth culture, 223, 224–226. *See also* Woodstock
Skiffle music, 214
Slayer, 304
Sledge, Percy, 204
Sledgehammer, 300
Slick, Grace, 227
Sly and the Family Stone, 162, *238*, 269, 270
Small's Paradise, Harlem, 107
Smashing Pumpkins, 311
Smith, Bessie, 15, *62*, 293
    Columbia recordings, 62, 64
    Goodman and, 113
    Hammond and, 121
    (B.) Holiday and, 123
    Joplin and, 80
    minstrel shows and, 58
    recordings, 60–61
    sample, 56
Smith, Buster, 110
Smith, Clarence "Pinetop," 67
Smith, Funny Paper, 44
Smith, Mamie, *58*, 59–60, 92, 127
Smith, Marvin "Smitty," 162
Smith, Patti, 272, 273, 309
Smith, Will, 343
Smith, Willie (the Lion), 107
Snider, Dee, 288
Snoop Doggy Dog, 337, 342
Snowden, Elmer, 107
Sobule, Jill, 39
Soft Cell, 285
Solomon Brothers, 333
"So Long, It's Been Good to Know Ya" (Guthrie), 30, 31
Songsters, 14, 41, 43–44, 51, 82
Songwriters, 182. *See also* Singer-songwriters
    Brill Building, New York, 191, 192, 193, 256
    Motown, 194, 195
Sonic Youth, 293, 307
Soul jazz, 145
Soul music, 199, 266–269
Soul Sonic Force, 322, 327–328
Soul Train, 268
Soundgarden, 305, 308
Sound of Jazz, The (TV show), 122
"Sound of Memphis, The" (Palmer), 203
Sound of the City, The: The Rise of Rock and Roll (Gillett), 191, 213, 214, 236
Sound systems, Jamaican, 322
Southern rock, 251
Southern Syncopated Orchestra, 98
Spain, folk ballads of, 17
Spann, Otis, 73, 74
Spears, Britney, 313
Specialty (recording label), 167
Spector, Phil, 192–193, 212, 338
Spice Girls, 293

Spirituals, 45, 207
Spivey, Victoria, 62, 80
"Springfield Mountain," 10, 13
Springsteen, Bruce, 40, 260, 296, *297, 298*
    Berry covers by, 173
    Dylan and, 271–272
    rock and, 283
    Vision Shared, A (W. Guthrie tribute album), 25, 299
SST (indie record label), 308
Stacy, Jess, 114
"Stack O'Lee Blues" (Hurt), 44
"Stagolee," 15, 17
Stanley, Paul, 265
Stanza formats, in Anglo-American ballads, 2
Staple Singers, 246
Starr, Ringo, 78, 216, 220
Stax Records, *201, 202*, 203–204, 267
Steely Dan, 162
Steig, Jeremy, 162
Stein, Gertrude, 91
Stein, Kevin, 187
Steinbeck, John, 40
Stephney, Bill, 318, 338
Steppenwolf, 254
Stewart, Dave, 292, 293
Stewart, Rex, 102
Stewart, Rod, 281
Stewart, Teddy, 144
Stills, Stephen, 234, 257, 348
Sting, 283, 348
Stipe, Michael, 307, 309
Stitt, Sonny, 140
Stockhausen, Karlheinz, 261
Stokes, Geoffrey, 223, 227–228, 238
Stoller, Mike, 182, 193, 256
Stompin' the Blues (Murray), 317
Story, James, 83
Storyville, New Orleans, 83, 90
Storz, Todd, 183
"Straight No Chaser" (Monk), 138, 140
Strayhorn, Billy, 117–118
Streckfus, Johnny, 88
Streisand, Barbra, 96, 293
Stride piano style, Harlem, 107
Strong, Barrett, 197
Strophic form, 4
Strummer, Joe, 278
Studio 54, New York, 281
Sub-Pop (indie record label), 305, 308
Sugar Hill Gang, 281, 317, 323
Sullivan (Ed) Show, 38, 179, 180, 195, 213–214
Sumlin, Hubert, 78, 237
Summer, Donna, 280, 293
Sunnyland Slim, 67
Sun Ra, 159, 270
Sun Records, 178
Superfly (film), 267
Supergroups, 234, 236
Supremes, *195*

Surf music, 210–212
Sweet Soul Music (Guralnick), 199, 204
Sweet-Tee, 323
Swing Era
    Basie, 115–118
    big bands, 125–126
    Ellington, 116, 118
    Fitzgerald, 125
    Glenn Miller Orchestra, *112*
    Goodman's band and, *109,* 110–111
    Holiday, 122–124
    racial segregation and, 111, 113
    radio and, 107–108
Swinging Blue Jeans, 219
Sykes, Roosevelt, 67
"Symphony Sid" (New York DJ), 140, 144–145
Synthesizers, 261, 266–267
    Roland TR-808, 327–328
Synth-Pop groups, 283

Tales of the Jazz Age (Fitzgerald), 91
Talking Heads, 261, 271, 272, 273, 293
TAMI (Teen Age Music International) Show, 210, 212
Tamla (record label), 194
Tampa Red, 71
Tate, Greg, 338
Taupin, Bernie, 263
Tavares, 280
Taylor, Cecil, 156, 162
Taylor, James, 40, 256
Teagarden, Jack, 126
Technology, audio, 261
"Techno" music, 328
Teenagers, 165, 167, 173, 304. *See also* Sixties youth culture
    as teen idols, 186, 188
Television. *See also* MTV (MusicTelevision)
    of the 1850s, 166
    American Bandstand, 182
    Armstrong and, 96
    Partridge Family, 253
    Presley and, 180
    rock band of, 233
    Saturday Night Live, 305
    TAMI (Teen Age Music International) Show, 210, 212
Television (punk group), 272, 273
Tell Me a Story, Sing Me a Song: A Texas Chronicle (Owens), 19
Temptations, 195, 197, 267
Tennant, Neil, 285
Tequileros, 19, 22
Terrasson, Jackie, 162
Terrell, Tammi, 197
Teschemacher, Frank, 101
Texas blues, 46, 51
Texas Flood (Vaughn), 80
Texas Mexican Cancionero, A (Paredes), 18
Theater Owners Booking Association (TOBA), 58

Theodore, Grand Wizard, 320
3rd Bass (rap group), 333
Third Stream, 147, 148
"This Land Is Your Land" (Guthrie), 23, 24, 40
Thomas, Carla, 203
Thomas, Henry ("Ragtime Texas"), 51
Thomas, Rufus, 178, 203
Thompson, Richard, 259
Thompson Twins, 283
Thornton, Big Mama, 80, 168
Thrayil, Kim, 305
Threadgill, Henry, 162
Three Deuces, on 52nd Street, 126, 136
Three Dog Night, 259
"Three O'Clock Blues" (King), 76, 78
Thriller (Jackson), 286
Times They Are A'Changin', The (Dylan), 38, 217
Timmons, Bobby, 162
Tin Pan Alley, 58
Tizol, Juan, 117, 118
T.L. Records, 281
TLC, 343
Toasting, Jamaican, 322
"Tom Dooley," 31–32, 217, 218
Tommy (rock opera), 245
Tommy Boy Records, 327, 333
Tone-Loc, 343
Toop, David
    on disco and rap, 327
    on disco DJs, 319–320
    on Kool DJ Herc, 322
    on male-domination of rap, 323
    on rap roots, 13, 328
    on Run-DMC and Aerosmith, 332
    on Salt-N-Pepa, 343
    on urban violence, 333
"Top Forty" playlists, 183, 184
Tosh, Peter, 276
Tough, Dave, 101
Townshend, Peter, 162, 242
Trammps, 280–281
"Trans-Europe Express" (Kraftwerk), 327–328
Travers, Mary, 39. *See also* Peter, Paul, and Mary
Travolta, John, *279,* 280–281
Trent, Alphonso, 110
T-Rex, 262
Tribe Called Quest, A, 343, 343
Tristano, Lenny, 156
Trumbauer, Frankie, 101
Tucker, Ken, 254, 256, 274, 302
Tucker, Sophie, 59
Turner, Big Joe, 168, 199
Turntables, in rap music, 320
20/20 (ABC-TV news magazine), 323
Twin-Tone (indie record label), 308
Twisted Sister, 288, 301
2 Live Crew, 340
Tyner, McCoy, 152

U2, 25, 40, 283, 299–300, 302
Ulrich, Lars, 304
Ultravox, 283
Underground rock, 272–274
Uptown Records, 343
"Urban Contemporary" format, 270
U Roy, 322
US3, 343
Us Girls, 323
UTFO, 332

Vai, Steve, 301
Valens, Richie, 186, 295
Van Dyke, Earl, 197
Vanguard (record company), 32
Van Halen, 300, 301–302
Van Halen, Eddie, 286, 301, 302
Vanilla Ice, 333
Van Ronk, Dave, 32
Varèse, Edgar, 145
Variety, rock 'n' roll warnings in, 181
Vaughn, Stevie Ray, 49, *76,* 80
Vega, Suzanne, 39, 260, 298–299
Velvet Underground, 265
Victor Company (recording label), 62, 90, 91, 98
Vietnam War, 217, 237
Village People, 281
Village Vanguard, 30
Vincent, Gene, 173
Violence, in lyrics, 29, 323, 333–335, 361
Virgin Records, 275
Vision Shared, A (Guthrie/Leadbelly tribute album), 25, 40, 299
Vocalion (recording label), 22, 62

Wainwright, Loudon, III, 259
Walcott, F. S., 64. *See also* Rabbit Foot Minstrels
Walker, T-Bone, 49, 77, 168
Wallace, Christopher, 343
Wallace, Sippy, 62, 80
Waller, Fats, *104,* 105, 136
Wallflowers, 298
Walser, Robert, 254, 301, 302
Ward, Hart, 44
Warhol, Andy, 265
Warner Brothers, 288, 290, 341
Warner Communications, 249–250
Warwick, Dionne, 293
Washboard Sam, 71
W.A.S.P., 301
Waters, Ethel, 62, 102
Waters, Muddy, 69, *70,* 71–72
    Dixon and, 74–75
    guitar playing of, 237
    in *The Last Waltz,* 220, 246
Watts, Jeff "Tain," 162
Weather Report, *157*
Weavers, 15, *29,* 30
Webb, Chick, 111, 121
Webster, Ben, 117, *123,* 124

Weill, Cynthia, 192, 193
Weinstein, Deena, 301, 302
"Well, You Needn't" (Monk), 138, 140
Wells, Dicky, 119
Wells, Evelyn K., 7
Wells, Mary, 195
Wenner, Jann, 223
Wexler, Jerry, 198, 203, 205–207
Wham!, 285
Wheatstraw, Peetie, 55
"Where Did You Sleep (Stay) Last Night?," 16, 93
White, Armond, 333
White, Barry, 267, 343
White, Bukka, 51, 56
White, Josh, 30
White blues, 54, 55
Whiteman, Paul, 101, 103
Whitesnake, 302
Whitfield, Norman, 197, 267
Who, 204, 227, *242*
"Who Wants to See Ten Niggers Play Basketball?" (White), 333
Wiggins, Ella May, 29
Wiggins, Keith (Cowboy), 323
Wild One, The (film), 171
Wild Style! (film), 318, *319,* 322, 323
Williams, Bert, 118
Williams, Cootie, 116, 117
Williams, Fess, 107
Williams, Hank, 171
Williams, Lucinda, 39, 299
Williams, Martin, 123, 138
Williams, Mary Lou, *106,* 110, 129–130, 158
Williams, Paul (rock critic), 223
Williams, Paul (saxophone player), 145
Williams, Tony, 151, 161, 162
Williams (Clarence) Blue Five, 98
Williamson, John Lee "Sonny Boy," 71, 75
Williamson, Sonny Boy, II (Rice Miller), *73,* 75
Willis, Ellen, 234, 242, 244
Wilson, Ann and Nancy, 293
Wilson, Brian, 211, 212
Wilson, Cassandra, 147, *161*
Wilson, Teddy, 114, 123, 126, 135
Wilson, Tom, 259
Winter, Johnny, 74, 242
Winwood, Steve, 78, 236
With His Pistol in His Hand (Paredes), 19, 20
Wojahn, David, 231
Wolfe, Tom, 194, 249, 281
"Wolverines," Beiderbecke and, 101
Women
    ballads of, 9–10
    blues singers, 58
    folk music revival, 298–299
    with guitars, 293
    heavy metal and, 302
    hip-hop culture and, 322–323, 343

Women *(continued)*
  indie-label, 308–309
  in jazz, 109–110, 122–124, 125
  on MTV, 285, 292–293
  pop divas, 293–294, 296
  pop rap, 343
  rap answer records, 332
  rock 'n' roll, 312–313
  singer-songwriters, 227
"Women Writin' Rappin' Breakin'"
  (Guevara), 323
Wonder, Stevie, 197–198, 266–267, 269,
  276, 328, 348
Woodstock, 240–241, 243, 244

Woody Guthrie: A Life (Klein), 40, 298
Work songs, 42, 45
World Saxophone Quartet, 162
Worrell, Bernie, 271
Wright, Eugene, 148
Wu-Tang Clan, 343
Wymouth, Tina, 293

X (band), 274, 275

Yancy, Jimmy, 67
Yardbirds, 72, 236, 253
Yarrow, Peter, 35. *See also* Peter, Paul, and
  Mary

Yellow Magic Orchestra, 327
Yes, 261
Young, LaMonte, 261
Young, Lester, 114, 119, *123,* 124, 135
  (B.) Holiday and, 122, 126
Young, Neil, 220, 234, 246, 257, 275,
  311
Young Man with a Horn (Baker), 101
"You Shook Me," 74, 77
Youth culture, Sixties, 223
Yo-Yo, 343

Zappa, Frank, 270, 288
Zawinul, Joe, 162